SACRAMENTUM MUNDI

VOLUME THREE: HABITUS — MATERIALISM

SACRAMENTUM MUNDI

An Encyclopedia of Theology

Edited by

Karl Rahner SJ, Münster
and
Juan Alfaro SJ, Rome
Alberto Bellini, Bergamo
Carlo Colombo, Venegono
Henri Crouzel SJ, Toulouse
Jean Daniélou SJ, Paris
Adolf Darlap, Munich
Cornelius Ernst OP, Oxford
José Fondevilla SJ, Barcelona
Piet Fransen, Louvain
Fergus Kerr OP, Oxford
Piet Schoonenberg, Nijmegen
Kevin Smyth, Paris
† Gustave Weigel SJ, Woodstock

© Hermann-Herder-Foundation, Basle–Montreal

Published by Herder and Herder New York · Burns & Oates London · Palm Publishers
Montreal · Herder Freiburg · Éditions Desclée de Brouwer Bruges · Editorial Herder
Barcelona · Edizioni Morcelliana Brescia · Paul Brand Hilversum

SACRAMENTUM MUNDI

AN ENCYCLOPEDIA OF THEOLOGY

VOLUME THREE

HABITUS
TO
MATERIALISM

BURNS & OATES

HERDER AND HERDER NEW YORK
232 Madison Avenue, New York, N. Y. 10016

BURNS & OATES LIMITED
25 Ashley Place, London S. W. 1

1st Edition 1968
2nd Impression 1968
3rd Impression 1969

General Editor: Adolf Darlap

First published in West Germany © 1969, Herder KG
Printed in West Germany by Herder
SBN 223 97644 X

ABBREVIATIONS

The following list does not include biblical and other well-known abbreviations. Whenever an author, not listed below, is cited in an article by name only, followed by page number(s), the reference is to a work listed in the bibliography at the end of the article.

AAS   *Acta Apostolicae Sedis* (1909 ff.)

ACW   J. Quasten and J. C. Plumpe, *Ancient Christian Writers* (1946 ff.)

Billerbeck   (H. L. Strack and) P. Billerbeck, *Kommentar zum Neuen Testament aus Talmud und Midrasch,* I–IV (1922–28; reprint, 1956), V: rabbinical index, ed. by J. Jeremias and K. Adolph (1956)

CBQ   *Catholic Biblical Quarterly* (1939 ff.)

Chalkedon   A. Grillmeier and H. Bacht, eds., *Das Konzil von Chalkedon, Geschichte und Gegenwart,* 3 vols. (1951–54; 2nd enlarged ed., 1962)

CIC   *Codex Iuris Canonici*

CIO   *Codex Iuris Canonici Orientalis* (Unless stated otherwise, the references are to the law relating to persons.)

Collectio Lacensis   *Collectio Lacensis: Acta et Decreta Sacrorum Conciliorum Recentiorum,* ed. by the Jesuits of Maria Laach, 7 vols. (1870–90)

CSEL   *Corpus Scriptorum Ecclesiasticorum Latinorum* (1866 ff.)

D   H. Denzinger, *Enchiridion Symbolorum, Definitionum et Declarationum de Rebus Fidei et Morum* (31st ed., 1957); see also *DS*

DB   F. Vigouroux, ed., *Dictionnaire de la Bible,* 5 vols. (1895–1912)

DBS   L. Pirot, ed., *Dictionnaire de la Bible, Supplément,* continued by A. Robert (1928 ff.)

DS   H. Denzinger and A. Schönmetzer, *Enchiridion Symbolorum, Definitionum et Declarationum de Rebus Fidei et Morum* (33rd ed., 1965); see also *D*

DSAM   M. Viller, ed., *Dictionnaire de Spiritualité ascétique et mystique. Doctrine et Histoire* (1932 ff.)

DTC   A. Vacant and E. Mangenot, eds., *Dictionnaire de théologie catholique,* continued by É. Amann, I–XV, *Table analytique* and *Tables générales,* XVI ff. (1903 ff.)

ABBREVIATIONS

Enchiridion Biblicum	*Enchiridion Biblicum. Documenta Ecclesiastica Sacram Scripturam Spectantia* (3rd ed., 1956)
ETL	*Ephemerides Theologicae Lovanienses* (1924 ff.)
GCS	*Die griechischen christlichen Schriftsteller der ersten drei Jahrhunderte* (1897 ff.)
Hennecke-Schneemelcher-Wilson	E. Hennecke, W. Schneemelcher and R. McL. Wilson, eds., *New Testament Apocrypha*, 2 vols. (1963–65)
HERE	J. Hastings, ed., *Encyclopedia of Religion and Ethics,* 12 vols. + index (1908–26; 2nd rev. ed., 1925–40)
JBL	*Journal of Biblical Literature* (1881 ff.)
JTS	*Journal of Theological Studies* (1899 ff.)
LTK	J. Höfer and K. Rahner, eds., *Lexikon für Theologie und Kirche,* 10 vols. + index (2nd rev. ed., 1957–67)
Mansi	J. D. Mansi, *Sacrorum Conciliorum Nova et Amplissima Collectio,* 31 vols. (1757–98); reprint and continuation ed. by L. Petit and J. B. Martin, 60 vols. (1899–1927)
NRT	*Nouvelle Revue Théologique* (1879 ff.)
NTS	*New Testament Studies* (1954 ff.)
PG	J.-P. Migne, ed., *Patrologia Graeca,* 161 vols. (1857 ff.)
PL	J.-P. Migne, ed., *Patrologia Latina,* 217 vols. + 4 index vols. (1844 ff.)
Pritchard	J. B. Pritchard, ed., *Ancient Near Eastern Texts relating to the Old Testament* (1950; 2nd revised and enlarged ed., 1955)
RGG	K. Galling, ed., *Die Religion in Geschichte und Gegenwart,* 6 vols. + index (3rd rev. ed., 1957–65)
RHE	*Revue d'histoire ecclésiastique* (1900 ff.)
RHPR	*Revue d'histoire et de philosophie religieuse* (1921 ff.)
RSPT	*Revue des sciences philosophiques et théologiques* (1907 ff.)
RSR	*Recherches de science religieuse* (1910 ff.)
RSV	Revised Standard Version of the Bible
TS	*Theological Studies* (1940 ff.)
TU	*Texte und Untersuchungen zur Geschichte der altchristlichen Literatur. Archiv für die griechisch-christlichen Schriftsteller der ersten drei Jahrhunderte,* hitherto 62 vols. in 5 series (1882 ff.)
TWNT	G. Kittel, ed., *Theologisches Wörterbuch zum Neuen Testament,* continued by G. Friedrich (1933 ff.); E. T.: *Theological Dictionary of the New Testament* (1964 ff.)
ZAW	*Zeitschrift für die alttestamentliche Wissenschaft* (1881 ff.)
ZKT	*Zeitschrift für Katholische Theologie* (1877 ff.)

H

HABITUS

1. *The general notion.* The notion of *habitus* is used to explain the special nature of human action. Since man is spirit realizing himself in freedom, he comes upon himself not merely as a neutral entity, but primarily as a task imposed. Through and in his action he must make himself what he is and ought to be. But this power to make himself does not mean that he is totally indeterminate, as if he had to make an absolute beginning at each moment. On the contrary, the free action of man as spirit always starts from a determinate state of the subject, which is prior to any given act and enters into it as a determining factor. We call this subjective disposition *habitus* — insofar as a) its nature cannot be deduced from a formal definition of the essence and hence could have been otherwise, and b) the act in question is related to man as a totality, that is, to his being good or bad. If we call bodily constitution a habit *(habitus),* this can only be in a transferred sense, as when we speak of a "sickly" or healthy habit. The spiritual, free action of man is only determined by those modes of being which refer this action to the absolute of truth and love. Thus these modes of being are characterized by the fact that they are orientated to the absolute itself: they are the modes of existence, and a habit *(habitus)* is a determinate quality of existence insofar as it is orientated to man's action. With this, the notion of *habitus* approximates to that of the existential. For by existentials we also mean the basic structures of existence, that is, of the orientation to the absolute which

takes place in the world, which structures are not comprehended in an abstract, formal definition of man's essence but are found in the concrete being of man. Insofar as existence itself is an orientation to action, the existentials are *habituses.* But since the *habitus,* unlike the existential, indicates not only a basic structure but its individual differentiation in each person, the *habitus* has more sharply defined characteristics than the existential.

This description of the *habitus* differs somewhat from the classical definition given by Aristotle: "The *habitus* (ἕξις) is an acquisition whereby something is better or worse off as regards itself (i.e., its own nature) or another (i.e., the final end of its nature)." (*Meta.,* V, 20; 1022 b, 10 ff.) Aristotle's more static view sees the *habitus* primarily as a further determination of the subject, and only then as related to action, which is not confined to human action. We take it more dynamically and strictly, primarily as the basic possibility of specifically human action, spiritual and free and also part of the world process. Only when taken in this sense can it help to explain the specific nature of human action.

2. *Definition in detail.* In view of what has been said above, the further determination of the notion of *habitus* must begin with the characteristics of existence, insofar as they determine human action.

a) Existence is orientation to the Absolute. This orientation is set on foot by the self-bestowal of the Absolute itself. Existence as thus founded is the being of man in its inmost

1

core, which is the primary determinant of his action, though an interiority not consciously grasped. In this merely formal consideration of the core of being as source of action, it is not yet *habitus,* since it has no particular determinations beyond its essential constitution. It is only *habitus* when it is considered in its intrinsic determination. This determination of the substantial being (which *qua* produced does not yet formally imply relationship to the world) is brought about by the fact that the Absolute bestows itself (by giving rise to the being in question) and in the way in which it bestows itself. In the pre-Christian and non-Christian realms, this self-bestowal remains veiled in an anonymity which, though not indeterminate, is still ultimately inexplicable. For Christians, it is characterized as Jesus Christ, in whom the living God turns to us in love, ordaining our being to Christ through the offer of salvation, transforming and determining it in Christ. It is a self-bestowal which enables men to share profoundly, though gratuitously, the possibilities of God's own self-existent being. This determination, which is the adaptation and ordination of existence to Christ, since it is part of existence and yet is only intelligible in view of Christ, is the "supernatural existential" of man (K. Rahner). As the acquisition which in Christ affects man in the core of his being, elevating and changing him, it is sanctifying grace. Both of these, supernatural existential and sanctifying grace, had to be called by scholastic tradition *habitus infusi,* because absolutely inexigible by man and only implanted by God, and *habitus entitativi* because determinative of the core of man's being — though as a rule only sanctifying grace is designated as an entitative infused *habitus.*

b) The orientation to the Absolute takes place in the world, that is, the substantial interiority of man is only there as related to the world. Fundamentally, it is the spiritual faculties which realize this relationship. But since of themselves they do not specify the relationship any further, they must themselves receive a further determination, so that each act of man has not to be accomplished as an absolute beginning (cf. 1). In contrast to the entitative *habitus,* which did not formally include such relationship to the world, the determination in question, in which the relationship to the world is crystallized, implies an immediate relationship to the action of man in the world. Hence tradition calls this determination of the faculties *habitus operativi.* There are two such operative habituses:

(i) The relationship of the Absolute to the world in general, accomplished through the operative faculties, is consciously grasped in the act of existence, that is, in the free action of the spirit, though such knowledge does not necessarily take the form of articulate statement. But this relationship is the structurizing of worldly beings by the Absolute as they are brought about, and it is formulated initially and in general by means of the first principles of being. Since this relationship is grasped in every spiritual activity of man, the operative faculties are at once materially determined in their first act by insight into the first principles — which insight is not simply a logical deduction, but presupposes the factualness of the world in general. Hence the scholastics termed this *intellectus principiorum* the primary *habitus* of the human spirit.

(ii) This primary insight which is always present gives human action a certain (general) relationship to the world, but not to history, which being action accomplished in freedom is never complete. And here it is not only a matter of the history of the individual; for his history only takes form in his reaction to history in general, which offers him, and imposes on him, its harvest of thought and experience and is thus a prior factor determining each action. The individual action must be made an organic part of one's own history and hence of general history, if one is to take a responsible attitude to one's own and others' acts. Hence the condition of possibility of responsible action is that the operative faculties both end and preserve this history by taking it over as a determination. And this determination, being the imprint of personal and general history (insofar as the individual is concerned with it), makes the actions of the individual characteristic of his personality — and makes them good or bad. Such determinations of the operative faculties are then the more intellectual virtues of science, wisdom and prudence (or their absence) or the more practical moral virtues (or vices), which equip each action of man for its exercise of freedom, where the life of man is gathered up into one, as Yes or No to the Absolute, hence really to the living God of Jesus Christ.

3. *Conclusion*. The importance of the *habitus* is not merely that it can give rise to habits, favouring an economy of effort in certain ordinary courses of action. First and foremost, the *habitus* may not be regarded as a lessening of freedom. Its specific character makes it an invitation and outline for our freedom, which can only be exercised by virtue of it and in reaction to it. Hence the importance of the *habitus* is that it is the means whereby man is inserted into history, including his own, which is always history of salvation. And this organic link enables him to confront reality as a whole comprehensively, and to give the actuation of his freedom a deeper and fuller reality in this confrontation.

See also *Man* I, *Freedom, Essence, Existence, Human Act, World, Principle, History* I.

BIBLIOGRAPHY. J. Chevalier, *L'Habitude, Essai de métaphysique scientifique* (1929); P. de Roton, *Les Habitus, leur caractère spirituel* (1934); A. Arrighini, *L'abitudine* (1937); J. Valbuena, "De significatione specialis Praedicamenti 'habitus'", *Angelicum* 22/23 (1945/46), pp. 172–7; R. Garrigou-Lagrange, *De beatitudine, de actibus humanis et habitibus. Comment. in S. Th.,* I, II, qq. 1–54 (1951); G. Funke, "Gewohnheit", *Archiv für Begriffsgeschichte,* III (1958); K. Rahner, *Theological Investigations,* I (1961), II (1964).

Oswald Schwemmer

HEALTH

I. Physical Health. II. Psychic Hygiene.

I. Physical Health

1. There is no simple, generally accepted definition of health and disease. "Health" can indeed, as an ideal norm, be described according to the definition of the World Health Organization as a "state of perfect bodily, mental and social well-being". This definition is, however, neither useful in practice nor entirely acceptable in theory. Health can be defined only with reference to sickness and only to the extent that the concepts are mutually exclusive when they refer to a particular individual (one is either sick or well, never both at the same time), but a broad neutral area is left, where the individual feels himself neither entirely well nor yet sick. Why this is so becomes clear if we analyse the facts.

2. For the terms "well" and "ill" there are apparent synonyms, e.g., the concepts of normal and abnormal. Norms are to be found in biology and medicine alike. They divide into three groups. a) The essential qualities of the species and breeds are their "norm", deviations from which (6 fingers, albino, for example) are abnormal. Yet such abnormalities do not necessarily connote sickness. b) The average of a group already classified as healthy could be defined as the norm in relation to individually widely distributed qualities (blood pressure, basic metabolism, etc.). Yet variations from the standard are by no means unhealthy in every case (e.g., great size of body). They are so only when the averages concern vital functional values such as, for example, blood pressure. Such values always include the *mandatory standards* of a regulative mechanism, any considerable change in which is consequently unhealthy. c) In human life there are norms of behaviour stemming from social custom. They are of special importance to the notion of mental illness. "Unhealthy" is the adjectival determination of a state or process which injures the health of individuals, and so makes them ill. The terms "wounded" or "injured" denote illness following a wound, the term "damaged" refers to the permanent result of a wound. It too need not be identified with illness.

3. The problematic nature of the concepts health and sickness is seen from the fact that modern medicine by its fight against disease in the last hundred years has doubled life expectation (to an average of seventy years), whereas the number of days' illness of the insured has increased roughly threefold.

4. Our notions of health and sickness are derived from daily experience, especially that of doctors. The first guide to understanding these concepts must, therefore, be the *phenomena* or actual manifestations. The basic phenomenon is how the person feels: when he falls sick he becomes a "patient" (*pati* = suffer). Pain drives him to the doctor. Subjective discomfort, however, accompanies many "physiological" processes and arises with innumerable adaptive manifestations: after use of the muscles in the form of stiffness, in adapting to heat as a feeling of fatigue and inability for heavy work, etc. "Feeling" can therefore be considered as a sign of illness

only when it points to disturbances that are, in the widest sense, a threat to life. Every sickness "has death for its aim" (Jores). Thus a disturbance in the way one feels is to be taken all the more seriously the more it seems to be justified by bodily indications ("symptoms") which mark a departure from the normal. Symptoms give support to the diagnosis which starts from the way the patient feels (e.g., fatigue through lack of blood pigmentation); they are usually, though not always, sufficient to establish the presence of an illness. They can be absent even where there is considerable subjective disturbance (e.g., headache); they can be a threat to life without any subjective disturbance (cancer).

5. The patient is ill when he himself believes he is no longer able to work. He alone makes this decision, he "goes sick"; yet his decision calls for confirmation by the doctor who "signs" to that effect. Health is therefore in the first place capability for work in accordance with the individual's own judgment. The threat of future inability to work can, however, also constitute illness (e.g., cancer or arteriosclerosis). The question of whether and to what extent the patient is justified in going sick is one that cannot always be objectively answered. Even the words of the doctor can so alter the way a patient feels that he can feel sick without any objective cause (medically induced illness).

6. The diagnosis of the actual presence of an illness is complicated by the fact that the spiritual and bodily elements in man react on each other so that he can be understood only as a unity of body and soul ("psychosomatic" approach). This mutual influence has recently been experimentally confirmed in animals. Animals too can be psychosomatically ill (most recent literature in Baust-Golenhofen-Zanchetti). Man's mental condition is also strongly influenced by his social position and environment, rises on the wings of hope and success; lack of prospects, monotony of work, isolation, loneliness make him depressed and so affect him that not only has he less resistance to feeling ill but he is also more subject to such feelings because of the changes in the sympathetic nervous system. We speak of "sociosomatic" indications and illnesses and of "social health". Neuroses and psychoses are very much subject to social influences of this kind (Mitscherlich). The religious factor makes itself felt in this area and the loss of religion in the rapid structural change in society and the world of work has contributed greatly to the rise of sociosomatic disturbances. The ability to "put up" with things has dwindled more and more.

7. Here it becomes apparent that there is a moral aspect to health and to sickness in the social sense. Most "illnesses" in medical practice are minor and are never fatal. Many could be endured without work stoppage. They would then be regarded as "subjective-objective" disturbances but not as "illnesses". Thus classification as illness is the result of a complex judgment. A person who is indisposed will have a place somewhere along the scale between absolute health and fatal illness, and he will be all the nearer to illness the more he feels himself subjectively threatened, the worse his objective symptoms are, or at least appear, and the more inclined he is by temperament to take his symptoms seriously. The significance of social norms in this case is obvious: society formerly had fixed ethical limits to what one should endure. Today conventions fail or have become flabby for the most part: man considers himself or others sick at every minor indisposition. The rate of illness of the insured (i.e., the number who are sick at any one time as a percentage of the total employed) is thereby increased and determines the statistical level of the nation's health.

8. The moral problems of sickness and health have become more extensive as a result of the great economic importance of these phenomena. Because of the rate of illness and of early invalidity every year, a large part of the Gross National Product is lost. The individual has a *duty to his health* and especially to preserving health since the community has to provide for him when he is ill. There is to be sure the corresponding right to health: the community must do all it can to protect the individual's health and in case of illness to provide relief. Both the right and the duty can, however, be positively established only with difficulty. That they are so much emphasized today is the result of the modern way of thinking with its strong orientation towards society, partly no doubt as a consequence of the Christian tradition (the idea of charity as a duty).

9. Sickness is nevertheless not a primary moral phenomenon despite the fact that in the Middle Ages it was frequently seen in that light and the etymology of many languages points to it (ill from evil, *malade* from *mal!*). This has not been entirely overcome in respect to mental illness. Here the role of convention as a basis for judgment is very much in evidence: in matters of the mind what is unusual is frequently regarded as illness (genius and madness according to Lombroso). It seems misleading to regard illness as the consequence of sin. Illness can indeed be the result of a lively consciousness of sin (e.g., the scrupulous conscience) and would in such a case be classified as psychosomatic. It can also be the natural consequence of sinful behaviour (venereal diseases). But for the most part the theologian underestimates the considerable effect of emotions and suggestibility on the human body and the compulsive nature of biological phenomena.

10. Health is a guarantee of freedom and every illness implies a loss of freedom, i.e., a loss of possibilities (Jores, Mitscherlich). The sick person is unfree because sickness imposes on him a reduction in performance, forces him to take precautions, or (in the case of psychosomatic or mental illnesses) results in abnormal, socially unacceptable behaviour. But health can also be the cause of mental and moral mediocrity, whereas sickness can be the source of mental development won through suffering. All suffering enriches the world of psychosomatic experience and leads to mental and moral reactions that are of the highest social importance. For that reason too, the definition of health quoted above from the World Health Organization is unbiological: man without suffering is a man without adaptation to a world in which suffering of all kinds has a great social, political and religious significance. In particular a long, severe illness inclines the patient to call on his mental and moral resources and can lead to a considerable strengthening of these.

11. The terms health and illness are also frequently used of higher units: the family, the State, humanity or certain social or political structures (Kütemeyer). Since the concept of health is scarcely capable of definition even in the case of the individual human being, there is much less possibility here. It merely serves to give a judgment as to how far the social structure under consideration tallies with the bias of the viewer, that is, corresponds with his views of what is right and normal. Accordingly, every judgment on the health of social institutions is a political judgment, to be made only on the basis of a pre-existing concept of social order.

See also *Illness, Death, Freedom, Body, Soul*.

BIBLIOGRAPHY. A. F. Bonnar, *The Catholic Doctor* (1938); C. H. Best and N. B. Taylor, *The Physiological Basis of Medical Practice* (1940); P. T. Young, *Emotion in Men and Animals* (1943); W. Sargant and E. Slater, *Somatic Methods in Psychiatry* (1944); H. F. Dunbar, *Mind and Body: Psychosomatic Medicine* (1947); R. Frazer, *The Incidence of Neurosis among Factory Workers* (1947); E. Weiss and O. S. English, *Psychosomatic Medicine* (1949); A. J. Carlson and V. Johnson, *The Machinery of the Body* (1954); A. Jores and others, eds., *The Fourth European Conference on Psychosomatic Research, Hamburg* (1959); A. Jores and H. Freyberger, eds., *Advances in Psychosomatic Medicine* (1960); A. Mitscherlich, "Methods and Principles of Research on Psychosomatic Fundamentals", *Culture, Society and Health, Annual of the New York Academy of Science* 84 (1960), pp. 783–1060; W. Kütemeyer, *Die Krankheit in ihrer Menschlichkeit* (1963); H. H. Wolff and P. Hopkins, eds. *Principles of Treatments of Psychosomatic Disorders,* pub. by the Society for Psychosomatic Research (1965); W. Braust, K. Golenhaufen and A. Zanchetti, *Verhandlungen der deutschen Gesellschaft für Kreislaufforschung* 32 (1966), pp. 23–56.

Hans Schaefer

II. Psychic Hygiene

Mental health is a state of harmonious functioning in our personality, wherein we perceive ourselves and the world around us with a sense of accuracy, alertness and dynamic awareness, by meeting stimuli and responding with a measure of urge and initiative for action, or with a restful sense of satisfaction; by enjoying the confrontation, and enduring reverses with a sense of challenge marked by commitment to action or resolution to patience according to the circumstances of the situation and the nature of our person; recognizing limitations and emphasizing endowments and the need to express ourselves as individuals freely yet in keeping with divine law.

As the personality functions, it unfolds and develops towards a maturity which is reached on the average around the age of 30, leading with continued growth to the emergence of character and finally to the development of a philosophy of life which crystallizes with advancing age. Essentially, the parts or spheres unfolding in the personality are the emotional, the intellectual and the spiritual. The emotional, which is primarily of an instinctive type at and shortly after birth, is the predominant frame of reference in the life of a child. Around the age of seven the intellectual capacities are displayed more prominently, ready for schooling, and also permit the appearance of a simple logic, essential to the first manifestations of reason, conscience and will. Around the age of fourteen the intellectual equipment of the individual reaches the adult level with full potential for abstraction, induction and deduction, and it is then that the spiritual activities may begin to unfold in the full sense. This is the time when the sense for a religious vocation may be experienced more clearly; also when scrupulosity may first become a problem. The individual learns to manage these three spheres in the personality in a practical sense in the next decade or more and shows maturity around the age of thirty regarding choice, decision and effective independent and interdependent responsible action.

From birth onward a series of problems make their appearance at certain successive stages in life, keep recurring thereafter and often pose conflicts pertaining to passivity—aggressivity, good—evil, masculinity—femininity, dependence—independence, anonymity—prestige, pride—humility. The healthy individual acquires proficiency in handling them. As life-roles are defined, the formation of character follows in the fuller sense of the word. Maturing requires, in brief, a transition from self-centeredness to self-giving.

Mental health permits us as individuals to realize our worth with dignity and to participate in the social scene, helping to resolve family and sociological issues while engaging in the many aspects of the expression of charity as St. Paul wonderfully described it.

Our person is active in three spheres, emotional, intellectual and spiritual, harmoniously interrelated in the psychologically mature adult according to a hierarchical precedence: the spiritual, the intellectual and the emotional. It is essential to recognize that, in addition to our conscious life guided by reason, discerning through conscience and acting through will, there is also unconscious mental activity in us, vast and concealed from

our immediate knowledge. Analysis of the unconscious points to the fact that even here man is true to his basic nature, which is good. Relative shifts in hierarchical precedence occur during sleep, dreams, conditions of hypnosis, brainwashing and passion, but at no time can our moral concept of good be opposed without conflict. When we act maturely our motivation is to do good and avoid evil, whether for ourselves or for the sake of others; in attaining our objective, we proceed with intelligent dispatch, and seek pleasure while avoiding pain insofar as possible. These are considerations of the spiritual, intellectual and emotional order. Disregard of this hierarchy in action denotes immaturity. When immature, we may inadvertently or erroneously become involved with evil. Wilful involvement with evil does not make spiritual sense; evil action is unhealthy and *per se* immature.

In practical living, we must realize the need for commitment to action, yet not any action, but rather that which is good or is apprehended as good in keeping with the principle of double effect. In making healthy judgments, pride both conscious and unconscious (narcissism) is the greatest obstacle. Acceptance of the divine will with humility is the greatest asset. The pitfall is the urge (often unconscious) to get even (seek justice vengefully through one's own hand). This represents regression to primitive, law-of-the-jungle behaviour. Also practical is the need to appraise observable personality differences on a constitutional basis, distinct from those environmentally conditioned and interpersonally determined. There are definite contrasts between the faster-to-act, intense person with multifaceted, superficial thinking and the slower-to-act, sensitive person with precise, detailed thinking. They are related to matter and energy factors, and they point to a natural tissue predominance of the fast and solid (tachysteric) or the slow and delicate (bradyleptic) kind, biologically inherited at different somatic levels, which determine various degrees of personality activity in the emotional and intellectual spheres (reflecting in turn on spiritual activity). Consequently, various types of reactions and attitudes regarding work, social performance, personal habits, etc., result.

The appreciation of personality differences is of paramount practical importance but will not be construed ethically as requiring a relative rather than absolute spiritual norm of conduct, for it merely broadens the understanding about pace of living, tastes and values, susceptibility to temptation, the meaning of communication and culture and the conception of character and ideals. It should facilitate co-operation between persons and render human relations more fruitful, especially in marriage.

BIBLIOGRAPHY. G. Bergsten, *Pastoral Psychology* (1951); W. Carrington, *Psychology, Religion and Human Need* (1957); G. Vann, *The Paradise Tree* (1959); J. Dominian, *Psychiatry and the Christian* (1962); L. de Lavareille, *Psychologie et christianisme* (1962); *Research in Religion and Health*, pub. by the Academy of Religion and Mental Health, Fordham (1963); H. A. Carroll, *Mental Hygiene* (4th ed., 1963); D. Brink, *Readings in Mental Hygiene: Principles and Practices* (1965); M. Leach, *Christianity and Mental Health* (1967).

Edward L. Suarez-Murias

HELL

I. Doctrine. II. Descent of Christ into Hell.

I. Doctrine

1. In the history of revelation the notion of hell as the place and state of those who are finally lost goes back to the OT notion of Sheol as the place and state of the dead — the "underworld". In a long, slow process of theological reflection, the state in question came to be understood differently of the good and the bad, in keeping with their life on earth. The "sheol of damnation" (*1 Q Hodayot* [Qumran Thanksgiving Hymns], 3, 19) was the final lot of the wicked (Gehenna; cf. *LTK*, V, cols. 445 f., with bibliography). The notion of the fire of judgment burning in the Valley of Hinnom (Gehenna) (Jer 7:32; 19:6; Is 66:24) also influenced the development of the theme.

2. In keeping with the theology of his time, Jesus, like the Baptist, spoke in his eschatological menaces of hell as the eternal place of punishment, prepared not only for the devil and his angels (Mt 25:41) but for all who have rejected the salvation offered by God. It is the punishment of their unbelief and refusal to repent (Mt 5:29 par.; 13:42, 50; 22:13, etc.). He speaks of hell as a place where eternal, unquenchable fire burns (Mt 5:22; 13:42, 50; 18:9, etc.), where there is darkness, howling and gnashing of teeth (Mt 8:12; 22:13; 25:30, etc.). A similar description is found in Rev 14:10; 20:10; 21:8. St. Paul speaks of hell in abstract theological terms as eternal destruction, ruin and loss (2 Thess 1:9; Rom 9:22; Phil 3:19; 2 Thess 2:10, etc.).

3. In its official teaching, the Church has defined the existence of hell (*D* 16, 40, 429, 464, 693, 717, 835, 840) (on the interpretation see below, 4c) and its eternity against the doctrine of the apocatastasis as put forward by Origen and other ancient writers (*D* 211). Asserting implicitly an important principle of hermeneutics, the Church eliminated temporal patterns from the existence of the dead, by affirming against the doctrine of an intermediate state of the lost before the general judgment that entry into hell takes place immediately after their death (*D* 464, 531). A certain distinction is made between the loss of the vision of God *(poena damni)* and the pain of sense *(poena sensus)* (*D* 410), but apart from this there is no official declaration on the nature of the pains of hell, though the difference of punishments in hell is mentioned (*D* 464, 693).

4. In speculative and kerygmatic theology, the following points should be noted:

a) For a proper understanding of the matter, all the rules for the hermeneutics of eschatological assertions are to be observed, as must also be done in all preaching on hell. This means that what Scripture says about hell is to be interpreted in keeping with its literary character of "threat-discourse" and hence not to be read as a preview of something which will exist some day. Insofar as it is a report, it is rather a disclosure of the situation in which the persons addressed are actually to be found. They are placed before a decision of which the consequences are irrevocable. They can be lost for ever if they reject God's offer of salvation. The metaphors in which Jesus describes the eternal perdition of man as a possibility which threatens him at this moment are images (fire, worm, darkness, etc.) taken from the mental furniture of contemporary apocalyptic. They all mean the same thing, the possibility of man being finally lost and estranged from God in all the dimensions of his existence. Hence it can be seen that the question of whether the "fire" of hell is real or metaphorical is wrongly put, since "fire" and suchlike words are metaphorical expressions for something radically not of this world. Hence they can never be described in terms proper to their own "phenomena" and even when they seem to be expressed in the most abstract terms, they can only be spoken of "in images". Even such a term as "eternal loss" is in the nature of an image. This does not mean that "fire" is to be given a "psychological" explanation. It indicates the cosmic, objective aspect of loss which is outside the consciousness. Just as the blessedness of the immediate vision of God also involves an openness in sharing love and bliss with the glorified environment, so too loss means a definitive contradiction of the abiding and perfected world, and this contradiction will be a torment. It also follows that speculations about the "place" where hell is to be found are pointless. There is no possibility of inserting hell into the empirical world around us.

b) As regards preaching, the following considerations are important. "Hence, the theological exposition of the dogma cannot be primarily devoted to an objectivating speculation on the other world. It must apply itself above all to bringing out the real relevance of the affirmation of hell to human existence. Hence it cnnot be the task of theology to go into details about supposed facts of the next life, such as the number of the damned, the severity of their pains and so on. But it has the task of maintaining the dogma of hell in all the severity of its realistic claim. For without this claim it cannot fulfil its task as part of revelation, which is to bring men to control their lives in the light of the real possibility of eternal failure and to recognize revelation as a claim of the utmost seriousness. This salutary purpose of the dogma must always set bounds to and provide the guiding lines for all speculation in this matter." (J. Ratzinger in *LTK*, V, col. 448.)

c) Even in his "judgment-discourses" Jesus gave no clear revelation about whether men are actually lost or how many may be. That he restricts himself to the possibility follows from the real nature of these discourses, which is to be a summons to decision. For this reason, there are no decisions of the magisterium on the matter,

since these prounouncements are to be read in the same way as the judgment-discourses of Jesus, which they reiterate. Hence the preacher who mounts the pulpit must not appeal to visions of the saints or private revelations in these matters. To deny or to affirm that any or many were lost would be to go outside the terms of reference set by these summonses to decision and would be an immediate contradiction of the statement involved in the discourses. We must maintain side by side and unwaveringly the truth of the omnipotence of the universal salvific will of God, the redemption of all by Christ, the duty of all men to hope for salvation and also the true possibility of eternal loss. Hence too light-hearted appeals to the dogma of hell, as for instance when preaching on sin, are to be deprecated, especially if they only induce a servile fear which is insufficient for justification and which is unconvincing today. Hence the preacher must try to bring home to his hearers the seriousness of the threat to eternal salvation, with which the Christian must reckon without any sly look at a possible apocatastasis. Nonetheless, the emphasis on the possibility of hell as perpetual obduracy must be paralleled by insistent encouragement to rely with confidence on the infinite mercy of God.

d) It is possible, and indeed necessary today, to explain the eternity of hell (with Thomas Aquinas) as the consequence of the inward obduracy of man, and not either as cause of it or as an independent element. This inner obduracy, the rejection of the grace which inspires a salutary act, springs from the essence of freedom and is not in contradiction to freedom. Freedom is the will and the possibility of positing the definitive. It is not the possibility of constant revision of decisions. And "eternity" is not the continued duration of time after the history of freedom, but the definitive achievement of history. Hence hell is "eternal" and thus a manifestation of the justice of God. Hell is not to be thought of as a most drastic but merely additional punitive measure of God's vengeance, punishing those who would improve but for the infliction of this punishment. The just God is "active" in the punishment of hell only insofar as he does not release man from the reality of the definitive state which man himself has achieved on his own behalf, contradictory though this state be to the world as God's creation. Hence the notion of vindictive punishment, such as inflicted by political society on those who infringe social order, is not at all suitable to explain the doctrine of hell.

See also *Apocatastasis, Eschatology, Last Things, Apocalyptic, Salvation* I, IV A, *Freedom, Mercy.*

BIBLIOGRAPHY. COMPARATIVE RELIGION: Billerbeck, IV, pp. 1016–1165; F. Cumont, *Lux Perpetua* (1949); J. Jeremias in *TWNT,* I, pp. 9 f., 146–9, 657 f. BIBLICAL: P. Volz, *Eschatologie der jüdischen Gemeinde im neutestamentlichen Zeitalter* (2nd ed., 1934); W. Eichrodt, *Theology of the Old Testament,* I (1961). THEOLOGICAL: J. B. Agar, "The Doom of the Lost", *Expository Times* 22 (1910/11), cols. 207 ff.; J. P. O'Connell, *The Eschatology of St. Jerome* (1948); F. von Hügel, "What Do We Mean by Heaven and What Do We Mean by Hell?", *Essays and Addresses on the Philosophy of Religion* (1949–51); G. Bardy and others, *L'enfer* (1950); M. Pontifex, "The Doctrine of Hell", *Downside Review* 71 (1953), pp. 135–52; M. Schmaus, *Katholische Dogmatik,* IV/2 (5th ed., 1959), pp. 452–510; A. Winklhofer, *The Coming of His Kingdom. A Theology of the Last Things* (1963); A. Roets, "De hel", *Collationes Brugenses et Gandavenses* 9 (1963), pp. 190–210; K. Rahner, "The Hermeneutics of Eschatological Assertions", *Theological Investigations,* IV (1966), pp. 323–46.

Karl Rahner

II. Descent of Christ into Hell

In the article of the creed "the descent into hell", one must distinguish between the mode of expression and the statement intended. The expression makes use of terms borrowed from accounts of descents to the underworld in various ancient religions. But the statement intended is a genuinely Christian one.

1. *Descent into hell as assertion of death.* "The descent into hell" (Apostles' Creed, *D* 6) or "the descent into the underworld" (Fourth Lateran Council, *D* 429; Second Council of Lyons, *D* 462) means first of all that Jesus truly died. This article of the Creed points beyond the act of dying to the state of death. For Christ this meant that while he was still connected with the world, it was nevertheless withdrawn from him. In this state of death (a state and not a geographical place) he was no longer, in his created

spirit, united with his body in a fully human manner: he was no longer in the earthly state and not yet in the heavenly. As man, he no longer possessed his humanity as a pilgrim; but neither had he it in its glorified state (although he possessed the beatific vision as he did during his earthly life). The redemption was not yet completed, for he was not yet glorified. In the Creed, the descent into hell is mentioned among the Christological mysteries. It follows upon his death and burial, and precedes the resurrection and ascension. The words heaven and hell are here used to indicate the absolute extremes: for Christ, the condition of death, his being less than a full human being, was his most radical self-emptying; the ascension in his glorified humanity was his fulfilment. As the mystery of Christ was unfolded in the course of the liturgical year, the descent into hell, the state of death, was given its place in the liturgy on Holy Saturday.

2. *The descent into hell as a salvific event.* The descent into hell does not mean a new redemptive act of Christ beyond his death. Nonetheless, as the state of death it is significant for salvation. a) *Anthropologically.* By his death, Christ entered the state of the dead and thus experienced this further element of our human lot, which is natural to us by reason of our being creatures, but should not have happened to us according to the concrete order of things. In this way Christ became one with us even in the loss of the preternatural gift of immortality, in order to unite us with himself through a solidarity comprehensive enough to include even dying and the state of death. Thus our death, which is a consequence of sin, has been "redeemed", so that the vision of God can be experienced in death, though only perfectly at the resurrection of the flesh. b) *Cosmically.* By submitting to death, by thus allowing his human nature to be rent asunder (as happens to all who die), Christ surrendered himself in the most complete way possible to the nothingness of all creation. And thus, beginning with his own resurrection, he could emancipate it from this nothingness — both of being fallen and of being "mere creation". c) *Historically.* In the history of salvation, the descent into hell is a special event, since it brought the vision of God to those who died in grace. Even though those who lived before Christ

could have had sanctifying grace (grace of Christ), so that they could live and die as redeemed and justified, still, from the purely temporal point of view of our life on earth, no access to the glory of the Father was possible until the historical completion of the Christ Event — from the incarnation to the exaltation. For us human beings, the vision of God is possible only "in the glorified Lord".

At his descent into hell, Christ identified himself with the dead, but unlike them, had the vision of God; he was victor over death, on the threshold of his glory, about to bring with him those who had died in the state of justice and were ready for the vision of God. But his entry into glory and hence the entry of the saved into the blessed vision of God took place only after his resurrection and ascension. Hence this aspect of the descent into hell points of itself to the exaltation. Hence the significance of the descent into hell in the order of salvation is that of the whole paschal mystery.

In the Fathers, this aspect of the descent into hell appears in three themes, that of "the preaching to the dead", in which Christ proclaimed the completion of his work of salvation, that of "baptism", in which he bestowed salvation to those who were under the earth, and that of "the harrowing of hell" in which he conquered the hostile powers.

In the liturgy, the descent into hell is celebrated as a salvific event whenever the paschal mystery is recalled in its unity: at the end of Holy Week, but also at each celebration of the Eucharist and above all at baptism, in which we die, are buried and rise with Christ (cf. Rom 6:3–11).

The teaching of the Church on the descent of Christ into hell is the answer given by revelation to the human questions which are behind the various descents into the underworld of which the various religions speak. It is not an addition to the kerygma of the death and resurrection of Christ, but is already contained in it, since the descent into hell is part of the *mysterium paschale*. It is part of the "passage from mortal life into the glory of the Father" for our salvation.

See also *Salvation III A, IV A, Ascension of Christ, Resurrection, Original Sin, States of Man (Theological), Beatific Vision.*

BIBLIOGRAPHY. O. Rousseau, "La descente aux enfers, fondement sotériologique du baptême chrétien", *RSR* 40 (1952), pp. 273–97; O. Simmel, "Abgestiegen zu der Hölle", *Stimmen der Zeit* 156 (1954/55), pp. 1–6; O. Rousseau, "La descente aux enfers dans le cadre des liturgies chrétiennes", *Maison Dieu* 43 (1955), pp. 81–84; K. Rahner, *On the Theology of Death,* Quaestiones Disputatae 2 (1960); J. Galot, "La descente du Christ aux enfers", *NRT* 83 (1961), pp. 471–91; W. J. Dalton, *Christ's Proclamation to the Spirits. A Study of 1 Peter 3: 18 – 4: 6,* Analecta Biblica 23 (1965); H. Vorgrimler, "Christ's Descent into Hell: Is It Important?", *Concilium* 1, no. 2 (1966), pp. 75–81.

Robert Lachenschmid

HELLENISM AND CHRISTIANITY

A. GENERAL FEATURES

Hellenism, the language and thought-forms of which influenced reflection on Christian revelation and the formulation of dogma from the 2nd to the 4th century, must not be taken as a homogeneous philosophical system, such as that of Plato, Aristotle or the Stoics. It consists of syncretist structures — neo-Pythagoreanism, middle Platonism, neo-Platonism — in which Platonism predominates but nearly always permeated by Aristotelian and Stoic elements. The unanimity with which the Apologists one after another affirm the as it were necessary convergence of Platonism and Christianity is very striking. Justin speaks of the similarity between Moses and Plato in their doctrine of the Logos and the Spirit (*Apol.,* I, 59f.), Plato being the plagiarist, according to a theme that was to become classical. Justin also accepts Plato's definition of God (*Dial.,* 2f.). Following Clement of Alexandria (*Strom.,* V, 14), Eusebius (*Praeparatio Evangelica,* XI, 17, 20) and others find the Christian doctrine of the three hypostases anticipated in Plato (*Ep.,* II, 312d–e). Plotinus (*Enneads,* V, 1, 4ff.) is also invoked. Theodoretus (*Graec. aff. cur.,* VI, 13) finds allies in Plato (*Laws,* II, IV, X) and Plotinus (*Enneads,* III, 2) for the doctrine of providence.

Augustine is not quite so downright, but he is no less clear on the point. He claims to have found in "certain writings of the Platonists" (*Confessions,* VII, 9, 13) the whole doctrine of the prologue of St. John on the eternal Word, though not his incarnation and humility. As regards the vision of God, he goes so far as to affirm of these same Platonists, particularly Plotinus, that Christians are entirely in agreement with them: "Non est nobis ullus cum his excellentioribus philosophis in hac quaestione conflictus." (*De Civitate Dei,* X, 2.) He finds in Porphyrius "the shadow of a faint notion" of the final end, the Trinity, and even some notion of the necessity of grace, but not of the means of attaining the end, the redemptive incarnation (*De Civitate Dei,* X, 29, 1). Augustine's last words, as cited by Possidius (*PL,* XXXII, col. 58), are a literal quotation from Plotinus (*Enneads,* I, 4, 7, 23f.) of which the content is Stoic.

The influence of Stoicism was widespread, though often not recognized as such, and attributed to other sources, as modern research has revealed (Theiler, Hadot, Spanneut). Aristotle was mostly regarded as an adversary by Christian writers (for his denial of providence); cf. J. de Ghellinck in *RHE* 26 (1930), pp. 5–42. But important exceptions were made, as when the distinction between "substance" and "quality" (*Categories,* 6, 11a, 15) was adopted in the controversy with the Homoiousians (Athanasius, *De Synodo,* 53; Marius Victorinus, *Adversus Arium,* I, 20, 53), and when the concept of "relation" was applied to the persons of the Trinity (perhaps Alexander of Alexandria or his orthodox fellows, *PG,* XXVI, col. 709 c; esp. Augustine, *De Trin.,* V). Albert the Great and Thomas Aquinas then became disciples of Aristotle ("the philosopher"). Epicureanism, which denied the existence of the gods and the immortality of the soul, was unanimously rejected (as by Origen, for instance, *Contra Celsum,* I, 21), or simply ignored.

B. The Problems

1. The explicit testimonies of Christian writers to the pagans whom they name and quote are only a small part of what has to be investigated, though it has the advantage of being well defined. A much more extensive, complicated and far-reaching matter is, of course, the actual — unacknowledged — influence of the Greeks on Christianity. It is nearly always very difficult to estimate, since the manuals in which Hellenism was passed on are lost, or preserved only in fragments. Critical research has often nothing else to go upon when reconstructing these missing links except the authors who are dependent on them, so that the coefficient of uncertainty is high. But some general results may be considered as assured.

2. In general, the relationship of Hellenism to dogma poses three sets of questions: a) What are the topics which (i) tend to coincide with Christian dogmas, (ii) are incompatible with it, (iii) are represented only in the Bible and were developed solely by Christian theology? b) (i) Did the themes adopted by theology and dogma remain unaltered, or were they transposed and even given an opposite meaning? (ii) Did these transformations or novelties become part of the strictly philosophical thinking of the West, perhaps in a totally secularized form, and if so, under what aspects? (Cf. the able investigations of H. A. Armstrong, *An Introduction to Ancient Philosophy* [1947].) c) What were the reactions, conscious or unconscious, of orthodox theologians and the Councils, and again, of heretics, with regard to Hellenism, especially from the 2nd to the 4th century? The great heresies of the 5th century onward, and their opponents, paid far less attention to philosophy than to the tradition of the Fathers and the Councils. Here Chalcedon is typical.

3. To illustrate the effects and extent of this influence we propose the following four working hypotheses as guiding lines. (For a more precise enunciation of their nature and limits, and for detailed proofs, see P. Henry, *The Christian Idea of God and its Development* [1961].)

a) Some main themes of Hellenism, especially those of "Platonism", were naturally sympathetic to Christian thought: God, the soul and their mutual relations, especially in mysticism. In this sense Pascal was right in saying: "Platon pour disposer au christianisme." Under the pressure of the heresies, orthodox doctrine as elaborated by the theologians and confirmed in the Councils was "forced" (Athanasius, *Decreta Nicaeae,* 19; *Ad Afros,* 5–6; *De Synodis,* 45) to go beyond the affirmations of Scripture and use the terminology and even the ideological schemas of the suspect "Greeks", though the vocabulary is often restored to its pre-scientific meaning, as for instance in "one person in two natures". This gives us the right and the obligation to fill out

11

silences by analogy (cf. Marius Victorinus, *Adv. Arium*, II, 7, 12, "de lectis non lecta componere", a principle of Hellenistic law quoted by Cicero in the form "ex eo quod scriptum sit ad id quod non scriptum pervenire", *De Inventione*, II, 50, 152).

b) In the attempt to reach a rational synthesis of dogma, the slavish repetition of contemporary thought-forms was often the source of heresy. In this sense Tertullian was right in saying that Plato was the source of all heresies ("doleo Platonem omnium hereticorum condimentarium factum", *De Anima*, 23). The latent philosophy of a heresy makes it conformist; it tries to be conservative in theology and there is nothing revolutionary in its speculation.

c) Orthodoxy, on the other hand, while on principle avoiding philosophy, is in fact mostly original and creative. Under the pressure of biblical revelation and its frequently existential categories, themes derived from Hellenism were modified, corrected, completed and made more precise. Distinctions previously unknown were introduced, as for instance between "image" and "likeness", cf. Clement of Alexandria, *Strom.*, II, 22, 131, 5; Origen, *De Principiis*, III, 6, 1. Terms are given new meanings, as in "homoousios" and quite new but fundamental concepts are formed.

d) Such new creations often survived in the philosophy of the West, sometimes even in a secularized form. The most significant examples are the three allied concepts of creation, history and person, which are absent from Hellenism but make themselves heard in Scripture and were developed and systematized in Christian thought, especially by Augustine in his *Confessions, City of God* and *Trinity*. The common basis of the three concepts is the notion of freedom and creative power (implying uniqueness, irreversibility and so on; cf. P. Henry, *Augustine on Personality* [1960]).

C. FUNDAMENTAL PRINCIPLES OF THEOLOGICAL METHOD

1. *Reason and tradition.* It has been shown by C. Andresen in his *Logos und Nomos. Die Polemik des Kelsos wider das Christentum* (1955) that philosophers like Celsus, in spite of their prescinding from historical process in their religious philosophy, none-theless admitted the value of the argument from authority and antiquity. It appears in Augustine in the form: "Ad discendum necessario dupliciter ducimur, auctoritate atque ratione." Hence at least at this period the ideological atmosphere was less remote than is usually thought from biblical Christianity, with its basis in prophecy and history. Plotinus appeals to the *philosophia perennis* (*Enneads,* V, 1, 8; IV, 8, 1) and blames the Gnostics for "breaking with Greek antiquity" in order to be "innovators", whereby "they abandoned the truth" (II, 9, 6, 5–12).

2. *Allegory.* The parallels in the "allegorical" methods of exegesis between paganism, Judaism (in Philo and others), and biblical and patristic Christianity are hotly debated. The discussion is carried on mostly by three writers and centres on Origen. J. Pépin (*Mythe et Allégorie, Les origines grecques et les contestations judéo-chrétiennes* [1958]), while maintaining the "unquestionable originality of Christian allegory" (p. 479), stresses the borrowings from Greek allegory and the identity of method and accuses both Celsus and Origen of "inconsistency" (*ibid.,* p. 261). His thesis is radically rejected by H. de Lubac (*RSR* 46 [1959], pp. 1–43; cf. esp. *Histoire et Esprit* [1950]) who tries to show that the "spiritual" exegesis of the Fathers is of a totally different inspiration and orientation from pagan allegory. The intermediate position of J. Daniélou (*Origène* [1948]) is a distinction between patristic "typology" which is theologically valid and Jewish or Hellenistic "allegory" which is to a great extent untenable. Here one may well ask, with de Lubac (*op. cit.,* p. 34), whether this distinction "takes all the texts into account and corresponds to the terminology of the ancient writers", especially Origen.

Along with the "spiritual" exegesis of the Alexandrians and the "literal" exegesis of the Antiochenes, there existed a third trend, less widespread and hardly noticed by historians, which aimed at the literal sense and paid little or no attention to symbolism, but sought a metaphysical content in biblical expressions and categories, often doing violence to the sense. It is represented in particular by Marius Victorinus Afer in the first Latin commentaries which have survived on Gal, Phil and Eph (*PL,* VIII, cols. 1145–294).

D. Hellenism in Dogma and Theology

1. *The attributes of God.* In early Christian times there took place, even in philosophy, a profound alteration in the concept of God. New attributes are mentioned and the meaning of others is modified. Infinity as an attribute of God — not clearly affirmed in Scripture — was rejected by ancient philosophers, for whom the infinite, indeterminate and formless was essentially the material (ὕλη). Origen still maintained (*De Principiis,* II, 9, 1, undoubtedly a true rendering of the original Greek) that the divine power was not infinite, since otherwise it could not know itself. Philo, however, and perhaps his sources, then middle Platonism and Plotinus – for whom, however, the Absolute is rather potency than act (*Enneads,* IV, 4, 4; cf. III, 8, 10; V, 4, 2) — like Christian theology (cf. II above), considered God and the world of forms as infinite (cf. É. Gilson, "L'infinité divine chez St. Augustin", *Augustinus Magister,* I [1954], pp. 569–74; A. H. Armstrong, "Plotinus' Doctrine of the Infinite and Christian Thought", *Downside Review* 73 [1955], pp. 47–58). This is the basis of the doctrine of the divine incomprehensibility and the "negative" theology.

In Plato, the world of the divine was characterized as immutable, to distinguish it from the visible world subject to change, though even this was held to be eternal. This moderate dualism was retained in Christianity but completed by the concepts of divine freedom and creation. But immutability becomes so essential an attribute of God that in the Arian controversy the opposition of ἄτρεπτος - τρεπτός was used to distinguish creator and creature. And for Augustine, the main content of the concept of God was not "the Good" of Plato, the "Pure Thought" of Aristotle, the "One" of Plotinus or the *"Esse"* later suggested by Thomas, but immutability *(Sermo 7 in Exod 3:14).*

The allied attribute of eternity is stressed, as among the Greeks, but with the difference that a cyclic time as image of eternity is eliminated in favour of the linear time of history, which Christians contrast with the eternity of God (cf. Cullmann).

Philosophy knows — and this may be true of all "pagan" philosophy — only two categories of beings: those without beginning or end, eternal, and hence immutable, and those with beginning and end. Christianity took over this division but added a new category, that of beings and events, such as the created soul and the incarnation, which go "from beginning to beginning" and do not end. Gregory of Nyssa applies this category even to the vision of God (*In Canticum, hom.,* 8), where he supposes constant progress, on account of the infinity and incomprehensibility of God.

The attribute of omnipotence evolved slowly. In Scripture and the early creeds it meant primarily God as Lord of history, παντοκράτωρ, but gradually came to be used as an attribute of God's absolute being. The transition in Marius Victorinus (*Adv. Arium,* II, 3, 18) has been described by Hadot. Of the eight attributes enumerated by the Fourth Lateran Council (*D* 428), and given in fuller form by the First Vatican (*D* 1782), at least four were elaborated and defined under the influence of Hellenism, mediated to a great extent by Augustine, while two (omnipotence and eternity) were transposed from the plane of history to that of immutable essence, to some extent under the same influence.

The really new and central attribute is that of creator, unknown to classical antiquity and only implicit in Scripture, though not so remote from the Greek notion of demiurge as is usually supposed (cf. H. Wolfson; also H. Junker, "Die Chaosvorstellung Gen 1", *Mélanges Bibliques pour A. Robert* [1957], pp. 27–37). The clear and explicit notion of creation only developed slowly in the 3rd century (Denis of Rome, *D* 49f.; to some extent in Origen), with the three distinctive notes of freedom, *cum tempore* and *ex nihilo.* It was given full expression at Nicaea through the sharp opposition between γεννηθέντα and ποιηθέντα which Arius and the Greeks found unthinkable. Meanwhile, without undergoing any discernible influence from Christianity, Hellenism came "asymptotically" to a similar concept. Atticus (cf. Eusebius, *Praeparatio Evangelica,* XV, 6, fr. 4) gives a "fundamentalist" interpretation of Plato (*Timaeus,* 41b, etc.) which ascribes a beginning to the world without denying the eternity of matter (so too Plutarch, in Proclus, *Timaeus,* I, 381; II, 153). He affirms that the world will remain eternally, but by the will of God (cf. Justin, *Dialogue,* 5, 4), which is compared to the creative will of man. The monist tendencies of Plotinus, however, lead him to a position which is revolutionary even with regard to middle Platonism. Matter emanates from the Absolute (*Enneads,* IV, 8, 6, 21), necessarily and eternally, as the result of a gradual descent.

2. *The Trinity.* a) *The Nicene (Nicaea-Constantinople) Creed,* the confession of faith put before Alexander by Arius and the neo-Platonic schema of the "three chief hypostases" (*Enneads,* V, 1, title) are at one in affirming the strict oneness of God, a certain trinity of supreme principles and their being united by emanations or "processions", which are often described by the same words and prepositions, as for instance ἐκ. But the two Christian creeds always see these principles in their relation to the history of creation and salvation — in contrast to the "essentialist" *Quicumque* — and provide the whole confession of faith with temporal coefficients, affirming, for instance, that the Son created, became and remains incarnate and will come again. But in Platonism causality and "salvation" remain outside time. The conformist heresy of Arianism succeeded as little as Plato (*Timaeus,* 28 b) in distinguishing between πατήρ and ποιητής, or as Plotinus in distinguishing between γεννάομαι and γίγνομαι. It applied slavishly the scheme of descending degrees of causality to Father, Son and Holy Spirit. Orthodox thought worked out a hitherto undreamt-of distinction and rejected such inequalities (between the divine persons).

The key-word of Nicaea, ὁμοούσιος, does not come from Plato, Aristotle, the Stoics or from middle Platonism or neo-Platonism, but from the great adversaries of "Greeks" and Christians, the Gnostics, who used it to describe the generation of the first natures. It was rejected by Arius as Manichaean and materialist. According to Basil of Ancyra (cf. G. L. Prestige, *God in Patristic Thought* [1936], pp. 209–9; Athanasius [*De Synodis,* 41–45], Basil [*Ep.,* 52], Hilary [*De Synodis,* 77–84], Marius Victorinus [*Adv. Arium,* I, 28 f., II, 10]), an attempt was made at Antioch to give a Platonizing interpretation ("substantiam praeexistere et sic ex ipsa patrem et filium esse", cited by Victor, *op. cit.,* I, 29, 10), but it was rejected by both parties. In spite of all these dangers, the term was adopted at Nicaea.

A third novelty appears during the quest for an analogy which would help to formulate and explain the divine processions. The fundamental analogy ceased to be the production of the world "outside God", which had occasioned pre-Nicaean subordinationism, and became the spiritual processes in the mind of man himself. This explanation, which had been begun by the Greek Fathers and sketched by Marius Victorinus ("esse — vivere — intelligere") was given its classical expression in the psychological theories of Augustine (*De Trin.,* VIII–XV), which took several forms. The Logos, primarily directed *ad extra* even in the prologue of St. John (מֵימְרָא, λόγος προφορικός) is now seen as primarily God's self-expression for himself, and the Holy Spirit the perfect unity (through consciousness or love) of the immanent life of the Trinity (cf. Augustine, *De diversis quaestionibus,* 63; *PL,* XL, col. 54).

b) *The Logos* is also the site of the forms, the archetypes of this world; all the exemplarism of the order of being and knowledge stems from the Logos. From Plato to Augustine the development went in two stages. The first transferred the forms, against Plato but along with Platonism, into the νοῦς and identified the demiurge with his creative forms. This was as early as Posidonius, but remained a debated point among the "Platonists" for a long time (cf. Porphyrius, *Vita Plotini,* 18, 10–19). The notion was taken up by Christians, who were alone in taking it a stage further. Since the Logos is of the same substance as the Father, the forms are in the Absolute itself, in the first order of existence, while in philosophy they remain in the "second God". But Christians avoided speaking of the forms as being in the Father, though the Son was in the Father (cf. Origen, *In Jo.,* I, 22).

c) *The Holy Spirit.* Explicit reflection started later (about 360) and the influence of Hellenism is at once noticeable, though less strong than in the doctrine of the Logos. One instance will suffice. When attempting to express "in accordance with Scripture, the concepts by which the Spirit is to be described" (*De Spiritu Sancto,* 9), Basil has recourse almost exclusively to terms used by Plotinus (*Enneads,* I, 6; V, 1; VI, 9), which he also uses in *Hom.* XV, *De fide* and elsewhere. And a short treatise *De Spiritu* (*PG,* XXIX, cols. 768–73), probably by Basil but certainly from his time, is so much a mosaic of texts from Plotinus that it can be used to restore the text of Plotinus himself. But Basil is quite clear (*De Spiritu Sancto,* 16, 38) on what separates him from the doctrine of the "three hypostases" (*Enneads,* V, 1, title).

3. *Christology.* The system of Apollinaris, which is known from fragments and pseud-epigrapha, is perhaps the most profound and consistent effort ever made by the East to come to grips with the psychological problems of Christology. It was a sort of Kenosis-theory in reverse. It was also the most thoroughly penetrated by contemporary thought, which, however, Apollinaris had not thought out creatively enough. His "metaphysical" exegesis of the ὁμοίωμα (Phil 2:7) is already a piece of Platonizing, emphasizing, in contrast to Paul (Rom 1:23; 5:14; 6:5; 8:3), the formal dissimilarity and inferiority. Like Arius, who used the same philosophic intuition as the basis of the contrary heresy, he pushed the scheme of the Logos-Sarx, which was latent in Alexandria and even in Antioch, to the utmost extremes, and applied the Platonizing Stoic vitalism, according to which man is "a spirit in a body", with absolute rigour, to the incarnation of the Logos.

4. *Christian anthropology.* a) *The immortality of the soul.* Here again Plato is an ally of Christianity, though a dangerous one. Like all the Platonists, Origen accepted too slavishly the pre-existence of the soul — whereby the existence of a rational soul in Christ appeared in Origen in a heretical context. To explain man's final destiny, he transformed the Stoic doctrine of the final conflagration of the universe into his theory of the apocatastasis, thus undermining the authentic freedom which he defended so vigorously elsewhere. Orthodox Christian thought corrected Platonism on two points. It affirmed that souls had a beginning, and that according to Christian revelation survival is that of the whole man, soul and body, partaking through grace of the true life which is God.

b) *Grace and mystical union.* Here it will suffice to recall briefly the profound influence of neo-Platonism on Christian mysticism. Without citing Plotinus, Gregory of Nyssa (*De Virginitate,* 10; *PG,* XLVI, cols. 361 D – 372 C), took his whole vocabulary from two mystical treatises of Plotinus (*Enneads,* I, 6; VI, 9). So too Augustine, when describing the famous vision at Ostia, uses structures and terms from Plotinus (*Conf.,* IX, 10, 23–26) and quotes (*ibid.,* 25) a sentence from the *Enneads* (V, 1, 2, 14–17). But just as the "dark night of the soul", a classic theme from Gregory of Nyssa to John of the Cross, was unknown to Plotinus, so too Augustine departs from Plotinus on two essential points. The Enneads (I, 6, 9, 23–24) call on man "to have confidence in himself and fix his gaze (on the One) with help from no one". Augustine, inspired by this page of Plotinus (*Conf.,* VII, 10, 16 — "inde admonitus"), contradicts his source explicitly and takes his stand on the doctrine of the necessity of grace: "et potui quoniam factus es adiutor meus" (cf. Ps 29:11). Further, though Augustine is clearly neo-Platonic in his theory of mystical experience, he differs from most mystics in allowing scarcely any place to the theology of negations (cf. V. Lossky, "Les éléments de théologie négative dans la pensée de St. Augustin", *Augustinus Magister,* II [1954], pp. 575–81). This is again a proof of the independence which was possible because his thinking was dominated by the central dogma of Christianity, the incarnation of the Son of God.

See also *Revelation, Dogma, Apologists, Occident, Antiochene School of Theology, Alexandrian School of Theology, Arianism.*

BIBLIOGRAPHY. L. Laberthonnière, *L'idéalisme grec et le réalisme chrétien* (1904); P. Henry, "Kènose", *DBS,* I, cols. 65–75; R. Arnou (Platonism of the Fathers), *DTC,* XII, cols. 2258–392; P. Camelot (Clement of Alexandria and Greek philosophy), *RSR* 21 (1931), pp. 541–69; W. Theiler, *Porphyrius und Augustin* (1933); P. Henry, *Plotin et l'Occident* (1934); E. Hoffmann, *Platonismus und Mystik im Altertum* (1935); M. Richard ("Hypostasis" in the theology of the incarnation), *Mélanges de Science Religieuse* 2 (1945), pp. 5–32, 243–70; id. (Athanasius and the psychology of Christ), *ibid.* 4 (1947), pp. 5–54; E. von Ivánka, *Hellenistisches und Christliches im frühbyzantinischen Geistesleben* (1948); P. Hadot, "Typus, Stoïcisme et monarchianisme au IVᵉ siècle", *Recherches de Théologie Ancienne et Médiévale* 18 (1951), pp. 177–87; W. Kamlah, *Christentum und Geschichtlichkeit* (2nd ed., 1951); T. Boman, *Das hebräische Denken im Vergleich mit dem Griechischen* (1952); C. Andresen, "Justin und der mittlere Platonismus", *Zeitschrift für die neutestamentliche Wissenschaft* 44 (1953), pp. 157–95; P. Hadot, "Epistrophè et Metanoia", *Actes du XIᵉ Congrès international de Philosophie* (1953), pp. 31–36; H. A. Wolfson, *The Philosophy of the Church Fathers* (1956); A. Fox, *Plato and the Christians* (1957); H. J. Waszink, *Platonismus und antikirchliche Gedankenwelt,* Entretiens Hardt 3 (1957), pp. 137–79; M. Spanneut, *Le stoïcisme des Pères de l'Église de Clément de Rome à Clément d'Alexandrie* (1957); H. Rahner, *Griechische Mythen in christlicher Deutung* (2nd ed., 1957); E. F. Osborn, *The Philosophy of Clement of Alexandria* (1957); A. H. Armstrong, "Salvation, Plotinian and Christian", *Downside Review* 75 (1957), pp. 126–39; Marius Victorinus, *Ecrits théologiques,* ed. by P. Henry, with intro. and notes by P. Hadot, 2 vols. (1960); J. Barr, *Semantics of Biblical Language* (1961); J. Daniélou, *Message évangélique et culture hellénique* (1961); A. Momigliano, *Conflict between Paganism and Christianity in the Fourth Century* (1963); J. Pépin, *Théologie cosmique et théologie chrétienne* (Ambroise) (1964); O. Cullmann, *Christ and Time* (new ed., 1964); W. Beierwaltes, *Proklos, Grundzüge seiner Metaphysik* (1965); H. Jonas, *Gnosis und spätantiker Geist,* I (1934; 3rd ed., 1964), II/1 (1954; 2nd ed., 1966).

Paul Henry

HERESY

I. Concept. II. History of Heresies.

I. Concept

1. *In the Bible.* The Bible does not always use the word αἵρεσις, αἱρετικός (from αἱρέομαι, choose) in the same sense. It can stand for the choice of a certain doctrine which puts forth claims to authority, which is the Greek sense of the word (Herodotus, *History,* IV, 1), and is thus used of the Sadducees in Acts 5:17, for the Pharisees in Acts 15:5 and 26:5 and of the Christian community (by the Jews) in Acts 24:5, 14 and 28:22. But the word is also applied to a heretical doctrine which is a departure from that of the Church. But this last usage again is not yet clear in St. Paul. In 1 Cor 11:19 he uses αἵρεσις in the same sense as σχίσμα to designate a division in the Church of Corinth, but without making it clear whether there is a religious cleavage, or whether it is merely a lack of discipline and self-control among individual members of the Church. Gal 5:20 includes heresies among the works of the flesh. In Tit 3:10 there is a warning against a "heretic" (αἱρετικός), who is to be avoided if he does not reform after one or two warnings. But it is not clear what is meant by "heretic" here. In 2 Pet 2:1, the αἵρεσις means the activity of teachers who introduce false and harmful doctrine and deny the Lord. But no precise heresies are described.

Nevertheless, 2 Pet already uses the word heresy to indicate a departure from Christian teaching, and this is the sense of the word which was to become predominant in the course of history.

2. *In Church history.* The early Church, after 2 Pet 2:1, used the word heresy in the sense of a departure from the doctrine of the Lord as preached by the apostles (*Didache,* 8; *Barnabas,* 9, 4). The Fathers warn against the dangers of heresy which represents a departure from Christian truth. Thus Ignatius of Antioch warns the Trallians against Docetism (*Ad Trallenses,* 6, 1). He congratulates the Church of Ephesus on having no room for heresies, since Christ himself had taught it the truth (*Ad Ephesios,* 6, 2). Irenaeus of Lyons describes a heretic as one who falsifies the word of God (*Adv. Haer.,* I, 1, 1). The heretic prefers his own personal views to the word of God (*ibid.,* III, 12, 11f.). To remain in the truth, the Christian must follow the doctrine of the apostles and the preaching of the Church (*ibid.,* III, 12, 13). Cyprian affirms that to preserve the true faith it is necessary to live in the unity of the Church (*De Unitate*). According to Ambrose, heretics are enemies of the truth and opponents of the true faith (Sermon 13, on Ps 118).

From the very beginning, heresy was regarded as a grave crime in the ancient Church, because it meant falling away from the unity of the Church's faith. Those who fell into heresy were regarded as public sinners, and the full severity of ecclesiastical penance was meted out to them (Innocent I, *Epistle,* 14, 4, 8; Augustine, *Epistle,* 93, 53; Synod of Elvira, can 51; Synod of Laodicaea, can. 6, 7, 31). Falling into heresy was not punished by perpetual exclusion from the Church. The principle was rather that repentant heretics should be received back into the Church. Only Tertullian rejects the possibility of pardon and reconciliation for heretics. But this rigorism was an innovation, a breach with the normal practice of the Church.

Since to fall into heresy was considered as one of the gravest of sins, heretics could only be received back into the Church through the normal channels of penance: they were restored to membership of the Church by the imposition of hands, mostly after a long period of penance. Those who had themselves re-baptized in a heretical group were received back after a more severe penance (Felix III, *Epistle,* 7, 1; Innocent I, *Epistle,* 2, 8, 11). Bishops, priests and deacons who had themselves re-baptized in heresy had to do penance for the rest of their lives and only received Communion, as administered to lay people, on their death-beds (Felix III, *Epistle,* 7, 2). The re-baptized could not become clerics (*ibid.;* Augustine, *De Baptismo,* 1, 12, 20). The penance decreed by Felix for those who had been re-baptized was that they should lose their rights of full membership of the Church for three years, during which they were treated as catechumens; for seven years they remained in the class of penitents, while at each liturgical service the priest imposed hands upon them; for two further years they were excluded from the offertory procession, that is, from the eucharistic table. This is a typical instance of the severity with which the ancient Church viewed heresy. When the Roman emperors had been converted, the State began to use force against heretics (cf. *Code of Theodosius,* I, XVI, titulus 5, "De Haereticis").

While those who fell into heresy were submitted to the penitential discipline of the Church, those who came to the Church after being born in heresy were treated differently. Since there was no personal guilt (Augustine, *Epistle,* 43, 1; *De Baptismo,* 5, 23, 33), they were received into the Church by the imposition of hands, without any penance.

The *Pontificale Romanum* contains a rite for the reconciliation of heretics. The rite first appears in the Pontifical of Durandus, Bishop of Mende (d. 1292), but it is based on earlier texts of various types. The most important elements in the rite are the leading into the Church, the profession of faith, the invocation of the Holy Spirit and the imposition of hands. The Gallican rite contained an anointing with chrism (Gregory of Tours, *History of the Franks,* II, 31, 34) which betrays Eastern influence (cf. First Council of Constantinople, can. 7; Second Council in Trullo, can. 95). This rite shows how problematical it was felt that the sacrament of confirmation, received in heresy, should impart the Holy Spirit. According to the Fathers, the Holy Spirit is so intimately united with the Church that outside the Church, in a heretical group, no transmission of the Spirit was possible.

3. *In canon law.* According to the present law, a baptized person is a heretic if while retaining the name of Christian he contumaciously denies or doubts a truth which ought to be accepted by virtue of divine or Catholic faith. The heretic does not abandon the whole truth or a fundamental truth of the Christian faith, in contrast to the apostate (cf. can. 1325, para. 2). According to this definition, the crime of heresy comprises three elements. First, only a baptized person can be a heretic. Those who are not baptized and hence are not persons in the Church of Jesus Christ cannot be heretics (can. 87). The existence of heresy depends on error or doubt with regard to revealed truth. Can. 1323, para. 1, defines the meaning of "fides divina et catholica": all truths which are contained in sacred Scripture and in tradition, and which have been proposed to the belief of the faithful by the Church, as revealed truths, either by the ordinary magisterium or by a solemn definition. The existence of heresy also depends on the contumacious will to remain in error or doubt. Error or doubt alone would not constitute heresy, for which *error voluntarius* is required (Thomas Aquinas, *Summa Theologica,* II, II, q. 11, a. 1). Hence there must be the free and deliberate will to reject a truth proclaimed by the Church, in spite of its being known. The ecclesiastical penalty for heresy is only incurred when contumacy in error or doubt is expressed externally, by words or signs. Inward denial of the truth is a grave sin against the faith (2 Pet 2:17; Jas 2:12 ff.). Along with the penalty of excommunication laid down in can. 2314, the heretic suffers further notable restrictions on his rights of membership (can. 167, para. 1, no. 4; 188, no. 4; 542, no. 1; 646, para. 1, no. 1; 731, para. 2; 765, no. 2; 795, no. 2; 985, no. 1; 1060; 1240, para. 1, no. 1; 1453, para. 1; 1470, para. 1, no. 6; 1657, para. 1). The absolution from the excommunication in the inner forum is reserved in a special way to the Holy See, in the outward forum to the Ordinary (can. 2314, para. 2).

The distinction between those who were culpably outside the doctrinal fold of the Church and those who adhered inculpably to false doctrine was already familiar to the ancient Church (see Augustine, above). The principle of penal law, "nulla poena sine culpa", had to be applied to those who did not accept fully, but without deliberate contumacy, the truths which should be accepted by virtue of divine or Catholic faith. Thus the Church distinguishes between material and formal heresy or heretics. Material heresy is a denial of the truth which is not deliberate and conscious. There can be no contumacious adherence to an error in faith where a Christian, baptized outside the Catholic Church, has no knowledge and understanding of the doctrine of the Church. It is to be assumed, as experience teaches, that in the case of Christians living in a community separated from the Catholic Church there is no contumacy. Hence the Ecumenical Directory (14 May 1967, no. 19) points out that non-Catholic Christians who come to the Catholic Church as converts are not subject to the penalties mentioned in can. 2314. Hence there is no need to absolve them from excommunication. After their profession of faith, they should be at once admitted into the full communion of the Catholic Church, according to a rite laid down by the local ordinary. The provisions of can. 2314 hold good only for those who have culpably separated themselves from the Catholic faith and the Catholic fellowship.

Vatican II avoided completely the words heresy and heretic. The decrees speak only of separated non-Catholic Christians or of separated brothers. In view of the *Directorium Oecumenicum* it may be assumed that the notion of heresy and heretic have changed since Vatican II. The view upheld by Augustine that those who are born (Christians) outside the Catholic Church are not to be spoken of as heretics seems to be prevailing once more. Hence the only heretics would be those who deliberately departed from the doctrine of the Church of Jesus Christ, and these would then be subject to the penalties of canon law.

See also *Docetism, Council, Constantinian Era, Baptism* I, *Penance* II.

BIBLIOGRAPHY. A. Michel in *DTC,* VI, cols. 2207–57; H. Schlier, "αἵρεσις", *TWNT,* I, pp. 180–4; A. Lang, "Der Bedeutungswandel der Begriffe 'fides' und 'haeresis' und die dogmatische Wertung der Konzilsentscheidungen von Vienne und Trient", *Münchener Theologische Zeitschrift* 4 (1953), pp. 133–46; E. Wolf, G. E. Hartlaub and H. Köster in *RGG,* III, cols. 13–21; H. Heinemann, *Die rechtliche Stellung der nicht-katholischen Christen und ihre Wiederversöhnung mit der Kirche* (1964).

Heribert Heinemann

II. History of Heresies

1. *Basic considerations.* a) The history of heresies is to a large extent parallel to the history of dogma. Most of what has to be said about it is in substance said in the history of dogma. It can therefore be regarded as historical writing about the historical course, doctrinal content and historical effects of heresy, and this historical writing in turn has its own history. It can, however, mean the actual course of the heresies themselves. If the word is used in this second sense, the question immediately arises whether, how and from what points of view this series of heresies can be conceived as one single history with an at least to some extent recognizable structure. If we recall that the history of dogma and the history of heresies are mutually dependent, it immediately becomes clear that this question is identical in the concrete with the similar question which arises in the history of dogma. The history of heresies is the critical and threatening factor in the history of dogma, its merely human side.

b) The real theological problem of a history of heresies is only apparent, however, when the ambiguous nature of heresy is taken into account. In the first place it is difficult to draw a precise dividing line between heresy and the complete denial of Christianity (apostasy). Heresy is defined as false doctrine, rejected by the Church and declared to exclude from the Church, held by baptized persons within "Christian" doctrine ("retento nomine christiano"). On that basis one cannot clearly determine what belongs to a history of heresies and what does not. All the more so because even an apparently totally unchristian ideology (within the domain formerly occupied by Christianity) has not really succeeded, since the coming of modern times or in the post-Christian era, in being anything but the heretical and at the same time secularized counterpart to the Christian understanding of the world and of man. It can of course remain an open question whether that must be so and whether it will remain so. Leaving aside the distinction between heresy and apostasy, it is also possible to lay down that heresy is present when a doctrine meets with definitive rejection by the Christian magisterium. This appears readily to determine the subject-matter of the history of heresies. But then two things have to be taken into consideration and they once more complicate the problem of the history of heresies.

(i) A serious and historically influential heresy has a long prehistory and history in the history of the theology and dogma of the Church itself before it is rejected by the magisterium and leads to schism on the part of the heretics. And this prehistory and history of the heresy within the Church will always or almost always be intelligible only as a (humanly speaking) unavoidable crisis of growth in the development of the history of dogma and in awareness of the faith in the Church itself. As a consequence, often the most tragic and guilty element in this history consists in its moving out of the Church's unity and its history of faith, and becoming isolated in ecclesiastical bodies of its own. This may come about through the heretical, schismatical impatience of those immediately involved, or through a justified but to some extent impatient reaction on the part of the teaching Church. For this history, in spite of its onesidedness and problematical questionings, should really attain its proper goal, namely a real growth in the *intellectus fidei,* within the Church. The positive function of heresy for the Church and its growth in the faith does not entirely come to an end for the Church if after mutual anathema the heresy accomplishes its history outside the Church. Now if all this is taken into account, a Catholic theological history of heresies (not one simply designed as a history of ideas) cannot regard that history as anything but a part of the history of dogma, treated separately for convenience. Otherwise such a historical account would miss the real nature, origin and significance of heresy in sacred history. This is particularly clear if we remember that God-given faith can never regard itself as merely in antithesis to a human error. It must see itself as the higher, more comprehensive truth, against a part of which an error shuts itself off by "selecting" (heretically) and "separating" (schismatically). Moreover, the historical influence of a heresy is never explained by the error as such (as a firmly held negation), but by the truth contained in the error, though onesidedly stressed. The Church has reason to confront its own full truth with the partial truth which is showing itself in a historically influential way in the heresy.

(ii) It is self-evident to a Catholic under-standing of the faith that "in itself", i.e., for man in general (and so — realizing this abstract norm — for many individual men), the Catholic Church is recognizable in actual fact as the bearer of the one complete truth of Christian revelation. This does not mean, however, that that is evident to all men and for all Christians, when their actual historical and individual circumstances and limited span of life are taken into account. By "recognizable" here we are not referring only to a quality in the reality itself but are taking into account that the knowing subject's own characteristics contribute to constitute the reality known. For to be recognizable means to be recognizable by someone. To deny this would imply that no one without grave subjective guilt could fail to find the Catholic Church by the end of his life. But that is certainly an assertion which on a variety of grounds is absolutely to be rejected. A man's inculpable failure to attain a moral goal which in itself is binding demonstrates the impossibility of its attainment for the man in question, even if that impossibility is attributable to the subjective guilt of others, e.g., the first heresiarchs (though their guilt also is ultimately impossible to establish), and in this respect may be merely "permitted" by God. Even so a positive salvific meaning can be acknowledged in this impossibility of recognizing the Church permitted by God in an innocent person, without thereby contesting the importance for salvation of the unrecognized truth or denying that it is recognizable in itself. To some extent it is possible to understand the positive meaning for salvation, under God's providence, of this particular unrecognizability. Having regard for the "hierarchy of truths" in Catholic teaching which "vary in their relationship to the foundation of the Christian faith" (Vatican II, Decree on Ecumenism, art. 11), it is clear that certain human beings (by their general historical and psychological make-up) more easily succeed in fact (not *per se*) in grasping the most central doctrines important for salvation when they are not confronted with the whole of explicit Catholic Christianity. From this point of view, however, the history of heresies assumes yet another quite different aspect, provided it is not regarded simply as a history of ideas. The formal rejection of a Catholic truth as such cannot be approved, but in most cases it can be presumed to be only objectively erroneous, not subjectively guilty. When it lives on in the history of heresy, it embraces the various individual and collective forms in which *genuine* Christianity finds realization. This is analogous to the way in which various mixed forms of *fides explicita* and *fides implicita* arise as modes of the Catholic faith, even within Catholic orthodoxy, which vary widely when compared with the *per se* valid doctrinal system of Catholic Christianity. Thus the history of heresies becomes once again, in its historically important manifestations, an element in the history of dogma within the Catholic Church, showing what shifts of emphasis in concrete personal attitude and degrees of realization are possible in relation to the manifold reality presented by faith. In fact, of course, it is not very difficult to match the various heresies (particularly if envisaged from the point of view we have just described) with homologous structures within the Catholic Church (e.g., an orthodox Christology can be indicated which is akin to Nestorianism or to Monophysitism, and so on).

c) It is therefore clear that the history of heresies is best dealt with in the context of the history of dogma itself. There it has the positive significance of throwing light on dogma in its actual history both as regards its content and the actual religious and personal attitude adopted to it in the concrete. Insofar as a structure can and must be discerned in the history of heresies (which cannot be deduced *a priori,* yet is not a mere enumeration of errors), this structure and its principle are those of the history of dogma.

Furthermore, certain formal aspects can be seen to recur constantly in the history of heresies. One feature of heresy is that the whole of Christianity is still virtually contained in it, or in its whole conception of Christianity. On this basis the idea of a purely verbal heresy might be formed (cf., for example, certain forms of Monophysitism). This is in fact an erroneous non-conformity with the linguistic usage of the Church. It is really schismatic, linked with sectarian distrust that in the language of the great Church, genuine Christianity may not find plain and unmistakable expression. It is also quite conceivable that in the course of its history a real heresy may, unwittingly, work itself back into a purely verbal one. Then, because doctrine and practice go together, there is

another important aspect. (The patristic theology could not take it into account, because of the short period during which heresies had existed.) The possibility has always to be borne in mind that within the history of a heresy as a historically developing non-Catholic denomination there can be forms of Christianity in teaching and practice which are indeed always preserved and present potentially in the Catholic, i.e., true, comprehensive and historically legitimate form of Christianity, but which have not yet reached there the same explicit level of realization. These can form a stimulus to the development of doctrine and practice in the Church itself.

In this way they can exercise a positive function in redemptive history in relation to the Church. According to Paul, heresy comes under the principle of something which "must be" in redemptive history. Man's at least objective guilt in diminishing and narrowing God's truth remains comprised within the will of God for his revelation and its bearer the Church. And from this fact (which does not legitimate it as a human act) heresy receives a positive meaning which it has not in itself. It is the way in which God's truth, to the extent that it is man's truth, remains subject to lowliness and in fact grows in the mind of men as the "inevitable" basis of leading the Church into all truth. In that way it assumes a position in relation to the saving history of believed and known truth analogous to that of Israel in relation to the Church (Rom 9–11). Consequently it is not true that in face of heresies the Church merely statically defends truths which it has already grasped adequately. The Church learns to know more clearly its own truth by hearing and rejecting contradiction of its own truth and of its growing self-understanding.

A further aspect, however, is that the history of truth and its development (the development of dogma) is the history of discernment. It is the progressive, fuller and clearer rejection of heresy by the Church, the necessary discernment of spirits, the initial stage of God's judgment which sifts the truth and the error of men. The Church's judgment, however, concerns the historical expression of man's attitude to truth (an expression always ambiguous as regards the interior faith), and not the attitude itself and hence not man. In accordance with the genuinely historical character of the knowledge of truth even in the Church, and the dependence of the Church, in its struggle, on God's unforeseeable designs (cf. Lk 21:14), a genuinely *a priori* (not purely formalistic) outline of possible heresies, a corresponding anticipatory sketch-plan of the history of heresies and an unambiguous *a priori* exposition of the history of heresies which have already occurred (in the style of Hegel's philosophy of history) are not possible. That does not mean, however, that the history of heresies is simply an arbitrary list of contradictions of the various articles of the faith. It is also to a large extent a function of the general history of ideas (and their political and social presuppositions) the structural pattern of which is to some extent intelligible. Heresies, therefore, are almost always to be understood as views of the truth from a certain angle, which are given a falsely radical character and then "split off". They are formally comparable to the different theological schools within the Church, which even in their plurality, have a lasting function in the Church and its theology and to some extent an indispensable place in the whole. Furthermore, there are certain fundamental formal heresies which are continually recurring in concrete cases (e.g., the denial of the analogy of being; of the Chalcedonian principle of "without mixture, without separation"; of the principle of the incompleteness of all human intellectual systems in face of the "ever greater God" [cf. *D* 432]; of the analogy of faith, etc.).

These and similar points of view fully permit us to go beyond a merely positivist inventory type of history of heresies. Though the question of the most appropriate terminology remains open, it must be admitted that even within the Church and for considerable periods of time there can be tendencies, attitudes, emphases, etc., perhaps in theory, but above all in spontaneous practice, which can only be characterized as latent, inarticulate but real heresies or, as leanings to heresy (cf. the theological note: *sapit haeresim*). Such latent heresies and heretical leanings should really form part of the history of heresies, especially as they may generate similar or opposed heresies of an explicit kind. However plainly the history of theological schools within the Church is to be distinguished from that of heresies, the homology of their history with the history of heresies should be noted,

because important insights follow from it for both.

2. *Some pointers on the history of heresies.* a) *Principles of arrangement of the history of heresies.* As stated above, the really theological principles of structure are those of the history of dogma, but negatively applied. They need not, therefore, be repeated here. The specific ways in which heresies accompany the movement of dogma (retarding or accelerating it) can perhaps, however, be formally distinguished, though in the same heresy several such modes may be simultaneously at work. There are "reactionary" heresies which shut themselves off from a historically necessary development in the Church and its teaching (so for example Montanism or Novatianism, which wrongly wished to retain systematically a severer previous practice of penance; an Augustinianism which was given a heretically absolute status in Jansenism and Baianism). There are heresies by "reduction", which seek either to give Christianity an existentially radical character or to relieve it of doctrines that are "not modern", by restricting it to doctrines declared to be the only important ones. A heresy by radical reduction was the older Protestantism with its triple "sola" *(scriptura, gratia, fides)*, "Fundamentalism", heretical existentialist demythologizing, modernism, etc., seek to relieve Christianity of unwelcome burdens. There are (as has already been noted) verbal heresies which think they cannot recognize their faith in a particular ecclesial formulation, although they in fact say the same thing or advocate an interpretation of an article of faith which is tenable inside the Church (e.g., certain forms of Monophysitism). We might also speak of "contact heresies", i.e., attempts to assimilate non-Christian ideologies into Christian doctrine or to subordinate the latter to the former (e.g., the phantom heresy of Americanism). If we extend to some degree the concept of heresy, there is cryptogamic heresy (K. Rahner, *On Heresy,* Quaestiones Disputatae 11 [1964]), i.e., what is in fact a heretical attitude inside and outside the Church consciously or unconsciously evades reflection and conceptual formulation. Not every heresy in its history or in its doctrine leads to the formation of a Church, although many have done so. It is therefore possible to distinguish between Church-forming and

non-Church-forming heresies. The latter are usually called "particular" heresies, because they concern a single particular point of doctrine. Church-forming heresies usually start (explicitly) from some particular heresy but generally develop into a fundamental conception which colours their understanding of Christianity as a whole. They become "universal" heresies.

If we remember that a true statement about God must always concede that God is greater than can be directly stated in analogous mundane terms, i.e., that any statement about God must be a dialectical one and cannot say anything positive which, taken by itself, could serve as an adequate principle of deduction for all other statements in that domain, we see that there can also be "anti-dialectical", systematically one-directional heresies. One of these was Predestinarianism and another Pelagianism, in the question of sovereign grace and human freedom. On the frontier of mere heresy, or already beyond it, are "secularizing" heresies, which retain more or less some formal structures of Christianity and of its doctrine, but transpose them into attitudes and doctrines which are secular, i.e., without relation to God. This is to forget that such formal structures ultimately wither away if deprived of their real historical manifestation and concrete embodiment (which was and is Christian). Many forms of modern humanism are secularizing heresies of this kind.

b) *On the history of heresies*. Obviously not all particular heresies are to be listed here, nor is it a question of a precise distinction between heresies and totally anti-Christian doctrinal systems and philosophies (within the limits of the historical domain influenced by Christianity). (i) At the beginning stands the reactionary heresy of Judaism (which Paul was the first to combat); this was a denial that Christianity should be detached from the religious situation in which it appeared. The extreme contrary of this is found in Marcion with his denial of any continuity between saving history in the Old and New Testament. (ii) The great heresies of the 2nd to 4th centuries, Gnosticism and Arianism, were contact heresies, which endeavoured to fit Christianity into existing mental perspectives. In the panentheistic view of the God-world relationship common in Hellenism, the history of the created world becomes the history of a God who lives through his destiny in a dualistic world (Gnosticism), and the self-communication of the absolute God to created history distinct from him becomes the communication of lesser principles, only half-divine (Arianism: the Logos and the Pneuma are not really God himself). (iii) The Christological heresies of the 5th century (Nestorianism, Monophysitism, Monotheletism) were primarily particular and anti-dialectical heresies which tried to systematize onesidedly the mystery of the relation between world and God, either rationalistically (Nestorianism) or undialectically in a mystical philosophy of identity. (iv) Pelagianism (5th century) and Predestinarianism (5th, 8th centuries; Calvinism) were likewise anti-dialectical heresies, at first particular ones, which in the grace–freedom relation attempted to dissolve the mystery in favour of one of the two poles. (v) As Protestantism has no unified, closed doctrinal system, but exhibits very many radically divergent ones, what they have in common might perhaps best be described as a universal reduction-heresy. Either, as in early Protestantism in particular, a reduction to the threefold *sola (scriptura, gratia, fides)* is undertaken so that everything else becomes unessential to Christianity, or is felt to be radically opposed to it. Or else other elements are rejected as unessential, especially those concerning the constitution of the Church (episcopacy, papacy, sacraments). (vi) Other forms of reduction-heresy are Modernism and the many forms of Protestant liberal theology: Christianity is reduced to the interpretation of man's experience of himself.

c) *The formal basic structure of the possibility of heresy*. Although the historical order of heresies cannot be deduced, all heresies can be understood as the possible ways of deforming the mysterious fundamental relation between God and world which can only be stated dialectically and can never be comprised in a single formula. Either the true reality of the creature disappears (the human reality of Christ, human freedom, the significance of ministry in the Church, etc.), in face of the sole causality of God, or the reality proper to the creature is deistically misconceived as independent (e.g., in Nestorianism or Pelagianism), so that God in the ultimate resort becomes the radiance of man himself as absolute (as in Modernism).

See also *Dogma* III, *Heresy* I, *Apostasy, Theology* II, *Schism, Arianism, Gnosticism, Monophysitism, Predestination, Calvinism, Protestantism, Modernism.*

BIBLIOGRAPHY. See bibliography on *Dogma* III and on the other related articles mentioned above; also: F. Oehler, *Corpus Haeresiologicum,* 3 vols. (1856–61); J. E. Rahmani, *Documenta de antiquis haeresibus* (1909); A. S. Turberville, *Medieval Heresy and the Inquisition* (1920); L. Cozens, *A Handbook of Heresies* (1945); M. Menéndez Pelayo, *Historia de los heterodoxos españoles,* 8 vols. (1946–47); R. A. Knox, *Enthusiasm* (1950); H. E. W. Turner, *The Pattern of Christian Truth. A Study in the Relations between Orthodoxy and Heresy in the Early Church* (1954); G. L. Prestige, *Fathers and Heretics* (1954); G. Isely, *Chrétiens, sectaires et mécréants* (1954); J. W. C. Wand, *The Four Great Heresies* (1955); L. Cristiani, *Brève histoire des hérésies* (1956); H. Grundmann, *Ketzergeschichte des Mittelalters* (1963); H. Hilgenfeld, *Ketzergeschichte des Urchristentums urkundlich dargestellt* (1884; reprint, 1963); W. Bauer, *Rechtgläubigkeit und Ketzerei im ältesten Christentum* (1934; 2nd ed., 1964); K. Rahner, *Theological Investigations,* V (1965).

Karl Rahner

HERMENEUTICS

A. The Notion and Problem of Understanding

Hermeneutics is an aid to the *understanding* of something which is not — as in matters which are to be "explained" — indifferent and external to the mind, but which is pervaded by individual, collective, permanent and historically conditioned elements and thus belongs to the world of intersubjective agreement. This universal and primordial phenomenon of understanding as it occurs in general, scientific and inter-human experience should not be disguised by the much more striking forms of disagreement which are the occasion for the development of a hermeneutics. As long as "tradition" is accepted and transmitted without question — prescinding for the moment from the re-interpretations possibly concealed therein — individual "misunderstandings" and many "errors" arise, rather than fundamental difficulties of interpretation. But the sense of the passage of time, changes in vocabulary, concepts and thought-forms can bring about a break with tradition, which will now appear as "strange" and questionable. To ensure against particular mistakes and to provide the relevant application or normative repetition of tradition a regional hermeneutics is then worked out, as, for instance, in the rabbinical interpretation of Scripture. This hermeneutics has a concrete way of understanding in mind, for which it draws up a canon of rules with which to approach the tradition, especially the texts. In this sense there exists a (special) hermeneutics in the normative sciences of ancient and medieval theology and law. There were rules for "application", "spirit and letter", allegory, for filling in gaps in codified law, for the scholastic interpretation of authorities: *reverenter exponere* and so on. But such hermeneutics were simply the sum of concrete guides to right understanding derived from experience, and were mostly applied to fixed systems, of an acknowledgedly authoritative character, which aimed at right practice. They aimed at an elaborate "art" or technique of understanding, which is far from what is meant by a "theory of understanding" such as constitutes the modern concept of hermeneutics. Profound spiritual upheavals (as between the Sophists and Plato, or "la querelle des anciens et des modernes") and a break with all inherited tradition (as between OT and NT; between the Old Faith and the Reformation) are the necessary prerequisites for a clear sense of the great problems of hermeneutics.

B. Origin and Purpose of Modern Hermeneutics

1. While the Reformers still maintained on principle the unity of the canon of the Bible on dogmatic grounds, the 18th century began to consider sacred Scripture as a historical document, which was therefore to be understood according to the mind of the authors who wrote the books and in the light of the ancient environment. Hence the interpretation should prescind from the immediate interests of later readers (so, e.g., J. S. Salomo, A. Ernesti). This "critical and historical" interpretation is the logical outcome of the Protestant principle of Scripture explaining itself *(scriptura sui ipsius interpres).* The return to the "historical" understanding of Scripture was used at first to get rid of traditions and to disown a present Church supposedly alienated from its origins. The history itself thus remained subordinated to

an application which felt sure of itself. The demonstration of the historical gap reached its climax in the 19th and 20th centuries, when the interpreter could no longer identify himself "naively" with the contents and purpose of the text. When the interpreter became fully conscious of his task, the Christian thing itself became problematic.

2. The universal hermeneutical problem was felt more acutely as it became clearly necessary to find the broader historical contexts of statements which could no longer be treated in isolation. It was seen that a whole complex world of experience and the individual components of it had to be used to throw light on each other. Once Romanticism had ended in a total alienation with regard to tradition, a radical means of overcoming this alienation and the universal possibility of misunderstanding was called for. Only a sincerely methodical and scientific attitude can take the finished article from its original context in world history and reproduce it faithfully, by means of a sympathetic divination which enables one to imitate the creative act. The difference between linguistic-historical and theological hermeneutics vanishes. Schleiermacher designates special hermeneutics as an "aggregate of observations", while general hermeneutics is a "mighty motive for linking the speculative with the empirical and historical". This relationship between conscious knowledge and the living totality which is inseparable from it must always be kept in mind and then leads implicitly to freeing hermeneutics from being confined to history and theories of knowledge. "It is difficult to define the role of general hermeneutics" (Schleiermacher).

3. It was left to W. Dilthey to bring to light the profoundest philosophical role of general hermeneutics. The concrete cognitive subject is linked *a priori*, by identity of life and possibility of experience, with the past which is being expounded, though man's having to rely on creations ("expression") other than himself gives rise to real history and hence finally to a disclosure of the meaning of life. The first stage in leaving behind the psychological intentions of Schleiermacher's hermeneutics and in arriving at an expansion of the domain of hermeneutics is found in the term "expression". This now includes — along with the texts and the oral discourse which Schleiermacher favoured — anything and everything, even wordless happenings and the actions of history-making man. But Schleiermacher and Dilthey bog down in an obscurely pantheistic conception: that of the pre-established harmony and free union of all individuals, each of whom represents an epiphany of the "Living All", whose basic unity makes a connatural sympathy of understanding possible. This is a tendency which the "historical school" also fails to avoid. Its ultimate aim is not the "emasculated objectivity" of a fully depersonalized individual, but conscious alliance with the great permanent moral forces which guarantees a secret share in the totality of world history and allows one to sense the hidden meaning of the whole.

4. This is no longer as in the speculative dialectics of Hegel the transformation of the mind's objectivations into the original spiritual reality. But in the mind of the modern historian there are the same presuppositions — those of the absolute self-transparency of the spirit and the supreme capacity of the reason to explain itself to itself. Hermeneutics thus becomes the great effort of a totally lucid universal understanding and only thereafter is it a "methodology". But the question is whether the historian, for instance, by virtue of the presence of the same "spiritual nature" in all human behaviour, can have an inward sense and sympathy even for the most distant past. Can the creative process be so imitated and re-constructed subjectively and objectively that the original purpose of a work re-appears once more? The work thus fetched back from its alienation in the past remains after all a mere concept and it is precisely the necessary communication with the present which is left unachieved. Hegel saw clearly the impossibility here involved. Further, it is doubtful whether the justifiable purpose of excluding or controlling the "prejudices" of one's own historical situation, in order to have an "objective" view of ancient testimonies, can be successful when essential phenomena in particular are involved. If understanding is arrived at to some extent through the concrete situation of the interpreter at the present day, the whole depth of the historical experience actually undergone could not be represented in the self-understanding of the historical method. But then the basic problem of

hermeneutics, the relation of the thinker to the subject-matter, remains unsolved.

5. A radically new approach was that of M. Heidegger, whose critique of the ontological premisses of modern notions of subjectivity disclosed the intrinsic infinity of this basically idealistic notion of spirit in the midst of the "finite-historical-empirical" understanding. Heidegger refuses to admit that the historicity of existence poses limits to understanding or threatens objectivity. Hermeneutics is now justified as ontology. Prior to all philosophical and methodological interests, existence has already "understood" the world. Hence to understand, being "ability to be", "potentiality", is a primordial characteristic of the being of human life itself. Understanding, as "sketch-plan", implies no detached self-possession of existence; it must always find itself limited by the inescapable facticity of its being and moulded by history and historicity.

This basic principle of a "hermeneutics of existence" was then taken further, independently, by H. G. Gadamer. An adequate hermeneutics deals with history thus efficacious in the very act of understanding. It must therefore demonstrate how the thinker stands therein in a manifold complex of tradition (*Wirkungsgeschichte* — "the effective history" or history as impact). It must make the thinker acknowledge this presupposition consciously before turning to the individual objects and "objective" analysis. Hence every affirmation can be regarded as an answer to a question which is the more or less definable horizon of a "prior understanding" (mostly unconscious) and which implies a vital relationship of the interpreter to the matter involved. This "prior understanding" is provisionally acknowledged and then itself submitted to criticism in the further process of understanding. The thinker always finds himself caught up in a world which is in process of explicitating itself in detail. When this open horizon takes in a new experience which cannot be subsumed into familiar expectations and tendencies, it upsets the older "pre-understanding", accepts and assimilates the "alien" and thus expands and enriches the realm of its own experience of the world ("the merging of the horizons"). This inescapable interplay of an efficacious tradition and the movement of the understanding itself is a relationship which no longer falls under the categories of "subjective" and "objective". Even the formal characterization as the "hermeneutic circle" is misleading (though there is no question of a logical or methodological [vicious] circle).

The decisive point has still to be made clear, that the circle, by virtue of the acknowledged finitude of the mental horizon, leaves an opening through which one can be the victim of something "alien" which impinges on one from the realm of history. Such an experience is not to be explained as the action of the subject, or subjectivity actualized — nonetheless, it does not come about without the thinker, as may be seen from the fact that the true understanding of what has been thus appropriated only results from the interpretation translated into one's own language. Such "knowledge of the known" contains an element of self-conscious analysis (which is, however, never exhaustive), and hence may not be regarded as naive spontaneity.

The universal medium of such hermeneutics as the basic movement of finite-historical existence in general is language. For language conveys, conceals and reveals a whole understanding of the world and other unobtrusive anticipations and conditions which affect the understanding. Its structure, which is not independent of ethical and political action and public life, can convey to a certain extent phenomena like power and social interests which seemingly lie outside the scope of speech. Hence formally, language can provide the truly universal aspect of a hermeneutics.

It has been said (e.g., by E. Betti) that the transformation of the classical hermeneutics, which aimed at objectivity of understanding, into a hermeneutic of existence is a subjectivist denial of the independence of the object of hermeneutics. But this objection is a fundamental misconception with regard to the hermeneutics in question, since "being conscious of historical impact is inevitably rather being than being conscious" (Gadamer). In practice, however, the hermeneutical principles of Gadamer and Betti are very much alike, though Gadamer does not try to produce a methodology of such "sciences of the spirit" as history. W. Pannenberg and (to some extent) J. Habermas try to extend on principle the horizon of the new hermeneutics to make it take in, hypothetically or theologically, an anticipatory theology structured in terms of universal history or again, a philosophy of history of a concrete type. The relevance of hermeneutics for the theory of the sciences is still to be examined (K. O. Apel).

C. Modern Hermeneutics and Catholic Theology

The working out of a regional hermeneutics in the individual theological disciplines is as necessary as the hermeneutical task of theology in general. The transcendental or phenomenological and hermeneutical horizon which gives the conditions of possibility for the dogmatic truth, and also the receptivity of man with regard to such truth, must be treated much more carefully and expressly — in spite of the positive concrete nature of the history of salvation and of the Church (K. Rahner). A thorough-going confrontation of Catholic theology with modern hermeneutics is a task still to be accomplished, for which the following guide-lines may be suggested.

1. The term "hermeneutics" must not be used in a sense which fails to do justice to the present-day problems of philosophical hermeneutics. It must try to grapple critically with the questions there posed.

2. Since theological discourse has to uphold an "objective reality" which limits, integrates and transcends the universal historical flux and relativity of changing views of the world, it cannot take over inconsiderately the post-Kantian ontology which is the recognized basis of modern hermeneutics. The crisis in metaphysics cannot be solved by falling back upon hermeneutics. Hermeneutics as the one universal ontology is still an impasse, or a poor substitute for metaphysics.

3. To explain the biblical texts simply as expressions of the human understanding of existence, by the use of a hermeneutics which blunts the edge of the affirmations about God, the world and history is always — in spite of the bearing of self-understanding on such affirmations — an illegitimate restriction of the biblical "pre-understanding", which is not merely anthropological. It also fails to do justice to what Heidegger originally meant by "existence".

4. Hermeneutics may not be used to favour limited formal categories such as "de-cision", "communication", "word-event", "language-event", to the exclusion of the concrete contents of the Christian message. In theology, the efficiency of hermeneutics is measured by its power to re-state in undistorted form the actual truth of faith.

5. Hermeneutics can give rise to an intellectually justifiable rehabilitation of Church tradition and authority, as necessary functional elements in the thinking out of the faith. A constant recall of the traditional and free acceptance of authority are the prerequisites of a "dogmatic" form of thought.

6. Within a theological hermeneutics, "tradition", being the all-encompassing hermeneutical horizon, must be given a concrete historical orientation, with all its constitutive elements.

7. While adhering as it must to the methodical scholarship of each individual theological discipline, hermeneutics can show what is prior to all the understanding attitudes of the subject, including the methodical approach of science, and what is "skipped" or "blurred" by such understanding: the original claim of the gospel and its truth. This claim, and the original understanding experienced in faith may not be subjected to a process of total alienation in scientific study. On the contrary, they must become fully articulate in a fundamental theology (of the phenomenological type). Hermeneutics is not exhausted by the immanent scientific function of the theological disciplines as known hitherto.

8. Once we have conceded that the hermeneutic problem is a universal one, the question remains as to whether present-day hermeneutics provides a universally valid basis for all understanding of being (including action and the religious reality) and whether language, as a universal hermeneutical medium, is the key to the understanding of all that can be understood. Some indispensable test-cases in theology would be: sacramental structures, miracles, the action that goes beyond the word, the definitive nature of the truth with which theology is concerned.

In the discussion of these and other problems the hermeneutical task imposes itself on all theological work with an urgency which it would be hard to overestimate. And the difficulties which it presents by reason of the subjects and the mental processes involved should not be underestimated or evaded by short-sighted "solutions".

See also *Historicism, History, Experience, Language, Science* II, *Apologetics, Dogma* IV, *Faith* I, *Demythologization* II, *Tradition, Phenomenology.*

BIBLIOGRAPHY. See bibliography on *Biblical Hermeneutics;* also: G. Ebeling in *RGG,* III, cols. 242–62. PHILOSOPHICAL: J. Wach. *Das Verstehen,* 3 vols. (1926 ff.); K. O. Apel, "Verstehen", *Archiv für Begriffsgeschichte* 1 (1955), pp. 142–99; E. Betti, *Teoria della interpretazione* (1955); F. Schleiermacher, *Hermeneutik,* ed. by H. Kimmerle (1959); M. Heidegger, *Being and Time* (1962); W. Dilthey, *Gesammelte Schriften,* V (4th ed., 1964); H. G. Gadamer, *Wahrheit und Methode* (2nd ed., 1965); P. Ricœur, *De l'interprétation* (1965); J. Habermas, "Zur Logik der Sozialwissenschaften", *Philosophische Rundschau,* supplement 5 (1967); E. A. Burtt, *In Search of Philosophical Understanding* (1967); E. Hirsch, *Validity in Interpretation* (1967). THEOLOGICAL: H. W. Bartsch, ed., *Kerygma and Myth,* 2 vols. (1953, 1962); E. Fuchs, *Hermeneutik* (2nd ed., 1958); R. Bultmann, *Essays Philosophical and Theological* (1955) = *Glauben und Verstehen,* II; id., *History and Eschatology* (1957), ch. viii; id., *Existence and Faith* (1961) = *Glauben und Verstehen,* I and III; W. Pannenberg and others, *History and Hermeneutics* (1961); G. Ebeling, *Word and Faith* (1963); J. M. Robinson and J. B. Cobb, *New Frontiers in Theology,* I: *The Later Heidegger and Theology* (1963); II: *New Hermeneutic* (1964); C. Braaten, *New Directions in Theology Today. History and Hermeneutics* (1967); R. Marlé, *Introduction to Hermeneutics* (1967); R. Lapointe, *Les trois dimensions de l'herméneutique* (1967); K. Rahner, "Demythologization and Preaching", *Concilium* 4, no. 3 (1968).

Karl Lehmann

HIERARCHY

1. *Concept.* Etymologically hierarchy means holy origin (ἱερὰ ἀρχή), holy dominion and, since the time of Denis the Areopagite, it has been used to signify the order given the Church by the Lord. In ecclesiastical legal language the hierarchy is the structure composed of those who, according to the principle of unity of head and body, are called to represent the invisible Lord; more precisely, it is, in the objective sense, the institutional order within this structure, and, in the subjective sense, the totality of those holding sacred authority.

2. *Basis.* To sum up the teaching on the Church as offered by Vatican II in a short formula, one could say that the Church is the new people of God living in hierarchical order in the service of the kingdom of God. The hierarchical order which goes with the distinction between clergy and laity is essential to the Church; therefore one speaks of the hierarchical structure of the Church, which excludes the acceptance of a charismatical structure. The hierarchical structure is a constitutive principle of the people of God and has its theological basis in the sacramentality of the Church. The Church is the sign of salvation erected by Jesus Christ for all men, "in Christ as it were, a sacrament, i.e., a sign and instrument for the innermost union with God as well as for the unity of the whole of mankind" (Vatican II, *De Ecclesia,* art. 1). This sacramental significance of the Church is bound to the hierarchical structure proper to the Church, i.e., the Church is only a sacramental sign by reason of the fact that the Lord, who is the invisible head of the Church, is visibly represented in the Church by men: for without a visible head the Church cannot be a visible representation of the Lord's body. This order of the Church is based on the will of the Lord who has determined to continue his work of salvation in the Church by means of authorized representatives. He instituted the twelve apostles, made them, as the word shows, his representatives in a legal sense and placed Peter at the head of the Twelve. With the continuance of the Lord's mission guaranteed by the apostolic succession, Jesus Christ himself lives on in the Church and is the animating and ruling head of all the members of the people of God, not only by reason of the invisible rule of the Holy Spirit, but also in the visible activity of the servants chosen and authorized by him.

3. *Unity in duality.* The ultimate purpose of the hierarchy is to represent the one Lord. It therefore seems strange that the hierarchy is divided into a hierarchy of orders *(h. ordinis)* and a hierarchy of jurisdiction *(h. iurisdictionis).* Corresponding to this two-fold hierarchy is the differentiation between the power of orders *(potestas ordinis)* and the power of jurisdiction *(potestas iurisdictionis),* which are to be seen as complementary elements of the one sacred ecclesiastical authority. The *C.I.C* speaks in the singular of

sacra, or *ecclesiastica hierarchia* (can. 108, no. 3; 109), a point which is rarely noticed, and thus testifies to the unity of the hierarchy, which, in regard to orders and office *(ratione ordinis — ratione iurisdictionis),* is differentiated into a hierarchy of orders and one of offices. The constitution *Lumen Gentium,* which presents the hierarchical structure of the Church's constitution in its third chapter, avoided mentioning expressly the distinction between the hierarchy of orders and that of offices; nevertheless it offers all the elements which are essential to the distinction. Therefore one cannot say that the distinction between a hierarchy of orders and one of offices has been abandoned. What stopped Vatican II from expressly making the distinction, besides the lack of clarity concerning the relationship of the power of orders and the power of jurisdiction, was an urgent concern for the unity of the hierarchy as well as of ecclesiastical authority; this unity had been overlooked to a great extent in the Latin Church and had been distorted to some extent into a real separation. The Council emphasizes, in contrast to this separatist trend, that ecclesiastical authority is sacramentally based on orders, but does not deny that the canonical mission is still needed in order to make the power which is ontologically based upon holy orders a power capable of being exercised. The distinction of the two hierarchies, which in the last analysis aims to guarantee the unity of the hierarchy, must be seen in this context.

The hierarchies of orders and offices are basically distinguished by the fact that entrance into the ranks of the hierarchy of offices — except for the supreme authority of the Pope and the college of bishops — is through canonical mission (can. 109), which is primarily the transmission of an office, though it also includes delegation of jurisdiction. On account of the indelible character which is given with holy orders, enrolment into the hierarchy of orders is irrevocable; in contrast, the canonical mission can be lost at any rank and can be withdrawn by the competent ecclesiastical authority. The fact that a consecrated minister can be deprived of his office and be completely excluded from the hierarchy of offices protects ecclesiastical authority, called to represent the invisible Lord, against human failings; and because the only true wielders of sacred authority are in both hierarchies, the ecclesiastical hierarchy preserves precisely through its duality its intrinsic unity.

4. *Ranks within the hierarchies of orders and offices.* Within the bounds of the hierarchy of orders as well as of the hierarchy of offices one must distinguish between the ranks of divine and of ecclesiastical law. In the hierarchy of orders the three sacramental orders (episcopate, presbyterate, diaconate) are ranks of divine law; the other ranks of orders, together with first tonsure, which precede holy orders, are of ecclesiastical law (in the Latin Church: subdiaconate, acolyte, exorcist, lector, porter; in the Eastern Church: for the most part the subdiaconate, plus one or the other of the minor orders). Within the hierarchy of offices the supreme pastoral office of the Pope, as successor to St. Peter, and of the college of bishops, which has succeeded the college of the apostles and which has the Pope as its head (Vatican II, *De Ecclesia,* art. no. 22), as well as the episcopal office which is subordinated to the two bearers of supreme ecclesiastical power mentioned above and which is related to the guidance of a particular Church, are of divine law. All other offices are derived from these and go back to ecclesiastical institution. The offices of the Pope and the college of bishops are, with their divine institution, concretely present in the Church and do not need either an ecclesiastical erection, nor are they capable of such; on the other hand, the episcopal office, related to a particular Church, necessarily needs an erection by the competent ecclesiastical authority because it demands an ordination to a particular flock. The particular episcopal office is of ecclesiastical law, but the tasks and powers which belong to episcopal office thus made concrete flow from the episcopal office as instituted by God and are not derivable from the primatial power of the Pope (Vatican II, *ibid.,* art. 27; Decree on the Bishops' Pastoral Office in the Church, art. 8).

The presentation of the Church's constitution in *CIC,* which still does not take into consideration the doctrine of episcopal collegiality — except for the ecumenical council — is based on the notion of the Pope as supreme authority and of the bishop as ruler of the diocese. Derived from the office of the Pope are: a) its auxiliary organs for the administration of the whole Church

28

(college of cardinals, Roman congregations, Curia offices and courts, papal legates); b) archbishops (patriarchs, primates, metropolitans); and c) the bearers of episcopal power for those areas in which an episcopate has not yet been installed (apostolic vicars and prefects, apostolic administrators, abbots and prelates *nullius*), as well as the heads of exempt orders of priests. Derived from the office of bishop are: a) the auxiliary organs for administering the diocese (vicars-general); b) the deans or archpriests as local organs of inspection for greater areas within the diocese; c) the parish priests as the responsible leaders of the parish communities.

Over and beyond all the ranks within the hierarchy of orders and of offices, we find both hierarchies connected indissolubly with one another in the episcopacy. The various ranks of episcopal service are based upon the office alone, and not upon the episcopal ordination, which is the same for all. The Church's constitution is thereby so constructed that the supreme pastoral office of the Pope and every archiepiscopal office (patriarch, major archbishop and metropolitan) is connected with a particular see. This characteristic of the Church's constitution, which has no secular parallels, is based upon the fact that a particular Church is not only a part of the whole, but represents the whole Church in its area; at the same time it is an expression of a collegial element in the Church's constitution, which has found its legal expression in the institution of the synod. The collegial element is an important complement of the hierarchical principle of the ecclesiastical constitution. It connects the individual bishops not only with the Pope, but also with all the members of the college of bishops. The vertical component expressed in the relationship of Pope to bishop is complemented by the horizontal union of all bishops who represent, in unity with the Pope, the whole Church.

See also *Church* III, *Clergy, Laity* I, II, *Ecclesiastical Authority, Bishop, Pope* I, *Apostolic Succession, Orders and Ordination.*

BIBLIOGRAPHY. L. M. de Bernardis, *Le due potestà et le due gerarchie della chiesa* (2nd ed., 1946); K. Mörsdorf, "Die Entwicklung der Zweigliedrigkeit der kirchlichen Hierarchie", *Münchener Theologische Zeitschrift* 3 (1952), pp. 1–16; id.,"Weihegewalt und Hirtengewalt in Abgrenzung und Bezug", *Miscelánea Comillas* 16 (1951), pp.65–110; id.,"Zur Grundlegung des Rechtes der Kirche", *Münchener Theologische Zeitschrift* 3 (1952), pp. 329–48; id., *Lehrbuch des Kirchenrechts,* I (11th ed., 1964), pp. 244–8; id., "Einheit in der Zweiheit — Der hierarchische Aufbau der Kirche", *Archiv für das katholische Kirchenrecht* 134 (1965), pp. 80–88; id., "Die hierarchische Verfassung der Kirche, insbesondere der Episkopat", *ibid.,* 134 (1965), pp. 88–97.

Klaus Mörsdorf

HISTORICISM

1. *Concept.* By historicism we understand "a view of man, his culture and his values which is on principle historical" (E. Troeltsch). It replaces a generalizing concept of man's changeless nature by knowledge of his concrete individuality in history. "The State, law, morality, religion, and art are dissolved in the flux of historical change; they can only be understood by us as elements of a historical development. This helps us to see better how the contingent and personal is rooted in broader, supra-individual contexts . . . But it destroys all eternal truths." Historicism, in its typically modern form, was largely formulated in the 19th century, though the groundwork was already laid in earlier stages of the cultural history of the West. It gained in importance and influence from the time that the concept of history gave up the image of man typical of the Stoic-Christian philosophy, took up the particularizing methods of a descriptive anthropology and ceased to divide history according to the periods of redemptive history. It did not thereby relinquish all thought of an inner relationship between historical events, and hence the possibility of a speculative grasp of those relations, as in the philosophy of history. With this emancipation from the earlier framework (in which, however, the formal structure of personal and teleological history-writing was preserved), a "purely immanent interpretation of social and historical life" became possible (W. Dilthey) which is the new element in modern history, as opposed to the older treatment as a mere chronicle or as theological history of salvation.

The adoption of the word historicism is more recent than that of the outlook it represents. It was first used by K. Werner in 1879, primarily in a polemic fashion against the "Historical School" of economists, and later against the historical and positive theology of A. Ritschl. It was only after World War I that it gained universal significance as a criticism of the inadequacy of mere scholarship and the disintegrating forces of historical relativism. E. Troeltsch then took the first step towards a philosophical explanation of the controversial phenomenon in his work on historicism, *Der Historismus und seine Probleme* (1922). His views, which went beyond mere polemics and explained the historical view of the world in the perspective of modern science, were systematically developed by K. Mannheim and B. Croce. Historical research into "historicism" dates from F. Meinecke's book on the origins of historicism (*Die Entstehung des Historismus* [1936]), where it is seen as a spiritual revolution in Western thought from which sprang a new interpretation of human life as well as the impulse to modern historical research.

2. *Historical development.* The first attempts at modern historical criticism were made in the 16th and 17th centuries; they were closely bound up with the advance of empiricism in the post-scholastic sciences. Significant progress was made on the way towards historicism when history was freed from biblical chronology and world epochs (J. Bodin), and when the first sketch of a science of history was given by Vico in the 18th century. The historical thinking of the Enlightenment was, by contrast, decidedly retrograde, though it promoted the emancipation of profane history and the scientific analysis of its methods. It gave to historicism the concept of progress (Turgot, Condorcet) which became the immanentist principle of interpretation of history, instead of the older eschatology. Yet the Enlightenment failed to achieve a comprehensive historical view of the world, since it was unhistorical enough to make the present the measure of the past, while it also tried to compensate for the break-up of classical anthropology by having recourse to a decidedly unhistorical concept of the natural law.

Hence the break-through of historicism proper, which was effected in the late Enlightenment and the Romantic period, was decisively stamped by opposition to the rationalism of the Enlightenment and the soulless governmental policies of the absolutist State. It gave rise to a more profound view of the realm of history, which was to have far-reaching effects on the politics and the science of the 19th century. In opposition to the concept of an unchanging human nature where the historical phenomenon was relatively unimportant, Herder championed the originality of individual peoples and replaced the pragmatic concept of progress by a view which stressed the autonomy of each epoch. With Möser, Burke and Savigny and their studies in the history of law, the organic development and natural growth of States took the place of mechanistic causality and planned performance. In aesthetics, the will of the genius replaced the rules (Shaftesbury, Diderot). The transformation of the idea of revelation into that of development (Lessing), and the notion of peoples as "thoughts of God" (Herder) engendered an understanding of history which saw the historical process as the gradual realization of the spiritual life sent down by God to man. The culmination of this universal view of history was reached in the work of Ranke, who saw humanity as "unending variety of developments which appear little by little", while each epoch stands "in direct relation to God". Contrary to Hegel's interpretation of history, which proceeded from the context of the Enlightenment, this type of historicism did not understand history as a gradual self-realization of the absolute Spirit to which the movements of individuals is subordinate. The notions of development and of individuality are in a fertile tension, which prevents everything being treated as of equal value, while it also excludes a historical determinism destructive of the individual.

With the decline of Idealism and Romanticism, the historicist synthesis based on the Christian and humanistic tradition also yielded to new sketch-plans of history. This change led in part to the imposition of a deterministic pattern upon history with the help of Hegelian dialectic or the positivist concept of progress (Marx, Comte, Buckle), and in part to a purely passive response to the charm of historical phenomena, with no attempt at historical theory or evaluation. The appearance of new sciences in historical form, the application of the historical approach to the plastic arts and poetry, made the late 19th century a *saeculum historicum*. At the same time, the problems set by a history which moved aimlessly through a wealth of data were felt more and more acutely. Nietzsche sought a justification for historical research in his "Life-Philosophy", while others like E. Troeltsch and M. Weber sought to restore some sort of order among the political and social anarchy of values in historicism. Philosophical attempts to integrate the methods and objectives of the historical school into the whole of scientific study (Dilthey) gradually became, after World War I, comprehensive ontological enquiries.

3. *The results and problems of historicism.* The dominance which history exercised over the thought of the 19th century has given way today to a marked restriction of the value allowed to historical thinking, when it is not disregarded completely. In public life as well as within the world of scientific scholarship, history lost its influence. In Western countries "a historicism with an exclusive claim to insight" (O. Brunner), such as existed in the 19th century, is hardly conceivable today. Even in communist countries, the postulate of a historical interpretation of human existence in general can be maintained only artificially.

Modern criticism (K. Löwith, E. Topitsch) is inclined to find the roots of historicism chiefly in the secularizing of the concepts of the history of salvation and the transfer of speculation on the order of the cosmos into the sphere of history. But this transformation of the sacred into the secular was the cause, as is now clearly seen, of the later crisis in this type of thought. The failure to find a comprehensive interpretation of "the world as history" is not only due to the inability of history, as an empirical science, to deliver a view of the historical cosmos as a whole and hence a philosophy of history. It is also a necessary result of the theological impossibility of resolving the divine plan of salvation into a metaphysical movement of the spirit (Hegel) or of reducing it to an unlimited continuum of a general history of the spirit (Dilthey).

Though historicism has thus failed as a system of total interpretation of the world, as a substitute metaphysics and "the last religion of the cultured" (Croce), the effects of the historicist view of the world cannot be simply annulled. Questionable as would be any generalization of the relativity of existence disclosed by historicism, it would be equally wrong to evade the recognition of factual historicity by an unhistorical treatment of the nature of man or a cyclic interpretation of ever-recurring history. Historical thought, setting a limit to non-historical sketch-plans and theories of political absolutes remains valuable when it refuses to treat history, as historicism did, as the key to the ultimate significance of all that is human; it can then fulfil its role as a corrective of an autonomous will to world-making.

See also *History* I, II, *Enlightenment, Idealism, Romanticism, Marxism, Secularization.*

BIBLIOGRAPHY. SOURCES: J. G. Herder, *Auch eine Philosophie der Geschichte zur Bildung der Menschheit* (1774); G. Vico, *Principi di una scienza nuova intorno alla natura delle nazioni* (1725), E. T. (abridged): *The New Science* (1961). LITERATURE: B. Croce, *History: Its Theory and Practice* (1916); E. Troeltsch, *Der Historismus und seine Probleme* (1922); K. Mannheim, *Archiv für Sozialwissenschaft und Sozialpolitik* 52 (1924), pp. 1–60; B. Croce, *La storia come pensiero e come azione* (1938); id., *Dallo storicismo alla sociologia* (1940); id., *Filosofia e storiografia* (1948); E. Topitsch, "Der Historismus und seine Überwindung", *Wiener Zeitschrift für Philosophie, Psychologie, Pädagogik* 4, no. 2 (1952); K. Löwith, *Meaning in History* (1949); H.-I. Marrou, *De la connaissance historique* (1954); G. Barraclough, *History in a Changing World* (1955); F. Meinecke, *Die Entstehung des Historismus,* 3 vols. (3rd ed., 1959); P. Rossi, *Storia e storicismo nella filosofia contemporanea* (1960); R. Aron, *Dimensions de la conscience historique* (1961); H. P. Rickman, ed., *Meaning in History: W. Dilthey's Thoughts on History and Society* (1961); G. Rand, "Two Meanings of Historicism in the Writings of Dilthey, Troeltsch and Meinecke", *Journal of the History of Ideas* 25 (1964).

Hans Maier

HISTORY

I. History and Historicity: A. Terms and Concept. B. The Development of the Notion of History. C. Basic Structures of Historicity. D. History and Historicity. II. Philosophy of History: A. The Main Approaches. B. The Great Modes of Experiencing History. C. Development of Modern Philosophy of History. III. Theology of History: A. Problem. B. Basic Theological Assertions. C. The Categories of the Theology of History.

I. History and Historicity

A. TERMS AND CONCEPT

The words used throughout Europe for history come through the Latin *historia* from the Greek ἱστορεῖν, to know, investigate, except the German *Geschichte*. The former group indicates rather the study or science of history, while the German envisages rather the event itself, first the individual occurrence and then the individual life-process and the total world-process. The humanists used the German *Geschichte* in the definitely scientific sense of *historia*. But *Geschichte* always retained a special nuance of its own (which has become important in modern theology, and is often rendered by simply transcribing the German word as it stands into English and other literatures). The special connotation of *Geschichte* is that of the irresistible working of historical forces (almost like that of the ultra-modern sense of "happening") which is more emphasized than the sense of research and knowledge. The word is used in the singular (in the plural it simply means occurrences), but not in the sense of a single science. There is always the connotation of the one great comprehensive event, the *one* History (of which the differentiations, the historicity and transcendentality will be discussed in C below).

This history is one, being the one world of man in his historicity (the world being understood not just as a setting, but as a reality coming into being, not just as space but as order). Here historicity means the peculiar nature of human existence (gathering up world and time into one) by which man stands between a past which is imposed on him, with enduring effects and yet beyond his reach, and an outstanding future on its way to him which he must try to procure. It is only in this interaction of beginning and end, the essentially inter-personal tension of freedom and determinism that man attains his (contingent) selfhood and essence. By reason of this essential structure, man can only become aware of his history and historicity in the course of history and can only accept it and take it over in the historical struggle with it. As a spirit-being he possesses his history only by understanding it (a truth which is the basic unity of the two senses of history, as event and historical knowledge, *Geschichte* and *historia*). But this understanding has itself its history and its very change is a moment of the history in which man lives out his historicity. Throughout this article, the word history will be used predominantly in the sense of (total) event.

B. THE DEVELOPMENT OF THE NOTION OF HISTORY

Since man is inextricably involved in history and historicity, there are no peoples completely without a history, even where the origins and the future of a people (and the world in general, of which it sees itself as the centre) are presented in mythic narratives. In the Occident, this self-understanding became *historia* in the "Father of History", as Cicero termed Herodotus (*c.* 484–425 B.C.). Herodotus tries to trace one consistent law throughout the multiplicity of all that was said and done. He sees the decisive force in history as the confrontation of man who recognizes his limits with man who is carried away by the arrogance of his *hybris*, which always leads to the destruction of the immoderate by the gods. A different view is taken by Thucydides (*c.* 456–396 B.C.), who confined himself to a description of the Peloponnesian War and was the founder of political history as such. For Thucydides, history consisted of the conflict of interests, in which the stronger always imposes his law as the right — though even the stronger is not exempt from the hazards of inexplicable catastrophes. Hence the lessons to be deduced from this one war can be seen as a "possession for ever".

Polybius (*c.* 201–120 B.C.) uses the same approach to write the first great history of Rome. He links the effects of geography, climate and other impersonal causes with the initiatives of men and demonstrates for the first time how the destinies of the various nations are interwoven. Polybius also makes it clear that the writing of history can be made to serve a purpose. By displaying the rise of Rome as a sort of natural law, he tries to legitimate the power of the Empire and to justify the practical politics of his day. Sallust (86–35 B.C.) on the other hand uses history as a criticism of the decadence of his times, as does Tacitus (A.D. 55–120). But the moral appeals are of no avail. The natural experience of flowering and fading, transposed from the start to the succeeding epochs of civilization, leads to a pessimistic renunciation of the senseless recurrence of rise and fall.

This attitude is then confronted by Christianity with a completely different notion of history. For Israel, history is above all else the history of the covenant lived out along with the God of the covenant (as is discussed more fully in the article *Old Testament History*). The history of the world itself is the pre-history of the covenant towards which it moves. The covenant itself will finally be one with the history of the world. All the successes and reverses of history are phases of this dialectical process: sin, punishment, forgiveness, fidelity and fulfilment are the categories in which history is understood. In the experience of the messianic fulfilment of this history through Jesus Christ its dialogal interpretation is again confirmed. This event was first regarded as the end of history, but when the expectation of the imminent end was disappointed, a new and comprehensive conception of history was outlined, even in the books of the NT, especially in St. Luke's Acts of the Apostles. In the light of the Christ-event, world history from Adam to the hoped-for parousia was seen as the history of salvation, centred on the death, resurrection and missionary mandate of Jesus.

This interpretation found its great spokesman in St. Augustine (354–430), whose historical thinking *(De Civitate Dei)*, as much as anything else, made him the "Teacher of the West". But it may well be asked whether his influence here was not due in part to a misunderstanding. The two cities *(civitas Dei — civitas terrestris)* are founded through the two-fold Fall before all history in the ordinary sense. And their *finis sine fine* lies outside all inner-worldly happenings. But even their advance through history is not historical, that is, demonstrable, in the sense of *historia*. Just as the *Confessions* describe the conversion of the individual, so too the great historical work tells of the inward way of man before God, and this way cuts right across the historical events. Hence either the whole political sphere is in the power of the demons (Cain the first founder of a city, leading on to Babel, to Babylon and Rome); or the contrast between the two cities is itself seen in terms of polities, and then the Church, which is really the earthly Jerusalem, the image of the heavenly, becomes a theocratic power. Or again, the contrast is made in non-political terms, and then the history of the State ceases to have any significance for religion. In Augustine, this is all left undecided. But one can see how various developments were left open to his successors in the writing of the "theology of history". For Augustine at any rate the facts formed a sort

of text whose spiritual sense he worked out according to the patristic method of interpretation. He sees in temporality, sin, death, the present duty of love and eschatological hope the existentials of human history.

The work of St. Augustine's disciple Orosius, *Historiae adversus Paganos* (417/18) was richer in concrete historical detail. Then, at the height of the Middle Ages, Otto of Freising (*c.* 1115–58) transposed the Augustinian concept on a grand scale to recent history, in an attempt at justifying the Hohenstaufen imperial ideas. The last great work on these lines was the "Universal History" of Bossuet (1627–1704).

But in the meantime, the understanding of history had undergone a decisive change. The notion of progress had taken the place of providence. The Renaissance and the Humanists discovered the delights of experience, the value of the extraordinary, the special rank of the earthly. Observation and experiment, doubt and testing are to make knowledge a pliant instrument of power. History, in spite of its duties to the Church, is pressed into the service of national and political interests. The notion of nationality becomes associated with the will to discover new worlds. Thus the ancient world's approach to history could once more be adopted, though again, in spite of the abandonment of the notion of providence, the question of the total meaning of history could never be totally silenced.

Humanist historiography differs from that of antiquity and the Middle Ages above all by its conscious attention to sources and ancient documents. But the quantity of the collected materials was far too great for the scholars' powers of synthesis. Highly imaginative and eclectic outlines of universal history and philosophy of history went hand in hand with thorough-going and accurate collections of sources, though these could not yet be put into any comprehensive order. There were critics of culture like Rousseau as well as its admirers, but nowhere was a real sense of the proper nature of past or foreign cultures. And though history was acknowledged to be of immense value in education and regarded as part of the bedrock of all culture, of the individual and of society — as for instance by Voltaire — what was sought in history was the universal rationality which it was supposed to display in ever increasing measure, in spite of passing set-backs, and not the uniqueness of each particular epoch as such. G. B. Vico, for instance, whose philosophy of history and historical insights, in spite of much that was arbitrary, anticipated the progress made in the 19th century, remained uncomprehended and without influence.

Nonetheless, the growing perception of the differences of cultures and of the distance of each historical culture from the ideal norms laid down by reason was preparing the ground for a new approach. There was a dawning sense of the historical relativity of every form of society, and also of every standpoint from which they were viewed. (Thus Leibniz attributed a peculiar perspective to each monad within the totality. This was taken over by M. Chladen [Chladenius, 1710–95] in his work on the "Universal Science of History" [*Allgemeine Geschichtswissenschaft*] and explicitly said to be the "viewpoint", the "inner and outer condition" of the historian.)

The humanist view of all history as the process of educating man to the attainment of his true humanity was given its supreme expression in Herder, Goethe and W. von Humboldt. And at the same time, romanticism was finding its joys in the richness of individuality in persons and peoples, and bringing out the proper intrinsic value of the Middle Ages, so long neglected in favour of classical times.

Savigny and Hegel may be named as exponents of both trends, which united to give rise to the 19th century as the century of history. The mental paradigm of the first line is the living individual organism. History is the life of a "body of people" or rather "a body politic" and culture the expression of the people's soul. Hegel too, especially in his earlier writings, made use of the notion of the organism. But Hegel's basic term was "spirit". Just as the individual, even the "great man" serves the spirit of the people, so too the various national "spirits" are moments in the self-explicitation of the spirit as such — which is Hegel's way of contemplating world history. Thus every figure has its own proper value, though not strictly speaking as an independent organism. It is there as a moment which is merged and merges of itself into the totality of the self-realization of the world-spirit. World history is the growing consciousness of freedom — a progress which has to be recognized as a process of necessity. Its goal is the freedom of the knowledge of the spirit — the manifest identity of reality and reason. It is therefore the freedom of the universal, into which the freedom of the individual, freed from *itself*, passes. Hegel's was a grandiose effort of historical thought, which took in all the riches of the concrete historical material then known in an effort to comprehend it. But it provoked immediate criticism, because the individual, his freedom and history could only be comprehended at the cost of dissolving them into an idea. That is, they were grasped in precisely what was not their own nature.

Thus the Hegelian understanding of history was challenged by a positivist philosophy (such as Schelling's), the claim of the individual to existence (as in Kierkegaard), the effort to understand the concrete (as in modern hermeneutics). The place of speculative interpretation and neat arrangement is taken by the demand for "the naked truth without adornment", the effort to show things "as they really were" (L. von Ranke). The classical perfection which von Ranke's descriptive work aimed at was methodically attained in the history-writing of J. G. Droysen. Rejecting mechanistic natural causality and the organic thinking of the romantic movement, Droysen brought out the creative independence of the (ethically-minded) spirit. And this spirit cannot be grasped by disregarding the self of the researcher. It is attained by its being totally committed to "enquiring understanding".

The synthesis thus reached contained too many disparate elements to be stable. Positivism tried to reduce history to a natural science, after the analogy of the "natural history" of biological evolution. For Marxism, history is likewise an event determined by natural laws, but still the history of freedom coming to consciousness of itself. But freedom is not that of the Hegelian Absolute, it is that of man in his working struggle with nature and between the classes. Knowledge of history is itself an instrument in this warfare, at the end of which lies the perfect society without a history. Then there were the various interpretations of culture: a social and political notion of culture (L. von Stein, H. von Treitschke), a humanist view of culture (J. Burckhardt), a rejection of culture (A. Schopenhauer,

F. Nietzsche), and the morphology of cultures (K. Lamprecht and others).

Towards the end of the 19th century all this merged into the problem of historicism. W. Dilthey undertook the task of producing a "Critique of the Historical Reason", in order to understand "life" by virtue of life itself, in a "psychology" which aims at grasping the historical developments and inter-connections of life as the mode in which man really is. His thought was undoubtedly fruitful and has provided extraordinary stimulation down to the present day, but it cannot be said that he is entirely free from biological or rationalist approaches and he did not succeed in laying stable foundations in the flight of change. What Dilthey aimed at with his ultimately vague concept of "life" or "life-philosophy" was attempted by E. Troeltsch in theology, while P. Yorck von Wartenburg tried to work out the categories of a genuinely historical thinking. M. Heidegger, in the main statement of his thought, *Sein und Zeit,* stated that his programme was "to cherish the spirit of Count Yorck, in order to serve the work of Dilthey" (E. T.: *Being and Time,* p. 404).

With this, the problem of history was freed from the restrictions of a mere theory of the (human) sciences and made an analysis of man as such. The search for man's history was extended to take in the search for his historicity. (It is only on this basis that even a theory of the human sciences can be envisaged, since they deal with *de facto* particulars and hence cannot be validly based as long as the historical forms are understood merely as the second-rate, supplementary realization of a universal.) Thus with the search for historicity, an ontological question is raised prior to an epistemological one. It is the effort to attain a new ontology which will not eliminate the ancient ontology of meta-physical essences but seeks to get "the better" of it, in a mode of thought which does full justice to the concrete and individual and which therefore does not strive to grasp and master by technical methods, but accepts its own historicity and allows itself to be grasped and mastered by the "destiny of being".

To develop these brief indications, however, would be not merely to register the history of thought, but to discuss systematically and on its intrinsic merits the problem itself. (This is in fact one of the permanent acquisitions from the logic of Dilthey, that in philosophy — and in theology — the historical and the systematical approach cannot on principle be kept separate.) The discussion may begin with a consideration of the singular existence of man, since being is not only there principally *in* him, but only *for* him — and *hence* principally in him.

C. BASIC STRUCTURES OF HISTORICITY

1. *Historical man.* Man has his essence (not as an abstract notion of essence, but as the concrete basic reality), the essence which dominates his history as norm and end, only inasmuch as he fetches it in by bringing it about. His essence is the law "according to which he proceeds", the previously demarcated ground of his history of freedom. It is also that which is at stake for him in his history — that for whose realization he has "to be concerned". In this sense, not in the psychological sense of being troubled and oppressed, his existence is characterized by concern. Here there is displayed an ontological dialectic between what is imposed as a prior datum and what is imposed as a task, where no absolute equilibrium is possible. In this simultaneity of life assigned and life to be assumed — of *datum* and *mandatum* — man cannot simply be thought of as self-sufficient and autonomous.

Not only can he not give himself what is given him as himself — as follows from the analysis of the terms — he cannot of himself achieve the fulfilment of the task which the gift of himself imposes — though it is he who must fulfil the task. The reason for this is that it is the gift (he himself) with which alone he can master his task, which imposes on him the task: because, therefore, the gift is only "incipient". Thus the dynamism of his essence, its goal and its force, must belong to him intrinsically but still cannot be a constitutive element of his own self. He is man, before he fulfils his task, indeed, precisely as he on whom this task is imposed. And at the same time, this task, which has still to be fulfilled and hence is still outstanding, is nothing else than his being man.

This peculiar structure of human existence is its temporality, in the three dimensions which are generally known as past, present and future. Since man always experiences himself as a given, finding himself in a given world reality and situation, he experiences in himself a "has-been" which determines his "essence" now by virtue of the past (as something derivative). Thus the past has not simply gone by but continues to be effectively present as what has been. But it is present as escaping him, as the ground of the present disposition over which one does not dispose. But the past is likewise present as within one's grasp, since the present decision is not concerned merely with this thing or that but ultimately with freedom itself, that is, with freedom as an arrival from the past. That past demands to be accepted. Its origin arrives at man as a task, so that it displays and opens up to him his future. Thus the future comes as a demand, one that has still to be achieved, and furthermore, as something which surpasses his capacities of achievement and therefore must be bestowed on him as a gift in spite of all his efforts. In this sense the future is present only as something still outstanding. In this way, freedom experiences the present as the unity of a past that is out of reach and within one's grasp, and a future which is arriving and outstanding. The two-fold character of the two dimensions explains the possibility of different attitudes towards them.

Thus man can repress the past by way of protest or take it over freely in remembrance and re-collection. This re-possession takes place in an immediacy mediated by tradition, so that the original reality of the past — individual as well as collective — is not disguised but is permanently visible, in order that it may in fact be a task (to which the response may be either acceptance or the rejection of [self]-criticism). The "necessity" of history does not mean here only the fact that what is done cannot be undone. It also means that existence is in possession of itself only in constant recourse to what has happened (not independently thereof in a plan based on an abstract notion of essence). Finally, necessity signifies the inevitability with which the past in each new back-reference receives a new configuration — though precisely in order to remain itself. Historical recourse *(anamnesis)* is not a matter of a *per se* neutral existence returning arbitrarily upon a mere past event, as historicism supposes, but considering and accepting the claim of what has come to be. Hence the identity of the past does not

consist of its being always described in the same way but in the fact that its claim is always different — and hence to be described differently — in keeping with the actual present situation, while remaining the same. This is the basic notion of the truth of tradition. There is therefore a certain relativity, not in the sense of relativism, but in the literal sense of the word — as forming part of a relationship. Impartially, what has come to be addresses each hour of history differently. In doing so it displays new "visages" — whereby no doubt misunderstandings arise, creative as well as destructive. But the most infertile of all misunderstandings would perhaps be the effort to register the past once for all in the colourless, dispassionate archives which would fix it finally. But these visages or aspects, being part of its "effective history" (H. G. Gadamer) also belong to the event. The future of the event belongs to the event itself — even though it is never brought about by the event alone but is co-effectuated by the concrete situation of this future and by the free act of remembrance. And conversely, the event itself belongs to this its future. And so one cannot — as actualism or existentialism suppose — live in the present as a completely new beginning. One cannot really repress the fact that the moment of the present is always the future of what has come to be.

Just then as the past demands to be accepted as something beyond one's reach and yet within one's grasp and imposed on one as a task, so too the future at the same time, as arriving and yet as outstanding, that is, in hope and openness. For it is not just the past that arrives in it but also the claim to its fulfilment. This opens up the possibility of holding the actual past at a distance, the possibility of taking it over in repentance and revolution, that is, in rejection of it.

If one denies the derivative nature of this future, the result is the mistakes of utopianism and permanent revolution, while if one denies the true futurity of the origins, the result is restorative tendencies and timid or comfortable conservativism. Hence the right attitude to the present is obedience to the summons of what has been preserved but is still on its way, and relaxed tranquillity as regards the hoped-for gift of what is out of reach and outstanding. This unity of obedience and tranquillity avoids both the activism which sacrifices the present to the future and the dilettantism which remains irresponsive.

2. *Historical being*. In the way thus described, man has never to do merely with himself. The individual is never really left to himself: a situation always involves others, the "hour" is the hour of other people's claim on him; past and present are never just mine, but always and primordially ours. And again, man has not merely to do with man. One and all, men have to do with truth, with goodness, with being. Change of the condition of the self, the environment and the world is always and indeed primarily a change in the relation of being. And here one must distinguish the change of the articulation of this relationship — as expressed, for instance, in the theses of an ontology — from the basic change of the relationship itself (in existence).

A certain detached knowledge of history is part of the essence of history, and since this aloofness is only possible by virtue of the transcendence towards being (the true, the good), the transcendence towards the Absolute and Unconditional is a constitutive moment of historicity. Knowledge of history and historicity can only be there — even when only implicitly apprehended — when sustained by absolute knowledge. But man "has" not this absolute knowledge, he cannot dispose of it, but lets himself be disposed of therein by the Absolute — to be thus enabled to dispose of himself and things to a certain extent. Being thus withdrawn from man's control, absolute knowledge is knowledge of being forced to rely on the incomprehensible mystery.

This knowledge is not a purely speculative act but a basic option in personal openness — a laying hold of while allowing oneself to be laid hold of. It is itself the historical free action: the constantly original event of history. Philosophy as reflection on such historical primordial attitudes (individual as well as age-long) is again itself historical free action. Hence metaphysics is always thought out within a certain horizon which while becoming historical remains beyond the control of metaphysics and of man himself.

The historical event, interpreted by the metaphysical pre-understanding, comes within a pre-determined mental horizon, but determines and modifies in turn, according to its capabilities, the horizon within which it is understood. Where the absolute mystery becomes absolute proximity in concrete history and itself effects its acceptation through the obedient openness of historical existence, the historical horizons of this acceptation are not stripped of their cultural diversity. They are surpassed and redeemed into an absolute proximity to the absolute mystery as such. Their unity, in spite of the impossibility of an adequate positive expression, is positively fulfilled — it is not the empty unity of merely being referred to the mystery.

But even before this incomparable fulfilment — and in any case "taught" by it — thought can affirm, on principle and in general, the real unity of the manifold of history as historically suprahistorical. Its suprahistorical character is expressed in the non-historical character of the laws of thought and of the prohibitions of the natural law. But these abstractions are not the essence of being, any more than the abstract definition of the nature of man *(animal rationale)* are his fundamental concrete reality. But it is part of the concrete reality of being (truth, goodness) to be known by man. If this knowledge is historical, then, inasmuch as the *cognitum* and the *cognoscens in actu* are identical, being, truth and goodness are likewise historical.

But this consideration must be taken still further. No doubt the traditional metaphysic of essences recognized that our knowledge has its history. But it made a sharp distinction between the historicity of this our concept of being (truth, goodness) and the non-historical character of being, truth and goodness in themselves. In this perspective, the affirmation just put forward, that historicity can be asserted of being itself, is guilty of s switch in suppositions. But it is only relativism which denies the *in se* of what is intended by these concepts. A historical ontology aims at grasping the concept, not just as produced by man, but also, and prior to this, as produced by the "sending" of being, especially as being does not here mean the *esse subsistens* but primarily the reality which is at the base of the "concept" of the *esse commune*. However, even with reference to the supreme mystery itself the affirmation has a good sense. The "hour" is not just the hour of our "willing or running" — our more or less successful exertions — it is an hour disposed and sent. Thus the "Lord of the hour" is suprahistorical but he is so in a sovereignty which may not shrink from the *kenosis,* the "death of history" but founds history as its Lord and hence may rightly himself be called historical. (The word is not used univocally but analogically, as is true of all terms used in natural theology. Nonetheless, it may be used because in the ontology now in question it is not identical with the negative, finite temporality of the traditional metaphysics, but is prior to such a concept.) His transcendence is so "immanent" to history that the message of the incarnation always remains unfathomable, a marvel and a scandal, but not an impossibility. It represents a fulfilment — even in the guise of a superabundant fulfilment — of a potentiality which may be predicated of creator and creature. And it is not merely the centre, as the supreme instance of creation, history and historicity at its culminating point. It is also the recapitulation of history, that is, where it comes to a head and finds itself once more in its summary.

Thus historicity is not merely the seal upon the finiteness of man, the experience of his non-identity, the pain of the futile and destructive *pour-soi,* and above all, not the painful laborious way of an absolute which has yet to come to (consciousness of) itself. It is much rather the seal upon the dignity of man as "freedom called out", as a person. And it is the only way in which God can exist, not merely *in* "the other of himself" but also *for* the other, positing out of himself purpose and multiplicity-in-unity, freely diffusing the suprahistorical "processional" character of his trinitarian life as the *bonum diffusivum sui.*

Thus the concept of historicity, which was necessary to the discussion of the concept of history, leads back once more to the latter, since historicity appears as the potentiality and actualization of history, as the existential structure whose meaning and content must be found in concrete, factual history.

D. History and Historicity

The meaning of historicity cannot be found there, but must be sought in history. The story of the philosophy of history is the story of the quest for this meaning. But the pure factualness of an (eternally) recurring set of cycles of history cannot answer the question, any more than a linear concept — either of ascending progress or of descending depravation — once the past is seen as merely the past. The growing conviction of the inadequacy of attempts — to say nothing of the ideological short-circuits of totalitarianism, racialism and the like — has led to a phenomenon not unlike that of ancient Stoicism with its ideal of "opting out" (λάθε βιώσας). There is at present an interpretation of existence-philosophy which suggests a withdrawal into the individual and his own personal decision. But such evasions do not eliminate the question. And it is also unsatisfactory to affirm that the meaning consists of "endowing the meaningless with meaning" (T. Lessing) by our own interpretation. Meaning cannot be decreed but demands to be found.

There is, however, some element of truth in this last conception, since the finding of meaning is not a speculative experience, but a giving and receiving. Meaning is experienced inasmuch as this experience is one of the factors which go to make up this meaning. Decision and knowledge penetrate one another in a way which admits of no rational demonstration. Nonetheless this does not represent an irrational decree, but an experience based on its own luminousness. Thus the experience of the meaning of history is itself a historical event where the structures described above are once more verified. The meaning of history itself is present as at once out of reach and within one's grasp, as arriving and still outstanding. This is true of the meaning of the individual history (of one's "life") and equally so of epochal history and of the one history which is the unity of the various regions of history. (Even the unity of the one history which we spoke of at the start is only consciously explicit historically, and its manifold changes — from mere neutral juxtaposition to the conflict of spheres of power within the "one world" and new differentiations within each of these very spheres — is characterized by the same dialectical double structure as is the meaning of any given history.)

But if this is so, the meaning of history can only be experienced and known — and also to some extent effected — in the double act of remembering and hoping. The duality of this attitude can be seen in the interpretation of national histories (see, for instance, the *Aeneid* of Virgil, or indeed the national feasts of the present day), and hence it is also true of the acceptance of the meaning of the history of man (as an individual but no less essentially as a totality), of salvation through the self-communication of the divine mystery. Just as Israel lived in the tension of *anamnesis* of the Exodus and expectation of the Day of the Lord, so too and above all the community of Jesus the Christ lives in the *anamnesis* of his death and resurrection, "till he comes", in the hope of the parousia.

The certainty and finality of this experience of salvation does not mean that history is already abolished — obvious though the temptation to quietism is — but that history is at last really set free to be itself, because it is only the certainty of meaningfulness that frees man for historical action. And since it is the certainty of faith and hope it actually demands action, since the meaning thus given must be assimilated in freedom by us and thus at last fully accomplished.

In this way historicity is fulfilled by a history which is incalculable, that is, not just in fact unpredictable, but nowhere predetermined even ideally, proceeding only from interpersonal event and its primordial decision. And not only is it fulfilled, it is also transformed (since the formal structures of historicity are not its concrete reality, any more than in the case of being, truth, goodness or man). And in transforming historicity, history is again historical: history is always the one thing, the history of man in this world and of his gift of transcendence towards the mystery, but never uniformly the same, just as man and his history in their identity are never the same.

There is a short-sighted way of applying categories to this identity which reduces it to a manageable uniformity where the differences are ignored as accidental. Against this, historicism takes a relativist view and denies the "transcendental" unity and identity through all categorical change. Against this denial again the Baden school of Kantianism (Windelband, Rickert) tries to safeguard the permanent in a world of values. But historical ontology tries to preserve the balance of the transcendental and the categorical, demanding that the transcendental be thought of not as non-historical sameness but as historical identity.

It renounces the effort to distinguish neatly between identity and difference not merely because the distinction is not adequately accessible to us, but because it does not exist "in itself": the core of reality is not univocal but of itself analogous, that is, relational: the self-relationship of freedom. The identity-difference which runs through history and historicity is a sign of such freedom.

See also *World, Creation* IV, *Myth, Jesus Christ* I, *Salvation* III A, *Progress, Renaissance, Humanism* I, *Enlightenment, Rationalism, Romanticism, Hermeneutics, Positivism, Marxism, Historicism, Existence* II, *Essence, Freedom, Tradition, Revolution, Mystery, Identity, Relativism*.

BIBLIOGRAPHY. See bibliography on *History* II and III, *Historicism;* also: M. Heidegger, *Sein und Zeit* (1927), E. T.: *Being and Time* (1962); T. Lessing, *Geschichte als Sinngebung des Sinnlosen* (1927); A. Toynbee, *The Study of History*, 12 vols. (1935–61); abridged ed. by D. C. Somervell (1947–61); R. C. Collingwood, *The Idea of History* (1946); K. Löwith, *Meaning in History* (1949); P. Geyl, *From Ranke to Toynbee* (1951); P. Gardiner, *Nature of Historical Explanation* (1952); H. Butterfield, *Christianity and History* (1950); K. Jaspers, *Origin and Goal of History* (1953); E. Husserl, *Die Krisis der europäischen Wissenschaften und die transcendentale Phänomenologie* (1954); E. Troeltsch, *Protestantism and Progress* (1958); M. Müller, *Expérience et histoire* (1959); J. G. Droysen, *Historik* (4th ed., 1960); M. Heidegger, *Nietzsche*, 2 vols. (1961); E. Fackenheim, *Metaphysics and Historicity* (1961); W. Dilthey, *Pattern and Meaning in History* (1962); R. Bultmann, *History and Eschatology: the Presence of Eternity* (1962); H. Rickert, *Science and History, a Critique of Positivist Epistemology* (1962); A. Darlap, "Geschichtlichkeit", in H. Fries, ed., *Handbuch theologischer Grundbegriffe*, I (1962); H.-G. Gadamer, *Le problème de la conscience historique* (1963); A. Darlap, "Fundamentale Theologie der Heilsgeschichte", *Mysterium Salutis*, I (1965); R. C. Collingwood, *Essays in the Philosophy of History* (1965); K. Löwith, *Nature, History and Existentialism* (1966); J. Splett, *Der Mensch in seiner Freiheit* (1967); id., "Vérité, certitude et historicité", *Archives de Philosophie* 30 (1967), pp. 162–86; J. Robinson and J. Cobb, eds., *Theology as History* (1967).

Adolf Darlap and *Jörg Splett*

II. Philosophy of History

The term "philosophy of history", coined by Voltaire, is used in modern times for a large number of philosophical and historical sketches. Hence we shall first consider the various ways in which the philosophy of history is understood, then consider the main historical movements which a philosophy of history must suppose, and finally sketch the development of the philosophy of history.

A. THE MAIN APPROACHES

1. Philosophy of history is in general the effort to penetrate the meaning of the past and orientate oneself to the future, without being tied to the traditional patterns of the theology of history. It is therefore characteristic of modern man's effort to understand the world and his own autonomous place in it. History takes on the character of a process with a definite direction, either in the form of a development or a cyclic, spiral ascent. History is always considered "as" something — such as the progress of civilization, while the question of history as history does not arise. This is because in this type of the philosophy of history man, conscious of his autonomy, presupposes his own existence, as an individual or as a society, prior to history, and by this presupposition determines the meaning in the light of which history is interpreted. History can be judged on the basis of an unequivocal measure. This type of the philosophy of history includes such diverse approaches as the *Essai* of Voltaire, the *Positive Polity* of Comte and Spengler's *Decline of the West*.

2. In contrast to this "immanent" type of analysis of history, there is another approach based rather on the critiques made by Kant. It tries to work out a critique of the historical reason which will enable it to deal with a multiplicity of historical events which cannot be reduced to a system. It enquires into the conditions of possibility of historical knowledge in general, in order to define the nature and scope of historical research. This type of philosophy of history takes history essentially as a succession of facts from the past. The transcendental reason, as the *a priori* ground of historical knowledge and action does not offer the possibility of fixing an ideal in the light of which history could possibly be explained. But since meaning is disclosed only in the succession of past events — the reason being only the ground of possibility — the meaning

of history can only be worked out by history itself. The notion of a universal key to history is a guiding-line only, a limit notion which can never be realized. The philosophy of history is the "construction of the historical world in the sciences of the spirit" (Dilthey). This type of philosophy of history is found above all in the sphere of influence of neo-Kantianism. But it is also the basic attitude of many historians and theologians who do not recognize its provenance. This position is found in reverse, as it were, in structuralism, which offers a sort of objectivation of the transcendental reason. All the historical data which are accepted as such are treated in isolation from one another and examined individually for their proper constitutive laws. By reducing each element to its laws, the historical data are transformed into a "simultaneity of perspicuousness" — they are as transparent as they are contemporaneous.

Philosophy of history takes on a meaning different from that given it in 1 and 2 when man or reason is no longer pre-supposed as prior to history but when he begins to consider his own real historicity. All knowledge and action is then drawn into the ambit of history, in which man encounters the world in his knowledge and action. Hence history here is the all-encompassing, including the existence of the world as well as that of man. Everything is stamped with the mark of historicity, and history is no longer regarded "as" something. It is not the set of events which can be registered in the light of the transcendental reason. History is thought of as history where man is always in motion in self-awareness and in action, where the world is disclosed to him and where he can converse with men and the inner-worldly reality.

When history is regarded in this way as the all-encompassing, there are two modes of the philosophy of history, according to the aspect from which the relationship between history and thought is viewed. (Here "thought" is not taken in the sense of theory in contrast to practice, but as the luminous act of existing in which that which is becomes lightsome to man.) Since thought is always the act of existence, self-conscious and lucid, the philosophy of history can be understood as history dawning in thought, concentrating itself in concepts (see 3 below). Or history is world and worlds, man and mankind, being given into self-hood, and thus is the immemorial endowment of thought with the power to actuate in history all that is (see 4 below).

3. The basis of the concept of philosophy of history in the first of these two senses is the grasp of the conceptual character of thought. Since man when thinking is there with that which is, he actuates it in regard to its being. Thus that which is actuated is brought in the luminousness of the act into the selfhood of thought and thus grasped as concept. In the concept the thing comes to light and thought takes possession also of itself. This process of the spirit's becoming master of itself in the all, which is the assertion of the purpose of the spirit, is history. Thus history coincides with thought. It is the "actuation" of the spirit as it encompasses and becomes aware of itself and so of all things. Thought, as self-realization of the spirit, takes place as the sending to self of all that there is, in a series of historical dispositions. In the light of such a philosophy of history, history always has a universal character. Its course is composed of a series of major meaningful complexes which succeed one another while at the same time essentially comprising one another. For Hegel, whose philosophy of history is the great prototype of such explanations, world history is essentially the "explicitation and realization of the universal spirit" (*Grundlinie der Philosophie des Rechts,* para. 342, E. T.: *Philosophy of Right* [1942]).

4. The second of the latter two types is a correction of the third in which the basis is modified. Thought is still regarded as constructive: it produces beings. But this production, in which that which is dawns on man, is in itself something assigned to man, because it comes forth, in an incalculable way, from its own nothingness: *ex nihilo sui.* Man and the world, man and man encounter each other in an openness which is a supremely sovereign and unfathomable act of giving. Since man in his mundane existence is presented with himself to be taken over freely, he is intrinsically — like his world — ek-static in structure: he is always stepping out of the past, and his taking over of himself in the world has always the character of a surge forward into the future. Thinking is essentially thinking over, thought is always

after-thought. In its identity each being which is thought of affirms itself as other than that very concept, by reason of its immemorial origin. All comprehension is based on a self-bestowal which changes the grasp, from within, into a grateful acceptance. In this way thought is both historical and dialogal. In this thinking, which is in the nature of an event which comprises within itself, as a derivative mode, all thinking which registers and calculates, the structure of the world and the worlds, of man and mankind, is disclosed. But this structure is released by and does its work in that openness which while giving still retains the structure within its immemorial concealment. History, being this structure, presents itself as the self-interrogating question put to the mystery which is the ground of all that is.

This basic understanding of history would comprise such approaches as Heidegger's notion of the history of being, Jaspers's concept of transcendence and Rosenzweig's dialogical thinking. This type of philosophy of history opens up perspectives which are based on the event of the openness in question as the lay-out of history. This philosophy of history finds its justification in the light thrown on such concepts of history by the event which they themselves attest, of creative openness.

B. THE GREAT MODES OF EXPERIENCING HISTORY

1. *Myth and metaphysics.* The ancient view of history, as attested by Herodotus, Thucydides, Plato and Aristotle, forms a remarkable contrast to the preceding experiences of history among the Greeks. Earlier, God (θεός, a word without a vocative case) was the supremely primordial event, history. Θεός is expounded through verbs in the infinitive (Diogenes of Apollonia, Frg. 5, Diels [Pre-Socratics]); cf. Wilamowith-Moellendorff. In the *Helen* of Euripides, Helen cries out: "O gods! For it is God, when the loved ones are known." The event of recognition is θεός. It is only when one looks back on the occurrence that the gods appear with name and contour. History comes about in events, in each of which all is concentrated — world, men and gods.

Greek metaphysics takes the opposite view. There everything is traced back to the supreme ἀρχή, the principle beyond time, ground of all beings, itself conceived of as a substance. From this ultimate principle comes the all, as a well-ordered beautiful cosmos which is grasped by inerrant knowledge ("science" — ἐπιστήμη). In contrast to ἐπιστήμη, we have ἱστορία, the story of the item qua item, told in terms of what has been seen and heard (Aristotle, *Poetics,* 1451 b). It includes accounts of plants and beasts as well as news of men and events. History, as sheer multiplicity of items, is ἀμέθοδος ὕλη, *materia invia* (Sextus Empiricus, *Adversus Mathematicos,* I, 12, 254). Hence the aim of Greek history writing was to give instruction about the universal which manifests itself in the individual items: the power of the gods which brings everything into balance (Herodotus), the immanent laws of politics (Thucydides). History as a whole is the fragmentated, blurred appearance of the cosmos, its purpose is the ascent to the principle (ἀρχή) in which history is left behind (Plato, allegory of the cave).

2. *The OT covenant.* Unlike Hellas, Israel experienced history as a covenant. The covenant is not, as it were, within history, it is the primordial, incalculable opening of history. Israel proclaims Yahweh as its God, the God who had turned to the fathers, rescued the people from Egypt and promised to be its God for ever (historical Credo, Deut 26 : 5–9). The event of the covenant throws open future and past in a special way: in view of the utterly unfathomable election in grace, Abraham is nothing but a man, called out of the ranks of mankind. Before Yahweh, the peoples combine into mankind. The universal history of Gen 1–11 forms the necessary background to the history of Abraham and the covenant. But God's promise of well-being which throws open the future is not confined to the people of the covenant. It is also the guiding-line and the norm of history in general (Dan 7). The God of the covenant is, in retrospect, the creator God, in prospect the judge of history, its promise of well-being. The justification of such hope is seen by Israel again and again in its own continued existence. Throughout the many worlds and world-pictures which come and go, throughout judgment and grace, the people survives at least as a remnant, and hence may understand itself as the people founded on the covenant and willed by God.

Here history takes place as the one enduring history of the covenant in the one but manifold history of mankind.

3. *The fullness of time.* The Christian community affirms that the Christ-Event is the fullness of time, where covenant history and world history are merged, submerged and subsumed. The salvation come in Christ is the salvation of all the world and all worlds, not a thing of the distant future but something to be grasped in time. Above and beyond all the ambiguity and obscurity of history, overflowing all its bounds in death and sin, God has bestowed himself as blessed fulfilment. Thus all time becomes his time, in all times hovers the fullness of time. This is attested by the Church, as the one Church of Jews and Gentiles which sees itself sent to the whole world and understands itself to be most fully at one with the poorest and the most abandoned. Hence in the fullness of time the fellowship of men from the most diverse worlds, world-views and views of history is an event which takes place in a way of unmistakable significance. At the same time, this one world history, as the history of many worlds, is totally given over to man, "desacralized", because God, the salvation of history, abandoned all historical form — in the death of Jesus.

C. DEVELOPMENT OF MODERN PHILOSOPHY OF HISTORY

The Christian thinkers of antiquity and the Middle Ages took an essentially theological view of history. They were more concerned with the meaning of the whole than the investigation of historical facts, as may be seen from the historical judgments of Augustine, Bonaventure or Thomas Aquinas. But with Descartes the traditional concepts of the world and of history began to be radically challenged. Basing himself on Descartes but reversing his conclusions, G. B. Vico sketched his *Scienza Nuova.* Combating incidentally the pretensions of science, he affirmed that all history was explicable beyond doubt or hesitation by virtue of its origin, its human positing. Fixed principles were at work in this positing of history by man. Hence Vico sought for "an ideal, eternal history, according to which the histories of all people follow their course in time". A little later Voltaire, in his *Essai sur les Mœurs et l'Esprit des Nations* sketched a new outline of human history. Its goal is the enlightened man. Voltaire began with China, rejected the chronology of the OT and spoke as a historian and philosopher, that is, as a man who did not believe in revelation.

The Encyclopaedists, Turgot and Condorcet, continued with the philosophy of history as the philosophy of human progress, while Rousseau defined history as the process of depravation of natural man, and his true nature. Comte's *Cours de la Philosophie positive* (1830–42) was the basis of all succeeding positivist and sociological interpretations of history, with its three stages of human history — theological, metaphysical and positive or scientific. History, for Comte, is a sort of social physics, to be grasped scientifically by sociology.

Examples of German philosophy of history during the Enlightenment include Lessing's "Education of the Human Race" (*Erziehung des Menschengeschlechts*) and Kant's "Plan of a Universal History in Cosmopolitan Perspective" (*Idee zu einer allgemeinen Geschichte in weltbürgerlicher Absicht*). In both of these, the notion of progress was predominant, to which Herder then added his discovery of the "inner-directedness" of the individualities of various peoples and eras. A unifying central meaning and impulse in history is the key to human life. W. von Humboldt described the goal and structure of world history as the revelation of the power of the human spirit. In his essay on the task of the historian (*Aufgabe des Geschichtsschreibers*) he gives the principles of historical method as they result from his own view of history. History writing is the re-creation of reality, inspired by the human forces which unite past and present.

Hegel went beyond the tentative efforts of Herder, Humboldt, Fichte and Schiller to interpret history as the manifestation of the spirit as it comes to comprehend itself in its various forms (see A, 3, above). The systematic character of universal history which resulted from this approach led historians in particular, like von Ranke and Droysen, to reject it. While Marx, in spite of his opposition to Hegel, retained his systematic approach to the interpretation of history,

Droysen's *Historik,* a philosophical consideration of the nature of history and the methods of modern historicism, formulated the principle: "The essence of the historical method is to reach understanding through research."

Hence there is felt to be a contradiction between historical understanding and the ideal of scientific objectivity. Windelband and Rickert sought to escape the dilemma by their appeal to a theory of values, while Dilthey sought for a solution in hermeneutics (strongly tinged by psychology). In Dilthey, and even more so in P. Yorck von Wartenburg, the link between the scientific ideal and the tradition of metaphysical thinking is affirmed. In the light of Heidegger's notion of the historicity of the understanding of being, the previous sketches of a philosophy of history seem to be nothing but metaphysical interpretations of history (see B, 1, above), which presuppose the Jewish and Christian affirmations of history as salvation but distort them by making them metaphysical. The development of a non-metaphysical, historical thinking in more recent philosophies of history opens up a new approach to the understanding of the affirmations of faith. But the latest developments of a structuralist philosophy of history offer, on the contrary, a new reduction of history to metaphysics.

See also *Historicism, History* I, III, *Progress, Structuralism, World, Concept, Sociology, Hermeneutics* I.

BIBLIOGRAPHY. See bibliography on *Historicism, History* I, III; also: R. Rocholl, *Die Philosophie der Geschichte* (1878); R. G. Collingwood, *The Idea of History* (1946); K. Löwith, *Meaning in History: The Theological Implications of the Philosophy of History* (1957); J. G. Droysen, *Historik* (4th ed., 1960); W. Dilthey, *Gesammelte Schriften,* I, III, V, VII (1960); M. Heidegger, *Nietzsche,* 2 vols. (1961); K. Löwith, *Nature, History and Existentialism* (1966); P. Hünermann, *Der Durchbruch geschichtlichen Denkens im 19. Jahrhundert* (1967).

Peter Hünermann

III. Theology of History

A. PROBLEM

1. *History.* History is one of the basic categories of biblical revelation. Revelation does not merely throw light on history, it also gives rise to it. The absolute gratuity of

revelation brings with it its character of historical contingency. As an event which can neither be foreseen nor influenced revelation sets up new historical reality and gives a promise of a future. The new conditions of salvation thus brought about demand on the part of men conversion of heart and the decision of faith, and thus revelation also leads to a knowledge of the intrinsic historicity of man. It is this character of historical event which distinguishes the OT and NT revelation from the non-Christian epiphany religions, where revelation is understood merely as a hieratic manifestation of the eternal ground of being, and still leaves history as the cyclic return of the eternal self-same. According to biblical revelation, history is not a moment of the cosmos, but the cosmos is a part of history. The metaphysical and cosmological notion of "nature" is replaced by the thought of a universal "history", in movement towards a future.

Elements of a theology of history are to be found as early as the first Christian apologists. Justin and Clement of Alexandria defended against Jews and pagans the continuity and the pedagogical purpose of the salvific action of God, while Irenaeus upheld the unity of creation and covenant against Gnosis. Origen used the doctrine of the Logos to depict history as a unified whole. Eusebius and Orosius had a theology of the empire based on the *Pax Romana,* while Augustine stressed the ambivalence of political power in his *De Civitate Dei.* In the Middle Ages, as for instance by Charlemagne, the doctrine of Augustine and the theocracy of the OT was again applied to the actual course of history.

Along with a speculative tendency, some starts at a theology of the history of salvation may be noted in Scholasticism (Otto of Freising, Rupert of Deutz, Petrus Comestor, Stephen Langton and others). More important efforts were made by Alexander of Hales, Bonaventure and Thomas Aquinas, though their thinking is mostly dominated by cosmological and metaphysical categories.

Patristic and scholastic thinking was more interested in a theology of the history of salvation than in a theology of history in the present-day meaning. This only became possible when history in general was detached from the framework of history of salvation (Voltaire, Vico), and when history had also become a philosophical problem.

This was furthered by a process of secularization which began within theology as the expectation of the imminent end was disappointed. Other factors were the influence of Joachim of Fiore, the resumption of non-Christian trends, as from Gnosis and the Kabbala (the theme of fall and restoration to pristine perfection occurring in J. J. Rousseau and romanticism), the collapse of the antique and medieval picture of the cosmos (Copernicus), and a historicizing view of a world brought under man's control, to which modern science and technology contributed. In Scripture, history had been part of revelation, but now revelation often became a moment of history, and history itself was seen as revelation (Herder, Lessing, Schelling, Hegel).

The theology of history must now be prepared to maintain itself against the competition from modern philosophies, ideologies, Utopias and programmatic views of history. In contrast to a theology of the history of salvation, it provides the framework of a theology of earthly realities.

At present there are various trends in Catholic theology. One, more optimistic, is orientated towards the incarnation (G. Thils, P. Teilhard de Chardin), another, more critical, is orientated towards eschatology (P. L. Bouyer) or a *theologia crucis.* Most theologians strive for a theology of history which will be an adequate synthesis (H. and K. Rahner, J. Daniélou, Y. Congar, H. U. von Balthasar).

2. *Method.* In the dialogue with modern philosophies and ideologies of history, theology must draw its inspiration from its own sources. This means that it must try to understand world history in the light of the history of salvation as interpreted by the word of revelation. This excludes on principle any theological interpretation of individual historical events outside the history of salvation. We may not draw any conclusions, for instance, as to wars, natural phenomena, etc., from their coincidence or combination with Church feasts or the like, since revelation in fact tells us nothing about them. For the same reason it is impossible to divide up the history of the world and the Church into periods with definite theological significance.

The prophetic charism of the Church, however, obliges it to address its message to each *kairos* as it comes. It must therefore speak in such a way as to be adequate to the times and do justice to history. It is not enough to be objectively correct. The Church must read the "signs of the times" (Mt 16:4). This calls for a logic of existential thought and of insight into each *kairos,* a discernment of spirits which can hardly be reduced to a hard and fast method. It can only be achieved by continuous obedience to the cross and by the daring of love.

In contrast to such legitimately prophetical views of history, the theology of history is a form of fundamental theology which ponders the basic, intrinsic structures of the history of salvation and tries to grasp their implications for the theology of history. Since it looks back constantly to the words of revelation, it is different from the philosophy of history, which must on principle regard the history of revelation and its understanding of history merely as one group of phenomena among others. Since the theology of history is based on faith, it must continue to build on faith, hope and charity, and not merely on knowledge.

B. Basic Theological Assertions

1. The *starting-point* is the primary mystery of the grace of the self-communication of God to man and hence to history. This has taken place once and for all in Jesus Christ, and will be fully manifested in a real future yet to come. This affirmation about the end of history is necessarily veiled, because it sees the fulfilment as the sovereign act of God, whose mystery cannot be anticipated by human knowledge. Both the apocatastasis and double predestination run counter to this principle.

But God is the end of history in the sense that he is also end-term and completion, because he assumes and affirms it "inconfusedly and undividedly" (*D* 302). This means that the consummation of history must not be regarded as coming only from on high, in the sense of a one-sided theology of the incarnation. It must also be regarded as a process of self-maturation accomplished from below. The acceptance of history by God in the incarnation has as its counterpart the acceptance of God by Jesus Christ in historical obedience and self-abandonment unto the death of the cross, which God takes up again in the resurrection and glorification.

History only reaches its fulfilment by the way of the cross; its fulfilment is the passover mystery of Easter, a possibility of surpassing itself provided by grace. But this obedient Exodus out of history to God is not a negation of history, but again the fulfilment of historical *ex-sistentia,* man's power to be outside and beyond himself. The cross is also his exaltation.

2. *Extension by a theology of creation.* The theological doctrine of creation is given not at the beginning but within the description of the history of salvation. It is there to justify the universal and total claim of the history of salvation and the absoluteness of the promise. Because God is Lord of all by his creative word, he can expect the answer of faith from within history. History then appears as a dialogue composed of divine offer and response or refusal by man's belief or unbelief. History has the character of summons and decision. But since it is founded only on God's free word, its contingence is not the hazard of blind fate, but the expression of a historical providence which is responsible for everything that is. The voice of history is a doxology.

Like assertions about the last things, assertions about the first (protological) are not historical descriptions of paradise, original justice, etc., but pointers to God's primordial and therefore all-embracing and therefore eschatological plan of history. Protology, therefore, also remains wrapped in obscurity and mystery, being an aetiology and not a report on externals. It gives the basis and horizon of our present order of salvation.

The power of sin is also a factor in our present situation, and it has been one of the determinants of history from the start. It is the refusal to go out of oneself to enter into the dialogue, and hence a refusal of authentic history. It comes to a head in the principalities and powers, in original sin, death, suffering, concupiscence and law. Awareness of the presence of sin should be a warning against an unduly optimistic view of creation, but also against a grinding pessimism, since sin too has been caught up in God's plan of salvation in Christ, to which the whole of history moves.

The intrinsic unity of human history is based on its protology and eschatology. This unity (peace) is eschatological expectation, symbolically proclaimed already in the unity

45

of the Church composed of Jews and gentiles, which charges Christians with a special responsibility for peace in the world.

3. History has its *ultimate roots in God*. The eternity of God does not mean primarily timelessness, as it did to the Greeks, but a time positively master of itself, and freedom to set up and enter into history, without being submerged in it. The Supra-temporal is, therefore, the Ever-present, immanent to each instant of time. All history is encompassed and determined by God, but not as a necessary pantheistic evolution. It is God's free decision, the *concretissimum universale* of the divine plan of salvation, on which all history rests, and which cannot be reconstructed in definable terms, without turning the theology of history into a determinism. God's plan of history is in accord with human freedom, without being dependent on it. Thus the relationship between time and eternity should not be taken as a static one. It unfolds historically. Though "each age is as close to God as any other", history is still only on the way to the point where "God is all in all" (1 Cor 15:28). This is the justification of a well-considered pluralism of the history of salvation, the history of the world and the history of religions. The effort to homogenize ("integralism"), to separate here and now the weeds from the corn, to turn the world into a monolithic Church, is basically presumption.

C. THE CATEGORIES OF THE THEOLOGY OF HISTORY

1. *Time and times:* see *Time, Aeon*.

2. *Factors of history:* see *Original Sin, Death, Concupiscence, Law, Law and Gospel, Angel, Demons;* but also *Spirit*.

3. *Periods of history:* see *History, Salvation* III, *Religion* II A, *Natural Law, Law and Gospel, Covenant, Church*.

4. *Patterns in the theology of history*. The best known are the pattern of the circle for the Greek view of history and that of the straight line for the biblical. But both are ambiguous and inadequate. The circle can depict the non-historical, the meaningless and the aimless (Origen, Augustine) or again, the course of history from God and to God (Thomas Aquinas). The line can indicate eschatological purposefulness and continuity, but not the

discontinuity of sin and of the cross. Points could represent contingence and the element of decision, but not the prolongation; the swing of the pendulum could stand for the antagonisms of apocalyptic but with the risk of importing a dualistic misunderstanding; the spiral could recall the element of continuity and progression, but not that of decision; the image of the widening circle in water unites some of these elements (point, line of movement, extension and circle), but lacks the moment of dialogue; the triangular movement of dialectic fails to represent freedom. All these diagrams are better ignored, because there is an element of distortion in all of them.

The most suitable theological pattern is that given by the typological and sacramental thinking of Scripture and patristic theology. Like the history of the world and the history of salvation, individual events are related to one another like anticipation and realization. We may thus deduce three fundamental laws of the theology of history: a) the law of continuity throughout and in spite of sin and the cross, by virtue of the divine fidelity; b) the law of orientation to a new and greater future. The antitype is always greater than the type; the last things are not just the restoration of the first, but their Easter transformation; c) the law of solidarity between the particular and the universal. The individual is always called as one with and representative of the whole of humanity. History cannot be simply divided between salvation and disaster; before God, humanity forms a single whole, for weal and for woe.

5. *Basic attitudes*. This three-fold law brings about three groups of basic attitudes when the Christian looks at history: a) Faith: through the eschatological act of God's salvation, his triumphant power has intervened definitively in history and has redeemed it from dissolution and failure, in the death and resurrection of Christ. History cannot now be basically a nightmare. The basic Christian attitudes are not anxiety and scepticism, but calm, courage, humour and alertness. b) Hope: this means yielding oneself boldly to the ever-changing newness of history, instead of clinging timidly, like men of little faith, to over-rigid and ultra-conservative traditions. But it also means patience and willingness to wait; it is a confidence in

God which excludes a naïve belief in progress as well as the fanaticism of the revolutionary millenarist. c) Love and solidarity: this means dutiful co-operation in the humanizing and pacification of the world, testimony in word, life and suffering, as representative of humanity.

D. Concrete Questions

1. *Historical understanding of the world:* see *World, Nature, History.*

2. *Historical shaping of the world:* see *Work, Culture, Science, Technology, Sociology, Politics.*

3. *The future within history:* see *Progress, Christianity* II.

See also *Revelation, Creation, History* I, *Apocalyptic, Apologists, Gnosis, Original Sin, Monogenism.*

BIBLIOGRAPHY. GENERAL: R. Aubert, "Discussions récentes autour de la Théologie de l'Histoire", *Collectanea Mechliensia* (1948), pp. 129–49; L. Malevez, "La vision chrétienne de l'histoire, II. Dans la théologie catholique", *NRT* 71 (1949), pp. 244–64; id., "Deux théologies catholiques de l'histoire", *Bijdragen* 10 (1949), pp. 225–40; G. Thils, "La théologie de l'histoire. Note bibliographique", *ETL* 26 (1950), pp. 87–95; M. Flick and Z. Alzeghy, "Teologia della storia", *Gregorianum* 35 (1954), pp. 256–98; J. David, "Theologie der irdischen Wirklichkeiten", in J. Feiner and others, eds., *Fragen der Theologie heute* (1957), pp. 560–67. BIBLICAL THEOLOGY: O. Cullmann, *Christ and Time* (1951; revised ed., 1964); G. von Rad, *Old Testament Theology,* 2 vols. (1961–65); J. Daniélou, "The New Testament and the Theology of History", *Texte und Untersuchungen* 73 (1959), pp. 25–34; T. Boman, *Das hebräische Denken im Vergleich mit dem griechischen* (3rd ed., 1959), pp. 104–33; J. Barr, *Biblical Words for Time* (1962); id., *Old and New in Interpretation* (1964); O. Cullmann, *Salvation as History* (1967). SYSTEMATIC THEOLOGY: K. Barth, *Church Dogmatics,* vols. I–III (1956–60); R. G. Collingwood, *The Idea of History* (1946); E. Rosenstock-Huessy, *The Christian Future or the Modern Mind Outrun* (1946); L. Bouyer, "Christianisme et eschatologie", *Vie intellectuelle* 16 (1948), pp. 6–36; E.-C. Rust, *The Christian Understanding of History* (1948); R. Niebuhr, *Faith and History* (1949); H. Butterfield, *Christianity and History* (1949); N. Berdyaev, *Meaning of History* (1950); E. Castelli, *I presupposti di una teologia della storia* (1952); W. Pannenberg, ed., *Offenbarung als Geschichte* (1961); R. Bultmann, *History and Eschatology. The Presence of Eternity* (1962); H. Urs von Balthasar, *Theology of History* (1962); P. Teilhard de Chardin, *Future of Man* (1964); J. Mouroux, *Mystery of Time* (1964); K. Rahner, *Theological Investigations,* V (1965); W. Kasper, *Das Absolute in der Geschichte. Philosophie und Theologie der Geschichte in der Spätphilosophie Schellings* (1965).

Walter Kasper

HOLINESS

1. The ultimate source of all holiness is the holiness of God, whereby he is the "wholly Other". But even in the OT, God the inaccessible, "the holy one of Israel", is also the joy, force, support and salvation of the chosen people (Is 10:20; 17:7; 41:14–20). In the righteousness brought by the "holy servant Jesus" (Acts 4:27, 30), who "sanctifies himself" that his own may be "sanctified" (Jn 17:19), God imparts himself to man. He draws him by grace into his own personal life, gives himself as the Holy One, and makes him holy through sanctifying grace in the Holy Spirit, called to "the holy city, the new Jerusalem" (Rev 21:2). Man is enabled to accept this self-communication of God and to respond to it through the supernatural ("infused") virtues, especially faith, hope and charity. These virtues direct his religious and moral action towards immediate participation in the life of the Trinity. Through them and in them God himself in his self-communication brings about the possibility and the free realization of participation in his life. Here the basic option for God which was already involved in baptism (*viventes autem Deo,* Rom 6:11) is constantly renewed as man dedicates himself totally to God and to an unqualified answer to God's offer of grace. This free self-dedication of man of whom God has taken possession in baptism (and substantially sanctified) is also moral self-sanctification, which, however, again presupposes the grace of God for its realization. This actual dedication to God, which makes the life of the Christian a cultic sacrifice (cf. Rom 12:1; Phil 2:17; 4:18; Heb 13:15, 16; 1 Pet 2:4f., 9) is, through Christ, service of God, union with him and assimilation to him who "hallows his (own) name".

2. More precisely, this self-realization of the Christian is love, which is found in all the diverse acts of Christian life (Mt 22:40), which is "the fulfilment of the law" (Rom 13:10) and includes the fulfilment of the other precepts (Gal 5:14) which it "sums

up" (Rom 13:9). Only love can assign man totally to God, because only love binds the multiplicity of his being into inner unity and dedicates it to God. For man is only fully himself when he turns in love to the Other. It is in love that man is given to himself and in it alone can he truly fulfil himself. Love alone is the full answer due to God as person.

3. But man who responds to God in love is a being of many dimensions. Hence his moral and religious perfection takes on many different forms, in virtues such as justice, virginity, humility, love of the neighbour, etc. For God does not speak merely in the commandment of love. There are a number of particular precepts which correspond to the manifold nature of human reality. These virtues may be there without the full expressiveness of love, but only come to their full perfection in love. Though they imply at once a total commitment, this is only gradually achieved, and it is only in personal action that all human faculties and domains are fully integrated according to the potentialities of the individual. From this point of view, love is always pressing forward to a stage beyond what it has reached at a given moment. The individual is called by God in his uniqueness and cannot know beforehand what God may demand from him in the future (K. Rahner, *Theological Investigations,* V, pp. 494–517). The more love has found itself and informed the other virtues, the more perfect is holiness.

4. God, the goal of life in love, does not remain hidden as he acts on man in grace. His self-communication brings about in man the response of knowledge as well as love. This action of God in grace does not remain beyond the bounds of consciousness, but is experienced, not indeed as an object, not as something "seen", not in the sense of Ontologism, but as an unobjectivated light which illumines the "objects" of the supernatural acts. But it is not itself the object of such acts. Hence God cannot be attained through psychological introspection, but only as a concomitant experience linked with the objects of faith, hope and charity which are given objectively and linked with the sense of faith of the Church. The experience is all the stronger, the more man is familiar with and knows how to practise the natural transcendence of the spirit towards being in

general, inner recollection, ethical action, aesthetic experience and so on. This experience, however, gives no certainty about the state of grace.

5. The love of God, as well as being "other-worldly", that is, the love with which God in his immanent trinitarian life loves his own perfection, is also "worldly", that is, God's redeeming love of the world (Jn 3:16). The supernatural love of man is participation in the love of God. Hence the Christian who really loves God also necessarily participates in God's love of the world. Hence love of God, sharing in God's love of the world, is primarily directed towards men. These are loved in the absolute love of God, but for their own sakes, in keeping with the commandment which makes love of God and love of man run parallel. But since man is loved as a person, and hence by reason of an absolute moral decision, love of the neighbour necessarily includes love of God, which is its foundation and support. In a certain sense this love of the world also includes the irrational creation and material reality, insofar as they are "goods which we wish to others . . . So too God loves them *ex caritate*" (Thomas Aquinas, *Summa Theologica,* II, II, q. 25, a. 3). They are lovable insofar as they are seen in combination with the beloved person.

6. Since true love cannot remain inward only but strives to express itself in action, to embody itself, as it were *(caritas effectiva),* true love of the world will also try to act visibly in an effort to order human society with regard to things and things among themselves. Thus love is exercised in "profane" action in the world as well as in the "cultic" action of the liturgy in its various sacramental forms. Thus all appropriate action of the man who loves, in work and leisure, in action and meditation, is love and holiness, since the basic intention which sustains and shapes this action is the supernatural dynamism of love, which radically alters man and hence his action (*D* 799f., 821). If love is the basic principle which forms, moves and guides all being and action, it is also implicitly actuated here and also finds its fullness of being in such modes of life (work, service of the world — as *caritas implicite actuata*). It too participates in the "knowableness" of grace as described above,

which is concomitantly the consciousness of the presence and action of God (light, force, joy, tranquillity). Thus the ontic world of categories is met as a form of the ontological and transcendent reference to God, which is or can be experienced as such in an eschatological prolepsis — which is the Christian way of "flight from the world". The reason for this harmony between the natural and objective relationship to the world and a life of love and holiness is ultimately the fact that the natural order of creation is a presupposition and intrinsic moment of the order of redemption — since in the incarnation the redemptive reality provides itself with the natural order in order to be itself, and by giving it an ultimately supernatural meaning confirms it in its naturalness and heals it where it is wounded (K. Rahner, *Mission and Grace*, I, p. 63). Hence holiness is not rejection of the world but, of necessity, holy action on the world. When he makes love manifest, the Christian is fulfilling the task which is given him as a member of the Church which is in the world to give testimony in history to the grace of God.

7. Since holiness is a participation of the self-communication of God, in man it is a grace-given listening to God and a commitment to him, wherever his summons is heard. Hence it is very necessary to learn to understand the "language" of God, which has its own "idiom" corresponding to the transcendence of God, for which the discernment of spirits is important. Scripture tells us that there is such a thing as growth in grace (Mt 13:8; Jn 15:2; Eph 3:16–19), which is both granted to and demanded of man (Eph 4:15; *D* 803). Because of the danger of a self-centred perfectionism, the focus of all holiness must be God himself, who rouses and sustains man's effort as he encounters him in grace and is ultimately the goal of this dynamism ("hallowed be thy name"). But here precisely God wishes man to co-operate freely (*D* 799, 850), so that the unity of creation and redemption may be preserved, without the natural structures being disguised, displaced or distorted. The natural values of thought, desire and feeling are to be sought after and realized as a condition and inner moment of grace. What is naturally valuable is not in itself a condition or inner moment of grace, since nature can never be a positive ground for grace. It is only such

insofar as God freely pre-posits and accepts it as the condition for his action in grace. It is only in this sense that nature is the antechamber and place of grace. As experience shows, psychosomatic health is not always the point of insertion for grace. It is often linked with bodily illness and mental strains. But the Church struggles against the disruptive forces of temptation (the devil, evil, sin, etc.) by orderly thinking, helps to the will, etc., that is, by directing creation to its natural fulfilment. In the justified, natural values are of course sustained by grace and when they are achieved they are already elevated by grace and are the fruit of the Spirit (Gal 5:22–23).

Love as self-dedication to God is necessarily allied to Christian self-denial in the work of sanctification, as an anticipation of death along with Christ; it sustains this work and realizes itself there *(caritas crucifixa)*. Since holiness involves many attitudes whose immediate goals diverge, it must be a dynamic equilibrium of many dialectical tensions, which must find their inner harmony in love: self-development and crucifixion of the "natural" strivings, renunciation of the world and formation of the world, self-respect and humility, the prudence of the serpent and the simplicity of the dove, freedom and obedience, resistance and patience, total confidence and anxious effort.

8. When man's response to the gift of grace is approximately total, so that while still an individual effort it is an epoch-making moment in the holiness of the Church as a whole, then the holiness of Christians reaches the height which is called "heroic virtue" in the process of canonization.

9. All Christians are called to holiness. "The great commandment of charity knows no bounds ... everyone is commanded to love God as well as he can" (Thomas Aquinas, *Contra Retrahentes*, 6), according to the measure and nature of his gift of grace (cf. Rom 12:3; 1 Cor 12:11), in the concrete realization of love to which they are individually called. The "rich young man" was called to total renunciation of his possessions, others were called to other forms of unconditional following of Christ. A double morality which attempts to assign a minimum Christianity to the laity is theologically indefensible.

10. Vatican II's Constitution on the Church (*Lumen Gentium,* art. 15) affirms the existence of great holiness outside the Church. So too it is above all the Church itself, and not any particular institution in it, which is the great state of perfection, "established by Christ in fellowship of life, love and truth" and as "instrument of the redemption" (art. 9), including that of its members, to which it offers "so many great means" of sanctity (art. 11). Christians are "equipped to bear increasingly rich fruit of the Holy Spirit" (art. 34). The holiness of the Church expresses itself in various forms, though in a special way *(proprio quodam modo)* through the evangelical counsels (art. 39). The way in which holiness appears in this way of life is only one particular and special way. All Christians are to grow in holiness "according to their own special calling" (art. 35), "the ways proper to each" (art. 41), using the means proper to each (arts. 11, 41) and above all by serving in love, which "guides, animates and makes efficacious" all means of holiness (art. 42) and is therefore the one great means, the "more excellent way" of 1 Cor 12:31. In the Church, all Christians are "most intimately united with the life and mission of Christ" (art. 34). The whole Church must be "virgin", "true to the truth which it has pledged to the bridegroom, pure and inviolate, imitating the mother of its Lord in the power of the Holy Spirit and preserving virginally a faith undiminished, a confidence unshakable and a love sincere" (art. 64). All Christians must "dedicate themselves to God alone with a single-minded devotion", though this is easier in celibacy *(ut facilius corde indiviso)* (art. 42). All share in the priestly, kingly and prophetic office of Christ (art. 31). All are "consecrated to Christ" (art. 34). The eschatological age is anticipated in all of them through the beginning of the future transfiguration which comes in grace; all are also witnesses to this grace and the future glory, which the Christian family proclaims "with a clear voice" (art. 35). They are not only guided by the outward institution of the Church, they are also "inwardly impelled by the Holy Spirit" (art. 40), and also enriched by charisms (art. 12), so that they may embody in their lives in ever growing measure the Church's evangelical message and hence the essence of Christianity (arts. 31, 38, 41).

See also *Holy, Grace, Grace and Freedom, Faith, Hope, Charity, Nature, Death, Saints I, III, Charisms, Evangelical Counsels.*

BIBLIOGRAPHY. O. Procksch, "ἅγιος", *TWNT,* I, pp. 87–116; B. Häring, *Das Heilige und das Gute* (1950); K. Barth, *Church Dogmatics,* II/1; G. Thils, *Théologie des réalités terrestres;* H. Küng, "Rechtfertigung und Heiligung nach dem NT", in M. Roesle and O. Cullmann, eds., *Begegnung der Christen* (2nd ed., 1960); M. Schmaus, *Katholische Dogmatik,* I (6th ed., 1963), pp. 562–67; G. Thils, *Christian Holiness* (1961); C. V. Truhlar, *Antinomiae Vitae Spiritualis* (2nd ed., 1961); id., *Structura theologica vitae spiritualis* (2nd ed., 1961); K. Rahner, "The Church of the Saints", *Theological Investigations,* III; G. Thils and K. V. Truhlar, eds., *Laics et vie chrétienne parfaite* (1963); K. Rahner, *Schriften zur Theologie,* VI, pp. 277–98.

Karl Vladimir Truhlar

HOLY

I. History of Problems. II. Phenomenology and Philosophy. III. The Holy in Revelation.

I. History of Problems

Through the writings of E. Durkheim, N. Söderblom and R. Otto, "the holy" became a central concept in comparative religion. But the unique and primordial notion of the holy has always been part, not only of human experience but of man's conscious convictions. It became a major subject of thought as soon as the interpretation of the holy given in religious worship and in myth ceased to be sufficient.

Plato was the first Western thinker to deal with the holy, after the struggles of the pre-Socratics. He calls it "good", "divine" and "God" (ἀγαθόν, θεῖον, θεός); its image is the sun, the giver of all light and life, but it is not merely an unchanging star. It is also the shining-forth of "the sudden", and it is so uniquely "worthy of awe" that man should be ready to be its "toy". (*Laws,* 803 b, c). In Aristotle, the holy has ceased to be "startling" and has rather been absorbed into the eternal, absolute truth and goodness. In spite of its transcendence as νόησις νοήσεως, it has to some extent been "brought into line" as the first principle of the world. Just as the Platonic view was given its radical expression in the neo-Platonism of Plotinus, so too the attitude of Aristotle in the Stoic doctrine of the world as permeated by reason.

Christianity comes from the experience of the holy in revelation, but it interprets revelation by means of Greek thought. This interpretation, Aristotelian, one might say, in the schools, Platonic in mysticism, saw the absolute grounds of metaphysics and the absolute manifestation of the holy as combined in Jesus Christ, without, however, posing explicitly the problem of the mode of this unity. The debate on universals provided some hints of the problem.

The initial posing of the problem and an effort at synthesis characterize the writings of Nicholas of Cusa. The process here signalled came into its own in modern philosophy, where the transcendentality of the holy was affirmed with ever-increasing vigour. While the speculative theology of Hegel claimed to "comprehend" the holy, Fichte and Schelling, in their later thought, made it absolute being and life, where knowledge founders and man fulfils himself in personal act.

The students of religion mentioned in the first paragraph sought to defend the holy against its being deformed in terms of psychology, biology or sociology. So too M. Scheler and the philosophy of values defended it against its being transposed into a category of culture, as in the Baden school of neo-Kantianism, and also against certain failures to keep its nature clearly in view in neo-Scholasticism.

Both sets of defenders allowed too little weight to one of the decisive traits of the biblical revelation of the holy: its impact on history. This was emphasized by M. Buber in his own writings and in the translation of Scripture which he undertook along with F. Rosenzweig. A similar line of thought was pursued by M. Heidegger, who had good reasons for appealing to Hölderlin, the "mythic" poet of the story of Western faith. It was Heidegger above all who showed that the holy was not to be juxtaposed, much less opposed to being or the transcendentals, as had been done in the course of controversy — so much so that a special organ or sense had been supposed for the apprehension of it. Appealing to the fathomless originality of the holy, he does not speak of the God of Abraham, Isaac and Jacob like Pascal, but in contrast to the God of the philosophers, he evokes the "divine(r) God". He maintains, however, that we can only speak meaningfully and honestly of God when we once more have experience of the holy, or rather, when it presents itself once more to our experience.

Is the holy in fact withdrawn from us or only given to us in the guise of its absence? Or is it merely that its presence is taking on a new and still unwonted form? There seem to be signs (cf., for example, bibliography: H. U. von Balthasar, B. Welte) that even today thought need not end in anxious question.

Jörg Splett

II. Phenomenology and Philosophy

1. *The question of the holy.* a) To reflect on the holy is not to think of holiness as an attribute of God or of holy beings, places, times or things; what is in question, therefore, is not the meaning of the adjective holy as a predicate that can be applied to someone or something. Nor is the holy a neutralizing collective name for the different forms whether personal or impersonal in which the highest principle is conceived. Concern with the holy rather means seeking the domain or dimension proper to the divine encounter in which the supreme principle shows itself.

b) But how, then, is the holy important for Christian theology? That theology knows where the divine principle manifests itself: in the unique and definitive revelation which takes place in Jesus. Nevertheless it needs to understand the holy. It would be useless to draw a system of correct propositions from revelation whose very correctness left the essential and appropriate encounter with the divine God and the grace of his redemption unexplained, or even threatened to obscure it.

c) The question of the holy is of its nature not something confined to Christianity. It is bound up with man's awareness of being and of himself, and develops in many human ways and forms. This very multiplicity is significant from the Christian point of view, for revelation presupposes an ontological openness of man to God's self-revelation, in other words, the horizon of the holy. Revelation addresses itself to this horizon, makes use of its particular human form. Within this horizon the one enduring message takes on the manifold forms of its historical expression.

2. *Manifestation of the holy.* Not every concept of being and of man is open to the manifestation of the holy.

a) The holy does not reveal itself to a purely theoretical interest. The fact that attention is directed away from itself towards measurable and verifiable results does not exclude *a priori* the knowledge that finite being is not its own ground. But it is not of itself capable of being affected by the holy. A new dimension of man's cognitive life is reached as soon as he comes to sense the inexorable and in fact absolute impact of truth.

b) Similarly the holy is not perceptible to purely aesthetic contemplation. The enchantment of the beautiful gives aesthetic activity certain features akin to those of religion. Where, however, it is a game to be enjoyed to the full without regard to the earnestness of personal existence, there is no sense of the other quality, the holy, which is nevertheless close to the surface of the beautiful.

c) The holy remains closed even to a purely ethical attitude. When faced with the inviolable and incalculable majesty of the good, the will turns back to itself as its own measure, the good does not reveal itself as holy.

d) The simultaneous presence of two apparently opposite characteristics distinguishes the religious attitude, which is open to the holy. One is the seriousness of personal existence: what is at stake is not any particular thing, but everything, myself, my salvation. But then the gravity of the concern for salvation causes the self to turn away from self, to transcend self and to trust to the infinitely other than itself. Where serious concern for self and open-hearted detachment from self coincide, access is thrown open to the holy. This, however, does not force the holy to appear. It gives itself only as a free gift.

3. *Fundamental characteristics of the holy.* In the many forms in which the holy appears, two polarities are generally present simultaneously.

a) It is the intangible which touches me deeply. The basic religious attitude reflects this polarity. The holy is in itself sublimely transcendent through its own inexplicable, independent and unconditional primacy and majesty. But this very sublimity makes it anything but neutral. It concerns me deeply. It is self-subsistent — but bears down on me. Of itself, that is, unrelated to me, it is the totally other and prior, but thus it comprises me, though not like a general concept of which I would be an individual instance. It moves me and knows me in my inmost depths. To move and to know are not additional activities of the holy but its own primordial force. It is not because of something it does that the holy concerns me, but because it is the holy. The precedence of the holy raises it beyond my grasp; it is intrinsically a limit and inviolable, once again not in virtue of external adjuncts such as a prohibition, for example, but simply because it is holy and inaccessible as that which is the prior concern of all.

b) It is awesome and beatifying. The first polarity, which is simply the force of the very nature of the holy, also includes a second, as the fundamental religious attitude also testifies. The holy both rejects and attracts. It withdraws itself inaccessibly from my grasp and as it comes it opens up the insuperable difference of the otherness at whose mercy I am and before which I am silent. Yet nothing but this other can reach and fulfil me interiorly; it is only in contact with the holy that I am blissfully and intimately liberated from the ambiguity and vacuity of my self. The duality of abyss and close presence once again does not signify a disharmony in the holy, but the oneness of its holiness where I am both a stranger and at home.

4. *The concept of the holy.* How is our understanding of being to do justice to the coming and the summons of the holy? Not by counting the holy among the topics which it has comprehended, but by submitting itself to the holy. With the coming of the holy, it is "beside itself" but at the same time still itself, for otherwise the coming would merely be a blind impact. But it is a gift which endows me anew with itself and with myself and with my grasp of being. My understanding gratefully transcends itself and thus finds itself at home with the holy, which it still recognizes as the prior and transcendent. This understanding follows the normal lines of all questioning — to ask after nature and purpose.

a) When the question of the nature or essence goes beyond individual beings to ask what is the being of beings in general, it comes upon such primordial and universal notes as the true, the good and the beautiful. Is the holy to be numbered with these? Its closeness to them is apparent from the fact that it transcends all beings and yet pervades them all. It differs from them, however, more than they differ among themselves. Truth, goodness, beauty and the corresponding being are not exhausted by the beings to which they are communicated, but their immediate orientation is towards beings; they tend to become predicates of beings and hence to become that which beings are. But beings are not holy of themselves, but only inasmuch as they point beyond themselves. The true and the good and so on are reflected and re-presented in beings. But the holy is merely commemorated there. That beings should be, in face of the holy, is not obvious, it is a marvel. Beings, in this ambit, are what are allowed to be. The holy is not the comprehensive essence of being, it is not prior to beings, but being's grateful memory of the hidden origin of all.

b) This backward thrust of being, in which the holy shows its might, even goes beyond the question of "why", which is itself a step further than all questions about beings. In the question, "Why?", beings cease to be taken for granted, but the purpose of this incomprehension is to look for the cause. Once the cause is clear, so is the being which was in question. If the why leads to an answer, I know what is "behind" things, in their cause. But there is no "getting behind" the holy. As the memorial to the holy, as the site which testifies that it intervened, beings remain unfathomable, wonderful; thus and only thus am I content. In the domain of the holy, the question "Why?" is answered only by remaining an open question; the source is not a first thing, but a mystery disclosing itself out of free and incalculable favour. The reversal of being which occurs in the holy manifests the difference between the "God of the philosophers" and the living, the divine God.

III. The Holy in Revelation

Attestation of revelation is in essentials, if not in words, attestation of the holy.

a) Gen 28 and 32, Exod 3 and 19, and Is 6, for example, display the typical combination of remoteness and proximity, fear and joy in the holy. Peter's cry: "Depart from me, for I am a sinful man, O Lord" (Lk 5:8), and the other, "It is well that we are here; let us make three booths" (Mk 9:5), indicate the tensions within which the domain of the

holy is revealed and in which meeting with the divine takes place. Similarly the OT passages referred to. This "domain" is the irruption of the divine God, his action itself. It contains nothing but himself, but he is there present as he who goes beyond himself, filling this "extra space" and showing himself there, but still, as the origin, always "behind" it.

b) In the definitive divine revelation of salvation in Jesus Christ, all becomes the one comprehensive holy place (cf., for example, Acts 10 and 17, 1 Cor 3:22f.; 10:26), while losing all "magical quality". It is given into the hands of men to be at their disposition (as what has been truly sanctified). The sacred and the profane character of the world become identical in the Christian view.

c) The domain of the holy in which the definitive memorial to God's coming is placed and where his coming is constantly to be re-enacted, is revealed in Christianity by the love of the Son of God giving himself to us in death: it is the human partner universally (Mt 25:40) and especially the fellowship of believers united in this love (Mt 18:20; Jn 17:22ff.; Acts 21).

See also *Religion* II, *Worship, Myth, Revelation* I, II, *Value, Attributes of God, Transcendentals, Mystery, World, Being.*

BIBLIOGRAPHY. R. Otto, *The Idea of the Holy* (from the revised German ed.) (1950); B. Häring, *Das Heilige und das Gute* (1950); M. Scheler, *Vom Ewigen im Menschen* (4th ed., 1954); R. Caillois, *Man and the Sacred* (from the 4th French ed.) (1959); M. Eliade, *The Sacred and the Profane* (1961); B. Welte, *Heilsverständnis* (1966); H. Urs von Balthasar, *The God Question and Modern Man* (1967).

Klaus Hemmerle

HOLY SPIRIT

I. Pneumatology. II. Gifts of the Holy Spirit.

I. Pneumatology

The teaching on the Holy Spirit developed very slowly in the faith of the Church from the indications of Scripture. Pneumatology always lagged behind Christology. This is all the more surprising because, according to Paul, the possession of the Spirit is characteristic of the justified and distinguishes him from those who are not justified. In general, Scripture speaks more of the Spirit's function in our salvation than of his nature. The activity of the Spirit (in inspiration) joins the OT and NT together as a unity.

1. *The Old Testament.* The OT speaks of the Spirit in many different ways which create a number of tensions, which cannot be reduced completely to a system. The terminology differs from that of the NT; the OT does not speak of the "Holy Spirit", but of the "Spirit of God" (Yahweh), whereas the NT uses "Holy Spirit". There is, however, no difference in meaning. The change of terminology is probably due to the efforts of late Judaism to avoid using the name of God and to use instead one of his attributes. The "Spirit of God" is a spirit different from the world and therefore rightly named "Holy" Spirit. "Holy" here means "of God"; it indicates the transcendence of the Spirit. In the OT, the "Spirit of God" means a divine power active in the world, or rather God himself insofar as he is acting in man and in the universe, in history and in nature. As the divine power is evident in a special way in the bringing forth and the maintenance of life, the Spirit of God is considered as the source of life (e.g., Gen 1:2; 2:7; 6:3; Ps 33:6; 104:29f.; 146:4; Job 12:10; 27:3; 34:14f.; Ezek 37:7–10). The Spirit of God works powerfully and holds sway in history (e.g., Exod 33:14–17). In the majority of the texts, the Spirit is imparted to specially chosen individuals, men equipped with tasks that affect the course of history, such as Joseph, Abraham, Moses, Gideon, etc. (Gen 41:38; Num 11:17; Exod 31:1–5; Jg 6:34; 14:6), and especially the Prophets (1 Sam 10:6; 16:14; 3 Kg 17–19; 22:22ff.; Mic 2:7; 3:8; Hos 9:7; Ezek 2:2; 3:12ff.; 8:3; 11:1ff.; Wis 1:4f.; 7:7; 9:17). Now and again the Spirit is praised as the cause of salvation for all the members of the people of God (Ps 51:12f.; 143:10). While the original expectations of the Spirit were centred on heroic feats, especially in war, on physical strength and special prudence, these hopes were later transferred more and more to the religious sphere. The Spirit plays a special role in the description of the coming Messiah, the prince of peace (Is 11:1f.; 32:15–18; 41:1ff.; 42:1ff.). In the period which he inaugurates, the possession of the Spirit will be a gift given to all (Ezek 11:19; 36:27; 37:14; 39:29; Jer 31:33; Is 32:15; 35:5–10; 44:3; Joel 2:28f.; Zech 12:10).

The Spirit of God imposes the loftiest demands upon the people of Israel, but he also comes upon the people as a blessing (Is 44:3). God's fidelity to his covenant is guaranteed by the promise of his Spirit (Is 59:21). Because the Spirit of God is in the midst of his people, there is nothing to fear (Hag 2:5). Among the Rabbis and in the Targums, the Spirit of God is above all the spirit of prophecy. The Spirit is mentioned many times in these writings as the pledge of the bodily resurrection of the dead.

The most emphatic pointer to the new Messianic age is given by Joel (3:1–5). Salvation will be accomplished with the outpouring of the Spirit upon all. The meaning of this prophecy is, as the NT texts show, not that the Spirit comes upon all men, but that he is imparted to all the faithful within the believing community.

2. *The New Testament.* Corresponding to this prophecy, we find in the NT the conviction that the redeemed community (the Church) is constituted by the Holy Spirit. First, John the Baptist resumes the inspired prophetic ministry of the OT. But he differs from the earlier prophets inasmuch as he saw the Messiah already present as the bearer of the Spirit and the giver of the Spirit to all (Jn 1:26). The incarnate Son of God was conceived through the Spirit; he was equipped with the Spirit at his baptism. He was driven into the desert by the same Spirit for his first decisive struggle with Satan. The Spirit is the moving power behind every activity of Christ. The opposition of men to the Spirit is called by Christ the unpardonable sin (Mt 12:31f.; Lk 12:10; Mk 3:29f.). According to Acts, Christ promised the Spirit to his own during the time of his absence (Acts 1:8). In the power of this Spirit they were then to be his witnesses in Jerusalem, in Judaea, in Samaria, and to the ends of the earth. In fulfilment of this promise, the fundamental gift of the Spirit was given on the first Pentecost. In the miraculous events that accompanied it, it was manifest that the saving action of God in the world was pressing forward irresistibly (Acts 2:1–11). Those partaking in the event experience it as the definitive bestowal of salvation. Peter interprets it as the fulfilment of the OT promises. The pentecostal outpouring of the Spirit is the beginning of the communication of the Spirit which continues through all time. The

Spirit henceforth leads and guides the Church and inspires all within it. He chooses Paul to preach the gospel to the heathens (Acts 13:2ff.). He is the unseen power behind the apostolic missionary activity. He sends the Apostle from the harvest fields of Asia to those of Europe (Acts 16:6f.). The Spirit foretells to Paul the sufferings of his imprisonment (Acts 20:22f.; 21:10f.). The Spirit will tell the faithful what to reply to their judges in the time of persecution, so that they need not be anxious about their answers (Mk 13:11; Mt 10:19f.; Lk 10:11f.). Because the redeemed community is led by the Spirit, the lie of Ananias and Saphira is an offence against the Holy Spirit, and is severely punished (Acts 5:3, 9).

It is the Pauline writings which contain the most comprehensive and impressive testimony to the Spirit. In the Pauline theology, the word covers a wide field and it is impossible to define exactly what Spirit (πνεῦμα) meant to Paul. The functions which the Apostle ascribes to the Spirit form a number of sharp contrasts. They were not invented by Paul, but were experienced within the community. The new and revolutionary element was that the baptized experienced effects which clearly come from God. Paul sought to describe in orderly fashion the rich variety of this activity. With O. Kuss, we may begin with the most striking phenomena to interpret Paul's notion of the Spirit and gain a general picture of it. The most strange and surprising gift of the Spirit is glossolalia, the gift of tongues, an unintelligible stammering in the enthusiasm of faith, in praise of God. Paul judges this phenomenon in a basically favourable light, but demands that it be exercised in an orderly way in the community. This demand supposes that the Spirit does not overwhelm the recipient, but leaves him free to control the effects of the Spirit. But then the danger arises that the Spirit will be deprived of his effectiveness by human opposition. The difficulties of the communities in this matter caused Paul to issue the anxious warning: "Do not quench the Spirit" (1 Thess 5:19). But there are other "charisms" of the Spirit which are better than these enthusiastic cries which no one could understand. One of the most important is inspired prophecy, i.e., the explanation of the word of God. These gifts bring about more easily and effectively the edification of the community which is the goal of all the functions of the Spirit. Strongly though the Apostle feels that the work of the Spirit should not be restrained, when he is faced with the confusion caused by the charisms at Corinth, he points out insistently that the Spirit works for unity and order. In this connection, Paul develops his personal doctrine of the Church as the body of Christ which the Spirit produces and animates as vital principle.

Even when the faithful are not gathered for worship, it is the Spirit who keeps alive their sense of dependence on God and urges them to live a life of the imitation of Christ. Paul teaches that the Spirit moves them to express their thanks and joy even in unintelligible sounds (Rom 8:26f.), but, above all, to call God "Father" (Gal 4:6). But the work of the Spirit is not confined to these extraordinary gifts. He is also active in the everyday life of the faithful. He is the foundation of a totally new life and activity. The baptized are a temple in which God dwells (1 Cor 3:16). Both the Church as a whole and the individual Christian are temples of the indwelling Spirit (1 Cor 6:19). The Spirit is a force which is active not only in passing moments of ecstasy, but everywhere and always in the life of the baptized. He is the first-fruit, the pledge, the handsel, the anticipation, the guarantee of the eschatological fulfilment. He moves and guides the preachers of the message and all other Christian believers. Paul too sees the possession of the Spirit as the fulfilment of the OT promises. The notion that the Spirit is already a foretaste of final salvation gains more and more importance in Paul as it becomes clearer that the resurrection of Christ which the disciples experienced was not identical with his parousia, but that there was to be a long interval between the resurrection and the consummation of all things. With the giving of the Spirit a beginning at least has been made of the final consummation.

In the life of the believer, the Spirit grants all the gifts of salvation for which the believer longs. He is the giver of life (Rom 8:10), a life which partakes of the dialectical tension between present and future (Gal 6:8; Rom 1:17; 2:7; 5:17; 8:11ff.). The Spirit gives life, but full life will come only in the future (Rom 6:4, 11, 13; 2 Cor 3:6). The Spirit brings about freedom, liberation from the servitude of the law, from sin and from death: the eschatological freedom (Rom 8:2;

Gal 5:15; 2 Cor 3:17), the freedom of the children of God.

He brings about holiness (2 Thess 2:13), so that the believer "thinks the things of God". The believer lives in the Spirit. This is opposed to the sphere of "the flesh"; he who lives in this realm thinks of the "things of the flesh". But the believer is under the influence of the Spirit who dwells within him (Rom 8:11). There is still something "fleshly" in the believer, who is under the influence of both powers. But the Spirit is the predominant influence, and it is only a question of time until the "flesh" is completely eliminated.

The fact that the faithful are moved by the Spirit, that the whole redeemed community is constituted by the Spirit as its principle of life, is manifest in their behaviour. There are ethical criteria for the discernment of the possession of the Spirit (Gal 5:19–31; Rom 11:17; Gal 5:19; esp. 1 Cor 13). The sign of the new life is a new morality (Rom 8:6–11; 1 Cor 6:9ff.; 15:9ff.; Gal 1:13–16; 5:9–23; Eph 1:17ff.; 1 Tim 1:12–16). The gifts of the Spirit are an unforeseeable, heavenly, marvellous and overwhelming intervention into human life. But they must be accepted, and given effect to by men. Their purpose would not be fulfilled if they did not impel men to corresponding action. The deepest purpose of the Spirit is to be a Spirit of joy, of love, of service. Characteristic of Paul is the combination of assertion and exhortation, of indicative and imperative (Gal 5:25; 2 Thess 2:13–17) which has often been noted. There are two questions which especially arise with regard to the Pauline teaching on the Spirit: what is the relation of the Spirit to Christ? Is the Spirit to be understood as personal or impersonal?

In respect to the first question, the Spirit is called both the Spirit of God and the Spirit of Christ. Gal 4:6 asserts: "To prove that you are sons, God has sent into our hearts the Spirit of his Son, crying 'Abba! Father!'" "Spirit of God" and "Spirit of Christ" are interchangeable (as can also be seen from Rom 8:9ff.).

Christ is for the baptized the principle of life, since he gives them the Spirit (Eph 4:11–16). The meaning of the formula: "The Lord is Spirit" (2 Cor 3:17) is disputed. According to the obvious sense of the words it seems to identify Christ and the Spirit. But as Paul usually distinguishes Christ from the Spirit (e.g., 2 Cor 13:13; Rom 5:1–5; 1 Cor 12), this should only be interpreted as a dynamic and not an ontological identity. Christ is active through the Holy Spirit, so that Christ and the Spirit do not constitute two separate principles of activity, but combine as one. Christ accomplished his work of redemption "in the Spirit" and is present in the Church in the Spirit as he exercises his saving power. For in the resurrection, he himself became "spiritual". As regards the personal nature of the Spirit, Paul does not of course use the developed concepts of the later teaching of the Church and of systematic theology. He attempts again and again to describe the Spirit from different approaches, primarily his function, not his nature. However, one can infer the nature from the functions of the Spirit, especially when combined with the Pauline texts in which the Spirit is named in the third place beside the Father and the Son, and hence in which the Trinitarian structure of the divine life is hinted at (especially 1 Cor 12:4–11; 2 Cor 13:13). At any rate, the Pauline theology contains the kernel from which the Church's doctrine of the Holy Spirit as the third divine "person" could be developed. Paul's teaching is thus in agreement with the baptismal formula given by Mt (26:28), the Spirit is the third person along with the Father and the Son. We find an echo of the Pauline teaching on the Spirit in the First Letter of Peter (e.g., 1:1f.).

In Jn we find the personal nature of the Spirit more in evidence. According to Jn, Christ promises his own in the farewell discourse "another comforter", who will be his representative during his absence. He will remain with the disciples till the end of time and help them to continue the work and the words of Christ (Jn 14:16f., 25f.). He will convince the world that there is sin, righteousness and judgment (Jn 16:5–11). The Spirit gives testimony to Christ, makes his work continually effective and explains it (1 Jn 2:1).

3. *Tradition.* In the patristic period, the Spirit is named in the baptismal formula with the Father and the Son, and he is also mentioned with the Father and the Son in reply to the accusation that Christians were atheists. As in Scripture, the Spirit is still seen dynamically, as for instance in Irenaeus. He says (*Adv. Haer.,* II, 6, 4): "Lord, Thou the one true God, beside whom there is no other

God, grant that the Holy Spirit may rule in us through our Lord Jesus Christ." Similarly, he explains in the "Proof of the Apostolic Preaching" (1:1, 6f.): "And the third article is the Holy Spirit, through whom the prophets prophesied and the patriarchs were taught about God and the just were led in the path of justice, and who in the end of times has been poured forth in a new manner upon humanity over all the earth, renewing man to God. Therefore the baptism of our rebirth comes through these three articles, granting us rebirth unto God the Father, through his Son, by the Holy Spirit. For those who are bearers of the Spirit of God are led to the Word, that is, to the Son; but the Son takes them and presents them to the Father, and the Father confers incorruptibility. So without the Spirit there is no seeing the Word of God, and without the Son there is no approaching the Father; for the Son is knowledge of the Father, and knowledge of the Son is through the Holy Spirit. But the Son, according to the Father's good pleasure, administers the Spirit charismatically as the Father will, to those to whom He will."

Because of the unity of action of the Word and the Spirit in the work of redemption, it is not surprising that in this period while doctrine was still undeveloped, there were many uncertainties. Thus, for example, Theophilus identifies the Spirit and the Word, or the Wisdom of God (*Ad Autolycum*, II, 10; II, 15). Theological reflection turned in the 4th century to the Holy Spirit, as an after-effect of Arianism, which was condemned at the Council of Nicaea (325; cf. *D* 125 f. [54]). In a logical development of their views concerning the Son of God, the Arians taught that the Spirit was created by the Son. Athanasius attacked this view in his four letters to Bishop Serapion of Thmuis. Similarly, the Subordinationist interpretation of the Spirit was rejected by the Cappadocian Fathers, especially Basil, and by Ambrose. The main proponents of the false doctrine were Bishop Macedonius of Constantinople (362), and then Bishop Maratonius of Nicomedia. The decisive condemnation was pronounced by the Council of Constantinople (381), which affirmed the true divinity of the Spirit and his consequent significance for man's life of grace: "I believe in the Holy Ghost, the Lord and giver of life, who proceeds from the Father. Together with the Father and the Son he is adored and glorified.

He spoke through the prophets" (*D* 150 [86]; cf. also 152–77 [58–82], 151 [85]). A Roman synod under Pope Damasus I (382) gave a more detailed presentation of the Church's doctrine, which emphasizes the divinity of the Holy Spirit rather than his function in salvation. Thus the synod tended in the direction of a more metaphysical systematization of the doctrine (*D* 178 [83]). Later doctrinal pronouncements brought only one important change, the addition of the *filioque* to the creed of Constantinople, which was to be a source of discord between East and West, down to the present day (*D* 527 [277]; also *D* 188 [19]; 566 [294]; 573 [296]). The addition was first made in the 6th century in Spain (Synod of Braga, 675) and then in Gaul and Italy. When in 808 the monks of the Frankish monastery on the Mount of Olives near Jerusalem sang the *filioque* in the Creed, they were accused of heresy by the Greek monks. Pope Leo III declared that the procession of the Spirit from the Son was to be preached but that its insertion into the Creed was superfluous. Nevertheless, at the request of Emperor Henry I, the *filioque* was included by Benedict VIII in the Creed at Rome in the year 1014.

The Greek Patriarch Photius (1078) made the procession of the Holy Spirit from the Father alone a main dogma of the Greek Church. He thus supported with dogmatic grounds a division between the Eastern and the Roman Churches which was rather due to ecclesiastical politics. The obligation of faith with regard to the procession of the Holy Spirit from the Son was determined as follows by Pope Benedict XIV in the Bull *Etsi Pastoralis* in 1742: "Though the Greeks must believe that the Holy Spirit also proceeds from the Son, it is not necessary for them to acknowledge this in the Creed. However, the Albanians of the Greek Rite have commendably accepted the opposite custom. It is our wish that this custom be maintained by the Albanians and by all those other Churches which have already adopted it."

The foundation of the procession of the Holy Spirit from both Father and Son is seen by the Church as the unity of the Spirit with the Father and the Son in the economy of salvation. The sending of the Spirit by the Father and the Son proves the immanent origin of the Spirit from the Father and the Son. Greek theology teaches a procession from the Father through the Son, in which the Son is understood not merely as a transit channel but also as an active principle. There is no point in trying to find a real opposition between the two formulae. They express the same fundamental concept with a difference of accent. The Latin formula, which goes back to Augustine in content, if not in express terms, emphasizes that Father and Son form one single principle; but it does not mean that the Son did not receive from the Father his propriety as origin of the Spirit, as indeed, he ceaselessly receives it. The Greek formulation affirms that the Father is the origin of the two divine persons. It does not deny that Father and Son are one as principle of the Spirit. Augustine does justice to the Greek concept, in spite of his Latin approach, when he says that the Father is the origin of the Holy Spirit *principaliter*. What is foremost in the Latin formula is the unity; in the Greek, the difference of the persons.

4. *Later theology.* A closer description of the Holy Spirit was arrived at in Augustine's theology of the Trinity. By having recourse to the life of the Spirit and the soul in man, and also stimulated by some indications of Scripture, Augustine came to the concept of the Holy Spirit as the love which binds the Father and the Son. He originates therefore from the movement of love between Father and Son. The theology of the Middle Ages developed the basic idea of Augustine in an often very subtle fashion. The question was more clearly posed whether the Spirit originated from the mutual love of Father and Son or from the one love of the Father and Son directed towards the divine nature.

The theology of the Holy Spirit returned, once more, to the dimension of salvation when in medieval and modern theology the question of the Spirit's relation to grace was raised. This question is indissolubly connected with the problem of whether grace is to be viewed as an entity or as a more personal factor. Peter Lombard identified grace with the Holy Spirit. This thesis was thoroughly discussed in the 13th and 14th centuries. It was generally rejected; but it brought to the fore in the treatise on grace, that is, on the free self-communication of God to men, an aspect which could never be forgotten and remained a burning question. In scholastic theology it appears under the key-words *proprium* or *appropriatio*. Scholasticism, in view of the dogma of the unity of the divine operation *ad extra,* maintains that the indwelling of the Spirit in men which is attested by Scripture, is only an appropriation. It is questionable, however, whether the dogma referred to necessarily implies such a view. There have been many theologians since the 18th century, especially those with a historical bent of thought (e.g., Petavious, Thomassinus, Passaglia, de Régnon, J. M. Scheeben), who have asserted that each of the divine persons takes possession of the justified according to their personal proprieties. The Holy Spirit lays hold of him and thus grants him a share in the divine nature which is identical with each of the divine persons. In the Holy Spirit the justified are united to the Father through Christ. The Holy Spirit, therefore, only takes possession of man for the Son and for the Father. This is the deepest reason why his union with man is not a hypostatic union. The sanctifying function of the Spirit is also affirmed, when, in Greek as well as Latin theology, the Spirit is called the gift, not in an immanent process but in the perspective of the economy *ad extra.* According to Augustine, the Spirit is the gift of God to his creation from all eternity, because it is of his nature to be a gift *(donabile).* Augustine's doctrine of the Spirit seems to imply an immanent proximity of God to the creature, particularly in history, though this was not worked out by the Church Father. When the orientation to creation which according to Augustine was an eternal constituent of the Holy Spirit was realized through his mission to the world, and especially to the Church, he became involved in a historicity like that of the incarnate Logos, since he is the vital principle of the people of God. He is the eschatological force and the evolutionary factor which impels the people of God, and through them the whole of history, on to the fulfilment. His onward-urging power continues to work after the stage of fulfilment is attained, since the perpetual intensification of the dialogue with God in Christ continues in the Holy Spirit.

See also *Trinity of God, Trinity in Theology, Jesus Christ* III, *Inspiration, Church* II, III, *New Testament Theology* II, III, *Charisms, Arianism, Grace* II.

BIBLIOGRAPHY. M. Schmaus, *Die psychologische Trinitätslehre des heiligen Augustinus* (1927);

P. van Imschoot, "L'action de l'Esprit de Jahvé dans l'Ancien Testament", *Revue des Sciences Philosophiques et Theologiques* 23 (1934), pp. 478–90; P. Galtier, *Le Saint Esprit en nous d'après les pères grecs* (1946); K. Barth, *Church Dogmatics,* I/1, para. 12 (1949); IV/1, para. 62 (1956); IV/2, para. 67 (1958); L. Lebauche, *Traité du Saint-Esprit* (1950); J. E. Fison, *The Blessing of the Holy Spirit* (1950); T. Rüsch, *Die Entstehung der Lehre vom Heiligen Geist* (1952); A. Malet, *Personne et amour dans la théologie trinitaire de S. Thomas d'Aquin* (1956); G. Lefèvre, *L'Esprit de Dieu dans la Sainte Liturgie* (1958); E. H. Palmer, *The Holy Spirit* (1958); L. Dewar, *The Holy Spirit and Modern Thought* (1959); J. Galot, *L'Esprit d'amour* (1959); O. Kuss, *Der Römerbrief* (2nd ed., 1963; E. T. in preparation), Excursus; H. Kleinknecht and others, "πνεῦμα, πνευματικός", *TWNT,* VI, pp. 330–453; E. Käsemann, M. Schmidt and R. Prenter, "Heiliger Geist", *RGG,* II, cols. 1272–86; M. Schmaus, *Katholische Dogmatik,* I (6th ed., 1960); E. Brunner, *I Believe in the Living God: Sermons on the Apostles' Creed* (1960); K. Rahner, "Some Implications of the Scholastic Concept of Uncreated Grace", *Theological Investigations,* I (1961), pp. 319–46; H. Mühlen, *Der Heilige Geist als Person* (1963).

Michael Schmaus

II. Gifts of the Holy Spirit

In Catholic dogmatic theology the gifts of the Holy Spirit are one of the elements of justification. The Council of Trent explains the gifts *(dona)* as part of the "interior renewal" *(D* 799). The liturgy speaks of the seven-fold gift of the Spirit, e.g., in the hymns *Veni Sancte Spiritus,* and the *Veni Creator Spiritus,* and in the rite of ordination of deacons. The biblical basis is the description of the presence and activity of the Holy Spirit in the just (Acts, Paul, Jn). To be united in faith to Christ is to participate in his Spirit and hence to be bearer of the Spirit. The notion that participation in the Spirit of Christ as head of the Church takes effective form in the gifts of the Spirit is based on Is 11:2, which says that the Spirit of the Lord will rest upon the coming Messiah, the Spirit of wisdom and understanding, the Spirit of counsel and fortitude, the Spirit of knowledge and piety, the Spirit of the fear of the Lord (Vg — the gift of piety is not in the Hebrew). For an understanding of the gifts of the Spirit, it should be noted that in the ancient Church, in the theology of the East and of the West, the scriptural doctrine of the Spirit was understood to be that the Spirit himself was given to the just by God.

Augustine enriched this concept by noting that the Holy Spirit is the love which proceeds from the Father and the Son and, for this very reason, God's gift to man, since the first gift of love is always love itself. Augustine saw the difficulty of making the personal Spirit a gift to man, since the notion brought with it the danger of giving the Spirit temporal existence or quality. His answer was that the personality of the Spirit came from its eternal immanent propriety as gift, and not from its being actually given in time. That this view might also imply the attributing of the relationship to creation to the personality of the Spirit seems to have caused Augustine no misgivings. Later theology, where it did not lose itself in speculation, likewise adopted these views without misgivings. If the Spirit himself is the gift of God to man, then the seven "gifts" are the salutary consequences and manifestations of the basic gift of salvation. The question of the precise nature of these consequences and the exact number of the gifts was given various answers in the course of theology, till finally, in the 19th century, the number seven was generally accepted and one particular explanation, that of Thomas Aquinas *(Summa Theologica,* II, II, q. 8, etc.). Here the gifts are created qualities by which man is enabled to follow easily and gladly the salutary impulses given by God, especially in obscure and complicated situations, to enable him to come to the right decision in spite of the confusing clash of reasons for and against. Behind this theory of Aquinas is the doctrine of the *potentia oboedientialis,* according to which man is open and receptive to divine inspirations by virtue of his character of creature. Hence the gifts are special salutary modifications of the openness for God which is intrinsic to human nature. They also hold in check the forces of self-assertiveness, selfishness and sloth (concupiscence) which resist the inspirations of grace. Since God is ceaselessly active, these qualifications for the acceptance of the divine in man's own action are constantly being created anew. They exist as qualities by being constantly created.

This objectivating interpretation which is current in dogmatic theology needs to be supplemented by the personal component, which will also throw light on the earlier elements. The personal component consists of the fact that the Holy Spirit, as God's gift to the justified, brings about both the inclina-

59

tion to salutary acts as well as justification itself, though man does not cease to be the agent of his own action. The Spirit, as "uncreated grace", works throughout as the one Spirit. But he works in such a way that different effects ensue as the historical situation in which man has to realize his relationship to God demands. The plurality is not in the Spirit of God but in man.

The question of whether this effectiveness was a *proprium* (personal propriety) or an *appropriatio* (a mere attribution to the Holy Spirit) was discussed in Western theology. Scholastic theology in general held it to be an *appropriatio*. But in view of the indications given in Scripture and the doctrine of the Eastern Fathers one should rather speak of a personal propriety of the Spirit, on the understanding that in the work of salvation Father, Son and Holy Spirit act in a way corresponding to their personal propriety. Further, it should be affirmed that the Spirit, on the analogy of the incarnation of the Word, unites himself personally and dynamically (not personally and ontologically) with the Church and its individual members of which he is the principle of life. The doctrine that the divine action *ad extra* is one and common to all three Persons is not affected by this thesis, since it does not imply efficient but formal (or quasi-formal) causality.

As regards the domain of the gifts, dogmatic theology usually thinks of the individual as the main field of action. But we must not forget that the individual whose salvation is his own destiny receives, nonetheless, the gift of justification as a member of the Christian community, that he is bound to it by many bonds and can serve or harm it by his action. Since the community is the sociological *a priori* for the salvation of the individual, the gifts of the Spirit further the life and growth of the community in its understanding of Christ and its love of Christ in each changing historical era. In 1 Cor the gifts of the Spirit (wisdom, knowledge, prophecy, speaking in tongues, i.e., inarticulate cries inspired by the enthusiasm of faith, and its interpretation) are given an "ecclesial" interpretation, and seen as manifestations of the one body of Christ and helps to its building up. The charisms are within the domain of the gifts of the Spirit. These unpredictable but nonetheless always indispensable gifts are meant for special tasks in special situations of Church life. The systematic treatment of the gifts in theology brought with it the tendency to treat them as private and individual gifts, but their "ecclesial" origin and orientation should not be lost sight of. In theology, the gifts of knowledge were distinguished from the inspirations of the will, a distinction which made for precision and showed where the emphasis lay in each case. But in reality, the whole man is affected by the salutary illumination of the Spirit in his act of faith. The gifts of the intellect are understanding, wisdom, knowledge and counsel. They are all within the domain of faith and its actuation in the world and history, and do not claim to substitute for the effort of scientific investigation of the world and its technological mastery. They give insight into the mystery of salvation, they orientate the Christian in the world towards the horizon of God, they sharpen his hearing for the will of God in all the situations where law and precept are inadequate but where the conscience trained on law and precept must decide. The gifts of the will are piety, fortitude and fear of the Lord. They have nothing to do with naturalism or magic, but enable man to love and adore the Father Almighty and to combine with other men to build up a brotherly fellowship. With the help of these gifts, he is steadfast in hardships, trials, and dangers without sullenness or the flight into false mysticism or despair, and he follows the demands of his historical situations which he has critically sifted to see there the demands of God.

See also *Justification, Faith, Decision, Grace and Freedom, Charisms, Nature II, Magic, Mysticism I, Potentia Oboedientialis.*

BIBLIOGRAPHY. A. Gardeil, *Dictionnaire de Théologie Catholique*, IV, cols. 1728–81; F. M. Schindler, *Die Gaben des Heiligen Geistes nach Thomas von Aquin* (1915); F. Büchsel, *Der Geist Gottes im Neuen Testament* (1926); L. Billot, *De virtutibus infusis* (4th ed., 1928), pp. 155–75; J.-F. Bonnefoy, *Le St-Esprit et ses dons selon St. Bonaventure* (1929); B. Froget, *De l'habitation du Saint-Esprit dans les âmes des justes d'après la doctrine de S. Thomas d'Aquin* (1938); H. Schauf, *Die Einwohnung des Heiligen Geistes* (1941); P. Galtier, *Le Saint-Esprit en nous d'après les pères grecs* (1946); J. Trütsch, *Sanctissimae Trinitatis inhabitatio apud theologos recentiores* (1949); T. Fitzgerald, *De inhabitatione Spiritus Sancti doctrina S. Thomae Aquinatis* (1950); H. Kleinknecht and others, "πνεῦμα", *TWNT*, VI (1959), pp. 330–453; I. Hermann,

Kyrios und Pneuma (1961); J. Alfaro, *Fides — Spes — Caritas. Adnotationes in Tractatum De Virtutibus Theologicis* (1963); C. Baumgartner, *La grâce du Christ* (1963), pp. 25–39; I. Willig, *Geschaffene und ungeschaffene Gnade* (1964); M. Schmaus, *Katholische Dogmatik*, III/2, para. 195 (5th ed., 1956), with bibliography; H. Mühlen, *Una mystica persona* (2nd ed., 1967).

Michael Schmaus

HOPE

A. The Traditional Doctrine

1. The ordinary presentation of hope was in the framework of the theological virtues, in dogmatic and moral theology. The theology of hope was worked out above all by Thomas Aquinas (*De Spe, Summa Theologica*, II, II, qq. 17–22). Hope is directed to a future good which is hard but not impossible to attain. It is elevation of the will, made possible by grace, by which man expects eternal life and the means to attain it, confident of the omnipotent aid of God. Hope is *the* great virtue of man in his *status viatoris*. It comes after faith, from which it receives its object. It is akin to the love of desire *(amor concupiscentiae)* and precedes perfect love. Man can hope only for himself and for those whom he loves. The extreme threat and direct test of hope is death. The sins against hope are despair, as anticipated failure, and presumption, as anticipated fulfilment. In both these cases man seeks to break out of his pilgrim existence and have his life otherwise than from the hand of God.

2. In the outline of hope thus presented, there is little explicit mention of the gospel message, the redemption through Jesus Christ, his resurrection and his enthronement as Lord. The foundation and object of hope are as a rule not notably Christocentric. It is also notable that most dogmatic eschatologies fail to discuss the virtue of hope. Not enough attention is paid to the way in which the universal biblical promises correspond to Christian hopes, so that hope is reduced to a personal and private matter. In moral theology, the three theological virtues make up a set of themes along with others in special moral theology, and this obscures the fundamental and all-embracing importance of Christian hope. The intrinsic connection between faith and hope has been obscured since the Reformation by polemics against the *fides fiducialis* of Luther. The relationship between this world's hopes and Christian hope was either glossed over lightly or judged to be negative. Hence preaching on hope came too easily to sound like merely consoling oneself with the promise of a better life elsewhere, or a flight from this valley of tears and its tasks. This occasioned the reproach of Karl Marx that religion is the opium of the masses.

B. Biblical Theology

1. *Old Testament*. The structure of hope is determined in the OT by a wide range of concepts: בטח, to be confident, to feel secure, קוה, to wait for, be tense, יחל, to expect, hope, חסה, to fly to, take refuge in, חכה, to wait for longingly, שבר, to trust, and אמן, to be firm and consoled, to believe, trust, hope. Israel hopes for blessing, mercy, help, just judgment, forgiveness and salvation from Yahweh. False and empty hope builds on idols made with hands, on men, riches, power, religious practice. More important here than a list of texts is a grasp of the structure of the OT relationship to God. Israel's faith is based on historical experiences which it regarded as the *magnalia Dei*. Israel's hope was directed to a future in history of which the horizon was constantly broadening. The unifying bond between past and future was the fidelity of Yahweh. Israel recalled his *magnalia* in its liturgy, to reinforce its pleas for help and to strengthen its own hope. Thanksgiving for the mighty works of Yahweh which Israel has experienced becomes a confession of hope. Yahweh himself is the hope of his people (Jer 17:7; Ps 60:4; 70:5). The words in which the Protector God of the patriarchs presents himself: "I shall be [with you] as he who I shall be [with you]" (Exod 3:14) point to the future as the setting of man's knowledge of God. He who believes in this God is sent forth at his command to act mightily on history, with the hope of God's promised help. This faith enables man to take the risk of history with this God in the strength of hope. The bearer of the promises is not primarily the individual but the people, the covenant, the remnant (in the prophets), and only the loyal individual in apocalyptic. But at the same time the horizon of hope becomes more universal. Every hope ful-

61

filled opens up new and greater hopes, till the whole cosmos and all peoples are embraced. Hope is the bridge between the Old and the New Covenants, since hope does not try to determine how God will show himself but remains open for all new and astonishing manifestations of love.

2. *New Testament.* The range of concepts identifying hope in the NT include ὑπομενεῖν, be patient, endure, and γρηγορεῖν, be watchful, as well as ἐλπίζειν, to hope. In Jn and to some extent in the Synoptics, hope coincides with faith, in 1 Pet faith coincides with hope, in Rev, hope with patience. Hope takes on different forms in the NT writings according to the various eschatological concepts which are taken as models.

In the NT, likewise, a look at the structure of hope is more enlightening than a listing of the texts. The lordship of God which has come in Jesus Christ, in his life, death and resurrection, is the basic experience of faith for NT man. But he has not possession and control of this lordship, which is his only as a heritage, in the form of a pledge or handsel, through the Spirit. The power of death, sin, the elements of the world, the principalities and powers and fear have been broken by Christ. The new freedom to which the Christian has been set free is freedom to live the new life in the hope of glory. In spite of (and because of) the known love of God, in spite of (and because of) the gift of God's life and Spirit, the believer lives only in hope. The contact with salvation is so close that the believer feels keenly the contradiction between it and the present which still persists and must be endured, and so tries to make his hope concrete in the expectation of an imminent end or substitutes for it a fanatical enthusiasm. The various eschatological concepts and paradigms are to be explained in the light of this situation, and none of them is to be erected into an absolute. The tension between the experience of the present and the salvation believed in, like the tension between justification and sanctification, must be sustained in hope. The ordinary way of explaining this tension, with the help of the concepts "Already" and "Not yet" in combination risks dividing salvation in the sense of a *partim — partim.* The justification of the sinner is a definitive gift of God which takes man into God's service and starts him on the way of ful-

filment. Justification itself is thus promise of fulfilment. In the fellowship of Christ the faithful share the old experience that each stage of fulfilment is itself a new and greater promise: "Christ in you, the hope of glory" (Col 1:27). From this it follows that hope is identical with the New Testament relationship to God: a heathen can be described as one who is without hope (cf. 1 Thess 4:13; Eph 2:12). Faith is confidence and conviction about a hoped-for but unseen future (cf. Rom 8:24f.; Heb 11:1) which is described in terms of social well-being, such as peace, justice, forgiveness, conquest of suffering and death, resurrection of the flesh, marriage feast, heavenly Jerusalem, new heavens and new earth. Since his hopes are so universal, the believer is called upon to furnish an account of its justification before the whole world (cf. 1 Pet 3:15). The bearer of this promise and the provider of this justification is the community, the new covenant, the Church in inter-subjective structure. Hope does not finally become possession pure and simple. It remains intrinsic to the eschatologically permanent form of the relationship to God (1 Cor 13:13), since it is alsways openness for the "always greater God" and the free gift of his immediacy.

C. PROGRESS AND HOPE IN PRESENT-DAY THINKING

When Christians, distrustful of the future offered within the world, put their hope in God, they need not be surprised that others set out to realize the world's hope without reference to God. We observe today a widespread atheism with regard to the setting of man and his future. This has led to the "great schism" of the modern world, the schism between "religion and revolution, Church and Enlightenment, divine faith and future purpose, reliance on salvation and responsibility for the world" (J. Moltmann). Karl Marx maintained that religion had to be eliminated if man was to be liberated from his alienation, oppression and slavery.

Ernst Bloch sees "the principle of hope" as the driving force of all human initiative, and from it he looks for the coming of the new, the never-before, the undreamt-of (hardly even in men's religions). What is primarily decisive for the present is not the past but the future, since the present is the seed-bed of the tendencies and latent urges which open out on the future and which man must seize upon and develop.

The question still remains, however, as to whether Bloch's theory really explains the presence of the truly new in the future. Is not the future, as he explains it, still merely the unfolding of what is already latent? And does he explain how there is still hope for each personal human being, and not just for "humanity"? Is not God who as regards the world is always "in potency", the sole guarantor of a really new future, for men and for mankind?

The "evolutionary humanism" of Julian Huxley, which is generally accepted on an atheistic basis, presents itself as a new system of ideas, an order of values open to and in need of further development, which is the instrument to man's hand as he masters his great task of directing an evolution which he himself has taken over. Evolutionary humanism rejects all dogmatism of principles or rules, since it would hinder evolution. It sees its own efforts as an aid to the better development of man as he is today and will be tomorrow, to the provision of a wider space of freedom. These efforts include practical initiatives such as help to developing countries and regulation of births. This humanism is to some extent combined with a new form of faith in science, which relies on technology for the solution of all questions. In view of the risks which it involves as regards the positive course of further evolution, evolutionary humanism must be characterized as a system of "hopeful knacks".

In non-Marxist philosophy, hope is seen as a good by G. Marcel in his reading of man as *homo viator* and by O. Bollnow in his effort to go beyond existentialism, while it is rejected by K. Löwith, who sees progress as a menace and hope as an illusion. Hope is left its place in the open dialectics of T. W. Adorno.

The present conjuncture forces man to ask the question of the meaning of hope and of progress and to examine his motives as he tries to dominate a baffling future. A new relationship between theory and practice is taking shape, since the future cannot simply be contemplated, but must be channelled. It is not enough for theologians simply to point to the biblical origins of

hope and of the will to the future. The challenge to the Christian faith and the Christian hope which the modern consciousness contains is not thereby answered. The imposing and fascinating response attempted by Teilhard de Chardin suffers from the lack of an adequate distinction between evolution and history. He does not seem to take seriously enough the component of freedom, including the freedom of the will to evil and to self-destruction.

D. THEOLOGICAL PRINCIPLES

1. *General.* The basis and centre of Christian faith is the message of Jesus and its promises, and Jesus' being raised up by God. But these two things, the message and the resurrection, are not really themselves in their entirety without the return of Jesus, without the resurrection of all flesh (cf. 1 Cor 15), without the new heavens and the new earth (cf. Rev 21:22). Hence faith in the resurrection of Jesus means hope in the universal consummation which is promised and pre-figured by this resurrection. All theology is discussion of how the resurrection and future of Christ affects us (J. Moltmann). W. Pannenberg sees the end, the consummation or fulfilment, as already realized by anticipation in the resurrection of Christ, where it can already be deciphered.

In hope, the believer pierces the gap which has been opened up by the cross and resurrection of Jesus. Faith and hope are two inseparable moments of the one act, of which (initial) love is the integrating centre. The juxtaposition of the three theological virtues caused a certain amount of obscurity with regard to this intrinsic unity of the three theological virtues. There is no truth or blessing of faith which is already fully and finally complete in the past and which one can secure merely by a faith which looks backwards. Hence a treatise on God, his nature and attributes *(De Deo)* cannot be presented as complete in itself at the beginning of theology, since it is only from creation, redemption and fulfilment that we see who God really is. God is always the "God in front of us" (J. B. Metz). He is the "absolute future" for man (K. Rahner).

For the same reason, the treatise on creation can never be fully rounded off, since we will only see from the new heavens and the new earth what God really meant by the first creation. The reason why so many questions about nature and grace bogged down hopelessly was because creation has been so thoroughly thought out that grace could only come as an accessory, as it were from outside.

The incarnation is not understood when the formula of Chalcedon is interpreted statically. It must also include the thought of the future of this Jesus of Nazareth, cross and resurrection, second coming and lordship, the permanent significance of his humanity for the fulfilment of man (K. Rahner), if even the incarnation is to be given its true meaning.

The inclusion of the eschatological dimension preserves the Church from identifying itself wrongly with Christ or the kingdom of God and hence from all "triumphalism". It shows clearly the limits imposed on the Church by its provisional character, and prevents the sacraments from being misunderstood as magical signs.

Discussion of the meritorious nature of works could be formulated in more biblical terms, and thereby become more readily acceptable ecumenically, if one emphasized the element of confidence and hope which is inspired by God's promises and fidelity.

The full application of the structural principle here set forth would mean the excision of eschatology from theology as a separate treatise, but would restore the eschatological perspective to all the other treatises by being seen at last in its true and comprehensive character. Hope is the advocate of the immense openness of the promised future amid the reality of faith and the reality of salvation in history. These are the two dimensions — truth and history — in which the theology of hope must now be expounded more precisely and its consequences noted.

2. *Hope and truth.* The truth of faith can only be grasped in the perspective of hope, not just in the sense that hope only has the notion of its goal from faith, but rather in the sense that hope is the inner force of faith which enables man to give himself to the "ever greater God", in confident dedication, in view of the promised future. There is no formula of human language which can ever adequately express revelation as promise, or interpret it definitively. Not even Scripture can do this, or a summa of dogmatic theology.

Every closed system breaks down in face of the fullness and the futurity of the gospel. The whole of history will be needed, including its permanent fulfilment, to display this fullness. Dogmas are indications of the truth which is Christ, not the truth itself. This helps us to see what is meant by saying that all truths of faith are known by analogy. Hope is the safeguard of the *maior dissimilitudo* throughout all possible *similitudo* of the affirmations. The imagery of eschatological truth is a valid utterance, which cannot be wholly exhausted by demythologization and existential interpretation and is quite adequate to safeguard the openness for futurity, for the fullness of salvation — and hence to provide a new future for each stage of knowledge achieved. Through hope, faith avoids the mistake of taking the hiddenness of God for absence. Confidence in the fidelity of God enables faith to accept him as the principle and promise which sustains the immeasurable fullness. Through hope, the believer finds the strength to hold out even in the profoundest darkness, without despairing or giving up. Hope reminds the believer of the never-failing promise which was given in Christ. It is not hostile to past tradition but favours and promotes tradition as the "eschatologically-orientated transmission" of the redemptive works of God (G. Sauter). At the same time, it prevents tradition from hardening into an ideology, since it makes it impossible to take faith and Christian life for granted, as they are constantly threatened with being in the sphere of Christian traditions. Hope makes dialogue with unbelievers possible, because it recognizes that the believer himself is still on the way to the fullness and hence can make room for the experiences and findings of the unbeliever in its own discovery of truth. In the final fulfilment, hope is not eliminated but made fully manifest in its basic structure, as marvelling and trusting dedication to the ever greater God and the freedom of his love.

3. *Hope and history.* There is no truth for man except that which is mediated by his historicity. In this connection the distinction between history and evolution, between futurity and goal is of decisive importance. Not all that happens merits the name of history, and not all that is yet to come merits the name of futurity. Evolution is a fixed process. The pre-determined goal anticipates

the whole process and determines it as its final cause. Evolution can only bring out what is already present and latent. We can only speak of history when the specifically human intervenes: freedom, responsibility, decision, possible failure in the individual and inter-subjective spheres. Freedom is the key to the new, to the coming of what never was before. History is played out between the freedom of God, the ground of all, and the freedom of man. Christian hope fixes its gaze on the futurity which this play of freedoms makes possible and not on the predetermined goal of a development. Hope looks to history that is to come.

God gives salvation in such a way that it has also to be achieved by man. Hence man goes towards the future which he hopes for from God by advancing towards his inner-worldly future. His inner-worldly hopes are the place where he practises Christian hope and the channels through which it is bestowed on him. They are not merely rivals. Hope does not render effort superfluous, but demands it. It is the way in which hope realizes itself and takes on its responsibilities. Man hopes for God's justice and peace by striving now for their anticipation. The Christian "must constantly make the correctness of his faith come true in the correctness of an action determined by the last things" (J. B. Metz). Though hope is just taking the next step (K. Barth), each present step is weighty because it helps to decide the definitive future. Hope is not the opium of the people but an impulse to change the world in the perspective of God's promises, a revolutionary force which strives to create conditions favourable to the men most loved by God, the poorest and the weakest. Christian hope is the driving force of all inner-worldly hopes, which are penetrated and carried on beyond the scope of their own powers in reliance on the mercy and omnipotence of God. He who loses his life in such loving service gains it before God. Death itself, which still must be suffered in its bitterness, has been opened up inwardly by Christ to the fullness of God. Hope confirms man's right to seek salvation in the new, but frees him from the burden of having to create this newness himself while it takes him into its service on behalf of the promised future. J. B. Metz calls for a "creative eschatology" which will be conscious of the social and political responsibilities which flow from the universality of the promises. And here hope must reckon with the meagreness of its knowledge of the future. Often it can only aim at its desires by simply criticizing or negating existing conditions but without being able to put forward positive suggestions. This safeguards it from the danger of being a totalitarian ideology. The heavenly Jerusalem comes down from heaven. It is the gift of God. The peoples bring in their riches — the fruits of love active in hope (cf. Rev 21:10, 24). Hope abides in the fulfilment as readiness to accept these fruits of its own love and hence God himself as the eternal gift of his love.

See also *Faith* II, *Charity* I, *Virtue, Despair, Justification, Humanism, Evolution, Analogy of Being, Demythologization.*

BIBLIOGRAPHY. ON A: St. Thomas Aquinas, *Hope (Summa Theologica*, vol. XXXIII, pub. by McGraw); C. Kramer, *Fear and Hope according to St. Alphonsus Liguori* (1951); G. Dubuquois, *Hope* (1966). ON B: see the Theologies of the OT and NT.; also: H. Rengstorf and R. Bultmann, "ἐλπίς", *TWNT,* II, pp. 517–35; J. van der Ploeg, "L'espérance dans l'Ancien Testament", *Revue Biblique* 61 (1954), pp. 481–507; C. F. D. Moule, *The Meaning of Hope* (1963); N. Brox, *Die Hoffnung des Christen* (1965); H. Schlier, *The Relevance of the New Testament* (1968), ch. viii: "On Hope". ON C: G. Marcel, *Homo Viator: Introduction to a Metaphysic of Hope* (1962); O. F. Bollnow, *Neue Geborgenheit* (1955); E. Bloch, *Das Prinzip Hoffnung* (1959); T. W. Adorno, "Fortschritt", in H. Delius and J. Patzig, eds., *Argumentationen. Festschrift für J. König* (1964); J. Huxley, *Essays of a Humanist* (1964); R. Garaudy, J. B. Metz and K. Rahner, *Der Dialog* (1966). ON D: J. Alfaro, *Fides — Spes — Caritas. Adnotationes in Tractatum De Virtutibus Theologicis* (1963); W. Pannenberg and others, *History and Hermeneutics* (1964); G. Sauter, *Zukunft und Verheissung* (1965); J. B. Metz, *Gott vor uns: Ernst Bloch zu Ehren,* ed. by S. Unseld (1965); J. Moltmann, *Theology of Hope* (1967); F. Kerstiens, "Glauben als Hoffen", *Diakonia* 2 (1967), pp. 81–91; K. Rahner, "Zur Theologie der Hoffnung", *Schriften zur Theologie,* VIII (1967), pp. 561–79.

Ferdinand Kerstiens

HUMAN ACT

A. Origin and Primary Characteristics

1. When described empirically, "human" or moral action must be said to begin with the personal (free, conscious) reaction to the conflict between the urge to instinctive

self-satisfaction and the claims of society. It supposes the development of the consciousness of self as distinct from and opposed to the surrounding world, which is experienced as a set of claims contrary to the needs of an immanent self-fulfilment. The human act in the child occurs when it makes the experience of being loved, as it is accepted and helped by its milieu. Thus the child denies itself instinctive satisfactions if they are contrary to its affectionate union with its mother which it naturally values highly. Where the conflict is not felt, the coming of the moral act is delayed.

The next stage of consciousness is that the need of self-realization, to which the setting is felt to contribute, leads to an uncritical adoption of the views of the environment. There ensues, in fact, an ,,introjection'', by which the conduct of others, normally the family, is adopted as the pattern of behaviour, by a process of identification. As the child's world is enlarged and its critical faculties develop, new conflicts arise. He meets patterns of conduct which are mutually contradictory and must decide which to follow. Here his own needs are not the sole factor. He comes to see more and more the purposefulness of what is done and demanded of him. The strength of his affective attachment to certain models plays, of course, a large part.

Once the child can see that certain actions, such as telling the truth, are intrinsically rational and that they are demanded of him because they have a value of their own, he can accomplish inchoative human or moral acts. He is now able to demarcate immanent and spontaneous instincts so clearly that he can compare them with the claim of "duty" and react freely on the basis of this insight. In favourable family circumstances this occurs normally between six and seven years of age — the "age of discretion" when he "comes to the use of reason". But this stage can also be much delayed.

This critical detachment from the received norms of the environment and the instinctive urges of the ego is, of course, very restricted to start with and can only develop gradually, since conscious reflection and attitudes must always be a function of direct knowledge and deliberate decision, and these constantly change their character as the personality develops. They can never be fully perspicuous. Hence deliberate moral action cannot

be fully and clearly distinguished from uncritical reactions and always depends on the firmness of the development of the personality. And the personality itself is often influenced by the ethos implicit in the super-ego, so that genuine moral choice is harder, since absolute value may be ascribed to traditional notions without sufficient reason, sometimes merely as the result of education.

An essentially higher stage is reached when a young person can decide freely and responsibly not only with regard to individual acts, but also with regard to himself, when he takes an attitude — definitive so far as he himself is concerned — towards the essential aspects of his environment. For this he must first have an adequate concept of the bearings of his action and, secondly, the objective self-consciousness must be well enough developed to allow of a definitive subjective self-determination. And effective personal relationships must be strong enough to allow of a subjective grasp of the absolute nature of moral obligation, so that to go against it is felt as something which makes man himself bad and not just the individual act.

Personal maturity in this sense allows of the human act fully worthy of the name. It presupposes a) a sense of one's own irreplaceable identity, normally induced by the conflicts set up by the awakening of sexuality and its concomitant phenomena; b) the power to see sufficiently well the bearings of one's action as it affects definitively one's own life and one's relations with the world. The essential future implications must be seen. The adequacy of such insight depends on experience and education. c) It also presupposes a recognition of the dignity of the person. This must be strong enough to make the young person respect and love it for its own sake. He is so far emancipated from egoism that he can see and accept the claims of others as persons. But this power of discernment and, above all, this capacity to love do not usually coincide with the end of physical puberty and should not be ascribed too hastily to young persons.

2. From the point of view of philosophy, one can speak of moral action or human acts when the personally conscious subject acts as such by means of his free decision, as he takes on responsibility for himself and

others. Thus a human act demands consciousness and free will, regard for the other persons with whom the subject is always involved and responsibility with regard to their self-fulfilment. They are seen to have a right to an answer and an explanation. This means that there is no human act that does not involve an attitude towards the transcendental norm of morality, towards perfection and the striving after it. Thus it is always a summons to metaphysical faith, hope and love. In other words, the human act is formally good when it recognizes God as the supreme good, and hence believes, when it expects salvation from God and hence hopes, when it accepts God as the supreme good and hence loves.

For an act can be judged good or bad only insofar as it is seen to be in keeping with or contradictory to being. But this knowledge is only possible in proportion to the evidence with which being in itself appears. And this evidence summons us to believing acceptance of being in itself, because this is both the necessary precondition of all we know and yet is not grasped in itself, but is to be pre-supposed. Here it can be rejected by the will, though it is grasped by the reason as something which ought to be affirmed. This means that every morally good act is an act of faith.

It is also always an act of hope. For a conscious act can make man better or worse only insofar as it appears to him as reasonable or unreasonable and hence arbitrary. But this again is only possible insofar as a given line of action, which is in keeping with being, is recognized as absolutely obligatory. But knowledge of the reasonableness of action is a transcendental condition of conscious action, since this is necessarily purposeful. And the basic acknowledgment of the reasonableness of action in keeping with being is a free act of hope, since the proof of the rightness of this fundamental acknowledgment is awaited only from the future, and hence can be freely accepted or rejected.

Finally, when man makes a decision with regard to something recognized as obligatory, he is following or refusing to follow the moral summons, and hence to love the good in itself or to reject it wilfully and lovelessly. For in his conscious action man both necessarily strives after the perfect and hence the good in itself, and must still decide in favour of the good in itself, since the good in itself is only grasped by us in a limited way and hence can be rejected in favour of an arbitrarily chosen good.

Hence the starting-point for the determination of the human, moral action must be the transcendental relation to God. This relationship is only developed enough to enable us to speak of a moral act when man is so referred to God that he either accepts him in faith, hope and love in the moral decision, or rejects him in unbelief, arbitrarily and hence ultimately despairingly and selfishly. The relationship to God need not be consciously reflected on (in actu reflexo). It is enough that it be really there (in actu exercito) in the actual exercise of the act. This relationship to faith, hope and love is transcendentally necessary in the human act and in the present order of salvation it has been given in fact a supernatural extension. This three-fold transcendental and supernatural relation of the human act to God will be discussed in the following.

B. Relationship to the Transcendental Norm: Faith

1. It follows that the prerequisite of a human act is that it be recognized as good or bad. This means both the knowledge of the norm of morality and of the relationship of the act to the norm. All that is meaningful in itself and hence ought absolutely to be is immediately desirable and hence objectively good in the moral order. Hence the ultimate criterion of morality is the orientation to the perfection of God, in whom alone we can find our ultimate fulfilment. We are objectively fulfilled by the perfect love of God and subjectively by our perfect adaptation to his will.

Everything else is good insofar as it is ordained to a goal which transcends it and which itself has an immanent purpose within it. For in this way everything is affirmed and accepted insofar as it partakes of God's perfection, and hence striven after in keeping with (its) being. The perfection of God is participated in by beings endowed with spirit (angels, men) in such a way that they both have an intrinsic purpose which makes their self-realization meaningful, and that this self-realization cannot be attained except by their being ordained to their transcendent goal, that is, towards that which is meaningful in itself and hence has a character of absoluteness (and insofar as it has such a character). But this means that the morally good is what promotes man's being man in accordance with other men and this accord insofar as it is in accord with God. Hence directly good acts are those which perfect the agent in his relationship to God and to man. In other words, ultimately goodness is what promotes inter-subjectivity, persons in relation to one another, in all its dimensions.

But since infra-human creation has no other end than to serve the self-realization of man, orientation towards it is morally good objectively insofar as it can be made to serve the development of man. This means that the material reality which is infra-subjective and hence objective and hence categorized can only be indirectly good in the moral order — "materially".

Hence an act is morally good subjectively insofar as it is consciously ordained towards the self-realization of the agent in accordance with God and the neighbour, and takes material reality into the service of inter-subjectivity.

It follows that the first prerequisite for moral action is an adequate knowledge of the incommensurability of persons with the infra-human, and hence of human and material values. One who cannot sufficiently distinguish persons from objects is not morally responsible.

The required knowledge of the good in itself can be more or less clear. It need not be fully conscious and articulated. But it is there as soon as one has direct if confused knowledge of certain values — truth, perfection, justice and freedom — in a word, as soon as one sees that virtues are desirable for their own sake. The virtues are always values which serve the development of "inter-subjectivity". Thus they are necessarily transcendent values. This means that the subject who aims at them is necessarily perfected, conditioned as he is by this "inter-subjectivity".

It follows that man cannot err in his grasp of virtues and vices. They always make him receptive to the good as such. By their very definition, that is, of their very nature, they point out a well-ordered or disordered inter-personal relationship. This means that man can never go wrong in deciding whether an act is permitted, forbidden or com-manded, since he is necessarily ordained by his reason — and instinctively or freely by subjective disposition — towards the truth as such, in an act of the will; and he has evidence of his personal and inter-personal character ("inter-subjectivity") in spite of this being given him as the experience of objects ("objectivity"). For thus lawfulness or otherwise is referred directly to the subjective acceptance or rejection of persons, that is, to attitudes which are good or bad in themselves. Like the act of faith in the assent of faith, the moral act, in its intrinsic attitude to the norm, to the good as such, has a formal structure and is correspondingly certain. It is self-authenticating, because it is an act of direct inter-subjective communication, the structure of which is directly known by man — though not necessarily brought before the articulate consciousness — just as is the communication itself. Since it aims at the true and the good, the absolute in other words, it is directly ordained to God, even if something else is expressly affirmed, since the transcendental relation to the absolute is ordination to God, though its translation into propositions may be faulty.

But man has to interpret his inter-subjective attitudes in action. There must be external, objective and hence transcendent actions. This is achieved when man uses his bodily nature and the goods of this earth as means of self-expression and self-realization, referring them for this purpose to the demands of "inter-subjectivity". Here he is involved in the proper laws of these realities and their categories, but influences them so personally that he determines what they must be, and they are no longer simply the results of causes independent of him.

When man comes to weigh the proper laws of things he can err. In other words, he can err about the things which he permits, forbids or commands, that is, in the concrete objectivation of his attitudes. That his "objective" interpretation of his "subjective" attitudes can be erroneous is due to the necessity of abstraction and the necessity of forming a judgment. The former is by definition an imperfect knowledge of the essence of things, since the essential unfolds only in the historical process and thus is not definitively displayed. We grasp it selectively, by prescinding from certain characteristics. In the judgment, we pass a transcendental verdict on what comes under categories, since by means of the copula we link the transcendental concept with its realization in categories. Error is possible here, since the identity between subjective and objective is grasped by us only in their difference.

Further, though the mind is of itself necessarily ordained to truth, knowledge depends to some extent on the disposition of the subject. Our grasp of the truth is limited and "objectified", and we are always free in the attitude which we adopt to the truth as concretely grasped, since it is something open to interpretation. Hence our actual grasp of truth depends to some extent on our instinctive attitudes and our love of truth — which is a free act. Hence failure to grasp the truth can be due not merely to the limitations of reason, but also to the disposition of the will.

We conclude that moral judgments can adequately render the morally permissible etc., or more exactly, the will of God. They are imperfect because they are abstract, and because of the limitations of the mind's ordination to truth in its actual efforts. And they are sometimes erroneous. But they render infallibly the will of God insofar as we are ordained to the truth as such. This ordination to the will of God, being a free act, always implies a "metaphysical act of faith", because the acceptance of the true and the good, though within the framework of the transcendental conditions of our knowledge and will, can only take place in an act which is not transcendentally necessary and hence is free.

2. Thus our assertions about the nature of objective realities and the purpose of our dealings with such categories can be positive, but can never be exclusive or definitive. In the same way, our assertions about the goodness or badness of such actions, being general and objectivating, can be positive assertions, but they cannot be exhaustive or definitive. We can define them materially, but not formally. In other words, the nature of an action concerned with categorized objects, of an *opus operatum,* may have been rightly grasped, but may still have an aspect which has escaped us, and the act may have a purpose which we have not grasped. This means that there are external acts of which on principle we cannot say that they are always and under all circumstances formally good or bad, morally speaking. It can only

be said that they are materially so. And this means again that the act once done has an aspect materially good or bad which it does not lose even if it must be regarded as possibly objectively ambivalent, morally speaking, on account of other possible purposes in it.

According to the subjective intention, an act may be called objectively and formally good or bad, and not merely subjectively and formally so, though this does not eliminate the material finality of the act, which may be to the contrary. Hence, for instance, unjustifiable homicide is objectively and formally always murder. But homicide in legitimate self-defence has an objectively ambivalent moral finality, one which formally justifies the act and one which is materially bad, not formally but nonetheless objectively intended. Hence that murder is always formally bad is not due to the objective external act of homicide, but to the inward attitude, which is necessarily bad because by virtue of its presuppositions it is unjust. We must distinguish further the materially indifferent acts which in the concrete are objectively — and not merely subjectively — good or bad. This depends on the end which they are made to serve by the actual intention of the doer.

C. Relationship to Transcendental Perfectibility: Hope

1. If an act is to be a moral one, it must appear as good or bad for me. The recognition that an act, the good in itself, is suitable or unsuitable on the level of personal action and reaction does not at once mean that it is recognized as what ought to be done. Its obligatory character ensues only from the recognition that the act seen as good or bad is beneficent or pernicious for the doer or for others and hence that the doer must account for it to himself or others. He sees that the act ought to be done and that he is thereby responsible. Responsible action is, in fact, deliberately rational action. But deliberately rational action is only possible when one refers oneself to an acknowledged goal which is meaningful in itself and hence is an end in itself. Deliberately purposeful action is not necessarily responsible action because one could aim at arbitrary goals. The deliberate choice of an arbitrary end is, however, not only pointless, but irrational

and absurd, since conscious intention is always directed to the fully self-comprehensive and self-justifying. Hence if the deliberate choice of a goal is to be rational, the goal must be grasped as something of itself desirable to the doer. The goal must be its own sufficient reason and the pursuit of it must be appropriate to the seeker.

It follows that man can only have responsibility with regard to the order of things which are amenable to the categories insofar as these things, with their physical laws which man cannot abrogate, are brought into the sphere of inter-personal relationships by the personal action of man. The realities of categorized experience have of themselves only the function of means to the self-realization of man. They cannot ordain themselves to an end, but must be given a direction by man to help him fulfil himself, since otherwise they would be pointless. If they are given arbitrary goals by man, a potential sinner by reason of his limitation, they are pointless insofar as they are referred to no rational end, but they are not absurd, since they retain their own proper meaning, which is to serve the self-realization of man. But man has responsibility with regard to selfhood consciously grasped, since this "subjectivity" is always meaningful of itself. Further, he must have grasped in the concrete the rationality or otherwise of the act with regard to himself or others, whereby he also recognizes its obligatory character.

It follows that there is a transcendental necessity that "subjectivity" should always strive for self-fulfilment. By definition, the realization of the subject is always self-realization. And hence deliberate self-realization is self-realization in responsibility to oneself. Thus even selfless love is only possible when it is seen as meaningful for the man himself and tending to perfect him. Indeed, he could only commit suicide with the intention of finding therein a self-fulfilment corresponding to his circumstances.

The ultimate reason for this is that all our potentiality can only be actuated by what is actual on at least as high a level, and ultimately by the activation imparted by God which alone makes our self-realization possible. Thus our productive activity consists in grasping the offered potentialities and not in primordially creative achievements. The only possibility is that bestowed on us, and our originality comes into play only in each attitude which we take up to the ever-changing possibilities. Thus it is that man is radically an individual and a social being, a creature who can only say "I" insofar as he can say "You" and ultimately "my God", original only in his unique self-realization in the historical process.

Hence self-realization can only mean the right ordering of life in dependence on others. This becomes moral purpose only when the action involved is seen to correspond to the meaning of life in general and when it is recognized as something that ought to be done. This is the case when persons and their attitudes to persons and categorized reality are referred to persons. But we know our subjectivity in an interplay of persons ("inter-subjectivity") which is channelled by objectivations whose transparency is limited because temporal-spatial. Thus we know our subjectivity and our inter-subjective dependence only by distinguishing it from objectivated past, present and future and at the same time referring it to the changing realities of such objectivation. But since moral action is always that of the subject, it can only exist insofar as the doer, in his objective action, can take an attitude towards subjectivity — which, by the nature of things, cannot be fully at one's disposition but which can dispose of the objective reality. Hence every moral act has a unique aspect, since every objective situation to be confronted is unique by reason of the persons involved, and every action stems from the uniqueness of the subject.

This means that man can only give an account of his action where his subjective attitude, mediated by objective reality, is referred to subjectivity. Responsibility can only exist where man has grasped the purpose of his own or others' subjectivity and the relationship of his own action to this end.

If man is to grasp and aim at such a goal, his future must appear meaningful in a certain manner, and his answer likewise. This presupposes transcendental hope of a meaningful and hence "salutary" future. Man must expect something from the future and so welcome it, while also recognizing that he can make this future his own by a certain personal attitude. If he freely affirms and accepts this ordination to salvation, he has the virtue of hope. This is the prerequisite of free, selfless and hence virtuous love, since man can only give himself insofar as he has become master of himself and accepted himself.

If he rejects the future as allotted to him and tries to give it an arbitrary meaning, he acts irresponsibly. His action does not correspond to the meaning of subjectivity and inter-subjectivity, which is known and demands acknowledgment. It corresponds to his own wilfulness and hence is irrational.

2. Insofar as one is responsible to oneself, we speak of autonomy, while where responsibility exists with regard to others, we speak of heteronomy. But since man is responsible both to himself and others, he is at once autonomous and heteronomous, though under different aspects.

Man is autonomous insofar as he must render an account to himself, to show that his subjective action corresponds to the acknowledged end of his subjectivity. The reason for this sense of being responsible to himself is that his free and deliberate action on his instinctive desires is such that they are no longer determined as such by causes independent of him, but become expressions and fulfilments of his self-understanding and autonomy. The sense of responsibility to self also arises from the fact that man's moral action is decided on the basis of his existing past and his links with the present, in view of a future which he sees as significant for his own well-being. Being thus original and goal of his action, he is responsible towards himself.

Man is heteronomous in so far as he must render an account to his neighbour and to God, to show that his subjective action corresponds to his subjectivity. Referring his actions to others, he discloses — within the range of his moral responsibility — the effects on the well-being and personal development of those involved and hence on his own salvation, which he can only hope for in reasonable accord with others. He is therefore heteronomous by reason of his dependence on others, since his self-realization demands that the proper laws of other beings be respected where he is dependent on them.

The human act is always part of the unique historical process. Hence the necessity of being able to take moral decisions in the light of conscience, which is legitimated by the love of truth as such and the resulting ordination of the judgment to the good. For in the verdict of conscience the act is judged, in the light of the good as such, subjectively, that is, as it is for the doer in its uniqueness. Thus in the measure in which truth is loved, knowledge is ordained to the good as such and the act to rational self-realization. This does not mean that objective error is excluded or deprived of its objectively evil effects, but it must first be regarded as the expression (though an inadequate one) of a good and loving attitude and a true and purposeful self-realization. The possibility of error always remains. This does not mean that the value of conscience is diminished (Vatican II, Pastoral Constitution on the Church in the Modern World, art. 16) because its ordination to the true, meaningful and good in itself remains.

If, however, the error in conscience is due to culpable lack of ordination to the truth, and hence to culpable lack of love of truth on the part of the agent, self-realization is striven for in a disordered and irresponsible way. Man's disordered love has failed to actualize the love of truth which he knew to be due and proper. The error was willed in the cause.

When man responds to his necessary ordination to truth and consciously refers himself to the truth, he orientates himself to the good as such, and consequently grasps, as the meaning of his existence, that it is his task to adapt his actions and his whole life to the claims of futurity. This is done by taking a responsible attitude to one's acknowledged duty with regard to self-realization in dependence on others. Hence, objectively, there is a morally responsible action in the strict sense when one takes a definitive subjective attitude, a morally responsible action in the broad sense when this subjective attitude is provisional. The first case is concerned objectively with a righteous deed — or grave sin — or an act which changes substantially one's own personal condition or intersubjective relationships (as in sin or repentance). In the second case we have an act which causes only a partial change in subjective or intersubjective relationships, that is, under certain aspects, but without affecting them radically.

Subjectively, there is a moral act in the strict or in the broad sense, according to whether one uses a fundamental sketch-plan or merely a partial one to implement or alter one's subjectivity — and hence inter-subjectivity. We have a fundamental plan when one decides about one's subjective final end in connection with one's intersubjective dependence. Thus fully moral action is only possible where one has grasped subjectivity or inter-subjectivity and their goals so well that one can take up a definitive attitude to them. This does not of course exclude the possibility of future objective conversion or perversion. We have a partial plan, when one decides about a particular act in relation to an existing fundamental plan; or again, when the definitive relationship to one's own subjectivity (or to inter-subjectivity) is fixated by emotional urges, but individual aspects of subjectivity or inter-subjectivity are well enough grasped to make a responsible attitude to them possible.

D. Relationship to Transcendental Perfection: Love

1. The human act by which man aims at salvation ordains man to perfection, since perfection ordains him to the fullness of reality. But if man is to realize himself as this fullness demands, the moral act must be free. Only where it is possible to take up an attitude freely is it possible to free oneself from the slavery of the various urges which one finds within oneself and which of themselves demand immediate satisfaction without regard to the total perfection of the person. With the help of reason, we can hold ourselves aloof from the fascination of these individual urges, and so liberate ourselves from their claim to satisfaction. This is done by refusing to act and then deciding on the basis of considered motives. Hence our freedom lies radically in our reason. This freedom makes it positively possible to ordain individual urges to the needs of subjectivity and intersubjectivity insofar as we know them. Thus we are free to make them serve love or sin.

As the freedom to serve love and hence perfection, moral freedom is essentially a dynamic entity and never a static achievement. It ordains autonomy to heteronomy and hence knows no limits, but bursts out of the limits set by immanent necessities and external coercion, giving access to an existence which is all the more human, the more fully it is realized. For thus man strives more

and more strongly for self-realization, not as simple identity with himself, but as acceptance of inter-subjective and objective dependence, and hence in accordance with the fullness of reality.

In sin, however, man refuses to accept himself as he is and hence says No to the full reality. He seeks his perfection only in identity with himself — where it is not to be found. He undertakes an effort which is foredoomed to failure, since he tries to transcend his contingence by claiming to be absolute.

What is the condition of possibility for such sin, which erects itself arrogantly into an absolute? It is a sufficient knowledge of the truth that man is a value in himself, that the dignity of the person is inviolable, claiming and meriting our reverence and loving protection and aid. We cannot dispose of its destiny arbitrarily. Thus we are fully morally responsible only to the extent in which we are capable of recognizing the inalienable rights of man as such.

Hence moral freedom imposes no external limitations on psychological freedom. It merely excludes misuse of this freedom, by giving a validity to the structures of transcendental freedom and so enabling this freedom to develop dynamically, it being its own end, since it is the transcendental presupposition for the fulfilment of love.

2. Man makes his individual urges serve love by orientating them as well as he knows how to, to the perfecting of his own subjectivity. This he does by directing this subjectivity to the affirmation and promotion of existing inter-subjective relationships within the framework of justifiable subjective interests. This means promoting subjective interests insofar as they are compatible with intersubjective claims.

It follows that the various virtues are virtuous insofar as they ordain certain modes of personal conduct to love. Obedience is virtuous insofar as it submits one's own will, as love demands, to that of another who has authority over one. In this sense, love may be termed the form of all virtues. Sins, on the other hand, are sinful insofar as they are offences against love. For the distinction between theological, cardinal and other virtues, see the article *Virtue*.

The good as such, to which man is ordained by love for the truth, is inexhaustible, because the objective possibilities of man's perfection are of themselves unlimited, on account of his being ordained to being as such. But the concrete possibilities of perfection and hence of moral decision are limited, on account of the limited nature of man. Hence responsible action must always be directed in accordance with these concrete possibilities, while maintaining the mental orientation to the absolute possibilities, through love of the true and the good as such. Thus moral action continually opens up new and unforeseen possibilities of perfection, which ultimately are bestowed on man as the gratuitous gift of God.

E. Summary

The human moral act opens up to man the possibility of subjective personal fulfilment. This man achieves by turning to God and his neighbour as he makes his external works serve the subjective and inter-subjective perfection of those whom his acts affect — by their performance or omission. Here we must remember that when he turns to God in love, he can only "perfect" him *ad extra*, which is the way in which man himself attains his own supreme perfection.

Hence the human act is at once egocentric and altruistic, and formally good insofar as the transcendentally necessary self-affirmation is transcended in free outgoing ("ekstatic") love for the persons affected by the act. The human act is formally bad when the necessary self-affirmation of free self-transcendence is made an absolute, so that man himself, his neighbour and God are only affirmed insofar as they are made to serve a self-realization which is arbitrary because in contradiction to reality.

In this formal structure, the moral act, *qua* immanent, is infallible in its commands, permissions and prohibitions, because here it necessarily takes a free, responsible attitude to consciousness, the claim of the person and perfection. The transcendent act arising from this moral stand has its formally moral quality from the intention of the doer. He can contradict its objective and material quality because of the human possibility of error in judging the laws of categorized reality, which man can bend freely to his service in an irrational way, precisely because he is finite and contingent. The human act, through its transcendental orientation, is capable of being informed by grace.

F. The Theology of the Human Act

To describe the human act theologically, we must start from its relationship to union with God in grace in the vision of God, to which all men are called according to the universal salvific will of God. This means that an act is human or moral insofar as it is proportioned to salvation.

Theologically speaking, therefore, deliberate, responsible and free acts which are not informed by grace can only be called moral in an indirect sense, since they provide at most an indirect disposition *(dispositio negativa)* with regard to grace and hence with regard to salvation. The question of the existence of such merely natural moral acts is generally answered in the affirmative by theologians. This is because they feel bound to maintain the distinction between the natural and the supernatural order, and particularly, the distinction between faith in the broad sense *(fides late dicta)* and the acts preparatory to faith *(initium fidei)*. But this answer need not be taken as final, since the assertion that there are moral acts which have no significance for salvation is not without its problems from the standpoint of a theological anthropology.

Hence the starting-point of the theological determination of the moral act will be that the degree of the information of the act by a sufficient grace determines its positive morality, while its relationship to the supernatural virtues of faith, hope and love determines its inner structure. Thus a moral act in the broad sense will be one which makes possible a positive disposition to justification, or a modification of some particular relationship to salvation in the justified. A moral act in the full sense will be one which makes justification possible or can essentially alter the relationship of the justified to salvation.

The attentive consciousness required for the moral act begins with the possibility of the *initium fidei,* and attains the maturity required for a fully moral act when the faith required for justification is possible. Such requisite moral consciousness is present insofar as salvation is expected from God's turning to man in grace, insofar as the response to God's will to grace is recognized as an absolute "must", and hence insofar as man becomes capable of hope. Finally, the requisite moral freedom is there to the extent to which man is capable of supernatural love.

Here it should be noted that this ordination to the supernatural end need not necessarily be consciously articulate. It may be there merely implicitly, without being reflected upon — though it can be actually accomplished by "atheists".

The moral act implies an attitude to the order of creation in its incarnational and historical process of salvation. Thus it has an ecclesial structure corresponding to authority in the Church. Man's natural power of moral action is brought to fulfilment in a supernatural and hence incarnational way. Hence the moral act presupposes and implies this natural power.

Theologically speaking, therefore, the good moral act is always a matter of the reasonable obedience of faith, conscious of its radical obligation to the God who imparts himself in grace and comes to us in the incarnation, and responding in the love of God which embraces men as brothers and is thereby full of hope of salvation. A morally bad act is always a type of unbelief, rejecting in arrogant self-assertion God's offer of grace and hence the comradeship of mankind and so placing itself in a situation of menace and disaster.

See also *Experience, Education* I, *Person, Freedom, Decision, Responsibility, Morality, Truth* I, *Holiness, Justice, Virtue, Conscience, Existence* I, *Rights of Man, Atheism.*

BIBLIOGRAPHY. V. Frins, *De actibus humanis,* 3 vols. (1897–1904); J. de Blic, "La Théorie de l'option morale initiale", *Revue des Sciences Religieuses* 13 (1933), pp. 325–52; H. de Mesmaecker, *Tractatus de actibus humanis* (5th ed., 1939); P. Lumbreras, *De Actibus humanis* (1950); G. P. Klubertanz, "The Unity of Human Activity", *The Modern Schoolman* 27 (1950), pp. 75–103; O. Lottin, "Pour une réorganisation du traité thomiste de la moralité", *Acta Congressus Scholastici Internationalis Romae a. 1950* (1951); id., *Morale Fondamentale* (1954); J. Bécaud, *L'action, instrument d'évangélisation* (1955); S. Pinckaers, "L'acte humain suivant Saint Thomas", *Revue Thomiste* 63 (1955), pp. 393–412; F. Böckle, "Bestrebungen in der Moraltheologie", *Fragen der Theologie heute* (3rd ed., 1960), pp. 425–46; J. C. Ford and G. Kelly, *Contemporary Moral Theology,* I: *Questions in Fundamental Moral Theology* (1962); K. Rahner, *Theological Investigations,* I (1961), pp. 377–414; II (1963), pp. 227–46; R. Robidoux, "Les aspects psycho-théologiques du premier acte humain", *Studia Montis Regis* 5 (1962), pp. 83–124, 133–84; P. Engelhardt, ed., *Sein und Ethos,* Walberger Studien, Philosophische Reihe, I (1963); R. Schnackenburg, *The Moral Teaching of the New Testament* (1964); J. Maritain, *Moral Philosophy* (1964); R. Hofmann, *Moraltheologische Erkenntnis- und Methodenlehre* (1963); M. Scheler, *Der Formalismus in der Ethik und die materiale Wertethik* (3rd ed., 1966); J. Pieper, *Reality and the Good* (1967).

Waldemar Molinski

HUMANISM

I. General. II. Anthropocentrism.

I. General

1. *History of humanism.* Humanism as the deliberate effort to justify the Renaissance arose in the 14th and 15th centuries as an intellectual movement among the nobility, especially the merchant aristocracy of the Italian city-states. Within the traditional framework of the medieval order, this new social class did not regard itself as bound to any existing pattern of life and could therefore develop its courtly patrician style of life into an original and autonomous mode of vigorous intellectual existence (alongside the scholastic culture of the clergy and the chivalric culture of the court). This mode of life (connected with the medieval tradition of the *artes liberales*) was based on a scholarly, religiously neutral and hence unprejudiced contact with the culture of antiquity, in a form untouched by Scholasticism. It regarded itself and its ideal of the *uomo divino* as a revival of the classical *humanitas*. Petrarch, the real founder of humanism, appealed to Cicero and his efforts to "humanize" the Roman *virtutes* by means of Greek music, mathematics, and especially literature, which was regarded as the model in both form and content, and thus produce the virtues of philanthropy, tolerance, and wisdom.

This direct aestheticizing embodiment of the classical spirit (differing to this extent from the medieval classical revivals, which had been much more strongly influenced by Christianity) dominated the private culture of the aristocratic and episcopal courts, even north of the Alps. It gained entry to the Papal court under Popes Nicholas V, Pius II, Sixtus IV, Julius II, and Leo X. An appreciable stimulus was given to humanism by the confrontation of the Western intellectual world with the original texts of Greek philosophy, to which it was introduced by Greek scholars at the Union Council of Ferrara-Florence (1438), and above all after the fall of Constantinople (1453); this encounter resulted in the revival of every variety of classical philosophy (of special importance was the Platonic Academy of Florence — Giovanni della Mirandola and Marsilio Ficino) and thus introduced the new intellectual attitude into the universities.

By the time of Erasmus of Rotterdam, humanism finally dominated the cultured world of Europe. It had ceased to be simply the cultured view of life of a new social stratum and was now a far-reaching scholarly movement. This movement not only led to a considerable intensification of linguistic and literary education in the *studia humanitatis* but also opened the way to a fresh start in many other fields (natural philosophy, historical research, political theory and practice — see article on *Renaissance*). Above all, abandoning the scholastic synthesis of Christianity and philosophy and relegating this synthesis to the status of a "middle age" in the essentially continuous history of thought from ancient to modern times (a threefold scheme which first appears in Flavio Biondi), humanism posed afresh the problem of reconciling the autonomous culture of classical paganism with the Christian culture based on revelation. In this connection not only Plotinian and Cabbalist mysticism (in the Florentine Platonists) but also the ancient Church Fathers down to Augustine acquired new relevance; in Petrarch, for example, who based his mediating formula, *Christus est Deus noster, Cicero autem princeps nostri eloquii,* on Augustine; even more so in Erasmus's efforts in the direction of a *philosophia Christi*. This effort to link up with Plato, the Stoa and Cicero, which had already been made by Origen, was intended not to provide a system but to point to a certain means of self-education as the divinely-willed preparation. By reaching back behind Scholasticism to the sources of faith (the efforts to provide exact original texts of the Bible were typical) humanism paved the way for the Reformation and also demonstrated the ambivalent relationship between itself and the religious approach. The absolute religious confidence of the Reformers, based upon a sense of being laid hold of by God's Word and not upon a linguistic, aesthetic interest in the Bible, is in the sharpest contrast with the humanist basis in a scholarship of an aesthetic trend, and with a correspondingly conciliatory diplomatic view of religion (cf. Luther's controversy with Erasmus). As an independent movement, humanism ended with the Reformation. The controversy between the new confessions left no room for any neutral ground of esoteric neo-classical intellectual culture. Although the rival parties adopted certain humanistic principles and educational methods (cf. Calvin's Stoic humanism as "handmaid" of the new theology, Melanchthon's humanistic Aristotelianism as framework for Lutheran dogmatics, and, on the other side, the use made of humanist education in the baroque scholasticism of the Jesuits), these hardly constituted any longer an independent form of intellectual life.

2. *Enlightenment and neo-humanism*. Following developments which may be termed humanist in a broader sense — the *humanisme dévot* (an anti-Jansenist movement in France) and French classicism — the philosophical and theological problem of humanism, how to reconcile autonomous self-understanding with the understanding imposed on man by revelation, was raised anew in the Enlightenment. But now the criterion was "reason" rather than the ideal of ancient *humanitas*. At times the Enlightenment did no more than merely rationalize theology in favour of or in opposition to religion. But as early as Lessing, and still more in Kant and the transition to German idealism, it made a considerable contribution to the problem by its study of the human spirit in action, of the "practical reason" as the sphere of religion and the judge of its truth, i.e., of its compatibility with responsible self-understanding. It was, however, in the aesthetic theory and the philosophy of history characteristic of German classicism and romanticism that humanism, in reaction against the rationalism of the Enlightenment, experienced a conscious renaissance in the late 18th and early 19th century (in Winckelmann, Herder, Schiller, Goethe and F. Schlegel). This neo-humanism, with its wholly new understanding for Greek culture, took as its ideal the blending of all the manifold riches of the human individuality into a harmonious work of art in which artist, creative process and

product are one. In contrast to the one-sidedness of rationalism, the "humanity" of the Greeks became the norm. With W. v. Humboldt and others (e.g., F. J. Niethammer, who in 1808 coined the term "humanism"), this educational ideal (in opposition to the utilitarian education in the non-classical secondary schools of the Enlightenment which was designed to produce functionaries for society) became influential in secondary schools and so spread widely (but very thinly) a humanist outlook among the middle classes down into the 20th century.

In the form known as the "third humanism", there was a further flowering of the West's enthusiasm for classical antiquity during the period between the World Wars (W. Jaeger, K. Kerényi).

3. *Marxist humanism.* To some extent related to this neo-humanistic self-understanding, a philosophy of history developed among the radical Hegelians which, without reference to classical *humanitas,* regarded itself as humanism in virtue of its hope in man's complete realization of all given possibilities (the thorough penetration of matter by the spirit being seen as the medium of man's self-realization).

This new movement acquired the form in which it remains influential to this day following its fusion with political economy in the work of Karl Marx. According to Marx and modern Marxism (chiefly represented outside the Soviet Communist area by R. Garaudy and E. Bloch), man is his own creator in the sense that all objective reality (including man's own reality) is simply the product of his own labour. (This production is achieved through the division of labour; in pre-communist forms of society it is taken away from the creating agent and thus alienated.) This state of affairs determines the task: namely, so to remove this "dehumanizing" alienation (of the subject from the objective world and so of men from each other) that each may find in social relationships the adequate medium for the mutual affirmation of all men (who acquire in this way their *raison d'être*). Humanism thereby becomes the successful implementation of "the ways of life through which the inward can become outward and the outward the inward" (Bloch); or, in concrete terms, humanism becomes social policy

which, by purposeful planning of production, prepares the soil for the ideal of the person at one with himself and in harmony with others — the "total" man.

This classical Marxism is at present experiencing a further development in the "second Enlightenment", as represented for example in T. W. Adorno and M. Horkheimer. Their humanism rejects as inhuman the elaboration of any positive social goals at all, on the ground that man never adequately projects the truth about himself in such abstract ideals but simply the distorted counterpart of his own alienated situation. The really humanizing achievement is a persistently negative criticism, which will use all the tools of modern sociology in an incisive demonstration of the symptoms of self-alienation in society. (This important development is often echoed among a wider public in such groups as the Humanist Association and in sociological currents which, by their "militant humanism", convert the methodical principle of critical de-ideologization into a new ideology.)

4. *Existentialist humanism.* In part closely related to this neo-Marxist theory and in part as a reaction against it, "existence" philosophy also regards itself as humanism. Sartre, for example, dissociates man's freedom (as responsibility for himself) from any sort of belief in pre-existent norms and makes it wholly dependent upon itself. It is to produce its own concrete expression in freedom and as freedom, in the resolve which recognizes its absolute responsibility to all in face of a given decision. From this initially purely formal principle of a heroic, tragic humanism, Sartre develops formal and material criteria for testing the authenticity of the exercise of freedom. He finds in these criteria the way from complete arbitrariness in the content of self-creation to Marxism as the only possibility of genuine self-fulfilment of freedom in the present situation. Heidegger ("Brief über den Humanismus") discusses this concept in terms of the being of selfhood. And here the strict logic of the absolute freedom of the individual culminates in the absorption of subjective existence into the self-realization of the truly authentic self of being. The I, at the most radical moment of its "ek-sistence", that is, at its greatest openness for being as pure "it-self", is now the scene of the apparition of the being which

is absolutely prior to all metaphysical disjunction between being and essence. In the light of "humanum" in this sense, where it is the realm of the event of being — situated, according to the later Heidegger, less in the vital resolve than in language, the purest revelation of being — true humanism is allowing oneself to be opened up to the "thereness" of "being", to the "realm of the coming of the wholly sound".

5. *Christian humanism*. To basically non-Christian varieties of philosophical humanism, other variants could be added, from the positivist religion of Comte to the medico-biological "evolutionary humanism" of the Ciba Foundation. Indeed, they could be increased, also almost at will, since every new standpoint taken up in the present discussion of practical philosophy claims to be a form of humanism because of the general terms of the dialogue. Christianity could never be uncritical in their regard, because it regards the truth of human existence as the eschatological transformation of man by God which surpasses even the greatest possibilities of man's self-realization within history. (In this sense, humanism in the Christian view is also, in the words of Karl Barth, the humanity of God, namely the kindness whose free gifts alone enable man to be really himself.) But Christianity could not remain neutral and indifferent to non-Christian humanism, for Christianity does not see itself as an extrinsic alien imposition upon man but rather as God's summons to man which is mediated through, and begins its transformative work at the very point where the hearer of the call is most authentically and responsibly himself, and hence "human" in the highest sense. Hence in striving for a Christian humanism, in face of the present state of the problem and aware of the ambivalence of its task, Christian thought is following a law of its own being as the incarnation of salvation. It is also following a tradition which reaches back to Erasmus (explicitly) and (in substance) to the early Christian apologists and the medieval syntheses, and goes on, down to J. H. Newman in the English-speaking world, E. Przywara, T. Haecker and H. U. v. Balthasar in the German-speaking world, and J. Maritain, H. de Lubac and Y. Congar in the French-speaking world. In this sense, Christian philosophy (G. Marcel) as well as Catholic (K. Rahner) and Protestant (R. Bultmann) theology accept the humanism of the philosophy of existence which affirms that *humanitas* (and therefore the place of revelation) is realized not in the fact as such (i.e., in particular social orders) but in the act, i.e., in the resolve in which freedom is both realized and exteriorizes itself in the fact; in the (unobjectifiable) proper being of the self.

Christian theologians have also entered into discussion with Marxist humanism, not only as individuals, but on a wider scale (as in the "Paulus-Gesellschaft"). Like Moltmann in discussion with Bloch or Teilhard de Chardin in the field of natural philosophy, they have attempted very far-reaching syntheses of Christian eschatology with the Marxist hope of a salvation within history. They have sought for a synthesis of sacred history with an evolution aiming at universal integration.

To remain at the height which discussion has now reached, Christian humanism must undoubtedly use the various types of humanism which consider themselves atheist to correct one another. This means that it must clearly face the truth that the inability of man to achieve his humanity (and hence his openness for God) except in dialogal confrontation with others and in an integrated society poses an inexorable dilemma. For man has no other medium of interpersonal harmony than social reality, since freedom never exists purely as such, but can only be concrete and communicated through its objects. And this is why the humanism of the social utopia has a certain claim to be considered. But then again, man can never sublimate this social reality into unmistakable fact. There will never be a successful "communion of saints". And this is why the consistent reduction of the significance of the factual to the intention behind it has a certain justification. On the basis of this insight a Christian humanism — at one in this respect with the "second Enlightenment" and with Sartre as possibly the most honest presentation of the human predicament — must accept this dialectical oscillation between a positive mediating reality (which, if it is turned into an independent fact, is distorted into an ideology and actually hinders understanding) and a critical rejection of that reality (which, as mere negation can, of course, exist only in virtue of the positive). On the other hand, by accepting such criticism of the real (of the supreme attempt of humanity to secure its own salvation for itself dialectically), Christian humanism, being *Christian* humanism, will not fall into the absurdity of an endlessly open dialectical future. On the contrary, in the light of the cross, it is precisely this unending, impotent process of self-sanctification in a society in search of its *humanitas* which is seen to be an initial stage of the absolute judgment upon history and its illusory efforts to end man's self-alienation. The negative criticism (made very real by the very course of history) is interpreted by Christians as an element in an absolute judgment, which assesses particular forms of alienation as expressions of an alienated condition impossible to end within history and thereby, in principle, relativizes every form of humanism. And hence, the future appears as the hope of an absolute infinity in which the ambivalence of interobjectivity and the fragility of intersubjectivity therein revealed are finally removed (and it would be ideological naivety to expect this in human history itself). Christian humanism looks to a personal mediator in whom the reality of love between persons is definitely presented in an adequate social reality (bodiliness) and imparted as universal integration.

This salvation, the transformation of man himself, is the absolutely transcendent goal of our continuously self-judging history, and as such is certainly not purely other-worldly. On the contrary, despite the utter impossibility of expressing it concretely in any particular system or in any utopian programme for the future, it provides a point of reference for present action in the actual world; it is the real partner already present in the dialogue between each particular present and its future. Its presence makes it possible for the *humanum* to come about as it patterns itself (in faith, in the hope against all hope, and in love, in spite of all disappointment and tragedy) on the true *humanitas* of God.

See also *Renaissance, Reformation, Protestantism* I, *Enlightenment, Rationalism, Marxism, Education* I, II, *Existence* I, II, *Salvation* II.

BIBLIOGRAPHY. RENAISSANCE HUMANISM: R. Weiss, *Dawn of Humanism in Italy* (1947); G. Sauter, *Il pensiero italiano nell'umanesimo* (1949–51); G. Toffanin, *Storia dell'Umanesimo* (1950); M. P. Gilmore, *World of Humanism 1453–1517* (1952). ENLIGHTENMENT HUMANISM: F. Haecker, *Vergil, Father of the West* (1932); W. Rehm, *Griechentum und Goethezeit* (1936; 2nd ed., 1949); W. Jaeger, *Humanism and Theology* (1943); W. Bruford, *Culture and Society in Classical Weimar 1775–1806* (1962); G. Wilson Knight, *Christian Renaissance* (1962); C. Bowra, *From Vergil to Milton* (1963). MARXIST HUMANISM: E. Fromm, *Marx's Concept of Man* (1961); E. Bloch, *Gesamtausgabe* (1964 ff.); R. Garaudy, *De l'anathème au dialogue* (1965); T. Adorno, *Negative Dialektik* (1966); M. Horkheimer, *Zur Kritik der instrumentellen Vernunft* (1967); V. Martin, *Marxism and Humanism* (1967). EXISTENTIALISM: J. P. Sartre, *Existentialism and Humanism* (1948); K. Jaspers, *Man in the Modern Age* (1957); id., *Über Bedeutung und Möglichkeit eines neuen Humanismus* (1962); M. Heidegger, "Brief über den 'Humanismus'", *Wegmarken* (1965); J. P. Sartre, *Critique de la raison dialectique* (1967). OTHER FORMS: J. Huxley, *Knowledge, Morality and Destiny* (1960); B. Russell, *New Hopes for a Changing World* (1960); J. Huxley, ed., *Humanist Frame* (1962); B. Russell, *Has Man a Future?* (1962); R. Perry, *Humanity of Man* (1956); A. Silbermann, *Militanter Humanismus. Von den Aufgaben der modernen Soziologie* (1966). CHRISTIAN HUMANISM: J. Maritain, *True Humanism* (1938); H. de Lubac, *Drama of Atheistic Humanism* (1949); G. K. Chesterton, *The Everlasting Man* (new ed., 1955); R. Bultmann, *Essays Philosophical and Theological* (= *Glauben und Verstehen*, II) (1955); N. Berdyaev, *Destiny of Man* (1960); K. Barth, *Humanity of God* (1960); R. Guardini, *Power and Responsibility* (1961); Q. Breen, *Christianity and Humanism* (1967).

Konrad Hecker

II. Anthropocentrism

God as the Creator is likewise the goal of all that he has called into being. Creation is therefore theocentric, and this finality of the visible world is at its most intense and expressive in man, who is called to bring the objective and material glory of God to its perfection by the conscious acts which make it subjective and formal. But this radical self-dedication is only possible to a being which can possess itself completely, dispose of itself, be present to itself and be at one with itself. The more fully transcendence "comes to *itself*", as transcendence, the more perfectly is it directed towards God. There is no way of separating clearly origin, activity and goal in this movement of the being. Man is concerned with God only insofar as he is concerned with himself — as someone intent on God — and when he is concerned with himself, it must be with regard to the meaning and goal of his nature and existence: which is God. There is only one single basic act, which, rightly understood, is both theocentric and anthropocentric, under different aspects, and is such that it expresses the unity of the two great commandments, love of God with all one's powers and love of man after the norm of love of self (Mt 22:38f.).

Just as in knowledge the transcendental is linked to categories, and thought to the senses, so too the exercise of freedom cannot escape this duality, which the creature must accept in proper humility. Just as he cannot speak of God except in anthropomorphic images and concepts, so too he cannot seek God's glory except by looking to his own salvation and that of others (in the fear and trembling which self-oblivious love is, Phil 2:12), he cannot serve the Lord except by developing his own possibilities and "talents" (Mt 25:14–29). The effort to escape from this order of things for the sake of a "pure" love is bound to fail, and it also fails to do justice to the greatness of the Creator, which is not enhanced by the (self-)depreciation of the creature, but is manifested incomparably better as the creature grows in greatness and splendour.

This order of things comes to an unsurpassable climax in Christ, the God-man, in whom, by the way of obedience and death, the visage of man has become the eternal visage of God, so that the Father is seen unmistakably in him (Jn 14:9).

But since man in this world and age must still seek for the fulfilment of his being — which he can only attain by accepting it as a gift — he is in danger of lessening the tension of this two-fold orientation and of denying it: he can set himself against God, in a false humanism. This can be theoretical or practical: as a general principle in the position which makes man "the measure of all things" (individuals, nations, classes, races or man in general) and in the concrete particular case: in every (grave) sin, since there man tries to make himself his own law. The danger of a "humanism without God" extends from an express denial of God and the rejection of his claims to the sublimest forms of a religious asceticism and self-seeking mysticism. And even in the exercise of love itself, the primacy of the first great commandment over the second which is "like to it" must always be preserved: all anthropocentric service is ultimately in the service of the glory of divine love. If then, by a radical process of reduction, Christianity may be formulated as something fully anthropocentric (Mt 25:31–45), this reduction is inevitably Christocentric, whether the individual

makes it consciously or not, and thus ordained "to the glory of God the Father" (Phil 2:11).

See also *God (Glory of)*, *Transcendence*, *Charity* I, *Man*, *Anthropomorphism*.

BIBLIOGRAPHY. H. de Lubac, *The Drama of Atheistic Humanism* (1949); F. Michaeli, *Dieu à l'image de l'homme* (1950); K. Rahner, *Theological Investigations,* I (1961), pp. 215–45, II (1963), pp. 15–28, IV (1966), pp. 105–20; J. B. Metz, *Christliche Anthropozentrik* (1962); H. Urs von Balthasar, *Herrlichkeit,* I–IV (1961ff.); J. B. Metz, "Nochmals: Christliche Anthropozentrik", *Theologische Revue* 61 (1965), pp. 13–16; H. Urs von Balthasar, *Theological Anthropology* (1967).

Jörg Splett

HUMILITY

1. *The term.* The English word "humility" derives from Latin *humilis,* "lowly" ("near the ground", *humus* = earth). In the OT (LXX: ταπεινός) the dominant note is the elemental human experience of not having given ourselves existence, and therefore of not being necessary, which thrusts itself upon man in the pointlessness of life (cf. the sapiential books), in guilt, sickness, and death.

2. *Scripture.* a) *Old Testament.* Since Yahweh, the Creator God, has given man existence and keeps him in being, since Yahweh also rules the history of the Jewish nation and of the individual, and imbues the history of his chosen people, of each individual and all mankind, with meaning as the giver and the gift of eschatological salvation, humility is the only fitting attitude before him. Thus humility is one of the basic characteristics of the pious in the OT; cf. Num 12:3: "Now the man Moses was very meek, more than all men that were on the face of the earth." The prophets call again and again for humility towards Yahweh lest his wrath be kindled against Israel (Amos 6:8; Jer 13:16; Is 49:13; 61, 1f.; Mich 6:8). The bearer of eschatological salvation is pictured as a humble figure: "Lo, your king comes to you, triumphant and victorious is he, humble and riding on an ass" (Zech 9:9). Since here, as with Moses, humility is demanded even of those who share God's authority, the NT notion of humility is already signalled. The Psalms too abound with the assurance that

Yahweh upholds the humble (Ps 25:9; 131; 149:4). In the sapiential books humility chiefly means fitting into Yahweh's cosmic order (Job 22:29; Prov 3:34; 11:2; 18:22; 4; Ecclus 3:17ff.; 3:20; 19:26), so that humility also means forming a just estimate of oneself: "My son, glorify yourself with humility, and ascribe to yourself honour according to your worth" (Ecclus 10:28).

b) *New Testament.* Faced with the dawning kingdom of God and God's free condescension to him, man can only be humble as a child (Mk 10:15 par.) if he would be justified (Mk 12:38 par.; Lk 1:48; 14:11); and no man has any more merit than another unless it be the merit of greater humility (Lk 18:9–14). Jesus himself shows the right attitude: just as he, the envoy of the Father, humbly does the Father's will, so men must be humble before the Lordship of God which came with him: "Learn from me, for I am gentle and lowly in heart" (Mt 11:29), "For I have given you an example, that you also should do as I have done to you. Truly, truly, I say to you, a servant is not greater than his master; nor is he who is sent greater than he who sent him" (Jn 13:15–16). Decisively new here — though hinted at, undoubtedly, in the prophets' message about God's unfailing concern in Hosee and Ezek 16 — is that God himself showed himself humble in Jesus Christ. This gnosis is the reason why Christians must strive for the same attitude towards each other (Phil 2:5–11). Humility, which is intimately bound up with love (1 Cor 10:24; 13:4), must become a basic attitude towards the brethren (Rom 12:9f.).

3. *Theology.* Christian doctrine on humility grew out of constant struggle with the contempt for humility which prevailed in the ancient world (doubtless to be accounted for by social conditions). St. Augustine's profound definition, based on the sinfulness of man, "Tu homo cognosce quia homo es. Tota humilitas tua ut cognoscas te" ("Human, know that you are human. Your whole humility is to know yourself") (*Tract. in Joh.,* 25:16), exposes the shallowness of the ancient idea of humility. St. Thomas tried to link up humility with Aristotle's doctrine on magnanimity (*Summa Theologica,* II, II, q. 129, a. 3 ad 4). And in fact, Christian humility should be defined not in terms of lowliness but of selflessness. Christ is the supreme and inimitable model of humility in the inimitable greatness of his *magnanimitas* ("greater love has no man . . ."). Since all human virtues can become vehicles of self-assertive pride as well as of self-emptying love, humility is the peculiarly Christian virtue. This does not exclude the truth that charity is the *forma omnium virtutum,* since it merely declares that humility is the distinctively "Christian aspect" of charity. This is already suggested by the contrast between *eros* as the love which strives upwards and *agape* as the love which humbly condescends. The attitude of the ancient world to humility was passed on to the modern world (cf. Nietzsche) chiefly by means of the Renaissance. Man's growing power to master and manipulate his destiny and the pressing need to do so in this age of technology, nourish a cast of mind which gravely obscures the values of humility. But they could also pave the way to a comprehensive humility of a Christian inspiration, since man also experiences more clearly his limitations and his perilously exposed state.

See also *Virtue, Old Testament Ethics, New Testament Ethics.*

BIBLIOGRAPHY. J. van der Ploeg, "Les pauvres d'Israël et leur piété", *Oudtestamentische Studiën* 7 (1950), pp. 236–70; P. Adnès, "L'humilité . . . d'après S. Augustin", *Revue d' Ascétique et de Mystique* 18 (1952), pp. 208–23; 31 (1955), pp. 28–46; R. Bultmann, *Theology of the New Testament* (1952–55), I, p. 345, II, p. 182; P. Blanchard, "S. Bernard docteur de l'humilité", *Revue d'Ascétique et de Mystique* 29 (1953), pp. 289–99; A. Gelin, *Les pauvres de Yahvé* (1953); R. Guardini, *The Lord* (1954); G. Mensching, E. Kutsch, A. Benoît and R. Mehl in *RGG,* II, cols. 76–82; Bernard, Abbot of Clairvaux, *Steps of Humility* (1963); F. Hauck and S. Schulz, "πραΰς", *TWNT,* VI, pp. 645–51; R. Schnackenburg, *The Moral Teaching of the New Testament* (1965); B. Häring, *Law of Christ,* III (1966); W. Grundmann, "ταπεινός", *TWNT,* VIII, pp. 1–27.

Alvaro Huerga

HUSSISM

Hussism in Bohemia was born from a movement for reform which in its beginnings was of Catholic inspiration. It started with an attempt by Archbishop Ernest of Pardubice (1343–64) to reform his diocese. Among the measures he took there was one which was to be of great consequence. He called to

Prague a well-known German preacher, Conrad of Waldhausen, who had as a disciple the Czech Milíč of Kroměříž, soon to be followed by a whole line of Czech reforming preachers. The most famous among them was John Huss who caused the reform movement to take a decisive turn. While Archbishop Ernest had fought against the evil morals of his flock, Huss directed his attack principally against the wealth and the simony of the higher clergy. Huss and the preachers of his generation had come under the influence of John Wycliffe (d. 1384), the Oxford theologian, but paradoxically Huss, the most prominent among them, had been less affected than the others. Unlike Wycliffe he always maintained the real presence, auricular confession, absolution, and the sacrament of orders with its traditional degrees. Huss did not follow Wycliffe in his denial of the very principle of indulgences, but he did, however, attack the alleged indulgences which the antipope John XXIII had granted to those who took part in his "crusade" against Pope Gregory XII. He also insisted, sometimes indiscreetly, on the evangelical idea of the *true* bishop, that is, of the *good* shepherd. While he admitted the traditional notes of the Church on earth, he followed Wycliffe in defining the Church *properly so-called* as the society of the predestined or of the "good". The theological connection between the hidden Church of the just and the visible Church remained obscure. Finally, he denied the divine institution of the primacy. Huss was burnt as a heretic by the Council of Constance on 6 July 1415, only a few weeks after this same Council had declared its own superiority over the Pope. Huss had come to Constance of his own free will, convinced that frank discussion would have vindicated him. He was deeply disappointed by the proceedings of the Council Fathers and was convinced that they were not a genuine ecumenical assembly. He died like a martyr, calling upon Jesus Christ and reciting the Creed in a loud voice. From the drama at Constance later generations in Bohemia retained little of the Catholic sympathies of the man who perished in the flames, but the memory of the Council which burnt him, and which in addition condemned the use of the chalice by the laity, was to remain. And so another decisive step had been taken. From 6 July 1415 a large section of the Christians of Bohemia became and were to remain anti-Roman. What started off as a reform movement was now definitely changed into Hussism. The Hussites began by demanding the use of the chalice by the laity, freedom to preach the word of God, the punishment of mortal sins, those of the clergy included, and the confiscation of the temporal goods of the clergy. They successfully defended this programme (the Four Articles of Prague) against the Crusades organized in vain by Popes Martin V and Eugenius IV under the command of the Emperor Sigismund (1420–1436). When arms had failed, the Council of Basle, with the approval of Eugene IV, decided to negotiate. After the moderate Hussites had assisted the imperial troops to defeat the extremist sects at Lipaný in 1434, peace was ratified at Jihlav on 5 July 1436 on the basis of an amended version of the four articles (the Compacts): the chalice was granted to those laity who desired it; freedom to preach was assured to those who were duly authorized; mortal sins were to be punished by legitimate authority; the Church had the right to temporal goods, but also the duty of administering its property with due regard to justice. The Czechs, moreover, recognized as their king the Emperor Sigismund, the brother of their dead king, Wenceslaus IV. The Compacts established the rather ephemeral existence in the country of a Catholic Utraquism.

Then the Bohemian Brethren *(Unitas Fratrum)* took up the succession to Hussism. They were founded by Brother Gregory Krajči in 1457 at Kunvald, a village in the east of Bohemia. The Brothers were families, grouped in colonies, striving to observe the law of the gospel with order and discipline and most of all with efficacious faith in the Lord Jesus. In 1467–68 they chose for themselves priests and a bishop whom they had ordained and consecrated by the Waldensians. Two of the Brethren became famous: Chelčický, their "precursor", between 1425 and 1450, and most of all Komenský (Comenius), their last *senior* and a truly talented spiritual writer who after the battle of the White Mountain (1620) went into exile with the Brothers. The energy of the Counter-Reformation practically put an end both to Catholic Utraquism and the *Unitas Fratrum* as well as to the Protestant confessions which in the 16th century had spread all over the area now known as Czechoslovakia. When

Joseph II proclaimed an edict of toleration in 1761 there remained hardly any organized non-Catholic Christians in the Austro-Hungarian Empire. They then regrouped themselves into many confessions, all of which, over and above the Scriptures and the traditional confessional books of the Reformation, invoked the patronage of John Huss, the Four Articles and the Bohemian Brothers. The latest in date and the most numerous of these confessions is the "Czechoslovak Church" (1921).

See also *Conciliarism, Protestantism* III, *Communion under Both Kinds, Schism* IV, *Reform* II D.

BIBLIOGRAPHY. M. Spinka, *John Huss and the Czech Reform* (1941); M. Vischer, *Jan Hus. Aufruhr wider Papst und Reich* (1955); P. Brock, *The Political and Social Doctrines of the Unity of Czech Brethren in the Fifteenth and Early Sixteenth Centuries* (1957); P. de Vooght, *L'Hérésie de Jean Huss* (1960); id., *Hussiana* (1960); H. Kaminsky, *History of the Hussite Revolution* (1967).

Paul De Vooght

HYLEMORPHISM

1. Hylemorphism is strictly characteristic of Aristotelian scholastic philosophy. It is an effort to explain the nature of inner-worldly things. All bodies are essentially composed of matter (ὕλη) and form (μορφή) which in the concrete thing combine to make a unified whole. Hence hylemorphism is opposed to the various forms of atomism and dynamic monism which ultimately assume one single essential basis of beings. It is also opposed to a dualism which would suppose in living beings, and especially in man, two entities united to each other by mutual causality but nonetheless independent substances.

2. Hylemorphism is a fundamental element in Aristotle's theory of being and is a direct consequence of his doctrine of act and potency. Aristotle arrives at this duality-in-unity of things on the basis of ordinary observation. Changes can be seen to take place. In the realm of art, for instance, a statue is formed out of a block of marble, and in the realm of nature water becomes vapour. Since such changes are not completely new creations and not annihilations — notions which would be hard to imagine, since there is always something to start with and some-

thing always remains — all changes of a thing must be based on a common substratum which remains throughout. This *materia prima* is itself completely undetermined but is determined as this or that through the form which it receives and the cause which produces the form. — Aristotle comes to a similar result from reflection on the judgment: something is always predicated of something. And once more, all assertions suppose an ultimate substratum which is completely indeterminate, of itself pure indetermination but in potency to all possible determinations (forms).

Medieval Scholasticism adopted this view and developed it systematically. The accent, however, was displaced from the perspective of Aristotle, which was naive in the best sense of the word, to metaphysical discussions and speculation. But since even in Aristotle the notion of matter and hence the definition of the form was not quite clear, differences of opinion soon arose. Grave difficulties appeared above all when living things were considered and the question of the soul and entelechy arose. While Thomas Aquinas and the Thomists adhered strictly to the pure indeterminateness and potentiality of matter, Scotus and then Suarez allowed matter a certain actuality, which needed, of course, further determinations. Hence Aquinas maintained the unicity of the form from which all actuality and essential determinations flowed, while the others admitted a multiplicity of essential forms in living things.

In the Kantian and post-Kantian philosophy of the subject hylemorphism was not explicitly considered. It was not till the present century that renewed efforts were made to understand it, when dialectical materialism and the theory of evolution brought up the problem of matter and consciousness in all its acuteness. Mention should be made here of the view of Teilhard de Chardin that every "corpuscle" has two aspects, that of complexity externally ("matter") and the inward aspect of centering ("consciousness"), the inward aspect, which corresponds to some extent with the classical "form", "ascending" constantly in the course of evolution.

In theology, hylemorphism was invoked from the 12th century on to explain theological data, since medieval theology was strongly influenced by scholastic philosophy and found it applicable to the Eucharist, grace, the body-soul relationship, and so on. In sacramental theology in general, the sign was analyzed strictly in terms of hylemorphism: the material element (water, bread, oil) and the ritual gesture were considered the "matter", which was only constituted as a full sacramental sign by the "form" of the words, which determined the matter and gave it its meaning.

3. The history-centred thinking of modern times finds considerable difficulty in the way of a sympathetic understanding of hylemorphism, which is undoubtedly a somewhat static concept of reality. Not merely does the terminology appear hard to justify, but the Aristotelian concepts themselves, which have a certain justification in a limited field, seem to be transferred indiscriminately from one field to another. A distinction may be made between the matter and the form of a statue, but the application of these terms to other spheres only causes confusion: "matter" is not considered in a meta-physical sense but merely as an empirical datum ("ultimate substratum") which seems to exist in the same way as matter is understood to exist in ordinary conversation and in the sciences. Then too, the designation "form" seems to provide a world of degrees of being where each essence is neatly demarcated from all others. But this is a model of reality in which there is no place for evolution and a dynamic interweaving of things. But in spite of such justifiable criticism from modern philosophy the real concern of hylemorphism still has something to teach us. Underlying it is the question of the condition of the possibility of finite beings and of the finite spirit. Such beings, according to hylemorphism, are not "simple" but "mediated", at once active and passive. We can see most clearly what this being mediated means if we start from our own human action and production. We remark that there are always two aspects: the action is my action but it necessarily affects others. This identity which involves non-identity at the same time is verified in all acts, even the most "inward". Man is forced back upon this outgoing, this self-estrangement, in order to be able to express himself as man, that is, in order to realize his essence.

Merely to turn in on himself would be the equivalent of emptiness, loss of selfhood. Thus it is of the essence of man to be referred to the other than himself and to be determined by it on the vegetative and biological plane as on the mental plane. His essence brings with it something which makes it possible for man to go out of himself and exteriorize himself in this way. But since in this expression of himself he is determined by others and causes himself to be determined by others, the principle in question can only be receptive or potential, that is, it must be material, the possibility of being-with-others. This material nature of man is expressed in his bodily and sensible structure which is the necessary pre-condition of his action. The predominant characteristic of the bodily sphere is its passivity, its capacity to receive and accept what comes "from without". However, man never surrenders himself totally to the other because he remains, after all, identical with his own action. He has given himself over to others, but always in such a way that he still is in possession of himself. For even the seemingly total receptivity of the sense is conscious, that is, even in his sensible acts man betakes himself back into himself. This is the aspect of recollection, of self-possession, where man is actively "with himself", spontaneous, self-determining. This principle is, as it were, the formal (i.e., form-giving) element which penetrates and stamps all action (thought, will, and work). The individual activities, which take man out of himself, are gathered to the centre of the conscious selfhood. Man is, indissolubly, both: receptivity to determination from outside and self-determination from within. Man as spirit mediates himself to himself by expressing himself in outward, perceptible action, in order to come to himself through (and only through) this self-alienation. "Matter" as man's being outside himself and "form" or spirit as his being within, aware of and in possession of himself, form a polar tension which cannot be reduced either to one extreme or the other. Both are equally primordial, since we never come upon ourselves except as body-soul. In spite of their being equally essential, there is a certain difference of rank: spirit as the determining element stamps matter as the determinable. Sensible knowledge, as self-mediation of the spirit is always dependent on and formed by the consciousness. Nonetheless, it must not be forgotten that the receptivity of the senses demands a mediation of the human spirit through the material.

For in this way consciousness, as constitutive principle of man, remains a human, finite consciousness, not purely creative and spontaneous, not pure self-transparency, but receptive spontaneity, a self-possession which is mediated by the non-self.

If these considerations, which arise immediately from our knowledge of human action, are applied analogously to other things, a certain parallel appears in the realm of living things. The determinative principle, the form, diminishes in range and function the lower we descend the scale, till it has entirely vanished in otherness in inorganic things. Self-possession is reduced to being merely different from other things, which are no longer fetched back into a self. Since these things are the objects of human action, they must also be hylemorphic in structure.

See also *Aristotelianism, Scholasticism, Spirit, Matter, Marxism* II, III, *Evolution* I, *Monism, Dualism.*

BIBLIOGRAPHY. Aristotle, *Physics,* I, 7–9; *Metaphysics,* VII, 3; XII, 1–5; Thomas Aquinas, *In octo libros physicorum Aristotelis expositio,* ed. by P. M. Maggiolo (1954); id., *In XII libros metaphysicorum Aristotelis expositio,* ed. by M. R. Cathala and R. M. Spiazzi (1966); K. Rahner, *Geist in Welt* (3rd ed., 1964); E. McMullin, *Concept of Matter in Greek and Medieval Philosophy* (1965); E. Coreth, *Methaphysik* (2nd ed., 1964).

Herbert Scheit

I

IDEA

1. *History*. The idea, throughout all its changes of meaning, whether accepted or rejected, is one of the basic terms of Western thought, whose unity and differentiation it displays in the most concentrated form. Ἰδέα means first of all appearance, form, character. Plato uses it for the essence, first for that of the virtues in contrast to their distinctive modes of realization in the concrete, then for virtue as such and for the good in itself and the true reality of all beings. These essences (forms, ideas) are above change and perception and accessible only to spiritual insight. They constitute the κόσμος νοητός through which things are what they are by participation, and which man becomes aware of in "anamnesis", thereby coming to understand himself and the visible world. The later dialogues are specifically concerned with the intrinsic difficulties of the relationship between the world of appearances and of forms, and of the relationships of the forms to one another: their relation to the good, the form of forms, that is, not only the supreme form, but that which itself transcends the forms and alone makes them forms. But this tension is in fact the foundation of Western metaphysics, on which even the adversaries of Plato take their stand. Aristotle situates the εἶδος in the things, as μορφή and ἐντελέχεια, and not outside them, but still attributes to it, as the supra-temporal universal, the all-important role in the coming to be of the concrete individual. Nietzsche's polemic against the "world behind the world" merely reverses the traditional priorities. This is also true of dialectical materialism and to some extent of existentialism. The neo-Platonic solution of Plato's difficulty, that the forms were the content of the Νοῦς which proceeds from the One, was taken over by Augustine. He understands the forms as the exemplars of created beings in the mind of God. Things exist because seen by him, and our illumination by God enables us to know them according to their divinely-conceived essence. Thomas Aquinas then identifies these forms with the divine essence insofar as it is known by God as imitable *ad extra* in many ways. Nominalism sought to disrupt this order of things, by denying the universal and necessary character of the essences and putting them at the mercy of the absolute, arbitrary freedom of God.

Faced with this attempt at dissolution, modern thought strove to maintain the accessibility of things — as it had to do for the sake of life itself — by basing their forms or ideas in man. The first efforts in this direction still referred them ultimately to God (Descartes, Occasionalists, Leibniz). When this was criticized by the English empiricists, who reduced the *a priori* of the innate ideas to mental dispositions and ultimately to later associations of ideas, Kant undertook to provide a new foundation for the ideas in the transcendental consciousness. God, the world, the soul can no longer be the guarantee or place of the ideas, they are themselves rather the three ideas, principles of knowledge instead of knowledge, which is confined to the experience of the senses. Furthermore, they are not principles which enter constitutively the syntheses of knowledge as do the categories. They only represent the "rule" by which the movement of synthesis operates.

In German Idealism, however, the idea once more becomes constitutive. In Fichte it is the "image of God", the appearance of the Absolute in the world of reality; in Schelling it is the force in the coming to be of the Absolute itself; in Hegel it is the Absolute in itself, which exteriorizes itself into reality and thus comes to the truth of the total reality of the ideal and real. As the idea of freedom, the idea is also constitutive in the neo-Kantians Cohen and Natorp; in the philosophy of values it appears as the notion of "valid" essences; in Phenomenology it is a trans-historical essential form, while in Jaspers the three ideas of Kant become names for the "all-encompassing" which cannot be objectivated.

For Heidegger, the notion of the idea betrays the "oblivion of being" which beset Western thought. Instead of revelatory Being, only the disclosed beings (or essences) are kept in view. The beings thus presented to view give rise to the "representation", first of God, and then of the subject — from his innate ideas to his ideologies. In the course of this history the basic impulse in drawing up this sketch-plan is discovered to be the will to master the accessible forms. Similarly, especially by theologians, this Greek understanding of things seen is contrasted with the Hebrew, biblical experience of the world in the hearing of the word, where man does not try to grasp, but lets himself be grasped and mastered.

2. *Analysis.* Just as none of the senses may be attributed priority with regard to being, so too seeing and hearing, form and word are not to be understood as alternatives, but in synthetic polarity. The notion which would then transcend and comprehend both would be presence, thereness. The idea must then be understood historically. It means — beyond its ordinary usage, which vaguely treats as an idea every datum of consciousness — the essence, the essential form, which as such is neither universal nor individual, exists only in the concrete particular, but still expresses and guarantees the universality, the more than individual character of the individual. The idea, especially in man, is not a pre-existent, otherworldly "archetype", it is the "inscape" (G. M. Hopkins) of summons and responsive

hearing, towards which freedom develops in its single decisions.

Further, just as the idea helped in the elaboration of the doctrine of the Trinity (the Logos), the modern vision which takes together immanent and "economic" Trinity (the Trinity of the economy of salvation) leads to the same historical concentration: to Christ as the *universale concretum,* the idea and norm of history as a concrete person.

In this way the ideas are known not merely theoretically, by intuition (Plato), illumination (Augustine), abstraction (Aristotle, Aquinas), construction (Kant) or feeling (value-philosophy), but by the total act of free acceptance and adoption ("doing the truth"). In this way the notion of participation, which has been linked with the idea since Plato, receives a personal, historical sense. Idea and participation are thus moments of the finite spirit, or freedom, in action, as it realizes, analogously in each age, its own essential form and those of its world, in a process of self-shaping in which it also shapes as it sees and hears, and thus freely becomes what it is to be in its "hour".

See also *Knowledge, Metaphysics, Platonism.*

BIBLIOGRAPHY. C. Heyder, *Zur Geschichte der Ideen-Lehre* (1874); E. Dubois, *De exemplarismo divino,* 4 vols. (1898–1900); E. Husserl, *Ideas: General Introduction to Phenomenology* (1931); E. Garin, *La théorie de l'idée, suivant l'école thomiste* (1932); P. Wilpert, *Zwei aristotelische Frühschriften über die Ideenlehre* (1949); D. Ross, *Plato's Theory of Ideas* (1951); M. Heidegger, *Platons Lehre von der Wahrheit* (2nd ed., 1954); E. Husserl, *Erste Philosophie,* I: *Kritische Ideengeschichte* (1956); M. Heidegger, *Identität und Differenz* (1957); M. Scheler, *Die Wissensformen und die Gesellschaft* (2nd ed., 1960); M. Heidegger, *Nietzsche,* 2 vols. (1961); K. Jaspers, *Truth and Symbol* (1962); N. Hartmann, *Das Problem des geistigen Seins* (3rd ed., 1962); M. Müller, *Existenzphilosophie im geistigen Leben der Gegenwart* (3rd ed., 1964); H.-G. Gadamer, *Wahrheit und Methode* (2nd ed., 1964).

Jörg Splett

IDEALISM

A. General Notions

In philosophy, idealism is the general term for the speculative position which may be described as follows:

1. When considering the similarities and diversities, the identities and the differences

of which reality is composed, its intention is always directed to the universal, to what is common in the manifold individuals. It looks to the dominant factor which embraces the many and subsumes them into the whole of reality. It aims on each level at the single concept which will make the multiple comprehensible. It regards the universal as the permanent and essential in contrast to the transitory and contingent individual and hence assigns it priority in being as well as in knowledge.

2. On the analogy of bodily sight, it interprets this universal as *form (eidos, idea),* the immutable basic pattern which underlies its many manifestations, the permanent aspect disclosed to the spiritual gaze which looks beyond the sensible world. Thought is regarded primarily as pure vision, in contrast for instance to the biblical "hearing", and the concept is the fixed outline of the essence as it presents itself to the spiritual view. The insight thus immediately presented to thought in sensible experience renders it possible and necessary to link the objects of experience in mutual relationships. And the relationships discovered between the individual things serves once more in its turn to make the order of essences "evident".

3. The attitude is based on the speculative supposition that sight and insight, conceptual essence and spiritual vision, thought and form, are identical in act, because being itself, as spiritual being, is the "light" which illuminates both the form and the thought. Being diffuses and limits itself in the many "essences" which are the basic modes of existent reality: but in face of this reality, that is, in the ontological reflection which philosophy calls "spirit", being restores itself at once to its unity and illimitation. This still leaves open the question of the place where being and spirit hold sway in the supreme fullness of their identity, that is, to whom the form shows itself primarily as such, and who the thinker primarily is (the divine, the transcendent God, the thinking subject in the world and so on).

In this general sense, idealism is the basic form of Western metaphysics. When this philosophy asks about the being of beings, it looks — by virtue of the light of "being" or "reason" — beyond the existent being to its sufficient reason, and seeks above all to trace the essence of beings and establish the order of their essences as a whole. In this sense, idealism includes what is called "realism", insofar as realism considers the existent being as "res", that is, as the individual realization, in independent subsistence, of a universal entity. See St. Thomas Aquinas, *1 Sent.,* 25, 1, 4 c: "a quidditate sumiture hoc nomen res." This idealism also determines such reactions as conceptualism and nominalism, which put a radical cleavage between the order of being and the order of human thought, and treat the universal merely as a concept framed by finite thought, or as a generalizing name used to cope with the multiplicity of reality. But these systems remain tributary to idealism, because they still accord binding force, of a secondary order, to concept and name, which remain necessary for the ordering of human existence. The radical contrary to idealism is "materialism", whose dependence on the idealistic mode of thought may be seen in its attempts to understand itself and trace its own foundations, as in dialectical materialism. This denies that spiritual being is the real foundation of, and is prior in rank to, material reality. But by reversing the relationship, it retains the formal difference and the mediatory function of the ideal order. The basic forms of reality and its mutual relationships are no longer the ideal *a priori* aspects of a spiritual principle prior to and transcending the world, but the reflection of matter in human consciousness, as it attains self-awareness in the medium of human thought ("ideology"). This reflection remains more or less distorted till it is perfected in the dialectical-materialist truth.

B. Historical Survey

The history of idealism begins with the ontological idealism of Plato. For Plato, the changing sensible things in the world of perception (κόσμος αἰσθητός, the region of coming to be γένησις), which are only imperfect representations of their forms, do not really deserve the name of "beings". The real beings, in complete separation (χωρισμός) from these, are the forms themselves (idea = ὄντος ὄν; Platonic or extreme realism). The forms receive essence and reality from the supreme form of the good (the ἀγαθόν as εἶδος εἰδῶν) and form together the eternal intelligible world which is the true object of spiritual vision (κόσμος νοητός, the region of being, οὐσία). In the light of the good, and according to the model of the forms, the corporeal world was moulded from spatial chaos. Knowledge is only possible in the light of the good, and as a recall (ἀνάμνησις) of the pure forms originally present to the soul. Thus knowledge is a purgation (κάθαρσις) which frees the soul from the distraction and impediment of the senses and leads it to the pure contemplation where alone the soul can find its happiness. All action too is determined by this last end, especially in the social form of the State, which corresponds exactly in its hierarchical structure (ruler, guardians, workers) to that of the soul (reason, courage, desire) and must serve the common good by educating the citizens for happiness. This Platonic view of the State, which made it strictly subservient to an ideal order, became the foundation of the many Utopias of Western political philosophy.

The theological idealism of St. Augustine links up partly with neo-Platonism, partly with Stoicism, transforming both in the light of the Christian experience of God and revelation. It considers the forms as the eternal thoughts *(rationes aeternae)* of the transcendent God (the form of forms). As such, they are the source of all temporal things, and the reason why these are really knowable, in the light of the truth with which God enlightens man. (St. Thomas Aquinas combines this theological idealism with Aristotelian or moderate realism: the universal is prior to the thing, *ante rem,* as an exemplar in the mind of God; cf. *2 Sent.,* 3, 3, 2 ad 1; *Summa Theologica,* I, 44, 3 c, in the thing, *in re,* as in the singularity of the existent being, consequent to the thing, *post rem,* as the conceptual universal which the human spirit attains by abstraction.) The forms (eternal thoughts) as a whole constitute the plan of creation and salvation, now understood as the provident provision made by God, who created the world and wills to lead men by his grace from the one beginning to the one end: to see God himself as the Truth, "face to face".

Modern philosophy is largely the secularization of Christian ideas about God and thinking about history. Psychological idealism separates radically the "world of consciousness" from the "real world" beyond consciousness, and treats the forms as innate (R. Descartes) or as acquired by experience (empirical idealism, J. Locke, D. Hume), but in any case, as subjective "representations". Questions can now be asked for the first time about the criteria of certainty. Epistemological idealism asks whether and in what conditions the idea corresponds correctly to the "external" object, and acosmic idealism can go so far as to deny the reality of the so-called "external world" (G. Berkeley). For the first time also, the philosophy of history can see the natural process of human thought and action as "storia delle idee umane" (G. B. Vico), with terms of reference different from the realization of the divine plan of salvation in history.

The transcendental or critical idealism of I. Kant "goes beyond" the world of consciousness of the empirical subject, but not to the ideal order either of an "external world" (of beings in themselves) prior to human consciousness, or of a "higher world" (of the thoughts of God) which surpasses the external. Kant goes back to the structure of the finite subjectivity of each human subject, to reach the pre-conscious subjective conditions of possibility of human thought and action. Knowledge does not attain existent beings as they are in themselves, by virtue of their essence or their form, but only as they are met with as objects, that is, in the unity given each by the categories — conditioned by the understanding — which determine them. When Kant speaks of the "idea" he means a non-objective totality, "the world", for instance, which cannot as such be the object of experience and hence cannot be theoretically known. It remains, however, a regulative idea, a principle of order, for the theoretical reason, and so a necessary condition of possibility for progress in intellectual knowledge. In the field of moral action, the ideas are "postulates" of the practical reason, which, to give meaning to morality, demands belief in freedom, immortality and God, as guarantees of the "highest good", the unity of perfected morality and merited happiness in the "kingdom of God". History consists of an unending progress to this "ideal" end.

Developing the movement launched by Kant, German idealism takes the subjectivity to be the infinite principle of unity, from which then proceed the empirical subject and object, the ideal and the real order, spirit and nature, thought and being. In the subjective idealism of J. G. Fichte, in the Ego, in a primordial "pre"-historical act, the Ego poses itself and the non-Ego, being or the world. This is the concrete, palpable sphere of duty, where moral action has to prove itself historically in freedom. In this conquest it returns to itself in act, once it has understood itself as that which it necessarily is, in intellectual self-contemplation, on the level of pure reflection.

The objective idealism of F. W. J. v. Schelling takes an absolutely undifferentiated subject and object as the source from which proceed freedom and necessity, consciousness and unconsciousness, spirit and nature. Just as nature is the self-revelation of the absolute in manifold forms, so spirit is the medium of the self-contemplation of the absolute, the total identity where all finite forms are comprised and absorbed. In the absolute idealism of G. W. F. Hegel, the principle of unity is the idea, which realizes itself by becoming other, that is, nature, and returns to itself from this otherness, as spirit. The supreme mode of this spiritual return is the absolute knowledge of philosophical "logic", in which the absolute idea understands itself as such through its historical manifestation (the phenomenology of the spirit). There, delivered from all exteriorization and from all the historical effort of its return, the idea achieves absolute selfhood, as logos.

The neo-idealism of the late 19th and the first quarter of the 20th century sought to overcome positivism and empiricism by a new effort of thought. Sometimes it linked up with Fichte, as in Rudolf Eucken's philosophy of the absolute life of the spirit as the unity of consciousness and action. Or it linked up with Hegel, as for instance Benedetto Croce and Giovanni Gentile in Italy, F. H. Bradley, B. Bosanquet and E. McTaggart in England. In Germany, the universalism of O. Spann is a noteworthy example of a doctrine influenced by the Hegelian notion of the absolute spirit. But the major impulse came from the transcendental philosophy of Kant, though indeed its metaphysical basis and horizon were deliberately disregarded, since Kant was seen only as the philosopher who had conquered and destroyed metaphysics. The neo-Kantianism of the Marburg school, founded by Hermann Cohen and Paul Natorp, took the exact sciences as its model and sought to establish the logical conditions for true — in this case, correct — knowledge and will. These conditions, normative of all experience, were supposed to be pre-contained in the structure of the "pure consciousness". Interest was thus centred on "theoretical reason" but this approach also dominated the treatment of aesthetic, religious and moral problems. Cohen had already stressed the importance of the social elements in Kant's doctrine, and Karl Vorländer took up the point, trying to form a synthesis of Kantian ethics and Marxist socialism. On the basis of the doctrine of the conditions of possibility of knowledge Rudolf Stammler outlined a philosophy of law which proposed a doctrine of "correct law" or "the right rights". The Baden school in South-West Germany, under the leadership of Wilhelm Windelband and Heinrich Rickert, attacked directly the questions arising from the "practical reason". The decisive elements in real life are not logical pre-conditions but duties based on judgments of value. The consciousness recognizes that it is orientated to absolute values and summoned to realize them. Hence they are not merely "subjective", that is, they do not derive from the consciousness itself. But since they are not real, neither do they "exist" objectively. But they "hold good" absolutely. The distinction was made between natural sciences which took no account of values and cultural sciences which were determined by values. And the cultural sciences which used generalizing (Rickert) or nomothetic (Windelband) methods, trying to establish laws, were distinguished from the cultural sciences which used descriptive or individualizing methods. These distinctions came to be important for the theory of sciences, especially the human sciences. The influence of the Baden school was decisive in the philosophy of E. Troeltsch and M. Weber.

C. THE CHARACTERISTICS OF IDEALIST THINKING

To form a judgment on idealist thought, the following basic characteristics must be kept in mind.

1. Its principle ("ideation") allows it to see the question of the essence of any reality whatsoever as the quest for its "idea". Thus it can ask what idea is verified in

things, groups of things, and their mutual relationships. It can also ask what is the idea governing human attitudes and relationships such as law, love, the State, marriage, and so on. It can ask what is the idea of man and what happens to him, with him and through him in time — the idea which directs his history. Finally, it can ask after the idea of the whole and the highest, of being and of God himself.

2. The ideas are the basic determinants and relationships of the realm of reality. But they are also ordained to each other in a set of reciprocal determinations and delimitations, which may be called an "ontological" systematization. This has as its counterpart, on the level of reflective thought, the logical systematization of idealist thought. Such thought displays itself as the constructive force of the concrete intelligent consciousness, which must learn to know *the* world as *its* world, use this knowledge to construct itself and direct its action according to the knowledge.

3. A difference is experienced between the perfection of the basic form and the finite reality, between the measure and what is measured, between the order of things and the elements inserted into that order, between the absolute pure idea and the imperfect reality. This experience gives rise to the idealist ethic which recognizes in the idea the obligatory ideal, that which ought to be, the "value", and dedicates itself with all its might to the realization of the ideal (practical idealism). Now the pure idea is the measure and principle of order which allots the real its place in the whole. But the idea itself, in its perfection, can never be met with in any place accessible to immediate experience. It is "homeless" with regard to space and time — and therefore can be denied, when its mode of being is misunderstood. In this sense, therefore, idealist thought is essentially "Utopian", and in this type of thinking the man who goes beyond immediately perceptible reality *(mundus sensibilis)* to return to the region of its ideal causes *(mundus intelligibilis)* remains necessarily a "Utopian being".

The significance of the idealist position may be described as follows. Against all forms of irrationalism, it maintains that the nature of reality is intelligible. Against all forms of relativism, it defends the uncondi-

tional obligatoriness of a clearly recognizable order (and hence all thinking which recognizes norms and orders of things in natural law and social relationships is tributary to idealist thought). Against all forms of analytical positivism it retains the power of a synthetic vision of the whole and asserts the meaningfulness of the world and of human existence. And above all, against all forms of pragmatism, it affirms that the truth of the whole, knowledge of being, idea and value, are not merely means whereby man becomes in fact master of his existence in his struggle with the individual realities which he encounters. It recognizes that man is meant to transcend himself and individual entities in his orientation to the absolute, and that only in such transcendence can he hope to preserve his dignity and find his fulfilment.

The temptation besetting idealist thought is to try to conceive as an idea that which can never be an idea: the absolute and incomprehensible mystery which is at the root of being. And it may forget that man, since he is essentially referred to this mystery for his origin and meaning, must likewise remain a mystery and be incomprehensible. It is further tempted to take the order of essences, which comprises and determines all things, as itself a comprehensible whole. Hence, while looking to the ideal order, but being "blind" to reality, it often tries to force into a final "closed system" that which can never be coerced or encompassed.

The proper limits of idealist thought are set it by its experience of history, when this is taken seriously. History is not the accidental and somewhat unsatisfactory realization of the eternal, unchanging ideal order. Nor may it be conceived of as the reality which is the necessary self-understanding and self-development of the absolute idea. It is the activity of human freedom in its world, an activity obscure in origin, open and indeterminate as to the future. Hence history is a process of change which is utterly unamenable to theory and irreducible to concepts, the continuous remoulding of man himself, of his world, and of the whole order of beings, which never ceases to present new aspects. And here the question arises as to how the history of man and his "world" may be conceived, without dissolving the intrinsic enchainment of the changing, epoch-making order of things into the mere happenings; cf. article on *Historicism*. It is the question of the unconditional claim of the essential, the idea, the order and the norm, and of how this claim can be reconciled in each age with the insight that in the historical process of the "world", the order of essences itself, in things and in man, is always changing.

See also *Being* I, *Reflection, Spirit, Metaphysics, Platonism, Marxism* II, *Ideology, Idea, Irrationalism, Pragmatism, Positivism, Nominalism, Historicism.*

BIBLIOGRAPHY. W. Dilthey, *Gesammelte Schriften*, IV *(Abhandlung zur Geschichte des deutschen Idealismus)* (1921); N. Hartmann, *Philosophie des deutschen Idealismus*, 2 vols. (1923–29); J. H. Muirhead, "The Platonic Tradition in Anglo-Saxon Philosophy", *Studies in the History of Idealism in England and America* (1931); H. D. Gardeil, *Les étapes de la philosophie idéaliste* (1935); C. Ottaviano, *Critica dell'idealismo* (1936); R. Jolivet, *Les sources de l'idéalisme* (1937); A. C. Ewing, ed., *Idealistic Tradition* (1957); id. *Idealism: A Critical Survey* (3rd ed., 1961); F. C. Copleston, *History of Philosophy*, VI: *Wolff to Kant* (1960), VII: *Fichte to Nietzsche* (1963); M. Müller, *Existenzphilosophie im geistigen Leben der Gegenwart* (3rd ed., 1964).

Alois Halder

IDENTITY-PHILOSOPHY

1. *The principle of identity.* The identity of each thing with itself is taken to be the most simple and obvious principle of all logic and philosophy. Without the principle of identity (A = A) there could be no unambiguous and consistent thought and language. Nonetheless, identity is not an experience reflecting external objects. It is given in the self-experience of the human subject. In the consciousness of self, the Ego knows itself as the self which persists throughout all the changes which affect it, as the individual self in contrast to all others, even in contrast to the states, attitudes and actions which come and go within itself. The "I think" which is always concomitantly thought in all experience gives all man's functions their unifying term of reference and intrinsic connection. This is what Kant called the "transcendental apperception" (*Critique of Pure Reason*, B 116–169). It is intrinsic to the systems of German idealism and indeed to all modern philosophy of the subjectivity to affirm that the experience of things in their identity is part of the experience of the selfhood of the Ego. "It is only the I . . . which lends unity and consistency to all that is. There is no identity except that which appertains to what is posited in the I" (F. W. J. Schelling, *Vom Ich* [1795], p. 178). But even nonidealist philosophies affirm that the existence and nature of things in true identity can only be grasped by virtue of the experience of being, reality, identity, in the experience of selfhood, for pure empiricism denies such identity to things – or rather, to the complexes of phenomena which are called "things".

No knowledge or science can ultimately be founded on another rational, conceptual truth. There is no way of defining everything, that is, of always demarcating it in terms of another: this would lead in the end to a vicious circle. An ultimate justification of truth is only possible if there is a type of pre-rational, non-conceptual knowledge which is self-certifying and has not to appeal to anything else. This is the primordial knowledge which refers only to itself: self-experience, presence of the self to itself, identification of subject and object, *reditio completa in seipsum* (Thomas Aquinas), *Beisichsein* ("self-possession", Hegel), *Selbstgelichtetheit* ("autolucidity", Heidegger), which is "spirit" in act. Hence all knowledge and all science is ultimately bound to look for its justification in the human spirit's experience of identity. The *cogito — sum* of Descartes, the implications of which were worked out in different ways by Fichte and Husserl, is the secret focus of all knowledge (see W. Kern, "Das Selbstverständnis der Wissenschaften — als theologisches Problem", *Grenzprobleme der Naturwissenschaften* [1966], pp. 111–41).

2. *The appearance of difference in identity.* Identity is not the sameness of the inarticulate and immaterial, as may be seen from the intrinsic structure of the relationship of identity, which is characterized by differentiation. The self knows itself. A tension of subject-object, in the widest sense, a duality in unity appears in this experience. Man's self-possession always appears as a coming-to-himself *(red-itio)*. This holds good on the wider scale of the phylogenesis and ontogenesis of man's evolution as a whole and of man as an individual. It is also true on the smaller scale of each individual act of

consciousness. The being and the becoming of the self can only take place as a permanent transition through the other. The character of identity is primordially dialectical or even dialogal. All consciousness of self depends for its realization on the impulsion from "without": the other, the empirical object, or, more precisely, the claim of the other, of the other person, is indispensable. Self-consciousness can develop only in exteriorization, in a self-expression which goes "outside" of itself. Man's destiny is to be a pilgrim, his way always takes him through territory which is apparently strange. Return into one's own self goes hand in hand with outgoing into the world. The self and the world are fundamentally correlated. As Hegel says: "The power of the spirit is measured by its outgoing, its depths by the depths to which it entrusts itself in its self-explication" (*Phenomenology of the Mind*, p. 9).

The indissoluble link with the other makes it possible for the self to fall a prey to the other, the extrinsic, the alienated, but also to maintain itself and prove its quality in fruitful contact with the other. The space opens out in which man decides upon himself and perfects himself in freedom. Freedom is in fact the power to be detached and thereby to commit oneself. Since it is free choice *(liberum arbitrium)*, it presupposes various attitudes to the objects in the world with which the I can identify itself, and among which one must be chosen to the exclusion of all others in the exercise of freedom. This may be regarded as a dynamic identity, the movement of identification (with the world). Here is the place of the efficacious display of the profound essential freedom of man, which is always a matter of a choice of self to be made in the personal acceptance of the natural being of man with all its historical and social conditions and characteristics. It is a radical and universal self-identification of man in and with the world. Here too appears a final differentiation in identity, that of a happy or a deprived selfhood. Identity with the world is the "sacrament" *(sacramentum naturale)* of man's identity. His selfhood is always an identification in face of and in differentiation.

3. *Is identity in difference confined to the finite?* The situation in which differentiation in identity has hitherto been considered suggests that identity in difference is a charac-

teristic only of the finite. It seems to concern only man and his reason and freedom within his own world. No doubt the element of difference in identity is due in some measure to the conceptual and abstract nature of human knowledge, which has to parse the self-reference of identity in a series of words and even phases of thought. Hence it could be concluded that this "diastatic" relationship, being merely a *relatio rationis,* pertains rather to the mode of expression (the *modus quo* of the Scholastics) rather than to the real statement (the *id quod*). But this does not take us very far. There must be an irreducible difference between rational knowledge and free will if freedom is not to be totally undermined and relapse into the necessities of completely logical and ultimately purely rationalistic judgments — or if knowledge is not to disintegrate into a series of irrational impulses of the will. Since spirit is subject-object, it must necessarily — in order to avoid both rationalism and the irrationalism of voluntarism — have a two-fold orientation. Its act is a duality in unity, as the relationship of the object to the subject (in knowledge) and the relationship of the subject to the object (in will and in love as the fulfilment of the will). The spirit is only with itself, in possession of self (see above, 1) when it achieves itself in its being-with-others (see above, 2). The two elements of the spirit's functioning, knowledge and will, condition and determine each other reciprocally — in a circumincession of the spirit, to use trinitarian terms — under the aspect of the "essence" (the form, species, quiddity, etc., the element of knowledge) and under the aspect of "existence" (being, act, reality, causality, etc., the aspect of will). This identity in difference is constitutive of the spirit as such, independent of its finite modes of existence. It represents an application to the metaphysics of the spirit of the scholastic doctrine of the transcendentals, according to which all that is is ontologically true (i.e., related to knowledge) and good (i.e., in keeping with the will). This follows from a consideration of the primordial infinite reality of God as spirit. The creation of the world is an act of the sovereign free love of God's will, which must be distinguished from the necessity of God's knowledge of the world. This demands a *diastasis* (a *distinctio formalis* [or rather, *functionalis*] *ex natura rei;* cf. Scotus) between the two basic elements of the one spiritual activity of God. Even God's knowledge of the finite multiple other, by virtue of his infinite essence or selfhood, seems only to be possible by virtue of a fundamental intrinsic differentiation in the absolute identity of the spirit which is God. Hence the Absolute should not be treated as "the night . . . in which all objects are black" (Hegel, *Phenomenology,* p. 14). This is only a prejudice which affirms that "a total sameness of the most absolute kind is the most perfect mode of being, which is therefore that of that which is absolutely" (K. Rahner, ed., *Mysterium Salutis,* II, p. 384). Identity in difference, as the fundamental nature of spirit as such, and hence also of being, must also be affirmed as the prerequisite of the processions of the Son and the Holy Spirit in the Trinity, and of its relationships to the world.

4. *History of the concept.* This dialectical differentiation of the concept of identity is confirmed by the history of philosophy. The problem is posed as the origin of all thinking by the pre-Socratics. As against the mythology of oneness ("but it is all the same", Frg. B 57, ed. by Diels), Heraclitus propounds the dialectic of the reciprocal, the multiplicity in unity (cf. Frgg. 8, 10, 51, 54, 59, 67, 88). Parmenides proves the truth by a *reductio ad absurdum,* when he affirms that on the plane of the true everything is simply identified with the one being (Frg. B 2–8, ed. by Diels). The later dialogues of Plato develop the dialectic of the one and the many, the same and the other, as fundamental concepts of the spirit (Theaetetus, 185f.; Parmenides, 139f.). Plato rejects a "wrong" notion of identity: "You will hardly say that the One is by nature indeterminate?" (Parmenides, 139d). In his discussion of act and potency Aristotle describes various forms of identity (*Metaphysics,* V, 9; VII, 11; X, 3, 8; *Topics,* I, 5). His notion of identity, in the accidental and in the proper sense (*Metaphysics,* V, 9; 1018a 7) comes very close to the identification with the self or the world discussed above under 2.

German idealism, using the transcendental method of Kant, sought to solve the problem of the finite and infinite, the many and and the one, in the sense of a monistic unity. In Schelling's "Identity-Philosophy" (1801–1804; the term is first found in his *Darstellung meines Systems der Philosophie* [1801]) the Abso-

lute is regarded as the identity of subject, object, spirit, and nature as elements of the universe, an identity which is simply non-difference. Hegel, however, took the force of the negative as a principle of research. True identity, that which is concrete and dialectical, is essentially "identity of identity and non-identity", opposition and unity at once. "Just as identity must be affirmed, so too must separation." Identity is in fact of itself non-identity. This is an expression of the movement of the spirit as the law of all reality, since spirit is the reconciliation of self with becoming other, reflection on self in otherness. It is by virtue of this mode of being, by which the world is constituted, that the absolute spirit is not merely the "cold indifference of isolation". But there is some justice in the objection made by Feuerbach, that the difference of the individual movements is ultimately swallowed up by the identity of the whole. According to T. Adorno, who has recently reiterated this objection, the philosophy of identity is the "archetype of all ideology" (*Negative Dialektik* [1966], p. 149). The too great emphasis laid on non-identity in the Absolute itself had as its consequence a blurring of the identity of worldly reality. When the world is absorbed into the Absolute, it is not set free to be itself. The adequate inner element of equilibrium in identity is not to be sought say in matter alone. It can only be found in the difference of freedom.

5. *Test cases for a differentiated concept of identity.* Man is a unity and a totality, as is now emphasized against all dualistic tendencies. Nonetheless, the identity of the human being supposes rather than excludes the difference between matter and spirit as intrinsic elements and principles of human being. To neglect this constitutive difference would be to take a one-sided, monistic view of man, materialist or spiritualist, either of which readily becomes the other by a natural reaction. Body and soul in man are the partial aspects, as it were, of the difference constituted by spirit-matter.

The body-soul relationship in man presents itself as a natural comparison for the incomparably close personal (hypostatic) union in Jesus Christ, which embraces in identity the infinite difference of godhead and manhood "without separation", since there is identity of person, and "without confusion", since the natures are different (Council of Chalcedon, *D* 148, *DS* 302). If this unity of tension is dissolved, it is replaced either by the heresy of the two persons, where mere difference obtains, or the heresy of the one nature, where there is "pure" identity. The incarnation of God, the central fact of revelation (cf. Jn 1:14) points back to the eternal primordial nature of identity-in-difference: God is triune in the most real distinction between Father, Son, and Spirit and in the supreme unity of the divine nature, which even of itself, being necessarily trinitarian, cannot be simply undifferentiated (see above, 3). The incarnation also points forwards through its soteriological and ecclesiological significance. Jesus "differentiates" himself as man from God, on the basis of identity with him. In Christ, God "identifies" himself with us men, in the tension set up by the infinite difference between God and man. There is a vicarious identification which does not become an innocuous levelling out of mere comradeship because it includes non-identity (cf. D. Sölle, p. 185). Only such an identification, which is permeated by differentiation, can be redemptive, that is, can help the sinful non-identical, the publican and the sinner, to self-identity, before God. Thus Jesus Christ is the way to truth and to freedom (which is the NT way of speaking of identity; see D. Sölle, p. 179) for man as he strives to be himself and at one with himself. He is the prefiguration and the driving force of man, his basic sacramental reality, the fundamental act which expounds and expands itself into the communion of the saints in general. "In being-for-others, the search for one's own identity becomes superfluous" (D. Sölle, p. 197). This is an affirmation which is likewise an imperative. To the world, the Church is in a relationship of identity-in-difference which is constantly growing closer. The Church is "the whole universe in a limited reflection" (H. Schlier, *Der Brief an die Epheser* [1965], p. 96). It is the world not only in a static partial identification but in an identity which is on the way to an eschatological totality (cf. Eph 4:13), since in principle the dimensions and goal of the universe and the Church coincide (H. Schlier, *ibid.*, p. 94). Here too, but now on the major scale, identification with the world appears as identification with self (see above, 2).

The differentiated notion of identity is also of importance in the methodology and hermeneutics of Christian theology. The various theologies found in the NT writings do not always say the same thing, but they still make the same point — affirming the identical in differentiated ways (H. Schlier, after M. Heidegger). The same is true of the doctrines proposed by tradition, of the formulations of dogma and so on. Identity-in-difference has a normative function as an approach to interpretation. Methodical postulates and objective structures come together in the key-problem of theology, which is the effort to see how the relationship of identity-in-difference is verified on various levels in nature and grace (ontologically), in faith and knowledge (gnoseologically), philosophy and theology (epistemologically). The theology of grace and of faith presupposes, each no doubt in its own way, a philosophy of nature and knowledge, but grace and faith would not be themselves if they did not posit and preserve their counterparts with their authentic reality, independence, value and laws, if they did not set them free to attain their own true nature. Such is the function of the one, in its comprehensive fullness, with regard to the self-identification of the other.

This notion of unity in diversity, without separation and without confusion, presupposes a long practice of methodical analysis in the attainment of knowledge, an attitude which cannot be abandoned, if the highly desirable unity is not to yield to an indifference on the level of ideology, if concrete identity is not to yield to the abstract.

See also *Consciousness, Idealism, Experience, Being* I, *Reality, Knowledge, Person, Dialectics, Transcendentals, Pre-Socratics, Monism.*

BIBLIOGRAPHY. See bibliography on *Dialectics;* also: G. Siewerth, *Thomismus als Identitätssystem* (1939); E. Coreth, "Identität und Differenz", *Gott in Welt, Festgabe K. Rahner,* I (1964), pp. 158–87; W. Kern, "Einheit-in-Mannigfaltigkeit", *ibid.,* pp. 207–39; D. Sölle, *Stellvertretung. Ein Kapitel Theologie nach dem "Tode Gottes"* (1965).

Walter Kern

IDEOLOGY

1. *Concept and problems.* The term ideology first appears in the discussions carried on by the French Enlightenment with Napoleon

Bonaparte. The "Idéologues" were looked on by the political reactionaries as unworldly doctrinaires. But the general view is that "ideology" has a history going back as far as Bacon. It is still hardly possible to give a strict definition of ideology. The term is used in many ways — from the popular way of identifying ideology with programmed lying, the sceptical treatment of all non-empirical knowledge as ideological to the later Marxist identification of the class-determined consciousness with ideology. A definition could be sought in terms of psychological studies of projections and wish-fulfilment, the sociological theses on the determination of all thought by its environment or the positivist definitions of the theories of the sciences. But in each case one would have to include the philosophical, sociological or psychological school in question. This is true above all when assessing criticisms of Christianity as an ideology. The formal notion of ideology is part of the critique of knowledge.

Long before the term was coined, there were phenomena which could have been treated as objects for ideological criticism, the union between religion and the ruling powers, for instance, and so too it can be said that a partial critique of ideology was practised as early as the age of the Greek Sophists. But the actual historical appearance of ideology and critique of ideology was a consequence of the modern approach to science and the analysis of the bases of political and social order in post-medieval thought. As long as there was a principle of unity for the world with a philosophical basis and a theological guarantee, a principle which could be held to be binding on all, it was possible to derive axioms for the natural sciences and norms for social life from the *a priori* deductions of contemplative knowledge. But when the assumed unity of subject and object was called in question by nominalism and finally rejected, the ensuing crisis opened up the way to ideology and critique of the same. The shattering of this unity brought down with it not only the systematic fundamentals, theological and philosophical, of the Christian *ordo,* but also the identity of method in metaphysical and scientific study. In France and England especially, the claims of the inductive, empirical, experimental method prevailed against the deductive and speculative. Hence knowledge was valued

not as theoretical contemplation, superior by reason of its intrinsic, non-utilitarian ends to *actio* and τέχνη, but as the analytical process of research into nature. Philosophy should in no way fall short of the natural sciences in its exactness, and for this new methods of reflection were necessary. Knowledge must prove itself in practice and thereby show its power: "tantum possumus, quantum scimus." This approach to the acquisition of knowledge influenced more and more strongly the political and social order as time went on. Principles of organization based on theology and metaphysics gave way to principles based on the pure light of reason which sought to press education and science into the service of the State and society. These non-theological, anti-metaphysical principles were called "ideas". The critical methods whereby grasp of the ideas could be safeguarded against inadmissible interference from outside and intrinsic sources of flaws were known as "ideology".

2. *History of the concept.* Francis Bacon (1561–1626) in his *Novum Organon* cast doubts on the methodical stringency of the traditional Aristotelian logic, since it seemed to provide no adequate protection against dogmatism and the distortions of the fallacies which he termed *idola.* The *idola* of Bacon were called *préjugés* by the French Enlightenment. Ideology is a doctrine of ideas, in the sense of being guidance as to how to distinguish correct ideas from false. Bacon acknowledged in the true ideas the "vera signacula creatoris super creaturam" — the hall-mark of the Creator — which were to be brought out by the inductive method and the critique of *idola: idola tribus,* the idols of the tribe, the sources of error innate in man's nature; *idola specus,* the idols of cave, the weaknesses inherent in the knowledge of the individual; the *idola fori,* the idols of the market-place, the confusions due to human means of communication and conventional terms, and finally the *idola theatri,* the idols of the theatre, the false maxims and syllogisms deriving from philosophical tradition. Bacon's criticism of religion was to have grave consequences. He distinguished philosophy from theology, no doubt, just as he distinguished theology from superstition. But unfortunately, in the time of the wars of religion of the 16th and 17th centuries, his theme of the idols proved to be an effective

instrument in the hands of irreligious criticism. This was not the only case where Bacon's theories were taken over and put to uses foreign to their original intent, by controversalists dipping eclectically into the *Novum Organum,* of which the chapters on the idols had been designated by Bacon as the "pars destruens". Unlike the approach of the French Enlightenment, Bacon's critique was confined to psychology. He did not deny the general correspondence between being and thought, nor did he affirm that consciousness was subject to a material determinism. He saw philosophical truth as the mirror of nature. But the human mind was a mirror with a rough surface and to counteract its distortions strict methodical rules were needed. Bacon did not foresee the application of his scientific method to theology and politics, but once he had laid down his principles for science, the theme of science and politics was already intoned. The Enlightenment did not keep theory apart from practice in this realm, as did Bacon, but affirmed that a rational order based on natural law could be discerned and put into practice with regard to State and society. Only prejudices stood in the way. With this transformation of the discussion of the "idols" into a general critique of prejudices, ideology entered the field of political and social struggle.

Condillac (1715–80) and de Tracy (1754–1836) began by giving the psychological critique of the "idols" the radical form of a sensualist materialism. The spirit consists of sensible perceptions which are co-ordinated by an associative psychological mechanism of the consciousness. If this "science des idées" could attain the pure knowledge of the ideas, it would at last be possible to set up a just and rational order among mankind, without having to have recourse to metaphysics and religion for the "mystère de l'ordre social". The institutions of Church and State, which were both equally affected, struggled fiercely against this rationalism. Hence Holbach (1723–89) and Helvetius (1715–71) logically recognized in the alliance of Church and State a pact in defence of their common interest in the maintenance of the existing order. The two institutions could only cling to power as long as they deliberately kept men in ignorance. Religion was said to sanction the rule of the State by invoking a God whose existence could not be proved. Since then, ideological critique has been polemics against religious and socio-political prejudices at once. The source of untruth is not now in the psychological shortcomings of man, but in manipulation from outside in the defence of various interests.

These are the presuppositions — along with the materialistic critique of religion and Hegelian idealism by Feuerbach — on which is based the ideology-critique of Marx, the most important hitherto produced. For Marx, ideology means a false concept of reality, the separation of theory and practice (activity), neglect of the material, social and historical conditioning of thought. Like Feuerbach, Marx saw Hegel's systematic conception of the unity of reason and reality as a paralogism. Reality as a whole is as little rational as reason has really realized itself. Where the idea has been separated from its concrete material, social situation, ideology has taken over. And the presence of ideology is a symptom of social disease. In bourgeois capitalist society ideologies coincide with the interests of the ruling class. But the whole process of existence, torn in several directions at once by the division of labour and alienation, results in a set of ideologies, since the mind of the producer cannot recognize itself and realize itself concretely in the wares produced. Thus an antagonism is set up between production and (mental) reproduction, between thought and action, subject and object, idea and reality. The Christian religion presents a classical form of ideology, because it tries to justify unreconciled reality by an unreal reconciliation. Such ideological fetters can only be burst asunder by revolution. This is not just an interpretation of reality but so radical a transformation of it that the whole process of the life of society can be accomplished rationally, perspicuously and hence freely. The agent of revolution in the 19th century is to be the proletariate, which is in such dire need of the revolution. It is impossible to say, however, how far Marx's critique of ideology contains deterministic traits. The later developments of the theory of ideology in Marxism take very different directions. In the orthodox communism of today, the Marxist dialectic of theory and *praxis* has been replaced by the schema of infrastructure and superstructure. Communist doctrine is the ideology of the proletariate and hence true doctrine, while bourgeois ideology is false by reason of its basis. Other Marxists, such as Lukács, Bloch, and Lefèbvre, distinguish between ideologies linked to the infra-structure and utopian ideologies, which are also to be found in bourgeois society. The valuable elements in art, science and religion, for instance, need only be set free to be themselves by Marxism. Neo-Marxists in the West, such as Adorno, Horkheimer, and H. Marcuse, criticize ontology, existence philosophy, and positivism in dialectical and psycho-analytical terms, treating them as modern forms of late capitalist ideology.

The characteristic link between ideology and revolution in Marxism, like its social and economic determinism of the consciousness, was modified by K. Mannheim and M. Scheler, and was now presented as a sociological history of the spirit which took place on a level superior to all parties. Scheler attributed different thought-forms to each social class, but from the point of view of history as of empirical sociology these theories of upper and lower class thought must remain mere hypotheses. Mannheim, however, with his affirmation of the determinism of thought by virtue of being and situation, which reminds us of Marx, represented in fact a sociological modification of historicism. To escape the relativist consequences of his theory, Mannheim demanded that all ideology should be deemed suspect and postulated a group of "free minds" hovering outside the range of determinism. Philosophies of value, Fascist doctrine to some extent and positivism tried to escape the dilemma presented by the sociological theory of knowledge. Thus Scheler, Husserl and N. Hartmann sought to give absolute values a philosophical bedrock. Pareto declared that all dominant social elites and values were merely reflections of whatever political party happened to be stronger for the moment. M. Weber and T. Geiger dismissed on principle all concepts of value and purpose as unscientific, non-empirical speculation. These are the presuppositions on which the present-day discussion of ideology is to a great extent based.

3. *Christianity and ideology.* Whether Christianity is called an ideology or not will be decided according to the concept of ideology which is presupposed. That certain particular ideologies have been and still are influential

in the activity of the Church cannot be doubted. But it is another question when the general suspicion of ideology is applied to theology and the faith. When ideology is taken to designate every thesis which goes beyond the realm of the empirically verifiable and linguistic analysis, the faith must lose the appearance of scientific demonstrability. But this does not eliminate the fundamental necessity of having to take radical decisions about the purpose and activity of one's own life. In this sense, Christian faith can be called an ideology. Since Christianity must be embodied in the concrete in historical and social forms, it is always involved in a certain ambiguity, where ideological elements in the strict sense cannot always be excluded.

The Marxist criticism of Christianity as an ideology is a consistent theory which offers no loopholes. It can only be refuted in actual political and social activity, by permanent criticism of all attempts to set static, finite bounds to man in his history, and by the practical effort to eliminate inhuman conditions. Christianity finds the justification and the criteria for such effort in its eschatological promises.

See also *Religion* I B, *Revolution and Restoration, Scepticism, Enlightenment, Science* II, *Knowledge, Nominalism, State, Society, Dogmatism, Marxism, Thought-Forms, Historicism, Value.*

BIBLIOGRAPHY. C. van Duzer, *Contribution of the Ideologues to the French Revolution* (1935); M. Horkheimer, *The Eclipse of Reason* (1947); T. Geiger, *Ideologie und Wahrheit* (1953); K. Mannheim, *Ideology and Utopia* (tr. from the 3rd German ed., 1953); T. W. Adorno, *Das Bewusstsein der Wissenssoziologie: Prismen* (1955); W. Martin, *Metaphysics and Ideology* (1959); C. W. Mills, *The Sociological Imagination* (1959); H. Lefèbvre, *Problèmes actuels du Marxisme* (1960); N. Birnbaum, "The Sociological Study of Ideology (1940–1960): A Trend Report and Bibliography", *Current Sociology* 9 (1960); R. E. Lane, *Political Ideologies* (1962); G. Lukács, *Realism in our Time: Literature and the Class Struggle* (1964); H. Marcuse, *One-Dimensional Man* (1964); A. Siegfried, *Routes of Contagion* (1965); K. Rahner, "Christianity and Ideology", *Concilium* 6, no. 1 (1965), pp. 23–32; F. Rempel, *Role of Value in K. Mannheim's Sociology of Knowledge* (1965); P. Corbett, *Ideologies* (1966); G. Lichtheim, *Concept of Ideology and Other Essays* (1967).

Werner Post

ILLNESS

I. Physical Illness. II.: A. Mental Illness. B. Psycho-pathology.

I. Physical Illness

1. *General considerations.* Sickness, which is an evil, must be distinguished from physical trials to which man is exposed from without, such as hunger, exhaustion, or cold, and from moral trials, such as grief and afflictions of the heart. Sickness affects the human organism from within and tends of its nature to destroy that organism. A certain parallelism, then, can be discerned between health and life on the one hand and sickness and death on the other. When a man is well, his life flowers in activity, harmony, contentment and security; whereas any kind of illness is an imbalance, a disorder, that shows us how delicate and insecure life is. Physical suffering generally entails moral suffering as well: the anguishing thought that sooner or later an illness must prove fatal, and meantime the consciousness that one is dependent on others and at their mercy; the sick person becomes a "patient".

Since man is a being composed of body and soul, he may fall a prey to mental illness — affecting those of his powers which are properly spiritual (insanity); or psychic illness — affecting the sensibility or the imagination or the realm of the unconscious which modern psychiatry tries to explore (psychasthenia, neurosis); or bodily illness — affecting an organ or a function of the body. Here it is essential to bear in mind the psycho-somatic unity of man, the influence of body on soul and soul on body, if we would understand sickness. For it is something truly human and deeply personal. "There are no diseases", it has been said, "there are only sick people."

Juvenal's phrase *mens sana in corpore sano* may express a true ideal, even a certain perfection, of our human state. But it is a perfection of the biological, not of the moral, order. One will remember, then, that too healthy a body may crush the soul, and that illness has been the lot of some very fine human types (the condition if not the cause of their nobility of character) — among the saints and mystics, for example. Certainly in these cases "being ill as a way of being human" (V. von Weizsäcker).

2. *Illness and religion.* The history of religions shows that man has always been aware of the religious problem posed by sickness, and that for this reason medicine and cures figure in close connection with religion and magic.

a) In the OT the religious problem of sickness is associated with that of retribution, originally conceived of in temporal terms (Deut 28:21 f.), and follows the same course of development. Thus sickness, like every other evil, is first regarded as divine punishment which must have been incurred by some sin (cf. Ps 38 and 107:17–20), either of an individual or of the community. Accordingly it is a subject of scandal if a just man is afflicted with sickness, until in the end reality forces the Israelites to think that sickness may also be a trial sent by God in order to manifest a person's virtue. Job, Tobit, Qoheleth, and the Psalmists make painful attempts to resolve the difficulty, and the book of Wisdom (3:1–8) adds a new element by positing a reward in the next world. Then Deutero-Isaiah (53:48) in an intuition too transcendent to be exploited by Judaism speaks of Yahweh's Suffering Servant and the sacrifice whereby he effects a vicarious atonement (cf. A. Lods, "Les idées des Israélites sur la maladie, ses causes et ses remèdes", *Festschrift K. Martin* [1925], pp. 181–93; J. Chaîne, "Révélation progressive de la notion de rétribution dans l'Ancien Testament", *Rencontres*, IV: *Le sens chrétien de l'histoire* [1941], pp. 73–89).

b) The ancient idea of sickness as a divine punishment is still to be found in the NT (Jn 9:2) but is no longer the only idea. Without systematically combatting it (Jn 5:14; Lk 13:1–5), Christ considerably modifies it (Jn 9:3). In accordance with prophetic eschatology (cf. Is 35:5–6 and 53:4 with Mt 11:5 and 8:17), the kingdom Christ preaches will do away with every illness and infirmity as part of its triumph over Satan and sin (Lk 5:17–25; 13:11; Jn 5:14) — a doctrine which corresponds perfectly to the Jewish notion of man as a psycho-somatic unity. The mission of the disciples includes a particular attention to the sick and is attended by cures (Mk 6:13; Lk 10:9; Mt 10:1), Jesus himself, above all, is constantly working miracles of healing, to show that the messianic age has indeed come and that it means deliverance from every ill for the body as well as for the soul (cf. O. Cullmann, "La délivrance anticipée du corps humain d'après le Nouveau Testament", *Hommage et reconnaissance* [1946], pp. 31–40). For Jesus, the cure of sickness and the forgiveness of sins go hand in hand (Mk 2:1–12; Jn 5:1–15). It has been pointed out that Jesus never failed to heal any sick person whom he encountered. Nowhere in the gospels do we find him merely exhorting a sick man to derive spiritual profit from his suffering. Though the perfection of his human nature seems to have prevented his having any personal experience of illness, he invariably shows great compassion for the sick; indeed he goes so far as to identify himself with the sick so as to encourage everyone to treat them with a practical charity (Mt 25:34–45).

3. *The Christian approach.* Sometimes pagans were able to rise above their illness, as Epicurus did, by sheer determination. Nietzsche accuses Christianity of rejecting human values by glorifying weakness and suffering through the cross.

As to *theory,* centuries of meditation on the teaching and example of Christ gradually enabled the Christian soul to see how the fact of sickness is related to certain basic truths of faith: the creation of man and his supernatural destiny, the power of the devil, the fall of man and sin, redemption by the cross, the resurrection of the body, and so forth. In the light of these truths sickness remains an evil; but it is transfigured, endowed with positive values, fitted into the economy of salvation; and the history of Christian spirituality reveals a most suggestive growth in our understanding of this mystical reality.

It was plainly recognized from the very beginnings of the Church that sickness is essentially a consequence of sin (original sin, if not necessarily personal sin) and that it presents new temptations, since the sick person has been weakened both physically and morally. There is no surprise that sickness still remains while we await the Lord's return (1 Cor 11:30; Phil 2:26; 2 Tim 4:20; Jas 5:14–15), but a realization that it must disappear, with all the devil's control of this present aeon, when the kingdom is definitively established; meanwhile it is combatted, like every manifestation of the devil's power (sickness is often assumed to go with diabolic possession), in an eschatological perspective. At the same time the sick person is urged to practise resignation (St. Augustine), confidence in God (St. John Chrysostom), patience (St. Gregory the Great), and penance (St. Bede; Fourth Lateran Council, can. 22).

Illness is now regarded less as a punishment than as a means of expiation and reparation, or a trial permitted by God in view of some greater good (2 Cor 12:9). True, nowhere in the ancient Church do we find it included among the "equivalents of martyrdom" or the means to perfection. But without ever forbidding the sick person to pray for good health (cf. St. Gregory of Nazianzus), Christian piety tends more and more to admonish him that his sufferings offer him something of the sufferings of, even a mystical identification with, the crucified Christ, a share in the redemptive sacrifice that can be an apostolate (cf. Col 1:24) and a means of glorifying God. Examples of this kind of sublimation abound in the history of spirituality, though they are not commonly met with before the Middle Ages; and a whole devotional literature, either religious discourses written on particular occasions (for example, St. John Chrysostom) or general treatises (for example, Gérard of Liège [?], *De duodecim utilitatibus tribulationum,* or Pascal, *Prière pour demander à Dieu le bon usage des maladies*), sums up this doctrine, certain maxims of which ("If man but knew the benefits of sickness, he would wish never to live without it"; "sickness is the normal state of the Christian") seem a trifle paradoxical.

As to *practice,* the Christian attitude is above all one of charity towards the sick. They are no longer despised (Ps 38:12; 88:9), but honoured and served as Christ himself. That is why care of the sick ranks among the works "of mercy" (cf. the touching arrangements for the sick prescribed by the medieval custom-book of Cluny); that is why there are so many institutions (hospitals, nursing homes, foundations, religious orders) devoted to helping them. If a few heretical sects will not use human means to treat the sick, genuine Christianity has always fostered the science of medicine and permitted any remedies that did not involve superstition or magic (cf. St. Joan of Arc's saying: "If it can be done without sin, I am quite willing to have my wound healed").

Moreover, the Church prays for the sick,

for their recovery, their steadfastness in affliction, their supernatural welfare as they face an uncertain future (restoration to health, or death). A whole liturgy intercedes for them at the various stages of their illness; a multitude of blessings and rites exists for them; and it is not too much to say that one of the most constant intentions of the Church's prayer is that health of body and soul may be preserved, or restored, to all its children. Miraculous cures (like those of Lourdes) are not unknown, but normally Christ's work for the sick, and the charismata of the primitive Church, are now channelled through the sacraments. Baptism is able in principle to banish all the consequences of sin (St. Thomas, *Summa Theologica*, III, q. 69, a. 3), including sickness, and the historian Socrates relates that a Jew of Byzantium was freed of paralysis, as well as of his sins, upon being baptized. The common doctrine holds that the Eucharist is a remedy for both soul and body and commends it as such. Finally, the anointing of the sick — rightly regarded as representing, at least to some extent, the original charism of healing — is designed to combat bodily sickness as well as that of the soul (Jas 5:14–15); and sooner or later every priest can see for himself the effectiveness of this *medicina ecclesiae* (St. Cesarius of Arles).

The consequences for pastoral work are inescapable: this sacrament should be conferred at the onset of any serious illness, so that its healing power may operate to the best effect; it should not be made a mere preparation for death.

Aware as it is of the spiritual dangers involved in illness, the Church desires close co-operation between priest and physician, and makes visiting the sick one of the primary duties of those who have the cure of souls (*CIC* can. 468; Roman Ritual, tit. 5, cap. 4). On no account must the sick person feel cut off from the society of the parish when he is most in need of its support and when his sufferings enable him in turn to offer the parish incalculable spiritual benefits. It is for this reason that we have Masses and pilgrimages of the sick, etc., and within a wider framework certain forms of the religious life or the apostolate appropriate for the sick and infirm.

See also *Health, Death, Body, Soul, Anointing of the Sick*.

BIBLIOGRAPHY. See bibliography on *Reign of God* and *Anointing of the Sick;* also: J. Leclercq, "Du sens chrétien de la maladie", *La Vie Spirituelle* 18 (1937), pp. 136–43; E. Sutcliffe, *Providence and Suffering in the Old and New Testaments* (1953); H. Leenhardt, "L'Église et les malades", *Études théologiques et religieuses* 32 (1957), pp. 329–79; F. Lovsky, *L'Église et les malades depuis le IIe siècle jusqu'au début du XXe siècle* (1958); J.-C. Didier, *Le chrétien devant la maladie et la mort* (1960); G. Fourure, *Les châtiments divins. Étude historique et doctrinale* (1959); B. Häring, *The Law of Christ,* III (1966).

J.-C. Didier

II. A. Mental Illness

The term mental illness is applied to morbid states in which the patient loses touch with reality and his judgment is disturbed (whether in relation to other people and outward circumstances or in relation to himself), so that he will often end by behaving in an asocial or anti-social way. This type of illness has been studied with particular care during the past hundred years. Given the great difficulty of ascertaining the precise causes of mental illnesses and the pattern of their inter-relation, classical psychology has tried to work out a classification based on the main symptoms and syndromes (characteristic "clusters" of symptoms) that are exhibited in patients' behaviour. Disturbances with an organic basis (whether congenital, like feeble-mindedness [idiocy, for example], or caused by lesions, functional disorders, various intoxications, or infections, and so forth, as in the case of epilepsy, *delirium tremens,* etc.) are distinguished from those which have no known organic cause — psychoses in the strict sense. Psychoses are generally classified as paranoia (delusions of persecution, of grandeur, etc.); schizophrenia (more or less complete withdrawal from all human contact, ending in definite autism); the manic-depressive psychosis (alternating states of great elation and profound gloom); and endogenous depression (for which no outward cause can be discovered).

For the past few decades psychologists have been especially concerned with psychosis in the strict sense. They have realized — as has been so well described by Dr. Henri Ey — that these illnesses, which always entail a loss of intellectual or emotional competence, are in fact forms of human existence that have been buried in the unconscious and the imagination of the person. Accordingly dynamic psychiatry has tried to ascertain the psychic structures that are at work in these illnesses. Without denying that there may be somatic factors involved in the cause of the disease, it seeks to arrive at the cause by taking a total view of the human psyche — a view that varies according to each man's approach and the school of depth psychology to which he adheres. If there are many such approaches and schools, the reason is that the psychiatrist, unlike the somatic physician, is not dealing with organs or parts of the body which can be objectively determined, but has to infer the general nature of the psyche from painstaking observation and delicate cross-checking.

Therapy too, thanks to our better understanding of mental illness, has made great strides. On the one hand there are the shock treatments (insulin, and electric shocks, used especially in cases of schizophrenia and endogenous depression) and neurosurgery, the technique of which is constantly being improved. And on the other hand dynamic psychiatry has developed psychotherapeutic treatment which helps the patient find himself by re-integrating the elements of his personality on a sounder basis. Quite often these various treatments, prudently applied, will happily complement each other.

Needless to say, only persons with advanced training in medicine and psychology should treat mental cases. But the priest, without attempting to assume the role of the specialist, should know what the treatments are. It is of great importance, from the pastoral point of view, that the priest should be able to distinguish roughly between persons suffering from psychoses and those with neurosis or a neurotic reaction. As a number of the symptoms can be similar, it may be helpful for the priest to have a rule of thumb: the neurotic generally remains aware that his sufferings are a morbid state, or at least are out of proportion to whatever occasions them. Thus the neurotic wants help and accepts it. But (except in the early stages of certain illnesses) the psychotic generally denies that he is sick, and roundly declares that his sensations correspond to reality. When a person takes this uncritical attitude, and thus becomes impervious to all efforts at communication with him — though perhaps only in a given sphere — his state is plainly psychotic. That is something a priest will do well to remember, since it

commonly happens that relatives or friends will send him (as a man of discretion who can counsel them) some one whose odd behaviour is causing them concern. Obviously the priest cannot directly help. But he must get the afflicted person to see a psychiatrist (or advise those who can assume that responsibility to do so), if psychosis is involved. In a case of neurosis, on the other hand, he should advise consulting a psychotherapeutic physician or a depth psychologist.

The priest must carefully avoid argument with the sick person, whose state is such as to make any exchange of views, indeed any human dialogue at all, impossible. Attempting to persuade the sufferer that his ideas are mistaken or foolish will only strengthen his conviction, by forcing him to defend it. This must be borne in mind when certain religious subjects, symbols, acts, or postures figure prominently in the world of fantasy which the sick person has created. Religious delirium (delirium centred on one religious theme or several) is by no means uncommon: one finds psychotics appealing to religion or morality in defence of their abnormal behaviour, or using religious terms to describe their fears and distress. We must never forget that these elements of religion are simply the fancy dress (or expression in a sphere which is particularly important to a given patient) of the psychotic's interior confusion, disorder, or helplessness. A frontal attack is quite pointless. First the structure underlying the illness must be dealt with.

On the other hand one must also remember that mental illness does not necessarily eliminate all valid human acts. Certain psychoses are more or less confined to one sphere, while others abate at times (periods of remission or relative tranquillity). Accordingly a priest must not refuse patients ministrations to which they are entitled. First of all, patients should be given the sacraments if their demeanour suggests that they are more or less consciously asking for that consolation. Then the priest must try to help patients accept their state, trial though it is, as a means of sanctification. Obviously this ministry cannot be offered those in the grip of acute crisis or utter mental confusion. But it is often possible with patients who are seriously ill, and if it does not cure the psychic trouble, at least produces a genuine resignation based on an attitude of faith and a truly religious hope in God and love of him.

One point, finally, calls for the perspicacity of the priest. He is repeatedly asked about the effect of mental illness on a person's moral responsibility. At the present time there is a better awareness — and even non-specialists will commonly agree — that asocial or anti-social behaviour resulting from the morbid condition cannot be considered sinful. Still it must be borne in mind that mental illness does not simultaneously produce the same ravages in every sphere of psychic life, so that it would not do to deny that a mental patient can ever take a free and moral decision. Furthermore, by declaring the patient totally irresponsible one would be likely to aggravate his disorder.

What shall we say of possible guilt "in causa": can the morbid condition have been brought on more or less voluntarily, if only indirectly? The possibility cannot be excluded *a priori*. But be that as it may, the morbid condition remains a fact. It must be remedied with all speed, whatever part the patient may have had in bringing it about. Besides, endless speculation on this question of guilt is usually a feature of the illness itself. If a real sin, deliberately committed, is involved and there is genuine conscious contrition, then the upshot will be a liberation, thanks to admission of the fault and the sacramental pardon and absolution that follow.

To sum up, then, we may say from the pastoral point of view that the priest must know when to advise consulting the specialist for efficacious help, and must duly appreciate how many a mental illness will trick itself out in the guise of certain elements of religion. Thus he will be able to provide a real priestly ministry, as regards both the sacraments and spiritual direction, for souls grievously afflicted by mental disorder.

See also *Psychology* III, *Psychotherapy*.

BIBLIOGRAPHY. J. Vanderveldt and O. Odenwald, *Psychiatry and Catholicism* (2nd ed., 1957); R. Hostie, *Religion and the Psychology of Jung* (1957); A. Terruwe, *The Priest and the Sick in Mind* (1959); G. Vann, *The Paradise Tree* (1959); J. Dominian, *Psychiatry and the Christian* (1962); N. Autton, *The Pastoral Care of the Mentally Ill* (1963); L. Beirnaert, *Expérience chrétienne et psychologie* (1964); G. Bergsten, *Pastoral Psychology* (1964); J. Goldbrunner, *Realization. The Anthropology of Pastoral Care* (1966); T. Oden, *Kerygma and Counseling* (1966); id., *Contemporary Theology and Psychotherapy* (1967); M. Leach, *Christianity and Mental Health* (1967).

Raymond Hostie

II. B. Psychopathology

Psychopathology is the study of psychical disorders. As such it is an empirical science, the foundation of psychiatry. Schneider uses the term "clinical psychopathology". There are two basic types of psychical disorder.

a) *Aberrations* from mental normality, such as abnormal personalities (including the category of psychopathic personalities), abnormal social reactions, neurosis, and abnormal intellectual (certain cases of feeble-mindedness).

b) Psychical *disorders* caused by illness or organic malformation (disturbances of the consciousness, disintegration of personality, dementia, and certain features of psychical illness which range the latter under two headings: schizophrenia, or the manic-depressive).

As an empirical science psychopathology works with the data provided by the various branches of psychology. But two of those branches have always had a special connection with it: one is *phenomenological* psychopathology and the other is *dynamic* psychopathology. Though Hegel uses the word "phenomenology", Husserl really made it a psychological term, in the two senses of "descriptive psychology" and *Wesensschau*. The phenomenological psychopathology that dates from the publication of Jaspers's book (*Allgemeine Psychopathologie* [1913]) is such in the first sense; it is the purest possible description of abnormal psychical experience. The main methodological difference is that which exists between "explaining" and "understanding": the former is the method of natural science, the latter the method of the cultural or historical sciences. In mental illness we encounter psychical symptoms which cannot be understood but can be explained. For example, the dementia of general paralysis is explained in terms of the pathological anatomical development that lies at the bottom of it. Then there are causal relations. Of course these can only explain the *presence* of the psychic symptoms, not their whole *nature*. On the other hand some symptoms that occur in mental pathology can be understood — for example, social reaction after a traumatic psychical experience. In such a case understanding is genetic: one discovers motives rather than causes.

This methodological distinction has proved very useful in psychiatry, enabling us to fix the notions of psychic process and psychosis. Psychoses are psychic illnesses. Some of these are connected with a known organic disorder, as in paralytic dementia, or senile disorders, or epilepsy, or the psychic by-products of cerebral tumour or a wound or other physical cause. But there are other psychoses, verified by analogy with the foregoing, which so far have not been accounted for by any somatic disorder (somatosis). We may suppose that there must be one, because the person's psychic life is as completely altered as in organic psychosis (those which have a known somatic basis). His psychic life is broken and rent. The results of this wreckage are not like the variants of normal psychic life, such as neurosis.

The presence of such psychopathological symptoms cannot be understood, and yet must be explained as we explain the symptoms of organic psychosis. What has been wrecked is, as K. Schneider says, "die Geschlossenheit", "die Sinngesetzlichkeit", "die Sinnkontinuität der Lebensentwicklung" (the sense that one's life is a whole, with a consistent meaning and direction). Now only illness in the somatic sense can produce an effect of this kind.

Dynamic psychopathology is the child of psychoanalysis. Psychoanalysis affirms that the psychic experience which we cannot understand is incomprehensible because it belongs to the unconscious, not to the conscious. The unconscious, for psychoanalysis, is something dynamic. No doubt the unconscious does account for neurotic symptoms (obsessions, phobias, melancholia) and certain somatic symptoms (reverse reactions). Psychical energy that is not used in the psychical sphere drains into the areas that control the viscera, sense perception, and bodily movement; so psychic trauma gives rise to motor paralysis, sensory anasthesia, or visceral disorders. In recent years this dynamic interpretation has been extended to the psychoses, especially schizophrenia and the manic-depressive psychoses. Freud was hesitant about doing this, but Schneider has gone so far as to include general paralysis.

Dynamic psychopathology is a "depth pathology", being based on the existence of the subconscious. Such success as it has had is due to the fact that it does not merely describe, like phenomenological psychopathology, but attempts a cure.

Undue claims for it have led some to deny the validity of psychiatric nosology. Some even deny that mental illnesses are *mental* illnesses, calling them instead peculiar forms of human relationship (sociosis). Dynamic psychopathology flourishes in the United States. Phenomenological psychopathology is cultivated mainly in Central Europe, though there are some important schools in Latin countries. Advances now being made in pharmacology support the thesis of phenomenological psychopathology, which has enabled us to establish our present psychiatric nosology. The latest research on the structure of neurosis shows that we do not understand all about it after all, that a physio-dynamic structure underlies the psycho-dynamic structure of neurosis. It seems that neurosis is in some sense an illness, as was thought in the days of Cullen, who introduced the term.

As a system, psychopathology classifies and organizes clinical data. Phenomenologically, these data may be classified: a) according to the mode of the experience (sensation, perception, imagination, thought, feeling, values, impulses, voluntary acts); b) according to the main characteristics of the experience (experience of the self, of time, of memory, capacity for psychic reaction); and c) according to the "scope of the experience" (the attention, the consciousness, the mind, the personality). In dynamic psychopathology the system of classification is based on the metamorphoses of psychic energy (complexes, archetypes, conversion, transference) and the typical structure of the personality (id, ego, super-ego).

There are other interesting schools of psychopathology at the moment. One, the experimental, tries to produce disorders like those found in clinical work (intoxication by mescalin, lysergic acid, etc., which cause a schizophrenic condition). There are several types of anthropological psychopathology (von Gebsattel, Binswanger, Zutt, and others). Transcultural psychopathology studies the form that psychic illness takes in various cultures, etc. Present-day psychopathology has benefited considerably from the contributions of other fields like *Gestalt* psychology, behaviourism, animal psychology, etc.

See also *Psychology, Psychotherapy.*

BIBLIOGRAPHY. See bibliography on *Illness II A*; also: L. London, *Basic Principles of Dynamic Psychiatry* (1952); K. Schneider, *Clinical Psychopathology* (1959); K. Jaspers, *General Psychopathology* (7th ed., 1963); J. J. López Ibor, *Psychiatrie der Gegenwart (Psychosomatische Forschung)* (1963); N. Cameron, *Personality Development and Psychopathology: A Dynamic Approach* (1964); S. Frazier and A. Carr, *Introduction to Psychopathology* (1964); A. Buss, *Psychopathology* (1966).

Juan J. López Ibor

IMAGES

The image is a figure which is so constructed that it enables something to be really present. Hence the concept of image is not identical with that of a work of art. It is philosophically more comprehensive. In its theological form the concept is very close to that of a sacrament, since the sacrament likewise uses an outward sign to bring about the presence of another reality, grace. In the history of thought, the notion of image has been of paramount importance at one time: it was the point at which human minds diverged.

The metaphysical meaning of image is clear at once when the heathen worship of divine images is considered. The response of the Bible is to forbid the making of images: "You shall not make yourself a graven image, or any likeness of anything that is in heaven above or that is in the earth beneath, or that is in the water under the earth; you shall not bow down to them or serve them" (Exod 20:4f.). But the Bible also says: "God created man in his own image, in the image of God he created him" (Gen 1:27). St. Paul writes that Christ "is the image of the invisible God" (Col 1:15, cf. 2 Cor 4:4). And he also declares that "now we see in a mirror dimly, but then face to *face*" (1 Cor 13:12).

The essence of the image may be considered to be a created reality (man or heaven), the Word made flesh, or simply a work of art. The character and significance of the image will change accordingly. An idol has its own intrinsic value (it is "ad se ipsum"). The Christian image points to something else

("ad aliquid"). This was the distinction made by apologists in late antiquity and the early Middle Ages, which, while it does not always do justice to the heathen image of God, correctly describes the essential traits of idolatry. The idol tends to have an independent life of its own (for a people or a locality), while the image determines the nature of man, according to Gen 1:27 and 1 Cor 13:12. This structure of the image gives rise to a debate which has lasted to the present day.

The first stage of the conflict (in the history of salvation) starts with the prohibition of images in the OT. This precept did not forbid works of art. There were works of art of one type or another all through the history of Israel: decorated veils such as the veil of the temple depicting cherubim, images on coins and seals, wall-paintings (Ezek 41:17–20; 25:1; cf. the catacombs and the synagogue of Doura Europos) and even images of God (Exod 32; Jg 17; 1 Kg 12:28; 2 Kg 21:7; Ezek 8:3). The prohibition affected above all monumental statuary and cultic images. The intention of the law was to reserve the character of image to the primary realities of creation, man and heaven — in contrast to the secondary reality of the work of art. Plato and Plotinus also understood by image not the work of art but the cosmos and the heavens in particular. They were suspicious of the "shadow-like images" produced by the artist (Plato, *Republic,* 598b).

The early theologians accepted this view in principle. Hence Irenaeus (*Adversus Haereses,* I, 25) condemned the images in use among the Carpocratian Gnostics, and Origen told the pagan Celsus: "Christians and Jews are mindful of the commandment, 'Thou shalt not make thee an image' ... Hence they detest temples, altars and images and are even ready to die if necessary, rather than debase the notion which they have of God Almighty by any unlawful action" (*Contra Celsum,* VII, 64). Along with the decalogue, theological reasons from Christology are invoked to reject images. Writing to Constantina, the sister of the Emperor Constantine, who had asked for an image of Christ, Bishop Eusebius explained that Jesus, who had been radiant with divine majesty even in his earthly life, could not be represented "by means of lifeless colours" (*PG,* XX, col. 1545). But under the influence of Plato, Philo, and Plotinus and inspired by the symbolism of the ancient East and of Hellenism, a theory of images was developed which gave a theological foundation to religious art, especially to painting. The mystery of the incarnation was the starting-point of the theory, which regarded knowledge of images as of the essence of the human spirit. "The Son is the perfect image of God, the Holy Spirit is the image of the Son. Ideas of things are images, man is the image and likeness of God; the word is the image of thought; memory of the past and preconception of the future are images. Everything is an image and the image is everything" (A. Harnack, *Dogmengeschichte,* II, p. 457). This type of speculation distinguishes between likeness (ὁμοίωμα), relationship to origin (ἐκτύπωμα), and revelatory character as elements of the image.

This predominantly Byzantine theory which flourished in the early Middle Ages underestimated the proper value of created things. In the West, St. Gregory the Great rejected the *adoratio* of images, though without distinguishing between *dulia* and *latria* (reverence for images and adoration of God alone). St. Gregory stresses above all the educative value of images: "The image is to the illiterate what Scripture is to those who can read, for in the image even the illiterate can see what they have to imitate: there those who have never learned to read are able to read" (*Ep.,* 11, 13). The thesis formulated by Nilus was meant to mediate between the two positions: images should exist "so that those who cannot write and who are also unable to read the sacred Scriptures may by contemplating the images be reminded of the justice of the true servants of the true God and so be inspired to imitate the great and glorious works of virtue by which these exchanged earth for heaven, as they preferred the invisible to the visible" (*Ep. ad Olympiodorum,* 4, 61; *PG,* LXXIX, col. 577). According to these theories, the image determined relationships to God. The growth of the cult of images finally brought on the conflict about the image.

The iconoclast controversy in the Byzantine Church began with an edict of the Emperor Leo III in A.D. 726 and came to an end with the "Feast of Orthodoxy", instituted by the Empress Theodora in 843. The controversy came to a climax in the General Council of Nicaea in 787, which approved the reverence paid to images (Mansi, XII/XIII). The theologians of Charlemagne wrote against this council in the *Libri Carolini,* 790 (*Monumenta Germaniae Historica,* Concilia, II, suppl.). Along with political rivalry against Byzantium, the starting-point of the conflict was the concept of adoration. The Carolingian theologians rejected adoration of images but paid too little attention to the fine distinction between *latria,* the adoration due to God alone, and *proskynesis,* the reverence paid to the image. So too the West emphasized more strongly the proper value of the work of art, though negatively, to begin with. According to the *Libri Carolini* the image has no relation to the *forma prima:* it is non-spiritual and material (lib. II, c. 16; lib. I, c. 7; lib. II, c. 30). In Bishop Claudius of Turin we meet a Carolingian iconoclast, who was opposed by Dungal and Jonas of Orleans (d. 843). This discussion brought the Carolingian theologians closer to the position of Nicaea. Thus the Romanesque period which followed saw a flowering of the production of sacred images.

A new conflict began with St. Bernard of Clairvaux. He looked on the riches of Romanesque art as the quintessence of luxury and a danger to the spiritual life. Poverty is strongly urged. The observation of social distinctions is counselled: works of art are permitted for bishops (cathedrals), but restricted for monks (as in the austere forms of Cistercian art). St. Thomas Aquinas distinguishes between a *latria absoluta* due to God alone, and a *latria relativa* which is accorded to the image of Christ (*Summa Theologica,* III, 25, 3). This classical solution is endangered by the over-abundance of works of art in late Gothic spirituality, and by the new evaluation of art in the Renaissance. Discussion of the theological problem is accompanied by the conflict in the philosophy of art ("il paragone") about the priority of the word or the image. Leonardo could still describe painting as a science: "Painting in the true and scientific sense begins by ascertaining what is the body that casts a shadow, and what are primordial and derivative shadows, what is lighting, that is, darkness, light, colour; what is body, figure and posture, what is distance and nearness, what is movement and rest. These things are grasped by the spirit alone without the hands being engaged, and that is the science of painting, which remains in the spirit of those who meditate upon it" (*Libro di pittura*, I, 33 [19, 2]).

The Reformation provoked a new controversy about images. But the attitudes of the Reformers varied. In his *Abtuhung der Bilder* Karlstadt called for their removal (1522). Calvin condemned them in his *Institutio* (1529). For Zwingli (in his 'Answer' to Valentine Compar, 1525, and his *De vera religione*) an image in Church is equivalent to idolatry. In Switzerland, France, the Netherlands and also in Germany, numerous works of art were destroyed. Luther's initially hostile attitude was directed rather against the false idea of faith which thought it could amass merit by endowments for churches and images (v. Campenhausen). He treated images, even in Church, as "adiaphora", "neither good nor bad".

The Council of Trent, while striving to suppress the abuses connected with images, retains the traditional doctrine. "I firmly hold that images of Christ, of the ever-virgin Mother of God and of the other saints, are to be kept and preserved, and that they are to be paid due honour" (Tridentine Profession of Faith). St. Robert Bellarmine (*De reliquiis et imaginibus sanctorum*, cc. 5–25: *Controversiarum liber*, IV/2) distinguishes between reverence paid to the image and reverence paid to the person represented. In contrast to St. Thomas, he holds that reverence for images is inferior to reverence for persons. Commentaries on Trent dealing with the theory of art (J. Molanus, *De picturis et imaginibus*, 1570; G. Paleotti, *De imaginibus sacris et profanis*, 1594; G. Ottonelli e. P. Berettini, *Trattato della Pittura e Scultura*, 1652; Interian de Ayala, *Pictor christianus eruditus*, 1730) demand that images should be perfectly true, and that "venustas spiritualis" should replace "procax venustas".

The most important attack upon images was launched in modern times by the Enlightenment. In the French Revolution, a number of churches and their contents were destroyed, and the goddess "Reason", a woman, was installed in the cathedrals as the embodiment of the modern concept of the world and science. Very many works of art were destroyed in Germany during the Secularization (three hundred monasteries and eighteen universities were suppressed). The world is no longer looked on as the image of a creator. It is understood by

scientific observation as a storehouse of energy. The theological and mythological programmes of the baroque period were abandoned. Realism erects the visible into the norm of artistic work. Art itself becomes autonomous and loses contact with theology, even in the Church. Its reality is based on society and the person. The personalism of the artistic will brings about the isolation of the artist from society. The era of mental breakdown and suicide sets in for artists. In the course of the 19th century, the artistic mentality finds itself more and more in conflict with official taste (in a society of the masses). About 1910 the artistic movements of the 20th century begin, with Cubism, surrealism and abstract art, which de-personalize art and make it anonymous. In Germany, the iconoclasm of National Socialism launches a merciless campaign against "inartistic art", as does Soviet socialism in the East. Inspired by the idea of a Gothic supposed to remain eternally valid, or searching for a basic religious style (Beuron, French symbolism), Church circles likewise opposed the modern forms. After 1945, there was a swing over to the opposite attitude. The productions of abstract art, cubism and surrealism — often tastefully embellished — are admitted into the churches, which now become miscellanies of the various styles. Thus the most recent writings and projects call for a Church art without decipherable content. It means the disappearance of the Church tradition. And the replacement of the great personal art of the moderns by a manneristic formalism at second hand. Modern art, which tries to mould its experience of materials and of energy along with its unconscious processes, calls for a re-appraisal of the notion of image in Christian circles also. To give it a proper basis, it will be essential to recall that the world is the vehicle of a communication of its creator to his creatures.

See also *Sacraments* I, *Secularization, Revelation, Symbol*.

BIBLIOGRAPHY. G. J. Martin, *A History of the Iconoclastic Controversy* (1930); H. Leclercq, *Dictionnaire d'Archéologie Chrétienne*, VII, cols. 180–302; G. von Rad, G. Kittel, H. Kleinknecht, "εἰκών", *TWNT*, II, pp. 378–96; A. Grabar, "Plotin et les origines de l'esthétique mediévale", Cahiers d'Archéologie 1 (1945), R. Bernhard, *L'image de Dieu d'après St-Athanase* (1952); L. Ouspensky and V. Lossky, *The Meaning of*

Icons (1952); H. Crouzel, *Théologie de l'image de Dieu chez Origine* (1956); H. Schade (Libri Carolini), *Zeitschrift für Katholische Theologie* 79 (1957), pp. 69–78; P. Alexander, *Patriarch Nicephorus of Constantinople: Ecclesiastical Policy and Image Worship in the Byzantine Empire* (1958); L. Bréhier, *La querelle des images, VIIIe et IXe siècles* (1964); K. Rahner, "The Theology of the Symbol", *Theological Investigations,* IV (1966), pp. 221–86.

Herbert Schade

IMMANENTISM

Immanentism is the name given to the doctrine or attitude which excludes transcendence, that is, the reference to "the other" in any form whatever, on the grounds that this other is to be found equivalently in the subject itself. Immanentism, therefore, substitutes a false concept of "inwardness" or of commitment to the world, to eliminate the authentic religious attitude, which is the adoring recognition of God as the "wholly other", and the thankful acceptance of the surprises of his grace throughout history.

1. *The forms of immanentism.* The normal distinction is between epistemological and metaphysical immanentism. The former ("gnoseological") holds that human knowledge only attains the thought of its contents, not their being; the latter refuses to consider God as the wholly other beyond the world. Both forms have been chiefly developed in modern philosophy, by an exaggeration of the notion of immanence fostered originally by Christian thought.

a) The concept of immanence is derived from a twofold train of thought. One element, based on such texts as 1 Jn 4:12, was the indwelling of God in the Christian sanctified by grace, and then that of the creator in the creature (the *Deus interior intimo meo* of St. Augustine). The other element was the concept of *actio immanens,* which was chiefly worked out from the consideration of living beings as whole units realizing themselves from within themselves as their own proper ends. Knowledge is *actio immanens* in the fullest sense (as is also will), since it makes no changes in the thing known, but assimilates the knower himself to the thing as known — which again can only be done by an act of self-realization on the part of the knower. Since all knowing involves this inner self-realization, the act of faith includes among its presuppositions the ra-

tional *praeambula fidei* and the inner light of faith — neither of which are possible except by virtue of immanence in the first metaphysical sense. Thus the Christian doctrine of immanence stands or falls with transcendence, that is, with the existence of "another", which is so fully self-subsistent that it remains "other" when it subsists in another. It would be immanentism, however, to hold that the "one" and the "other" within man are only two aspects of the one reality, or two poles of the same act of thought.

b) Epistemological (gnoseological) immanentism is of only indirect interest for theology. It includes the relativist theory of knowledge on which Modernism is based, the term immanentism having apparently been forged in connection with Modernism. This theory of knowledge invokes the stage of philosophical reflection arrived at with Descartes and Kant, according to which knowledge is originally concerned only with the content of thought, so that henceforward the necessary ("transcendental") structures of thought itself must be the object of philosophical investigation. Modernism sought to escape the resulting agnosticism by a vitalist theory of religious knowledge which made it a matter of psychological attitudes. Instead of transcendent, authoritative truths, "religion" now becomes the norm, religion being understood as a vital urge within man. Reflection discloses that "the divine" is needed to satisfy this urge. "Impelled by our need of faith in the divine", as the modernist programme says, we can accept historical facts as unavoidably necessary for religious experience, and are enabled to "re-mould" them accordingly, and thus make progress in the knowledge of faith and in dogmatic formulations. The essence of this immanentism consists, therefore, of the fact that the true direction of religious dependence is inverted. "The God who matters to me" now becomes dependent on the religious needs of man — a perversion present in its initial stages wherever the acceptance of religious truths or the performance of practices commanded are made to depend on their "meaning something to me".

c) Metaphysical immanentism strictly speaking is pantheistic in tendency, because it assumes that worldly reality is ultimately self-sufficient. In this form it can hardly be said to exist today. Much more widespread, however, is "historical immanentism", which recognizes nothing beyond and outside history and the time of the world, and holds that history and human life, if they reach their goal at all, do so within history. Thus Marxism expects to arrive at a final happy period through a series of dialectical switches which are all forms of the one reality; so too all types of evolutionary theory, insofar as the end-term is regarded, not as a pre-existing goal, as in Teilhard de Chardin, but as already contained in germ in the process of development; so too, finally, the denial of immortality, in theory or practice. The seeds of such immanentism can also be present in Christianity, wherever so much stress is laid on the salutary force of quasi-sacramental signs, such as brotherliness, the eucharistic meal, the preaching of the word of God, that Christians forget that these things point on beyond themselves and are efficacious only through the free intervention of God's grace. As the industrialized world grows more and more self-sufficient, and the sense of metaphysical realities is blunted by a predominantly "matter of fact" education and outlook, this historical immanentism is likely to continue to spread in the future.

2. Theologically, *immanentism is to be overcome* by the vigorous affirmation of the Christian doctrine of immanence, which must appear less as a sort of impersonal indwelling of God (which could easily degenerate into immanentism) than as a Christological truth. The doctrine of the two natures is a guarantee of transcendence, while incarnation and transubstantiation give genuine value to the whole reality of the world. In philosophy and apologetics, the effort to arouse a sense of transcendence must be made a sort of propaedeutic to the faith. The method of immanence must be used to alert men to their primordial and continual orientation to the absolute You.

See also *Transcendence, Faith* IV, *Modernism, Reflection, Agnosticism, History* I, *Marxism, Apologetics* II.

BIBLIOGRAPHY. *Dictionnaire Apologétique de la Foi Catholique,* II, cols. 569–79; W. Temple, *Nature, Man and God* (1934); J. B. Lotz, *Scholastik* 13 (1938), pp. 1–21, 161–72; G. Bianca, *La filosofia morale nei sistemi immanentistici* (1950); W. Schulz, *Der Gott in der neuzeitlichen Philosophie* (1957); S. Breton, "Philosophie moderniste", *Divinitas* 2 (1957), pp. 104–23; *DTC,* Tables II, cols. 2214–18.

Peter Henrici

IMMORTALITY

By immortality is meant, in general, endless life. It is said absolutely of a being who cannot die (gods, God) and then of a being who survives in a changed form after death. This survival can be thought of as personal or impersonal (supra-personal), as bodiless or in some way bodily, as a lower or a higher plane of existence.

1. *Comparative religion.* Belief in life after death is attested, even before the funeral rites and the cult of the dead in primitive religions, by the burial procedures of the earliest cultures. In view of the burial gifts, the "books of the dead" and the myths, the life in question seems mostly to have been considered as an only slightly altered form of earthly life. Differences were supposed also to continue among the dead. The rank after death could be determined by the moral qualities of the dead person or by those of his relatives, by the burial rites or the type of sacrifice offered, by the nature of his death or simply by the rank he had held in earthly life. Rewards and punishments, linked with the notion of gradual purification, are the specific features of the doctrine of the transmigration of souls, though the ultimate end may differ — entry into *Nirvana,* into the *Brahma* or into a state where the soul is free of everything corporeal, as in Orphism.

2. *History of philosophy.* The Orphic tradition was adopted by Plato, who laid the foundations of the Western thinking on immortality by defining the soul as the element which survived the dissolution of the body at the moment of "separation of soul and body". But the soul was not merely part of man. "Man is nothing else than his soul" (*Alcibiades,* 129e, 130c). The immortality of the soul, according to Plato, is based on the cyclic character of nature in general and the doctrine of anamnesis: the survival of the soul corresponding to its pre-existence. More stringently, Plato argues from the simplicity of the soul, which cannot therefore be dissolved, and from its ability to grasp the eternal forms of the true, good and beautiful. Since like is known only by like, the soul must be of the nature of the forms. Finally, he argues from the nature of the soul as principle of life, in the *Phaedo* — an argument also

taken up in the *Phaedros*, 245c–246a. The Aristotelian notion of matter and form guaranteed a closer and more organic unity of body and soul, but made it more difficult to accept the immortality of the soul. According to Aristotle, only the supra-personal intellect (νοῦς) was immortal.

The Platonic and Aristotelian approaches were combined in various ways in later philosophical schools. Plato was the great master here for Christian thought. Augustine, for instance, proves the immortality of the soul from its faculty of grasping the truth. The theological (and ethical) arguments also are emphasized. The adoption of Aristotelianism then became the mainspring of the strictly philosophical discussion, but with the rejection of Averroism by Albertus Magnus, Thomas Aquinas and the Fifth Lateran Council (*D* 738, *DS* 1440) the hylemorphism of Aristotle was given a Platonic interpretation. At the time of the Renaissance, the immortality of the soul was one of the major subjects of debate between the Platonists and the Sceptics, as it was among the Aristotelians between Averroists and Alexandrists. But with Leibniz in particular, it was treated as the "central dogma" of the Enlightenment, at least in Germany. In France, as represented by Voltaire and the *Encyclopédie,* and in England as represented by Hume, the Enlightenment showed itself rather sceptical and hostile to the notion of immortality. The reaction gave currency in Germany to the influence of Swedenborg, whose "dreaming" was attacked by Kant. Kant rejected the rational value of the traditional proofs as paralogisms, but postulated immortality on ethical und practical grounds, since man could only attain the end of his nature by endless progress and because the moral order of the world demanded that man's destiny should correspond to his virtues. For Fichte, immortality is already there with the acceptance of truth, which is the "blessed life", whose outcome can only be understood as transformation into still more perfect love. As against the more emotional humanism or personalism of a Herder or a Goethe, and the theosophist speculation of the later Schelling, the thought of Hegel was later influential — or rather, the interpretation of his own ambiguous position as the denial of personal immortality in view of the history of the World-Spirit. This Hegelianism of the left and the crude materialism of a mainly biological type were opposed by the Hegelians of the right and speculative theism. In the philosophy of the present day, death is one of the predominant themes, but no more interest is taken in proofs of immortality than in proofs of the existence of God, whether immortality is rejected, left an open question or accepted.

3. *Theology.* The key-word here in the anthropology of biblical theology is not immortality but the resurrection of the flesh. Thus in the OT, there is survival in Sheol. But what survives is not the soul as part of man and still less the soul as the real being of man. Only man's "shadow" survives, and this might possibly be called immortality. But this mere survival is completely insignificant in comparison with the loss of earthly life, as also in comparison with the growing hope of being raised up by God. The influence of Hellenism can be already noted in the post-exilic period, and then patristic theology took up explicitly, as has been noted above, the Platonic conception, which it combined with faith in the resurrection as expressed in the later books of the OT and in the NT. But just as the descriptions of the body-soul relationship by the magisterium in terms of hylemorphism do not erect Aristotelian philosophy into dogma, so too the official declarations on eschatology (*D* 530, *DS* 1000) and against Averroism (*D* 738, *DS* 1440) do not give any particular philosophical explanation of immortality any status as part of the faith. While rejecting false interpretations of the faith, they used a ready-made philosophical terminology as a handy way of allowing the faith to find self-expression.

Present-day Protestant theology has to a great extent rejected all such aid. H. Engelland, in the *Evangelisches Kirchenlexikon,* III, cols. 1579 f., gives three reasons for refusing to work with the concept of immortality: "For the sake of the divineness of God, who alone has immortality" (1 Tim 6:16; cf. 1 Cor 15:53); "because of sin", of which the origin is not in the body but in the soul; "because of the unity of man". But there are also signs of a more moderate position (cf. *RGG*, VI, cols. 1177f.). And in fact, faith in immortality is not necessarily linked with a dichotomy between body and soul. It could be shown that the classical proof from the incorruptibility of a simple spiritual being, and from the necessity of eternal sanctions, is only a certain way of articulating the immanent basic experience of freedom itself. Freedom experiences itself in the experience of the unconditional claim of truth and of good. It recognizes that it could never escape itself, not even in death, and hence that it must resolve and decide, and that it must be fully itself by definitively accepting itself. At the same time, it experiences the "dialogal" nature of its situation. Immortality in the full sense of the word is not within its power, nor even merely a task to be laboured at. It is also a gift to be hoped for — a point at which it is well to recall the analogy with the proofs of the existence of God. That immortality is beyond man and yet man's gift is not a contradiction and not even a mere paradox. The two are indissolubly one, an identity in difference, by virtue of the essentially interpersonal nature of freedom as seen above all in the body and in language. In this sense, therefore, without any concessions to a rationalistic self-assurance or to an irrational hope which can give no "account" of itself (1 Pet 3:15), one can accept the quotation from Kierkegaard with which J. Pieper ended his book on death and immortality: "The question of immortality is of its nature not a scholarly question. It is a question welling up from the interior which the subject must put itself as it becomes conscious of itself" (*Concluding Unscientific Postscript*, p. 164).

See also *Afterlife, Transmigration of Souls, Body, Soul, Platonism, Aristotelianism, Materialism, Death, Resurrection* II.

BIBLIOGRAPHY. See bibliography on *Resurrection* II, *Body, Soul, Death;* also: E. Rohde, *Psyche: the Cult of Souls and Belief in Immortality among the Greeks* (E.T. from 8th German ed. [1925]); F. Heiler, *Unsterblichkeitsglaube und Jenseitshoffnung in der Geschichte der Religionen* (1950); A. Wenzl, *Unsterblichkeit. Ihre metaphysische und anthropologische Bedeutung* (1951); M. Scheler, *Schriften aus dem Nachlass,* I (2nd ed., 1957), pp. 9–64 (Death and survival); N. Luython, A. Portmann, K. Jaspers and K. Barth, *Unsterblichkeit* (1957); G. Marcel, *Présence et immortalité* (1959); H. Grass, "Unsterblichkeit", *RGG,* VI, cols. 1174–78; A. Ahlbrecht, *Tod und Unsterblichkeit in der evangelischen Theologie der Gegenwart* (1964); K. Rahner, "The Life of the Dead", *Theological Investigations,* IV (1966), pp. 347–54; J. Splett, *Der Mensch in seiner Freiheit* (1967); J. Pieper, *Tod und Unsterblichkeit* (1968).

Jörg Splett

INCARNATION

A. INTRODUCTION AND PRELIMINARY REMARKS

1. The teaching on Jesus Christ is the central mystery of Christianity, which of course takes its name from him. The doctrine of the one God who, as an infinite transcendent person creates, conserves and guides the world to its goal, the doctrine of the nature and dignity of man as a free person with an eternal, blissful destiny, and the doctrine of the unity of love of God and the neighbour as the ultimate purpose and saving activity of human existence, are also of course doctrines which are fundamental to Christianity and the Church and are fundamental to the hierarchy of truths which constitute the one message of Christianity. Yet these three doctrines receive their specifically Christian content and their ultimate ground from the message regarding Jesus Christ. Only in him, and in the union and distinction between God and the world found in him, is the God-world relationship and, as a consequence, God's very essence, made clear as self-communicating love. In Christ man's highest dignity and ultimate nature as radical openness to God is manifest, together with the guarantee and historically tangible demonstration that man's destiny is attained. In Christ the love of God and the neighbour acquires in the person of the one God-man an "object" of the highest unity, and as a consequence love for man attains its supreme dignity.

2. The connection between the doctrine of the Incarnation and Christian belief as a whole may be made still clearer at the start. Christianity is the eschatologically historical event of God's self-communication. This means that the really fundamental Christian conception of the world (including spiritual persons) and of its relation to God is not to be found in the doctrine of creation, fundamentally important as this is. It is based on the history of salvation, which shows that the absolute, infinite and holy God wills in the freedom of his love, to communicate *himself* by grace *ad extra* to what is not divine. That is why he has creatively brought the world into existence as the recipient of his self-communication in such a way that this self-communication is God's fundamental purpose, but is not something to which the

finite creature has a right. It remains a free grace of God's love. God creates the *ad extra* in order to communicate the *ad intra* of his love. This *ad extra* is not something presupposed and independent of God, but the possibility, effected by his own freedom, of his own self-communication. Its difference from himself has its origin in himself. Like the world and the spiritual creation, God's self-communication has a history. This self-communication is indeed the basis of world history because it is its ultimate meaning and its (grace-given) entelechy from the beginning. But it also has its own history within world history, attains clearer and clearer manifestation in it and reaches its culmination and irreversible manifestation precisely in the eschatological phase of the history of salvation which is constituted by Jesus Christ.

a) Viewed in this light Jesus Christ as the incarnate Logos of God is God's supreme self-communication. This takes place in the Incarnation. For here God is so much the self-bestower that the "addressee" of God's self-communication is posited by God's *absolute* will to his effective, i.e., accepted, self-communication (*ipsa assumptione creatur*, as Augustine says). The self-communication itself posits the act of its acceptance (as a created spiritual substance and its free and definitive act) and thus appropriates this latter wholly and makes it the manifestation precisely of God's will — identical with God himself — to self-exteriorization. (Further and more detailed treatment of this is to be found in Section D.)

b) Since this created spiritual reality, posited by the very acceptance which itself receives, is by its very nature a part of the *world,* this self-communication of God as accepted by the creation in Jesus Christ means that the world is in principle accepted by God for its salvation. And this acceptance by God in Christ has become historically tangible and irrevocable. In the Incarnation (which also includes Jesus' human life, his death and resurrection), the history of the world has been decided as a victorious history of salvation, not of perdition, and has been made manifest as such.

3. The Incarnation is a mystery because the possibility of God's self-communication to the finite is a mystery. It is also a mystery that the possibility of such self-communica-

tion can find its culmination in the Incarnation. Finally, the irreducibly contingent fact of the Incarnation's having occurred precisely in Jesus of Nazareth is an aspect of this mystery in the concrete. Yet the freedom of the Incarnation can certainly be regarded as one and the same freedom as that of God's-gracious self-communication to the world. For the essence of the assumption of a reality belonging to the world and its unity, in the Incarnation, itself implies God's fundamental will to sanctify and redeem the world as such. And conversely (cf. Section C below) the historically definitive manifestation of God's will to a self-communication to the world accepted by the world, that is, the absolute, eschatological mediator of salvation already implies Incarnation.

4. That the historical Jesus' self-awareness was materially identical with what is meant by the Incarnation of the Logos, is expounded in the article *Jesus Christ* (cf. also the article *Trinity of God*). It is hardly necessary to stress that the experience of Jesus' resurrection was of essential importance for the interpretation of the witness Jesus had borne to himself. That is, of course, the reason why in the account of his words and deeds the pre-paschal Jesus' interpretation of himself is rightly given from the standpoint, and as a part, of the kerygma concerning the risen Christ. The resurrection is not to be understood merely as an external miraculous attestation of Jesus' words, without any intrinsic connection with them. It is itself the eschatological, fundamental saving event which, if precisely and fully interpreted, shows Jesus to be the absolute bringer of salvation and hence implies what is meant by Incarnation.

B. JESUS IN THE NEW TESTAMENT

1. The doctrine of the NT regarding Jesus (beyond the historical Jesus' own witness to himself) need only be presented briefly here. It is not a particularly difficult problem to verify the identity of the Church's dogma with the Christology of the NT. For on the one hand the latter expressly teaches Christ's pre-existence, and on the other all the NT "Christology of Ascent" (Jesus as the Servant of God and Messiah raised up by the Father through the Passion and Resurrection) is certainly implicitly contained in the classical doctrine of the Church,

provided this is not misconstrued in a more or less Monophysite way.

This does not mean, however, that within NT Christology there are not very different, though not mutually incompatible, fundamental Christological conceptions according to whether an ascent or descent schema is preferred (gnoseologically and ontologically), and according to the precise way in which the starting-point is determined within such a schema. It goes without saying, too, that within the history of Jesus and NT Christology, certain terms (Son of God, Son of man, Messiah-Christ, etc.) themselves have a history of more precise interpretation, deepening and unfolding, and cannot therefore be taken as having everywhere the same meaning.

2. For the rest, cf. the articles *Jesus Christ* and *Christology*.

C. The Official Teaching of the Church

1. *Its preparation in the history of dogma*. The NT texts regarding Christology of Descent, e.g., Gal 4:4; 1 Cor 2:8; Phil 2:5–11; Col 2:9; Heb 1:3; Rom 1:3f.; Jn 1:14, etc., show how increasing experience concerning the man Jesus was translated even in the NT period into the article of faith regarding the pre-existent Son of God coming in the flesh. It is therefore not difficult to understand that while early Christology down to the 4th century had no difficulty in overcoming an ancient *truncated* Christology of Ascent (in which Jesus was, ultimately, merely a human Messiah, as for the Ebionites), the Christological controversies of the first centuries, surprising as this may seem, were more concerned with the question of the relation of the pre-existent Son to the Father (in Arianism, Sabellianism, Modalism) — which does not concern us here — or else raised the question of how exactly we are to think of the "flesh" in which God's Son appeared as revealer of the Father and mediator of salvation. In Docetism this is volatilized entirely. In the East the Logos-sarx theory whether extreme (Apollinarianism) or moderate (Athanasius), either denied the human intellect of Jesus or at least did not do justice to it as a theological reality. In the West, from Tertullian to Novatian, Ambrose and Augustine, the explicitation of the mystery of Christ in theological concepts developed relatively

without friction into the standard formulation of Leo I in the middle of the 5th century. The one *persona* (Tertullian already uses the term) has a double status (*spiritus* [divinity] — *caro:* Tertullian) and is *unus,* even though possessing (Ambrose) *utrumque (divinitas — corpus, caro, nostra natura)*, and even though it was still often said (without thereby denying the unity of person) that the Word of the Father had assumed a "man" where we today would simply say a "human nature". The course of development in the East was more difficult. It is true that as early as Origen we find the axiom that man is only completely redeemed if the whole human reality, *soul* and body, is assumed by the Logos. But the conceptual grasp of the union between the Logos and the "flesh" (man, humanity), and consequently the communication of properties, caused considerable difficulty. The distinction between ὑπόστασις and φύσις was only slowly worked out in the theology of the Trinity and it was even longer before this distinction came into general use in Christology. Πρόσωπον (as principle of union in the school of Antioch) could easily be misunderstood as a principle of merely "moral" unity, in which statements about Christ would have to be divided between two subjects different in substance. This tendency found decisive expression in Nestorianism. On the other hand the older conceptual models which represented the union of divine and human as a "mixture" or thought of it on the pattern of the union between soul and body (as Augustine did in the West; cf. *D* 40) were not really very suited to bring out with equal force the union and distinction of the divine and human in Christ. In the struggle against Nestorianism, Alexandrian theology endeavoured to express the real substantial unity of the one identical Christ, God and man, by means of the term φύσις (or by other words which at that time were still identical with it: ὑπόστασις, πρόσωπον). And so in a formula which derives from the Apollinarian Logos-sarx Christology, Cyril of Alexandria and to some degree the Council of Ephesus could speak of the one physis (nature) of the incarnate Logos or of his incarnate nature, of a ἕνωσις φυσική (cf. *D* 115; 117), without any intention of denying his complete humanity and its distinction from the divinity. But the formula was then misused by Monophysitism (Eutyches). Not until the Council of Chalcedon was the terminology clarified: πρόσωπον, ὑπόστασις, *persona* were taken as identical in meaning and used of the substantial subject and (in this case) the principle of union of the natures; φύσις (οὐσία, *natura*) from the point of view of terminology was no longer taken to have the same sense as hypostasis or person but (as in Trinitarian doctrine) was understood as signifying the principle of objective specification of an ultimate subject and as the principle of specific activity. At the same time it must be observed that this terminology was not precisely fixed and methodically developed, but was employed forthwith as occasion offered in Christology.

As a consequence it is not surprising that much remains obscure even to this day and is left to the philosophical and theological interpretation of individual schools and theologians. Consequently if the *theologically* binding meaning of these terms is to be rightly ascertained, positively and negatively, we must repeatedly take our bearings from the simple insight of faith that precisely this concrete individual who acts and encounters us, is true God and true man, that these two predicates do not mean the same, yet both are the reality of the one and the same being. The history of Christology after the Council of Chalcedon includes the dogmatic conflict with Monotheletism; otherwise, however, it is almost solely history of theology, not of dogma. Efforts are made to define more precisely the terms made use of. Subtle variations can be observed between a Christology which stresses the difference of natures and one which stresses the unity of both in a single person. The consequences of the hypostatic union for Christ's human nature are considered — his grace, his knowledge, the mode of influence of the hypostasis on the human nature, the question of Christ's "consciousness", the possibility of a human freedom under the dominion of the Logos, etc. There are attempts to conceive the "unity" of the divine person as the consequence of some other ontological reality, e.g., in modern Thomism, where the existence of the Logos itself confers real existence on (achieves or brings into the real order) Christ's human nature and thereby unites this to itself. All this, however, only concerns the pastor to the extent that it shows that while the formula of Chalcedon remains the standard and valid statement, theology,

preaching and piety should nevertheless not consider that all they are permitted to do is to repeat that standard formula.

2. *The actual official teaching of the Church.* a) *General characteristics.* The Church's official doctrine is formulated objectively and ontically, i.e., it is a concrete factual statement about Jesus Christ in himself. There is no explicit reference to the question of how we meet him in historical experience and in faith, or how this peculiar encounter (as the ultimate and absolute encounter with God, as he is in himself, in the midst of our history at its most concrete) can be used to establish this ontic Christology and understand it better. The key concepts of Church doctrine are the distinction between person and nature and the doctrine of the hypostatic union, as expressed by the Council of Chalcedon in terms which have never been improved on.

b) *The basic doctrine.* By the hypostatic union (*D* 148, 217) the eternal (and therefore pre-existent) Word (Logos), the Son of the Father as the second person of the Trinity, has united as his nature with his person in a true, substantial (*D* 114ff.) and definitive (*D* 85f., 283) union (against Nestorianism) a human nature created in time with a body and spiritual soul from the Virgin Mary, his true mother. The effecting of this union is common to the three divine persons (*D* 284, 429), but the union of the human nature is with the Word alone (*D* 392; against the Patripassianists). Even after the union the unmixed distinction between his divine and his human nature is not affected (against Monophysitism). Thus the Word became true man. Consequently to one and the same person, the Logos, there belong two natures, the divine and the human, without mixture and without separation (*D* 143f., 148); one and the same person is God and man. We can affirm of one and the same subject the realities of both natures and consequently, in a communication of properties (perichoresis: *D* 291), we can predicate of this one subject named on the basis of one of the natures, the characteristics of the other nature. This hypostatic union belongs to the absolute mysteries of faith (*D* 1462, 1669).

c) *The true divine sonship of Jesus Christ.* If this one and the same Jesus Christ is named, therefore, we must say that he is true God (*D* 54, 86, 148, 224, 290, 994, 2027–2031); the consubstantial (*D* 86, 554) Son of the Father

(*D* 1597); his Word (*D* 118, 224), God from God, begotten not made (*D* 13, 39f., 54), the only-begotten (*D* 6, 13, 86); a person of the Trinity (*D* 216, 222, 255, 708); creator of all things (*D* 54, 86, 422), eternal (*D* 54, 66), incapable of suffering (*D* 27); because he is true and consubstantial Son, he is not (in addition) an adopted son (*D* 299, 309f., 311ff.) like us (against Adoptianism, and a certain form of Assumptus-Homo-theology). The divinity of Christ is the presupposition of his role as mediator in the redemption, of his offices and of the privileges which distinguish him from us even in a human nature essentially identical with ours, and even though these characteristics also belong to him inasmuch as he is man.

d) *This same Jesus Christ is true man.* (i) He has a true body capable (before his resurrection) of suffering (*D* 13, 111a, 148, 480, 708), not an apparent body (*D* 20, 344, 462, 710) or a heavenly one (*D* 710). This was united to the person of the Logos from his conception (*D* 205) and has a rational spiritual soul as its essential form (*D* 216, 480). Accordingly he possesses a human, sensible and spiritual soul (*D* 13, 25, 111a, 148, 216, 255, 283, 290, 480, 710), created, not eternally pre-existent (*D* 204). Consequently all forms of Docetism and any extreme Logos-sarx Christology (e.g., Apollinarianism: *D* 65, 85) are heretical. Jesus Christ is, therefore, consubstantial with us (*D* 148), a son of Adam, born of a mother in true human fashion, related to us by blood, our brother (*D* 40, etc.). In contradiction to Monotheletism, therefore, we must acknowledge the real free created will, energy and operation (*D* 144, 148, 262–269, 288–293, 710) of the man Jesus Christ, a will distinct from the divine will of the Logos but fully in harmony with it (*D* 251ff., 288ff., 1465). In its activity he stood truly God-fearing (*D* 310, 343, 387) under God's rule (*D* 285).

(ii) In this humanity (not in virtue of it), Jesus Christ is the natural Son of the Father, worship is due to him (*D* 120, 221, 1561) (also in regard to his heart: *D* 1563; so too the blood of Christ). In his humanity he also possesses impeccability (*D* 122, 148, 224, 711; *Collectio Lacensis,* VII, cols. 560f.), holiness (substantial by the hypostatic union and accidental by sanctifying grace) and integrity (freedom from concupiscence), power to work miracles (*D* 121, 215, 1790, 2084) and an infallible knowledge

appropriate to his mission (including the vision of God from the beginning: *D* 248, 1790, 2032–2035, 2183ff., 2289; against the Agnoetes), but not, before the resurrection, an absence of the capacity to suffer (*D* 429, 708) or the *defectus Christi naturales* (Aphthartodocetism). In his humanity certain offices or functions belong to him.

e) *Official pronouncements* of the Church's solemn magisterium concerning the life and work of Christ are relatively few, except as regards the doctrine of the redemption. They are mostly dealt with by the ordinary teaching of the Church in its transmission of the statements of scripture.

D. The Doctrine of the Incarnation in the Preaching of the Faith at the Present Day

1. The Incarnation is a mystery of faith and therefore involves all that a mystery implies: the impossibility of compelling the free assent of faith, the "paradox" involved in any formulation of such a mystery, the character of being a stumbling-block to the pride of a rationalism autonomously accepting only what is fully comprehended. But a mystery is not a myth or a miracle, i.e., it is not, and ought not to be understood and preached as something which within a man's own realm of experience cannot seriously be taken as possible and believable even by one who does not arbitrarily restrict the range of experience in a rationalist and scientific way to what can be experimentally demonstrated. That means that the mystery must possess for man a genuine intelligibility and desirability, even if in some cases this mental framework must first be brought to light precisely by actual encounter with the mystery and its proclamation. In presenting the faith we must to a greater degree than in earlier times avoid giving a mythological flavour to the expression of this mystery. But that always happens if Christ's human nature is made to look like God's livery, which the Logos puts on to make himself known, or if it seems to be a sort of passive marionette manipulated from outside and used by God like a mere thing or instrument to attract attention on the stage of world history.

2. This, however, presupposes that the human nature of Christ, of the person of the Logos, must be understood in such a way that Christ in reality and in all truth is a man

with all that this involves: a human consciousness which is aware in adoration of its own infinite distance in relation to God; a spontaneous human interior life and freedom with a history which, because it is that of God himself, possesses not less but more independence, for the latter is not diminished but increased by union with God. For union with God and independence are in principle realities which grow in direct, not inverse proportion, as Maximus Confessor already emphasizes (*PG*, XCI, col. 97 A). The divine act producing the union is itself formally one which posits the created reality as free for its active independence in regard to God. This means that present-day Christology (in preaching and theological reflection) must as it were re-enact (and preach!) that history of the Christology of Ascent which in the NT itself, between the experience of actual contact with the historical Jesus and the descent-formulas of Christology in Paul and John, was transformed with remarkable speed into a doctrine of the Incarnation of the pre-existent Son and Logos of God. Preaching must speak of the Incarnation in such a way that experience of the actual historical Jesus is so profound and radical that it becomes the experience of that absolute and definitive presence of God to the world and to our human reality in Jesus, which is only consciously accepted without diminution or reserve when the classical formulas of Christology remain valid and are properly understood. It is, therefore, quite possible at first to come to know and regard Jesus as a human "prophet", who in a creatively new way was moved by the mystery of God and at the same time lived as a matter of course with his roots in the history of his own world, who preached God as the Father and announced the impending coming of God's reign. Even within orthodox Christology we can and may perceive in Jesus a genuinely historical consciousness, because the ultimate spiritual, ever-present transcendence of his being towards the immediate presence of God (in scholastic theology: the immediate vision of God by Jesus' soul), as the ultimate horizon and fundamental disposition of his human existence, does not exclude a genuinely historical character from his religious life in relation to God. But this "prophet" knew that he was not merely one of the many who

had time and time again during a history open towards an indeterminate future, perpetually come to reawaken a genuinely religious and radical attitude to God. He knew himself to be the final and absolute bringer of salvation, in whose person, death and resurrection the definitive covenant between God and man was realized, and was known as such through his resurrection. He knew himself to be not merely the prophet of a still awaited, purely future "reign of God", nor of one which would constitute salvation independently of his person and about which he could therefore only speak. He himself *is* the reign of God, so that the relation to his very self is what is decisive for the salvation of every human being. A saviour of this kind, however, implies precisely what we mean by Incarnation. For "salvation" is understood here as the eschatological finality of history against the background of a history which in itself could always be different and continue indefinitely and in the presence of a God of, "in himself", unending possibilities. Why the concept of an absolute saviour implies God's "Incarnation" will now have to be discussed rather more closely under another aspect (under point 3).

3. In the history of ideas the situation since the beginning of modern times has been characterized by a turning away from Greek cosmocentrism, with its thought based on things, objects, to modern anthropocentrism which in the question of being in general takes as the paradigm case the subject who knows and wills things. In order the better to understand classical Christology, therefore (without annulling it or doubting its permanent validity), it is possible and advisable to transpose ontic Christology into a transcendental, onto-logical Christology. Expressed as simply as may be, this means that man from the depth of his being *is* the absolutely limitless question regarding God. He does not merely pursue this question as one particular possible occupation among others. That is seen by the fact that his transcendental ordination, in knowledge and freedom, towards God — as a possibility permanently opened out by God, not as autonomous "subjectivity" — is the non-explicit but ever-operative condition of the possibility of all human knowledge and free action.

115

This transcendence finds realization, it is true, in a multiplicity of "accidental" human acts in space and time which constitute his history, but this very multiplicity itself is grounded in the fundamental act of transcendence which constitutes the essence of man. This fundamental act (insofar as it is antecedent to the exercise of man's freedom) is at once total origin from God and movement of return to him. It is the openness to God perpetually opened out by God in the act of creation, an openness which is a question addressed to the freedom thus constituted as to whether it will accept or refuse its transcendence. That openness is also the *potentia obedientialis* for God's *self*-communication as the possible but free and radically highest answer of God to the question which man himself *is*.

In this perspective, what is called in ontic terms the hypostatic union may be expressed in onto-logical terms as a union of question and absolute answer, on the following suppositions. The positing of the question which is constitutive of man, and the acceptance of this interrogative character, come creatively from God himself in such a way that the question is posited precisely as the condition of the possibility of the answer being given by God's self-communication to mankind. Moreover, this happens in such a way that the will to this self-communication and to its acceptance on the part of man, being absolute, not merely conditional, itself posits the *potentia obedientialis,* the unlimited question, because the will to answer is absolute. Finally, it happens in such a way that the absolute conferring of the divine self-communication on the spiritual creature (which implies its formally predestined acceptance) appears in a historical, irreversible manifestation. Then if all this is the case, the "question" (which man is) is an intrinsic component of the answer itself. In fact if this answer is not something which simply comes from God as its author but is most truly God himself, and if the question (as self-accepted in freedom, receiving the answer, allowing itself to be answered) is posited precisely as an element in God's giving of *himself* as answer (by self-communication), then the positing of the "question" as intrinsic component of the answer is as such a reality distinct from God and yet one which most strictly belongs to him, and is proper to him. On this basis it

could then be shown in greater detail that the difference "without mixture" between divine and human in Christ derives from the unifying will of God's self-communication, that the creation of what is human here (as Augustine already says) takes place through the "assumption" itself, and that the "covenant" is the ground of the creation (as Karl Barth is in principle correct in stressing). What has just been said can only be rightly understood and judged when taken strictly ontologically. Mind, self-consciousness, freedom and transcendence are not accidental epiphenomena "in" something which happens to be there (which at bottom is thought of in a reified way), but form the real nature of being, which in the individual existent is only hindered from attaining its true identity by the "non-being" of matter: "actus de se illimitatus limitatur potentia realiter distincta", the Thomist would say (cf. *DS* 3601 ff.; 3618). On that basis it is also understandable that God's self-giving (his irreversible and victorious self-communication) takes place to the *world* (in divinizing grace) and so has its historically irreversible and victorious manifestation and presence in redemptive history in the unique God-man. It then becomes clear that the God-man belongs to the one history of redemption precisely as a unique event (God's descent into the world happens "propter *nostram* salutem"). But it is also true that the God-man does not represent a special "degree" of divinization, without which the divinization — through grace — of others, on a lower level, should still be conceivable. Finally, in this way it is also clear that the mystery of the Incarnation fundamentally lies on the one hand in the mystery of the divine self-communication to the world, and on the other in the fact that it took place in Jesus Christ. The former aspect, however, is "thinkable" through man's fundamental tendency towards absolute closeness to God, a tendency based in fact on God's self-communication. This preserves the mystery of the Incarnation from giving the impression that it is a sort of marvel or something heteronomous.

4. It is also possible to attain an understanding of the Incarnation (which does not of course evacuate the mystery) from another point of view, which must be taken into account when this mystery has to be an-

nounced to the unbelieving "heathen" of the present time. People today live an evolutionary view of the world. They see themselves and mankind inescapably immersed in the current of history. The world for them is not a static reality, but a world in process of becoming. Natural history and human world-history form a unity. And this single total history is experienced and regarded as a history with an upward orientation, however the formal structure of each higher phase of this history is in fact described, e.g., growing interiority in self-consciousness; increasing mastery of reality as a whole; growing unity and complexity of individual beings. If this history is to produce something really new (i.e., higher, of greater ontological intensity, not merely different) and yet do so by its own action, then the transition from one form and phase of history to another can only be characterized as "self-transcendence". This self-transcendence in the direction of what is higher, although *ex supposito* it is produced by historical beings themselves, can, however, take place only in virtue of the absolute being of God, who without becoming a constituent of the essence of the finite existent in process of becoming, produces the self-transcendence of the finite being as the latter's own action. He does this by his creative conservation and concursus and as the future which impels and is aimed at at least asymptotically. If this idea of self-*transcendence* is conceived as a divine motion and the divine motion is conceived as conferring *self*-transcendence, the development of the material-spiritual world can be understood as a single history, without its being necessary on this account to deny or overlook the essential difference of kind within this one world and history. As we know from God's revelation expounding man's ultimate experience of grace, the highest, absolute and definitive self-transcendence of created being which is the foundation of all preceding acts of self-transcendence and gives them their ultimate meaning and goal, is the self-transcendence of the created spirit into the direct reality of the infinite mystery of the being of God himself. This self-transcendence requires God's "concursus" in an absolutely unique sense. From this point of view, such a concursus is God's gracious self-communication. The history of the

world and of mind which takes place in hierarchically ordered self-transcendencies of created beings has its ground in God's self-communication. A factor of this, which posits what it requires as its own condition, is the actual creation of what is other than God. Then in the world as it in fact exists, God's self-communication itself is the first cause and last goal. The ultimate and highest self-transcendence of the finite, and God's radical self-communication, are the two sides of what happens in history. In this regard two things must always be remembered. In the first place the goal of this ultimate self-transcendence is always the unfathomable mystery of God. This characteristic of the goal therefore contributes to determine the whole way into the future. It is a path into what is unknown and open. All self-transcendence is therefore hope and loving self-abandonment to what is absolutely beyond man's control and communicates itself as incomprehensible love. Furthermore, the history of self-transcendence is a history of freedom, and therefore a history of the possible, and actually realized, guilt and refusal of this dynamism of history, or of the false (i.e., autonomous) interpretation of self-transcendence, a history of the possibilities of the absolute and final failure to attain the last end. Within such a double possibility in the history of freedom, renunciation, the "Cross", and death have a necessary place.

This history of God's self-communication and of the creature's self-transcendence, which is the history of the increasing divinization of the world, does not take place only in the depths of the free conscience, but because of man's unity in plurality and the dynamic tendency of grace towards the transfiguration of all creation, has an actually concrete historical dimension. It is manifest and assumes concrete form in what we call history of salvation in the proper and usual sense, and this latter, a concrete history in space and time, is the history in which God's self-communication and the self-transcendence of the creature (i.e., man) takes place. Where God's self-communication and man's self-transcendence reach their absolute and irreversible culmination, i.e., where God is simply and irrevocably "there" in time and space and consequently where man's self-transcendence also attains a similarly complete self-giving to God, we have what in Christian terms is called the Incarnation. This indicates the Christocentricity of the world both on the cosmic plane and on that of the history of freedom. Not that the world attains its absolute self-transcendence "only" in Christ. It attains it as a whole, insofar as all that is material transcends itself into the domain of the spiritual and personal and will finally exist in the final fulfilment only as a factor of what is spiritual (in angels and men), and insofar as absolute closeness to God, to the absolute, infinite being, will be attained in the perfected spiritual creation. And so Christ does not really represent a "higher stage" of the spirit's self-transcendence and of God's self-communication. If this were so, we should have to ask why it only occurred once and why it is not attained in all spiritual creatures in a "panchristism". The incarnate Logos is the culmination and centre of the divinization of the world rather because as an "individual" he is necessarily present when the divinization of the world in grace and glory reaches its irreversible culmination and historically manifest victory. Because God gives himself to the *world,* there is Christ. He is not simply a possible mediator of salvation if he wills to accomplish this mediation, but is this mediation itself as irrevocable and as historically manifest. And this does not render the event of the cross and resurrection superfluous but actually implies them (see *Salvation* IV A).

5. As regards the question why Christian dogma declares that the Son of the Father, the divine Logos as the second person of the triune God, and not another divine person, became man, reference must be made to the article on the *Trinity of God.* The two statements mutually condition one another's intelligibility. Because the Trinity of the economy of the redemption *is* the immanent Trinity (and conversely), the "Word" in which the Father (God without origin), without ceasing to be the uncircumscribable, utters *himself* to us (so that the Word must be consubstantial with the Father) is necessary for our understanding of the immanent Logos of the Father and the converse is also true.

6. By these and similar considerations which it has only been possible to indicate very inadequately here, because of the present state of theological reflection, preaching today must create in the hearer of the Christian message the necessary presuppositions so that the doctrine of the Incarnation can "make an impact" and not give the impression of being a merely mythological conception.

See also *Jesus Christ, Christianity, God, God-World Relationship, Man, Creation* I, *Salvation* I, III, IV, *Mystery, Trinity of God, Resurrection, Arianism, Modalism, Nestorianism, Monophysitism, Docetism, Monotheletism, Rationalism, Myth, Experience, Person, Nature* I, *Transcendence, Potentia Oboedientialis.*

BIBLIOGRAPHY. See bibliography on *Jesus Christ,* I, III, IV, and the text-books of dogmatic theology and history of dogma; also: A. Michel, "Incarnation", *DTC,* VII/2 (1923), cols. 1445–539; A. Grillmeier, "Die theologische und sprachliche Vorbereitung der christologischen Formel von Chalkedon", *Chalkedon,* I (1951), pp. 5–202; V. White, "Incarnations and Incarnation", *Dominican Studies* 7 (1954), pp. 1–21; D. M. Baillie, *God was in Christ* (new ed., 1955); R. Haubst, "Probleme der jüngsten Christologie", *Theologische Revue* 52 (1956), pp. 146–62; A. Grillmeier, "Zum Christusbild der heutigen katholischen Theologie", in J. Feiner and others, eds., *Fragen der Theologie heute* (1957), pp. 265–300; J. N. D. Kelly, *Early Christian Doctrines* (1958); E. Gutwenger, *Bewusstsein und Wissen Christi* (1960); K. Rahner, *Theological Investigations,* I (1961); P. Smulders, "De ontwikkeling van het christologisch dogma", *Bijdragen* 22 (1961), pp. 357–424; M. Schmaus, *Katholische Dogmatik,* II/2 (1963); O. Cullmann, *The Christology of the New Testament* (rev. ed., 1964); W. Pannenberg, *Grundzüge der Christologie* (1964); G. Martelet, *Problèmes actuels de la christologie* (1965); K. Rahner, "On the Theology of the Incarnation", *Theological Investigations,* IV (1966), pp. 105–20; id., "Christology", *ibid.,* V (1966), pp. 155–215; B. Lonergan, *Verbum: Word and Ideas in Aquinas,* ed. by D. Burrell (1967).

Karl Rahner

INDIFFERENCE

Indifference is an aspect of the Christian's attitude to the world.

1. There is no single word in Scripture to designate indifference. But the attitude grows from Christ's liberation of man from the powers of this world, so that he lives in expectation of the Day of the Lord (cf. Rom

8:18–39; 14:8–12; 1 Cor 4:9–13; 7:27–39; 2 Cor 4:16–5:10; Tit 2:12f.; Heb 10:32–39). Expectation of the eschatological event implies a freedom which enables the Christian to keep his correct distance from inner-worldly things and still be involved in history as he ought (see especially the ὡς μή formulas of 1 Cor 7:29–32).

2. In the spirituality of the Fathers, less emphasis was laid on the biblical and eschatological aspects of indifference. The influence of contemporary philosophy, such as the Stoic doctrines of indifference to pleasure or pain (ἀπάθεια), impassivity under pleasure or pain (ἀταραξία) led to indifference being presented rather as a taming of the passions, which was to bring about the dispassionate repose of the soul which claimed to guarantee full freedom from created things in the vision of God.

3. In medieval German mysticism, the notion of indifference was rendered as "composure", "unconcern", which was essentially correct, but still could suggest a misunderstanding of indifference as a Stoic detachment, a cold aloofness from all that was not God.

4. In Ignatian spirituality indifference became a key-term. In the *Spiritual Exercises* of St. Ignatius Loyola, indifference is the indispensable pre-condition for going on to the central and decisive moment of the Exercises, the "Election" or choice (*Exercises,* no. 179; cf. also no. 166). The theology of indifference is indicated in the "Principle and Foundation" which is placed before the Exercises proper. From the end of man and of all created things it follows necessarily that "we must make ourselves indifferent to all created things, insofar as this is allowed to our free will and is not forbidden" (no. 23). If one notes the examples where indifference is to be brought into play according to Ignatius (the urge to be strong, to possess, to dominate, to exist, nos. 23, 166), it will be seen that these are fundamentally concentrated in man's effort at self-assertion within this world as a closed system. The object of "indifference" is to break through this shell, so that man can come face to face with the will of God (in the resolution or decision taken, for instance, in the "election" of the Exercises). But

indifference, in the sense of detachment, is not the last word on the relationship of Christians to the world. The sphere and function of indifference are limited by the second conclusion drawn in the "Principle and Foundation", which is that we must "choose that which brings us more fully to the end for which we were created", and also by the link between indifference and decision ("election"). When the theses of the Foundation are interpreted Christologically, in keeping with the basic principle of Ignatian spirituality, it is seen to contain the eschatological perspective of the dynamism of history which Scripture uses to determine the Christian's attitude to created things. Hence indifference is the negative aspect of a courageous and confident commitment to history, of a definite position taken up in the dimension of the visible, in Church and world. This commitment is the choice to be decided on in the "election". The "outward gaze" which the Christian is to practise integrates indifference into Ignatian spirituality as a whole. Hence it is not a neutral aloofness from history but a constant effort to go beyond the restrictive set of circumstances which hedge in every human decision and to reach a greater openness for the purpose of all created things. Indifference means being wholly open to the claim of God's will, which is disclosed to the believer by the movement of his history towards its eschatological goal. In the vital integration of indifference and choice, of freedom and active, decided commitment to history, of hearing and of loving response, this detachment is the opposite of a cold and aloof scepticism, or a weary resignation, and is absolutely contrary to all indifferentism.

See also *World, Stoicism, Spirituality* III D, *Indifferentism.*

BIBLIOGRAPHY. J. Calveras, "Indiferencia", *Manresa* 6 (1930), pp. 195–201, 303–316; 12 (1936), pp. 36–44; E. Przywara, *Deus Semper Maior,* I (1938), pp. 126–38; I. Iparraguirre, *Práctica de los Ejercicios de San Ignacio de Loyola en vida de su autor* (1946), pp. 194–207; R. Cantin, "Indifference", *Sciences Ecclésiastiques* 3 (1950), pp. 114–45; K. Rahner, *Spiritual Exercises* (1965); J. Robert, *Companion to the Spiritual Exercises* (1966); D. Stanley, *Modern Scriptural Approach to the Spiritual Exercises* (1967).

Ernst Niermann

INDIFFERENTISM

The notion of indifferentism became important in ecclesiastical usage in the 19th century, when it was used to designate pejoratively the religious and philosophical trends of modern times, especially of the Enlightenment, which rejected exclusive (dogmatic) forms of religion and ethics while accepting certain general principles. Indifferentism therefore may sum up the trends which allow more or less the same rights to the various forms of religion and ethics, and thereby leave them all without binding force, though the "universal" values underlying these forms and making them possible are acknowledged. This type of indifferentism was explicitly rejected by Pius IX in the Syllabus (*DS* 2915–18), and is what is meant in ecclesiastical discussion when indifferentism is said to be a danger, e.g., at Vatican II. Four main forms may be distinguished. a) Certain forms of atheism and radical deism treat all religions and all ethics based on religion as indifferent, while acknowledging the existence of an ethics based on intramundane motives. b) Natural religion and ethics are allowed for, while all supernatural religion and morality are treated as indifferent. c) The exclusive claims of the religions of revelation may be rejected while the religious and moral values of these religions are recognized. d) The exclusive character of the Catholic Church is rejected and all Christian denominations are treated as of equal value (relatively).

Indifferentism is less an explicit ideology than a by-product of ideological criticism of concrete forms of religion and morality. Its philosophical roots are to be traced ultimately to Nominalism, and more precisely, to the scientific and historical thinking of modern times, with its rationalistic basis, which favoured positivism and its derivatives of relativism, agnosticism and scepticism. It is sometimes influenced by the desire to free religion from an integralism which is foreign to its nature but nonetheless frequent. But its results are negative because it also comes forward with claims to exclusiveness. It erects reason, science, experience, etc., into absolutes and thus falls into the trap from which it seeks to free others.

There is also a sort of practical indifferentism with regard to the claims of one's own religion, whose claims to exclusiveness or superiority are allowed in theory but denied in practice. It shows itself in emancipated gestures, in disregard for the rules of *communicatio in sacris,* wrong views on the value of denominational education and group-formation, tolerance of error on principle and not merely practical tolerance with regard to those who err, etc.

Hence indifferentism is not really scepticism, but indifference to religious values, which are either left unheeded or rejected. The immediate cause of such lack of comprehension is religious and moral immaturity, which can be caused by defective or wrong upbringing or by moral failures. Thus the relationship of certain religious and ethical matters to religious and ethical values is lost sight of. The lack of response is due to the inculpable incapability of grasping religious and moral values as such, or the culpable rejection of known values. Thus indifferentism always means an inculpably or culpably wrong attitude in the intellect or the will to religious and moral values or matters involved in them. Hence indifferentism is not merely objectively contrary to the character of truth, revelation, and the Church, it is also — where consciously accepted — subjectively wrong, since it takes the illogical step of evading the binding character of truth, revelation and the Church and the testimony to it, and hence represents an offence against reason or faith.

The problems posed by indifference, arising out of the context of reason and history in which religion and ethics are inserted, have been considered more and more closely by theology and the Church as time went on. The main findings are as follows. a) Tolerance, it is seen more clearly, demands indirectly a certain tolerance of error as well as of the persons in error (see Vatican II, Declaration on Religious Freedom, art. 14). Thus it is not indifferentism if the State, insofar as is compatible with the common earthly good, remains neutral with regard to various religious and moral convictions, out of respect for conscience and religious freedom. b) More emphasis is laid on the positive significance of the non-Catholic Christian Churches and the non-Christian religions (see Vatican II, Decree on Ecumenism, Declaration on the Relationship of the Church to Non-Christian Religions). The conviction is now gaining ground that one is justified in co-operating with those whose philosophy of life is different, insofar as there is agreement on fundamental convictions and differences of opinion are left aside, so that common interests may be pursued without detriment to one's own convictions. c) More attention is being paid to the historicity of revelation and of knowledge of it. A better understanding has been gained of the limitations and sociological components of human knowledge, especially as regards its role in the development of dogma. This is not to call in question the absolute (though limited) truth of articulated dogma, which is a sufficient but non-exhaustive statement of the fundamental truth of God's self-communication in Christ.

Further, theology and Church are taking up an attitude of more complete detachment towards the proper laws of the categorial world, while striving to throw light on the transcendent relationships of this reality. This is in fact a tendency to a sort of indifferentism with regard to truths and values which are not immediately of a religious and moral nature, in order to be able to criticize all ideologies which strive to turn categorial realities into an absolute.

See also *Atheism, Deism, Nominalism, Rationalism, Positivism* I, *Relativism, Integralism, Church and World*.

BIBLIOGRAPHY. D. de Lamennais, *Essai sur l'indifférence en matière de religion*, 4 vols. (1829); J. H. Newman, *Discussions and Arguments* (1872); P. Richard, "Indifférence religieuse", *DTC,* VII, cols. 1580–94; R. Ostermann, *Les hommes d'aujourd'hui devant la religion et l'église* (1948); A. Oddone, "L'indifferentismo religioso", *Civiltà Cattolica* 102 (1951), pp. 519–30; A. Desqueyrat, *La crise religieuse des temps nouveaux* (1955); O. A. Rabut, *Vérification religieuse. Recherche d'une spiritualité pour le temps de l'incertitude* (1964), E. T.: *Faith and Doubt* (1967). See also bibliography on *Tolerance*.

Waldemar Molinski

INDIVIDUALISM

Individualism can stand for a large number of highly divergent views and attitudes, of which the highest common factor is the effort to make the individual stand out in bold relief against the background of society, community, group, collectivity and general setting. The meaning of individualism in any given case must be sought in the actual context. There is no systematic philosophy of individualism which the representative upholders of individualism possess. It is rather a matter of individualistic tendencies appearing in the train of other philosophical conceptions such as eudaemonism, nominalism, scepticism, subjectivism and existentialism. Here to some extent the individual is taken to be the goal and norm of ethical, political and anthropological knowledge in general and to some extent the individuality, in the metaphysical and logical sense, is given pride of place in contrast to the universal and the ideal, being considered as objectively prior, or as the only thing knowable or even real.

Individualism, however, is not necessarily at work every time that stress is laid on the individual or the individuality. It would be foolish, for instance, to see the Sophists and Socrates as representative stages on the way to individualism; it is even more aberrant to see Jesus as "the real initiator of religious individualism" (cf. *HERE,* VII, p. 219). Nonetheless, Socrates, the prophets, the Buddha, Confucius and Jesus (cf. K. Jaspers, *Socrates, Buddha, Confucius, Jesus* [1966]) and many others after them belong to the great individual figures of humanity; it is true to say that a history could be written of the flowering of consciousness as the personal self-awareness of the individual. But its stages would not be initial forms of individualism or preludes to it. Individualism, as a theory or as an attitude to life, is rather a one-sided overemphasis laid on the individuality. Abelard, St. Thomas Aquinas, Eckhart, Luther, Calvin and St. Ignatius Loyola are not "individualists", though they were — also — great individual personages. Hence the term individualism is unsuitable and should not be used to characterize the appeal to the individuality or personality in the metaphysical or ethical sense, that is, the appeal to the dignity, responsibility and freedom of man. For this it would be better to use the word personalism, in the metaphysical sense, though this again should be filled out by the (newer) concept of personalism, understood as an existential activation of the personality.

Though the term individualism cannot therefore be used for any philosophical theory, the concept seems to be most enlightening and useful, to characterize a certain attitude to life and way of behaviour. In this sense, individualism is a modern phenomenon, which is usually associated with the Renaissance the Reformation, the rationalism of the Enlightenment and the great revolutions. The individualistic attitude can express itself in an astonishingly large number of variations. It includes the appeal to reason, conscience, personal freedom as well as a total or partial resistance to traditional culture, beliefs, political and ecclesiastical institutions.

To show the whole wide spectrum of possible individualist attitudes in all their shades of colour, one could quote such names as Montaigne, Hobbes, Locke, Rousseau as well as Kant, Goethe, W. von Humboldt, Schiller and the economists A. Smith, Bentham and Ricardo; then there are figures like Bakunin, Carlyle, M. Stirner and Nietzsche and finally Christians like Schleiermacher, Kierkegaard and Newman. The term individualism is hardly applicable here because it is so equivocal. The above should be contrasted with figures like Hegel, Comte and Marx, as well as the upholders of socialist and collectivist theories in general and of fascist nationalism, and also those whose philosophy of history and especially of the State is dominated by an organic determinism. "Individualism" is often reproached with depreciating the State and society, whereas it gives in fact their proper value to State and society, which is a relative one. Liberalism, the "social contract" and democratic institutions are not simply to be branded as symptoms of individualism. On the contrary, they voice powerfully an understanding of the individual which can be ultimately justified only on biblical and Christian principles, and uphold the individual against the pressure to conform unduly to the anonymous mass, whether in the State and society or in the Church regarded merely as an institution. Where, however, emphasis on the individual becomes rejection of political responsibility, anti-social and egoistic (cf. its extreme form in M. Stirner, *Der Einzelne und sein Eigentum* [1845]), it leads ultimately to anarchy and the absurdity of solipsism.

The solution of the conflict between individualism and collectivism — in the fields of (social) ethics, politics, pedagogy, culture, religion and law — is to be sought in a correct understanding of personalism and solidarity. Actually, there is still plenty of room for individualist attitudes in the mass society of a technical age, and this type of "individualism" should be encouraged today. It is not the preserve of the rich, nor of the intellectuals and artists. At the present day, everyone has to foster a certain individualism or search for privacy, as a necessary and possible line of self-defence against the encroachments of publicity and the world of work. And such an individualism is one of the conditions of reciprocal personal relationships. The rights of the individual need to be stressed today as much as the rights of the person, if man is really to be himself.

From the theological point of view it should be noted that individualism, whatever its form, can only exist by virtue of the intervention of Christianity, since the consciousness of selfhood and individuality has its bases in the biblical experience of man's relationship to God. Within Christianity, however, it has happened that too much importance was attached to the subjective effort to attain salvation. The Christian thing is not the individual but the universal character of salvation. Piety, liturgy, the self-understanding of the Church, pastoral care and moral direction are now turning more and more away from individualism to enter more deeply into the spirit of eschatological brotherhood. Basic words like "the individual", "the heart" and "the person" point indeed to the inviolable dignity of each single historical human being, which can never be renounced and which sets up within the Church a fruitful and sometimes painful tension between authority and freedom. Theologically therefore an extreme individualism is also absurd, though the dignity of the individual can only be fully recognized in the light of faith.

See also *Society* I, II, *Nominalism, Scepticism, Subjectivism, Existence* II, *Personalism, Renaissance, Reformation, Rationalism, Enlightenment, Collectivism, Social Movements* IV B, *Authority, Freedom*.

BIBLIOGRAPHY. E. Fournière, *Essai sur l'individualisme* (1901); V. Basch, *L'individualisme anarchiste. Max Stirner* (1904); H. Wolf, *Geschichte des antiken Sozialismus und Individualismus* (1909); J. Dewey, *Individualism Old and New* (1931); E. Ehrhardt, "Individualism", *HERE*, VII, cols.

218–22; F. Hayek, *Individualism True and False* (1946); R. Devane, *The Failure of Individualism* (1948); M. Niemeyer, *The One and the Many in the Social Order according to St. Thomas Aquinas* (1951); A. Läpple, *Der Einzelne in der Kirche. Wesenszüge einer Theologie des Einzelnen nach John Henry Kardinal Newman* (1952); B. Russell, *Authority and the Individual* (1960); G. von Rad, *Old Testament Theology,* 2 vols. (1962–65); E. Cassirer, *Individual and Cosmos in Renaissance Philosophy* (1964); W. Ullmann, *Individual and Society in the Middle Ages* (1966); U. Viglino, *Enciclopedia Cattolica,* VI, cols. 1856–60; G. Morra, *Enciclopedia Filosofica,* II, cols. 1356 ff.; A. Knoll in *LTK,* V, cols. 653 f.; K. Jaspers, *Socrates, Buddha, Confucius, Jesus* (1966).

Heinz Robert Schlette

INDULGENCES

The question of indulgences offers dogmatic, psychological and pastoral difficulties. To have a sound basis for discussion, we begin with the teaching of the Church, always bearing in mind, however, that most of the declarations of the magisterium (all, in fact, except the Council of Trent, which is very reserved) are not irreformable decisions and that they are often the echo of a theology which is not in all respects of a strictly binding character. As regards the notion of temporal punishments due to sin, reference must be made throughout to the article on "Sin II, Punishment", since otherwise misunderstandings would be almost inevitable.

A. Official Teaching of the Church

The fullest description of indulgences by the magisterium is found in *CIC*, can. 911 (similarly Leo X: *D* 740a): the remission before God of a temporal punishment for sins of which the guilt has been forgiven (at least by the end of the work to which the indulgence is attached: can. 925), granted by ecclesiastical authority out of the Treasury of the Church, to the living by way of absolution, to the dead by way of suffrage. Though the details of this description have not been defined, it has been defined as a doctrine of the faith against Wycliffe, Huss and the Reformers that the Church has authority *(potestas)* to grant indulgences and that they are to be retained in the Church and are salutary for the faithful (Trent: *D* 989, 1471; cf. also *D* 622, 676–8, 757–62).

The pronouncements of the magisterium also indicate that in addition to the state of grace (cf. *D* 551, 676), further conditions are required for the gaining of an indulgence: baptism, freedom from excommunication, performance of prescribed work, and at least a general intention of gaining the indulgence (*CIC,* can. 925). Indulgences relate not only to the Church's canonical penalties but to the punishments due before God for sins (*D* 759, 1540). They are granted by the Church out of the "Treasury of the Church", which consists of the merits of Christ and of the saints (this was first declared by Clement VI in 1343: *D* 550–2; cf. 740a, 757, 1060, 1541, 2193). The power of the Pope (and, in dependence on him, that of other ecclesiastical authorities: *CIC,* can. 912, 239 § 1 n. 24; 247 n. 2; 349 § 2 n. 2) to grant indulgences is designated simply as *potestas* or as "power of the keys" (*D* 740a), which last term must doubtless (because of indulgences for the dead) be understood in a broad sense. There is no binding official declaration of the sense of the terms "per modum absolutionis", "per modum suffragii".

Theologians interpret the first in various ways (formerly, by reference to the remission of what are now hypothetical ecclesiastical penalties from which "absolution was given"; "payment" *[solutio]* of punishments in purgatory out of the Treasury of the Church; direct release from punishment, etc.). As regards the "per modum suffragii", cf. Sixtus IV: *D* 723a. The practice of the Church shows that there is a scale of indulgences, some of which are characterized by the provisions of the ancient canonical penances of the Church and are called "indulgentia partialis" (*CIC,* can. 921 § 2), while the others are called "indulgentia plenaria" (l. c. and can. 926). A strictly official definition of the precise sense of this distinction has never been given by the magisterium. It is still disputed among theologians whether the plenary indulgence is simply the remission of all canonical penalties with an effect in purgatory which cannot be determined more precisely (Cajetan and a few others) or is intended directly to remit all punishment for sin before God (most theologians), though whether this intention is fully achieved in the individual instance remains quite undecided (cf. *CIC,* can. 929; Gregory XVI, in Cavallerra, n. 1273).

It is certain that indulgences for the dead are of benefit to them "per modum suffragii" (Sixtus IV, 1476: *D* 723a; 740a, 762, 1542; *CIC*, can. 911). No authoritative decision has been given regarding *the way* they help the dead. In order to understand indulgences, reference must also be made to the doctrines of the temporal punishment due to sin and of purgatory. The Council of Trent defined that guilt *(culpa)* and punishment incurred by sin *(poena)* are not identical and are therefore not necessarily remitted simultaneously (*D* 535, 807, 840, 904, 922–925). There is no official explicit and definite doctrine regarding the more precise nature of punishment due to sin.

B. Scripture

As will become even clearer later, it is not correct to try to draw a scriptural proof in the proper sense from Mt 16 and 18. These passages, which are classical texts for the sacrament of penance, would prove, if they proved anything about indulgences, that in the sacrament of penance all punishment for sin can be remitted judicially, which is heretical. It is rather to be noted that a) it is a familiar idea in Scripture that the overcoming of the whole culpable alienation from God of a human being in his whole many-sided nature can be a long moral process ("to seek" the Lord; long practice of penance; penitential liturgy; dependence of the remission of all "guilt" on subsequent manner of life, etc.). This is all the more so, because guilt can have consequences which are not simply extinguished by conversion to the God of mercy, so that the seriousness of penance can even consist precisely in the humble, deliberate acceptance of judgment (1 Cor 5:5; 1 Tim 1:20; 1 Cor 11:32; Rev 2:22f.), which one does not simply escape by conversion, for in fact the latter can even be the consequence of the former (*TWNT*, IV, p. 983). If according to Scripture there are in fact punishments imposed by God for sin which are not cancelled when the guilt is forgiven (cf. Gen 3:17–19 with Wis 10:2; Num 20:12 with 27:13f.; 2 Sam 12:10–14), then at all events it cannot be a fundamental and consistent norm that God's forgiveness of guilt involves *ipso facto* remission of the consequences of guilt and therefore of punishments due to sin. b) The Church can

support this long process of reconciliation by its prayer. This is shown by the liturgical penitential prayers of the OT including those for the dead (2 Macc 12:43–46). The NT also bears witness to this (Mt 6:12; 1 Jn 3:20–22, 5:16; 2 Tim 1:18; Jas 5:16, etc.). c) A prayer of the Church as the sacred community of God's victorious mercy, made in the name of Jesus, has the firm promise of being heard (Mt 18:19f.; Mk 11:24; Jn 15:16; 1 Jn 5:15; Jas 5:16, etc.), to which the only limits are those set by the nature of God who hears prayer in his own sovereign way, and the willingness of the person for whom the prayer is offered.

C. Tradition

As the nature of indulgences is complex, having grown historically from various factors, we must first see how indulgences arose in the course of history (and were not simply discovered).

1. The Church's most ancient theology of penance clearly implies that a) the blotting-out of post-baptismal sins is not simply "remission" of sins, as in baptism, but presupposes a severe personal penitential activity of the sinner, even though (as Augustine clearly states) this activity absolutely requires to be based on the grace of Christ. Though in antiquity no terminological distinction was yet drawn between guilt and the penalty it entails, the foundation for the distinction was laid, for from the very beginning of a man's conversion no more doubt was felt about his salvation, yet a long penance was considered necessary (the distinction is in fact found substantially in the Protestant distinction between justification and sanctification). At least from the 2nd century onward, the Church supervised this subjective atonement by the sinner and regulated it according to the gravity of his guilt, and so the consciousness of possessing authority to determine works of penance, individually or generally, and to adapt them to the individual sinner, was very early taken as a matter of course. Severe penances being the rule for each sin, the coming of frequent confession in the early Middle Ages brought with it the counterpoise of "redemptory" works in individual cases. b) This process of purification could be supported by the prayer of the Church (whether of a more official, or

a more private kind, the intercession of the martyrs). Such intercession took place in an officially regulated liturgical manner (by bishop and people) and was certain of being heard, insofar as the hearing depended on it. This intercession was not primarily the "form" of the sacrament of penance. That form consists of reconciliation with the Church and so with God. The intercession supported the subjective endeavour of the sinner to make atonement.

2. In the period of transition from public to private penance (6th–10th century), a) reconciliation was gradually brought forward to the beginning of the Church's sacramental penitential discipline and yet a personal performance of penance was required, subsequent to reconciliation. That inevitably underlined the distinction between guilt and punishment. b) Even independently of the actual penitential proceedings, the sinner was assured of the Church's intercession in solemn but not in the proper sense jurisdictional forms (the original meaning of the absolutions from Gregory the Great onwards). c) Through the practice of commutations and redemptions of canonical penances (scale of penances), which was not a purely disciplinary measure but concerned the Church's insistence on undergoing the punishment due before God for sin, there was inevitably an increased awareness that the various ways of promoting the process of recovery of spiritual health and of sanctification are interchangeable.

3. Through the amalgamation of these traditional elements, the first actual indulgences appeared in practice and at first without theological reflection in France in the 11th century. The Church (bishops, Popes) assured believers in solemn and general form of its official intercession, and on that account, by an act of jurisdiction, simply remitted part or all of the particular person's canonical penance. The latter is not replaced by some other work of penance, even a more lenient one, as had been done in the remissions of penance for pilgrims to Rome in the 9th century. These must be regarded as redemptions. In contrast, the indulgenced work must rather be regarded merely as the ground of the special intercession-*absolutio*. The indulgence took place outside the sacrament of penance by a general offer, in the conviction that the efficacy of the intercessory prayer for propitiatory sanctification of the sinner, was the same as would have resulted from his doing penance on his own behalf.

In this sense the first actual indulgences were on the one hand a true act of jurisdiction (remission of a real canonical penance) and yet from the start were regarded (on account of the "absolution"-intercession linked to this act of jurisdiction) as effectual non-sacramental remission before God of temporal punishment due to sin. From the point of view of historical development it is the linking of these two acts which constituted indulgences as such. The connection of indulgences with the priest's intercessory prayer in the sacrament of penance and with the practice of redemptions and commutations explains why indulgences were not at first regarded as the Pope's prerogative but were granted by bishops and confessors in carrying out their office. The slow transition from redemptions conceded very leniently, to indulgences, explains why the performance of some work was always insisted on as an indispensable condition of an indulgence. It also explains why even into the 13th century indulgences were regarded as a concession to the imperfect, which better Christians should not claim. In the transitional period it is not always possible to distinguish between a lenient commutation and an actual indulgence. Once the various elements had coalesced to form the firm concept of an indulgence, it was no longer to be expected that attention would be explicitly directed towards the *intercessory* absolution. There was simply an awareness of the power to remit punishment due to sin, without much reflection on the mode of its operation.

4. It was not till the 12th century that theological reflection was focussed on indulgences. At first it was opposed to them. Abelard contested the bishops' right to grant indulgences. The Synod of Sens censured him on that account but on grounds that are not clear. Similar opposition was shown by Peter of Poitiers and other early scholastic theologians. From the end of the 12th century onward the attitude of theology gradually became favourable, the chief argument being actual practice. With Huguccio (d. 1210) indulgences appear for the first time as an act of jurisdiction regarding the

actual punishment due before God to sins. For a long time it was not clear why the suffrages of the Church were an adequate substitute for the effect that would have been produced in the next world by the remitted canonical penance. Nor was it clear what relation there was between the good work imposed as a condition, and the efficacy of the indulgence. Was it to be regarded as a redemption, or as a mere condition of an effect which itself derived exclusively from the power of the keys? Before the great age of Scholasticism the prevailing opinion seems to have been that indulgences possess their transcendent efficacy not because of a direct power of the Church to absolve, but only *per modum suffragii*. A new phase in the doctrine of indulgences arose when the idea of the Treasury of the Church was explicitly worked out (it is found in Hugo of St.-Cher, 1230). This made it possible to indicate more clearly what replaced the remitted penance. When it was added that the Church had a lawful claim to this Treasury and had jurisdiction to carry the claim into effect, the former difficulties appeared at an end, and the doctrine of indulgences as we still know it today could be developed. Previously the Church had only prayed for the remission of temporal punishment due to sin, and had excused a canonical penance on that account. Now, however, the remission of punishment could be regarded as occurring in an act of jurisdiction administering the Treasury of the Church authoritatively — as an owner disposes of his property — and consequently with unfailing efficacy (Albert, Bonaventure, Aquinas). On this basis it was possible for the relation between indulgences and the remission of canonical penances gradually to become so tenuous that at least some theologians (Billot, for example), excluded it entirely from the essence of an indulgence. For the same reason, after St. Thomas's time, the granting of indulgences became increasingly independent of the sacrament of penance, and a prerogative of the Pope, because only the Pope (or those empowered by him) could administer the Treasury of the Church. Earlier, when it had also (not solely!) been a question of remitting canonical penance, all who imposed such penances (confessors or, at least, bishops) could grant indulgences on their own authority. On the other hand, if the Church can administer the Treasury of the Church juridically, it becomes more difficult to solve the problem why and to what extent some good work is required as a condition for gaining an indulgence. This was really only intelligible in connection with the old commutations and redemptions of canonical penances, but not in the new jurisdictional theory.

5. Subsequent development of practice in the Middle Ages bears the following marks. a) Multiplication of indulgences accompanied by continual lessening of the indulgenced works. It is true that it was maintained that some work was a necessary condition on the part of the Church, though any reasonable cause could be considered sufficient for granting an indulgence (*Summa Theologica*, Suppl., q. 25, a. 2). b) The appearance of "plenary" indulgences. Towards the end of the 11th century the Church began to promise the Crusaders complete remission of punishment for sin (Urban II; Mansi, XX, 816), and in this way plenary indulgences arose (Boniface VIII: first Jubilee plenary indulgence, A.D. 1300). c) Since theologians and canonists from the 13th century onwards had been teaching the application of indulgences to the dead (cf. St. Thomas in IV *Liber Sententiarum*, Dist. 45 q. 2, a 2 sol. 2; *Summa Theologica*, Suppl., q. 71, a. 10), genuine papal grants of indulgences for the dead are made from the middle of the 15th century. d) The use made of indulgences for fiscal purposes. In view of the biblical and traditional praise of alms-giving, there could be no intrinsic objection to alms-giving as the good work prescribed for gaining an indulgence, and in fact indulgences for alms-giving are found as early as the 11th century. In the later Middle Ages, however, on account of their material usefulness for Church purposes, such indulgences were multiplied beyond all measure, and were regarded as a convenient source of money to be tapped at will. This was often exploited simoniacally by those who preached indulgences in a theologically frivolous and exaggerated way, as the Council of Trent expressly observes (Mansi, XXXIII, 193f.; cf. also *D* 983).

D. THEOLOGICAL INTERPRETATION OF THE NATURE OF INDULGENCES

It is permissible to doubt whether an adequate theological interpretation has yet been achieved. That is not surprising, because practice was in advance of theory and the reality involved is a many-sided one.

1. Negatively it may be said, contrary to the view of the vast majority of present-day theologians, that the Church's power of granting indulgences (even to the living) is not a power of jurisdiction in the strict sense, as regards the temporal punishment due to sin in the eyes of God, and that the appeal to Mt 16 is, therefore, not well-founded. Otherwise as regards the punishment due to sin, the Church would be able to do more outside the sacrament of penance and its judicial power than within it, yet the remission of such punishment is one of the very purposes of the sacrament. Nor would it be clear why the Church should not link the two powers so as to remit guilt and punishment entirely in every sacramental act. But that is contrary to tradition and to the teaching of the Council of Trent. Besides, indulgences for the living and for the dead would be different in kind. That does not mean that we deny that an act of jurisdiction was originally involved in indulgences, i.e., the remission of canonical penance. Nowadays, of course, this is merely hypothetical, and simply serves to express the different degrees of intensity with which the Church promises its intercession. It would also follow from the jurisdiction theory that the remission of punishment for sin in the sacrament of penance is less extensive, less certain and less readily to be assumed, than in indulgences. But that is contrary to the dignity of the sacrament and contrary to the fact that an indulgence, historically speaking, is simply that part of the sacrament which the Church can perform apart from the sacrament, and which consequently can be given distinct form. Besides, the theory which we are rejecting had to accept the difficulty and improbability that an *(ex supposito)* independent jurisdictional authority of the Church, derived from Christ (cf. *D* 989), was not exercised at all during 1000 years. For the regulation and mitigation of canonical penances, which always existed, is not the same thing as the granting of indulgences.

Finally, we must bear in mind that two formally and totally distinct causes cannot be assumed for the one effect. But it cannot be doubted, and has always been admitted in theology, that a charity which is perfect in all respects, which is not merely initially present in the intention but strives to integrate into itself the manifold dimensions and efforts of man's being — and hence is not necessarily there even at the death of the justified — means the remission of all the "temporal punishments due to sin". But if this principle is correct, then an indulgence can be nothing else than a (very important) aid accorded to the repentant sinner, to enable him to attain this charity which blots out everything but which is not necessarily present at the moment of justification. It is an (intercessory) aid for the gaining of the grace needed for such charity. In this way an indulgence ceases to be envisaged as a juridical process which is completely or to a great extent independent of the progress of man to maturity in morality and holiness and which would therefore deal with a restricted relationship of man to God. The notion of such a partial relationship was unhappy, since it implied that it could be regulated independently of love of God, whereas in reality the whole relationship to God is determined by charity. This way of integrating indulgences into the one process of faith and love which embraces the whole man and is therefore multi-dimensional, does not diminish the significance of indulgences, as will be made still clearer below. But this interpretation can resolve the justifiable inhibitions which are often felt today with regard to the conventional theology of indulgences — and a resulting practice which is often a matter of crude calculations. This approach also enables us to see clearly — as is *not* the case in the ordinary theory in spite of its well-intentioned efforts to do justice to this view-point — why indulgences are not in any way detrimental to the true spirit of works of penance. This last is what the help of the Church precisely aims at, because the integration of the whole reality of man into charity, which is perfected in this way, necessarily implies penance in the sinner.

2. The nature of an indulgence consists, then, in the special intercession continually made by the Church, in its liturgy and in the prayers of its members, on behalf of the complete reconciliation of its members, an intercession which by an indulgence is solemnly and in a special way applied to a particular member. Because that intercession is the prayer of holy Church itself and concerns a benefit which is indubitably in har-

mony with the will of God, it is in itself always certain of being heard, unlike the prayer of an individual sinful human being who does not know whether he is asking as he ought for what he ought; its only limit, but a real one, is therefore the receptivity of the person for whom it is made. If one remembers that even a "prayer" — as in the case of the anointing of the sick — can be an *opus operatum,* that only "actual" graces are asked for in indulgences, that every *opus operatum* is limited by the disposition of the recipient, then in the theory of indulgences here put forward there is nothing to prevent our granting the character of an *opus operatum* to an indulgence, as is generally done today in theology — though without making it sacramental.

On this basis, too, there is a difference between indulgences for the living and for the dead. The latter are not only beyond the Church's jurisdiction, but in other respects are in a special position, which means that the efficacy of the Church's official expiatory intercession for them is of a different kind. It is only indirect, through the merit of the living gainer of the indulgence, and through the recipient's merit, acquired earlier in life but no longer susceptible of increase, in relation to this indulgence (cf. Sixtus IV in *D* 723a).

3. On this basis the role of the "Treasury of the Church" in indulgences becomes clear. If we were to suppose that it is utilized by an act of jurisdiction, this would amount to "paying off" the individual items of punishment due, by partial reparations thought of in an equally fragmentary way (cf. Billot). On closer examination, such a conception is an impossible one and is rejected nowadays (e.g., by Galtier). But when the Church intercedes, it necessarily does so as the Body of Christ in union with the dignity and sacrifice of its head, and as the Church which is holy in all its "saints", that is, it "appeals" to the Treasury of the Church. Nothing is in the proper sense "paid out" of that Treasury, but appeal is always made globally, and consequently it is not lessened but increased thereby. Galtier is therefore right in emphasizing that the recourse to the Treasury of the Church is made in every case of remission of guilt and punishment, and is therefore not something peculiar to indulgences. Hence the "Treasury of the Church" is nothing else

than the salvific will of God, which aims at bringing all men to perfect charity. And such charity includes reparation and the elimination of the "punishments for sin", since this salvific will exists as centred on the redemption wrought by Christ and the holiness of the whole Church which depends on this redemption but is also present through it. And this holiness implies a dynamism which tends to the perfect charity which eliminates all the consequences of sin in every member of this Church.

4. The manner in which this intercession of the Church is to be considered efficacious in remitting the penalties of sin, and how exactly the certainty of an indulgence's efficacy is to be estimated, essentially depends on the precise idea formed of the nature of punishment for sin. If this is viewed solely as retribution, brought about by the justice of God specially for that purpose, but without significance for the moral purification and perfection of man, its remission would have to be viewed as God's simply waiving its actual infliction. As regards the way of representing the efficacy of indulgences, that would mean that on the part of the person gaining them, the only condition to be taken into account would be the cessation of actual attachment to sin. In that case indulgences would be an easier and more certain method of effacing the penalties of sin than personal penance and growth in holiness. If, however, the penalties of sin are regarded as various features of a person's interior and external condition brought about by sin, which are not removed or overcome by the first conversion (remission of the stain of guilt), and if these, through their disharmony with the whole objective, divinely-created reality (as the external instrument of punishment), both here and after death, produce suffering which is both retributive and in itself medicinal, then the remission by indulgences of the temporal punishment due to sin must be regarded as a divine help to discharging more rapidly and salutarily the "real" penalty of sin, in the sense defined. On this view, more conditions have to be fulfilled for this laborious conquest and total inner purification. And this latter does not necessarily imply an increase of merit and grace, but simply their increased influence on a person's whole state, such as can also be thought to occur in purgatory. An indulgence is only effective

inasmuch as the willingness is there to undertake an ever deeper and sanctifying purification of the whole person, over and above the remission of the stain of guilt as such. This view makes it clear why indulgences and personal penance are not detrimental to each other, because an indulgence is seen as the Church's help to more intensive and consequently more rapid and salutary penance, not as a substitute, lessening the need for penance.

E. Consequences for Pastoral Theology

1. The first thing is to note the fact, soberly, that interest in indulgences is largely diminishing in the Church, even in circles where religion is devoutly practised. The genuine religious concerns of Catholics have profoundly changed in form, being transferred to the celebration of the Eucharist, personal prayer and a truly Christian steadfastness in face of the tragic hardships of ordinary existence. It may also be noted that people today find it harder to feel a share of responsibility for their dead relations and friends. This may be due to the individualistic attitudes of modern culture (cf. K. Rahner, "Verehrung der Heiligen", *Geist und Leben* 37 [1964], pp. 325–40). It is unlikely that official commendations of indulgences or the granting of new ones would do much to change this situation.

2. Nonetheless, if indulgences are to be really retained, as the Council of Trent teaches, and not just officially upheld, the following points should be noted.

a) Efforts in this direction, justifiable though they be, should be prudently restricted, since otherwise too much pastoral time and energy would be consumed which should today be devoted to other objects.

The actual forms of the granting of indulgences (their frequency, the use made of them to recommend other secondary goals such as particular devotions, the number especially of "plenary" indulgences) need to be courageously though prudently revised. An obvious question, which should not cause much alarm, is whether the distinction between plenary and partial indulgences should not be abandoned. In any case, the various degrees of partial indulgences seems to have lost all religious significance today, though they still have a strange vogue, behind which no genuine principle can be

discerned. Plenary indulgences at any rate — supposing indeed that the term should be retained — should be linked with an act of religion which really corresponds to the significance of such a grant.

b) The doctrine of the communion of saints, of the veneration of saints, of the punishments of sin, of the necessity and blessing of personal penance and finally of indulgences should be preached in such a way that it fits into the whole framework of the Christian life. The doctrine of indulgences should be made really intelligible in this whole context and hence "practicable". A formal juridical notion of indulgences would not lend itself to this end.

c) Forms and practices should be devised, such as prayer of intercession, penitential devotions, etc., which will help the faithful to recognize through their concrete experience that the Church, as the body of Christ and fellowship of seekers of salvation, is always interceding by its prayers for the individual members in their perils and struggles. Once this task of the Church, which is also that of the individual, is brought home to the faithful in the concrete, they will once more be able to see the meaning and the blessing of what we call indulgences. For they are one way in which the Church, in its concern for their salvation, thinks of them and prays for them.

See also *Ecclesiastical Penalties, Sin* II, *Penance, Works, Purgatory, Salvation* IV A, *Communion of Saints, Saints* II.

BIBLIOGRAPHY. Thomas Aquinas, *Supplement,* 25–27; Suarez, *Opera Omnia,* XXII, pp. 979–1185; P. Galtier, "Indulgences", *Dictionnaire Apologétique de la Foi Catholique,* II, cols. 718–52; E. Magnin, "Indulgences", *DTC,* VII, cols. 1594–636; B. Poschmann, *Der Ablass im Licht der Bussgeschichte* (1948); P. Galtier, *De Paenitentia* (3rd ed., 1950), pp. 517–48; S. de Angelis, *De Indulgentiis* (2nd ed., 1950); E. Campbell, *Indulgences* (1953); K. Rahner, "Remarks on the Theology of Indulgences", *Theological Investigations,* II (1963), pp. 175–202; W. Herbst, *Indulgences* (1956); P. Anciaux, "De significatione praxis indulgentiarum in Ecclesia", *Collectanea Mechliniensia* 29 (1959), pp. 270 ff.; P. F. Palmer, *Sacraments and Forgiveness: History and Doctrinal Development of Penance, Extreme Unction and Indulgences* (1960); M. Schmaus, *Katholische Dogmatik,* IV/1 (6th ed., 1964), pp. 678–94; M. Lackmann, *Überlegungen zur Lehre vom "Schatz der Kirche",* Arbeiten zur kirchlichen Wiedervereinigung 2 (1965), pp. 75–157.

Karl Rahner

INDUSTRIALISM

Industrialism has brought about such a fundamental change in man's way of living and civilization that modern anthropologists (A. Gehlen and others) compare it with the change that took place in prehistoric times in the transition from hunting and food-gathering to a settled agricultural way of life. With industrialism man has crossed a "second absolute threshold of civilization".

This transition embraces — for the first time in human history — not merely individual cultural groups, but the entire world including the "developing countries". It is thus global and universal (H. Freyer).

This change in human living is not to be ascribed solely to "technology". The ground had been prepared for it since the end of the Middle Ages by the separation of thought from purely religious foundations in secularization and humanism with the result that tradition was replaced by the application of critical reason *(ratio)* and experiment as the "natural" founts of knowledge. Corresponding to this, there arose the notion of a "natural" society, as, for example, that of liberalism. The *ratio* of the commercial era is also prior to that of the technological.

Seen from the purely external point of view, "industrial society" is characterized by a special technique of producing goods and organizing work. Its most important instrument is the machine (mechanization of production), its scene of operations the "factory".

The factory age had its first beginnings in England with the development of the steam engine (1765–85) and the almost simultaneous mechanization of the production of textiles (spinning-jenny, 1768, and mechanized loom, 1785). Before the end of the 18th century it had come to be known as the "industrial revolution" — a name that referred in particular to the social phenomena that accompanied it (proletarianization).

Industry was then introduced in rapid succession into the North-Western and Central European countries and into North America: it took its shape in the early period of extreme capitalism after the model of liberalism. Today, as well as Russia and some of its satellite states, Japan, Canada and Italy can also be numbered among the industrial countries. It may be said, however, that there is at the present time no continent and no developing country which is not seriously concerning itself with industrialization. Even in feudally organized and agrarian countries it is regarded as the road that is to lead them out of hunger and destitution (e.g., China, India, South America, large areas of Africa, etc.).

The industrial revolution will continue in the future, for three decisive reasons: first because of the ceaseless expansion of production throughout the entire world, then because of the continually increasing productivity, and, finally, because of the possibility of increase in the world's population such as has never before been experienced in the world's history. Effective counter-forces do not exist. It will therefore remain a distinguishing mark of the "present epoch" (H. Freyer).

1. The first wave of industrialization was confined to a few sectors of production: chiefly the textile industry, the machine industry and mining. The great increase in the productivity of human work through "mechanization" very soon led in these sectors to structural (technological) unemployment which was to last for almost a century and a half (most recently in the world economic crisis of the 1930s). It was only gradually that the oversupply of labour was balanced by the continuing expansion of production in the industrial countries. The development of technology brought ever new inventions, new processes, new products, new materials and new sources of power. A second great wave came (in the last quarter of the 19th century) with the practical application of electricity, both as a source of power and as a means of long-distance communication. The internal combustion engine (1876) came into general use only after the First World War (at present over 100 million motor-powered vehicles in the world). The chemical industry developed over the same period (dyes, artificial manures, etc.), then radio, television and household appliances (cookers, refrigerators, washing machines); in most recent times the industrial production of synthetic materials and electrotechnology. A continuously expanding power industry provides the needed sources of energy, both primary (coal, oil, natural gas and water-power) and secondary (electric current for power and light). Here there is a disequilibrium which is, in other respects too, a characteristic world-wide

phenomenon: half of the total world demand for energy exists in North America, one quarter in Europe, one-sixth in the Soviet block countries and only one-twelfth in the entire remainder of the world (Asia, Africa, South America and Australia). The expansion of every branch of industrial production has proceeded so rapidly in the leading industrial countries that the unemployment problem has been replaced since the end of World War II by a decided shortage of manpower especially in the countries of the European Economic Community (the Common Market).

2. The amount produced by an agricultural worker in the U.S.A. has gone up two to three times since 1870, while that of an industrial worker has gone up five to six times (on an average). This so-called productivity increase is nevertheless only an average figure. In certain sectors it is much higher. For the production of a car in 1910, 15,000 hours of direct labour were needed: in 1950 the figure was already less than 1,000.

The increase in productivity is the chief cause of the rise in the standard of living. It has made possible rising wages with hours of work shorter by half than those previously obtaining. It secured the effective liberation of the worker from poverty and distress. Even today it must in a developed economy exceed a minimum annual increase of 3 % to 3.5 % if it is to meet workers' expectations of a further increase in living standards. For this reason too — in spite of the considerable danger of exaggeration — "automation" is necessary since it is but the final step in mechanization. It makes possible too a large expansion in the work of the public authorities and the number of clerical workers as well as the development of a "second line" of industry in the services (transport, banks, insurance, self-service stores), as also in the sectors of industry devoted to leisure and entertainment. These taken together already employ, e.g. in the U.S.A., just as many workers as do the productive industries properly so called. This development too will spread to all industrial countries (including those of the Soviet block).

3. The most clearly visible result of industrialization and the changes it has brought about (as, for example, in modern medicine and hygiene) is the population increase that it has made possible. In less than two cen-turies (since 1770) the world population has quadrupled itself and, if the same trend continues undisturbed until A.D. 2,000, it will have doubled itself again and reached a figure of over 6,000 millions. The population is a cause of anxiety at present in most "developing countries" so that one can rightly speak of a "population explosion". Here too all hopes are put in industrialization. In the highly industrial countries — in the so-called second phase of industrialization — a considerable decline in the birth-rate took place. The white races have increased seven-fold over the past three hundred years, but in the future their further increase will be small. The "population increase" of the immediate future will take place largely among the "coloured" peoples.

The situation that arose in the first liberal-capitalist period of industrialization (proletariat) brought about a strong contrary social movement: socialist parties (mostly Marxist) and trade unions. Yet at the same time the scientific world (cf. the German *Verein für Sozialpolitik* founded 1872) and the Churches entered the lists on behalf of the destitute workers. Pope Leo XIII wrote his encyclical *Rerum Novarum* (1891) on the social question. Nevertheless a modern body of Catholic social teaching, capable of finding acceptance outside the Church as well, came into existence only in recent times. An essential part in this development was played by the publication of the encyclicals *Quadragesimo Anno* (Pope Pius XI, 1931) and *Mater et Magistra* (Pope John XXIII, 1961).

Since the beginning of the 19th century the State (starting with England) has issued protective legislation to eliminate the worst abuses (child labour from the age of five, the truck system, etc.). The miserable subsistence wages lasted until *c.* 1850. Structural unemployment too remained characteristic of industrialism up to World War II — but particularly in the period of world depression around 1930.

State social policy also helped to alleviate the lot of the proletariat. In this, Germany led the way: following on the Kaiser's message of 17 November 1881 there came in quick succession the introduction of health insurance, accident insurance, disability and old-age insurance, and later (1927) unemployment insurance. Today the resulting re-distribution of income comes to about 13 % of the German social product (in France,

Austria and England it is even higher). Especially the periods of inflation of the last four decades necessarily led to the welfare and social security State of today. As well as this, a continuously expanding system of industrial legislation (labour legislation, industrial council legislation, legislation on collective bargaining and collective agreements) further helped to remove the effects of the original disintegration of all social bonds. In individual countries far-reaching measures were also introduced on behalf of the family. In the past fifteen years (in the Federal Republic of Germany since the currency reform) the standard of living (especially of workers) has risen in the leading industrial countries in a way hitherto unforeseen. The average income of a worker increased in purchasing power in that period until it is now three times that of 1890 (there has been a similar increase in the U.S.A. between 1901 and 1956).

All this, however, cannot conceal the fact that modern mass society has not yet found its inner equilibrium. All too quickly — practically in three or four generations — the industrial revolution has changed not only technology and the economy but the entire inner structure of human society, its understanding of itself and its accepted moral standards. At any rate it is a fact today that industrial society, as well in its consumption patterns as in its use of leisure time, has fallen a victim to practical materialism, to no less a degree than has the East to theoretical materialism.

See also *Technology, Humanism, Secularization, Liberalism, Social Movements, Leisure, Materialism.*

BIBLIOGRAPHY. R. Tawney, *Religion and the Rise of Capitalism* (1926); T. S. Ashton, *The Industrial Revolution* (1948); A. Toynbee, *The World and the West* (1953); A. Zimmermann, *Overpopulation* (1957); E. H. Phelps Brown, *The Growth of British Industrial Relations* (1959); A. Gehlen, *Die Seele im technischen Zeitalter* (1959); N. Drogat: The Challenge of Hunger (1962); A. W. Gouldner and R. A. Peterson, *Notes on Technology and the Moral Order* (1962); P. Hoffman, *World Without Want* (1962); P. Moussa, *The Underprivileged Nations* (1962); F. Quinn, *The Ethical Aftermath of Automation* (1962); B. Hoselitz and W. Moore, eds., *Industrialization and Society* (1963); E. P. Thomson, *The Making of the English Working Class* (1964); S. G. Checkland, *The Rise of Industrial Society in England* (1965); H. Freyer, *Die Schwelle der Zeiten* (1965); E. J. Hogsbaum, *Labouring Men* (1965).

Max Pietsch

INFALLIBILITY

A. NOTION

The term infallibility very often is understood to imply also sinlessness, a mistake which had to be denounced by Bishop Gasser as the official *relator* at Vatican I (see Mansi, LII, 1219). "Inerrancy" might be better, but this is usually reserved for the same quality in Scripture. The positive content of the term infallibility is simply "truth" or "truthfulness". In the following exposition we continue to use the word infallibility.

Infallibility must be distinguished from inspiration, which is attributed only to the attestation of revelation in the Church of the Apostles and the canonical books of the Old and New Testaments. Infallibility is an element of the *"assistentia" Spiritus Sancti*, granted to the Church of post-apostolic times.

Since the closing of revelation does not mean that providence ceases to watch over the further progress of Church history and the history of dogmas, infallibility may be regarded as a corollary to the development of doctrine. If we further consider "truth" in its biblical sense of fidelity, the fidelity with which God makes good his promises in history, the infallibility of the Church can then be provisionally described as the historical form which the fidelity of God takes in being true to his historical revelation which was brought to its unsurpassable conclusion in Christ, since he uses the Church to this end.

B. THEOLOGICAL CONTEXT

Though infallibility is predicated of the Church, it should not be treated as one of the attributes of the Church, since it is rather the general condition of their possibility, especially of the indefectibility. Hence infallibility must be linked with the possibility of the Church in general. Since the Church is the recipient and mediator of revelation, which means that theological knowledge has an ecclesial dimension, infallibility is a transcendental element in theology. It is related to theological knowledge in general as the guarantee of dogmatic security. Hence the question of infallibility belongs to fundamental theology, from the point of view of theological methodology.

The relevant notion of truth here, and the

treatment of infallibility in fundamental theology prevent over-hasty applications of the notion in particular cases, either by restricting it to special regions in ecclesiology or to particular organs of the Church. In principle, the whole Church must be envisaged when infallibility is spoken of. When the concept is taken in this wide sense, limited only by its being distinguished from revelation and from the inspiration which is ordained to revelation, all the historical statements can be integrated with no need to range them at once under the heading of any specific notion of infallibility, such as that proposed by Vatican I.

C. BIBLICAL FOUNDATIONS

The starting-point can only be the promise of the Lord, who is himself the truth (Jn 1:14; 14:6; 1 Jn 5:20) and who entrusted to his community the word of truth. The farewell discourses in Jn, especially the promise of the Paraclete as the Spirit of truth (Jn 14:17; 15:26; 16:13), are the most important proofs. The Spirit leads the disciples to all truth, remains with them and enables them to remain in the word and in the truth (Jn 8:32; 14:17; 17:17; 2 Jn 1–3; see also Mt 28:19f.). Pauline theology provides the notion of the "Gospel", which is God's word and power (Rom 1:16; 2 Cor 6:7; 13:8; Gal 1:7; 1 Thess 2:2), and which may never be falsified (2 Cor 11:4; Gal 1:6; 2:5). According to 1 Tim, the Church is the "pillar and the ground of truth" (3:15). In the synoptic Gospels we read of the teaching commission given to the disciples, with whose words the Lord ultimately identifies himself (Lk 10:16) and whose faith is to be strengthened by Peter (Lk 22:32). To sum up, it may be said that the post-Easter community reflected on the reliability of its faith and preaching, and took cognizance of the promise and of its duty to remain in the truth.

Mt 16 + 18 are skirted??

D. HISTORICAL PERSPECTIVES

The history of the development of the notion of infallibility in dogma has yet to be written, though there are a number of special studies and surveys which open up valuable perspectives (see bibliography). Infallibility was not treated of for its own sake in the patristic age, though the allusions to the "rule of faith", the "deposit of faith" and the Apos-

tolic Succession show how closely the notion of "Church" and "truth" were linked, as also appears from the practice of excluding heresy (see especially Tertullian, Irenaeus, Vincent of Lerins). The obligation of the Church towards the truth of the Gospel is brought out in particular at the Councils. As regards medieval theology, the change of meaning in the terms *fides* and *haeresis* is to be noted, and also the rareness of the occurrence of the term infallibility, mostly used in a nontechnical sense. But the teaching of theologians on the reality of infallibility must also be noted (e.g., Thomas Aquinas, *Summa Theologica,* II, II, q. 1, a. 2, 10; q. 2, a. 6 ad 3; *Quodlibeta,* IX, q. 1, a. 7). The Councils of Constance and of Basle are of importance, not merely because of the respect in which they were held and their continuing influence, which can still be seen to be at work in the 19th century, but also because of their permanent intrinsic importance as a counterpart to Vatican I in the history of the Councils. In the Conciliarist controversy the word infallibility was used in approximately the modern sense (J. de Turrecremata).

The Reformation stimulated reflection on infallibility, not merely by its opposition, but also by such positive approaches as that of Calvin. The controversial theology after Trent developed dialectically the notion of infallibility, through the Gallicanism of a Bossuet as well as through the works of J. Driedo, M. Cano and R. Bellarmine (among others). At the beginning of the 19th century the infallibility of the Church was universally taught, though the infallibility of the Pope was considered an open question in some quarters. That the whole people of God, including the laity, was involved in the real infallibility of the Church was clearly seen by such great theologians as Möhler, Newman and Scheeben. In the years preceding Vatican I the attribution of the most unrestricted form of infallibility imaginable to the Pope became the most widely held position. Vatican I had prepared a schema on the infallibility of the Church (Mansi, LI, 542f.; cf. LIII, 312–14), but succeeded only in defining the infallibility of the papal magisterium, in the dogmatic constitution *Pastor Aeternus* (D 1832–40, DS 3065–75). This result was due to some extent to the influence of the minority and to what R. Aubert calls the "third party". For the definition was that of infallibility and not that of the infallibilists. After the Council both supporters of the text like Manning and opponents like Döllinger went beyond the definition to underline one-sidedly the doctrine of infallibility (as the infallibility of the Pope). Vatican II re-affirmed the doctrine of Vatican I, but integrated it into the doctrine of the collegiality of the bishops united with the Pope and the doctrine of the Church as the people of God (*Lumen Gentium*, arts. 12, 18, 25).

E. Theological Explanation

Theological reflection on infallibility may well start with the constitution of Vatican II, *Dei Verbum,* on revelation, which considers the whole Church as the "hearing Church", *ecclesia discens,* prior to all differentiation (of offices etc.). In this sense, the infallibility of the Church in general can be described as "passive": it is the fact of the Church being rooted in and living by the word of God in the eschatological revelation which will never be withdrawn from the Church, since God remains faithful. The primary activity of the Church is "hearing", accepting the revelation which was given in words and events and which still resounds in the present day. The preaching, and especially the definitive preaching, is the second stage. The preaching, along with the promise of infallibility, forms as it were a testimony to an auditive experience.

1. From this point of view we may now ask who is the subject or who are the subjects of infallibility. The classic formulation of Scheeben is of interest here: "Infallibility belongs *radicaliter* only to the Holy Spirit who animates the whole body. It flows from the Spirit both into the teaching body and the body of the faithful" (I, no. 182). Hence the human subject so to speak of infallibility is the Church as a whole, because the Spirit lives and works in the Church as a whole. Since there is a certain order in the Church, infallibility conforms to the structure of the Church: the *whole Church,* in the organic unity of its parts, is subject of infallibility. Basing itself on the general priesthood of all the baptized, the Church is the hearing and teaching Church, and therefore the infallible Church, in all its members and offices up to the college of the bishops and the visible head of the Church, the Pope. It is the organized Church, with its various structures, equipped with hierarchical offices and urged on or criticized by the charismatic, which has received the gift of infallibility.

At this stage of reflection the question of an "inadequately distinct" independent or dependent infallibility of the episcopate as a whole may seem to be already superfluous, and the unity of the subject to be granted. But if we have to name the particular organs of authoritative teaching (see below, 3), we can deduce from the structure of the Church that they are the episcopate as a whole, in union with the Supreme Pontiff (or the Pope in union with the episcopal college of which he is the head). When these organs of the Church teach, the Church recognizes that it is *represented* in them. This is true of the ordinary and universal magisterium, with regard to the *ecclesia dispersa*. But this representation of universal Church is verified also in a special way, with regard to infallible teaching in an extraordinary way, when the organs of the teaching Church gather together as the *ecclesia congregata,* that is, when the bishops meet in a General Council. Both as regards convocation and assembly analogies may be drawn between Church and Council. The General Council, being the assembly of all local Churches to represent the unity of the "hearing" and the teaching Church (see *Dei Verbum,* art. 1) possesses the gift of infallibility. This does not mean that every Council must culminate in infallible truths of faith, that is, must strive to reach the heights of infallible pronouncements, as may be seen from Vatican II. Since the Council is to be regarded as representation of the whole Church and of each local Church, the dioceses are represented in the bishops, in the sense of being personified there, not that the bishops are merely deputies of the dioceses.

Though the Councils have been considered as representations of the Church since Tertullian (*De Paenitentia,* 13, 6–7), this way of understanding the infallibility of the papal office was slow to find acceptance. The main reason for this is to be sought in the preludes to Vatican I, in the ambiguities of its texts and a one-sided exposition of its doctrines. But as long ago as the early part of the 19th century, J. S. Drey could affirm that the Pope was "the one factor representing the whole Church" (*Apologetik,* 2nd ed., III, p. 311), while even at Vatican I Bishop Gasser gave an "official" explanation of infallibility which affirmed that the Pope was infallible only when exercising his supreme doctrinal authority, "ergo universalem ecclesiam repraesentans" (Mansi, LII, p. 1213). When the Pope teaches infallibly (and certain conditions have to be fulfilled if the infallibility is to take the form of definitive infallible pronouncements), he speaks as an organ of the Church, which is represented, concentrated and manifested in him.

This throws light on the much-debated statement, "Romani Pontificis definitiones ex sese, non autem ex consensu ecclesiae irreformabiles esse" (D 1839; see *Lumen Gentium*, art. 25). Its anti-Gallican background and the actual teaching of the Church (see, for instance, on General Councils, *CIC*, can. 228, para. 1) allow us to bring this affirmation into line with our considerations on how the Church is represented, even with regard to the definitive truths of faith pronounced by a General Council. This helps us to understand better that such infallible pronouncements are testimonies to the faith of the Church, and so draw on the *sensus ecclesiae* whose norm is Scripture and the tradition which expounds Scripture. They can never be isolated from the Church. This is true not only of the source of these pronouncements, but also of their goal. The end and object of a truth of faith is "that you may believe" (Jn 19:35). And thus infallibility does in fact aim at the *consensus ecclesiae*, and lives by it. This means that the "non ex consensu ecclesiae" must be restricted to exclude only a juridically verifiable act of ratification, a consensus formally expressed by the whole Church which alone would make the pronouncement infallible. In view of the theological and historical context, the statement in question means more precisely "non ex consensu subsequenti formali ecclesiae". Understood in this way, Vatican I leaves the way open for a proper appreciation of the nature of the acceptance of an infallible doctrine by the believing Church. It takes place primarily as a "real consent" (Newman): it is a process of understanding which passes through the stages of reflection. There is a formation of consensus in a historical process, with theology having a hermeneutical function. The infallible pronouncements come from the whole Church, challenge it by their "ex sese . . . irreformabiles" and are assimilated by its conscious faith. This consensus develops in the historical framework of the Church's perception of revelation and its authoritative exposition, a situation which both promotes and demarcates the consensus. The infallibility of the Church as a whole is also shown by the fact that the *charisma veritatis* is given by the Spirit not merely to buttress the authoritative formulation but also to help the Church to understand the truth in question. This is also part of the general promise of assistance.

2. Though the Church is led by the Spirit of God and is infallible in its teaching on account of the divine assistance, it is still necessary to define as closely as possible the extent of this infallibility. Here too the historical development has been such that the most detailed treatment is to be found under the heading of papal infallibility. The application to General Councils and to the teaching of the episcopal college in union with the Pope in its universal and ordinary magisterium may be taken to be parallel. Vatican I affirms that in the cases considered the Pope possesses "the infallibility with which the divine redeemer wished to have his Church endowed for definitive decisions in matters of faith and morals (D 1839; DS 3074). Infallibility is promised for the preservation and the explanation of revelation. It is therefore concerned with revelation (cf. *Lumen Gentium*, art. 25), the content of which is indicated by the formula "matters of faith and morals". This is to acknowledge on principle that infallibility is determined by its object, hence that its importance and significance are determined not only by the subjects of infallibility but also by the object. When therefore the Second Vatican Council's Decree on Ecumenism bids Christians to bear in mind that there is "an order or 'hierarchy' of truths in Catholic teaching, since they vary in their realationship to the foundation of the Christian faith" (art. 11), more light is thrown on infallibility. A pointer is given to theological reflection, which is warned not to treat infallibility superficially by applying it to a series of truths all on the same footing. The point is to see how dignity accrues to infallibility from the heart of the kerygma, from "the foundation of the Christian faith".

This will help theologians to allott their proper places to the so-called secondary objects of infallibility, the "Catholic truths" which are closely connected historically, logically or practically with the truth of faith (dogmatic facts, theological conclusions, canonizations and so on). It follows that the Church does not teach authoritatively that infallibility includes such matters, though they are of great importance within the framework of the ordinary magisterium (*Lumen Gentium,* art. 25). As a corollary, the theological "notes" or qualifications need to be carefully considered.

3. The infallibility of the Church does not mean that every single utterance of the organs of the Church is infallible and must be believed "fide divina et catholica". The form in which Church doctrine is proposed is also decisive. In the ordinary case, in the "ordinary" teaching of the Church, infallibility is as it were built into the life and preaching of the Church, especially the liturgy, though not all the individual statements could claim infallibility. If one then recalls that kerygma is objectively prior to dogma, it is not surprising that there can be true and infallible preaching in the Church on many matters and over a long period, without this being affirmed in particular for given propositions. And since dogma itself is ultimately doxology and always aims at being such, the intention of dogmatic definitions to be believed absolutely by all may not be present — as for instance in the dogmatic constitutions of Vatican II.

Hence it does not seem advisable to give more precise form to the "general and ordinary magisterium", which is endowed with infallibility, than that which it has achieved in the last hundred years. The essence of this teaching is precisely its relative lack of formal precision, which makes it difficult to grasp in meditative detail, but in no way lessens the importance of such infallible doctrine. The classical example in this matter is the Apostles' Creed. The moral unanimity of the consensus of the whole Church does duty for the formal statement of a truth of faith.

Dogmatic definitions which are binding on all the faithful aim at posing limits, that is, at marking off true doctrine from false. Hence they have mostly been given in answer to a threat to the faith. They are pronouncements of the "extraordinary magisterium". The

infallibility of the Church comes to a head in them. They are "limit cases on the upper level" (M. Löhrer). They are linked to strictly defined conditions, each of which represents a limitation. They must be proclaimed by those who represent the whole Church, a General Council or the Pope speaking as universal teacher of the Church, *ex cathedra.* They are confined to matters of faith and morals. The definition must be addressed to the whole Church. This last condition shows that the infallibility in question is a matter of single acts, which are only made possible when all the conditions are verified. Finally, an utterance intended to be a dogmatic definition must be clearly recognizable as such. In contrast to a tendence observed in some quarters to extend the notion and application of infallibility beyond its due limits, especially with regard to the ordinary papal magisterium, the texts of Vatican I and II note that infallibility should not be ascribed too readily to papal documents. *Lumen Gentium* confines itself to urging a "religious submission of will and of mind" with regard to the authentic teaching authority of the Pope (*Lumen Gentium,* art. 25).

F. Ecumenical Aspects

The doctrine of the infallibility of the Church, especially in the form given it by Vatican I, has been subjected to much criticism by Christians separated from Rome, and expressed in a very pointed way by Protestant theologians such as K. Barth, E. Brunner, and G. Ebeling. Their general tendency is to denounce the apparent claim of the Church to be superior to Scripture, the "potestas Papae" over the gospel, the seeming identification of revelation and Church. Ultimately, however, many of the misgivings are connected only with the danger of abuse of papal authority and look for stronger assurances that the Pope and the teaching Church will not trespass beyond the limits and conditions laid down for them. A characteristic statement of the Protestant notion of infallibility may be found in P. Althaus: "What the promise of the Spirit to the Church means is this: God will never let the Church die of its own mortality, of its own sins and impotence. Somewhere in the Church the Spirit of God sends out truth and life anew for the whole Church.

Somewhere he raises up prophets and reformers. This is the 'evangelical' notion of the guidance of the Spirit and the 'infallibility' of the Church" (*Die Christliche Wahrheit* [4th ed., 1958], p. 526).

In ecumenical discussion of infallibility, a comprehensive historical and theological exposition of the Catholic position is necessary, but as regards particular points the following truths may be given special emphasis on account of their ecumenical relevance.

a) Absolute infallibility belongs to God alone. The Church cannot have infallibility at its disposition, as a "work" which it produces, since it is always a gift, the *charisma veritatis.*

b) The magisterium is not above the word of God, but is at its service (cf. *Dei Verbum,* art. 10). Infallibility is exercised in the service of the word, and dogma is under the word of God. This characteristic of service and the responsibility which it involves must also be clearly seen from the forms and language of the teaching Church. There is no room for "dogmatic imperialism" and "triumphalism".

c) Infallibility helps the Church to be *ecclesia vera;* it makes it the Church in which the gospel is truly preached.

d) The infallibility of the Church means that the members of the Church join together in brotherly service in the finding of the truth. In this way the Church sees itself to be the Church which sustains and is sustained (J. Ratzinger).

e) Even with regard to infallible decisions on truths of faith, the conscience of the individual Christian is not excluded. It remains the immediate norm for his decision.

f) The solemnity and the definitively binding character of a definition does not mean a "thus far and no further" in preaching and teaching. The language of the definition is conditioned by its times, and possibly "contaminated" (K. Rahner) by the world image of the men who pronounce it.

g) The history of the infallible Church and the treatise *De Infallibilitate Ecclesiae* must be balanced by a realistic view of the *fallibilitas ecclesiae.* It must be granted that alongside of and outside the scope of the promised and actual infallibility, there can also be human error within the Church (as in the history of religious freedom).

h) The infallible dogmatic definitions represent a climax and also an extreme case of ecclesial infallibility. They cannot be given at will and without pressing need. Infallibility was not given to the Church to enable it to transform the whole kerygma into infallible dogmatic propositions.

i) The infallible dogmas are not ultimates, but milestones in the development of Church doctrine. They are manifestations of the truth in provisional stages, as follows from the fact that the Church is on pilgrimage. Dogmatic definition cannot blind us to the fact that faith only becomes vision in the kingdom of God.

j) When the Catholic Church speaks of the universal Church and attributes infallibility to the Church as a whole, it undoubtedly means primarily its own Church, but it must always consider this in relation to the separated communities which Vatican II also declares to be "Churches".

See also *Inspiration, Revelation, Fundamental Theology, Theological Methodology, Apostolic Succession, Magisterium, Gallicanism, Pope* I, *Bishop, Ecclesiastical Authority.*

BIBLIOGRAPHY. C. Butler, *The Vatican Council,* 2 vols. (1930); E. Dublanchy, "*Église* IV", *DTC,* IV, cols. 2175–200; id., "Infaillibilité du Pape", *DTC,* VII, cols. 1638–1717; G. Quell, G. Kittel and R. Bultmann, "ἀλήθεια", *TWNT,* I, pp. 232–51 (E. T., 1964); D. Schmaus, *Katholische Dogmatik,* III/1 (5th ed., 1958); H. Barion, "Infallibilität", *RGG,* III, cols. 748 ff.; M. Caudron, "Magistère ordinaire et infaillibilité pontificale d'après la constitution Dei Filius", *ETL* 36 (1960), pp. 393–431; A. Chavasse, *L'ecclésiologie au Concile du Vatican. L'infaillibilité de l'Église: L'ecclésiologie au XIXᵉ siècle* (1960); J. P. Torrell, "L'infaillibilité pontificale est-elle un privilège 'personnel'?", *Revue des sciences philosophiques et théologiques* 45 (1961), pp. 229–45; U. Betti, *La costituzione dommatica "Pastor Aeternus" del Concilio Vaticano,* I (1961); J. M. Todd, ed., *Problems of Authority* (1962); John Henry Newman and William E. Gladstone, *Vatican Decrees,* ed. by A. Ryan (1962); K. Rahner and J. Ratzinger, *Episcopate and the Primacy* (1962), esp. pp. 86 ff.; H. Küng, *Structures of the Church* (1963); C. Butler, *Idea of the Church* (1963); J. Salaverri, *Sacrae Theologiae Summa,* I (5th ed., 1963); *L'Infaillibilité de l'Église. Journées œcuméniques de Chevetogne* (25–29 September 1961) (1963); R. North, "The Scope of Infallibility", *Continuum* 2 (1964), pp. 555–74; A. Lang, "Unfehlbarkeit der Kirche", *LTK,* X cols. 482–7; W. Kasper, *Dogma unter dem Wort Gottes* (1965); M. Löhrer, "Träger der Vermittlung", *Mysterium Salutis,* I (1965), pp. 545–87; K. Rahner, *Schriften zur Theologie,* VII, pp. 103–20; H. Vorgrimler, ed.,

Commentary on the Documents of Vatican II, vol.
I (1967), pp. 186–217 (by Karl Rahner) and pp.
297–306 (by Joseph Ratzinger); H. Küng, The
Church (1968); J. Finsterhölzl, Newmans Kri-
terien echter Lehrentwicklung und die heutige Theologie,
Newman Studien VII (1968).

Heinrich Fries and Johann Finsterhölzl

INFINITY

1. *Meaning and history of the concept.* The word
"infinite" appears for the first time as an
attribute of formless "first matter". Later it
became one of the most pre-eminent attributes of God. Anaximander is the first to
speak of the infinite (ἄπειρον), which he
makes the inexhaustible ground of the
becoming and passing away of things.
According to the Pythagoreans and Plato,
things are composed of one element which
is indeterminate (ἄπειρον) and another which
is a determination (πέρας, limitation). Aristotle undertakes to solve the difficulty
posed by the fact that material things are
limited and still divisible *ad infinitum*. He
uses the distinction between the infinite in
potency and the infinite in act, that is, between that which can be conceivably or
possibly multiplied or divided endlessly, and
that which is really and actually unlimited.
Nothing actually infinite exists. The potentially infinite is the endless multiple in
quantity and the endlessly divisible in space.
Time is infinite in both these senses. Since
along with time the movement of the
world is endless, the obvious thing would be
to deduce that the ultimate unmoved mover
of all that moves, God, is actually infinite.
But Aristotle does not take this step. The
reason for his refusal is to be sought in the
nature of Greek thought, as displayed
further in art and ethics, for which the perfect
is the measured harmony, while the formless
and undefined is the inferior. The real, which
is also the true and the good-beautiful, is the
well-defined and demarcated. This is a
type of thinking which is supremely confident of the power of reason with its conceptual definitions.

This assessment of the infinite was altered
as neo-Platonists and above all Christians
began to take a special interest in the pole
of being opposed to the materially infinite,
the divine. It was affirmed that the divine
could certainly not be finite. As a being

beyond our comprehension, it had to be
without limit, and the sum of all perfections
since it was the inexhaustible source of the
world's riches. The Greek Fathers made
"infinite" one of the pre-eminent attributes
of God. According to Thomas Aquinas,
(first) matter and form limit each other
mutually as they constitute individual beings.
But in this hylemorphism, the form perfects
matter, while matter is no more than the
limiting principle of form. Hence though
both principles are of themselves unlimited,
matter can only subsist in beings, while
the form is of itself capable of being. The
form of being subsisting purely in itself
(God) is therefore actually infinite by its
own virtue. Further, the infinite is not
only prior as being, it is also prior as known,
though only of and for itself and not to us.
But since being is the image of God and is
also that which is best known to our mind,
hence in a certain way, God is also the first
known for us. This conclusion was explicitly
enunciated by Descartes: the finite thing
and the indefinite world are knowable only
against the background of a pre-knowledge
of the infinite God. Hence the notion of
the infinite is essential to the human soul,
which is therefore itself in a certain way
infinite. A similar line of thought had
already led Nicholas of Cusa to place between
the infinity of God and the infinity of matter
a world really infinite in space and time,
which he regarded as the explicitation of the
richness of being existing in a compact way
(complicite) in God.

Subsequent thought brought the infinity of the soul and the world and God closer
and closer together, till they ultimately
came to coincide in the thought of Spinoza
and again in German idealism. Such efforts
to "hypostatize" the infinite by separating
it from the endless process of human enumeration or measurement were subjected to
criticism by Locke, which was followed by
the development of the infinitesimal calculus by Leibniz and Newton. Kant was
inspired by a similar line of thought when
he affirmed that all the objects given us were
finite, but that all the objectives imposed
on us were infinite — the task of continuing
the synthesis of condition and conditioned,
of dividing or enumerating. Hence the
infinite is never a real object of knowledge
but only the regulative idea of scientific
research or the postulate of moral striving.

Hegel was the last great philosopher of the infinite, his principle being that it would be a contradiction to assert the self-sufficiency of the finite, which he defined as that which was not identical with its concept. For everything finite is, as such, limited by another finite being and hence transcends itself. This shows that the finite strives to be once more that which it originally was, the infinite. But the true infinity is neither this endless process of going beyond the limit, nor a self-contained infinity with the finite outside itself — since such a "spurious" infinity would be in some way determined by the finite and hence again be itself finite. The true infinity is the identity of the divine being or idea (concept) with itself which is maintained throughout all dissociation and movement. In contrast to this type of the metaphysics of the infinite, Heidegger tries to delineate a finiteness of being and of man which can be understood in the light of its own nature, without the pre-supposition of an infinity, which would be in contrast to the finite.

The mathematician Georg Cantor (d. 1918) introduced into his set theory actually infinite (transfinite) numbers which designated a constant and yet augmentable quantum which is greater than any finite quantity of the same nature, and hence greater than the (non-existing) greatest number of the natural series 1, 2, 3, etc. — e.g., the multitude of all finite numbers. The "Platonizing" concept of number as an ideal object which seems to underlie the theory of multitudes is contested by a more Aristotelian, "operative" line of thought in basic mathematics.

2. *The significance of the concept of infinity in theology.* In sacred Scripture little attention is paid to the designation of God as "infinite". Where the notion occurs, it means that God's incomparable power is to be praised, as displayed in the works of creation and his beneficent action in the history of salvation. The attribute always has the connotation of the impotence of man to comprehend God. These two notions remained of primary importance when theological speculation took up the attribute of infinity. Theology, which has to transmit the message of revelation in our thought-form (which is fundamentally Greek) can hardly do without the important contribution made by the notion of God's infinity.

Without the doctrine of the infinity of God in the background, there is a danger that the message of God's loving care for us, expressed in personal categories, might lose its seriousness. Only a God whose being is infinite can be present to the limitless reach of man's spirit in such a way that he is still hidden. Only the infinite does not at once, like every finite object proportionate to man's knowledge, pass over into the state of appearance which must let itself be inspected whether it wishes it or not. That is, only the infinite can freely reveal itself and still, in the very act of revelation, preserve its supreme transcendence — as mystery — over all human knowledge. So too creation, which is the free active positing of finite being in its own independent subsistence, is only possible when the creator is so supremely and infinitely sovereign lord of all that is, that not merely can there be nothing which would be independent of him, but that the creature can exist in itself — not in spite of, but by virtue of this dependence.

See also *Hylemorphism, Matter, Act and Potency, Principle, Being* I, *Soul, Pantheism, Concept.*

BIBLIOGRAPHY. See bibliography on *Pre-Socratics;* also: Plato, *Philebus;* Aristotle, *Physics,* III, 4–7; Thomas Aquinas, *Summa Theologica,* I, 7; R. Descartes, *Meditationes,* III; I. Kant, *Critique of Pure Reason,* B 432–595; G. Hegel, *Logik,* E. T.: *Logic,* by W. Wallace (2nd ed., 1892); G. Cantor, *Gesammelte Abhandlungen* (1932); H. Heimsoeth, *Die sechs grossen Themen der abendländischen Metaphysik* (1934); A. Farrer, *Finite and Infinite* (1943); A. Darbon, *Une doctrine de l'infini* (1951); M. Heidegger, *Being and Time* (E. T., 1962); W. Brugger, *Theologia naturalis* (1964).

Gerd Haeffner

INQUISITION

I. Inquisition. II. Witch-Hunting.

I. Inquisition

As a judicial prosecution of heresy by a special court set up by the Church and acting on its behalf, the Inquisition conflicts sharply with the civil tolerance which has been customary for centuries and recently confirmed officially by the Church in the Second Vatican Council (Declaration on Religious Freedom, *Dignitatis Humanae*). It is strange that the Inquisition took shape in a Church appealing to the Gospel and enjoining love. This is not the place for a direct apology for the Inquisition; what is undertaken is an attempt simply to understand it in terms of the principles of the medieval world.

The Inquisition could only have arisen in a world unconscious of any duality between Church and State and regarding them as a single indivisible unity, i.e., in that Central and Western European world within whose borders the undivided Christian faith was not only recognized as the official and obligatory religion but actually ruled as such; a world in which the Church was a "perfect society" comprising spiritual and secular elements. The Inquisition did not proceed against Jews, Moslems and pagans; its competence was limited to the baptized. The decision of the Fourth Council of Toledo (633), "Nemini ad credendum vim inferre", remained in force even in the Middle Ages. Official interest in the legal prosecution of heretics can be discerned from the very beginning. In fact this concern of the State contributed much to the development of the Inquisition. It was rooted in a desire to defend public order against sects which appeared to threaten it. Its roots go back to the religious majesty of the Roman Emperor in antiquity as well as to Germanic views of law, but the immediate occasion for suspicion was the secret meetings of dissident religious groups. The State was prone to regard heretics as potential rebels and traitors, not because they were anarchistic in the modern sense but because they undermined the faith of Christendom on which, in the last resort, the whole social order rested.

From the evidence of the history of religion, measures against nonconformists do not appear to have been exceptional in non-Christian religions. Even the persecution of the Christians in the Roman Empire, by means of an official test involving sacrifice, may be regarded as a kind of preventive and punitive measure against the new religion which seemed to threaten the welfare of the State. It is not surprising, therefore, that with the conversion of the Emperor the roles were gradually reversed and the non-Christians regarded now as the political danger and threatened with similar measures. Constantine's successors saw the unity of the Christian belief as one of the guarantees of the unity of the Empire and issued several laws against heretics, reinforced by penal provisions such as dispossession, banishment, etc. In 407 Arcadius made heresy a civil offence. The death penalty was invoked against certain heretics for *crimen laesae maiestatis*. Two Constitutions of Justinian (V, 16 and 18) dealt with the duty to seek out heretics. The penalties appointed for them ranged from confiscation of property and disqualification for office to banishment, deportation and execution (by burning). There was no uniform attitude to these measures on the part of the Church Fathers. Whereas some defended the death penalty by appealing to the OT (Optatus), Hilary declared that God had no need of enforced worship. At first, the execution of Priscillian (385) was universally condemned, but in the following centuries some theologians approved it. Whereas in the East, Chrysostom certainly wanted to deprive heretics of the freedom to propagate their teachings, he spoke out vigorously against the death penalty. Augustine likewise rejected the death penalty, but in the Donatist controversy he came in the end to demand compulsory religious unity *(compelle intrare)* and regard the punishments meted out by the secular authorities, called in for this purpose, as salutary encouragements to conversion. His views became standard in the West.

After the barbarian invasions and the conversion of the German tribes to Christianity, the kings of these tribal kingdoms took over the role of the Roman Emperor in respect of heretics. The Visigoths threatened with banishment and confiscation of property any who refused baptism, Jews especially. Only through the influence of Isidore, who urged the conversion of Jews by persuasion, did it become possible to exclude compulsion of non-Christians. But for those who renounced Christianity the law prescribed the death penalty.

The collections of canon law transmitted the pronouncements of the Fathers and imperial decrees and, in the 8th century, these were familiar even in the Frankish kingdom, although at first no practical consequences were drawn from them. The collections of Germanic law, however, from the 9th century onwards, with the establishment of the law about the *Send* (from Gk. *synodos,* an ecclesiastical court for dealing with misdemeanours), with the regular visitation of dioceses by the bishops and the appointment of synodal officers charged with referring all misdemeanours to the *Send,* instituted a judicial procedure which provided an immediate model for that of the medieval Inquisition. The equation of simony and heresy during the Investiture Controversy again stimulated livelier interest in the legal prosecution of heresy. When, a century later, Roman law took on a new lease of life, the Church adopted from it the concepts of *causa publica* and *lèse-majesté.* In the decretal *Vergentis in senium* (1199), Innocent III officially equated heresy and *lèse-majesté* for the first time, although *Gratian*, in a crude exaggeration of Augustine's view, had already affirmed that it was the task of the Church to enlighten heretical minds and to break their resistance. When ecclesiastical means proved ineffective, appeal was to be made to the secular arm, which was bound in duty to punish.

These legal opinions at first remained purely theoretical. But from the 12th century onward (with preludes in the 11th century) they were confronted by the popular heresies of the Middle Ages which denied the central tenets of the Christian faith. These movements spread along the trade routes through the whole of Europe. The reaction of threatened society came slowly. Convoking the Synod of Orleans in 1022, King Robert II of France had convicted heretics burned (the German punishment for witchcraft). In Goslar in 1051, the Emperor Henry III, "with the assent of all", had a number hanged. In the 12th century, measures taken by individual bishops no longer sufficed. In 1157 a Synod of Reims instituted a regular procedure with various tests and punishments. The innocence of an accused person could only be proved by ordeal. In England in 1166 a law against heretics was introduced for the first time into a civil collection. In 1162 heretics in Reims appealed from the Archbishop to the Pope. The first death sentence pronounced by a bishop was in 1172 and the first joint action at law by Bishop and Count in 1182 at Arras.

In Southern France the people failed to react against the heretics. The Pope and the bishops attempted to meet the dangerous situation by a typically inquisitorial procedure (official searches by clergy for clandestine meetings). When the Catharists in Toulouse in 1167 banded together into a second Church, the suppression of heresy came to be regarded as a task as important as the Crusade.

Alexander III abandoned a Crusade in favour of a mission in the territory of the Catharists. Bishops, clergy and people were bound by oath to denounce heretics. A tribunal was in session for three months in Toulouse.

At the urging of the Kings of England and France, the Third Lateran Council summoned the princes to proceed against heretics with armed force, and extended the Crusade indulgence to cover participants in the war. While in Southern France, a papal legate was placed at the head of the "holy army", in Aragon it was the kings who initiated the persecution of the Waldenses. Peter II regarded the Waldenses as no better than traitors and threatened them and their protectors with death by burning. In Italy, any effective suppression of the sects had been made impossible by the struggle between the Emperor and the Pope. When peace was concluded, Lucius III and Frederick Barbarossa agreed at Verona that the Church, i.e., the bishops and their assistants, should search out suspects and that the secular power should punish them whether they were lay people or renegade priests. The episcopal Inquisition was thereby introduced into imperial territory. The Fourth Lateran Council adopted these regulations for the whole Church and required secular lords to promise on oath to proceed against heretics. In France, the experiences of the Albigensian War led to the general decree of the death penalty for the stubborn. From now on the penalties ceased to be medicinal and became purely vindictive. In Italy in 1224, Frederick II ordered all Lombard heretics handed over by the bishops to be burned by the secular authority or to have their tongues torn out. In 1227 the Pope required the Lombards to recognize this decree and in 1232 introduced similar regulations for the Papal State. In 1232 a new constitution dealing with the prosecution of heresy in Sicily was extended by Frederick II to the entire Empire. According to this constitution, heretics were to be sought out by the State, brought before a Church court and if judged guilty and proving stubborn, to be publicly burned. Gregory IX wished to reserve the search for heretics to the Church. He included his decree of 1234 in his collection of Decretals, and from 1231 onward chose Dominicans and Franciscans for the most part as his inquisitors to seek out heretics. They had to invite the suspects to appear voluntarily. After the period of grace had expired, denunciations were accepted. Two informers sufficed and the names of these were not made public. Accused persons who confessed were given works of penance or even prison sentences; the recalcitrant were handed over to the secular power to be burned. After the death of Frederick II, Innocent IV adopted the whole system of the Emperor in two Bulls issued in 1252. Of far-reaching consequence was the authority given to the secular power to extort confessions by torture. Even the death penalty was now expressly recognized. Soon the Inquisition's courts were holding regular sessions in the cities. Their competence now extended to a great variety of offences (including witchcraft and sodomy). Sentences were carried out with great formal ceremony. In addition to life imprisonment and burning, the punishments also included confiscation of property. Even persons already dead were committed to the flames.

At first, the death penalty met with some opposition from the theologians. Bishop Wazo of Liège declared that the bishops had not received the sword of secular power. Petrus Cantor and Gerhoch of Reichersberg objected to the execution of heretics. But from the middle of the 12th century, in face of increasing danger, the canonists and theologians began to tolerate it. Thomas Aquinas approved of a severer punishment for heretics than for those convicted of lèse-majesté or counterfeiting, and even Marsilius of Padua wanted the death penalty retained for them, subject, however, to the secular power.

For the most part, the Inquisition was only able to establish itself in France, Italy and Spain (see below); in England and Scandinavia its success was only sporadic. In Germany it experienced a long interruption from the murder of the fanatical Conrad of Marburg in 1233 down to the introduction of witchcraft trials in the 15th century. In France it was frequently a political weapon in the hand of the king (as against the Knights Templar). At the time of the Reformation, inquisitorial laws were revived everywhere. In France, secular tribunals condemned the Calvinists; in the Netherlands, papal inquisitors were employed who were nominated by the State and subservient

to it; in England, under Mary Tudor, the old laws were reintroduced; in Rome, in 1540, Paul III established the Congregation of the Inquisition (first death sentence in 1545; later trials of G. Bruno and G. Galilei). When in 1908 there was a complete reorganization of the Curia, the Congregation became the Holy Office, and in 1965 this in turn became the Congregation for the Doctrine of the Faith. Even the Reformers, in the spirit of the Inquisition, prosecuted Anabaptists and "heretics" and had them executed (Luther, Zwingli, Calvin, Elizabeth I). In these trials, it was for the most part the secular law that was invoked.

There was a special development of the Inquisition in Spain. Faced with the danger of an infiltration of Spanish society by Jews and Moors who had accepted baptism only in appearance, and pursuing a centralizing policy, the Kings of Spain requested in 1478 the establishment of their own Inquisition and the right to appoint their own General Inquisitor who should merely be approved by the Pope. All tribunals of the Spanish Inquisition came under his control. They acted at first with extreme severity (in the first eight years, there were about 700 death sentences in just over 5,000 cases). During the Reformation they proceeded against Protestants. About 300 were burned alive, or in effigy, or after death. The Inquisition, about whose ecclesiastical or secular character there has been much discussion, also dealt with humanists and *alumbrados*. Even Carranza, Archbishop of Toledo, was held prisoner for years by the Inquisition. The King's influence created the danger of abusing the Inquisition for political ends (Philip II: "Twenty clergymen of the Inquisition maintain my kingdom in peace"). At any rate, the Catholic character of Spain is due to the Inquisition as well as to internal reform. The Inquisition was finally dissolved in 1834.

Although from a formal legal viewpoint the Inquisition, by making it the duty of the secular power, by virtue of its office, to conduct trials and establish relevant legal facts, represented a forward step, and although the Inquisition itself testifies to the absolute value assigned by the Middle Ages to religious truth and unity of belief, nevertheless the practice and the abuses of the Inquisition must be acknowledged to be a great blot on the Church's record and an undeniable scandal, as well as a permanent warning against blind religious zeal.

See also *Heresy, Tolerance, Church and State, Constantinian Era, Inquisition* II, *Curia.*

BIBLIOGRAPHY. P. Hinschius, *Das Kirchenrecht der Katholiken und Protestanten in Deutschland* (1887–97), V, pp. 449–92, VI, pp. 328–96; H. C. Lea, *The History of the Inquisition in the Middle Ages,* 3 vols. (1888) (biased); P. Frédéricq, *Geschiedenis der Inquisitie in de Nederlanden,* 2 vols. (1892–98); E. Vacandard, *L'Inquisition. Étude historique* (1907); id., in *DTC,* VII, cols. 2016–68; A. Turberville, *Medieval Heresy and the Inquisition* (1920); A. Maycock, *The Inquisition* (1926); J. Guiraud, *L'Inquisition médiévale* (3rd ed., 1928); id., *Histoire de l'inquisition au moyen âge,* 2 vols. (1935–38) (apologetics); C. della Veneria, *L'Inquisizione medievale e il processo inquisitorio* (1939); A. Erler, "Inquisition", *RGG,* cols. 769–72; J. Lecler, *Histoire de la tolérance* (1955). SPANISH INQUISITION: L. Paramo, *De origine et progressu officii S. Inquisitionis* (1598); E. Schäfer, *Beitrag zur Geschichte des spanischen Protestantismus und der Inquisition im 16. Jahrhundert,* 3 vols. (1902); E. Llorca, *La Inquisición en España* (3rd ed., 1954).

Hermann Tüchle

II. Witch-Hunting

1. In the period between the Middle Ages and modern times, that is from the 14th to the 18th century, superstition, which is present under the surface in all religions, took the particular form of hysterical witch-hunting which was to lead to the death of several hundred thousand victims.

There was a conviction, irrational and therefore difficult to counter, that wicked people could establish contact with the devil and make a pact with him and that they were then able to harm others through secret powers (*maleficium,* evil spells). This belief really did induce some people to dabble in "witchcraft" with books of magic and witches' potions. In this sense there really were witches (both male and female) who, probably out of hate, attempted to do harm through magic. But it is quite certain that only a very few victims of the persecution really were witches. Not a single historical case is known in which diabolical witchcraft was proved. The devil is nowhere directly involved.

2. On the other hand, witch hysteria led to a fear of witches and a desire for protection from them; this took the form not only of "counter-magic", but also of regular persecution by ecclesiastical and secular authorities. Any modern persecutions of witches are due to mob-law and are of course illegal.

3. The origins of witch-hunting in the Christian West lie in the pre-Christian superstitions of Oriental races, such as the Chaldeans and Egyptians, and in old Germanic notions about spirits. Many synodal decrees of Carolingian times prove that these superstitions had not been entirely overcome. Witch-hunting was given a great impetus by the Christian teaching on the devil, especially after scholastics had taken the view that witchcraft and appearances of the devil were perfectly possible and could be real and not merely imagined. The many legends of miracles worked by saints found their natural counterpart in a belief in miraculous, uncanny, diabolical arts. Often it was difficult to draw the line between superstitious practices of religious origin and acts of magic.

4. However, the persecution of witches only started when magic began to be regarded as a crime endangering society. The Inquisition proceeded to punish any deviation from the faith, whether open or implied. Witchcraft implied a break with God and was therefore gravely sinful. The moral theology of Scholasticism looked upon any superstitious act as idolatry and an abandonment of the faith. Thus the Inquisition took action against both heretics and witches. At trials in the South of France at the beginning of the 14th century both accusations tended to merge into one another. But the punishment of witches was soon left to the secular arm because witchcraft was harmful and a crime against society. In the course of the 15th century witch trials were gradually taken out of the hands of the Church Inquisition, although at this time theologians — but also lawyers — began to spread witch hysteria through their writings. Thus credulity acquired the appearance of a doctrine. While the secular authorities began to persecute witches in earnest and laid down definite punishments for witchcraft, as for instance in the *Constitutio Criminalis Carolina* (1532) of Charles V, belief in witches was fostered by the Church authorities, including even the Pope, as in the Bull *Summis desiderantes affectibus* (1484) of Innocent VIII. The Reformers too proved themselves children of their time and looked

upon witches in the same light; the devil plays a great role in the teachings of Luther and Calvin. Persecution therefore did not diminish with the Reformation: on the contrary, both sides tended to persecute witches more actively, and Catholics and Protestants even accused each other of negligence.

After the publication of the *Malleus Maleficarum* ("Hammer of Witches") in 1489, the teaching on witches remained basically unchanged for two centuries. According to this "teaching" the witch sought first of all to establish contact with the devil by means of magic incantations. Thereupon the evil spirit appeared and both signed the evil pact. The devil promised the witch (or the wizard — such as Faust) every help in attaining riches, power and good fortune, in return for which the witch sold him her soul and abjured God and the Christian faith. The pact would be sealed through various rites and incantations and often sexual intercourse. The witch now possessed preternatural powers and was able to harm her fellow-men by means of magic formulas and potions (made *inter alia* out of the bodies of children who had died unbaptized). Sudden death, inexplicable diseases, epidemics, bad harvests and floods could be caused by a witch, even from a distance. Witches could bring about infestation by vermin, they could awaken sexual desire or make it impossible, they could call up the dead, make cows give no milk, they could poison food and make children lame through the "evil eye", and they could be behind thunderstorms, hail and fires. Witches could change themselves into cats or toads, while wizards could turn into wolves (werewolves).

At certain times, such as Hallowe'en and 1 May, all the witches in an area had to fly to the Witches' Sabbath to worship Satan. Witches were members of a kind of secret society. As they had placed themselves in Satan's hands of their own free will, they were not properly speaking possessed; up to a point they even had some control over the devil. There was a belief, however, that witches could make others possessed.

According to the general "teaching" on witches, it was mostly women who took to witchcraft because women were more inclined towards sensuousness and sin; even Eve had led Adam astray. (A cold, clerical anti-feminism shows through here, a neurotic fear of the attractions of the opposite sex which ascribes its own passions to its object and hence attacks it.)

Witchcraft, that secret, diabolical art, was difficult to discover and fight, for the devil protected and strengthened his own.

5. Hence witch trials were conducted summarily. The least suspicion could be enough reason for an arrest. If a confession was not made immediately, force would be used without hesitation. Any kind of torture was permissible where witches were concerned, for this was a fight against diabolical powers. Sentence, in accordance with old custom, was very often one of burning, sometimes preceded by beheading. In places where torture was not used so freely, as for instance in England, other means were used to unmask witches: the witch's body was searched for the so-called witch's mark, the devil's stigma, or else ordeal by water might be used when the witch would be let down on a rope but could not sink because the water (hallowed by Christ's baptism) would not accept witches.

This then was the "teaching" on witches and the way trials were conducted. For centuries witches were persecuted in Germany, France and England (not so much in Italy, Sweden and America, and rarely in Poland, Spain and the Netherlands). There were witches as long as there were witch trials. The custom to ask witches before execution for the names of other witches greatly increased their number. Threatened by renewed tortures, a witch generally named those who had already been executed or were already under suspicion. Those denounced would be arrested without any further investigation and tortured. Thus one trial led to another, sometimes until a whole village or area was depopulated and often such a chain reaction could only be halted by the personal action of a prince. The accused almost never escaped sentence of death. The more energetically guilt was denied, the more suspicious the judges would become: only the devil could give enough strength to withstand such tortures! Thus the trials made belief in witches almost "legal", and once the fires had been burning for some decades, no one dared speak out against witch trials.

There were, of course, always men who condemned this hysteria and doubted whether all the accused were really guilty. But such honest expressions of conscience were not infrequently silenced by force. Anyone who defended a witch or spoke out against this hysteria endangered his own life, for disbelief in witchcraft was regarded as one of its very signs.

The writings of these progressive minds, theologians, lawyers and physicians — often published anonymously — made a gradual change of attitude possible. Towards the end of the 17th century the number of trials in England, Germany and France were growing less; in other countries they had mostly ceased already.

6. The explanations for witch-hunting can be found in religious and social psychology. Whenever a people is struck by disaster it will look for someone to blame. The rulers who ruled by "divine right" could not be guilty. Therefore the fault lay with base powers, inimical to God: the witches. Times of great social, religious and political unrest were always times when fear of witches was at its peak. But as soon as the economic situation took a turn for the better, witch-hunting disappeared again.

The ultimate explanation can be found in the fact that man is superstitious, that is, he has more fear of the devil than trust in God. Soothsaying and astrology go hand in hand with witch-hunting. Religion becomes perverted to magic, and trust in providence to a fanatical aggressiveness against any supposed enemy. Witch-hysteria is therefore an inner perversion in Christianity: men gave way to the permanent temptation in any religion, to try to defend spiritual values through temporal power and to safeguard God's rights through human laws. There is a pharisaical arrogance in the fanatical punishment of the religious errors of others. Witch-hunters were often unbalanced neurotics. Popular witch-hunting had its roots in the desire for sensation, for the uncanny and the gruesome. A witch-hunt gave an outlet to sadism and the wish to see others guilty while one could think of oneself as righteous and safe. The somewhat inward-looking theology of the time defended witch-hunting almost as an article of faith. The lack of any understanding of psychic diseases and of the social psychological aspects of mass hysteria prevented for a long time a realization of the crass stupidity of this tragic delusion. This may well be the historic lesson of witch-hunting.

See also *Superstition, Devil, Inquisition* I, *Possession (Diabolical)*.

BIBLIOGRAPHY. W. G. Soldan, H. Heppe and M. Bauer, *Geschichte der Hexenprozesse,* 2 vols. (1912) (very comprehensive); M. Summers, *The History of Witchcraft and Demonology* (1926); G. L. Kittredge, *Witchcraft in Old and New England* (1928); C. L'E. Ewen, *Witch Hunting and Witch Trials* (1929); P. Sejourné, in *DTC,* XIV (part 2, 1941), cols. 2340–417 ("Sorcellerie"); F. von Spee, *Cautio criminalis, seu De processibus contra sagas liber* (1631; reprint 1950); H. Zwetsloot, *Friedrich von Spee und die Hexenprozesse* (1954); R. H. Robbins, *The Encyclopedia of Witchcraft and Demonology* (1959); K. Baschwitz, *Hexen und Hexenprozesse* (1963).

Hugo J. Zwetsloot

INSPIRATION

"In many and various ways God spoke of old to our fathers by the prophets; but in these last days he has spoken to us by a Son, whom he appointed the heir of all things, through whom also he created the world." This opening passage of the Letter to the Hebrews at once fixes the Christian idea of inspiration as a saving mystery. Christ is the centre — the total, definitive Word, the fullness of revelation — round whom we find the concentric circles of the Son's creative activity, his manifestation in the universe, and the many words God sent from time to time as forerunners of the Word that crowns them all. The revelation Christ announced is echoed by his apostles: "It was declared at first by the Lord, and it was attested to us by those who heard him" (Heb 2:3). Thus we must think of inspiration within the context of the central mystery, the Incarnation, as part of the mystery of the word, something bound up with the cosmic order that is eloquent of God its Creator. In Christ all things hold together, including the inspired books. It is the common teaching of the Fathers that the whole of OT revelation has to do with Christ: "In his igitur Verbum versabatur, loquens de seipso. Iam enim ipsum suus praeco erat" (Hippolytus, *PG,* X, 819). Just as the Incarnation is the work of the Holy Spirit (Lk 1:35), so the mystery of the many and various words is the work of the Holy Spirit's manifold activity: the very term "inspiration" refers us to the "Spirit". The inspiration of Scripture, then, must be something living, active, piercing. The "breath" of God that was breathed at creation, that gives man life, that raises up heroes of salvation, also inspires the prophet, the "man of the Spirit"; and since this Spirit is a living, life-giving one, the inspired word too is something living and active (Heb 4:12). Charisma is the name usually given to the action of the Spirit in the economy of salvation. Inspiration must be seen in the variegated setting of the charisms, as part of the total experience of Israel and the Church.

A mystery of the word and a mystery of life, inspiration can be more precisely defined as verbal revelation. Every operation of God *ad extra* manifests him on one of three planes. In nature, organized being, a little thought enables us to trace the finger of God, a certain reflection of himself. (St. Paul calls this kind of thought *nooumena*, Rom 1:20). On the vast stage of creation God intervenes in human history, working signs and wonders, doing specific things, so that man may gain a closer knowledge of his Author. And within history God speaks to man: this is the fullest manifestation of God, revelation by his word. Nature tells us something about the being and attributes of God; from history we learn something of the ways of God with men; but verbal revelation gives us personal access to him. The personal revelation of the word sheds a flood of light on nature and history: they become transparent, God's revelation through his word unlocks the secret of the universe (cf. Ps 104, for example); in God's word man knows himself for what he is, so limited, torn between two poles (Ps 139), a sinner (Ps 51); that word shows beyond a doubt that history is the history of revelation.

We could imagine God causing the air to vibrate at the frequency of an address or a poem: words would sound in human language, Hebrew or Greek, but they would not be spoken by men; they would be appropriate to a particular age and society but transmitted mechanically. (Anyone who feels that such a revelation would be simpler and purer lacks an incarnational cast of mind.) The mystery of inspiration is precisely that God has chosen to speak through men, to "incarnate" his word: the word of God is truly a human word, it is spoken — not merely repeated — by men of a particular age and society, with a personality of their own.

A human word. Even in his language, man is the image and likeness of God. The creation of an orderly world shows us what God is like; and man, recreating the world through his words, shows what he is like. God incarnates himself in man, his image, he incarnates his word in language, the image of man and the second image of God. Language is communication, and the fullness of language is dialogue. This being so, language enables and compels man to know himself: having to express himself, man looks at himself, finds words for his experiences, thus taking reflex possession of them; stores them away in his memory, where they will be ready when needed. Dialogue is more than the sum of alternate communications, for in dialogue these communications become more and more enriched, more fraught with meaning. So it is with the language that God uses in his dialogue with men. This disclosure of God, of course, does not perfect him; but dialogue with God does exalt and perfect man, not only when he listens but also when he responds. The Psalms are a human response, one inspired by God, revelation embodied in dialogue: "Perpendat unusquisque nos per prophetarum linguam audire Deum nobiscum *colloquentem*" (St. John Chrysostom: *PG*, LIII, col. 119). When he must answer God, man comes to know himself; answering God in words that are inspired, divine, man knows himself in the light of God, of the divine word.

Language is a social and a historical thing. There are two ways in which it transcends the individual who speaks it. Since speaking actualizes language, when we speak we do not express our personal ideas by a process of elimination or purification, we take over the language of the society we live in with all its riches and variety, its overtones and atmosphere. In a sense the society speaks through the individual and the individual speaks in the bosom of his community — in its presence, on its behalf, for its benefit. This social dimension of language enters into inspiration. There is a second dimension, the historical one. A language both precedes and survives those who speak it; it endures and changes in strictly historical fashion, with its set forms, the evolution of its meanings, and the rest. This dimension too is subsumed by inspiration: when it appeared that the continuity of inspired language was going to be broken, that Hebrew would be displaced by Greek, God saw to it that a Greek translation of the OT provided a bridge between the two. We must not think of the inspiration of Scripture as a series of individual acts on the fringes of society, nor yet as isolated interventions on the part of God. Though the inspired writers are discontinuous in the sense that they are real individuals, inspiration uses them to express itself in language that is a social and a historical reality (and here one should not think merely of dictionaries and grammars, of Hebrew and Greek in the abstract).

We are acquainted with many inspired writers, men moved by the Spirit (2 Pet 1:21); some we know only through their books, others by name as well; and we must admit that the language they speak is thoroughly human, at times intensely so. Yet at the same time we believe that these words are literally the words of God, "qui locutus est per prophetas". How can one and the same word be both human and divine? Here is the great theological problem of inspiration, crucial because it takes us to the heart of mystery. The first thing to do if we wish to make sense of this mystery, or any other, is of course to refer it to the central mystery of the Incarnation, as the medieval authors recommend: "Verba quae multa locutus est, unum Verbum sunt; unum inquam quod et ipse caro factum est" (Rupert of Dietz, In Jo, 1:7). Pius XII himself follows their advice: "As the substantial Word of God became like man in all things except sin, so too the words of God, expressed in human language, are like human speech in all things except error" (Divino Afflante Spiritu).

The question still remains: what is the nature of this action of the Spirit that makes a human word a divine word? At what point does this action take effect? We cannot suppose that a purely human word becomes a divine word. Being acknowledged and received by the Church cannot make a divine word of what in itself is a purely human word (Vatican I); the Holy Spirit does not assume and elevate a human word that already has an independent existence, any more than God became man by assuming a complete human being already in existence. We must recognize that this word, this piece of language, is inspired from birth, indeed from the moment of its conception. The author's materials, to be sure, are another matter, whether these be experiences and intuitions, for example, that have not yet been formulated in language, or words already in existence which he turns to good account in new expressions, a new work of art. Like the sower's seed, the organic matter which the Spirit will form into the body of Jesus is not made out of nothing, nor even out of inorganic matter. It is in this way that we must think of inspiration, as operative from the moment when a concrete literary work begins to take shape. How does it take shape? This is not properly a theological question, having more to do with the psychology of language or literary creation. But these sciences can shed light on the way inspiration works.

Inspired writers. What immediately strikes us here is variety: inspiration is vigorous, complex, flexible. In the OT one first distinguishes between prophets and sapiential writers. The prophet receives a divine impulse, and contributes his own artistry to the work: the divine impetus may be like an unquenchable fire in one's bones (Jer), like a book that is digested before becoming a prophetic message (Ezek), like a lion's roar that is echoed in words (Amos), or a fleeting intuition (Jer 1).

The divine impulse sets the author to work on his book; and the whole task, from beginning to end, is guided by the spirit. No less so is the literary labour of the sapiential writer; but he is not conscious of the action of the Spirit; he feels no superhuman impulse, claims no divine revelation; he seems to proceed entirely on the basis of his own thought and experience. The historiographer may work in both these ways; relating events or studying official records, he may be enlightened from above as to their meaning. In any case, he too writes under the constant influence of the Spirit. What all three write is the word of God, and we must not make too much of the distinction between *verba Dei* and *ipsissima verba Dei*. In the NT we encounter a new factor, because all the preaching and writing of the apostles merely echoe the words of Christ (2 Cor 13:3; 2:17). If this is so, it is not because they were men with an exceptional memory. The apostles echoed Christ the Word, concretely embodied in the words of Christ, by the action of Christ's Spirit, who is sent by the Father and the Son (Jn 14:26; 16:13). Let us not make a fetish of the *ipsissima verba Christi* as though the rest were not really his word.

The inspired writers may also be classified according to literary genre. Examples abound in Scripture of the "many and various ways" God speaks. One book will be characterized by intellectual detachment, another by compelling emotion, another by traditionalism of form or content, yet another by literary artistry. Or we may distinguish these authors from the point of view of their social circumstances: some speak for the group to which they belong, others admonish rulers (Is), some are dogged fighters (Jer), some are men in advance of their time, some are isolated nonconformists (Eccles). But all offer scope for the operation of the Holy Spirit. We might set forth this plurality under the headings "intellectual element, volitional element, period of composition"; but perhaps pride of place had best be given to multiplicity, leaving us to marvel at the work of the Spirit that breathes where it wills.

Theologians have had recourse to various metaphors in an attempt to explain how a human word can also be a divine one. The metaphor of the instrument has enjoyed a great vogue (cf. *Divino Afflante Spiritu*): both *homo faber* and *homo ludens* know from elemental experience what an instrument is. The Fathers were very fond of the image of the musical instrument, with its suggestion of immediacy, of oneness with the artist, the blending of melody and tone. St. Augustine gives us the image of a bodily organ, such as the mouth or hand, alluding to the idea of the mystical body (*PL*, XXXIV, col. 1070). This image leads the Schoolmen into a metaphysical discussion of the efficient instrumental cause; St. Thomas himself, however, recognizes the limitations of the image and prefers to speak of a "quasi-instrumentum". The image of "dictation" is borrowed from the world of chancelleries and literature: it has not the modern sense of writing down what another says (something that will soon be done by machines) but means the intelligent assistance of a secretary, artistic collaboration in finding the exact wording desired (cf. the evolution of the word *dictare* into *indite*). Politics and diplomacy give us the image of mission: the sacred author is a messenger, he does not merely parrot what he has heard but conveys the message as a responsible person. Besides these three traditional images, there is one drawn from the world of literature that helps to illustrate the mystery of a word both human and divine: a poor novelist or playwright can put his own words into the mouths of his personages, which are nothing but marionettes; whereas the good novelist or playwright is not merely the creator but also the servant of his personages, he cannot do as he likes with them, what he has each one say must be "in character"; and the reader can rightly say that such words are both the personage's and the author's. Obviously if this analogy were strained it would lose its point, just as if we reduced the human instrument to an inert machine, the messenger to a parrot, the writer to a mere typist. But what these comparisons all show is that we are justified in saying that God is the principal author of the inspired books, and man their secondary author.

The inspired books. We have considered the nature and working of inspiration in its human term, the inspired writers (cf. 2 Pet 1:21). Scripture tells us, however, that the books they wrote are also inspired (2 Tim 3:16). Or rather we ought to say that the authors are inspired in view of the word, which is a communicable objectification that exists in view of some action, the final object of the whole procedure. The Fathers much prefer the second expression, "inspired Scripture". If we have dwelt upon the role of the human authors, it is in order to make it quite clear that inspiration is not something added later to a finished piece of writing. Next it behoves us to examine the inspired reality that is still preserved to us in the Church: "Now these things (that) happened to them ... were written down for our instruction, upon whom the end of the ages has come" (1 Cor 10:11). We profess our faith that God speaks to us, that his word reaches us; Pius XII tells us that God uses language which is "completely human, error only excepted" (*Divino Afflante Spiritu*); and therefore we feel justified in discussing God's word by analogy with certain aspects of the human word.

Language (according to K. Bühler) has three dialogal functions: to inform, to express, and to impress. In the first case the speaker states facts, ideas, doctrines; in the second he reveals his inner life, his feelings, his experiences; in the third he acts upon the person he is speaking to. These three functions are of course intermingled in practice, but it is useful to distinguish one from the other. Now if we consider the divine word, we may say by analogy that it informs by making known the deeds by which we are redeemed, the truths we must believe so as to be saved; that it expresses by disclosing to men God's nature and knowledge; that it impresses by exposing the hearer of the word to a divine influence. What we are considering here are only three aspects of a single reality, not three different phases or areas. It would not do to suppose that inspiration, in the Christian view, enters the picture only when doctrinal truths are formally taught: were such the case a great deal of the Bible, being repetitive, would be superfluous; indeed we could well dispense with the Bible altogether since the truths it teaches are more clearly stated in the catechism. When God instructs us, he does not lecture like a remote academician, he speaks to us lovingly as a father to his son (Deut 8:5). The human word possesses a native power to stimulate, move, impress the hearer (though not an infallible power, since the hearer may resist it if he chooses). At least the same efficacy must be granted the word of God, but on the plane of salvation where his word operates. This efficacy of the divine word should not be confused with that of the sacraments, nor explained as a parallel movement occasioned by reading Scripture in the proper dispositions; such an explanation falls far short of the lapidary formulae "able to instruct for salvation, profitable for training in righteousness" (2 Tim 3:15–17), "living, active, piercing" (Heb 4:12), and conflicts with the doctrine and practice of the Fathers. Scripture is efficacious on the plane of the word; its acceptance is efficacious on the plane of faith.

There are three basic levels of language: the common, the technical, and the literary. The common level is that of personal communication. When this kind of language has undergone a process of purgation in the interests of the utmost possible precision of thought and terminology, the result is technical language — impersonal, objective, in a sense absolute. Literary language, exploiting all the half-used or untouched resources of common parlance to dilate, enrich, intensify it, abounds in suggestive imagery. It is fair to say that literary language is much more opulent than technical language and much

less accurate. On which of these three levels do we find the inspired word? On all three, of course, since God has spoken "in many and various ways". A good deal of common parlance occurs in Scripture, and there are lengthy passages of technical language (ceremonial, legal, and so forth). On the whole, however, it is literary language that sets the tone, as we might expect. What more fitting to convey the riches of God's own life, his unfathomable designs, the plenitude of mystery, than an exalted imagery? Much mischief has come of treating biblical language as though it were technical (the language of astronomy, physics, or genetic history). Once we grasp the literary character of Scripture some important corollaries emerge, first of all the inexhaustible riches of Scripture. The delight of medieval writers (who called Scripture a treasure, a forest, a banquet, an ocean, a torrent, an abyss), they are now being rediscovered by the modern biblical movement. Secondly, we must do what we can to bring these riches to light and make use of them. That task, though a never-ending one, must be undertaken, in harmony with the Bible and the institutions based on it, under the guidance of the Spirit who inspired the Bible. Tradition is the name we give to this continuous, undeviating work of formulating, gathering, meditating on the treasures of God's "living, efficacious word", and the final guarantee of its soundness is the magisterium.

Language is either spoken or written. The spoken word is primary: writing is a convention that has become necessary in our culture if the works of men are not to be lost. Composition is either oral or written: neither lies beyond the scope of inspiration, and we may not suppose that a psalm, for example, that was not the word of God, became such merely because it was soon written down. On the other hand there is no reason why oral composition could not be supplemented by a composition set down in a different context. Scripture is the form in which God chose to have many inspired books written and to have them all preserved in the Church (2 Cor 10:11). But let us remember that Scripture is only notation, a score that needs to be interpreted, a word that returns to life through a new creation. When a person reads a literary text properly he revives it, calls it into existence once more: and when the reader gives the inspired word intellectual life, the life of the Spirit is imparted to him. It is well, too, to bear in mind that the utterances of the prophets were God's word before they were committed to writing; that a large part of the NT first existed as the word of Jesus, as the oral tradition of the primitive Church. Word of mouth does not die when it is written down; it goes on living parallel to, linked with, its written form.

As a rule biblical language hardened into literary works and did not remain an indeterminate flow of words. Together these works form a structure of massive proportions. A book of the Bible can belong to one literary genre, yet take up various traditional literary themes; blending artistic inspiration with the skill of many schools of writing, it may use a variety of styles; it speaks for the author, being his work, yet in a way transcends him because the language used evokes a whole society, a host of traditions; shut in upon itself as a complete book, it can nonetheless open the door to a new and higher context; though identical with itself, its character undergoes a change each time it is renewed by a reader's active co-operation; rooted in the life of one people and generation, it may be relevant to other peoples and generations.

These literary qualities are neither destroyed nor damaged by inspiration, which rather endows them with new vigour, meaning, and potency. Since the biblical book is a unit, it also follows that its parts exist for the whole and not vice versa. For this reason it is an error to regard the Bible as an enormous collection of propositions, each of which could be understood in isolation. Before we can expect to interpret any sentence, any word of the Bible, we must consider the book in which it is found, the character and intentions of the author, the age he lived in, and the whole context of divine revelation. Similarly, given the higher unity of Scripture, we must see each book as open to, in relation with, the rest, as part of a temporal process, a debate (Eccles, Job), and the whole of the OT as open to its fulfilment in the new.

The inspiration of the Holy Spirit has certain consequences (which some authors call "effects"). The first effect of inspiration is to make the inspired language the word of God: the expressions "inspired word" and "Word of God" are practically synonymous; the former merely draws more attention to the Spirit, the latter to the Logos. Since Scripture is the word of God, it has a saving power of its own which operates in liturgical observance, in the preaching of sermons, in reading when one receives in faith those things that are "able to instruct for salvation through faith" (2 Tim 3:15). Being the word of God, Scripture teaches the doctrine of salvation in its own particular way: this doctrine is sought out, formulated, explained, and proposed to our belief in dogmatic definitions, the teaching of the magisterium, the teaching of theologians, and the catechism. All this requires certain adjustments of language and constantly poses the problem of how far such change should go. How far may theologians depart from biblical language? Should the catechism use the language of the Bible or of dogmatic theology? Let us simply recognize both the need for modification and the dangers it involves, keeping in close touch with the language God has inspired. A Christian child nurtured in this language is in touch with the real religious world, with the language of true dialogue with God. Of course flexibility is necessary in this matter. But it seems very unwise to bring up children in peaceful ignorance of inspired language. Since Scripture is inspired by God, it follows that it cannot assert any falsehood: otherwise God himself would be commending falsehood to us on his own authority. In negative terms, this characteristic of Scripture is called inerrancy. The inerrancy of Scripture has always been taught by tradition and must, of course, be associated with its positive correlative, truth. Truth is a doctrine, a revelation, a light to our eyes: of the inspired word of God, too, we may say: "In thy light do we see light" (Ps 36:10).

See also *Charisms, Incarnation, Form Criticism* II, *Bible* I, III.

BIBLIOGRAPHY. J. B. Franzelin, *De divina traditione et scriptura* (4th ed., 1896); F. von Hummelauer, *Exegetisches zur Inspirationsfrage* (1902); C. Pesch, *De inspiratione Sacrae Scripturae* (2nd ed., 1925), with *Supplementum continens disputationes recentiores* (1926); A. Bea. *De Scripturae Sacrae Inspiratione* (2nd ed., 1935); P. Benoît, *Saint Thomas d'Aquin. Somme théologique: La prophétie* (1947); K. Rahner, *Inspiration in the Bible* (1961; 2nd ed., 1964); P. Synave and P. Benoît, *Prophecy and Inspiration* (1961); J. Levie, *The Bible, Word of God and Word of Man* (1962); O. Weber, in *RGG*, III, cols. 775–82; J. Beumer, *Die katho-*

lische Inspirationslehre zwischen Vaticanum I und II (1966); L. Alonso-Schökel, *La palabra inspirada* (1966).

Luis Alonso-Schökel

INTEGRALISM

By integralism, we mean the tendency, more or less explicit, to apply standards and directives drawn from the faith to all the activity of the Church and its members in the world. It springs from the conviction that the basic and exclusive authority to direct the relationship between the world and the Church, between immanence and transcendence, is the doctrinal and pastoral authority of the Church. In a word, integralism means that the world is to take shape only under the direct or indirect action of the Church. According to the integralist view, the Church is absolutely self-sufficient in all matters which are connected with faith and morals, so that these spheres are shaped according to their God-given laws only when the faith as proposed by the Church is taken as the positive norm. Integralism is therefore the effort to explain or master reality exclusively in the light of faith, instead of regarding faith as the key which makes the understanding or mastery of the world possible, but does not itself try to achieve it. Integralism tries to explain the faith and the life of faith in the light of an abstract and immutable system of doctrine, instead of trying to explain the dogmatic structure from the Holy Spirit's laying hold of the Church. Or it tries first to assure the political and social standing and power of the Church, to preach the gospel from this platform, instead of influencing the formation of society by the unprotected preaching of the gospel. Hence integralism is a sociological as well as a theological problem, since it is a question of integrating the preaching of the Church in a given order of society. Integralism tries to solve the problem one-sidedly, confining itself to the static and metaphysical, instead of also calling on the dynamic and historical.

In the course of Church history, this tendency came particularly to the fore in the early Middle Ages, in connection with the Gregorian reform. Legitimate efforts to free Church life from the alien power of the world were given an ideological substructure by notions of the Church's claim to rule the world and of claims of the hierarchy within the Church which were largely modelled on political power patterns. The tendency was shown in various ways. Philosophy was said to be the handmaid of theology. The Pope was said to have such direct or indirect power over the worldly authority that the duties of the latter were exhausted by its applying ecclesiastical directives or theological principles to the worldly realms of government. Blind obedience became the supreme virtue. Integralist thinking was also responsible for the view that the findings of natural science could be disregarded when contradicted by the Bible, and that theological notions should take precedence in economics, political science and cultural matters. The problem of integralism is also involved in the present-day discussion of the extent of ecclesiastical authority in matters of natural law, of the relative autonomy of earthly realities with regard to the faith and the independence of the laity in their tasks in the Church and the world.

The term integralism made its appearance in (ecclesiastical) jargon at the beginning of the 20th century, in the controversies connected with modernism, liberalism, laicism, and indifferentism. It seems to have first been used by the upholders of the "integralist" position themselves. These included Mgr. Umberto Benigni and the "Sodalitium Pianum" (named after Pius V), which had started with papal approbation and was turned by the Monsignor into an intransigent integralist organization. The main point of controversy at the time was the formation of supra-denominational Christian associations, parties and trade unions outside episcopal control. There were the Centre Party and the Christian trade union movement in Germany, the Christian democratic movement of the "Sillon" and the nationalist "Action française" in France, and the "social action" of Romulo Murri in Italy. The struggle became so extensive and sharp that Pius X found himself with no alternative but to sanction expressly "co-operation with non-Catholics for the common good" (Encyclical *Singulari Quadam* of 24 September 1912). Benedict XV dissolved the Sodalitium Pianum, which had turned into a sort of secret society.

Now that "pluralist" views of society are generally favoured, scientific approaches are better understood and the theology of earthly realities has been given official expression in the Pastoral Constitution of Vatican II on the Church in the Modern World, integralism as a theological thesis may be said to be fast disappearing. Nonetheless, it is still a force in practice wherever revelation alone is appealed to to throw light on reality, which means that it is wrongly treated as a sort of ideology. This integralism can take the form of a triumphalism which claims that the Church can solve all problems. Or it can take the defeatist form of bewailing the fact that the Church is not doing its duty and resolving all problems. As a practical attitude, integralism also takes the form of a tendency to fall back on a life "lived only by faith" and strictly within the Christian fellowship. It is unwillingness to accept in faith the inner-worldly efficacy of the world. It is a failure to respond in faith to one's own vocation insofar as it calls for a responsible integration of faith and reason, Church and society, as free and independent entities — not that this reconciliation can ever be complete, in view of man's weaknesses, his involvement in material realities and the constant changes of historical situations.

Integralism may also be used to describe the attitude which wrongly takes a given expression of the faith in a specific form of Catholicism, which must necessarily reflect certain personal and historical influences, and hence be one-sided, as the only possible expression of Catholic belief. For this is to neglect the dependence of faith on experience, which is a reality not to be deduced *a priori* from the faith, the dependence of the hierarchical office on the charisms, which are not confined to office-holders, and the dependence of society on the irreplaceable initiative of the individual member.

See also *Church and State, Reform* II C, *Obedience, Natural Law, World, Modernism, Indifferentism, Liberalism, Secularization* III, *Pluralism, Science* I, *Ideology*.

BIBLIOGRAPHY. See bibliography on *Church and World* and *Authority;* also: E. E. Y. Hales, *The Catholic Church in the Modern World* (1958); K. S. Latourette, *Christianity in a Revolutionary Age,* I: *19th Century in Europe. Background and Roman Catholic Phase* (1959), IV *20th Century in Europe* (1962); E. E. Y. Hales, *Revolution and Papacy* (1960); W. Ullmann, *Growth of Papal Government in the Middle Ages* (2nd ed., 1962); A. Latreille and R. Rémond, *Histoire du Catholicisme en France,* III: *La période contemporaine. Du XVIIIe siècle à nos jours* (1962); H. Urs von Balthasar, "Integralismus", *Wort und Wahrheit* 18 (1963), pp. 737–44; J. O. Zöller, "Integralismus heute?" *Wort und Wahrheit* 19 (1964), pp. 463 ff.; K. Rahner, "The Church's Limits", *The Christian of the Future,* Quaestiones Disputatae 18 (1967), pp. 49–76.

Waldemar Molinski

INTELLECTUALISM

This term was originally used in a derogatory sense, which it still often retains: the attitude which exaggerates the role of the intelligence in its work of abstraction, forming of concepts and use of logical reasoning, to the detriment of other activities such as observation, intuition, willing and feeling. Today, however, the term is frequently used in a good sense, to designate the attitude which recognizes the preponderant role of the intelligence in man's conscious activity. But the question of the role of the intelligence arises in various domains. We must therefore distinguish between several forms of intellectualism and try to form a judgment in their regard.

1. *Epistemological or noetic intellectualism.* This is the view of human knowledge which recognizes the basic function and value of the intelligence. As the faculty of being as such, as an unlimited capacity of transcendence, as the place of truth and certainty, the intelligence attains — at least to some extent — things in themselves, their necessary relations and their first cause. This form of intellectualism guarantees the possibility of metaphysics and natural theology. It is essential to Aristotelianism and all forms of scholastic philosophy up to the 14th century, especially Thomism. The principal exaggerations of intellectualism are idealism (which reduces all authentic knowledge to ideas, thought, intellectual activity, neglecting the contribution of the senses), rationalism (which exaggerates the role of discursive reasoning to the detriment of intuition), and panlogicism (which claims to deduce the whole order of things by the logical activity of reason). Intellectualism is opposed to all forms of empiricism, pragmatism and metaphysical voluntarism, such as that of Schopenhauer.

2. *Psychological intellectualism.* This is the theory which reduces all psychic functions to intellectual knowledge (Herbert) — an inacceptable position, universally rejected today.

3. *Ethical intellectualism.* This recognizes the primary role of the intelligence in moral action, especially a) in the exercise of liberty and b) in the attainment of man's last end. The doctrine is characteristic of Thomism. Exaggerated forms of it may be seen in Socratic intellectualism (which identifies moral good with knowledge of the good, and moral evil with error about the good) and in psychological determinism (where the motive presented most favourably by the intelligence is supposed to determine the will). Ethical intellectualism is opposed to voluntarism which a) accentuates the independence of the will in the free act and b) makes the attainment of the last end an act of the will. These are doctrines professed principally by Dun Scotus and the Franciscan school.

4. *Pedagogical intellectualism.* This overestimates the value of intellectual formation, to the detriment of other aspects of education; or makes too much of intelligence in the whole effort of education.

5. *Religious or theological intellectualism.* This accords the intelligence an essential directive function in man's religious life, or more exactly, recognizes that the intelligence can express revealed truths in dogmas or dogmatic formulas, that is, in precise conceptual assertions which are absolutely binding. This attitude, shared by the whole tradition of theology, was adopted by the Church in the dogmatic definitions which were imposed on the faithful. It implies the recognition of the essential function of the intelligence in man's moral action, and in particular, in the discernment of religious truth, the acceptance of divine revelation by faith and in the exercise of faith: the life of faith involves a humble but eager effort to understand God's message to man, according to St. Augustine's formula, "crede ut intelligas", and St. Anselm's "fides quaerens intellectum". It gives birth to theological knowledge, which is a human science worked out by the intelligence with the help of concepts and reasoning. Theology in turn is a precious aid to the magisterium in the elaboration of dogmatic formulas, to be promulgated by the Pope speaking *ex cathedra* or by a General Council, to define some element of revelation menaced by heresy or by grave theological error. Theological intellectualism was vigorously attacked by the modernists, on the grounds that it was a form of rationalism which perverted revelation and compromised authentic religious life. Theological intellectualism can indeed appear in extreme forms, as when the study of theology is given precedence over the religious life and the practice of virtues, especially charity; or again, when dogmatic formulas are identified with the truth and reality which they communicate. The greatest menace is a theological rationalism which assigns an importance to the intellect which casts a shadow on the sovereignty of faith.

See also *Experience, Will, Religious Feeling, Knowledge.*

BIBLIOGRAPHY. R. Garrigou-Lagrange, *Le sens commun, la philosophie de l'être et les formules dogmatiques* (3rd ed., 1922); P. Rousselot, *L'intellectualisme de St. Thomas* (3rd ed., 1936); É. Gilson, *Spirit of Medieval Philosophy* (1936); G. Siewerth, *Der Thomismus als Identitätssystem* (1939); K. Rahner, *Geist in Welt* (1939); M. Müller, *Sein und Geist* (1940); J. Maritain, *The Range of Reason* (1953); F. Van Steenberghen, *Epistémologie* (3rd ed., 1956); J. Maritain, *Distinguish to Unite or Degrees of Knowledge* (1959); H. Holz, *Transzendentalphilosophie und Metaphysik* (1966).

Fernand Van Steenberghen

INTERNATIONAL LAW

By international law is understood the sum total of all those norms which regulate relationships between States, federations of States and certain other so-called international law "persons" (see below) within the universal community of nations. The norms of international law bind States and statesmen in international intercourse: they lay down the rules to a certain extent for the great interplay of world politics. From another point of view they provide States and statesmen with a weapon — above all the weapon of the weak — in the interchange of world politics: to be able to use it is the art of the statesman. International law is the rule of law and order for the community of nations, i.e., a community which arose in medieval times from the idea of the unity of Christendom. It included at first only the States of the Western Christian world and gradually extended ever more widely (at the end of the 17th century with the inclusion of Russia and at the beginning of the 19th century with that of the United States, emerging as it did from European colonies and resting on the basis of European culture, and in the middle of the 19th century with the inclusion of Turkey and Japan), until today after the transformation of the former Asian and African colonies of the European powers into independent States, it embraces the entire world. The "natural" persons subject to the order of international law are the States; the "juridical" persons whose existence at any one time is dependent on the "natural" persons are the groups of allied States. The ultimate purpose of international law is to ensure the protection of man in his dignity and moral personality. The Apostolic See has a special position in international law. It — not the Catholic Church as such, which through it is introduced into international law without being otherwise subject to its norms — is likewise a "natural" person of international law with definite rights arising out of its duty to urge peace on the nations and act as possible mediator, appealing to the conscience of the nations. The norm of international law is seen partly in the content of treaties made between States, partly as customary law based on the agreed practice of States which derives in turn from the concepts of justice accepted among the nations. The heart of international law are those general principles of law which derive from the essence of law itself and which must be found in every system of laws if it is to merit any consideration as a "rule of law", as, for example, the principle of good faith or the proposition that agreements must be kept.

International law has in general no fixed form in which treaties must be made; if, however, to carry a treaty into effect requires the aid of intra-State laws, then the lawgiver in question must regularly "ratify" or give formal approval to the conclusion of the treaty. The position of States and groups of States in international law is characterized by the term "sovereignty", that is, self-government, externally or in relation to other States, and internally by means of a Constitution; the "sovereign State" is subject only to the norms of international law which guarantee and set the limits for its sovereignty. It is "immediately related to international law". The sovereign States are equal in this immediacy of relationship to international law, that is, *before* the international law; they have, it is true,

varying rights and duties in international law, according to whether they are great powers, which with their universal interests can assume the role of spokesmen for the community of nations and of guardians of the peace, or States without this position whose justified interests are naturally limited, or finally miniature States which can exist only in symbiosis with a larger State. Worldwide wars in modern times have regularly fostered the wish to secure peace through an organization of the community of nations; to this we owe the Holy Alliance at the end of the Napoleonic wars, the League of Nations after World War I and the United Nations Organization after World War II. The League of Nations and UNO were planned not only as worldwide organizations to safeguard peace and conciliate in disputes, but as instruments in the task of furthering the progress of mankind through economic and cultural co-operation. While UNO is worldwide and universal in its purposes, the so-called national federations such as the Council of Europe or the Organization of American States are essentially limited to a certain area, whereas the so-called specialized organizations, such as the World Postal Union, the World Health Organization, the Food and Agricultural Organization, etc., are directed only to a specific purpose. Even the manifold activities of the community of nations should not allow us to overlook the fact that international law is essentially a primitive form of law comparable to the law as known to primitive peoples. The individual State which feels itself injured in those rights derived from international law is for the most part compelled to establish its rights on its own account. Even the question as to whether a breach of international law has taken place is not always, and only relatively recently, declared by the judgment of a court. Since 1919 there is an international court in the Hague. States may bind themselves to submit all or certain issues to this court, but they are in no way obliged to do so. There are as well international courts for certain regions or certain tasks. Such is the international court of the European communities or the European court for the protection of human rights and basic freedoms. Before the creation of international courts the setting up of a court of arbitration was the only way of settling a dispute on the basis of justice;

disputes not amenable to a settlement, or which the parties are not willing to settle by judicial means, are even now dealt with by mediation, for which a third State can offer its services or special institutions of mediation are set up (tribunals). The central problem of international law has always been the prevention of the unjust use of force; that unjust use of force can, in certain circumstances, be prevented through the lawful use of force, is a fact of general experience not confined to international law. The widest use of force within the community of nations is war. Modern international law recognizes now only two forms of lawful war: the defensive war of a single State or the action of the organized nations against a State that has acted unjustly. While law in earlier times recognized in the case of individual States a monopoly of the right to use force, it is the mark of modern international law that it recognizes such a monopoly only on the part of the community of States. Here due notice must be taken of John XXIII on the destructive possibilities of atomic war: "Hence in our age, which boasts of being the atomic age, it is contrary to reason to continue to consider war as the proper means of enforcing injured rights" *(Pacem in Terris,* no. 127); and so too the declarations of Vatican II in the Pastoral Constitution on the Church in the Modern World (arts. 80, 82). If war does come, then the international norms for war come into operation — the norms of an exceptional order of things — in place of the prescriptions of international law in time of peace, i.e., the normal order of things. The norms of international law in time of war are also inspired by the idea of protecting the individual: it is forbidden to use weapons against the unarmed, i.e., against the members of the civilian population, who may not take part in the fighting, against the wounded and the sick who are unable to continue the fight and against prisoners who have given up the struggle. International law knows no war in which all is permitted. Even in a war of defence the nation is subject to certain norms. A substantially stronger sanction against the unlawful use of force than the fear of a lawful use of force is in international law the fear of international opinion which condemns a breach of international law: frequently the pronouncement of an organ of the community of nations has no other purpose than to mobilize this world opinion.

It is precisely the primitive nature of international law that brings it close to the natural law; since only a very small part of the norms of international law are codified in treaties, the dividing line between natural law and positive international law cannot be drawn as precisely as is attempted with State laws whose norms are codified in written statutes.

The relationship between natural law and international law has determined for centuries the teaching on the latter. The doctrine of international law began with the investigations of moral theologians, particularly on the just war. Of special significance in the history of international law are the two Spanish moral theologians Francisco de Vitoria and Francisco Suarez, the former of whom examines the Spanish conquests in the new world from the point of view of ethics and international law, while the latter placed international law in a comprehensive setting of law whose origin and source is God, the first and supreme lawgiver. The secularization of the theory of international law begins with Hugo Grotius, leading gradually from a natural law doctrine based on reason to a positivism hostile to natural law and finally to a denial of international law since it lacks the backing of force which came to be regarded as the only criterion of lawfulness, the power of coercion. It was only the experience of World Wars I and II that led to a revitalization of thought on natural law in international law theory, in Germany (Verdross), in France (Ives de la Brière, Lefur, Delos), in Spain (Truyol, etc.) and in the English-speaking countries (Brown-Scott). On the other hand the extension of the community of nations to a world community and the disintegration of the world into ideologically opposed camps has led to a crisis in international law, since the common basis which international law previously possessed in the commonly accepted moral teaching of Western Christendom, cannot be the basis for a modern worldwide international law in a secular world. Such law is nonetheless necessary, as John XXIII pointed out in the fourth part of *Pacem in Terris,* by virtue of the common good to which all States are bound. This is also treated of explicitly by Vatican II, in the Pastoral Constitution on the Church in the Modern World, ch. V, part 2.

See also *State, Law* III, *Occident, Rights of Man, War, Natural Law*.

BIBLIOGRAPHY. H. Grotius, *On the Law of War and Peace*, 3 vols. (1925); H. Lauterpacht, *The Function of Law in the International Community* (1933); L. Oppenheim, *International Law*, I: *Peace* (8th ed., 1955), II: *Disputes, War and Neutrality* (7th ed., 1952); D. Anzilotti, *Corso di diritto internazionale*, I (4th ed., 1955); W. Gould, *An Introduction to International Law* (1957); G. Schwarzenberger, *International Law*, I (1957); E. Reibstein, *Völkerrecht. Eine Geschichte seiner Ideen in Lehre und Praxis*, 2 vols. (1958–63); L. Cavaré, *Le droit international publique positif*, 2 vols. (1961); J. L. Brierly, *The Law of Nations* (1963); W. G. Friedmann, *The Changing Structure of International Law* (1964); H. Kelsen and W. Tucker, *Principles of International Law* (2nd ed., 1966); F. Suarez, *Selections from Three Works* (including: *A Treatise on Laws and God the Lawgiver*) (1944).

Friedrich August Freiherr von der Heydte

INVASIONS, BARBARIAN

Mass migrations have not been confined to any one period or to certain peoples. Various causes again and again set whole peoples on the move: oppression by neighbouring peoples or conquerors, natural disasters, overpopulation, love of pillage and adventure. But we are concerned here only with the Germanic invasions, beginning with the settlement of the Goths on Roman soil in the year 376 and ending with the Lombardic settlement in Italy in the year 568. These "Barbarian Invasions" brought to an end the *Imperium Romanum* in the West, but the subsequent unification of Christian, Germanic and Roman elements laid the foundations of a whole era of Western history. However, the arrival of the Slavs and the Arab invasions must also be reckoned among the migrations which influenced the history of the early West and its Church.

The Germanic invasions must themselves be divided into the migrations of the East Germans and the settlement of the West Germans. For the most part the East Germans spread out over wide areas and completely abandoned their connection with former territories. The West Germans, in contrast, by persistent invasion and penetration, occupied the immediately adjacent territories of the *Imperium Romanum* without ever losing touch with their former homeland. The East Germans had encountered

Christianity at an early stage, although in an Arian form, and remained for a long period, therefore, isolated from the Catholic world around them, whereas the West Germans, at first predominantly heathen, for the most part accepted Christianity in its Catholic form. The East Germans, whose migrations and military expeditions caused the disintegration of the Roman Empire in the West, were ultimately completely assimilated into the surrounding Roman world; the West Germans, on the other hand, maintained their traditional political, economic and intellectual inheritance from the Roman period alongside their Catholic Christianity, although in a modified form.

1. *East German migrations and founding of States.* Unceasing German pressure on the borders of the Roman Empire finally enabled the Allemanni, about the middle of the 3rd century, to occupy the Decuman (frontier) lands and the Romans were forced to surrender the areas beyond the Rhine and Danube. At about the same time there was a successful mass invasion of Dacia (Rumania) by the Goths. In the middle of the 4th century the Romans were forced to accept the Salian Franks in Toxandria (North Brabant). The real beginning of the Germanic invasions is, however, rightly placed in the year 375, when, under pressure from the Huns, the Goths moved westwards from their settlements around the Black Sea. In 376 the Visigoths crossed the Danube and, following the defeat inflicted by them on the Emperor Valens at Adrianople in 378, the Emperor Theodosius was obliged to settle them in the province of Moesia as *socii*. This, the first settlement of a compact Germanic people on the soil of the *Imperium Romanum* as *socii*, inaugurated a new era in Roman-Germanic relationships which ultimately led to the decline and fall of the Western Empire. The Visigoths, on one of their later migrations, invested and sacked Rome in the year 410, under their leader Alaric. This sensational event was seen by non-Christians as a punishment for the abandonment of the old religion; it was to counteract this view that Augustine wrote his great work on the city of God (*De Civitate Dei*). After an abortive attempt by the Visigoths to migrate from southern Italy to Africa, they were settled by the Romans in southern Gaul in the year 418 as *socii*. This Tolosanic

kingdom (so named after the capital, Toulouse) fell to Frankish attacks in the year 507. The Visigoths consequently shifted the centre of their kingdom south of the Pyrenees, making Toledo their capital. Here in 711 they succumbed to the Arab invasion.

In the year 406 the Suevi, Vandals, Alans and Burgundians poured across the Rhine. The Burgundians succeeded in settling in Gaul, establishing there a kingdom with its centre, it is thought, either in Worms or in Jülich. It was destroyed by the Huns in the year 437 at the instigation of the Roman General Aetius. Along with other events, this defeat of the Burgundians later became the nucleus of the *Nibelungenlied*. The remnants of the tribe were settled as Roman *socii* near Savoy. Here, in repelling the attacks of the Franks they found a support in the Ostrogoth king, Theodoric, but after his death were brought under Frankish sovereignty in 532–534.

After crossing the Rhine in 406, the Suevi, Alans and Vandals pushed on into Spain. From 408 the Suevi were firmly settled in the North West of the peninsula, at first as Roman *socii*. Finally, after struggles with the Alans, Vandals and Visigoths, they were restricted to the province of Galicia (Asturia); here, their kingdom fell victim to the Visigoths in 585.

The Vandals and the Alans ultimately moved into the southern peninsula, near Andalusia. Even here, however, the Vandals felt insecure, and in the year 429 they moved on to Africa, in the first instance with the agreement of the Roman governor, Boniface, under the title of Roman *socii,* but they soon turned against the Romans, and by 442 had conquered the Roman province of North Africa. During their siege of Hippo (the present Bône) in 430, Augustine, the bishop of the city, died. It was here under Genseric (d. 477) that there arose the first completely independent German kingdom on Roman soil not even maintaining the pretence of a federation with Rome. This represented a special threat to Rome since the corn supply for a large part of the Roman Empire depended on the rich province of North Africa. Vandal rule in North Africa ended in 533 when it fell to Belisarius, the Emperor Justinian's general.

In the year 476, following a revolt of the army in Italy, composed mainly of Germans, Odoacer had deposed Augustulus, the last West Roman Emperor, and begun to rule as king in Italy. The Emperor successfully used the Ostrogoths against him and his kingdom. The Ostrogoths had been liberated from the rule of the Huns following the collapse of the Hun kingdom in the year 454, and had settled in Pannonia as Roman *socii*. In 489 they were led by Theodoric to Italy, which they succeeded in wresting from Odoacer (d. 493) after bitter struggles. The Ostrogoth Empire, embracing the whole of Italy and parts of the provinces of Pannonia, Noricum and Rhaetia, was at the height of its power under Theodoric (d. 526). It fell during the reconquest of Italy by the Emperor Justinian, which was carried out by his generals, Belisarius and Narses, between 535 and 555.

This wave of East German migrations ended with the campaign of the Lombards (Langobardi), who settled in the province of Pannonia and parts of Inner Noricum, allocated to them by the Emperor Justinian. After wars against the Gepidae in the years 565 to 567, they abandoned their territories to the Avars and in the year 568 moved to Italy, most of which they succeeded in wresting from the Emperor. Their rule in Italy was finally ended by the Franks in the year 774.

2. *The Christian Church in the Eastern German States*. The East Germans had known Christianity since the 4th century. The missionary work owed its real beginning to the activity of Bishop Ulfilas (d. 383) among the Visigoths in Moesia. Since it was the Arian form of Christianity which was at this time dominant in Byzantium, it was as Arianism that it reached the Goths and thence the other East German tribes. In their migrations and conquests, these Arian Germans encountered a Christendom which dominated the entire Roman Empire and which had, ever since the Council of Constantinople in 381, rejected Arianism once and for all. But they also met with a Christian Church which, after prolonged persecution by the Roman State, had first been tolerated, from the year 313, and then, from 383, had become the official imperial Church and adjusted its organization to conform to that of the State. The result was persecution of Catholic Romans by Arian Germans, leading, especially in the North African Vandal kingdom, to

157

confiscation of Church property and deportations of Catholic priests. Further, even where there was no persecution, the Germanic invasions meant that the Church was deprived of the organizational support of the State and Church life suffered gravely. In any case, the different faith of the East German States established on Roman soil hindered assimilation between the German conquerors and their Roman subjects. It was only when it was already too late for the decision to have any political influence that these German States adopted Catholicism — the Burgundians at the beginning of the 6th century, the Visigoths under Reccared (d. 601), the Lombards towards the end of the 7th century — and so paved the way to becoming the most important factor in the history of the West. Even after their conversion to Catholicism the danger persisted that the Churches here might develop into relatively independent regional Churches only loosely subordinated to the Papacy. The danger was very real among the Spanish Visigoths, where the Bishops of Toledo and Seville acquired a dominant role and demonstrated a great measure of independence at the eighteen Councils of Toledo.

3. *Political importance of the founding of States.* The settlement of East German tribes as *socii* on the soil of the Roman Empire from 382 on still allowed the Emperor a nominal sovereignty over them at first and even the East German kings and princes, with the exception of the Vandals, respected at least the moral authority of the Emperor at Constantinople. It is doubtful that the Germans ever intended to carry out a thorough political remoulding of the Roman world; the words traditionally attributed to the Gothic king, Athaulf (Orosius, *History,* VII, 43, 3), asserting that his first intention was to obliterate the name of Rome and to turn "Romania" into "Gothia", are without parallel. Athaulf himself later repudiated such a plan, stating that he had rather tried with the assistance of the Goths to renew the Roman Empire. Neither he nor the other East German princes succeeded in this aim. The confessional division brought about by Arianism stood in the way of this, as did also the division in the State whereby military power was reserved to the Germans and civil power to the Romans. Theodoric

then tried in vain to make a feeling of solidarity among the German peoples and states of the West, reinforced by princely marriages, the basis of a new political order and a counterpoise to the Byzantine Empire. The Roman Empire, with its political, social and cultural institutions, thus remained for the most part no more than an admirable model for the East Germans. But the institutions which they admired were already condemned to death. The most important result came from the encounter with the intellectual world of antiquity, which produced a certain revival in the field of literature. Promising opportunities for an encounter between the Germans and the literary heritage of antiquity were opened up in particular by Boethius (d. 526) and Cassiodorus (d. 583). It was a tragedy that the East Germans should have gained access too late or not at all to the only power which carried the future in itself, namely, Catholic Christianity. Their kingdoms, founded during the Barbarian Invasions, though able to destroy the *Imperium Romanum,* nevertheless perished in and with the Roman world without ever having contributed anything of its own to that world or having preserved anything of importance from it.

4. *West German settlements and States.* The results of the migrations of the West Germans were more enduring. They pushed forward beyond the frontiers of the Empire adjacent to them without ever losing touch with their original homelands.

The Allemanni, who in 213 had breached the Upper German *Limes* and from 259 had settled in the frontier lands, from the middle of the 5th century on crossed the Rhine and Danube and occupied Alsatia and the Alpine foreland. After stubborn resistance they succumbed to the Franks at the end of the 5th century and from then on were mostly under Frankish rule.

Their neighbours in the East were the Bavarians in parts of the old Roman provinces of Noricum and Rhaetia, between the Alps and the Danube. There were no further migrations on a large scale; instead, at the beginning of the 6th century, under Gothic influence, there was a development of sovereignty leading to the tribal formation of the Bavarians.

The Franks, divided into two parts, the

Salian Franks and the Ripuarian Franks, living from the 3rd century on in the territory of present-day Belgium and parts of the Netherlands, conquered, in the middle of the 5th century, the Roman province of Gaul. In the year 486, with the conquest of the kingdom of Syagrius between the Somme and the Loire, the remaining portions of the Roman Empire came under their control. The Franks succeeded in either ousting the other German States in Gaul (as in the case of the Visigoths who moved on to Spain) or bringing them under Frankish sovereignty (as with the Burgundians). So too they were able after decades of fighting to extend their rule to the West German tribes to the east of the Rhine (Frisia, Saxony, Hesse, Thuringia, Allemania, and Bavaria).

From the middle of the 5th century, Angles, Saxons and Jutes from Lower Saxony and Holstein occupied Britain, now abandoned by the Romans. Their kingdom, which broke up into seven petty kingdoms, never extended to Wales, Cornwall and Scotland.

5. *Christianity among the West Germans.* As in the case of the other West German tribes, and unlike the East Germans, the Franks long remained pagan during their contact with the Roman world. In places where they came in contact with the inhabitants of the former Roman Empire, the division was between pagan and Christian, instead of between Arian and Catholic. While there was scarcely any direct persecution of Christians on religious grounds, the West German conquest severely shook the organization of the Christian Church in the occupied provinces. For example, episcopal sees in the present-day Belgium and Northern France had to be transferred from Frankish territory to "Romania" (e.g., from Tongeren to Maastricht, from Tournai to Noyon), while the dioceses of Arras and Cambrai were united. The same happened in the former Roman province of Rhaetia, where the see of Octodurum (Martinach) was withdrawn to Sion, or in the province of Ripuarian Noricum, ruled by the Bavarians, where the diocese of Lorch vanished altogether. In isolated instances, the Christian faith was maintained even without the support of Church organization, e.g., in Augsburg, the memory of the martyrdom of St. Afra, in Upper Austria, the memory of St. Florian. Over large areas, however, Christianity either perished or else was syncretized with heathen forms of religion, so that in such places there was new territory for cultivation by future missions.

The conversion of the Frankish king, Clovis, at the end of the 5th century, to Catholic Christianity was to have far-reaching consequences. The religious contrast with his Roman subjects was thereby eliminated and one of the vital conditions created for a reshaping of the Western world after the decline of the Roman Empire. Hence too the other tribes east of the Rhine, which the Franks added to their kingdom, found their way from the outset to Christianity in its Catholic form.

In Britain too, following the decline of the Christian Church of the Roman period, a new missionary start was necessary. It was undertaken by the Irish Church which, situated at the very edge of the then known world, had not only developed a remarkable scholarship but also, because of non-urbanization, had developed other forms of Church organization in which the cloister took precedence over the diocese. From the year 596 onward, this Irish mission was joined by another sent from Rome and directly initiated by Pope Gregory the Great. As a result of the latter mission, following great initial successes, the archbishopric of Canterbury became the ecclesiastical centre of the country. The very close relations between the Anglo-Saxon Church and the Roman Pontiff then became the heritage of the Frankish Church under the influence of such Anglo-Saxon missionaries as St. Boniface (d. 754). This prevented the emergence of a Frankish national Church. The close bond between the Germanic peoples and the Pope was to be an essential element in the stability and cohesion of the West.

6. *Slavs.* To this German-Roman synthesis resulting from the Barbarian Invasions there was added, as a third component of importance for the emergence of the West, the settlement of the Slavs. From the 5th century onward, these Slavs set out from their original homeland between the Vistula and the Dnieper and pressed on over the territories near the Don and the Donetz to Bohemia and Moravia. Their major thrust, however, came only in the wake of the Avars, a people akin to the Turks. Near the

middle of the 6th century the Avars advanced from Siberia over the Black Sea, first of all towards Thuringia, from where they thrusted southwards. After 568 they pressed into Pannonia which had been abandoned by the Lombards, roughly the Hungarian Plain. They were followed by the Slavs, who gradually occupied the Balkans, which had been abandoned by the Germanic peoples since the withdrawal of the Langobardi. The Slavs also pushed on into the Alpine valleys of the former Roman province of Inner Noricum and were only halted by the Bavarians at the exit of the Puster valley about the year 600. In Carinthia the first Slav State in these territories was still in existence at the end of the 6th century; at the beginning of the 7th century Samo the Frank set up a Slav State obviously centred on Bohemia. Finally, in the 7th century the Bulgarians, a Hunno-Turkish people, migrated into the Balkans and founded a kingdom there in 679. In these regions Christianity almost completely succumbed. These Slav settlements and States, occupying a decisive boundary position like a bolt shot home between the Latin Church of the West and the Greek Church of the East, also contributed to the estrangement between the two Churches which was becoming ever more evident. Even Christian missions to the Slavs and Bulgarians, reaching out from Aquileia from the end of the 7th century on, from Bavaria from the 8th century onwards, and from Byzantium from the 9th century onwards caused conflicts between the Eastern and the Western Church which finally ended with the assimilation of the Carinthian and the Bohemian-Moravian Church into the Roman obedience and the Bulgarian Church into the Byzantine obedience.

7. *Arabs.* A third migration which affected the history of the early West and its Church was the invasion of the Arabs after the death of Mohammed (d. 632). Syria, Palestine, Egypt, Persia, North Africa and, after the battle of Xeres de la Frontera in the year 711, even the Visigoth kingdom in Spain succumbed to Islam. A further thrust beyond the Pyrenees was stemmed by the victory of Charles Martel at Cenon between Tours and Poitiers in the year 732. In 751 the Arabs lost Narbonne, their last city beyond the Pyrenees. Although the Arab invaders as a rule did not persecute their Christian subjects for their religion, it was a severe blow to the Christian Church when not only Palestine, the original cradle of Christianity, but Africa as well, one of the most important Church provinces, which had produced Tertullian, Cyprian, Lactantius and Augustine and which consisted of about 700 dioceses, came under the rule of non-Christian conquerors.

It was also a great loss that the parts of Spain occupied by the Arabs could not for the time being be brought within the growing unity of the West. The final result of the Arab invasion was also the destruction of the ancient unity of the lands bordering the Mediterranean. This led in turn to a further estrangement between the Byzantine Empire in the East and the German States in the West, and this also had consequences in the continued conflict between the Byzantine and Roman Churches. This Arab irruption marked the end of the period of the Barbarian Invasions which made a fundamental contribution to the formation of the West.

See also *Occident, Constantinian Era, Arianism, Islam.*

BIBLIOGRAPHY. See bibliography on *Islam;* also: C. Previté-Orton, *Medieval History* (2nd ed., 1916); J. B. Bury, *The History of the Later Roman Empire from the Death of Theodosius I to the Death of Justinian,* A.D. *395* — A.D. *565,* 2 vols. (1923); A. Dopsch, *Wirtschaftliche und soziale Grundlagen der Europäischen Kulturentwicklung von Caesar bis auf Karl den Grossen,* 2 vols. (2nd ed., 1923–24); J. B. Bury, *The Invasion of Europe by the Barbarians* (1928); J. Ryan, *Irish Monasticism* (1931); F. Lot, *Les invasions germaniques* (1935); F. Pirenne, *Mahomet et Charlemagne* (1937), E. T.: *Mohammed and Charlemagne* (1955); C. Courtois, *Les Vandales et l'Afrique* (1955); H.-I. Marrou, *St. Augustin et la fin de la culture antique* (1958); C. R. Dodwell, ed., *The English Church and the Continent* (1959); C. Oman, *The Dark Ages, 476–918* (2nd ed., 1962); F. Dvornik, *The Slavs in European History and Civilization* (1962); C. Godfrey, *The Church in Anglo-Saxon England* (1962); J. Wallace-Hadrill, *The Barbarian West, 400–1000* (1962); L. Bieler, *Ireland, Harbinger of the Middle Ages* (1963); E. A. Thompson, *The Early Germans* (1965); C. Dawson, *The Formation of Christendom* (1967).

Kurt Reindel

INVESTITURE CONTROVERSY

The Investiture Controversy, which flared up in the 11th century over the question of investiture (i.e., induction into spiritual office and benefices), was but one phase in the struggle between the secular and spiritual authorities. Given the nature of the visible Church, this struggle is almost inevitable and has persisted throughout the centuries. Since spiritual office and secular authority were especially closely associated in the medieval Church of the German Empire, since feudalism influenced government more strongly in Germany than in England and Spain, since, above all, the very idea of the Empire was wholly bound up with the Church, the Investiture Controversy became mainly a struggle between the Church and the medieval German Empire. Problems similar to those in Germany were successfully settled in France and England, therefore, without such passions being let loose.

The Church of late antiquity which had to confront a politically vigorous Germanic culture, was a society which lived by its own conception of law. The leading officers (Pope and bishops) were chosen by the clergy and people and, once elected, assumed full authority in the Church or in their dioceses, without the intervention of other elements (except proof of election and the right of the Eastern Emperor to confirm the election, and, of course, apart from the illegitimate influence of party struggles and intrigues). The close connection between the Church in the new German kingdoms and the barter economy and land possession, the attempt of the original landowners to safeguard, even against the Church, full freedom to dispose of their own land property (*Eigenkirche* — medieval church in the possession of a landlord), the political importance accruing to the Church and its educated officials by reason of the scarcity of intellectual movements and forces, the quasi-priestly status of kings, a status stemming from a still influential old Germanic culture — all this led inevitably to kings taking a growing interest in the appointment to Church offices. In theory, the Germanic State-Church did not contest the religious precedence of clerical power based on *ordo;* but in practice, there was a spontaneous co-operation between the clerical and the secular, in which the kings' right was continually growing. The Ottonians in particular, under whom the ceremony of anointing and consecrating kings was equated with the *ordo* for the consecration of priests, had not merely secured their influence over the head of the Church, through the nomination of Popes. They also based for political reasons the kingdom as a whole upon the episcopate and granted it considerable secular power. That they and their successors should therefore have had more influence in the investiture of bishops and imperial abbots was only logical. Bishops and abbots continued to be elected but in this the king's agreement or influence was decisive. Candidates were not infrequently drawn from the king's court and it was only a short step from this to direct nomination by the king. In that symbol-loving age, investiture took place in acts performed by the king himself; he gave the new bishop his Church by handing him a staff. The royal authority reached its highest point when, from the time of Henry III, when kings even deposed and instituted Popes, the ceremony of presenting a ring was added, a clearly spiritual symbol.

From the modern standpoint, crude exaggerations were here involved which inevitably led to a reaction. For ultimately, not only might such an investiture practice be abused by a king no longer mindful of his religious responsibilities; it also carried within it the danger of a general misunderstanding of the source of the clergy's pastoral authority. The reaction did not at first come from reforming circles in the medieval Church. Neither the monastic reforms nor the Church princes influenced by them, not even Leo IX, sought to break with the system in use at the German court. What they aimed to do was to safeguard the Church's freedom by internal reform and by staking off the tyranny of the nobles.

The reaction was the result of innovations in canon law and a renewed sense of the meaning of the Church. After the middle of the 11th century, on the basis of comparisons with the Church's ancient order and under the influence of the pseudo-Isidorian decretals, voices were raised condemning the existing investiture practice as dangerously close to simony and therefore rejecting it on principle. The identification of simony and heresy, already made by Gregory the Great, was vigorously re-affirmed by Cardinal Humbert of Silva Candida, mainly envisaging the princes' influence in the election of bishops. Because of the Cardinal's position in the Curia, the struggle became uncompromising. Meanwhile, even the consecration of the king gradually declined in importance compared with that of the bishop; a new view of the Church as a hierarchically graded authority emerged, ranking the princes with the laity and condemning princely investiture as lay-investiture and as a perversion of the proper relation between priests and laity. A radical abandonment of its traditional practice would, of course, have threatened the Empire to its foundations.

At first, the struggle against lay-investiture was conducted at the level of legal theory. The general prohibition issued at the Roman Synod of 1059 contained no detailed penalties. Despite the cooling of relations between the Curia and the German court following the death of Henry III, the Papacy directed its efforts primarily against the French and German bishops who were hostile to reform, and even Gregory VII in his *Dictatus Papae* confined himself for the time being to simply declaring publicly his claim to supremacy.

The occasion for the outbreak of the conflict was not one which should have threatened the stability of the Empire. The Milanese reformers had put forward a rival candidate for the vacant see of Milan in opposition to the archbishop proposed by Henry IV. The Pope forbade the King to invest his candidate for Milan. When Henry did so, and at the same time nominated bishops in central Italy without even informing the competent archbishop (the Pope himself), Gregory threatened him in December 1075 with excommunication. This was the signal for battle. In the declaration of the Synod of Worms, the King and his bishops united in demanding the Pope's resignation. A month later came the excommunication and deposition of the King. The absolution at Canossa brought only a brief respite. When, after three years' neutrality, the Pope recognized the new King and once again deposed Henry, the latter responded by electing a counter-Pope and waging war on Rome. Henry was crowned at Rome by his counter-Pope and Gregory died in exile in 1085.

In this period of the Investiture Controversy, Canossa already represented the climax and the turning point. With the submission of the King and the moral victory of the Papacy, the radical conflict between *regnum* and *sacerdotium*, into which the Investiture Controversy had now developed, reversed the early medieval relation between the two powers. This conflict, with the Pope henceforth denying in principle the sacral kingship and conscious of his own mission, calling all the more vigorously for a just worldly order and for the freedom of the Church, alerted men to the danger of a complete destruction of the imperial structure and stimulated opposition over a wide front. This opposition sought to win public support by the first great literary polemic on the principles of Kingdom and Church. No solution was found to the investiture problem following the death of Gregory, for the German King continued stubbornly to support his counter-Pope, despite the conciliatory attitude of Victor II and the diplomatic skill of Urban II, though Henry IV lost supporters and the Pope's leadership of Christendom was made evident during the First Crusade.

Attempts at a solution were first advanced in France and England. Because of the altogether different principles of the French monarchy, the issues there concerned power rather than existence. In 1097, the canonist Ivo of Chartres distinguished between Church office and the possession of temporalities. Although conveyance of the office of bishop should be denied to the laity on the ground that a sacramental act is involved, installation into Church property could be conceded to the King, since it was a secular act and even the Church enjoyed its property as the gift of the King. The French King accordingly relinquished investiture with the staff and ring, and contented himself with an oath of allegiance following canonical election and with the conveyance of the temporalities to the person elected, without any ceremony, though reserving to himself the power to dispose of these temporalities. In England, the excommunication of the royal councillors and of those who had been invested by the King compelled Henry I to accept Anselm of Canterbury's mediation. A compromise ceremony was agreed on at the London Parliament of 1107. The King (*rex et sacerdos* according to the anti-Papal "Anonymous of York") renounced investiture with ring and staff, guaranteed canonical election witnessed personally by him, and required an oath of allegiance from bishops before consecration.

A similar compromise appears to have been impossible for Germany, however.

Here the temporalities were not simply lands, tithes, rents, but privileges of rank, earldoms and dukedoms carrying with them specific duties to the Empire. These it was impossible to regard as inviolate Church property and to renounce all influence over them. Thus all attempts to reach agreement in Germany failed, even when, following the death of the counter-Pope (1100), the main questions solved themselves. New possibilities only appeared with the Roman campaign of Henry V. But the utopian proposal of Pope Paschal II that the Church would renounce all *regalia* in return for the renunciation of investiture by the King (Sutri 1111) came to nought through the opposition of the parties involved. The captive Pope's acceptance, extorted from him by the King, of full royal investiture with ring and staff, provoked the protest of the Church party. But despite the hardening of positions, a compromise solution emerged, based on the views of Ivo. Calixtus II failed indeed to secure the renunciation of formal investiture into the temporalities. Yet the negotiations backed by the German princes resulted in a settlement. In the Concordat of Worms (1122) the Pope approved Henry V's presence at the canonical election, his right to decide in disputed elections, and investiture into the *regalia* by the secular symbol of the sceptre together with an oath of fealty. In accordance with the greater interests of the King, in Germany this investiture was to precede consecration, but in Italy and in Burgundy to follow it. This was not a concession to Henry V but the confirmation of an old imperial right after co-ordination with the just claims of the Church (Kempf). The Concordat was solemnly ratified at the Reichstag in Bamberg and at the Lateran Council of 1123.

The new dialectic with its distinctions made a settlement possible but produced only a solution in principle. Basically, Gregory VII's views on the freedom of the Church had indeed won the day; yet in practice the Church continued to be closely identified with the life and interests of the medieval State. For the most part, bishops developed into secular princes and the Church remained for centuries at the mercy of the secular power and subject to its benevolence or caprice. The Investiture Controversy had been settled at the summit level but the task of properly delimiting the changing forms remained.

See also *Reform* II C, *Church and State*, *Crusades*.

BIBLIOGRAPHY. G. Meyer von Knoau, *Jahrbuch des Deutschen Reiches unter Heinrich IV. und V.*, 7 vols. (1890–1909); R. W. and A. J. Carlyle, *A History of Mediaeval Political Theory*, IV (1922); A. Fliche, *La réforme grégorienne*, 3 vols. (1924–37); A. Fliche and V. Martin, *Histoire de l'Église*, VIII and IX (1950, 1953); L. Knabe, *Die gelasianische Zweigewaltentheorie* (1936); A. Fliche, *La querelle des investitures* (1946); E. Kantorowicz, *The King's Two Bodies* (1957); N. F. Cantor, *Church, Kingship and Lay Investiture in England* (1958); G. Tellenbach, *Church, State and Christian Society at the Time of the Investiture Contest* (1959); W. Ullmann, *Growth of Papal Government in the Middle Ages* (1962).

Hermann Tüchle

IRRATIONALISM

Irrationalism is the doctrine which holds that reality, in whole or in part, is not amenable to the conceptual thought of the intellect, or to reason or the spirit in general. Reality is said to be wholly incomprehensible or basically attainable only by acts independent of the intellect, such as feeling, experience, intuition, love, sympathy, attunement, faith, instinct or action.

1. *The main forms of irrationalism.* (i) The irrationalism which derives from nominalism and empiricism holds that it is impossible to have rational knowledge of the essence and metaphysical structures of the sensible world. (ii) Voluntarism sees the world as deriving from a purely arbitrary or impulsive will, to the exclusion of any spiritual structure of being. Reality is attainable by man only in the will or in love. (iii) Life-philosophy makes life the essence of reality, and holds that this life-force may be grasped intuitively but not conceptually. (iv) According to Kant and some of his followers, things in themselves and indeed reality as such are not attainable by the intellect. (v) The philosophy of values distinguishes being as known by reason from values, the latter being attained only by feeling. (vi) Existential philosophy, which holds that knowledge is an act of the whole man, makes it a pre-rational or supra-rational process, which according to many existentialists cannot be made explicit in rational terms. (vii) The extremist form of the situation ethics refuses to accept rational knowledge of universal laws as the norm of moral

action. (viii) Many schools of the philosophy of religion hold that God discloses himself only to intuition, faith or feeling. Propositions enunciated by reason (dogmas) are often treated as merely symbols for the divine incomprehensibility, which change indefinitely. (ix) The extremist form of dialectical theology takes revelation to be a paradox which contradicts any order of things recognizable by reason.

2. *The analysis of human knowledge* shows that irrationalism and rationalism are extreme positions, fundamentally defective, but with justifiable interests at heart, which have, however, not been properly envisaged. (i) Just as the personal unity of man is displayed in a rich profusion of mutually complementary forces, so too human knowledge must be understood as a basically unified structure, which is composed of various moments of knowledge, analogous to one another and differently accentuated according to object, situation and historical setting. (ii) The unity and the formative principle of all modes of knowledge is to be found in the transcendence of the human spirit which is orientated to the horizon of being; this primordial unity of the spiritual consciousness excludes an ultimate pluralism in knowledge. (iii) Since the human spirit addresses itself to the absolute in its affirmation of being and in the accomplishment of its free acts, it has knowledge of being as a whole. Hence the fundamental structure of reality and so everything in general is known initially to the spirit from the start. Everything therefore is knowable to the spirit in principle. The very fact of asking about "all things" and "the whole" presupposes a non-explicit foreknowledge of the whole: otherwise the question would not be possible. Hence a thorough-going irrationalism eliminates itself by an inner contradiction: it speaks as if it had knowledge of something which should be beyond the reach of knowledge. (iv) Since the human spirit is finite and primarily directed to objects in the world, human knowledge is poised in an irreducible tension between living insight and intellectually manageable but abstract concepts. Insight grasps initially the concrete fullness of the object but still lacks rational perspicuousness. Hence it strives for concepts, while still remaining unamenable to complete conceptual grasp. (v) Conceptual thought is therefore not an independent function of knowledge. Working with categories and abstractions, it is merely the objectivating stage of a still non-conceptual insight and experience. Hence every region of being is accessible to conceptual or to rational thought in the stricter sense (see, however, the articles *Revelation* and *Mystery*). (vi) As conceptual thought proceeds with its work of deduction and dialectic, it continues to live from the original act of insight. But since it knows along with its finite object the relation of that object to being in general — its ontological specification — it can go beyond that object to interrogate it about its metaphysical and theo-logical foundations. (vii) At the various levels, the relationship of the object to being is different and so too the relation between concept and insight: it varies from the almost total transformation of insight into exact concept to the mythic naming of the mystery. For this reason, the nature of rational knowledge must not be one-sidedly determined in terms of a preconceived ideal of knowledge or any particular branch of knowledge such as the natural sciences. It has a different stamp and a different language for each of the various fields of knowledge to which it adapts itself. But the conceptual style is all the apter, the more the thing known coincides with its functions and categorial specifications. (viii) On the necessary involvement of insight and thought with spiritual strivings, feeling and love see *Voluntarism*. (ix) For the human spirit, sensible knowledge is a part of itself which is external to itself. It is fundamentally akin to the spirit, and ordained to it, being its necessary starting-point and permanent complement. But being relatively independent and limited, it cannot be fully subsumed and transformed into spiritual knowledge and so remains an expression of the fact that human knowledge is a matter of perspectives and a finite thing.

See also *Analogy of Being, Kantianism, Religion* I C, *Religious Feeling*.

BIBLIOGRAPHY. R. Garrigou-Lagrange, *Le sens du mystère et le clairobscur intellectuel* (1934); R. Crawshay-Williams, *The Comforts of Unreason. A Study of the Motives behind Irrational Thought* (1947); K. Jaspers, *Vernunft und Wiederkunft in unserer Zeit* (1950); A. Alliotta, *Le origini dell'Irrazionalismo contemporaneo* (1950); E. R. Dodds, *The Greeks and the Irrational* (1951); J. Bofarull, *En el mundo de lo irreal* (1954); R. Masiello, *Intuition of Being according to the Metaphysics of Saint Thomas Aquinas* (1955); O. F. Bollnow, "Die Vernunft und die Mächte des Irrationalen", in K. Ziegler, ed., *Wesen und Wirklichkeit des Menschen* (1957); K. Rahner, *Theological Investigations,* IV (1966), pp. 36–76; *Enciclopedia Filosofica,* II, cols. 1553–64.

Klaus Riesenhuber

ISLAM

A. History and Spiritual Foundations

Islam is the name which Moslems give their religion (a combination of Arabian, Jewish, Gnostic and Christian elements), the political and social order connected with it and indeed the whole Islamic culture. Since they attribute their religion to Allah, and regard Mohammed only as his instrument, they reject the term Mohammedan which became current in Europe. The Arabic word *Islam* means total surrender to the will of Allah, who is the same God (though envisaged to some extent in the light of Oriental despotism) as the God whom Jews and Christians worship (Vatican II, Declaration on Non-Christian Religions, art. 3).

Islam began in the early 7th century with Mohammed's experience of his call to proclaim monotheism. His religious campaign started from Medina. As regards the religious situation in Arabia, it may certainly be assumed that in the time of Mohammed the native religions, some of which were still polytheistic, but included belief in the demiurge Allah or Rahman, had been affected by Jewish and Christian influences (from Jewish colonies, Christian Jacobites and Nestorians, etc.).

Little is known about Mohammed's early life. Tradition has it that he was orphaned at an early age, looked after by relatives of modest means, and worked hard for his living until an advantageous marriage left him comfortably off. Having had no formal education (it is not clear whether he could read or write), he is not impressive as a speculative thinker, but he had a highly receptive mind and was a brilliant organizer, as the extraordinary achievements of his public life demonstrate. As to Mohammed's sincerity, the question is not whether he did or did not have divine revelations but whether he really thought he had them. Today specialists in Islamic studies take his sincerity as a working hypothesis. In keeping with the Jewish-Christian tradition that revelation is communicated to the peoples by divinely-sent prophets, the conviction grew in Mohammed — inspired by his experience of his call — that he had received a message from an envoy of heaven, like the great figures of Jewish-Christian history before him, Noah, Abraham, Moses and Jesus. He gained only a few disciples at Mecca, where he began to preach. The aristocracy of the place felt itself menaced and made his life unbearable. The main emphasis in his preaching at Mecca was on judgment, the resurrection on the last day and faith in Allah, the one God. He also laid down a number of religious and social duties. After thirteen years of hostility in Mecca, he found a friendlier atmosphere in the neighbouring city of Yathrib, to which he then fled secretly from Mecca. This flight is the *hegira* ("abandonment of kindred"), the first event in Mohammed's life which can be accurately dated (15/16 July 622). With it begins the Moslem era. The Moslem calendar, being lunar, lacks about eleven days of our solar year. Henceforth Yatrib was called *Madinat al-nabi*, the city of the Prophet, or simply Medina. Here Mohammed displayed his capacity for leadership. At Mecca he had been a revolutionary, clashing with an entrenched established order. At Medina he figured as a representative of order, and within a few years' time had grown powerful enough to seize Mecca and make the Kaaba there the goal of pilgrimage for his own followers.

During his activity in Medina, Mohammed broke radically with Judaism. Even the direction of prayer was not towards Jerusalem but Mecca. He saw his task as the revival of the monotheism of Abraham which had been corrupted by Jews and Christians. In 632, death put an unexpected end to his preaching, leaving Islam an unfinished work. Mohammed's preaching was committed to writing in the Koran. Like the Scriptures of the OT and NT, the Koran was to be the sacred book containing Mohammed's revelations. It represents a collection of fragments which had either been written down by Mohammed's first disciples or memorized. The Caliph Othman had the various versions gathered, sifted and put into a canonical form, which he made obligatory. It comprises 114 chapters, called *sura,* which in turn are divided into verses *(ayat).* No logical or

165

chronological order is observed; a single *sura* may contain verses of very various dates, having to do with quite unrelated subjects. So as to minimize the difficulties this arrangement entails, a division was made between Meccan and Medinese *suras,* according to the time of their origin. When he preached at Mecca, Mohammed's great concern was to convert his countrymen to faith in Allah, the only God, who creates men and rewards them; in the resurrection, the last judgment, hell, and paradise. The Medina section of the Koran reflects the great change in Mohammed's life; now he is a person of authority and gives orders as he sees fit according to circumstances.

The Koran also reflects Moslem thought. It tells Moslems what they need to know in this life so as to attain happiness in the next. But it is not enough to know the Koran. Numerous situations arise that it did not foresee. But the Koran is the foundation of all other commandments and the definitive norm which guides the doctors of every age.

B. Historical Development

No provisions had been made for the succession to Mohammed. The period immediately after his death was one of the most critical in Moslem history. Eventually his closest associates gained the upper hand and appointed Abu Bakr first Caliph (*khalifa,* successor, representative). Thus arose the institution of the caliphate, nebulous in its purpose, powers, and mode of transmission, with no directives for it in the Koran. A revolt of the tribes that had allied themselves with Mohammed was put down in the bitter wars of the secession, the *ridda:* and then began a series of attacks on Persian and Byzantine territory which became a full-fledged invasion once the Arabs realized the wealth of these areas and the pitiful weakness of their defences. Syria was lost to Byzantium by the battle of Yarmuk, in 636; Persian rule on the banks of the Tigris ended with the battle of Qadisiyya, and the victory of Nihawand in 641 threw open the Iranian plateau to the Arabs. The first three Caliphs, Abu Bakr (d. 634), Omar (634–46), and Othman (646–56) ruled from Medina. During the turbulent caliphate of Ali the seat of government was removed to Damascus. Here the Umayyad dynasty reigned till 750, adding to the unparalleled triumphs of Islam, and by

711, in the time of the Caliph al-Walid, Moslem forces had reached the Atlantic coast of Morocco and the Iberian peninsula in the West, and in the East stood on the banks of the Indus and the Yaxartes.

The fall of the Umayyad caliphate heralded the dismemberment of its empire. The Caliphs of Baghdad had already lost Spain, which acknowledged the Umayyads of Cordoba. After a century of brilliant expansion, many other regions also broke away and became a mosaic of independent states. From time to time powerful states could conquer the smaller ones — the 10th-century Umayyads of Cordoba, for example, the Egyptian Fatimids, or the Oriental Ghaznawids. In the 11th-century the Seljuk Turks dominated the East and the Almoravids the West. The latter gave way in the following century to the Almohads, while Egypt was subject to the Ayyubis (1171–1250). Mongols ruled Persia in the 13th and 14th centuries, the Mamelukes Egypt. The power of the Ottoman Turks reached its zenith after the conquest of Constantinople in 1453 and then gradually declined until it vanished at the end of the First World War. Persia enjoyed a period of grandeur under Shah 'Abbās I, while the Great Moguls were at the height of their power in India. The Moslem countries today are Morocco, Algeria, Tunisia, Libya, Egypt, Mauretania, Senegal, Chad, Northern Nigeria, the Sudan (excepting its southern provinces), Eritrea, Somalia, the coast of East Africa down to Zanzibar, the whole Arabian peninsula, Syria, Turkey, Iraq, Iran, Afghanistan, Pakistan, and Indonesia. There are also strong Moslem communities in India, China, the Malay peninsula, and the Soviet Union. No reliable statistics are available. It is reasonably estimated that there are about 400 million Moslems.

C. Theology and Observances

1. The original theology of Islam did little more than affirm the existence and oneness of God, the prophetic mission of Mohammed, and the necessity of obeying the basic commandments known as the "pillars of Islam". On this foundation, in the course of disputes leading to much bloodshed, was erected a dogmatic structure that has not materially altered since the 8th century of our era. Dogma deals chiefly with the existence of Allah and his attributes. Allah is one

and there is no other. He is eternal, the first and the last. There is no distinction of substance or accident in him, he is not limited or composed of parts. His attributes are said to include wisdom, omnipotence, supreme majesty, life, will, hearing, vision, and speech. Allah is free to do as he pleases: he can perfectly well pardon all infidels or punish all the godly. Nevertheless whatever he decides to do is supremely just: there is no analogy between divine and human justice, for no one has any rights as against Allah. All the acts of creatures, whether good or evil, are pre-determined by Allah. Though passages can be found in the Koran both for and against free-will, determinism is the prevalent view in Islam. There are no secondary causes which have an action independent of the first cause. There is no necessary connection between cause and effect. Events simply succeed each other as Allah wills. Substance is the atom. When atoms combine, they form bodies, when they separate, the bodies decay. The accidental modifications of substances are created moment by moment by Allah and hence are contingent. Fire burns because Allah causes the burning.

As to human acts, since it cannot be admitted that anything happens against the omnipotent will of Allah and since man is also aware of being able to choose between two courses of action, it is said that Allah first creates in us the power of choosing between good and evil and then directly (and freely) creates the human act that corresponds to the choice we have made. One must also believe those whom Allah has sent when they are speaking in his name. Mohammed is the last of the prophets and his law abolishes earlier laws except where it coincides with them. Besides man, Allah created the angels, the devils, and the jinn (or genies). These are beings intermediate between angels and men, made of pure fire and endowed with supernatural powers. Some of them are Moslems.

It is also necessary to believe in a future life, the last judgment, paradise with its delights, and hell with its torments. Moral precepts admonish men to do good and avoid evil. There is no clear-cut distinction between grave and venial sins. All sins can be forgiven except that of apostasy. The Koran exhorts the faithful to relieve the necessities of orphans, pilgrims, prisoners, and the poor; it recommends prayer, loyalty to contracts and resignation under misfor-

tune. The existence of the soul is admitted, but the concept is not analysed. Generally it is believed that the soul survives the body. There is disagreement as to whether the soul dies with the body in order to rise again with it at the resurrection, and whether a soul is created for every new human being or has an independent existence before being united with the body.

The "pillars of Islam", the chief duties of the faithful, are prayer, the profession of faith, alms, fasting and pilgrimage. Moslems divide the world into two great camps: the countries that are Moslem and those that are not yet subject to Islam. At the end of the world all will be subject to Islam. A Moslem must pray five times a day: at dawn, at noon, in late afternoon, at sunset, and when night has fallen. He always prays facing Mecca. Almsgiving is a means of justifying the goods one has received from Allah, and of preparing to receive them. It quickly grew into a precise system of taxation. The fast of the month of *Ramadan* requires one to abstain from all food, drink, smoking, sexual intercourse, etc. from the first sign of dawn until sunset. Every Moslem in a position to do so must make the pilgrimage to Mecca at least once in his lifetime. Islam draws no clear distinction between the spiritual and the temporal. Even the most trivial of acts is ruled in some way or other by the will of Allah.

2. The *Šari'a* is the religious law of Islam. Its sources are: a) the Koran; b) the *Sunna,* that is, the example of Mohammed, his words and deeds as known by tradition and preserved in various compilations; c) in cases not covered by the Koran or the *Sunna,* reasoning by analogy *(qiyas)* and judgments based on prudent considerations *(ra'y);* d) the common opinion of the learned or the customary practice of the people. These factors, notably the last, have enabled Islam to assimilate new elements and discard the antiquated. In the 8th and 9th centuries, four great schools grew up around the *Sunna* which still exist today: that of Malik ibn Anas (d. 795), of Safi'i (d. 820), of Abu Hanifa (d. 767) and of Ahmed ibn Hanbal (d. 855). They disagree only on relatively unimportant matters. What Mohammed established is a community of brothers in faith, equal before Allah whatever their race or condition. Allah is sole judge in the internal forum, since he alone sees the heart. In the external forum a distinction is

drawn between acts relating to worship and those that have to do with the life of society.

3. Religion makes itself particularly felt in public life through various holy days and seasons. The most solemn of these are the lesser feast, celebrated at the end of *Ramadan* — the month of fasting — and the greater feast, with which all Islam marks the end of the Meccan pilgrimage. There are also ritual observances for all the decisive moments in a person's life. Circumcision is very common among Moslems, though contrary to the common opinion, it is not of obligation. The best known dietary rules are those forbidding the use of pork and alcoholic drinks.

Mohammed founded a theocratic State. Being the last of the prophets, he could leave behind no successors where religion was concerned; but a temporal ruler, the Caliph, was required to see to the interests of the community. Moslem law cannot be territorial, because it is based on religious conviction: it is personal and binds only Moslems. Other residents are tolerated in exchange for taxes and peaceful submission. On these conditions Christians and Jews could be allowed to practise their religion in private and be protected in their persons and property. But they belonged to a lower order of society. Only adult males enjoy full legal and religious rights. Women are subject to various restrictions.

4. It has been said that asceticism and mysticism are alien to the spirit of Islam. Certainly there is nothing in the Koran that could be called an obviously ascetical text, and Moslem tradition on the whole is non-ascetical. But from the beginning pious souls have practised asceticism and taken the way of mysticism. The names of Ḥasan al Baṣrī (d. 728) and Rābiʿa al-Adawiyya (d. 801) were famous.

In the 8th century the name *Ṣūfī,* a derivative of *ṣūf* ("wool"), began to be applied to ascetics who wore a mantle of coarse wool in imitation of Christians. The flourishing state of Sufism in the 9th century provoked the hostility of the orthodox Sunnites. The Sufis explained the ideal of Moslem life in quite a different way; and besides, the orthodox were sure that no sort of reciprocity was possible between exalted Allah and insignificant man. To love God, in the view of orthodox Sunnites, was simply to worship him and obey him according to the established rules. They found it detestable to

talk of love of Allah, and above all of union with him. The struggle between the Sufis and the orthodox Sunnites was long and bitter and has not altogether ceased even today. Thanks, however, to the efforts of al-Gazzāli, a modified Sufism was reconciled with orthodoxy and spread widely in Islam as a whole.

It is generally admitted that Sufism is at the base of Moslem ethics. Its influence remains notable in the Moslem world, partly as a result of the works of poets and classical authors, which encouraged the desire for a closer relationship with Allah. *Ṭarīqa,* associations of pious souls who accept the guidance of a director skilled in the ways of the spirit, had a similar effect. Their primary object is religious and ethical, but inevitably the larger and wealthier *ṭarīqa* became factors which governments had to reckon with in their internal and even their foreign policy. Suffice it to recall the influence which the *ṭarīqa bektāšsiyya,* to which the Janissaries belonged, had over the Sultans of Turkey, and the fact that the leaders of the *ṭarīqa sanūsiyya* have become the reigning dynasty of Libya. Invariably the *ṭarīqa* have been a religion within religion, almost a State within the State, earning themselves the hostility of ulamas and muftis, who feared them as dangerous rivals. At the present time those institutions are losing a good deal of their former influence, but in many areas still hold their own.

Islam, in the course of its continuous evolution, has been shaped by the work of theologians, lawyers, and Sufis. It has known a variety of opinion and emphasis, of jurisprudence, of philosophical and theological movements, and a wide range of mystical doctrines, so much so that the bounds of orthodoxy were sometimes blurred or abolished.

D. SECTS

Only those groups are considered properly heretical which dissent from the mainstream of Islam on fundamental issues and choose to live independent of it, in a completely separate society with rulers of its own. If the original unity of Islam was soon shattered, the cause was not theological controversy but the clash of human ambitions over the political legacy of Mohammed. The Chariji took a democratic view, declaring that any Moslem was fit to be chosen Caliph. The orthodox Sunnites maintained that the Caliph must be chosen from the tribe of Quraysh, to which Mohammed himself belonged. The adherents of Ali, Mohammed's son-in-law, rejected the principle of election and sought to keep the succession within the family. *Šī'a* in Arabic means party or sect, and this name was applied by antonomasia to the partisans of ʿAlī, the Shiites. Their constant failure in military and political matters points to the religious character of the demands of the Shia. Their unwarlike, pious nature also favoured a process of division into many small sects. The Chariji insisted on the necessity of works for faith. By grave sin one ceased to be a believer and became worthy of death. A branch called the Ibadites still survives in Oman and Zanzibar, and in certain parts of Algeria and Tripolitania.

Sunnites and Shiites are as deeply divided over the prerogatives of the supreme dignity in Islam as they are over its origin. For Sunnites the Caliph is simply the temporal ruler whose duty it is to protect religion but who has no magisterium or other religious privilege to raise him above other Moslems. But the Shiites believe that the Imam, their supreme head, endowed with a definitive magisterium and superhuman knowledge, is both infallible and impeccable. The Shiites flourished in the 11th and 12th centuries, when the Shiite dynasties of the Buyids ruled at Baghdad and the Fatimids in Egypt. Schisms troubled them from the outset. The oldest and most notable date from the 8th century, when the Zaidi set up a regime in the Yemen that lasted until 1963, and when the "Sevens" (Ismaëlis) separated from the "Twelves" (Imamites). The former are so called because the line of their hereditary Imams ended with the seventh, while the latter went on to the twelfth. Ismaëli followers of the Aga Khan are modern representatives of the "Sevens"; they are scattered across central Arabia, Iran, India, and East Africa. But the most numerous and important sections of the Shia are the "Twelves", who have ruled Iran since the Safawid dynasty (1502–1722) forced their doctrine upon the country. They are also numerous in Iraq, especially in the towns of Samarra, Baghdad, Najaf and Karbalā.

Passing over other sects of less importance, we should mention certain bodies which ultimately derive from Islam but can no longer be considered Moslem: the Druz (Druses) — a tiny group in South Syria and the Lebanon — are descended from the Shia, as are the Babi and the Bahai. The latter, whose main strength is in Iran, have also attracted adherents among Western neo-pagans, especially in the United States. They profess humanitarianism and universal brotherhood. In Iran the Bahais have sometimes been the victims of outbursts of intolerance, accompanied by bloodshed. Occasionally, they are called Wahabis, but in error, as the latter are a reform which seeks to restore Islam to its primitive form. The Aḥmadiyya sect, founded by Gulam Aḥmad of Qadyan, in the Punjab, at the end of the 19th century, is merely technically a heresy because its founder said he was a prophet (Mahdi). The sect actively propagates Islam not only in Moslem countries but also in Europe and America. Though these people sincerely claim to be true Moslems, the orthodox persecute them, putting them to death, whenever possible, if they will not recant. There are two branches of the sect, the Lahori and the Qadyani. The former desire an accommodation with orthodoxy; the latter hold firm to the teaching of their founder.

E. Islam and Christianity

1. Though at least from the point of view of the history and phenomenology of religion Islam appears in the context of the "religions of revelation" (Judaism and Christianity), its rejection of the basic truths of Christianity (the Trinity, the divine Sonship of Jesus and the "closing" of revelation which it implies, the redemption) brought it into sharp opposition to Christianity from the beginning. This was first reflected in Greek and Syrian theology (John Damascene and Theodore Abu Kurra), which regarded Islam, however, merely as a heretical movement of Judaism. Later, with the development of theology in Islam *(kalam)* in terms based on Greek philosophy, the possibility of real discussion ensued, as contacts multiplied with Christian theology during the Islamic penetration of the West, the *Reconquista* and the Crusades. Notable figures on the Christian side were Peter the Venerable, Raymond Lull and St. Thomas Aquinas (in his *Summa contra Gentiles*). Further political developments such as the wars against the Turks and the downfall of the Ottoman Empire resulted in the almost total cessation of dialogue. In spite of the lack of discussion

169

on the theological level, apart from the exceptions mentioned above, constant efforts to convert Islam were made by Christian missionaries. The Islam mission was begun in Spain in the 9th century and carried on in the 12th and later centuries by St. Francis of Assisi, Raymond Lull, the Dominicans, Franciscans, Carmelites and Capuchins, by the Jesuits from the 16th century on and in modern times by the White Fathers, Charles de Foucauld and the French associations, Association Charles de Foucauld and the Mission de Foucauld. The greatest difficulty facing the missions is the identity of religious, political and cultural life in Islam. The missionary effort of Islam, especially in modern times, has chiefly been directed to Africa and India.

2. Since the Renaissance, and more particularly in the last hundred years, there has been a growing interest in scientific study of Oriental literature and history, but these profane interests found little echo in theology. The "Islamic-Christian" dialogue, first signalled by Vatican II, has many implications which cannot be gone into here. Vatican II takes up the subject of Islam in two places. The first is in the Declaration on the Relationship of the Church to Non-Christian Religions (Nostra Aetate), art. 3: "Upon the Moslems too the Church looks with esteem. They adore one God, living and enduring, merciful and all-powerful, Maker of heaven and earth and Speaker to men. They strive to submit wholeheartedly even to his inscrutable decrees, just as did Abraham, with whom the Islamic faith is pleased to associate itself. Though they do not acknowledge Jesus as God, they revere Him as a prophet. They also honour Mary, his virgin mother; at times they call on her, too, with devotion. In addition they await the day of judgment when God will give each man his due after raising him up. Consequently, they prize the moral life, and give worship to God especially through prayer, almsgiving and fasting. Although in the course of the centuries many quarrels and hostilities have arisen between Christians and Moslems, this most sacred Synod urges all to forget the past and to strive sincerely for mutual understanding. On behalf of all mankind, let them make common cause of safeguarding and fostering social justice, moral values, peace and freedom."

Then, in the Dogmatic Constitution on the Church (Lumen Gentium), in art. 16, apropos of the various ways in which those who have not yet received the gospel are ordained to the people of God, the Council speaks of the Moslems, after first mentioning the Jews: "But the plan of salvation also includes those who acknowledge the Creator. In the first place among these there are the Moslems, who, professing to hold the faith of Abraham, along with us adore the one and merciful God, who on the last day will judge mankind."

The description of Islam given in the first of these texts omits such difficult questions as polygamy, repudiation of wives, etc. But serious efforts are being made in most Moslem countries to introduce reforms in these matters. Further, the description of Islam given by the Council really confines itself to Moslem theodicy, but does not take in the faith of Islam, which includes the prophetic mission of Mohammed. In spite of these shortcomings in the document, the solemn recognition of Allah as the one God and creator may be regarded as a foundation for future dialogue between Christianity and Islam.

See also Monotheism, Religion II A, B, Reconquista, Crusades.

BIBLIOGRAPHY. T. W. Arnold, The Preaching of Islam (1913); The Encyclopedia of Islam, 4 vols. and supplement (1913–38); R. Nicholson, Mystics of Islam (1914); id., Studies in Islamic Mysticism (1921); T. W. Arnold, The Caliphate (1924); A. Wensinck, Handbook of Early Mohammedan Traditions (1927); T. W. Arnold and A. Guillaume, The Legacy of Islam (1931); R. Levy, Introduction to the Sociology of Islam (1933); D. Donaldson, The Shiite Religion (1933); R. Hartmann, Die Religion des Islam (1944); H. A. R. Gibb, Modern Trends in Islam (1947); id., Mohammedanism (1949); F. M. Parejo and others, Islamologia (1951); W. C. I. Smith, Islam in Modern History (1957); J. Pearson and F. Ashton, Index Islamicus (1958 ff.); N. Daniel, Islam and the West. The Making of an Image (1960); P. Southern, Western Views of Islam in the Middle Ages (1962); J. Jomier, Introduction à l'Islam actuel (1964); K. Cragg, The Dome and the Rock. Jerusalem Studies in Islam (1964); J. Saunders, History of Medieval Islam (1965); R. Caspar, "Le dialogue islamo-chrétien. Bibliographie", Parole et Mission 33 (1966), pp. 312–22; 34 (1966), pp. 475–81. PERIODICALS: Revue du Monde Musulman (Paris, 1906 ff.); The Moslem World (New York, 1911 ff.); Die Welt des Islams (Berlin, Leiden, 1913 ff.); Islamic Culture (Hyderabad, 1927 ff.); Islamic Quarterly (London, 1954 ff.).

Felix M. Pareja

J

JANSENISM

Jansenism, a movement within the Catholic Church of the 17th and 18th centuries, especially in France and the Netherlands, represents one effort to solve the problem with which all Christian life is faced — that of reconciling the fundamental antagonisms inherent in Christianity. There is the acceptance of the world which has as its counterpart a condemnation of the world, and there is the necessity of working out one's salvation responsibly while always knowing it to be a freely bestowed gift, beyond all man's merits. The antagonism cannot be left as a dualistic discord, and it cannot be resolved into a monism where one or the other side alone remains in possession. The attempted middle position taken up by Jansenism was rejected as one-sided by the magisterium of the Church.

1. *Jansenistic doctrine.* The main initiator of this new effort to articulate the self-understanding of Christianity was Cornelius Jansen (the younger) (d. 1638), who had studied in Louvain and Paris, taught theology at Louvain and was Bishop of Ypres from 1636 on. His views were chiefly propagated through his *Augustinus seu doctrina S. Augustini de humanae naturae sanitate, aegritudine, medicina adversus Pelagianos et Massilienses* (published posthumously, Louvain, 1640 ff.).

This work took up the themes of the right notion of divine grace and its relationship to the free will of man which had become once more burning questions among Catholics, under the influence of the Reformation and the controversy between Molinism and Baianism. The argument, in deliberate opposition to scholastic tradition as well as to the humanist notion of man's shaping his own religious and human destiny, relied so exclusively on patristic theology and on St. Augustine in particular — especially his controversy with Pelagius — that Jansenists could call themselves "friends of St. Augustine". Indeed, the whole movement could be described as a modern form of Augustinianism. It was on an Augustinian basis that Jansenism developed its own theological system, in the light of a three-fold division of the history of salvation. In the first stage, the state of "innocent nature", "Adam" was so free and so much master of himself that he could freely bring about his own salvation — with the assistance of the *adjutorium sine quo non,* a grace indispensable for the supernatural end, but due to him and as it were at his disposal. But with original sin, man lost his self-mastery so completely that he has lost all sense of the religious and moral value of his actions, is totally incapable of a personal, responsible decision for the good and is completely at the mercy of "concupiscence triumphant". His will is therefore determined by the attractions of created things and so always sinful in all its actions. Every effort, no matter how well meant, to amend by his own forces, either in practice by the exercise of the virtues generally recognized as such, or in theory itself by the analyses of philosophy, can only be "splendid vices" in the service of evil desires, since man is so thoroughly at the mercy of the *libido sentiendi, sciendi, excellendi.*

Against this totally negative background

of the loss of freedom, redemption is not presented as the restoration of freedom and new responsibility, but as a new determination of the will. But this time it is the heavenly joy which is the determinant. This is a re-orientation of the will towards its salvation, towards love of the divine instead of love of the created. There is an *adjutorium quo* which is in no way mediated by human assent, but is efficacious by its very nature and absolutely irresistible. An extremely literal interpretation of the antithesis between the "slavery to sin" and "slavery to Christ" presents Christian freedom not as inner freedom in and before the freedom of God and his love, but at the very most as freedom from outside constraint. For his salvation, man is abandoned to a totally arbitrary election on the part of God. He is treated as an object, not as a counterpart (relatively) to the divine will.

The logic of this position brought with it a point which was to be one of the most essential and highly controverted of Jansenist views — the *a priori* restriction of the salvific will of God and the redemptive value of Christ's death to those who were in fact predestined to salvation. Thus there was a sharp contrast between human corruption — the total extinction of responsible self-determination — and redemption (the arbitrary determination of some people, through a "triumphant concupiscence" now directed to the divine). This dualism remained the basic conviction even of later Jansenism in France, where it was less a theological system than a practical way of life.

2. *The spread of Jansenism in France.* This view of the history of salvation became of practical importance first in France, where it was to be at its most influential. The large convent of Cistercian nuns of Port-Royal, with two foundations in and near Paris, adopted a reform inspired by the Jansenist understanding of Christianity, chiefly under the influence of Saint-Cyran (Jean-Ambroise Duvergier de Hauranne [d. 1643]), Abbot of Saint-Cyran, a friend of Jansen in his student days at Paris. The Abbess of Port-Royal, Angélique Arnauld (d. 1661), was mainly instrumental in implementing the reforms. "Petites écoles" were set up, and hermitages provided for those who wished to retire from public life to devote themselves entirely to God and his new creation which was the negation of the old world. From these bases Jansenism gained great influence on French society, among its most notable conquests being Racine and Pascal, who came into contact with Port-Royal through his sister Jacquéline who entered the convent in 1642. Controversy ensued, chiefly with the Jesuits, the Jansenist spokesman being the youngest brother of Angélique Arnauld, Antoine (d. 1694), sometime member of the Sorbonne and later head of the movement.

Thus Jansenism took on the contours of a party in the Church. In the realm of morals and asceticism, it strongly opposed the broad-minded "Probabilism" of Jesuit casuistry by putting forward the severest demands with no room for compromise. Jansenism called for complete certainty about the lawfulness of an action before it could be performed ("Rigorism"); for perfect contrition based on love of God, not merely on fear of the punishment of hell, as pre-condition for the sacrament of penance ("Anti-attritionism"); for supreme reverence for the sacrament of the altar, which was to be received only on rare occasions (contrary to the Jesuit recommendation of frequent Communion), while the priesthood was considered to be a task of enormous daring. These were the theses of the controversial writings of Arnauld, especially his *De la fréquente communion,* and of Pascal's *Lettres à un Provincial,* whose sharp and witty polemics did much to discredit the Jesuits. This ideal of strict religious observance was put into practice in small groups, which were kept as intimate as possible — parishes, monasteries and oratories. Jansenism followed the trend in Church politics which opposed the centralism of the religious orders, mostly of international character, which sought as far as possible to be exempt from all jurisdiction except that of the Pope. It favoured the relative independence of dioceses and parishes. Most of its numerous supporters belonged to the upper middle class. These had had in the Parliaments (courts with legislative powers to some extent competing with royal legislation) a certain political instrument, but they had been discarded by the monarchy as soon as the power of the common enemy, the ancient "military" nobles, had been broken. When the monarchy now favoured the court nobility, descendants of the ancient feudal nobles, but now entirely dependent on the king, the upper middle class lost all hope of political power and was ready, in its disappointment, to see all purely human religious endeavour discredited. It was ripe for a doctrine which sharply opposed the true order of values, that of grace, to the natural and worldly order.

3. *The stages of the controversy*. Conflict with the magisterium of the Church broke out with the publication of the Bull of Innocent X *Cum occasione* (1653), which condemned five propositions of Jansen on the relationship of grace and freedom (*D* 1092–1096, *DS* 2001–2007). These propositions were not taken word for word from the *Augustinus*, but were formulated in keeping with its principles. The Jansenists acknowledged the justification and authority of this decision, and hence the *quaestio juris*, but denied the *quaestio facti* — that the propositions in question were to be found in Jansen. They also refused to recognize the authority of the Church to decide on such "facts" which were not revealed facts, and claimed that in this matter the magisterium was entitled to no more than *silentium obsequiosum* from Christians. In 1657, the general assembly of the French clergy called upon them to subscribe to a formula of submission which acknowledged the *de facto* heretical status of Jansen and the authority of the Church in such matters of fact. A similar formula was also proposed by Pope Alexander VII in 1664. In the subsequent quarrels, many Jansenists, including Arnauld and Paschasius Quesnel, were forced to seek refuge in the Netherlands. There was a temporary peace after 1667 (the "Clementine Peace" of Pope Clement IX) and the conflict ceased to be a major preoccupation when the Roman and the French Church clashed on Gallicanism (the Jansenists being mostly on the side of Rome, defending the independence of the Church as regards the State). But after the settlement between the papacy and the monarchy, the conflict broke out again in still more acute form. The Bull *Vineum Domini* appeared in 1705 and led to the suppression and destruction of Port-Royal (1707–12). But the persistence of Jansenism may be seen from the condemnation of 101 propositions of Quesnel by the Bull *Unigenitus* (1713) and its counterpart — the demand for a General Council to decide this new controversy. The promulgation of the Bull *Unigenitus* as French law finally brought Jansenism to an end as a movement. Organized Jansenism survived only in the Netherlands, where it still exists as the "Church of Utrecht", now united with the Old Catholics.

The whole controversy between the Jansenists and the magisterium has a strange twilight element. The longer the controversy continued, the less was it concerned with definite doctrines. Jansenism was a complicated matter, based rather on a certain mentality and spirituality than on an explicit dogmatic theology. It was an effort at Church reform in the spirit of early Christianity, which was asked to declare itself heretical, though this was the last thing which it wished to be. It is hard to avoid the suspicion that the reaction of the magisterium to this undoubtedly very serious-minded effort at Christian self-understanding really created the opponents which it then condemned so severely as Jansenists.

4. *The relevance of Jansenism*. In the perspective of the great movements of the human spirit, Jansenism may be seen as a reaction, in line with that of the Reformation, affirming the Christian consciousness of election against the highly conciliatory intermediate position of Renaissance humanism. It undoubtedly highlights the central problem of Christian self-understanding — as Christian humanism did from the opposite standpoint — but seems as little helpful as the arguments of its opponents to the type of theological discussion which is now prescribed by the progress of philosophical reflection since the Enlightenment, transcendental philosophy, idealism and existence-philosophy. Above all, the great problem which is at the base of all the others, how to reconcile divine grace which is absolutely gratuitous and beyond merit with personal human responsibility, religiously as well as theologically, can hardly be solved along Jansenistic lines. The Jansenist abstractions concerned with an *adjutorium quo* effective of itself and of the nature of a "quality", and with a freedom of choice which is basically impotent, hardly allow us to pose the question properly, much less to solve it. It is a problem to which we can only hope to do justice if we treat it in the categories of interpersonal mediation, which will allow for the dialectic of individual personal originality within the

framework of interpersonal originality. We must recognize, in fact, that responsible freedom can only be brought into existence by the creation of this dialectical tension and harmony with its opposite free counterpart. This dialectic must be basic not only for the limit notion of a "pure state of nature" but above all for the theological exposition of the mystery of redemption (insofar as it is a summons to use the liberty which it alone confers).

See also *Augustinianism, Baianism, Grace and Freedom, Concupiscence, Moral Theology* III, *Gallicanism, Humanism* I, *Enlightenment, Existence* II, *Nature* I.

BIBLIOGRAPHY. G. Gerberon, *Histoire générale du Jansénisme* (1700); Anonymous (D. de Colonia), *Bibliothèque Janséniste ou catalogue alphabétique des principaux livres jansénistes* (4th ed., 1744); A. de Meyer, *Les premières controverses jansénistes en France* (1919); A. Gazier, *Histoire générale du mouvement janséniste* (1924); L. Laporte, *La doctrine de Port-Royal* (1923); N. Abercrombie, *The Origins of Jansenism* (1936); L. von Pastor, *History of the Popes,* XXIX (1938); J. Orcibal, *Les origines du Jansénisme,* 3 vols. (1947–48); L. Willaert, *Les origines du Jansénisme dans les Pays-Bas catholiques* (1948); L. Ceyssens, *Jansenistica,* 4 vols. (1950–59); J. Laporte, *La morale d'après Arnauld* (1952); P. de Leturia and others, "Nuove ricerche storiche sul Giansenismo", *Analecta Gregoriana* 71 (1954); J. Orcibal, *Saint-Cyran et le Jansénisme* (1961); H. de Lubac, *Augustinisme et théologie moderne* (1965); L. Goldmann, *Weltflucht und Politik. Dialektische Studien zu Pascal und Racine* (1967).

Konrad Hecker

JESUS CHRIST

I. Biblical: A. Questions of Fact. B. Problems of Method. C. Jesus' Message and Mission. D. Questions concerning the Passion and Easter. E. New Testament Christology. II. Quest of the Historical Jesus. III. Christology: A. Historical Survey. B. Christology Today. IV. History of Dogma and Theology: A. Jesus Christ in Classical Fundamental Theology. B. New Approaches. C. Preliminary Considerations of Principle regarding a Contemporary Christology. D. Perspectives in Dogma and the History of Theology. E. The Official Doctrine of the Church. F. Problems and New Questions.

I. Biblical

The following may be listed as assured findings of scholarship: a) No doubt is cast on the historical existence of Jesus by any serious scholar. Now that the debates raised by Bauer and Drews about Christ being a myth have died away, there is wide agreement about the historical fact of Jesus. b) The old-style attempt to construct "Lives of Jesus" has failed; even recent books of this kind (e.g., Stauffer's book on Jesus) are interesting for details but are no longer in harmony with the present state of scholarship as a whole. c) This is due to the character of the sources for the life of Jesus; the NT writings, even the gospels, being kerygmatic in purpose, are not strictly historical sources but testimonies of belief.

The present article assumes agreement on these points. It deals with problems of fact (A) and of method (B), the message and mission of Jesus (C), questions concerning the Passion and Easter (D), and NT Christology (E).

A. QUESTIONS OF FACT

1. The few non-Christian sources merely confirm that in antiquity it never occurred to any one, even the bitterest enemies of Christianity, to doubt the existence of Jesus (cf. Bornkamm, *Jesus of Nazareth,* p. 25). These sources are: Tacitus, *Annals,* 15, 4 (Christ condemned to death by Pontius Pilate under Tiberius), Suetonius, *Claudius,* 25, 4 (a certain "Chrestus" caused disturbances in Rome; uncertain whether Christ is meant), Pliny the Younger's letter to Trajan, *Epistola* 10, 96 (Christ revered as a god), Josephus, *Antiquities,* 20, 200 (James, the brother of Jesus who is called the Christ). The authenticity of the *Testimonium Flavianum* (Josephus, *Antiquities,* 18, 63 f.), which had long been recognized as a Christian interpolation, yet usually considered to derive in substance from Josephus, has been contested again recently. H. Conzelmann detects in the passage the Lucan pattern of the Christian kerygma and therefore considers that it was "subsequently interpolated in its entirety" (*RGG,* III, col. 622). The Talmud references and the apocryphal gospels likewise add nothing to our knowledge of Jesus.

2. The Christian sources comprise a few indications in early credal formulas (birth, death on the cross, resurrection), and above all the books which are expressly concerned with Jesus, i.e., the gospels. Nevertheless it is generally admitted that they do not

satisfy the ideas and demands of a modern historian. The classical quest of the historical Jesus still thought it possible to draw from the gospels a psychologically and historically incontestable picture of Jesus. When the special character of the fourth gospel was recognized and the Two Sources Theory was worked out for the Synoptics, the attempt was made to reconstruct a life of Jesus on the basis of Mark's Gospel. Wrede, however, showed that Mark himself possessed no clear picture of the life of Jesus but arranged his gospel from dogmatic points of view; Schmidt established the secondary character of the framework. This excluded the last "historical" source, i.e., Mark's Gospel in its present form, for a reconstruction of the life of Jesus. These conclusions still remain substantially valid. Form-criticism made it clear that the beginning of the tradition concerning Jesus — if we leave brief credal formulas out of account — is the independent pericope. This is not a section of a larger whole, but contains the whole revelation of Jesus. The intrinsic interweaving of report and confession of faith prevents direct access from the individual pericope to the historical, earthly Jesus (see below, B). The NT writings take into account the new situation after Easter; they do not describe Jesus κατὰ σάρκα and are only interested in his earthly life to the extent that it is the necessary condition of the confession that "Jesus is the Christ, the Kyrios". But even if the character of our sources is taken into account (message, not report), the following biographical details among others can be established: Jesus' Galilean origin, baptism by John, execution under Pontius Pilate.

3. The chronology of Jesus' life, like the routes of his journeys, is uncertain. The NT writers are not interested either in an absolute chronology or in synchronizing Jesus' life with the secular history of the age. Only the late passage Lk 3:1f. inserts at least the public ministry of John the Baptist into the framework of Roman and Jewish history. (The 15th year of Tiberius lasted according to Roman reckoning from 19 August 28 to 18 August 29, and according to Syrian reckoning from 1 October 27 to 30 September 28; the second is now regarded as the more probable.) The year of Jesus' birth is also uncertain. The difficulties can only be briefly indicated: Jesus is said to have been born under Herod the Great when Quirinius was governor of Syria (Lk 2:1). But there is no evidence that Quirinius was governor during Herod's lifetime. None of the explanations of this contradiction so far suggested is satisfactory. All that is generally accepted is that Jesus was born before 4 B.C. (death of Herod). More precise details cannot be drawn from the infancy narratives of Matthew and Luke.

The most important chronological problem is the date of Jesus' death and, as a consequence, of the Last Supper. The paschal lamb was killed in the afternoon and eaten in the evening of 14 Nisan, and on 15 Nisan the festival of the Pasch was celebrated in memory of the deliverance from Egypt. According to the Synoptics, Jesus celebrated the establishment of the new Covenant within the framework of a paschal meal (14 Nisan) and was executed on 15 Nisan; according to the Johannine dating, Jesus was put to death on the eve of the feast-day, i.e., 14 Nisan, and Jesus' Last Supper has no connection with the paschal meal, which in John's Gospel is not eaten until after the Crucifixion. The controversy over these conflicting data has not been resolved to this day. Even the solar calendar discovered in Qumran does not make it possible to harmonize the Synoptic with the Johannine chronology. Moreover, both in Mark's and in John's indications of time, theological interests have to be taken into account. For Mark, the old commemorative meal is replaced by a new one; Jesus himself is the paschal lamb which is eaten; for John, Jesus is the true paschal lamb which is slaughtered. Once this theological purpose of the dates is recognized, it becomes of secondary importance to fix the actual day. The majority of exegetes take 15 Nisan (= 7 April), A.D. 30, as the probable date of Jesus' death, but they are aware that this is hypothetical (cf. Trilling, *Probleme*, p. 64).

4. The person of Jesus must be seen against the background of his age and environment. Since 63 B.C. the Jews had been politically subject to Roman sovereignty. Although these foreign rulers made considerable allowance for the national and religious susceptibilities of the Jews, there was in Jesus' time a widespread expectation, fanned by the fanatical Zealots, of a political Messiah. It is evident from the gospels that Jesus took no stand on burning political

problems; they seldom mention a political group as hostile to him (except on the question of taxation), whereas they devote much space to religious controversy with the Pharisees. How far Jesus is to be brought into connection with the Essene movement on which new light has been thrown by the finds at Qumran, is still disputed. Scholars seem to be agreed that the points of contact are substantially fewer than was first thought when the discovery of the scrolls was announced. There is no longer any question of direct dependence on Jesus' part. The Qumran community regarded itself as an organized community of salvation with a hierarchical structure; by its obedience to the Torah and the observance of prescriptions of ritual purity, it was fitting itself to be the eschatological "remnant". Jesus, on the contrary, addressed himself expressly and without distinction to the whole nation.

The Jews jealously defended their religious and national traditions; Hellenistic influence was therefore very slight in Palestine as compared with the Judaism of the diaspora. Jesus shows no sign of Hellenistic influence. His speech is Aramaic, his parables are drawn from ordinary Jewish life, his controversies with opponents concern the OT idea of God, the interpretation and observance of the Torah. His actual home, Galilee, was despised by the purely Jewish population of Judaea and the capital on account of its mixed population, as was its half-pagan neighbour Samaria. Although the geographical outline of the earliest gospel belongs to the Marcan editorial stratum, it is very probable that Jesus began his public ministry in Galilee (Lake of Gennesaret, Capernaum).

B. Problems of Method

1. The first problem is where to insert Jesus' earthly life. What place does Jesus occupy in an account of NT theology? Whereas one school of thought among exegetes (e.g., Meinertz) places Jesus at the beginning of NT theology, another (e.g., Bultmann) puts Jesus before the beginning of NT theology, as its presupposition. Even if Jesus knew himself to be the Messiah and called for faith in himself as such, he cannot be described, according to Bultmann, as a sharer of the Christian faith, of which he is none the less the object (cf. *Verhältnis*, p. 8).

Bultmann therefore deals with Jesus among the presuppositions of NT theology, but as a historical presupposition within its framework. A third school, however (e.g., Schlier), excludes Jesus completely from NT theology. These exegetes recognize that the NT presupposes Jesus, his words and deeds, and that without them there would be no NT. But the theology of the NT writers is not simply a continuation of Jesus' theology. The historical figure of Jesus cannot be drawn from the gospels, which throughout are an interpretation of his history by believers. The historical figure is a condition of NT theology but as such should not be made a part of NT theology itself (Schlier, *The Relevance of the NT,* p. 11).

There would probably be general agreement that Jesus may be termed the presupposition of the development of the NT kerygma. The further question whether he is to be dealt with within the framework of NT theology, is of secondary importance.

2. A second, more important problem is the transition from the earthly Jesus to the Christ of faith, i.e., the problem of continuity and discontinuity raised by the dividing-line of Easter. The longer scholarship pursued the "quest of the historical Jesus", the more it emphasized the discontinuity between the "earthly Jesus" and the "Christ of faith". This development reached its culmination in Bultmann's theology. From the fact that only Jesus and the NT kerygma are historical elements, Bultmann concludes that only Jesus and the kerygma can be in continuity with one another, but not Jesus and the Christ of the kerygma, who is seen as outside history. Consequently no path leads from Jesus to the Christ of the kerygma. The kerygma is said to presuppose the sheer fact that the historical Jesus existed, the fact of his life and history on earth but this "fact that . . ." has no saving significance of any kind. Consequently it is said that the believer cannot believe in the earthly Jesus; the latter has no significance for one's own personal life; only the Christ of the kerygma can encounter the believer in the kerygma, in the word of the Church spoken today. The continuity between Jesus and the kerygma, which is inconceivable without Jesus' earthly existence, is acknowledged; but an agreement in content is not admitted, for the kerygma does not simply take over Jesus'

message, nor did Jesus' message already contain the NT kerygma (e.g., the Christological kerygma had no place in Jesus' teaching).

With Bultmann, who is here representative of other exegetes, emphasis on the discontinuity between Jesus and the kerygmatic Christ reached its culmination. Hand in hand with it goes a serious concern for continuity; continuity stands in the forefront of inquiry for a whole line of Bultmann's pupils. The problem is acute because an explanation has to be found why the disciples and with them the NT do not simply repeat Jesus' message. The faith in God's action in Jesus evoked by the appearances of the risen Lord led, in a long process of reflection, inspired to some extent by passages from the OT, to the interpretation of the death of Jesus as redemptive. As this understanding gradually became more explicit (cross — glorification — baptism or birth — pre-existence), the whole of Jesus' earthly life was drawn into the post-paschal proclamation of Christ. This process is visible, for example, in the increasing interest shown in Jesus' earthly life. To explain the continuity as a linear extension, so to speak, without taking into account the Easter events as a radical dividing-line, would not do justice to the significance of the Resurrection. In any case an explanation acceptable to all theological schools of thought is not to be expected in the present state of research.

C. JESUS' MESSAGE AND MISSION

In the centre of Jesus' message and mission is the reign and kingdom of God (1); its proximity determines the uncompromising demand for immediate conversion (2); it is the absolutely sovereign and freely offered gift of God's grace to his chosen people (3).

1. Jesus' teaching on the reign of God shows that God is the centre of his thought. Men do not have to do something first in order to receive God's gifts, nor is God under an obligation to reckon up man's precise merits and reward them accordingly. Jesus declares war on piety of that kind. God is the only actor who really matters. The "kingdom of God" or "reign of God" therefore does not mean a merely static condition, but God's dynamic action also. The reign of God is a reality opposed to the present aeon, and signifies that the dominion of Satan is ended (Lk 11:20 = Mt 12:28).

The reign and kingdom of God is the theme of many of Jesus' parables. The "parables of growth" (to which the term "contrast-parables" is now preferred because of their point) show that that reign can only be brought about by God, but that he will bring it about despite all obstacles (Mk 4:26–29, 30–32 par.; Mt 13:33 par.). These contrast parables are aimed in particular at the impatience of those who wish to bring about the kingdom of God by force (Zealots) or their own achievements (Pharisees). Such people are told that it does not depend on them, because the kingdom of God is the action and gift of God alone.

The controversy about Jesus' conception of the reign of God has led to agreement on a middle position. Neither thorough-going eschatologism (J. Weiss; A. Schweitzer) nor realized eschatology (C. H. Dodd) has prevailed. According to the first of these two extreme positions, Jesus expected the reign of God as a strictly future reality which would come in his lifetime (before the completion of the disciples' mission to Israel). According to the second, the reign of God is already present. With various modifications the prevailing view today is that Jesus regarded the essentially futuristic reign of God as extending into the present through his coming and as particularly manifest in his exorcisms and miracles.

From the post-exilic period onward Israel expected that God would inaugurate his reign with a day of judgment. The nations will be annihilated in battle (Joel 4:15f.; Ezech 38:22) or judgment (Dan 2:34f.; 7:9f., etc.) or must be subject to Israel (Psalms of Solomon 17). Israel as the chosen people of God enters into the kingdom of God. This self-confidence had already been opposed by John the Baptist (Mt 3:7ff.). Jesus even threatens that the kingdom will be taken from the Jews and given to others (Mk 12:9; cf. Mt 8:11f.).

2. The call for conversion inspired by the proximity of the reign of God leads to an intensification of the demands of the Torah and also to the suppression of certain precepts which misrepresent the genuine will of God. Jesus' attitude to the Law is the point which provoked the hostility of the Jews, because they saw in it an attack on God. Among the precepts which are made more radical are the prohibition of divorce (Lk

16:18; cf. Mk 10:1–12; Mt 5:31, against the practice of the note of dismissal), the honest observance of the fourth commandment (Mk 7:10–13, against the usage of the "Corban"), the antitheses of the Sermon on the Mount (Mt 5:21–42) and the unqualified requirement of love of enemies (Mt 5:43 ff.). Jesus is not concerned about literal fidelity in the fulfilment of a precept but about the will of God himself. Consequently he directly attacks the Law where that will was concealed by the "hedge about the Law". This is particularly clear in the disputes about the Sabbath (Mk 2:23–3:6); in this sense, Jesus' attitude is certainly correctly described by the saying, secondary in character, at Mk 2:27.

The insistence on the true will of God stands in direct connection with the message of the imminent advent of the reign of God. Jesus knows he is a voice calling at the last hour, consequently he lays down no law with detailed prescriptions but demands penance and conversion to God himself. This is seen in the herald's cry which sums up the whole of Jesus' proclamation (Mk 1:15). Because the reign of God comes solely by God's power and grace, man can only pray for it ("Thy kingdom come") and recognize the present as a sign calling for conversion (Lk 12:54–59; 10:23); it is now that the uncompromising decision for or against Jesus must be made.

The saying about confessing and denying (Lk 12:8 ff.) shows that the positive or negative response to Jesus' message and person is decisive for membership of the eschatological community of salvation. Anyone who accepts Jesus' message now, i.e., fulfils God's will to salvation and holiness now in the radical way proposed by Jesus, has qualified as an heir to the promises.

3. The expectation of the imminent advent of the reign of God also inspires Jesus' endeavour to prepare the whole of Israel to inherit salvation. Jesus regards the empirical Israel of his time as the chosen people of God, i.e., in accordance with the history of revelation, he respects the prior claim of the people of Israel as the bearer of the promise of salvation. Consequently Jesus restricted to Israel his own work and later that of his disciples who were co-operating in his own mission (Mt 10:5 f.; 15:24 ff.). All the more weight attaches to the cures of pagans which are reported as exceptions (Mt 8:5–13 par.; Mk 7:24–30).

The summons to the whole of Israel finds expression in characteristic features of his preaching. A first typical feature is that there is no trace of flight or separation from the world. Unlike John the Baptist in the desert, Jesus sought public places in order to reach all Israelites with his message. In contrast to many movements of the age (Essenes, Qumran), Jesus did not want to gather together the holy remnant and separate the pious from the sinners. For Jesus, all Israel is a scattered flock without a shepherd (Mich 5:3; Mt 9:36; 10:6). God's goodness is shown by his not excluding even sinners and outcasts (Lk 15), and so Jesus too converses with the religious outcasts and sits at table with them. Access to the kingdom of God is offered to all Israelites on the single condition of readiness for conversion. Jesus' refusal to segregate and gather together repentant Israelites into a special Messianic community is shown both in his words and his actions; he avoided all contemporary ecclesiological references and terms. Even on the supposition that there was a circle of the Twelve before Easter, this is to be regarded as representing not the holy remnant but the whole of Israel, the twelve tribes of the nation. The number twelve unmistakably expresses Jesus' claim to the whole of Israel. The refusal to divide the good from the wicked is explicitly emphasized by the parables of the fishing-net (Mt 13:47–50) and the weeds (Mt 13:24–30).

The reserve shown by Jesus in speech and action results from the fear of misunderstandings: a) to gather the remnant into an organized community (cf. Qumran) would merely have been regarded as entering into competition with the "sects" of the day; b) Jesus does not simply demand the correct observance of the Mosaic Law; going beyond and partly cancelling the old Law (especially the ritual precepts) he teaches an ethics which is clear and uncomplicated compared with legalistic casuistry; with a special separate community there would be a danger of a new sectarian juridicism; c) the refusal to set up a special community is also consistent with the new relation between God and man; whereas Jewish sects claimed to do more than fulfil the Law and viewed their relations with God in the categories of achievement and reward, Jesus wished to manifest God's justice and mercy; all men are sinners before

God. If Jesus had formed a separate community, this aspect of his message would have been less prominent; d) since Jesus laid down only one condition for entry into the eschatological community of salvation, namely decision for him here and now, the immediate urgency of this demand would have been unnecessarily weakened by the provisional foundation of a special community. These and other reasons explain Jesus' reserve with regard to an organized community of the heirs of salvation.

So far only the Israelites have been referred to as candidates for salvation, but something must also be said on Jesus' attitude to the pagans. Despite the recognition on principle of Israel's prerogative, Jesus' conception of salvation also has room for the pagans. Jesus excludes the idea of revenge from his teaching (cf. Lk 4:19 with Is 61:2) and at least in isolated cases allows pagans to know of the dawn of the reign of God which he has inaugurated (Mt 8:5–13 par.; Mk 7:24–30). Furthermore, it appears possible to show that Jesus had in mind the idea of the eschatological pilgrimage of the Gentiles (Mt 8:11; cf. J. Jeremias, *Promise to the Nations*). This would not imply a mission to the pagans, but would affirm their eschatological participation in salvation.

D. Questions concerning the Passion and Easter

It is possible to assume without serious difficulties that Jesus himself saw his passion coming as a reaction to his preaching about God and the kingdom of God, or even consciously went to meet it. Among the problems connected with the way Jesus regarded his death is the question of the historicity and origin of the λύτρον-saying (Mk 10:45), and the even more decisive question of the words used at the Last Supper on the pattern of various OT themes (Ex 24:8; Is 53; Jer 31:31–34). It is difficult to reconstruct the original form of words because the accounts of the Last Supper as we have them probably also reflect the post-paschal understanding of the Eucharist. Differences have long been observed between the Matthew-Mark version and the Luke-Paul version. Furthermore, two separate traditions concerning the Last Supper are involved: an account of the Supper which is eschatological in outlook, and an account of the institution (of the Eucharist). We can scarcely expect to reconstruct the original wording with certainty *in detail*. Nevertheless it is possible to follow the Semitic tradition very far back; at all events the themes of vicarious death and of the Covenant cannot be derived from Hellenism. It is also difficult to judge the prophecies of the Passion and Resurrection (Mk 8:31; 9:31; 10:32–34). These are considered by the critics to be *vaticinia ex eventu*; it is generally recognized that at least in their present form they are secondary in character. Consequently they cannot be quoted in isolation as evidence for the way Jesus envisaged his death. From the whole pattern of Jesus' claim to a divine mission, however, it appears at least probable that within the circle of his disciples Jesus spoke of his death as a divine "must" (Lk 12:50; 13:32f.) and accordingly understood it as a new means of salvation. It must also seriously be asked whether he cannot have been capable of discovering the divinely-willed meaning of his death in the function of the vicarious suffering of the Servant of God who suffers "for many" (Is 53:4–12), i.e., as a new gracious act of God for Israel and the Gentiles (Is 42:6f.; 49:5–8), especially as the thought of the vicarious and expiatory significance of the sufferings of the just man had been current since the time of the Maccabees (E. Schweizer, *Erniedrigung*, pp. 24–26). The idea of atonement can be supported at least by the logion of the baptism of death (Mk 10:38 par.) which is not open to suspicion of being post-paschal interpretation based on biblical theology.

The question of Jesus' understanding of his death is of secondary importance from the point of view of post-paschal faith, inasmuch as this death was overcome by God's action and the history of Jesus began anew on another plane. According to the convergent testimony of old formulas of belief and the Easter narratives in the gospels, the disciples were convinced by the apparitions that God had crowned Jesus' death by a new act of revelation, the miracle of raising him from the dead. He who had been executed shamefully was raised up to be the heavenly Kyrios. The markedly divergent Easter narratives of the gospels and Acts 1 are, of course, not to be regarded as a detailed report reproducing the actual course of events. But as "interpretations" of God's saving action they are valuable expressions of the primitive Church's belief in Jesus' resurrection and in its reality and significance for Jesus himself and for the continuation of the work of the redemption. Attention is rightly drawn to the contrast between the multiplicity of Easter accounts and the unity of the Easter message (Bornkamm, *Jesus*, p. 166). Catholic and Protestant theologians are agreed that not the Resurrection as such but the Easter faith, the disciples' personal conviction, is accessible as a historical event in the strict sense (Trilling, *Probleme*, p. 152; Kolping, in *Handbuch theologischer Grundbegriffe,* I, p. 141).

With faith in Jesus' resurrection there begins a gradual unfolding of the Christ-event and a retrospective interpretation of Jesus' life; these are visible very early, particularly in kerygmatic formulas and Christological titles, and are finally incorporated in the gospels.

E. NEW TESTAMENT CHRISTOLOGY

It is generally agreed that Jesus did not make his own person a main theme of his message, and that on account of the special nature of his eschatological claim, he could not apply to himself any of the existing terms used to denote bringers of salvation, at least not to the extent to which they are now found in the texts (e.g., Son of Man). It is therefore possible that titles such as "Messiah", "Son of Man", "Lord", perhaps also "the Son", were first used by the primitive community to characterize Jesus' consciousness of his mission or the claim which his mission implied, and to express its own faith in him. The resurrection of the crucified Jesus to heavenly power must be regarded as the basic starting-point and guide-line of NT Christology.

1. Probably the earliest stratum of the NT is the "Exaltation Christology". In conjunction with theocratic messianic prophecies (2 Sam 7:14; Ps 2:7; 110:1), the Resurrection was interpreted as installation as Messianic Son of God, as sitting at the right hand of God and as enthronement as Kyrios equal to God. It is a very instructive fact that the primitive community, according to the most probable meaning of *Maranatha*, prayed for the coming of the era of salvation, not directly from Yahweh but from the heavenly Jesus. This is only meaningful if the Resurrection or Exaltation was not regarded merely as a transitory assumption but as the installation of Jesus with heavenly power to save.

This faith in the Resurrection made Jesus the Saviour the centre of the preaching, instead of Jesus' message. In the light of the Exaltation Christology, the post-paschal message becomes the message about Jesus (the Gospel of Jesus, objective genitive [Rom 15:19; 1:9; 1:1–3]).

2. The message of salvation, first proclaimed on Jewish territory, spoke for missionary reasons in the first place of what God had done in Jesus. The divine confirmation of the Crucified was the primary reason for speaking about the redemptive meaning of this death (cf. the pre-Pauline formulation at 1 Cor 15:3f.). As well as the fact that the death was in accordance with the Scriptures (see also the OT allusions in the accounts of the Passion), the idea of atonement as well as the redemptive power of Jesus' death was also envisaged (Gal 1:4; 2 Cor 5:14f., 21; Rom 4:25; 8:32).

3. Another possible interpretation of Jesus' death is shown by the frequent linking of brief formulas concerning it (including the idea of atonement: Rom 5:6, 8; 1 Pet 3:18; being raised up by God: 1 Cor 15:3f.) with the title of "Messiah, Christ". The title of Messiah was not tied in Judaism to a particular bringer of salvation, and Jesus did not apply it to himself because of its political colouring. Even if the disputed saying before the Sanhedrin (Mk 14:61f.) is not historical, it may be considered certain that the Roman procurator condemned Jesus to death as a political claimant to Messiahship, at the instigation of the Jewish leaders (cf. the inscription on the Cross). Hence the apostolic preaching probably used the title of Messiah to affirm that the execution of Jesus as a messianic claimant was a divinely-willed redemptive death. Reserve regarding the title of Messiah consequently disappeared in the primitive community in the situation after Easter, and in fact "Messiah" became the most frequent way of designating Jesus' function. Then when it was used by Greeks for whom it did not designate a function, it became a proper name. Thus, to put it in a simplified form, the Palestinian profession of faith "Jesus is the Christ" became in Hellenism the proper name "Jesus Christ", and this then became an element in a new profession of faith, e.g., "Jesus Christ is Lord" (Phil 2:11).

4. The profession of faith in Jesus as the Messiah was linked in Palestinian circles with proof of his Davidic descent. The appeal to Jesus' ancestry, as in the ancient formulation at Romans 1:3, was used to prove the Messianic character of the earthly Jesus and this was linked with the Messianic enthronement as Son of God which took place in the Resurrection.

The reference to Jesus' Davidic descent in the oldest kerygma is due less to interest in biography than to the proof from prophecy (2 Sam 7:12; Is 11:1); it expresses the claim to the Messianic throne of David. On account of its strongly national colouring, this title meant little to Gentile Christians and soon disappeared.

5. Since the theological affirmation of Davidic sonship links Jesus' Messiahship with his ancestry and birth (cf. the opening chapters of Mt and Lk), the question of Jesus' pre-existence arose when recourse was had to what Jesus was before his birth. As the historicity of the Synoptic logia in which "the Son" is used absolutely (among others Mt 11:27 par.) is contested, as is the existence of the myth of the Anthropos *(Urmensch)* Redeemer at the time, preference may be given to the explanation that the Jewish-Hellenistic doctrine of the Wisdom which was prior to the world led to faith in Jesus' pre-existence (Phil 2:6ff.; Rom 1:3; 8:3, 29, 32; 1 Cor 8:6; 10:4) and so to the affirmation of the Incarnation (according to Phil 2:6–11, even before Paul). The pre-existence Christology, i.e., belief in divine being as always belonging to Jesus Christ, was more precisely expressed in Jewish-Hellenistic Christianity with the help of the title Son (of God); for genuine Jewish thought, this is only a messianic royal title. Whether the use of the title Son of God to denote the pre-existent only came in with Paul (Gal 4:4f.; Rom 1:3a) or was already pre-Pauline, must remain an open question. But it is certain that the OT concept of Son of God had no connection with pre-existence and certainly not with metaphysical sonship of God. It was rather the notion of election for a special task and of strict obedience to the divine call (cf. Cullmann, *Christology,* p. 281). Similarly the term "divine man" among the Greeks, even when birth from a God is mentioned, contains no hint of metaphysical sonship. The divine man (ruler, philosopher, poet, doctor, wonderworker) was a supernatural being (θεῖος) but not a god (θεός). But the primitive Church understood Jesus to be the true and only "Son of God" in an absolute sense, and on this account the apostolic message could also be termed "the gospel concerning his Son" (Rom 1:9; cf. the variant readings at Mk 1:1, which place the whole gospel under the confession of faith in Jesus as the Son of God). Even if Jesus did not use the absolute term "the Son" of himself, some explanation for the term may be found in the uniquely direct relation to God which Jesus claimed for himself as the final spokesman of God's will to save and sanctify.

6. Special problems are raised by the title "Son of Man" which historical research claimed most persistently for Jesus. Since it is improbable that Jesus used the title himself as frequently as it occurs in the texts, three groups of Son of Man sayings are now distinguished in the synoptics: sayings about his future coming, about his suffering and resurrection, and about his present work (Bultmann, *Theology,* I, p. 30). In the third group (Mk 2:10, 28; Mt 8:20; 11:19; 12:32), the title at least is almost universally regarded as secondary by exegetes (contrast E. Schweizer). In the second group (Mk 8:31; 9:31; 10:33 — not in Q) it is regarded as secondary by a large number of exegetes. At present the main debate is about the Son of Man sayings found in both Mark and Q (Mk 8:38; 13:26f.; 14:62f.; Mt 24, 27, 37, 39, 44 par.)

Until a few years ago the only question was whether Jesus meant himself or someone else when speaking of the *coming* Son of Man. But today distinguished representatives of critical scholarship point out that Jesus could not have announced the imminence of God's reign, while at the same time expecting a new mediator of salvation before the judgment (Vielhauer, Braun, Käsemann, Bornkamm). Hence they hold that the primitive Church was the first to draw on the apocalyptic image of the Son of Man coming from the hidden world of God and carrying out the judgment in God's name. These were the only terms in which to explain an advent of the saviour from heaven, in other words the parousia of the Messiah, Jesus, for the judgment, on the basis of an existing form of eschatological expectation. But even on this assumption, the belief of the primitive community in Jesus' parousia would be anchored in an act of revelation by God; once again the importance of the Easter faith for the post-paschal gospel would be exemplified.

7. The title "Servant of God" plays as prominent a role in critical scholarship as that of Son of Man, since it is used to prove that Jesus was conscious of making vicarious atonement (Cullmann; Jeremias).

Of the four Songs of the Servant of Yahweh (Is 42:1–4; 49:1–7; 50:4–11; 52:13 – 53:12) the last in particular is relevant because of the vicarious atonement of God's Servant. The traditional view claims that Jesus himself had this in mind ("παῖς-consciousness" instead of "Messianic consciousness"; cf. Cullmann, *Christology,* p. 81). On the other hand, one should note two texts of Matthew (12:18 = Is 42:1–4; 8:17 = Is 53:4) which emphasize Jesus' quiet activity or his miracles but not his expiatory sufferings. Would this theological interpretation have been possible for Matthew if Jesus had plainly regarded himself as the Servant of God making vicarious atonement? Nevertheless the other extreme must also be excluded, namely that Jesus could not have understood his violent death as expiatory in the sense of the Servant of Yahweh of Deutero-Isaiah.

It is to be noted that Judaism did not think of the figure of the Servant of God as a single reality; the Servant Songs were not yet recognized as a thematic unity. Judaism did indeed attribute expiatory power to the death of a martyr, but not on the basis of Is 53 (e.g., verse 10). Moreover, the thought of vicarious expiatory suffering was not yet linked with the Messiah (Cullmann and others, against Jeremias). On these grounds a vicariously suffering Messias could not have been deduced from Is 53. When the NT linked suffering with the Messiah, this was an absolute novelty, the explanation of the scandal of the Cross. It is also conceivable that Jesus selected the trait in Isaiah which corresponded to his special awareness of his mission (cf. Is 53:12; atonement). But even if Jesus did not regard himself as the Servant, this would not prove that he did not understand his death as espiation "for many" (Mk 10:45 and the words at the Last Supper, Mk 14:24; Mt 26:28; "for you", Lk 22:20, are secondary).

8. A frequently used title, particularly in primitive Christian worship, and one which expresses Jesus' installation as universal ruler, is the name Kyrios. Here we can trace in the texts the development from the Marē-(Kyrios) of the liturgical intercession *maranātha* to the absolute ὁ κύριος in Greek-speaking circles or to the form of confession which was possible there: "Jesus is Lord" (1 Cor 12:3; Rom 10:9). This development was probably due in part to the use of the term Kyrios in Hellenism to denote a ruler honoured as divine, as well as to its use as the name of God in the Septuagint, even if Jesus was not honoured as Kyrios-Yahweh in the full sense. At all events the liturgical invocation of Jesus as Lord facilitated the transference of the Septuagint title "Lord" to him. In contrast to the pagans, the Christian confesses only one God, the Father, and one Lord, Jesus Christ (1 Cor 8:5f.). The function of this Lord consists in the present guidance of his Church (1 Thess 3:12f.; Rom 10:12), in the exercise of a cosmic dominion over principalities and powers (1 Cor 15:25ff.) and in the last judgment on the "day of the Lord", which is now attributed to Jesus (1 Thess 5:2; 2 Thess 2:2; Acts 2:20). Profession of faith in the exalted Lord is given its most magnificent expression in the closing words of Matthew (Mt 28:18). Jesus is also retrospectively called "Lord" (1 Cor 2:8; 9:5; 7:10, 12), but on the whole it is the post-paschal profession of faith which this title summarizes (Acts 2:36; Phil 2:9–11). Brief indications of other bases of Christology: Paul contrasts Christ as the second Adam and ancestor of justified mankind with the first Adam and ancestor of sinful mankind (Rom 5:12–21). Hebrews compares Jesus' function as mediator to that of a heavenly high priest. The Logos-Christology of the Johannine prologue sets special problems, and its origin (Gnosis? Wisdom?) has not yet been fully explained.

9. *Summary.* NT Christology as it has been exemplified here on the basis of certain titles, inquires first and foremost not into the divine or human nature of Jesus Christ but into the significance of his person in the history of salvation; consequently most titles are words which denote functions and express some particular aspect of his activity as mediator of salvation. The full develop-

ment of the ontological concepts of dogmatic Christology is not to be expected from the NT, since its interests lay elsewhere and its language was still uninhibited.

See also *Bible* I A, 2, B, *Biblical Exegesis* II B; *Reign of God. New Testament Books* I-IV, *Eucharist* I, *Resurrection* I A, B, *Kerygma*.

BIBLIOGRAPHY. GENERAL: H. Conzelmann in *RGG,* III, cols. 619–53; A. Vögtle and R. Schnackenburg in *LTK,* V, cols. 922–40; K. Adam, *The Christ of Faith* (1934); M. Dibelius, *Jesus* (1949); G. Bornkamm, *Jesus of Nazareth* (1960); R. Bultmann, *Jesus Christ and Mythology* (1960); W. Trilling, *Fragen zur Geschichtlichkeit Jesu* (1966); A. Schweitzer, *The Quest of the Historical Jesus* (3rd ed., 1963). ON A 1: F. C. Burkitt, *The Earliest Sources for the Life of Jesus* (1910); J. B. Aufhauser, *Antike Jesuszeugnisse* (2nd ed., 1925); J. Klausner, *Jesus of Nazareth* (1925; new ed., 1964); E. Stauffer, *Jesus and his Story* (1960). ON A 2: W. Wrede, *Das Messiasgeheimnis in den Evangelien* (1901); K. L. Schmidt, *Der Rahmen der Geschichte Jesu* (1919); R. Bultmann, *The History of the Synoptic Tradition* (1962); M. Dibelius, *From Tradition to Gospel* (1965). ON A 3: H. Instinsky, *Das Jahr der Geburt* (1959); J. Blinzler, *The Trial of Jesus* (1960); A. Jaubert, *The Date of the Last Supper* (1965); E. Ruckstuhl, *The Chronology of the Last Days of Jesus* (1965); J. Jeremias, *The Eucharistic Words of Jesus* (1966). ON A 4: J. Robinson, *The Problem of History in Mark* (1957); A. Vögtle, "Das öffentliche Wirken Jesu auf dem Hintergrund der Qumranbewegung", *Freiburger Universitätsreden,* new series 27 (1958), pp. 13–20. ON B 1: M. Meinertz, *Theologie des Neuen Testaments,* 2 vols. (1950); R. Bultmann, *Theology of the New Testament,* 2 vols. (1952–55); R. Schnackenburg, *New Testament Theology Today* (1963); H. Schlier, "The Meaning and Function of a Theology of the New Testament", in H. Vorgrimler, ed., *Dogmatic versus Biblical Theology* (1964). ON B 2: E. Käsemann, "Das Problem des historischen Jesus", *Zeitschrift für Theologie und Kirche* 51 (1954), pp. 125–43; J. Robinson, *The New Quest of the Historical Jesus* (1959); H. Zahrnt, *The Historical Jesus* (1963); F. Mussner, "The Historical Jesus and the Christ of Faith", in H. Vorgrimler, ed., *Dogmatic versus Biblical Theology* (1964). ON C: E. Percy, *Die Botschaft Jesu* (1953); V. Taylor, *The Life and Ministry of Jesus* (1954). ON C 1: C. H. Dodd, *The Parables of the Kingdom* (3rd ed., 1953); J. Jeremias, *The Parables of Jesus,* (revised ed., 1955); R. H. Fuller, *Interpreting the Miracles* (1963); R. Schnackenburg, *God's Rule and Kingdom* (1963); A. Schweitzer, *The Mystery of the Kingdom* (1964). ON C 2: J. Behn and L. Würthwein, "νοεῖν", *TWNT,* IV, pp. 945–1016; see also bibliography on *Metanoia.* ON C 3: J. Jeremias, *Jesus' Promise to the Nations* (1958); A. Vögtle, "Ekklesiologische Auftragsworte des Auferstandenen", *Sacra Pagina,* II (1959), pp. 280–94; W. G. Kummerl, *Promise and Fulfilment* (2nd ed., 1961); F. Hahn, *Mission in the New Testament* (1965).

ON D: J. Schmitt, *Jésus ressuscité dans la prédication apostolique* (1949); A. Vögtle, "Exegetische Erwägungen zum Wissen und Selbstbewusstsein Jesu", *Gott in Welt, Festschrift K. Rahner* (1964), II, pp. 608–66; H. Schürmann, *Le récit de la dernière cène* (1965); E. Schweizer, *The Lord's Supper according to the New Testament* (1967); E. Lohse, *History of the Suffering and Death of Jesus Christ* (1967); see also bibliography on *Resurrection.* ON E: V. Taylor, *The Person of Christ in the New Testament Teaching* (1958); R. Casey, "The Earliest Christologies", *JTS* 9 (1958), pp. 253–77; O. Cullmann, *The Christology of the New Testament* (1959); R. Bultmann, *Existence and Faith* (1961 = *Glauben und Verstehen* I, III); L. Sabourin, *The Names and Titles of Jesus* (1966). ON E 1: F. Filson, *Jesus Christ the Risen Lord* (1956); W. Thüsing, *Die Erhöhung . . . im Johannesevangelium* (1960); E. Schweizer, *Erniedrigung und Erhöhung bei Jesus und seinen Nachfolgern* (2nd ed., 1962); R. Schnackenburg, *The Gospel according to St. John,* I (1968). ON E 2: see bibliography on E 7 below. ON E 3: J. Klausner, *Die messianischen Vorstellungen des jüdischen Volkes im Zeitalter der Tannaiten* (1901); S. Mowinckel, *He that Cometh* (1956); W. van Unnik, "Jesus the Christ", *NTS* 8 (1961–62), pp. 101–16. ON E 4: E. Lohmeyer, *Gottesknecht und Davidsohn* (2nd ed., 1953). ON E 5: L. Bieler, ΘΕΙΟΣ ΑΝΗΡ, 2 vols. (1935f.); B. van Iersel, *"Der Sohn" in den synoptischen Jesusworten* (2nd ed., 1962); A. Feuillet, *Le Christ Sagesse de Dieu d'après les épîtres pauliniennes* (1966). ON E 6: H. E. Tödt, *The Son of Man in the Synoptic Tradition* (1965); P. Vielhauer, "Gottesreich und Menschensohn in der Verkündigung Jesu", *Aufsätze zum Neuen Testament* (1965); G. Haufe, "Das Menschensohn-Problem in der gegenwärtigen wissenschaftlichen Diskussion", *Evangelische Theologie* 26 (1966), pp. 130ff. ON E 7: T. W. Manson, *The Servant Messiah* (1953); E. Lohse, *Märtyrer und Gottesknecht* (1955); W. Manson, *Jesus the Messiah* (1956). ON E 8: F. Mussner, *Christus, das All und die Kirche* (1955); E. Schweizer, "Der Glaube an Jesus den Herrn", *Evangelische Theologie* 17 (1957), pp. 7–21; W. Bousset, *Kyrios Christos* (5th ed., 1965). ON E 9: A. Vögtle, "Die Adam-Christus Typologie und 'Der Menschensohn'", *Trierer Theologische Zeitschrift* 60 (1951), pp. 309–28; G. Friedrich, "Beobachtungen zur messianischen Hohepriestererwartung in den Synoptikern", *Zeitschrift für Theologie und Kirche* 53 (1956), pp. 265–311.

Ingrid Maisch and *Anton Vögtle*

II. Quest of the Historical Jesus

Historical investigation of the life of Jesus is inspired by the desire to establish a critically reliable picture of Jesus. From the time of the Synoptics and John's Gospel onward there have been portraits of Jesus coloured by the spirit of their age and the theological perspective of their authors. The scientific quest for the historical Jesus is, however, a phenomenon of modern times. It has developed since the Enlightenment, side by side with historical criticism and in particular with the emergence of historico-critical theology. If lives of Jesus in earlier times can be called critical at all, the critique was theological, not historical. Theological critique even seems to have determined more strongly the mode of presentation in the gospels themselves than it did the later arrangements of the canonical writings into gospel harmonies, poetical adaptations of the gospel materials, epic, dramatic and edifying representations of the life of Jesus (Tatian, Juvencus, Sedulius, the *Heliand,* Otfried, Ps.-Bonaventure, Ludolf of Saxony). The discovery of the theological critique of the evangelists and, as a consequence, the different pictures of Jesus presented by them, belongs in its acute form to the most recent phase of research (form-criticism). The recognition of the evangelists' theological critique by the historical criticism of modern scholarship marks an important dividing-line or even the end of the scientific "quest for the historical Jesus" of modern times. A brief account of its course and chief stages must be traced by a retrospective glance at the history of scholarship, with a brief sketch of the pictures of Jesus proper to each period.

The course of research into the life of Jesus was described at the beginning of the present century by Albert Schweitzer in his *Quest of the Historical Jesus* (1st German ed., 1906; E. T., 2nd ed., 1926) "as the inspiring and splendid history of the consciousness of truth in Evangelical theology" (C. H. Ratschow, in *RGG,* III, col. 655). "The quest of the historical Jesus is a monument to the veracity of Protestant Christianity" (A. Schweitzer, Preface to 6th German edition, p. XVIII). It can be properly understood only in the wider perspective of the general history of ideas and of theology in modern times. "In the great debate on the meaning and significance of the Bible, which began with the emergence of modern Western thought, the chief positions were already marked out by 1680. The Enlightenment changed the historical stresses, but contributed nothing essentially new" (K. Scholder, p. 171). The Enlightenment, however, extended rational criticism, gave it a more radical tone and applied it to the gospels in order to attack the traditional dogmatic account of Jesus. The first important thrust against the orthodox biblical

conception of Christ came from the Hamburg Orientalist H. S. Reimarus in his *Apologie oder Schutzschrift für die vernünftigen Verehrer Gottes,* from which G. E. Lessing published the *Wolfenbüttel Fragments* (1774–74). Conflict between "reason" and traditional "faith" over the figure of Jesus set in and has continued (disastrously) down to our own times in the form of a controversy between historical science and traditional notions of faith. Its solution will require considerable efforts in philosophical and theological hermeneutics. In view of this, the history of research into the life of the historical Jesus may also be regarded as a history of biblical hermeneutics.

Reimarus and Lessing introduced into the rationalist theology of the Enlightenment the historical element which was to contribute to its downfall. Reimarus's criticism of tradition was intended to shock. He regarded Jesus as a Jewish national Messiah inspired by strong apocalyptic expectations, whose disciples invented the legends of Jesus' resurrection and ascension in support of their expectations of the Parousia. This raised the fundamental problem of the distinction between the historical Jesus and the dogmatic Christ. In one form or another it has remained decisive for subsequent research.

The next important impulse came from D. F. Strauss (cf. the title *Der Christus des Glaubens und der Jesus der Geschichte* [1865]), who in 1835–36 brought out in two volumes his *Leben Jesu, kritisch bearbeitet.* The advance of intellectual emancipation from religious and dogmatic conceptions allowed Strauss systematically to apply the idea of "myth" to the forces which shaped the evangelical picture of Jesus. For Strauss the idea of the God-man as the goal of humanity and of each individual is what is unshakably real in the person of Jesus and cannot be contested by historical critiscism of myths. The equally sharp criticism which Strauss applied both to the supernaturalist and to naturalist and rationalistic accounts of Jesus is, it is true, only made possible by a "mythical interpretation", but it opened out new paths to later research by its more complex view. The transformation of the tradition concerning Jesus into kerygma seemed to become intelligible, and a way had apparently been found to locate the "historical" Jesus. Strauss himself, however, drew a picture of Jesus on liberal lines in his *Leben Jesu, für das deutsche Volk bearbeitet* (1864), in which he rather clumsily spiritualizes the Jesus of the Synoptics. Here he followed the tendency of liberal theology to "modernize" Jesus and, with the help of psychological explanations, drew a great number of relatively consistent and often extremely subjective pictures of Jesus as exemplar, reformer and great man.

The pictures of Jesus in liberal theology were based on source-criticism. Since Strauss, this had become indispensable and was intensively pursued. The basis was recognition of the priority of Mark and of the importance of the older Palestinian Logia-source (Q). Mark's Gospel provides the outline of Jesus' life, Q that of his teaching. Historical imagination, the art of psychological composition and "the conviction that historical reconstruction can be the basis of present-day world-views" (H. Conzelmann, col. 620) guide the descriptions of Jesus as teacher and model for humanity. For Schenkel, Keim, Holtzmann, B. Weiss and Beyschlag, Jesus as a "personality" was primarily a "spiritualizer of the idea of the Messiah, a profound thinker and founder of a present Kingdom of God" (A. Schweitzer).

Trust in the sources for the life of Jesus was shaken at the beginning of the present century. In the course of the last sixty years, form-criticism and history of redaction have taught us to regard the Synoptics themselves as preachers and theologians, and their gospels as the theological redaction of kerygmatic traditions of many kinds. The framework of the story of Jesus presented in the gospels has proved to be a secondary, literary composition, from which no conclusions can be drawn with certainty about sequence of events in Jesus' life. Even until recently, research was dominated by the 19th-century picture of two periods in Jesus' work, the Galilean spring-time of success, and the subsequent crisis and the end in Jerusalem; but fundamentally judgment had been passed on "biographies of Jesus" by W. Wrede at the beginning of the present century: "Present-day study of the gospels starts from the assumption that Mark had more or less clearly before his eyes, though not without gaps, the real circumstances of Jesus' life. It presupposes that Mark thinks in terms of the life of Jesus, bases the various features of his story on the real circumstances of this life, on Jesus' real thoughts and feelings

and that he links the events which he describes in a historical and psychological sense ... This view and method must be recognized to be false in principle. It must be plainly stated that Mark no longer has any real picture of the historical life of Jesus" (p. 129).

The results of more recent criticism, supported by the school of history of religions, which rejected liberal attempts to modernize Jesus and opened out new ways to a deeper historical understanding of the NT, were regarded as destructive by the "life of Jesus" type of theology (whether of the liberal or the conservative kind). They were felt as a liberation by dialectical theology, however, which seeks to make the Christ of faith wholly "independent" of the historical Jesus. The abandonment of the "historical Jesus" by R. Bultmann must therefore at bottom be regarded as an ultimate consequence of liberal theology. Bultmann's book on Jesus (1926) no longer draws any picture of Jesus. It attempts to clarify and translate Jesus' call for decision, Jesus' significance. With Bultmann's programme of demythologization and existential interpretation of the NT, study of the life of Jesus has also reached its most important hermeneutical phase. The antagonism between "facts" and "faith" in regard to Jesus was suppressed by Bultmann onesidedly in favour of faith (or to its disadvantage). At the same time, however, the possibility of a more reliable solution was opened up through reflection on the nature of historical understanding. It will not be possible to overcome the "historicism" which still strongly influences NT studies by a fundamentally unhistorical "existential" interpretation, but only by a historico-theological exegesis determined by a new way of thinking. The question of Jesus can no longer be taken up again as a new quest of the historical Jesus in the same sense as the old. But in the form of inquiry into the figure of Jesus as this is critically accessible to us, into Jesus' programme, into Jesus' action as attesting and calling for faith, a question seems to emerge which is susceptible of historico-theological understanding. This question also preserves the rights of both faith and historical criticism; for the former needs the latter in its own interest. The theology which kept historical criticism at a distance, or the kind of historical criticism which in the form of a quest of the historical Jesus despised theology, are both at an end today in the light of the testimony to Jesus contained in the gospels. A new historical understanding guided by testimony must re-state the old question regarding Jesus.

See also *New Testament Books* I, III, *Form Criticism, Liberalism and Liberal Theology, Demythologization, Faith and History.*

BIBLIOGRAPHY. W. Wrede, *Das Messiasgeheimnis in den Evangelien* (1901); A. Schweitzer, *Von Reimarus zu Wrede* (1906), E. T.: *The Quest of the Historical Jesus* (1910); G. Baldensperger, "Un demi-siècle de recherches sur l'historicité de Jésus", *Revue de Théologie et de Philosophie* 12 (1924), pp. 64–84; E. F. Scott, *Recent Lives of Jesus* (1934); T. W. Manson, "The Life of Jesus. Some Tendencies in Present-Day Research", in W. D. Davies and D. Daube, eds., *The Background of the New Testament and its Eschatology,* studies in honour of C. H. Dodd (1954); J. M. Robinson, *The New Quest of the Historical Jesus* (1959); H. Ristow and K. Matthiae, *Der historische Jesus und der kerygmatische Christus* (1960); K. Scholder, *Ursprünge und Probleme der Bibelkritik im 17. Jahrhundert* (1966); F. Mussner in *LTK,* VI, cols. 859–64; H. Conzelmann in *RGG,* III, cols. 619–53; R. Ratschow, *ibid.,* cols. 655–63.

Rudolf Pesch

III. Christology

A. Historical Survey

1. *Early Christianity.* Though it is true that the Christian community broke out of Judaism by professing that Jesus is the Christ, that Jesus Christ is the Lord (Rom 10:9; Phil 2:11), and though it is also proper to say in this sense (but only in this sense) that the original profession is a "purely Christological formulation" (O. Cullmann), this profession of faith is nevertheless meant as an affirmation of the saving activity of the one God, who is the God of the OT and who established Jesus as the Christ and Lord (Acts 2:36). This profession is, therefore, embedded in faith in the one God of creation and of the whole history of salvation (and has thereby a higher unity); but it also indicates that the one God has his absolute and definitive representation in the world through Christ, and in the Church through his Spirit. And hence the whole proclamation of what God is for us can be articulated in a threefold scheme of a Trinity that is primarily conceived of in terms of the economy of salvation (Mt 28:19). In this scheme Christology is peculiarly subordinated to the profession of the one living God of the world and of

history, but contains within itself the whole, since it is the very centre of that profession. This is the abiding problem of the nature and place of Christology.

2. *The patristic age.* Though in the Apostles' Creed various originally Christological assertions are inserted into the part of the creed which speaks of the Son, there is no change in the old tripartite scheme. It rather underlines the proper (that is to say, the comprehensive) meaning of these assertions about Christ. Although this basic form is primarily simply that of the profession of faith in the three divine agents in the one salvific activity, reflection upon their relation to each other (which had already begun with the μονογενής of the Apostles' Creed) was bound to lead soon to the developing of *theologia* in distinction to *oikonomia.* And we already find in the *De Principiis* of Origen that the teaching on the Trinity (book 1), and therefore an immanent Christology, is separated from the teaching on the incarnation which is only treated at the end of the book 2, so that the two tractates are separated by those on creation and sin. The danger of a theology concentrated on the immanent life of God, and of a Christology that is only one part of an *oikonomia* instead of containing both *theologia* and *oikonomia,* is already very real. But the comprehensive view is already unmistakable, shortly before Nicaea, in Eusebius of Caesarea, though with a subordinationist tendency. The Council itself (325) rather emphasized the distinction between *theologia* and *oikonomia,* without, however, separating them absolutely. A more extensive survey of the doctrine of the Fathers would not change this picture very much, even though they differ so much otherwise (e.g., the great catechetical discourse of Gregory of Nyssa, *PG,* XLV, cols. 9–105; Theodoret, *History of Heresies,* book V: *PG,* LXXXIII, cols. 439–556; John Damascene, *De fide Orthodoxa;* Augustine, *Enchiridion*). The "total" Christology is divided up into a first part on the Trinity, without much elaboration in terms of the plan of salvation, and a Christology which only comes after the teaching on creation and sin. This division is in danger of isolating and levelling out Christology strictly speaking, especially when it is taught that each of the divine persons could "become man" (cf. *DTC,* VII, cols. 1466, 1511 ff.). Fulgentius of Ruspe

(*De Fide: PL*, LXV, cols. 671–706) presents, however, a unified doctrine of the Trinity and incarnation before speaking of creation, sin, baptism, and eschatology. The patristic scheme does not mean that its theology was not Christocentric, but only that its systematic presentation made this character less clear.

3. *Early and classical scholasticism*. a) The sequence Trinity-creation-fall-incarnation, etc., basically a historical sequence, was generally taken for granted and it became all the more significant with the beginning of systematic theology as such. This is evident as early as the *Elucidarium* of Honorius of Autun (where the mysteries of the life of Jesus are also dealt with) or in the *Sentences* of the school of Anselm of Laon. (Christology is treated in the 3rd book among the remedies for sin.) In the *Summa Sententiarum* of the school of the Victorines we find again the approach of Gennadius and Fulgentius. The Trinity and the incarnation come first, though now the teaching on redemption is almost eliminated. In the *Sententiae Atrebatenses* we have, as against the scheme of the *Sententiae* of Anselm, perhaps for the first time a clear emphasis on the section *De Christo Redemptore* which is here placed before the other aspects of the "redemption". It is, therefore, the beginning of the separation between Christology and soteriology (cf. R. Silvain), although at the same time there are *Sentences* from the school of Abelard in which Christology is treated under the heading of "beneficia", and thus seen almost from the point of view of the Reformation. In the *Sentences* of Peter Lombard Christology (in book 3) follows the teaching on the Trinity (book 1) and treats of how Christ (and the virtues, which are, however, hardly developed out of the Christology) leads man on from the "utilia" of creation to the "fruibilia" of God (Augustine). This Christology is notable for the fact that the mysteries of the life of Jesus are presented in historical order within a systematic theological survey. The teaching on the sacraments (book 4) refers back to Christ only in one sentence (dist. 1 c. 1). It is no wonder that the commentators on the *Sentences* made little effort to develop a Christocentric doctrine of the virtues and the sacraments. While Robert Pullus, Gandulph, Peter Lombard, *et al.*, at least placed the teaching on the virtues after Christology, the Christology of Peter of Poitiers in his *Sententiarum libri quinque* is preceded by the treatment of grace, justification and merit (though in the Christology Christ is represented as the *caput ecclesiae*) — a systematization which was taken up by others (Grabmann, *Geschichte,* II, p. 515).

b) In the *Summa,* part III, Thomas may be said to divide Christology — as usual, treated apart from the "theologia" of the Trinity — into two parts. There is an abstract and speculative Christology (one that was traditional, but better structured and hence valid to the present day) in which the inconsistencies of Peter Lombard are overcome with the help of a clear theory of subsistence. And there is a concrete Christology of the mysteries of the life of Jesus (entrance into the world, life, death, glorification). He represents, then, in his treatment of the person at the centre of Christology a sort of return to the early Christology, in which abstract *theologumena* are developed in the light of the life of Christ as depicted in the NT. For Thomas, the place of Christology within the whole is of course determined, as for the other Thomists, Henry of Ghent, Scotus, et al., by his conception of the object of theology (God as God: *Summa Theologica,* I, q. 1, a. 7). A different tradition which extended from Augustine through Cassiodorus to Robert of Melun, Robert of Cremona, Kilwardby, Robert Grosseteste, and finally to Gabriel Biel and Peter d'Ailly (cf. E. Mersch) saw the object of theology as the "Christus totus", "Christus integer". This could have prepared the way for a very Christocentric orientation of the whole of theology, though from this point of view it had in fact great difficulty in attaining a real synthesis. But when the object of theology, as in Thomas, is God in himself, and the God who is attainable by the creature in supernatural immediacy, theology and *oikonomia* are grasped as a unity. The going forth of all things from this God and their return to him, the triune fullness of life who communicates himself and not only created realities, can be taken also as the basic conception of the whole history of salvation. In such a system, a Christology could also be incorporated which would be conceived as absolutely neutral, as soon as Christ is clearly enough considered as he in whom all things proceed from and return to God. But the question is whether in the concrete development of this system Christology does not appear too late in Thomas, as the whole Christian anthropology and the teaching on grace and Christian life have been elaborated previous to the Christology. Here, of course, the question about the systematization is of necessity a question about the content itself, about the Christocentric nature of all reality and the precise explanation of the predestination of Christ.

The rest of Catholic Christology cannot be discussed in detail here. It is really a history of commentaries upon the *Summa* of Thomas, with new recourse to the patristic inheritance (Petavius, Thomassin) but without any change in structure. Christology and soteriology draw farther and farther apart. Suarez still has a detailed tractate entitled *De Mysteriis Vitae Christi*. But in the time of the Enlightenment it disappeared almost completely from the theology of the schools.

B. Christology Today

The impulses which led to the re-vitalizing of Christology came from inside and outside Catholicism (see Bibliography).

1. *The place of Christology.* a) *The present approach to the question.* In the course of its historical elaboration, Christology came to contain two parts which were not always very organically connected: Christology in the narrower sense (the doctrine of the person of Christ) and soteriology, which based its central theme — the satisfaction offered by Christ to God — upon the doctrine of the person of Christ as a divine subject of infinite value and dignity. This is only a part of Christology in the whole of Catholic theology. Fundamental theology treats of Christ as the bringer of revelation and the founder of the Church. Moral theology is trying (for the first time, or once more) to show how its teaching can be linked up with Christ and that it must develop its own approach (cf. J. B. Hirscher in the 19th century; and today, for example, F. Tillmann and B. Häring) since traditional Christology offers nothing explicit in this direction. Till recently, the theology of the life of Jesus has largely been left to pious literature on the margins of research (new attempts to treat of the life of Jesus specifically in dogmatics: B. M. Xiberta, *De Verbo Incarnato;* J. Solano, *Summa,* III). A part of Christology, then, has established itself outside of dogmatic theology.

It is also necessary to examine to what extent Christology is present or absent in the other treatises. The treatise *De Deo Trino* has, in its teaching on the processions and missions (and here precisely through the sending of the Son) a constitutive importance for Christology. However, the connection between these two important mysteries does not in general come clearly enough to the fore. There is a levelling effect resulting from the problematic assumption that any of the three persons could have taken on a human nature (cf. St. Thomas, *Summa Theologica,* III, q. 3, a. 5). Apart from the fact that reflection upon a purely "possible" order is very problematic, and that the possibility of incarnation in one hypostasis in God cannot be simply transferred to another, since "hypostasis" is precisely the source of differentiation in God, and cannot be applied univocally to the three persons, the relative proprieties of each person, as revealed in the *oikonomia,* must be given more weight in the solution of this question. Is it so clear that the *innascibilitas* of the Father is not incompatible with an earthly birth as Thomas asserts (*loc. cit.,* ad 3)? Does not the relation of the mission of Christ to that of the Spirit show that the one *oikonomia* has two totally different aspects? In the Son it is realized as a historical-objective work; in the Spirit that which was accomplished by the Son is inwardly appropriated by the redeemed. The roles are not interchangeable. The same is true of the Father, who would come appropriately as the "unborn" if a human reality could really become a presence that would be revelatory of him, insofar as such a "coming" (that is, outside of his coming in the Son) is at all conceivable. The human birth, therefore, has an inner and not merely a factual relation to the "Son", though it remains true that the incarnation as such is free. If there was such a thing as the incarnation of the Spirit, he could not accomplish the work of inner spiritual assimilation which is proper to the Spirit. Thus the order of the missions corresponds to the divine relations between the persons, and hence it seems that Thomas and his commentators could have linked the Trinity and the incarnation more closely.

The absence of Christology is especially noticeable up to the present in angelology and in anthropology (Suarez, however — contrary to Thomas — speaks of the grace of the angels as the grace of Christ). The teaching on the sacraments is fortunately taking on a new orientation. While Peter Lombard, for example, only mentions their institution by Christ, the sacraments today are seen more and more clearly as the sign of the effective continuation of the death of the Lord and thereby of his whole history (especially baptism, Eucharist and penance; cf. Thomas, *Summa Theologica,* III, q. 60, a. 3: *signa rememorativa*). And ecclesiology, which had already been treated of under its Christological aspect in the *Eludicarium,* is once more being developed in these terms, after many interruptions. The most complete example is perhaps that of chs. I and II of the Constitution *Lumen Gentium* of Vatican II, on which see the detailed commentary by A. Grillmeier in H. Vorgrimler, ed., *Commentary on the Documents of Vatican II,* vol. I (1967). The Council links Christology, soteriology and ecclesiology to an extent which had previously been unknown in such documents. The Christological re-moulding of eschatology is also given conciliar form in ch. VII of the same constitution. For earlier attempts see, for instance, J. Alfaro in *Gregorianum* 39 (1958), pp. 222–70. One of the most important tasks of present-day theology is, no doubt, to help to make good the claim of Christology to dominate the whole sphere of the *oikonomia,* from creation to the last things.

b) *Principles determining the place of Christology.* We have, at the very beginning of the history of Christology, had to do with the inter-relation of *theologia* and *oikonomia.* This relation means everything for Christology. The whole *oikonomia* is the Christ-event. Within it Christ does not share himself with the Spirit, but the whole belongs to him (as an objective, historical work, as described in the Creed), just as it then also belongs wholly to the Spirit who is the Spirit of Christ, as something which is to be imparted to the community of the redeemed. They were acquired in Christ and are now to be fully formed in the Spirit. This *oikonomia* derives its form and meaning from the very nature of its origin in the *theologia.* It is true that the early Fathers only came to the *theologia* by way of their analysis of the order of salvation. But then their interpretation of the *oikonomia* itself was reconsidered in a new light. In any systematic exposition, therefore, the treatises *De Deo Uno* and

Trino must precede Catholic Christology. In this anticipatory synthesis of what is experienced of God in himself in the course of the history of salvation, the theologians of the early Church had already — in their opposition to the Gnostics — accomplished one of the greatest and most lasting achievements in the history of Christian thought. Within this synthesis, they included the work of creation and the divine missions, though their thinking verged on subordinationism (cf. G. Aeby). Thus Christian theology was early on the way to a system of an interpretation of the world (relation between God and world) such as was aimed at — in their own way — by the neo-Platonists and later by Schelling and Hegel. It is only on the basis of a fully developed *theologia* (of course joined to the *oikonomia*) that Christianity can counter such competition, by putting forward a non-Gnostic and non-Pantheistic "system" (which is an actual personal exigency as well as a general Christian one). This great Christian tradition and unavoidable task will prevent theology being dissolved into a purely "ad nos" preoccupation or attempting a Christology without a preceding tractate on the triune God.

But the basic decision about Christology must already be made in the *De Deo Trino.* The clearer the precedence accorded to the (Thomistic) formal object of theology (and hence also of trinitarian theology), the more important it is to bring out "the undivided" element of both tractates. The interpretation of the processions within the Godhead must, then, also include their possible (free) relationship to the world and to history. On the exact nature of this relationship there are still great differences of opinion. They centre on the question of the "motive of the incarnation" and on the relation between creation and incarnation. K. Barth's standpoint is resolutely and radically Christocentric: creation (i.e., the order of nature) is the "extrinsic basis of the covenant" (Dogmatics, III/1, pp. 103–58); the covenant (i.e., the order of the incarnation and the redemption) is the "intrinsic basis (necessary or freely given?) of the creation" (*ibid.,* pp. 258–377). On these grounds, in a way which not all will find convincing, the article on creation in the creed is inserted in the second place (cf. above: Fulgentius, *Summa Sententiarum*) in a sort of Christological straitjacket. Since the light of knowledge is kindled only in the act of revelation in Christ — in the same way both for the knowledge of the Trinity and of the world — it follows that the "undivided" is preserved for *oikonomia* and *theologia,* in the strictest possible way. But the "unmixed" is endangered, because this obscures the fact that we encounter Christ within the totality of a history which reveals its Christocentric character only slowly, since otherwise the inner distinction between nature and grace within the one order of Christ is in danger of being lost. And so, no matter how strongly the Christocentric is stressed for the sphere of the *oikonomia,* one will always place the tractate on the incarnation after that on creation (which will, however, remain very formal for the moment).

The full Christological implications of the teaching on creation (angels, men, world) can also be indicated if it is retained in its historical place, and Col. 1:15 taken seriously. The second article of the creed does in fact throw light upon the first (Trinity) and subsumes it within itself, so that its contents are already Christology of "Advent". But then the tractate on the fall (of the angels and of man) which goes with *De Deo Creante* must also be developed in advance with reference to Christ. The supernatural elevation of man, which is presupposed by natural creation as the condition of its possibility (so that creation appears in fact only as the place where God communicates himself in Christ), is an inviolable covenant established in Christ from the very beginning. The same is true then for the Christological character of the remaining theological tractates which display in full the sphere of the *oikonomia.* This need not be further developed here.

2. *The structure of Christology.* Here there are two things to consider.

a) *The relation between Christology and soteriology.* As we have seen, the separation into Christology and soteriology has existed from at least the 12th century. It was above all the satisfaction-theory of Anselm of Canterbury which promoted this development. Here too the "unmixed" and the "undivided" must go hand in hand. Catholic theology — at least since Scholasticism, but in a certain sense also since Hellenism — likes to go from "being" to "action". Hence the strong development of Christology in the narrower sense. We must, however, advert to the fact that Western subjectivism, as it was expressed

in Augustine and then accentuated in the Reformation, opened up aspects which Greek theology, objective in spite of all mysticism, could not see (cf. A. Malet, *Personne et Amour* [1957]). The *pro nobis* characteristic of Christ was retained in Western theology from Augustine to the Scholastics, but only in modern times has it again been deliberately stressed, to some extent on account of the over-emphasis laid on it by R. Bultmann and F. Gogarten (cf. J. Ternus: *Chalcedon,* III, pp. 531–611, especially 586 f.). Catholic Christology can, without detriment to its tradition, bring out more clearly the *pro nobis,* if soteriology is already prepared in the stricter Christology (e.g., by the treatment of the knowledge and power of Christ, his Sonship, his offices, in the light of the history of salvation). Since Chalcedon, Christology in the East and the West has been built up on a few concepts — the two natures, the one hypostasis, and the assumption of human nature by the person of the Word. Doubtless, it was precisely through the elaboration of these concepts, together with the efforts to interpret the mystery of the Trinity, that the imposing structure of Christian theology took shape. Nevertheless, the danger of a narrowing of perspective must be avoided (cf. K. Rahner, *Chalcedon,* III, pp. 3–49) if all the riches of the Christological utterances of Scripture and tradition are to be fully exploited. We shall deal with this briefly, taking Christology and soteriology separately.

b) *The intrinsic characteristics of the two groups of notions.* (i) The bond of union between Christology and soteriology will be provided *ipso facto* by the notion of the revelation of God in Christ. But revelation must not be discussed merely in terms of fundamental theology. It must be given a strictly theological development, such as is provided by Vatican II in the first two chapters of the Dogmatic Constitution on Divine Revelation (see R. Latourelle, *Théologie de la Révélation* [2nd ed., 1966]; H. Vorgrimler, ed., *Commentary on the Documents of Vatican II,* vol. II [1968]). In keeping with tradition, the concepts nature and person will furnish the indispensable structural schema for Christology, in the ordinary Christology of "descent" in which a human nature is taken on by the person of the Logos. Yet these basic concepts must not be presented as abstractions which can be presupposed as clear and obvious, needing only to be applied to the question in hand. It must rather be demonstrated that they follow necessarily from the words of revelation in Christ and about Christ. Hence the history of the development of these concepts must be creatively re-traced. In this process it would be necessary to presuppose certain formulas of Christology (as they appeared in the course of history) which preceded this "nature and person" Christology. Just as we cannot confine ourselves to these earlier formulas (in order to eliminate the Christology of Ephesus and Chalcedon as a metaphysical aberration, or a Hellenization of Christianity or religiously irrelevant), so also is it impossible for the Catholic theologian to assume tacitly that this metaphysical formula is the primordial Christology. Scripture speaks very differently. It is very necessary to investigate carefully these original formulas, with regard to their potentialities, scope, their possible "full" meaning and content (in the light of the present nature-person schema), and their present kerygmatic adaptability. We too must pose the question of the "meaning of NT Christology", even though we do not answer it like R. Bultmann (cf. H. Braun in *Zeitschrift für Theologie und Kirche* 54 [1957], pp. 341–77).

The same is true for soteriology. The biblical categories should not be all swallowed up by the theory of satisfaction. The total situation into which man has been brought by sin must be considered, e.g., his being doomed to, his being a prey to "principalities" and "powers", to the law, etc., and the act of redemption and its effects must also be considered under all these aspects. A theological analysis of the existential ontology of death must show why we are redeemed through *death*.

Anselm here points the way to a very progressive theology. The (self-)sacrifice of death is of such supreme importance, because it is the total (irrevocable) dedication of human existence, Christ's, in fact, who is the man of the highest worth and dignity (*Cur Deus Homo?*, II, 11; see also K. Rahner, *On the Theology of Death*, Quaestiones Disputatae 2 [rev. ed., 1965]). This is the place for dogmatics to include the mysteries of the life of Jesus from his birth to his exaltation. Here too the theology of the offices of Christ must find a place, and in this regard we have much to learn from Augustine (cf. also Luther and Calvin). It is true at any rate of

Christology and soteriology that neither the mere "person and nature" schema nor the mere theory of satisfaction are sufficient to encompass all the riches of Christ and his actions as reported in the gospels and interpreted in both Scripture and the Fathers, though these aspects must remain directives for the thinking of the Church.

(ii) In such a presentation one will have to reckon with a tension which is typical of this tractate, the tension between Christology "from above" and "from below". It must first be shown how "God is in Christ" (cf. H. Vogel [1951]); Christology must be able to presuppose from *De Deo Trino* a real doctrine of the Logos and Son of the Father. He is not only "one" of the three divine persons, but he in whom "God" (as the unoriginated Father) expresses himself, if the Logos expresses himself within the world as the self-communication of God. "Word" and "Son" are capable of a reference *ad extra* and to birth, which is not proper to the other two persons. The Apologists of the 2nd century had already grasped this. To this Christology "from above" (which has also many other aspects) there must correspond another "from below". It still is so palpable in the gospels and the Acts that it often led to an Adoptionist misinterpretation. Here we have to show that we come to knowledge of the presence of the Son himself because this knowledge affirms something essential about the object of cognition itself. This knowledge is not only a conceptual acceptance of Christ's self-affirmation in his testimony to himself (though this remains an essential element in that knowledge). It also contains other elements which may not be merely characterized as the "knowledge of faith" in general. For in Christ and with Christ, man has an experience — on the cross and in the resurrection — which is not only external testimony to an affirmation, but is itself intrinsically connected with the presence of the God-man. The "experience-in-faith" in Jesus is here "a unity without confusion" which is both dogmatic theology of Christ and of the presence of God in the world, and a fundamental theology in the light of the real history of Jesus (since Christ is not merely the preacher but the object of the preaching; not only the motive of faith but also its content). The experience in faith reaches its culmination in Christ and is, as an experience of the real presence of God, not only one case of the general experience of faith but its comprehensive fulfilment.

Within such a Christology "from below", the affirmation that "Christ is man" cannot remain merely formal and abstract. He is a man, not a woman, not married, capable of suffering, in the middle of history and not at its beginning, etc. It is, therefore, impossible to deduce all that can be said about him either from the Godhead or from his humanity, taken in its formal sense. All further affirmations are about the Logos himself and must therefore be taken seriously. The Christology "from above" and "from below" brings with it a double form of soteriology. The redemptive coming, suffering and death of Christ, are first of all to be shown as the initiative of the merciful God, as 2 Cor 5:18 says: he has reconciled us to himself, so that in a certain sense, even before our own personal decision in Christ, we stand before him as "justified". This "from above" is also decisive for the work of Christ, so that every kind of soteriological Adoptionism is excluded. Nevertheless, redemption is the work of the man Christ, so that man has really satisfied the demands of God. This gives scope to a Christology which has taken the humanity of Christ seriously and which still derives all the value of his actions from his Godhead.

See also *Salvation* III A, IV, *Nature* I, III, *Man* II, III.

BIBLIOGRAPHY. ON A 1: D. van den Eynde, *Les normes de l'enseignement chrétien dans la littérature patristique des trois premiers siècles* (1933); J. Bissen, "De primatu absoluto Christi apud Col 1:13–20", *Antonianum* 11 (1936), pp. 3–26; J. N. D. Kelly, *Early Christian Creeds* (1950). ON A 2 AND 3: M. Grabmann, *Geschichte der scholastischen Methode*, 2 vols. (1909–11); J. Kaup, "Cur Deus Homo?", *Franziskanische Studien* 21 (1934), pp. 232–43; M. Müller, "Die theologische Gesamtsynthese des Duns Skotus", *Wissenschaft und Weisheit* 1 (1934), pp. 110–40; M.-D. Chenu, "Le plan de la Somme Théologique", *Revue Thomiste* 45 (1939), pp. 93–107; H. Berresheim, *Christus als Haupt der Kirche nach dem hl. Bonaventura* (1939); F. Stegmüller, *Repertorium commentariorum in sententias Petri Lombardi*, 2 vols. (1947); R. Silvain, "La tradition des Sentences d'Anselme de Laon", *Archives d'Histoire doctrinale et littéraire du Moyen-Age* (1947–48), pp. 1–52; A. Grillmeier and H. Bacht, eds., *Das Konzil von Chalkedon*, 3 vols. (1951–54; 2nd ed., 1962); A. Landgraf, *Dogmengeschichte der Frühscholastik*, vols. I/1–IV/2 (1952–56); Y. Lefèvre, *L'Elucidarium et les Lucidaires* (1954); G. Aeby, *Les missions divines* (1958); J. Bonnefoy, *La Primauté du Christ selon l'Écriture et la Tradition* (1959). ON B: L. Bellanti, "Christ the Centre of Christian Teaching", *The Month* 155 (1930), pp. 193–203; J. Bissen, "De motivo Incarnationis", *Antonianum* 7 (1932), pp. 314–36; E. Silva, "Rédemption", *DTC,* vol. XIII, cols. 1912–2017; G. Rocca and G. Roschini, "Ancora sulla ragione suprema dell'esistenza di Cristo in questo mondo", *Divus Thomas (Piacenza)* 20 (1943), pp. 271–82; M. Corvez, "Le motif de l'Incanation", *Revue Thomiste* 49 (1949), pp. 103–21; K. Rahner, "Chalkedon — Ende oder Anfang?", *Chalkedon* III, pp. 3–49; B. M. Xiberta, *Tractatus de Verbo Incarnato*, 2 vols. (1954); K. Adam, *The Christ of Faith* (1957); A. Grillmeier, "Zum Christusbild der heutigen katholischen Theologie", *Fragen der Theologie heute* (1957); G. Svenster, W. Pannenberg, P. Althaus in *RGG,* I, cols. 1745–89; K. Rahner, *Theological Investigations,* I (1961); E. Mersch, *Le Christ, l'homme et l'univers* (1962); E. Schillebeeckx, *The Sacrament of the Encounter with God* (1963); W. Künneth, *Glauben an Jesu? Die Begegnung der Christen mit der modernen Existenz* (2nd ed., 1963); W. Pannenberg, *Grundzüge der Christologie* (1964); J. R. Geiselmann, *Jesus der Christus,* 2 vols. (2nd ed., 1965); A. Grillmeier, *Christ in Christian Tradition* (1965); J. Solano in *Sacrae Theologiae Summa*, III (Biblioteca de Autores Cristianos) (5th ed., 1962).

Alois Grillmeier

IV. History of Dogma and Theology

A. JESUS CHRIST IN CLASSICAL FUNDAMENTAL THEOLOGY

1. Fundamental theology traditionally considered Jesus as *legatus divinus,* i.e., as one of many bearers of revelation who confirm their message by miracles and are therefore worthy of credence. The miracles of Jesus were invoked in the same way. Among these miracles added extraneously to the prophetic message, the miracle of his resurrection was certainly given particular emphasis. Nevertheless it was treated simply as one of many external "wonderful works", evaluated solely from the apologetical point of view and therefore in their formal character as miracles. The essentially unique character of NT miracles was not brought out, which consists in the unity of God's final eschatological saving act and its self-attestation. Jesus having been once recognized in this way as *legatus divinus,* the argument immediately moved to his founding a Church, and to its teaching authority (and that of holy Scripture). After that the actual doctrine concerning the divine and human reality of this *legatus divinus* could be left entirely to dogmatic theology strictly

so-called. The latter is based on the Church's magisterium and the Christology of Paul and John and is not a theme of fundamental theology itself. Within such a dogmatic theology the question is raised again, but at the most as a secondary one, whether it can be shown that the mind of the "Jesus of history", especially in the Synoptics and before them, was in continuity with ecclesiastical and NT Christology. This traditional method has of course the inherent advantage that in its own way it does distinguish between the Jesus of history and the Christ of faith. It is nevertheless open to considerable objections.

2. *Critical objections to classical fundamental theology.* a) Even on general grounds we must insist on greater unity between fundamental and dogmatic theology. The fact that a divine revelation has taken place (and in Jesus Christ in particular) can probably only be shown to be credible today by continual reference to what has been revealed and as such appears credible. In our context that means that the credibility *(credibilitas* and *credentitas)* of Jesus is from the start that of the eschatologically absolute saving event and bringer of salvation (see below F 2b). And the distinction between the notion of *legatus divinus* and that of the absolute bringer of salvation who is the "Son of God", though logically and formally conceivable, cannot in fact simplify the situation of fundamental theology.

b) The traditional method of fundamental theology underestimates the difficulty of establishing precisely how the Jesus of history regarded himself. Yet precisely in its character as fundamental theology (and therefore distinct in a certain respect from dogmatic theology, though this cannot be gone into here) it cannot evade that question. Even if the continuity between the self-understanding of the pre-paschal Jesus and the post-paschal Christ of faith is not denied (and precisely in fact because of the findings of historical inquiry; see *Jesus Christ* II), nevertheless it is only in the light of Easter that the scope and implications of the pre-paschal Jesus' conception of himself can become clear to us. This was the case for the original community itself.

c) From the start, therefore, Easter must not be regarded merely as the miracle of the restoration to life of some man or other, but which provides no indication of who this man really is. The Resurrection must be seen from the start as the event in which God by his self-communication victoriously and definitively accepts the world (in the fulfilment of the Incarnation). It must be understood as the event in which this eschatological action of God for the world is manifested, and in which — despite the knowledge we necessarily have of how the pre-paschal Jesus regarded himself — it only really becomes fully manifest who he himself is from the beginning. Even from the standpoint of fundamental theology, Easter is intrinsic to the revelation of Jesus as the Christ. It is not merely its extrinsic attestation.

d) The other miracles of Jesus have not the same rank in fundamental theology *for us.* Precisely because they are reported in the NT as manifestations (rather than as external attestation) of the fact that with Jesus the reign of God is present, producing a situation of absolute decision and making the most urgent demands, their character as miracles in the traditional sense cannot so easily be proved "historically" for us. As compared with the Resurrection, they have not for us here and now the same relevance to our personal existence in its fragility and its expectation. Consequently they have not the same central importance for our human reality as the Resurrection.

B. NEW APPROACHES

A contemporary fundamental theology of Jesus Christ must assume or take into consideration the following.

1. *Its purpose and the persons for whom it is intended.* Salvation and faith, being an all-embracing event of the whole human being in his unity and totality, cannot possibly be built up in their entirety by mere reflection (after the fashion of a particular branch of knowledge). By the very nature of the case reflection, whether everyday or scientific, cannot wholly capture and render explicitly conscious our existence, and man never lives solely by reflection. The same thing therefore also applies to Christology, if this is a central factor in Christian salvation and faith. In fundamental theology a Christology may not and need not proceed as if it had to synthesize faith in Christ *(fides qua* and *fides quae)* in the retort of scholarship by means of pure reflec-

tion (see the article *Faith* I). That does not mean that there can be a Christological fundamental theology *only* as "apologia ad intra", i.e., as justification of belief in Christ within faith itself, but not as "rendering an account of faith" to others, *apologia ad extra*. It means that the *demonstratio christiana ad extra* of fundamental theology is directed to a human being whom it presumes to be of morally good will. It therefore assumes him to possess the interior grace of God in Christ and to have already given an interior unanalysed assent to Christ. Moreover, it does not matter whether he knows this or not, or whether the *demonstratio christiana* has expressly taken this into account during its course, if this proves successful.

2. *Abstract Christology and Christology in actual practice.* It follows from this that the Christian may and must unaffectedly and courageously accept the "Christology" which he acts on in his own life: in the one faith of the Church, in the worship of its risen Lord, in prayer in his name, in sharing in his lot to the point of dying with him. The confession of faith of Gal 1:8–9 applies to this global experience, which certainly cannot be exhaustively analysed but which carries its own evidence with it. And in regard to it the Christian can still say, even today: "Lord, to whom shall we go? You have the words of eternal life" (Jn 6:68). Reflection on the liberation, vivifying support, and all-inclusive concentration of mysterious and unfathomable meaning which comes to the believer from Jesus Christ, may in the first place (as reflection) apprehend faith in Jesus Christ merely as one of several abstractly conceivable possibilities of coping with life and death. But reflection as such need not achieve more. It lays hold of this possibility as present, already realized, salutary; it sees no other better concrete possibility; that is sufficient for the believer, beyond the scope and possibilities of reflection, to allow himself to be laid hold of by Jesus' absolute claim which faith, not reflection, answers with an absolute assent.

3. *Christological arguments appealing to present-day conceptions of human reality.* From what has been said above, B 1, it also follows that the Christology of present-day fundamental theology, as well as using the traditional arguments which have always been and still

are valid, can also appeal in three ways to the global sense of human reality which through prevenient grace is already "Christian". It is not of course totally accessible to reflection, but it can be appealed to. This would mean carrying out one side of the "transcendental Christology" (see below, C 3; F 1–2) in a rather more deliberate and explicit way. These three arguments are all based on the principle that if man resolutely accepts his own existence, he in fact acts upon what may be called an "inquiring Christology". They all aim simply at making this anonymous Christology rather clearer. The conviction that this inquiring Christology will find what it seeks precisely in Jesus of Nazareth and is not simply "waiting for him who is to come", must of course supervene on this appeal to the spontaneous, unanalysed "inquiring Christology" really operative in each human being. In this respect we should simply have to ask where else an inquiring Christology of that kind is to find what it seeks, and what it affirms at least as a hope for the future, and whether Jesus and the faith of his community do not provide adequate grounds for the act of faith that he indeed offers what is always sought.

a) *The summons to absolute love of the neighbour.* Here we should have to take with radical seriousness what is affirmed in Mt 25. We should have to work this out from below, on the basis of actual love of the neighbour, not simply interpret it from above. If we do not turn Jesus' saying that he himself is truly loved in each of our fellow-men, into an "as if" or a mere theory of juridical attribution, then this statement when interpreted on the basis of the experience of love itself, means that an absolute love bestowed radically and unconditionally on a human being implicitly affirms Christ in faith and love. Now that is the case. For since a human being is merely finite and always untrustworthy, he cannot of himself meaningfully justify the absolute love bestowed when someone commits himself unreservedly and entrusts himself wholly to another person. Of himself he could only be loved conditionally, with a love in which the lover would either have reserves or else entrust himself absolutely to what may possibly be meaningless. To overcome this dilemma solely by recourse to God himself as guarantor and limit of the absolute character of such love would perhaps be possible speculatively and abstractly on the basis of the general concept of absolute love. But the love whose absolute character is experienced (even though it only becomes fully aware of itself in view of its radical unity with the love of God through Jesus Christ) involves more than a divine "guarantee" which remains transcendent to it. It requires a unity of love of God and of the neighbour in which love of the neighbour is love of God, even if only implicitly, and only thereby is fully absolute. By that very fact, however, it seeks the God-man, i.e., him who as man can be loved with the absolute character of love for God, and seeks him not as an idea (because ideas cannot be loved) but as a reality, whether present here and now or still to come. This argument presupposes of course that human beings form a unity, that true love does not shut itself off individualistically, but that in spite of its necessary particularity it is always ready to include all. Conversely it implies that love for all must always take concrete form in love of the concrete individual, and consequently that the God-man makes possible within the unity of mankind the absolute character of love for the concrete individual.

b) *The argument from readiness for death.* Ordinary preaching is too much inclined to treat Jesus' death, despite its radical importance for salvation, as a particular event in this world which took place along with many others on the world's stage. It presents it as an event with its own special features but not really as one which manifests and brings into operation very much of the innermost nature of the world and of human reality. This is so if for no other reason than that attention is too quickly directed to the external cause and violent character of that death, and the "satisfaction" theory then regards it as a purely external meritorious cause of the redemption. A theology of death, however, can link more closely the event of Jesus' death and the fundamental structure of human reality. Death is the one act, pervading the whole of life, in which man as a free being disposes of himself in his entirety. And that active disposition is (or should be) an acceptance of being absolutely disposed of in the radical powerlessness which is manifest and suffered in death. But if the free and willing acceptance of radical powerlessness by a free being voluntarily disposing of himself is not to be an acceptance of the absurd, which in that case might with equal justification be refused under protest, then that acceptance implies that man obscurely expects or affirms the existence of a death (whether it has already taken place or is hoped for in the future) in which the dialectic of activity and powerless suffering (which with us always remains an empirical fact) is reconciled in death. But that is only the case if the dialectic is resolved by being identical in reality with him who is the ultimate ground of its duality. For man does not affirm abstract ideas and norms as the ground of his nature, but a reality which is already, or which will be, present in his own, historical existence.

c) *The appeal to hope in the future.* Man hopes. He moves towards his future, planning it, yet at the same time exposing himself to the unforeseeable. His advance into the future is a constant endeavour to lessen his inner and external alienations from himself, and to lessen the gap between what he is and what he wills to be and should be. Is absolute reconciliation (individual and collective) only the eternally distant goal aimed at asymptotically, only exercising its attraction from a distance? Or is it a goal which is attainable as an absolute future, but which, even when attained, does not involve the suppression of the finite, swallowed up in God as the absolute? If God's absolute future is really our future, is that reconciliation the goal as something which still lies entirely in the future? Or is it the goal of history because history already bears within it the irrevocable promise of the goal, so that history even now, though still pursuing its course, is in this sense already moving within its goal? The human being who really hopes, must hope that each of these questions is answered by the reality of history in the sense of the second alternative. This hope provides the Christian with a certain understanding of what faith in the incarnation and resurrection of Jesus Christ professes as the *irreversible* inauguration of God's coming as the absolute future of the world and of history.

The content of these three arguments of a present-day Christology for fundamental theology can be summarized by saying that man is on the look-out for the absolute bringer of salvation and affirms, at least implicitly, in every total act of his nature directed by grace to the immediate presence of God as his goal, that he has already come or will come in the future.

C. Preliminary Considerations of Principle regarding a Contemporary Christology

1. *Its main apologetical purpose.* The most urgent task of a contemporary Christology is to formulate the Church's dogma — "God became man and that God-made-man is the individual Jesus Christ" — in such a way that the true meaning of these statements can be understood, and all trace of a mythology impossible to accept nowadays is excluded. The attempt may first of all be made radically to avoid mythological misunderstanding by the following operation. In the ancient and orthodox Christology of the Church, the meaning of the "is" — the predicating synthesis in the fundamental Christological statements — does not expressly represent that logical synthesis of two formalities which is normally taken for granted in affirmative statements, and which is founded on their real identity. The meaning of the copula "is" rests here on a unique union (such as is not found elsewhere and remains profoundly mysterious) of really distinct realities: Jesus in his humanity and in virtue of his humanity, is not God, and God in his divinity and in virtue of his divinity is not man. The sentence "Peter is a man", on the other hand, posits a real identification of the contents signified by the subject and predicate terms. Consequently the "without separation" (ἀδιαιρέτως) of the unity must only be understood in conjunction with the "without mixture" (ἀσυγχύτως) of the distinction (*D* 148), even though the "is" in the fundamental Christological formulas says nothing explicitly about this. This first consideration, which classical Christology already stated in essentials, does of course formally exclude erroneous identification which would inevitably involve mythological misconceptions. But it does not itself perform two other essential functions.

a) The centre of unity itself (in the sense of what gives unity and at the same time is the unity thereby constituted), namely the "person" of the Logos, remains very formal and indeterminate. This centre of unity may be called the "hypostasis" or "person" of the Logos. If the term "hypostasis" is used, which denotes the "bearer" of the divine and human reality ("nature") of the concrete One who "is" God and man, then what is meant by saying that the hypostasis is a "bearer" and "possessor" remains very formal and abstract. Or else when the attempt is made to elucidate it further, it easily reverts to the simpler fundamental affirmations of Christology so that nothing more is achieved than a verbal safeguard against the tendency to explain away these affirmations rationalistically. If, however, this centre of unity is termed "person", we must expressly state that this word is to be construed in the sense of the Christological "hypostasis" and this of course is then immediately forgotten. Or else the word "person", because of modern usage, represents a constant danger that the Christological statements will be misunderstood in a Monophysite or Monothelite sense. It would then be overlooked that the man Jesus in his human reality faces God with a creature's active and "existential" and absolutely distinct centre of activity (adoring, obedient, with a history and development, freely deciding, etc.). In this case, however, we should have a fundamentally mythological view of the Incarnation, whether this view were refused as mythology or "believed". Finally, there would also be the fact that if, as centre of unity, "hypostasis" or "person" makes intelligible and brings home to us the saving significance of this union "for us", it does so only with great difficulty and, at most, indirectly.

b) The Christological "is"-statements — "one and the same" is God and man — are exposed to the perpetual risk of false interpretation because of their resemblance to the "is"-statements of everyday life. The identity which the form of words suggests, but which is not really meant at all, is not excluded clearly and radically enough by the explanation, which inevitably comes second, and in any case because secondary is soon forgotten. That is not an argument against the justification and abiding validity of these Christological "is"-statements. But it is obvious that they involve the danger of a Monophysite and therefore mythological misunderstanding. If, for instance, someone says today, "After all I cannot believe that a man is God, that God has become a man", the immediate correct Christian reaction to such a statement would not be to think that a fundamental Christian dogma has been rejected. It would be to answer that the rejected statement and the construction apparently put upon it do not in fact correspond to its real Christian meaning. The true Incarnation of the Logos is indeed a mystery which calls for the act of faith, but it must not be encumbered with mythological misunderstandings. Though the Christian dogma has nothing to do with the god-men myths of antiquity, one can nevertheless admit without hesitation that some formulations of the dogma elaborated in terms of this particular historical form of thought (e. g., God "comes down", "appears", etc.) were used and accepted much more unquestioningly as helps to interpretation than is possible to us today. Even today Christology has an urgent task. It cannot be accomplished merely by verbal repetition of the old formulas and their exposition, which in any case is only carried on in the domain of specialist theological study. Nor, on the other hand, for many reasons which cannot be gone into here, can it consist in abolishing the old formulas. But a certain broadening of horizons, of modes of expression and viewpoints for the statement of the ancient Christian dogma is an urgent necessity, even if here we can only offer a few pointers and initial sketches which cannot be condensed into fixed formulas of a permanent kind (cf. K. Rahner, *Theological Investigations, I*).

2. On the *methodological and theoretical problems of Christology* in past and present, see above, *Jesus Christ* II.

3. *The double structure of Christology (transcendental and categorial) and its unity.* If a historical event is to mean the salvation of man in his entirety, it must possess an intrinsic structure which claims man in his entirety. This is so despite the event's historical character and despite the fact that it is freely effected by God and cannot be deduced. It must therefore concern man's essence, including his existentials, which in relation to his "nature" may be free dispositions of God. And it must therefore also be susceptible of elucidation by a "transcendental" method (see article on *Transcendental Theology;* cf. K. Rahner, *Schriften zur Theologie,* VIII, pp. 43–65). That does not exclude, on the contrary it implies, that man's "transcendental" orientation towards such a historical redemptive event is only explicitly reflected on when man meets with this event in history (cf. K. Rahner, *Theological Investigations,* V). That also, and primarily, applies to the Christ-event. For its complete comprehension it requires a "transcendental" Christology. In this the fact and intrinsic structure of the following truth must be elucidated: Thanks

to his essence qualified by the supernatural existential, man is a being who is oriented towards a saving event which is possible to expect; as an absolute and definitive saving event, its content is precisely what Christian faith professes as God's final promise in Jesus and as "incarnation" or "hypostatic union" (cf. Rahner, *Theological Investigations,* I). A transcendental Christology must, however, also endeavour as far as possible to make it clear how it is that Christ's human reality (his "nature") has a *potentia obedientialis* for the hypostatic union. For it is evident that not just anything at all in the category of "substance" has the possibility of "subsisting" in the hypostasis of the Logos. Nor can this *potentia obedientialis* be regarded as a purely negative absence of contradiction. It must be inherent in the essence of man himself to *be* this *potentia obedientialis,* at least in the line of a conceivable and hypothetical prolongation of a spiritual being who is essentially and ec-statically oriented towards God. These two aspects and conditions of a transcendental Christology of course belong together and mutually condition one another. On the basis of such a conception, the content of the Christological dogma might become more intelligible and existentially assimilable.

Conversely it also follows that such a transcendental Christology only becomes historically possible and necessary when man encounters the factual Christ-event in his own empirical, "categorial" experience. This categorial experience requires in the first place a Christology "from below", for man, of course, first meets the human being Jesus. If he believes in him as the Christ, he does not do so solely because he hears Jesus' spoken testimony to himself and recognizes it as confirmed by miracles, but because he comes to know him in his resurrection as absolute saviour, as simultaneously the object and ground of faith, and translates this realization itself — and rightly so — into the classical statements of Christology. From that standpoint, the classical Christology of pre-existence, of the one divine person and the two natures, of the Incarnation and the hypostatic union, is a sort of mid-point between a transcendental Christology (i.e., of a transcendental ordination of man in his history towards the absolute saviour) and a categorial Christology "from below". As a Christology of descent "from above" (such as is already found in Pauline and Johannine theology), that classical Christology involves more explicitly and more directly than a Christology from below various metaphysical notions, terms, presuppositions, which can practically only be verified by a transcendental method. Yet it concerns the concrete Jesus of Nazareth who is known *a posteriori*. In this sense it is a categorial Christology (i.e., thought in the ordinary categories of experience).

4. *The unity of ontic and soteriological, ontological and functional Christology*. It has already been pointed out that classical Christology in its explicit formulation (i.e., in the doctrine of the one divine "person" and the two "natures") does not clearly express the soteriological significance of the Christ-event (cf. K. Rahner, *Theological Investigations,* I). This applies particularly to the Western conception which, probably because of Western individualism, is, of course, rather far from the idea of the "assumption" of all humanity in Jesus' individual human reality. Consequently, in this intellectual perspective the hypostatic union consists in the constitution of a person who, if he posits moral actions and if his performance is accepted by God as carried out vicariously in the place of mankind, accomplishes a redemptive activity; but he does not himself in virtue of his very existence signify salvation as such (see *Salvation* IV A, C). On the basis of the statements of Scripture and our present ideas, however, even prior to any explicit and specifically soteriological affirmations, a formulation of the Christological dogma is desirable which would directly announce and express the redemptive event which Jesus Christ himself *is* (cf. Rahner, *ibid.*). And this in turn might help to avoid Monophysite and therefore mythological misunderstandings in the formulas eventually chosen.

5. *The starting-point of systematic Christology*. Pauline and Johannine Christology is already "theology" (cf. Rahner, *ibid.*, V), though of course binding on us. It is reflection in faith in the light of the Easter experience on the implications of the historical Jesus' own understanding of himself. Nevertheless, a systematic Christology at the present time cannot take as its starting-point this theological understanding of Jesus Christ as a matter of course. This also applies to the oldest pre-Pauline Christological statements of Scripture. A systematic theology adapted to the contemporary outlook must retrace the theological path to the point at which these Christologies themselves arise, however historically basic they may be. Nor can the starting-point simply be the statements of the historical Jesus about the Son. In later tradition and in scholastic theology, these were for the most part read too quickly — which need not necessarily mean falsely — in the sense of a pre-existent Son consubstantial with the Father. In the mouth of Jesus, however, they have a meaning which is much more difficult to grasp. Certainly we may not exclude from them from the start the man Jesus' relation as a creature to God. Nor, however, is their meaning to be restricted to what is common to all men in their relation to God. Jesus' historically ascertainable understanding of himself must not be heard and read on the tacit assumption that for one reason or another (e.g., adaptation to his environment) it was less clear and explicit than the Christological dogma of the Church. The believer himself would after all expect Jesus' own statement about himself to appear to us today to express his *homoousia* with God the Father less clearly and radically than the Church's dogma, because his words are more comprehensive and complex. For that very reason, however, they do not run the risk of a Monophysite, mythological misunderstanding of the classical Christological dogma. Because we are accustomed to think almost entirely on the basis of these dogmatic formulations, Jesus' statements seem less clear to us. But even apart from the impossibility of Jesus' having spoken in terms drawn from late Hellenistic philosophy, we cannot of course assume that the formulas of the ancient Church are the only possible and the clearest possible.

The starting-point of a systematic Christology cannot be a single biblical predicate applied to Jesus (e.g., Messias, Son of God, Kyrios, Son of Man, Logos, etc.). Such a single predicate taken by itself either cannot be shown to have been used by the historical Jesus or its exact sense is difficult or impossible to determine. The function of a systematic Christology is to show that classical Christology is well-founded, and to produce a sound and progressive understanding of it. But at the same time the whole of biblical Christology cannot be expressed in it.

It will be best to start from an understanding of Jesus' eschatological function in sacred history, attested by the OT and the historical Jesus. That is, we should start with the event which was brought to completion, and not merely externally confirmed by the Resurrection, namely, that in him God promised himself to the world in judgment and mercy, definitively, supremely and irrevocably. This could also be expressed by saying that Jesus by his Cross and Resurrection is the eschatological redemptive event, and in this sense is the absolute bringer of salvation because the Cross is not a mere passively endured occurrence but is his own act. It must not be overlooked that the historical Jesus understood himself in this way, and the full depth of that understanding of himself was disclosed and became credible to his disciples in the Easter experience. Such a starting-point is probably more assimilable today than if we simply say at the outset that God became man.

But when we say that "In Jesus, God's absolute, merciful self-communication to the world in a historical event is not only taught but in truth is eschatologically and definitively accomplished and present", such a statement depends for its understanding on the realization that man in virtue of his history and his temporal character seeks the ultimate and definitive fulfilment of his existence precisely in history (where the same things do not always happen and what is final can occur), and on the realization that such an ultimate fulfilment cannot take place without involving the abiding mystery of his existence. This starting-point is not open to the suspicion of mythology, unless of course any doctrine about God as salvation is regarded as mythology. And it has nothing intrinsically incredible about it. For this starting-point merely says that God exists, that he freely wills to be man's salvation, in himself, not merely by his finite gifts, and that this definitive and irrevocable gift of himself is made in history and has been accepted in history on man's part. The decisive question for a Catholic Christology which chooses this approach is naturally whether the classical, orthodox Christology can be arrived at on such a basis (see below, F 2).

6. *The relation between expression and reality in Christology.* What has been said so far, and in particular the distinction between an objective starting-point implicitly containing the whole of Christology, and the classical Christological statements, already points to a legitimate difference between the Christological formulas of the official pronouncements of the Church and the reality which they denote. And this concerns not only the reality in itself, but also the different ways in which that reality can be grasped by faith.

a) This is already evident in the fact that there are early Christological formulas, e.g., "Jesus is the Christ", "Jesus is Lord", which do not merely say the same thing as the classical formulas but in different words. Yet they do really permit the believer to attain the reality designated by the classical formulas.

b) Another variant of the distinction between formula and reality is shown by the difference already referred to between the "objective systematical starting-point" and the classical Christological formulas of the ancient Church.

c) A further point of legitimate difference is also found in the fundamental possibility of a "consciousness-Christology" in addition to the classical Christology (cf. K. Rahner, *ibid.*, I). There was of course in the Protestant theology of the early years of the present century a consciousness-Christology, a sort of new edition of the Nestorian "confirmation" Christology, which was in fact heretical. That is to say, wherever by reason of a merely human reality, secondary and therefore derivative contents of a human consciousness arise and can be combined (e.g., a particularly intense trust in God) and these attitudes or mental contents are asserted to be what is really meant in Christology, there is a rationalistic and therefore heretical Christology. As well as an "ontic Christology", i.e., a Christology which makes its statements with the help of terms ("nature", "hypostasis") which can also be derived from concrete realities, there could also in principle be an "ontological Christology", i.e., one whose concepts, patterns, etc., took their bearings from strictly ontological realities and the radical identity of being and consciousness. Here, in some respects it would be much easier from the start to avoid the danger of a Monophysite and mythological misunderstanding than in an ontic Christology. An ontological Christology of this kind presupposes the realization that being and consciousness in their ultimate meaning are identical, that being is present to the degree that a being is "intelligens et intellectum" ("ens et verum convertuntur"; "in tantum aliquid est ens actu, in quantum est intelligens et intellectum actu"; the degree of "reditio in se ipsum" is identical with the degree of "esse actu" and vice versa). This presupposition cannot of course be further justified here (see articles on *Consciousness, Spirit, Ontology, Being*). If it is legitimate, however, we can say that in principle an ontic Christological statement must be translatable into an ontological one. This principle is of practical importance, e.g., for the interpretation and justification of the scholastic doctrine that Jesus always possessed the immediate vision of God; probably much in the Johannine Christology (cf. the "I-sayings") could be made more precisely intelligible exegetically and objectively on the basis of a consciousness-Christology; similarly the connection between "transcendental" and "categorial" Christology could be demonstrated more clearly.

A more precise proof of these inter-connections would have to undertake the following analysis: The man Jesus lives in a unity of will with the Father which totally dominates his whole reality from the start in an obedience from which he derives his whole human reality; he receives himself purely and simply and permanently from the Father. Always and in every dimension of his existence he has given himself over totally to the Father; by this self-dedication he is able, under God, really to do what we cannot do at all; his fundamental attitude and condition (as radical unity of being and consciousness) is radically complete origination from God and dedication to God. If these statements were worked out in detail, it would certainly be possible to translate them back into classical ontic Christology. (This of course would need to be shown in detail.) On the assumptions mentioned and if properly understood, such statements would no longer be the expression of a heretical consciousness-Christology but of a possible ontological Christology. By virtue of the ontic Christology, it would always have to be true to its own ultimate consequences, but could itself legitimately translate the reality denoted by ontic Christology and could lead to a better understanding of the ontic statements.

The primary purpose of all this has been to show in some detail, from the possibility of a legitimate pluralism of Christological statements, that there is a legitimate difference between Christological formulas and the reality they denote. Consequently dissatisfaction with classical Christology, because the changelessness of its formulas may easily seem lifeless, need not represent the unvariable condition of an ecclesiastical Christology.

D. Perspectives in Dogma and the History of Theology

The actual development of Christology can only be outlined in essentials here (but see *Jesus Christ,* III). The survey which follows is chiefly concerned with the historical development of dogma regarding the centre of unity of God and man in Christology.

1. *The central problem of the incipient Christology of the ancient Church: the union of God and man in Jesus Christ.* a) The decisive step in the development of this truth was taken in the NT itself, for even though a Christology "of ascent" (knowing the man Jesus as the presence of God for us in the crucified and risen Christ) is presupposed, a Christology "of descent" is also present, though of course in various forms: the incarnation of the pre-existent Word of God in Jesus, of the "Son" absolutely (see above, A 3, and below, F 3).

b) As a consequence, Ignatius of Antioch already affirms that salvation is only ensured if Christ is truly man (against Docetism) but also truly God. The question how he can be true God without this conflicting with monotheism as a fundamental Christian dogma or without teaching Patripassianism in a Sabellian or modalist way, was a problem which had to be answered more precisely on the basis of the Nicene Creed in the struggle against Arianism in the history of the dogma of the Trinity (3rd and 4th centuries). The problem that Christ is true man and how this is so was the subject of the struggle against Gnosticism (2nd century) and Apollinarianism, the latter asserting that the Logos took the place of Jesus' human soul. Although Origen had already affirmed that the whole of man would not have been redeemed if God had not assumed the whole man, a Logos-Sarx-Christology (though not a heterodox one) is to be found even in

Athanasius and other representatives of the Alexandrian school of theologians. The central problem of Christology is how "one and the same" can be God and man. Since this problem involves the ultimate datum of faith in Jesus Christ, it cannot of course be solved in such a way that behind the unity affirmed by faith, another reality and mode is discovered from which the union appears to derive as a consequence and is thus explained. All the formulas which emerge in the course of the history of the Christological dogma are intended as a logical, not an ontic, explanation of the union (on this distinction in general see K. Rahner, *ibid.*, IV, pp. 300 ff.). That is to say, what is in question is the history of the search for formulations intended to maintain and defend more clearly and effectively the simple statement that this Jesus is God and man in the face of misunderstandings and theories which explain it away. It is important to realize this, so as not to underestimate older expressions or to overestimate more recent ones.

2. *The first more elaborate expressions of the unity of the God-man.* Down to the Council of Chalcedon (*D* 148), the Fathers always measured a Christological statement by the simple formula: "One and the same is true God and true man." This truth already had a basis in Rom 1:3 f. and Jn 1:14, and then in the Nicene Creed, and can be elucidated by the *communicatio idiomatum* which justifies the title Θεοτόκος (mother of God) and is itself further explained thereby. At the same time the unity itself was also expressed in formulas and images which later proved inadequate (e.g., "mixture", "glowing iron", "Logos in the flesh", "Spirit, pneuma [= divinity] in the flesh", etc.). As the terms of Trinitarian theology had been worked out earlier against Arianism, they could gradually come into use in Christology. Thus Tertullian already speaks (though only for the West) of the one *persona* in which without mixture, but linked, there is a double *status*, two *substantiae*. This line continued in the West through Ambrose, Augustine, Leo I: one person, two natures. At the same time, however, the problematical comparison with the union of body and soul was retained (*D* 40: Quicumque) or the formula that the Logos assumed a "human being". This was not far from a more Antiochene Christology which in Nestorianism became heretical and

lived on in the so-called "Assumptus-homo Christology".

In the East the development was more complicated. Πρόσωπον need not necessarily signify what "persona" means in the West (a subject ontologically one). On the other hand, φύσις was also used to denote the ultimately single subject and was not at first contrasted in Christology with ὑπόστασις. As a consequence, the Alexandrian school of theologians, influenced by Apollinarianism, speaks of an (incarnate) *physis* of the incarnate Logos in order to emphasize the identity of subject (cf. *Chalkedon*, I, p. 170). Even at the Council of Ephesus (*D* 115) expressions of this kind were used against Nestorianism, without any attempt at conceptual clarification of the unity and distinction in Jesus Christ.

3. *The classical Christological formula of Chalcedon.* At the Council of Chalcedon (451) the classical Christological formula of the ancient Church was established. The formula of Cyril of Alexandria (with its latent danger of Monophysitism) was replaced by a doctrine of two natures (φύσις) which are "unmixed", and respectively make Jesus identical in essence with God and with us, so that φύσις (and οὐσία) can no longer be used as synonymous with ὑπόστασις. The centre of unity in which the two realities meet and are therefore realities of the same subject, is called "ὑπόστασις" (πρόσωπον, *persona*). These terms are not given further philosophical explanations. No further attempt is made to elucidate how the hypostasis of the Logos assumes, appropriates and unites to itself the human φύσις (which of course cannot be thought of as if it were a thing, if we are not to think monophysitically or monotheletically). The difference between the relation of the divine hypostasis to the divine φύσις (real identity) and the relation of the same hypostasis to the human φύσις (real distinction) is not brought out by the formula "one hypostasis, two natures". The conciliar "unmixed and undivided" will always remain a fundamental (dialectical) formula not only of Christology but of the Christian conception of the relation between God and world generally. But because of the "and" which cannot be elucidated further and which links and opposes the two statements, it will always confront man with the mystery

of God himself. Consequently in that way it will always be a new starting-point for further theological reflection (K. Rahner, *ibid.*, I.).

4. *Later elucidations and refinements of the basic formulas.* a) In the late patristic period there was a (mostly purely verbal) Monophysitism and a simple maintenance of the formula of Chalcedon; the so-called neo-Chalcedonians interpreted the formula of Chalcedon more on the basis of Cyril's Alexandrian Christology. In East and West the attempt was made to grasp philosophically the more precise sense of "hypostasis" ("being *in se*"; "existence *in se*") and *persona* (Boethius: "persona est naturae rationalis individua substantia", a formula which raised problems of which Scholasticism was later conscious); the concept of *enhypostasia* was developed, and the idea of *perichoresis* taken from Trinitarian theology was put to good use in Christology.

b) On the problems of Monotheletism, see the article *Monotheletism*.

c) The post-patristic and scholastic period in the West slowly refined the terminology even further. The word *subsistentia* was coined as an equivalent to "ὑπόστασις", so that *substantia* and *essentia* were now generally used only as equivalent to οὐσία ; *persona* and *subsistentia* were made unambiguously equivalent. In the 8th century a form of Adoptionism was rejected; it was not in itself very virulent. Without influencing the official doctrine of the Church, Baroque Scholasticism speculatively investigated in particular the nature of the hypostatic union, inquiring into what constitutes this union itself. For Suarez, a substantial mode; for Cajetan, the actuation of the human *essentia* by the *esse* itself of the Logos; for Tiphanus, the referring of the *subsistentia* of the Logos to the real created human *essentia*. In modern times, the Church rejected rationalist and psychological theories in Christology, in opposition to Günther and Rosmini (e.g., *D* 1655, 1917). The Christology of early Protestantism was based on that of the early Councils, and differences from Catholic Christology mainly concerned soteriology. From the Enlightenment onward, within Protestantism the old Christology was increasingly rejected, with Schleiermacher in favour of a consciousness-Christology; K. Barth and E. Brunner, however, fully accept the dogma of the ancient Church. But they are rather exceptional as compared with the prevailing tendencies to demythologization of Bultmann and his school and to fundamental criticism of the Christology of the ancient Church (see the article on *Hellenism and Christianity*). Nevertheless the World Council of Churches (1948) professes its faith in Jesus Christ "as God and Saviour".

E. The Official Doctrine of the Church

Comparison must be made with the article *Incarnation* as regards the Church's official doctrine on the true divine sonship of Jesus Christ, his true humanity, his life and work. The meaning of the key terms "person", "nature", "hypostatic union", which were elaborated in the teaching of the Council of Chalcedon is not determined more concretely by the magisterium. The question of the precise sense of these terms must be pursued in a process which of its very nature is very complicated, and has to be guided by the meaning the terms possessed even before they were employed in Christology. At the same time it must be noted that when *philosophical* terms are taken over, and rightly so, they always revert to some extent to their meaning in common speech. Moreover, their further definition must also receive its orientation from the elucidation given to these terms by the Fathers and theologians, even though they are not always unanimous, and above all from the use made of them in the Christological statements themselves. This is possible if attention is paid to what they are designed to affirm, i.e., the one and selfsame in whom God and man are present for us.

Since the Council of Chalcedon and the rejection of Monotheletism, the official Church Christology in the narrower sense has undergone practically no development. Even Vatican II had scarcely anything to say on the question how the dogma of the ancient Church can be made credible to people today. Vatican II repeats the old doctrine, sees in confession of faith (in the Trinity and) in Jesus as God, Lord, redeemer and sole mediator — a formula similar to that of the World Council of Churches — the specific character of all truly Christian Churches (*Unitatis Redintegratio,* arts. 1, 20). It gives this doctrine a certain relevance to more recent problems: Jesus Christ as answer to the questions of existence (*Gaudium et Spes,* arts. 10, 22), as head of a renewed mankind

(*Ad Gentes,* arts. 3, 8), as linked to the whole of mankind by the Incarnation (*Sacrosanctum Concilium,* art. 83; *Gaudium et Spes,* art. 22), as culmination of sacred history (*Ad Gentes,* art. 3; *Gaudium et Spes,* art. 45). By these and other expressions the predominantly concrete, existentially Christocentric character, centred on sacred history, of most of the conciliar texts concerning Jesus Christ is plain. They also display a certain reserve in regard to the classical Christological formulas, though not of course any suspension of assent to them.

F. Problems and New Questions

Only a few of the new questions can be selected and presented here in outline. The exegetical aspect and biblical theology of such reflections must be assumed from the exegetical section of this article.

1. *Christology in a comprehensive view of man's reality in the perspectives of evolution and sacred history.* The miracle of God's incarnation is an absolutely free act of God himself. But once it has taken place and is known by faith, it is possible to recognize that that incarnation can be brought into positive relation with the perspectives of man's knowledge of himself and the world. It is true, of course, that by insertion into these contexts, the intellectual perspectives themselves are given a radically different character.

a) We assume that there is such a thing as an evolutionary view of the world and that it is objectively well-founded (see the article *Evolution* II). This presupposes a unity of spirit and matter. The essential difference between them is not denied, but in view of the common origin of both from the same creative ground (God as the one Creator of matter and spirit), matter cannot be a reality totally different in kind from spirit. The same conclusion follows from the substantial unity of spirit and matter in man and from the ultimate teleological unity of the history of nature and the personal history of spirit and freedom. The history of the one world of matter and spirit may be regarded as the temporal history of "self-transcendence". What is earlier and lower rises above and beyond itself into what is later and higher (higher through its greater complexity and through growing self-consciousness in the individual and therefore of the world

as a whole), and does so in virtue of the dynamism communicated to it by God's absolute being (*creatio continua*) as the innermost centre of the world (and therefore superior to it). If this is so, then the last, highest, unsurpassable instance of such self-transcendence — under the necessary divine dynamism which in this case is called "grace" — is the coming of the material-spiritual world into immediate relationship to God. This immediacy guarantees that God is not merely the original ground, the self-supporting dynamism of the world and its history, the ultimate goal which it always pursues, though only asymptotically. It shows that he does not merely create the world but that he himself is the perfect fulfilment of the world through his self-communication in grace and glory, that is, by a quasi-formal, not merely efficient causality. This divinization (which does not mean a pantheistic identification with God), in an absolute final culmination of the history of nature, spirit and freedom, is the self-transcendence of the world; and in it God himself (through his free act) is not merely the cause but the actual reality of the world's perfect fulfilment. (See the articles *Grace* and *Reign of God.*)

b) If that is so, the process of divinization of the world is the history of all mankind as a unity in space and time. The essence of its history is present from the start and consists in a movement towards the immediate presence of God through God's free self-communication by grace, in a history which is perfectly fulfilled and known by us in that history. Consequently there must be in that history an event — whether it has already taken place or is still to come is irrelevant here — in which the essence of history understood in this way becomes irreversible and is manifested to us. This event, since it has already occurred in history, is what we call, in Christian terms, God's incarnation.

c) This is equivalent to saying that the really fundamental purpose of God's incarnation should not be regarded as a new and higher level of self-transcendence, of the divinization of the world, taking place only in a single individual, but as the centre and irreversible manifestation of the divinization of the created (material) spirit as such. This indeed only occurs in an individual, and in comparison to other factors of the one divinized mankind and its history, it is higher in kind. But it is essentially a factor in the one history of mankind that is to be divinized through grace and glory. That is its definitive meaning. "Propter nos et propter nostram salutem." This conception presupposes that we assume the necessary unity of the divinization of the world and the Incarnation as two correlative factors of God's one free self-communication to the creature. It presupposes that the grace of the angels is *gratia Christi* and that the angels are essentially related to the material world, so that their salvific history too can and does culminate in the Incarnation. Thus the question cannot arise why God "only" became man and not angel as well.

2. *Christology "from below"*. a) In a "transcendental Christology" (see above, C 3), it is possible to develop the idea that man is the being who has the "desiderium naturale in visionem beatificam". It does not matter here to what extent and in what sense the ontological ordination *(desiderium)* to the immediate presence of God belongs to the nature of man as an abstract entity or to his historical nature elevated by grace (by the supernatural existential, which, however, is an ontological feature of his fundamental condition). It is also possible to develop the idea that this orientation, since it is that of man who experiences and realizes his deepest essence in history, must find historical manifestation, must await and seek God's promise in *this* dimension if it is to achieve its valid realization through God's free action (on the historical *a posteriori* realization of this "transcendental Christology" see above, C 3).

b) On this basis it is possible to arrive at the concept of the absolute saving event and of the absolute bringer of salvation, as two aspects of the one occurrence: a historical event of a personal kind, not merely a word added extrinsically to reality or a merely verbal promise, in which man experiences his essence (in the sense explained above) as really confirmed by God's absolute, irreversible ("eschatological") gift of himself. And every aspect of man is affected by it because only in this way is salvation a fulfilment of man as a whole. This personal and absolute saving event and the saviour who constitutes it, who *is* salvation and does not merely teach and promise it, must be God's actual and irreversible self-giving to mankind, not a

merely provisional and conditional one; and it must be historical, because nothing purely "transcendental" can be definitive, unless it is already the vision of God or unless it were possible for man's transcendent character to be fulfilled without affecting his history. At the same time that absolute event and saviour must also be a free acceptance of God's gift of himself, which must be effected by the latter itself. And it must take place not merely in thought but by the activity of a whole life. For this too belongs to the saving event. At the same time the latter and its structure must not be regarded as absolute in the sense that it is identical with the perfect fulfilment of mankind in the direct beatific vision of God. Otherwise history would have already reached its consummation. It must be a really irreversible movement towards this consummation, of such a kind that the future of the individual as such is left open.

c) We assume here in the first place (see sections A, B above) that Jesus of Nazareth understood himself to be this absolute saviour and that his resurrection established and manifested that he really is so. Of course he did not employ the abstract formalization by which we try briefly to define and suggest the notion of an absolute bringer of salvation. But he certainly did not regard himself as simply another prophet to be followed in the still indefinite course of history by other acts of divine revelation which in principle would call in question and supersede what had gone before, and open out new epochs in redemptive history. On the contrary, man's relation to him is decisive for the salvation of man as such, and his death founds the new and eternal covenant between God and man.

In the second place we also assume that this view of himself is worthy of belief (see articles *Faith* III, *Revelation*) and that its content is not only attested as credible by the Resurrection but that it there definitively fulfils its redemptive function and reaches completion.

d) Such an absolute saving event and the absolute redemptive mediatorship of a human being will mean precisely what the Church's doctrine calls the Incarnation and the hypostatic union, provided that the implications of the first of these terms are carefully thought out, and that the second is not misunderstood monophysitically and mythologically. We also have to be clear about the special nature of a "real" act of revelation by God. This is never merely in the line of the empirical, but always has an ontological character. That is to say, its existence is that of a created reality of self-consciousness and language, and therefore of conscious relation to God. God's saving action, his "behaviour" in contradistinction to his metaphysical attributes, is free, and as such has a truly infinite range of possibilities. Sacred history is therefore always open to advance, and therefore each event in it can always be superseded; each is conditional, subject to reservation. This is all the more so because saving history is also the history of created freedom facing a future which is unplanned and cannot be calculated with certainty from what has gone before.

It is therefore impossible to determine in advance what will follow from the interplay of these freedoms. A mere "prophet" (or a "religious genius" as effective pattern for a certain religious relationship between God and man) can in principle never be the last. If God nevertheless does posit his uttermost, ultimate, unsurpassable and definitive redemptive act (though of course finite, because it is only one of many possibilities), then this act cannot have the same essentially provisional, temporal character as other instances of his revealed "word" (which of course itself consists of action and language). And the provisional character itself cannot be eliminated by a mere verbal "declaration" by God that he will "not speak any more" but will rest content with what he has said. For such a declaration would itself be marked by the conditional and provisional character of an utterance of that kind. Moreover, such a declaration would decree that redemptive history is closed, without actually bringing it to a genuine intrinsic goal. It would allow that history to pursue its course as the mere implementation of what had gone before, and this would destroy its true historicity. An absolute (eschatological) redemptive action must therefore have a really different relation to God from any other saving act of God in the course of redemptive history. Unlike anything else that is other than God, it cannot consist merely in the difference between God and created reality or in the difference between something real, but more restricted, and something greater that would have been possible. It cannot simply be the history which we ourselves carry forward under God's guidance and by his power. In the absolute saving event, God must act out its history as his own and maintain it definitively as freely posited. Otherwise it will be provisional and not binding on him in any sense. Only if this event is his own history, definitively determined in itself (because posited by divine and, of course, also by created freedom) and therefore irrevocable, can there be any question of an absolute, eschatological saving event. God's gift of himself, manifested in history and irrevocable, must consist in his own reality, not merely as regards divine origin but in its created character. And precisely this reality which is his, which he cannot set aside as superseded, must stand on our side, as our real salvation, on this side of the difference between God and creature. This provides a first basis for a Christology "from below", but objectively identical with the Church's classical Christology "from above". And this can also help to display the unity of incarnational (ontic) and soteriological (functional) Christology.

3. *The question of Christ's pre-existence.* The question of the necessity of Christ's pre-existence for an orthodox Christology has been raised anew at the present time and doubt has sometimes been cast upon it, at least as a necessary implication of the Christological dogma or if it is intended to be more than simply a representational model. On this point the following may be noted.

a) If Jesus Christ is the absolute eschatological self-expression and self-giving of God — and without this a Christology is not Christian — and, in conjunction with this, is the free created acceptance of that gift effected by the gift itself in formal pre-definition, and if only in this way can he be the absolute saving event, then he who is giving and expressing himself, namely God, is "pre-existent". And this is radically different from the case when God pre-exists to some other temporal creature which is not his *self*-utterance.

b) Exegetes can and must be left free to inquire without hindrance whether what Jesus meant by Son of the Father is simply identical with the God who is expressing himself in time and therefore expressing himself as pre-existent, or whether it also contains a factor which is not identical with this God and so is not itself "pre-existent" (cf. *Mysterium Salutis,* II, cols. 356–9). Even the second possibility does not exclude the pre-

205

existence of the divine subject who is expressed and whom the classical terminology calls Son and Logos.

c) This question is a problem of Trinitarian theology rather than of Christology and is connected with the necessity and difficulty of speaking of three "persons" in God. If we understand by the three persons (i.e., more precisely the "person"-forming and "person"-distinguishing formalities) three ways in which the one God subsists, and regard the second as identical with God's historical expressibility which precisely as such is immanent to God and essentially belongs to him within the immanent Trinity (cf. *Mysterium Salutis*, II, cols. 327–99 *passim*), then we can and must speak of a pre-existence of the subject self-expressed in Jesus Christ. And this need not cause the difficulties which are obviously the cause of present-day hesitation and questions about pre-existence.

4. *The use of the term "person" in Christology*. The official statement of the Christological doctrine of the Church uses the term "person", "hypostasis" (of the divine Logos) to speak of the ultimate centre of unity of God uttering himself and the created utterance in which and through which the utterance takes place. That is legitimate, if for no other reason than that God's self-utterance in sacred history would not be conceivable at all if the unity of God and man in Jesus Christ were only the result of the uniting of two previously existing elements. Such an extrinsic union of two realities would be a third reality, not God's self-utterance. But we must also bear in mind the danger of misunderstanding. The fact of the single purely divine "person" has nothing to do with the heresy of Monotheletism, according to which Jesus' human reality was only the passively pliable instrument of the divine Logos. The *anhypostasia* of the human nature (or its *enhypostasia* in the divine Logos) must not be misunderstood. There does intrinsically belong to that nature as such, a personal (in the modern sense) centre of action of finite self-consciousness and created freedom. Created and "unmixed", this confronts God. The appropriation of this active centre by the divine Logos does not suppress its own character, if for no other reason than that closeness to God and active independence of a creature grow in direct, not in inverse proportion. Conversely, that means

that the freedom of the creature — even in its substantial ground — is perfected by being totally given over to God. And the radical measure of its appropriation by God is determined by the particular ontological relation of its ground to God. Consequently Christ's human nature is the most independent, the freest and, in the modern sense, the most "personal", in its actual humanity.

It should also be remembered that in the Trinity, "person" denotes what is absolutely incommunicable, in its radical uniqueness and distinction. This cannot therefore be subsumed under a genuine universal term as if it were realized univocally three times over. It follows that even if in Jesus Christ the hypostasis of the Logos is the ultimate subject, it cannot at all be inferred that a different divine hypostasis could be the "bearer" of a human nature, so that it was only because of a particular decision of God that in fact the second hypostasis in God took over the function. Even leaving out of account the variety of Scholastic theories on the precise nature of the *unio hypostatica*, the representational model in which the second hypostasis in God is the "bearer" of the human nature, must be employed with the greatest care. For even in general it is not very easy, especially in the Trinity itself, to think of the hypostasis as the "bearer" of a nature. (In the Trinity, of course, what is in question are three ways of subsistence, each of which is really identical with the divine nature. Now when two realities are identified in reality, it is very difficult to conceive of one as the bearer of the other.) In Jesus Christ, however, the reality (human nature) which is "borne" by the Logos is only too easily interpreted monotheletically as a thing, a passively manipulated reality. The hypostatic function of the Logos in regard to the human reality of Jesus Christ need not, however, necessarily be thought of as formally identical with what hypostasis means within the Trinity (Cajetan, for example, does not think of it in that way).

All this should make us realize that when the official Church doctrine speaks of the one divine person in Jesus Christ, we have not the right arbitrarily to attribute to the word "person" in this statement a meaning which is neither guaranteed and precisely defined by the magisterium nor really unanimously accepted in theology. Nor can we draw conclusions from it which lead us into conceptual difficulties or else wrongly make the matter too clear. Objectively the affirmation of the one divine person in Jesus Christ can with certainty only mean that the (in the modern sense) personal, human reality of Jesus Christ has entered into such a unique God-given union with God that it became God's real self-utterance and a radical gift of God to us. In other words, it was not merely made into a psychological unity subsequently. On this basis it also becomes intelligible that, correctly understood, a consciousness-Christology (an "onto-logical Christology") could be a serious aim of present-day Christology. It could describe and think the union between God (divine Logos) and Jesus as man (in his humanity) in categories which in a special way make unity and difference intelligible in an equally radical way (cf. *Mysterium Salutis,* II, cols. 331–99 *passim*).

5. *Jesus Christ's knowledge and freedom in his human reality.* An undefined doctrine of the Church attributes the direct vision of God to Jesus' human soul from the beginning of its existence. We can understand this thesis on the basis of the fundamental ontological condition which necessarily belongs to Jesus' human reality. For since being and consciousness are correlative, the ontic union of his humanity with God inevitably entails such an immediate relation to God. Even leaving out of account the fact that this direct vision of God must not simply be identified with the beatific vision of the risen Christ, such a fundamental and in a certain sense "transcendental" condition (existence on the basis of a most radical and unique link with God) does not entail that it must always have been explicitly reflected upon in all its implications and conceptually objectified. That would be simply incompatible with an honest exegesis of Lk 2:52; Mk 13:32; Mt 16:28. Nor does it mean that this fundamental condition, which is always the basis on which Jesus speaks, can be explicitly reflected upon, conceptually objectified and translated into language, except in contact with his historical experience, with the terms and concepts of his environment, and so with the human openness of his history. On that basis it is not impossible to assume a develop-ment in this "translation" of his fundamental condition, which may even still be recogniz-able in the Synoptics. Only in this way is it possible to attain a correct understanding of

Jesus' immunity from error, one which does not do violence to the texts. This is a problem analogous to the question of the inerrancy of Scripture. The texts in question, especially Mk 9:1; Mt 10:23; Lk 9:27, must be read in their whole context, which is not just a collection of statements. The context is the individual's temporal process of translating his radical self-awareness into language through encounter with his open history. In such a context an imminent expectation — similar to that of the primitive Church — may be the only way in which truth is historically grasped, i.e., in this case with a certain imprecision of outline. The statement must not be described as erroneous, because in it a truth appears which is essential even for Jesus' human consciousness, namely, that in Jesus Christ, the Son of Man, the Kingdom of God is irrevocably taking possession of the world.

God is not a force competing with others in the world; he is primarily the ground which establishes the world in its own reality. Consequently it should be clear that God's closer proximity does not absorb the creature but makes it more independent. It will also be plain that the absolute redemptive event requires a free acceptance of God's self-communication by man. If in this way all Monotheletism, even of a hidden kind, is avoided, then the created freedom of the man Jesus in face of God and his will presents no new problem (see the article *Grace and Free-dom*).

6. *Jesus' death as the death of God.* Christology at the present day must reflect more closely on Jesus' death, not only in its redemptive effect, but also in itself. Not in order to countenance a superficial and fashionable Death of God theology, but because it is called for by the reality itself. For death is not a merely biological event but concerns man as a whole. If it is said that the incarnate Logos died only in his human reality, and if this is tacitly understood to mean that this death therefore did not affect God, only half the truth has been stated. The really Christian truth has been omitted. The immutable God in himself of course has no destiny and there-fore no death. But he *himself* (and not just what is other than he) has a destiny, through the Incarnation, in what is other than him-self (cf. *Rahner, ibid.,* IV, pp. 112–20). And so precisely this death (like Christ's humanity)

expresses God as he is and as he willed to be in our regard by a free decision which remains eternally valid. In that case, however, this death of God in his being and becoming in what is other than himself, in the world, must clearly belong to the law of the history of the new and eternal covenant in which we have to live. We have to share God's lot in the world. Not by declaring with fashionable godlessness that God does not exist or that we have nothing to do with him. Our "possessing" God must repeatedly pass through that deathly abandonment by God (Mt 27:46; Mk 15:34) in which alone God ultimately comes to us, because God has given himself in love and as love, and this is realized and manifested in his death. Jesus' death belongs to God's self-utterance.

7. *Supplementary theses.* a) It has only been possible to indicate, not develop, the soteriological aspect of the Incarnation and hypostatic union as such (see *Salvation* IV).

b) However unacceptable the Nestorian confirmation-Christology may be, in which Jesus only became the Son of God in the course of his history, it must nevertheless be realized that God's saving will applies to Jesus Christ inasmuch as he carries out and suffers his history in accordance with the universal relation between essence and history. History is not a mere epiphenomenon of an essence which abides statically and unaffected; it is the history of the essence itself. Consequently the life, death and resurrection of Jesus are the history of the hypostatic union, even though the latter constitutes the real "law" of this history from the start.

c) A Christocentric view of all the reality of the world and of man (such as was at work in principle in Vatican II) cannot wholly succeed if the human reality which Jesus assumed and thus established with its own intrinsic reality and preserved "unmixed" is regarded solely as something intrinsically alien which the Logos merely "assumes". The Augustinian *assumendo creatur* needs to be taken seriously (cf. F. Malmberg, *Über den Gottmenschen* [1960], pp. 32f., 37ff.): Jesus himself is what comes to be if God wills to express and communicate himself "externally". God's self-utterance (as content) is the man Jesus, and the self-utterance (as process) is the hypostatic union. Christology is the most radical anthropology (effected by God's free grace).

8. *Christology and actual belief in Jesus Christ.* Some people who reject the orthodox formulas of Christology (because they mistake their meaning) may nevertheless in fact actually exercise genuine faith in the incarnation of the Word of God. If in view of Jesus' cross and death, someone really believes that the living God has uttered in Jesus his ultimate, decisive, irrevocable and comprehensive Word and so has delivered man from all the bondage and tyranny which are among the existentials of his imprisoned, guilty, deathward-bound existence, then he believes something which is only true and real if Jesus is he whom the faith of Christendom professes. Such people believe in the incarnation of the Word of God whether they explicitly realize this or not. That is not to deny the importance of an objectively correct formulary which is the ecclesiastical and sociological basis of common thought and belief. But only a heretic who equates the circle of those who really believe the saving truth in the depth of their heart with the circle of those who profess the orthodox formulas of the Church (the Catholic cannot do that) can deny *a priori* that someone can believe in Jesus Christ even though he rejects the correct Christological formula. In the living of human life, it is not possible existentially to adopt just any position, however theoretically conceivable. Consequently anyone who does allow Jesus to convey to him the ultimate truth about his life, and professes that in him and in his death God conveys the ultimate truth in view of which he lives and dies, by that very fact accepts Jesus as the Son of God whom the Church confesses. And that is so, however he himself expresses that active faith practised in his life, even if theoretically it is an unsuccessful formula, or even conceptually false.

It is possible to go even further. Some encounter Jesus Christ yet do not realize that they are coming into contact with someone into whose life and death they are plunging as their destiny. Created freedom always involves the risk of what has been overlooked, what is inwardly hidden in what is seen and willed, whether that is realized or not. It is true that what is absolutely unseen and purely and simply alien is not appropriated by freedom when it grasps something specific and clearly defined. Nevertheless what is unexpressed and unformulated is not necessarily absolutely unseen and unwilled.

God and Christ's grace are in everything as the secret essence of all reality that is an object of choice. As a consequence, it is not very easy to seek anything without having to do with God and Jesus Christ in one way or another. Even if someone who is still far from any explicit and verbally formulated revelation accepts his human reality, his humanity, in silent patience, or rather in faith, hope and love (however he may name these), as a mystery which loses itself in the mystery of eternal love and bears life in the very midst of death, he is saying Yes to Jesus Christ even if he does not realize it. He is entrusting himself to something unfathomable, for God in fact has filled it with the unfathomable, i.e., with himself, for the Word became flesh. If someone lets go and jumps, he falls into the depth which is actually there, not merely the depth he has measured. Anyone who accepts his human reality wholly and without reserve (and it remains uncertain who really does so) has accepted the Son of Man, because in him God accepted man.

We read in Scripture that those who love their neighbour have fulfilled the law. This is the ultimate truth because God himself has become that neighbour and so in every neighbour it is always he, one who is nearest and most distant, who is accepted and loved (cf. Mt 25:31–46). The reality which the Christian confesses to be that of Jesus Christ is not truth and redemptive reality for him alone, it is salvation for all, provided it is not rejected in personal guilt. It "holds true not only for Christians, but for all men of good will in whose hearts grace works in an unseen way. For, since Christ died for all men, and since the ultimate vocation of man is in fact one, and divine, we ought to believe that the Holy Spirit in a manner known only to God offers to every man the possibility of being associated with this paschal mystery" (Vatican II, *Gaudium et Spes,* art. 22).

BIBLIOGRAPHY. GENERAL: Catholic: M. Schmaus, *Katholische Dogmatik,* II/2 (6th ed., 1963); M. Premm, *Katholische Glaubenskunde,* II (1952); J. Solano, *De Verbo Incarnato* (5th ed., 1962); C. Chopin, "Le verbe incarné et rédempteur", *Le Mystère chrétien* 8 (1963). Protestant: K. Barth, *Church Dogmatics,* I/2, IV/1–3 (1936–62); E. Brunner, *The Mediator* (1934); R. Svenster, W. Pannenberg and P. Althaus in *RGG,* I, cols. 1745–89; P. Tillich, *Systematic Theology,* II (1957). Anglo-Catholic: E. L. Mascall, *Christ, the Christian and the Church* (1946); and see the bibliography on *Christology* in the *Oxford Dictionary of the Christian Church* (1958; reprint 1963). HISTORY OF DOGMA AND SPECIAL QUESTIONS: J. Rivière, *Le dogme de la rédemption. Étude historique* (1905); id., *Le dogme de la rédemption. Étude théologique* (1914); J. Relton, *A Study in Christology (1917)* (on "enhypostasia"); P. Crysostome, *Le motif de l'incarnation* (1921); J. Backes, *Die Christologie des hl. Thomas und die griechischen Kirchenväter* (1931); P. Galtier, *Unité du Christ* (3rd ed., 1938); P. Parente, *L'Io di Cristo* (2nd ed., 1955); B. Lonergan, *De constitutione Christi ontologica et psychologica* (1958); E. Gutwenger, *Bewusstsein und Wissen Christi* (1960); K. Rahner, *Theological Investigations,* I (1961), IV (1966), with bibliographies; H. Diepen, *La théologie de l'Emmanuel* (1960); F. Buri, *Das dreifache Heilswerk Christi und seine Aneignung im Glauben* (1962); A. Piolanti, *Dio Uomo* (1964); J. N. D. Kelly, *Early Christian Creeds* (3rd ed., 1965); K. Rahner, *Theological Investigations,* V (1965); A. Darlap, "Heilsgeschichte", *Mysterium Salutis,* I (1965); H. Riedlinger, *Geschichtlichkeit und Vollendung des Wissens Christi* (1966); K. Rahner, *Schriften zur Theologie,* VII (1967), pp. 123–96 (mysteria vitae Christi); VIII, pp. 43–65 (anthropology); id., "*Ich glaube an Jesus Christus*" (1968).

Karl Rahner

JOSEPHINISM

The State Church system of the Habsburgs had been built up systematically from the Middle Ages onward through political power as well as papal privileges; it helped the Church to make a number of improvements, especially in carrying through monastic reform after the Western schism, while later it was an obstacle to the advance of Protestantism and was even able to reconcile to the Church many who had deserted it. But it was also the most important force in building up the power of the modern State and this fact outweighs any advantages the system brought to religion and Church. The Enlightenment which gained ground steadily during the 18th century and the increased absolutism that went with it in Europe naturally led to greater control of the Church by the State and a significant change in the traditional system. The papal privileges which the rulers had been granted for the defence of the Church, and which had not always been interpreted as intended, now came to be regarded as superfluous and in the end these privileges, together with the provisions in canon law for Church property and personal immunity, were looked upon as incompatible with the sovereign power of the State.

Hence in June 1768 the Empress Maria Theresa of Austria, following the advice of her Chancellor, Prince Kaunitz, made a unilateral change in the relationship between Church and State, establishing the principle of State control, so that there should be henceforth only one supreme power in the land. Theory was then put into practice: the papal privileges which until then had limited the sovereignty of the State were now swept away altogether and all Church property was made subject to taxation; moreover, there was also serious interference in the purely ecclesiastical sphere, especially with religious orders, whose recruitment and activities were gravely hindered. This State Church system was most fully developed under the Emperor Joseph II (1780–90) from whom the system takes its name. Bishops could no longer communicate freely and directly with Rome, religious orders were withdrawn from the jurisdiction of superiors residing abroad and contemplative orders were dissolved altogether, because "as they were completely useless to their neighbour, they could not possibly be pleasing to God"; soon after, the monasteries and their entire property were ordered to be used for parochial purposes. The activities of the parish clergy were regulated down to the smallest detail and even the education of secular and regular clergy in the General Seminaries was submitted to strict State supervision. Even marriage legislation was withdrawn from the jurisdiction of the Church and in particular the various marriage impediments of canon law were abolished by the new marriage law of January 1783. The Josephine system which was laid down in many thousands of "imperial royal edicts in publico-ecclesiasticis" brought the religious orders to the verge of ruin. Very soon the upper classes were estranged from the Church, while already during the reign of the Emperor there was such a catastrophic falling off of vocations that the parishes and chaplaincies which had been added shortly before could often no longer be manned. After the death of Joseph II some particularly unpopular edicts and arrangements, such as the General Seminaries, were abolished, but the system as a whole remained in being. Thus rigid new regulations for religious services were laid down in 1791, and when, for instance, the parish priest of Baden, near Vienna, wanted to have a sung litany instead of a

recited one on a Sunday afternoon in 1800, he had to submit a special petition to the Emperor himself. In the decades that followed some small relief was granted regarding religious services and pastoral work, but inevitably such a long-lasting and total subjection of the Church to the alien spirit of the State was bound to leave deep and almost ineradicable traces in Austrian Catholicism.

Naturally, with State tutelage such as this, laymen could hardly have a feeling of co-responsibility for the fate of the Church, and anything like "Catholic Action" would have been quite unthinkable. Priests and even bishops, faced with these all-embracing, rigid State-regulations which made any pastoral initiative and adaptation to changed circumstances at least much more difficult, gradually became used to this state of affairs and were convinced in the end that this protective State control was better or more necessary for the Church than freedom. That is why the Austrian bishops did so little to regain freedom when the opportunity arose in 1848. And when Josephinism was actually abolished in 1850, the Archbishop of Vienna considered it necessary to write a special pastoral letter to reassure the faithful that the Church in Austria was not going to perish as a result.

See also *Absolutism, Church and State.*

BIBLIOGRAPHY. S. Padover, *The Revolutionary Emperor Joseph II* (1934); M. Goodwin, *The Papal Conflict with Josephinism* (1938); F. Maass, *Der josephinismus,* 5 vols. (1951–60) (with sources).

Ferdinand Maass

JUDAEO-CHRISTIANITY

The word Judaeo-Christian (sometimes Jewish-Christian) is used to describe two quite distinct entities. It can mean the whole corpus of the Old and New Testaments, and in this sense we speak of the Jewish-Christian revelation. It can also signify a form of Christianity whose habits of thought and social structures are specifically Jewish. If today there were a Christian community in Palestine which used Hebrew as its liturgical language, it could be called Jewish-Christian in the second sense. This is the sense used in this article, which treats of a special form of Christianity seen to be deeply committed to the structures of (early) Judaism. The Christians primarily concerned were those who continued to observe Jewish customs, especially circumcision and the Sabbath, and whose mental horizon was dominated by the Jewish culture of its day, that is to say, by an apocalyptic outlook.

1. *The history of Judaeo-Christianity.* The first Christians of Jerusalem were Jews who continued to observe the Sabbath, practise circumcision and join in the Temple worship after Pentecost. This is attested by the Acts of the Apostles (2:26; 21:10). The question of these practices being binding on Christians only arose after pagan converts began to enter the Church. At the outset, no one seems to have thought of imposing these rules on pagan converts. But the question was raised at Antioch in 48. It shows the reaction of a number of Jewish Christians who still maintained the solidarity of Christianity and Judaism. It was on this occasion that the Church of Antioch decided to put the matter before the Apostles in Jerusalem. The answer was that pagan converts were bound to follow only the Noachic prescriptions, that is, to abstain from food sacrificed to idols and to perform certain sexual purifications. It is clear, however, from 1 Cor that Paul did not attach much importance to these restrictions.

The decision of the Council of Jerusalem did not prevent Jewish-Christians from continuing their propaganda among pagans. Until the fall of Jerusalem in 70, the Jewish-Christian element exercised a considerable influence on the Church and tended to keep it within the framework of Judaism, in spite of the opposition of Paul, who found Jewish-Christian propaganda at work wherever he went, at Antioch, in Galatia, at Corinth, at Colossae and Rome. It was only after 70, and therefore after the death of Paul, that Gentile Christians were able to rid themselves completely of Jewish observances. It was only in the by-paths of Gentile Christianity that such practices survived for some time, as in Montanism, though they re-appeared sporadically at times in 3rd-century Africa, for instance, where a certain cult of the Sabbath was in vogue.

The story of Christian converts from Judaism is quite different. The local community of Jerusalem, presided over by James

"the brother of the Lord", followed the Jewish observance, and continued to do so till 70. No doubt it was for this reason that it enjoyed an increasing measure of tolerance. The community retired to Pella in 67 and returned to Jerusalem after 70. Eusebius tells us that all its bishops were of ancient Hebrew stock and that all its members were faithful Hebrews (*Hist. Eccl.,* IV, 5, 2). So it remained till the reign of Hadrian. Justin, who was a Palestinian, knew Christians who observed the Sabbath. After the time of Hadrian, the bishops of Jerusalem were of Greek extraction and the community was Gentile-Christian. But Judaeo-Christian groups persisted among the common people till the end of the Empire. Archaeological traces of them have been discovered by P. Testa (*Il simbolismo dei Giudei-cristiani* [1961]). These Christians of the Jewish observance were not confined to Palestine. Their missionary effort took in various parts of the East, and they were probably the first Christians to preach in Egypt, where Clement of Alexandria quotes from a Gospel of the Hebrews, and where in all probability the Letter to the Hebrews was written. Judaeo-Christian influence was particularly strong in Transjordan and Arabia, between Damascus and Bosra. These communities were still known to Epiphanius and Jerome in the 4th century. They used a Gospel of the Nazarenes, in Hebrew, of which Jerome has preserved some fragments. The communities survived till the coming of Islam in the 7th century. Mahomet was acquainted with them, and the Christian elements incorporated into the Koran go back to them. The evangelization of Osroene and Adiabene, whose language was Aramaic, must also be attributed to Judaeo-Christian missionaries. The Christianism of Edessa is strongly marked by Jewish influences, as has been shown by Vööbus in particular. Here Judaeo-Christianity was to find itself involved in the origins of Manichaeism in the middle of the 4th century.

2. *The diversity of Judaeo-Christianity.* It must not be thought that this Judaeo-Christianity was all of the same pattern. Judaism itself is known to have been a very complex phenomenon in the time of Christ. Some Christians, like Paul, came from Pharisaic circles. But it seems likely that most Jewish-Christians came from among the Essenes or from circles influenced by them.

Apart from the Essenian traits found in the Johannine writings, it is possible that the partly Judaeo-Christian works, the Testaments of the Twelve Patriarchs and the Odes of Solomon, were written by converted Essenes. Since these works come from Edessa, it seems probable that Osroene was evangelized by missionaries who were still Judaeo-Christians. This would explain the very marked asceticism of this Church, an asceticism which was a specific trait of the Essenian movement. Christian Essenes who had taken refuge in Transjordan must also have formed the sect of the Ebionites, who observed the Sabbath and turned towards Jerusalem for prayer. They had a gospel of their own which was known to Epiphanius. They acknowledged that Jesus was the True Prophet but did not confess his divinity. Here we have a heterodox Judaeo-Christianity, a Judaism which accepted Christ as a prophet but not as Son of God.

Other Judaeo-Christian sects were linked with marginal, heterodox movements of Judaism. Such were the Christian baptists of Transjordan, who stemmed from groups tributary to Judaism but kept only its monotheism. Their essential rite was a purificatory bath taken in the Jordan. The Elkasites of the end of the 1st century came from apocalyptic Jewish circles in Mesopotamia. More important is the encounter of Christianity, first at Samaria, and then at Antioch, with a dualist and syncretist type of Judaism. The Acts of the Apostles already mention Simon Magus. Here we are in the presence of a movement, Gnosticism, which was destined to take on very great proportions. Since the discoveries of Nag Hammadi, its Jewish roots are evident. But its essential characteristic will be to contrast the true God, who has nothing to do with creation, and who is manifested in Jesus, with the demiurge, the creator of the world. Gnosticism is therefore a form of Judaeo-Christianity. It must be distinguished, as a specific religious movement, from the apocalyptic Gnosis which is common to the whole of Judaeo-Christianity, orthodox and heterodox.

3. *Cultic and doctrinal structures.* We have sketched the origins and varieties of Judaeo-Christianity. We must now indicate, on the level of customs and ideas, some common features of this first expression of Christianity by means of a Semitic culture. Baptism is preceded by a two-fold instruction, dogmatic and moral. The first shows how the prophecies are accomplished in Christ, and is based on the collections of Testimonia already in use in the Judaism of its day. The moral instruction is an explanation of the "Two Ways", which is closely connected with what we find at Qumran. The obligatory fast preceding baptism has the character of an exorcism which it presented in Judaism. The cruciform sign traced on the forehead is the *tau* by which the members of the eschatological community are marked, following Ezekiel and the Apocalypse. The crowning with a wreath of leaves is a Jewish custom, which would be unthinkable in a pagan setting, where the rite had idolatrous connotations. The cup of water after baptism is also a Judaeo-Christian rite. The Eucharist is celebrated after the vigil on the evening of the Sabbath, that is, at dawn on Sunday, at cock-crow. It is preceded by a meal, by the reading of the OT and by a haggada. We must note the existence of a sacrament preparing the sick for death, which is not the anointing of the sick. It prepares the dying to encounter the demons who will try to bar their way to heaven. The existence of this sacrament has been proved by the researches of P. Orbe and P. Testa.

The Judaeo-Christians celebrated Easter on 14 Nisan, like the Jews. This custom survived in Asia Minor till the 2nd century and gave rise to the Quartodeciman dispute. But it was probably also in the same circles that the first Sunday after the Passover also began to be celebrated at the same time. This Sunday was in fact the beginning of the feast of Weeks, Pentecost, which ended also on a Sunday. On the vigil of the first Sunday the crossing of the Red Sea was commemorated, a custom which persisted in the later liturgy of the Christian Easter vigil.

As regards doctrine, we should note the designation of the Son and the Spirit by angelic titles: Michael and Gabriel, the two seraphims. More particularly, the Son is designated by expressions like the Name, the Law, the Covenant, the Principle. The mystery of Christ is represented as the descent of the Son through the angelic spheres and the ascension of the Word incarnate through the same spheres. Great attention is paid to the descent into hell, this being considered to answer the question of the salvation of the just of the OT. The cross is envisaged as a cosmic symbol. The Church is seen in an apocalyptic perspective as existing beside God since before the creation of the world. A visible reign of Christ is awaited, corresponding to the seventh millennium, the Sabbath, of the cosmic week. These examples show that though Judaeo-Christianity, as a community inserted into Judaism, has disappeared — to re-appear perhaps one day — it has left a considerable heritage to the Church, especially in the liturgy.

See also *Judaism* I, *Apostolic Church, Gnosis, Gnosticism, New Testament Theology* II.

BIBLIOGRAPHY. J. Marchal, *DTC,* VIII, cols. 1681–1709; M. Simon, *Verus Israel* (1948); H. J. Schoeps, *Theologie und Geschichte des Judenchristentums* (1949); S. G. F. Brandon, *The Fall of Jerusalem and the Christian Church* (1951); A. Vööbus, *Celibacy: A Requirement for Admission to Baptism* (1951); L. Goppelt, *Christentum und Judentum im 1. und 2. Jahrhundert* (1954); L. E. Elliott-Binns, *Galilean Christianity* (1956); A. Orbe, *Los primeros herejes ante la persecución* (1956); J.-P. Audet, *La Didaché, Instruction des Apôtres* (1958); R. M. Grant, *Gnosticism and Early Christianity* (1959); H. Kosmala, *Hebräer, Essener, Christen* (1959); W. G. Kümmel, F. Maier, and J. Leonhard, *RGG,* III, cols. 967–76; E. Peterson, *Frühkirche, Judentum und Gnosis* (1959); J. Blinzler, *LTK,* V, cols. 1171–74; J. Daniélou, *Theology of Jewish Christianity* (1964); W. Trilling, *Das wahre Israel* (3rd ed., 1964); J. Daniélou, *Primitive Christian Symbols* (1964); B. Bagatti, *L'Église de la circoncision* (1965); J. Daniélou, M. Simon and others, *Aspects du Judéo-Christianisme* (1965); J. Daniélou, *Études d'exégèse judéo-chrétienne* (1966).

Jean Daniélou

JUDAISM

I. Judaism from Ezra to A.D. 70. II. Origin and History: A. The Correct Approach. B. General Characteristics. C. The Main Divisions of the History of Judaism. III. The Religion. IV. The Philosophy.

I. Judaism from Ezra to A.D. 70

1. *The concept.* Early Judaism (sometimes called "late Judaism", by comparison with classical OT times) is understood in various ways. As a period, it is sometimes taken to run from about the date of the composition of the Book of Daniel (*c.* 160 B.C.) to the end of the Jewish wars under the Emperor Hadrian (A.D. 140). Others take a longer period — from the time of the activity of Ezra and Nehemiah in Jerusalem (*c.* 450 B.C.) to the final formation of the Talmuds (*c.* A.D. 500).

For others, early Judaism is the time of the second temple (*c.* 500 B.C. to A.D. 70). Others think of the period from the conquests of Alexander *c.* 330 B.C. to the fall of the temple. In any case, early Judaism is seen as a period which supplies Christian exegetes and historians of religion with much comparative material for the study of the OT and NT. It is relevant as a movement deriving from the OT, preceding, accompanying and opposing the NT and persisting after it.

But for many authors early (or "late") Judaism is not merely a way of speaking of a historical period. It is also a value judgment, depending on the notion that the only legitimate heirs of the OT are the NT communities — even on the plane of the history of religion. This is, however, to take an unjustifiably low view of Judaism after Ezra and Nehemiah. Hence the term "late" Judaism (mostly confined to continental scholars), though Judaism, as the religion and practice of the Jewish people, was still in an early stage of its evolution. Thus Bousset, *Religion des Judentums* (3rd ed., by H. Gressmann [1926]), can speak of "late Judaism" (the period now in question) as a time of inflexibility, petrification, legalism, ritualism, casuistry and superficiality, when the OT law was swamped by traditionalism and foreign influences. In this approach, Phariseeism and apocalyptic come in for some of the severest criticism. Very often this is done merely to bring out the uniqueness and absoluteness of the words and deeds of Jesus.

For a correct orientation here, it will be well to eliminate entirely the term "late Judaism" in this connection. Early Judaism is the correct term, and it is best taken as running from *c.* 500 B.C. to A.D. 500 (see above). It falls into two main periods, 500 B.C. to A.D. 70, the time of the second temple, early Judaism in the strict sense, and from A.D. 70 to 500, the age of the Mishnah and Talmud. This whole period is characterized by a growing tendency to centre religious life on the local synagogue, rather than on the central shrine at Jerusalem. Then, it will also be well to work out correctly the various relationships between OT, early Judaism and NT. As regards the NT, for instance, it should be noted that it must be read to a great extent in the light of early Judaism, while there is no correspondingly comprehensive view of early Judaism which can be gained from the standpoint of the NT. Finally, attention must be paid to the fact that NT statements on early Judaism are primarily and on the whole theological — not psychological, sociological or purely historical comment.

2. *Trends in early Judaism.* These may be distinguished as official, unofficial and separatist or heretical (early) Judaism. Official Judaism embraced those who were active in the government and religious life of the Jewish people. Unofficial Judaism held aloof. The others sharply opposed the official trend. It should be noted, however, that these notions apply differently before and after A.D. 70, since the hierarchical structure of early Judaism underwent a profound change after the destruction of the temple. Before that, the high priests, mostly Sadducees, were the hierarchical heads, while after A.D. 70, there was the patriarch in Palestine and the Resh Galuta ("Head of the Exiles") in Babylon. Before A.D. 70, no single party had been strong enough to force its own way of thought on the others as the prescribed norm. But after A.D. 70, the rabbinical schools, based on Phariseeism, became normative.

a) Official Judaism before A.D. 70 was represented above all by the religious policy of the Sadducees and Pharisees, and to some extent or for some time by the ruling families of the Maccabees and Hasmonaeans and the house of Herod. The two main religious parties had a common forum in the sanhedrin or council (of 71 members) which met in the precincts of the temple. The powers of the sanhedrin were, however, constantly more and more restricted by the actual rulers. Outside the sanhedrin, Sadducees and Pharisees had little in common. The Sadducees, according to Josephus at least denied that providence could be reconciled with human freedom (though here Josephus is probably importing terms from Hellenistic debate). The Pharisees, however, admitted providence and freedom, and also the resurrection of the dead, the existence of angels and the last judgment (cf. Acts 23:6–9; Josephus, *Antiquities,* 18, 16–17). Their views, perpetuated in the rabbinical schools, became normative for all Judaism after the calamity of A.D. 70, since Phariseeism had striven for peace with the Romans and had been severely critical of messianic pretenders and thus emerged less compromised from the war. But above all, its loyalty to the Torah and

tradition and its religion of the synagogue made it the only practical way of life once the temple was no more. The compilation of the Mishnah and the Talmud provides clear instructions on the keeping of the OT law, but it also shows the range and vigour of rabbinical Judaism in discussions of the problems of election and suffering, evils within Judaism, pagan oppression and eschatological hopes. As a consequence of the shattered economy of Palestine, the main centre of Jewish learning shifted more and more perceptibly from Palestine to Babylon.

b) Unofficial Judaism was composed of groups which held aloof from the religious policies of the ruling classes, though without breaking formally with them. They would include the Amme-ha-arez (literally, the country people), various apocalyptic conventicles and — before A.D. 70 — militant groups of rebels against Roman rule. Rabbinical literature describes the Amme-ha-arez as ritually impure, uncultured, careless about the Torah and hence "provincials" who were to be avoided as far as possible (Mishnah, Demai 2, 3; bBerachot 47b; bPesachim 94b; see also the commentaries on Mt 5:3 and Jn 7:49). As far as one can see, they were not simply the common people who were unfamiliar with the niceties of the law, but probably representatives of an interpretation different from the official one, and it was this which made them the object of polemics.

There were many apocalyptic circles in early Judaism where esoteric speculation was encouraged, and especially the hope of an imminent coming of the *eschaton.* The most important works of early Jewish apocalyptic were *Enoch* (Ethiopic) (2nd to 1st century B.C.), *4 Esdras* and the *Apocalypse of Baruch* (Syriac) (1st to 2nd century A.D.). Their influence can be traced in rabbinical writings, especially in the Midrash echa rabbati (on Lamentations) and the Pesiqta rabbati. — In spite of its radically negative attitude towards tense expectations of the imminent end, which it had inherited from Phariseeism, rabbinical Judaism of the second and third centuries A.D. could not always clear its mind of apocalyptic eschatological thinking, even in militant terms, though at first it was opposed to military action. The revolt of Bar-Kochba, for instance, had a messianic motivation which inspired it to take up arms (bSanhedrin 97b; pTaanit 4 [68d]).

The eschatologically orientated groups of

rebels who launched the Jewish war could not have been excluded from Judaism before A.D. 70, firstly because there was no "normative" Judaism, and secondly, because their theocratic ideals were firmly rooted in the OT. The uncompromising rebels were not the criminals whom Josephus described them to be. They aimed rather at establishing the absolute sovereignty of Yahweh over Israel in all its rigour. It was an ideal which necessarily included revolt against Rome as a religious duty, since Rome treated Judaea as the appurtenance of a pagan emperor. After A.D. 70, the number of the revolutionary-minded was so greatly reduced that all that rabbinical Judaism had to do to counter them was to give a spiritual and pacifist interpretation to the OT texts which the rebels had used as a military ideology. (Mechilta d'Rabbi Ishmael, Tractate Shirata 3, on Exod 15:2; Tractate Amalek 3, on Exod 18:1.)

c) Separatist Judaism comprised groups which abandoned voluntarily official Judaism as corrupt, or were "excommunicated" by official Judaism. The typical representatives of voluntary separation were the members of the Qumran movement, which was headed by dissident priests of a radically eschatological mentality. The Qumranites considered themselves the only legitimate inheritors of the religion of Israel, (1 QH 4–8; 1 QM 1; 1 QS 6–8, etc.), and hence may be regarded as a sect. After A.D. 70, certain groups and individuals were excluded from official and authoritative Judaism, and mostly given the somewhat ambiguous names of heretic *(min)* and Sadducee. The *minim* were chiefly the Samaritans, Judaeo-Christians and Gnostics (Mishnah, Sanhedrin 10, 2; bBerachot 28b; pTaanit 2, 1 [65b]). The Sadducees were considered as typically heretical on account of their denial of the resurrection of the dead and their rigid interpretation of the Torah (Mishnah, Makkot 1, 10; bJoma 19b).

Thus early Judaism appears as a composite movement containing various conflicting trends. Its historical development must be considered by students of religion and exegesis as a phenomenon almost entirely independent of the NT.

See also *Judaism and Christianity, Judaism* II, III, *Qumran, Apocalyptic.*

BIBLIOGRAPHY. See bibliography on *Judaism* II, III, *Judaism and Christianity*; also: W. Bousset, *Religion des Judentums,* ed. by H. Gressmann (3rd ed., 1926); J. Leipoldt and W. Grundmann, *Umwelt des Urchristentums,* 3 vols. (1965–66).

Clemens Thoma

II. Origin and History

A. The Correct Approach

Judaism is a very complex phenomenon, embracing religious, social, political, ethnic and historical elements. There are three main difficulties in the way of seeing it clearly as it really is. Firstly, each of the components mentioned cannot but involve the whole phenomenon of Judaism, so that there is an immediate danger of distortion if, say, the religion or the social structure of Judaism is taken in isolation — as is done by some authors who look on "early Judaism" as a religiously inferior form of the OT. Secondly, the whole notion of Judaism has undergone profound variations in the course of its history, and even today there is no general consensus as to how the nature, tasks and significance of Judaism are to be conceived. But thirdly and most important, ever since Judaism was born in OT times, it has been the object of fierce polemics from within and from without Judaism, so that a dispassionate and valid judgment is hard to arrive at. Existing Jewish and non-Jewish writing, either pro-Jewish or anti-Jewish, is to a great extent a reflection of attacks upon Judaism, or groups within Judaism, launched by religious or political movements, and of Jewish reaction to such attacks. Hence the most important prerequisite for a just and valid judgment is a correct estimation of biblical (and post-biblical) polemics. To avoid the temptation of either anti-Semitism or an uncritical admiration for the Jews, one must begin by forming a clear idea of the historically conditioned and hence relative nature of such polemics as occur in the Bible, and also of its formal nature, that is, of its function as a literary genre. The OT contains sharp denunciations of the Jews on the lips of prophets and teachers. Terms such as "a rebellious people" (Ezek 2:5–7) or "a stiff-necked people" (Exod 32:9; 33:3–5; Deut 9:6) are typical but stereotyped expressions of ancient polemics.

Nonetheless, the OT polemics is to some extent quite understandable, and can be positively evaluated as the frank and lofty self-criticism of the ancient people of God, and thus given its proper relevance. So too confusion is impossible when one observes critically the real intentions of the two parties involved in the opposition of paganism to Judaism which has flared up again and again from the 5th century B. C. down to our own times. But Jewish and anti-Jewish polemics always became overheated when it was a question of groups breaking away from Judaism and taking with them as their own inheritance the religious claims of Judaism (as in Qumran and indeed in Christianity). It is of particular importance today that Christians should take note of the historical conditions, the literary genres and the susceptibilities at work in general when they try to form a judgment on Judaism in the light of NT polemics. The importance of allowing for the historical situation can be seen from a comparison between Mt 23:35–39 and Ezek 22:2, 23–31. Both texts speak in similar tones of a blood-stained and sacrilegious Jerusalem, but in Ezekiel it is polemics within Judaism itself, while in Matthew it is the polemics of a Christianity in the process of freeing itself from Judaism.

B. General Characteristics

Judaism in the broad sense goes back to the establishment of the Amphictyony of the twelve OT tribes in the course of the conquest of Palestine (14th or 13th century B.C. onward). For its further development the history of Judah (after David) was of decisive importance. But strictly speaking, Judaism only exists from the 6th century B.C. on. The exiles who returned from Babylon were mostly recruited from the descendants of the tribe of Judah (see Ezra 1 and 2). They saw themselves as the purified "Remnant of Israel", that is, as the part of the Twelve Tribes which had survived the catastrophe of deportation and had submitted to it as the judgment of God upon their guilt. With this idea in mind, the Jews of the time sought to uphold the Mosaic traditions by a new Exodus which would bring them once more into the devastated land of Israel, there to make a new beginning in the hope of serving faithfully the God of the covenant. There is a very vivid expression of this feeling of being the "remnant" or true representative of Israel in Ezra 6:13–18. The consecration of the new temple included the ceremony of sacrificing "twelve he-goats as a sin offering

for all Israel, according to the number of the tribes of Israel" (v. 17). See also 2 Kg 19:31; Is 41–55; Jer 40:11; 42:15; 44:12; Ezek 9:8; 11:13, etc.).

The story of the foundation of Judaism as given here in Ezra already manifests the most central feature of Judaism. At all periods of its existence and throughout all adversities it saw itself as the people of the covenant in a special collective relationship of service and partnership towards the God of the covenant. The basic creed of the people may be expressed as follows: Yahweh is the God of Israel, Israel is the people of Yahweh (cf. Exod 19:4–6; Jos 24). The promises of descendants to the patriarchs are to be understood ultimately in the light of this covenant (Gen 13:16; 15:5; 26:4, 24; 28:14; 32:13, etc.). The thought of being the people of the covenant determines the nature of the historical activity of Judaism in the world. As the appointed heir of Israel, Judaism strives to embody and give testimony to the God-given doctrines, commandments and events of salvation. From this union as a people with God results the ideal of a political, social, cultural and economic solidarity among the beneficiaries of the covenant. There is a desire to see ordinary profane activities penetrated by the thought of the kingship of God, which is always present but must be realized more and more effectively.

Another general characteristic of Judaism is its relationship to the land of Israel as promised by the God of the convenant. Though the "land of Israel" has seen too many historical changes in its boundaries to be exactly described as a geographical entity, and although at all times there were Jews living outside it, either voluntarily or in forced exile, the claim to the promised land has never been abandoned by Judaism to the present day. It is inspired in this claim by religious and ethnic motives, and the land has often had extraordinary qualities attributed to it (cf. Deut 11:10–12; Judah Halevi, etc.).

A third characteristic which is generally observable is that Judaism tries to live out the present, especially when it seems dark and sorrowful through trials imposed on the faith, by reflecting on the glorious past of the people and the future salvation to be hoped for. Thus Judaism has a double perspective to inspire it – the hope of the restoration of the past and the hope of an eschatological salvation which goes beyond all human limits. Both memories of the past and hope of the future can take on various nuances. At times the nationalistic element prevails, at times the universalist, sometimes earthly and sometimes heavenly hopes. To illustrate these tendencies reference may be made to the biblical expositions of God's sworn promises to the patriarchs (Gen 24:7; 50:24; Exod 13:5, 11; Num 14:16; Deut 4:31; 6:23, etc.). Typical too are such rabbinical expressions as "for the sake of the merits of the fathers" (bRosh ha-Shana 11a, etc.) and discussions of the days of the Messiah and the world to come (bSanhedrin 97 a–b). We can see at once that the messianic hopes of Judaism are subordinate to the general eschatological expectations. Intense messianic expectations played a considerable part at times in Jewish history. This is particularly true of the period from about 170 B.C. (the time of the Maccabees) till A.D. 70 or 73 (suppression of the Jewish revolt by the Romans), and again of the rebellion of Bar Kochba (A.D. 132–5) and the period of the messianic pretender Sabbatai Zewi (1626–75). But in these and other periods of intense messianic expectation there was never any consistent or ideologically fixed notion of the concrete duties of the Messiah in the time of final well-being. As a rule, the Messiah appears only as the representative or protector of a well-being which has come or is about to come. He is not thought of as redeemer in the Christian sense.

One might also possibly adduce as a permanent characteristic the loyalty of Judaism to the languages of the Bible and the Talmud. No doubt many Jews, at all periods of the history of Judaism, did not know the languages in question (Hebrew and Aramaic, but above all Hebrew). But it was constantly felt to be a religious duty to learn Hebrew, and the modern slogan of "Yehudi, daber ivrit" (Jew, speak Hebrew!) was constantly given religious and national motives.

These essential bonds with covenant, land and past (and perhaps language) do not mean, however, uniformity, but leave room for strong polarities. The assertion of Leo Baeck, that Judaism has always been "bipolar" — he meant above all the polarity of diaspora Judaism to Judaism in the land of Israel — is true in many ways of the relationship of Judaism to the covenant. The people of the covenant feels itself, as the chosen people and the envoy of the God of the covenant, in a permanent state of tension as regards the peoples of the world. And at the same time, Judaism has to do justice to the fact that within the people and among those who profess the Jewish faith there are members who are not loyal to the covenant.

As regards the relationship of Judaism to past and future, tension arises above all from the different attitudes of various groups of Jews to their origins, present position and future fulfilment. The contrasts, for instance, between the strict orthodox in the present State of Israel and certain other groups, especially in the Kibbutzim, show that Judaism is elastic enough to allow one to feel oneself a Jew and still be without faith in God, attachment to tradition or messianic hopes. On the other hand, it is also possible to accept all that is genuinely Jewish in the religious sphere and still refuse to commit oneself to the concrete politics of the Jewish State.

Popular presentations of Judaism are very much given to ascribing peculiarities to Judaism for which there is little if any foundation. It is incorrectly asserted, for instance, that Jews are a homogeneous or singular race. It is common knowledge today among students of racial questions that within the Mongolian, Negro and European types of race only mixed forms occur or can occur. In any case, neither the Bible nor post-biblical Judaism gives occasion for affirming the superiority, inferiority or even unity of the Jewish race. There are, no doubt, strong tendencies to ethnic segregation in Judaism. The tendency was already prevalent in the 5th century B.C., in the age of Ezra and Nehemiah, and also in the age of the Mishnah and the Talmud. The existence of the Jewish ghettoes was not due solely to the desire of Jews to escape from anti-Jewish attacks. Their existence was due in part to the genuinely Jewish need for local isolation, in order to be more easily able to fulfil the mission of Judaism. But such tendencies always had their counterparts (even if we prescind from the divergent ethnic origins of Judaism) in outward-looking movements which sought for contacts and even assimilation with their surroundings. Thus at the same time that the group around Ezra and Nehemiah was dominant in Jerusalem, the

Book of Ruth was written, to praise a foreign (Moabite) woman as the ancestress of the Jewish king David. The Book of Jonas is also inspired by such universalist religious motives. The OT itself already denounces clearly and firmly the notion that precedence in election involved superiority on the human plane. The OT makes it clear that the people of the covenant was not chosen on account of its qualities, but rather in spite of its obstinacy and rebelliousness — merely by reason of the sovereign love of God (Deut 7:6–9; 9:4–9).

One must also be careful not to attribute an absolutely special and unique thought-form to Judaism. It is certainly quite wrong to affirm without qualification that Jewish thought is concrete, dynamic, lacking in speculative power, ethnically introvert and so on — in contrast to Greek (and hence the Christian) thought which is supposed to be abstract, static, speculative and universalist. There is still less justification for saying that there is little or no possibility of reconciling the two thought-forms. Even in OT times the Septuagint translation and such achievements as the very successful harmony of Jewish and Greek sapiential thinking in the Book of Sirach (Ecclus) tell strongly against such "psychologies" of religion and people. An even more telling example against the creation of such categories is the work of the Jewish philosopher, Moses Maimonides (d. 1204), with his notable contribution to classical scholasticism.

In conclusion, one could describe Judaism in general as an ethnic fellowship with the God of Israel, based on the covenant, looking on the possession of the land of Israel and the mastery of the language of Israel as its essential features, along with the constant actualization of past blessings and future hopes in each present moment. These features may include certain national peculiarities which are often designated as typically Jewish. But it should be noted that these secondary features are allowed relatively little value within Judaism itself and are often cancelled out by strong tendencies in the opposite direction.

C. THE MAIN DIVISIONS OF THE HISTORY OF JUDAISM

1. Early Judaism in the strict sense *began with the Babylonian exile (587* B.C.*) and ended with the fall of the second temple,* A.D. *70.* The earlier Jewish State became at the beginning of the Babylonian exile and in the course of the postexilic period an ethnic fellowship of worship (a union in prayer, sacrifice, religious study, meditation and assembly). The vitality of Judaism manifested itself in three main ways: as hierocratic restorative tendencies, as eschatological movements and as biblical learning. The restorative efforts were chiefly carried on by the priestly circles of Jerusalem and the ancient Jewish nobility. These strove to set up once more the conditions of liturgical and political life which had existed in particular under David and Solomon. Eschatological hopes were particularly lively from the end of the 3rd century B.C., as a result of the apocalyptic movement among priests and laity (especially those of the country-side, who were less well off).

As time went on, these hopes were expressed more and more forcefully. Among the Hasidaeans (cf. 1 Macc 2:42–48), the Qumranites (or Essenes) and other groups the notion of the imminence of final and universal salvation was less tinged with national and political hopes than among the Maccabees, the Hasmonaeans and many of the rebels in the first Jewish war against Rome (A.D. 66 to 70 or 73). The Scripture scholars, or rather "doctors of the law" in early Judaism, recognizing that inspired prophecy had ceased (i.e., prophecy acknowledged as inspired by the people, of the covenant) [b Joma 9 b; bSanh 11 a], that it was impossible to restore the past adequately and that the future was impenetrable, turned to the task of collecting national traditions and expounding the law for everyday needs (with the help, at times, of Wisdom speculation). It became clearer and clearer that study of the Scriptures, which was in fact mainly study of the law, provided the most solid basis for the shaping of Jewish social and private life. And here the Pharisees seemed clearly to offer the most desirable alternative to the Sadducees allied to the priesthood, temple and landed gentry, to the fanatical groups of eschatologically-minded "seers" (apocalyptic), the conciliatory Tobiades and Herodians, the uneducated masses of the people (am-ha-arez). Phariseeism must not be judged exclusively in the light of NT polemics. In the course of its history it strove constantly and vigorously to do justice to the law by bringing it into relevant relation with contemporary needs, it was a peace-making force and also the educator of the Jewish people at prayer and at study. Present-day Judaism is essentially based on the spiritual and religious principles of Phariseeism.

2. *Early Judaism of the period of the Mishnah and Talmud.* This was a period in which the Jews were without a temple and politically insignificant, under Roman and later under Persian rule. But Jewish life and religion flourished, especially in Galilee and in Babylon, and displayed its vigour above all in houses of prayer and of study, which to some extent were looked on as definitely replacing the temple (Pirke Aboth 5, 16; bMeg 29a; Mechilta Rabbi Ishmael, Tractate Bakodesh 11 [on Exod 20:24]). Leadership of Judaism was in the hands of the rabbinical sages, who imposed their pharisaical principles and norms on all Judaism. The synod at Jamnia (*c.* A.D. 90) became the basis of Judaism, which now sought to maintain itself, without temple and without political and religious independence and security, in the midst of the "peoples of the world" and in the face of new rivals in religion, especially Christianity and Gnosis. The most important products of Jewish efforts in late antiquity are undoubtedly the Mishnah and the Talmud (described under *Judaism* III). The repression of repeated Jewish revolts took a high toll of bloodshed. Judaism suffered very severe blows before, during and after the two revolts against Rome (A.D. 66–73 and 132–5), which were partly inspired by messianic hopes. They led to sharp religious and political persecution and to deportations. But there were also some successful efforts, especially in the 3rd century A.D., to work out a *modus vivendi* with the oppressive powers of the world.

3. *Medieval Judaism.* By this we understand the period from the end of the compilation of the Babylonian Talmud (6th to 7th century A.D.) to the Jewish "Enlightenment" of the 18th to 19th centuries. In Western Europe it took the form of individual assimilation, in Eastern that of a national Enlightenment movement, the Haskala. But there are authors who say that the modern period of Judaism should be considered to have begun with the expulsion of the Jews from Spain in 1492. Medieval Judaism appears on the one hand as stamped by the spirit of the Talmud, and a constant tendency to form groups, just as constantly repressed by external forces. But on the other hand, it also appears as a pioneering force in spiritual and religious matters, at least outwardly, since its debate with antiquity, Islam and Christianity helped it to work out a lofty religious philosophy (especially in Avicebron and Moses Maimonides). To a great extent, it was overshadowed and even oppressed by the medieval Christian world with its discriminatory legislation, ghettoes, persecutions and horror-stories. Late medieval Judaism was marked by the growing importance of East European trends such as those of the Chasidim and Mitnagedim and also by persistent messianic revivals in the middle of the seventeenth century (the Sabbatians and the Frankists), with no sense of political realities.

4. *Modern Judaism.* There are four main forces at work in modern times: a) Sacred Scripture and Talmudic tradition; b) Enlightenment and emancipation; c) Zionism and d) the foothold gained, not without new dangers, in the ancient land of Israel.

a) Traditionally-minded religious Judaism is chiefly represented by orthodox and conservative Judaism. But Scripture and Talmud play an important part in the thinking of all Jewish groups, even of Reform Judaism and of circles very far to the left.

b) The Haskala, the Jewish Enlightenment, was chiefly represented by Moses Mendelssohn (1729–86) (see, for example, Lessing's *Nathan the Wise*). It was chiefly inspired by a growing need for a relaxation of the traditional Jewish way of life with its quite totalitarian claims, and for closer cultural connections with the non-Jewish environment. It urged the Jews, especially in Central and Eastern Europe, to rid themselves of expendable elements of tradition in order to share fully the culture of the peoples among whom they lived. Since Jewish emancipation, especially in German-speaking countries, evoked anti-Semitic reactions, and since the Haskala in Eastern Europe did not meet with the desired success, the Zionist movement began.

c) Zionism may be divided into three main streams which are not entirely separate: (i) the Chibat-Zion Movement founded by Leon Pinsker (1821–91) which set out to organize all Jews who wished to go to Palestine; (ii) the political Zionism of Theodore Herzl (1860–1904); (iii) the Zionut Ruchanit, a religious Zionism, represented in particular by J. M. Pines (1844–1914) and Achad Haam (1856–1921).

d) The independent State of Israel (1948) may be said to be the fruit of the direst persecutions in history, under National Socialism in Germany. While it claims legitimation to some extent from its ancient rights, Judaism recognizes that in the eyes of the world this claim can be fully legitimate only if Israel extends to the non-Jewish inhabitants the toleration and citizenship rights which it so energetically defends for itself. There is also a hope among the Jews that the State of Israel is the "beginning of the dawn of redemption".

See also *Judaism* I, III, *Zionism, Covenant, Eschatology, Apocalyptic.*

BIBLIOGRAPHY. T. Reinach, *Textes d'auteurs grecs et romains relatifs au Judaïsme* (1895); E. Schürer, *History of the Jewish People in the Time of Jesus,* 4 vols. (E.T., 1898 ff.); S. Wittmayer Baron, *Social and Religious History of the Jews,* 10 vols. (2nd ed., 1952–65); C. Roth, *History of the Jews* (revised ed., 1961); id., "The Pharisees in the Jewish Revolution of 66–73", *Journal of Semitic Studies* 7 (1962), pp. 63–80; G. Scholem, *Judaica* (in German, 1963); S. Grayzel, *A History of the Jews from the Babylonian Exile to the Establishment of Israel* (5th ed., 1964); J. Maier, "Die messianischen Erwartungen im Judentum seit der Talmudischen Zeit", *Judaica* 20 (1964), pp. 23–58, 90–120, 156–83, 213–36; J. Parkes, *A History of the Jewish People* (2nd ed., 1964); J. Neusner, *A History of the Jews in Babylonia,* I: *The Parthian Period* (1965); C. Roth, ed., *The Dark Ages, 700–1096* (1966).

Clemens Thoma

III. The Religion

1. *The situation of Jewish religion.* In contrast with Christianity above all, with Islam and with Buddhism, the Jewish religion remained throughout its history almost exclusively the property of one people, the Jews. This concrete link with a definite people and the resulting fewness of the adherents makes it impossible to designate Judaism as a world religion. All that can be said is that it is not merely a national religion, since it possesses some emphatically universalist traits, and has attained world-wide significance through its "offshoots", Christianity and Islam.

The term "Mosaic religion", coined during the Enlightenment, does not go to the heart of Jewish religion. Jewish tradition looked on Moses as the founder of the Jewish religion, as prophet, teacher and leader of the people, but as such he was only a pointer to the heart of the religion, which was neither a human personality nor human nor even divine doctrine, but the historical presence of the God of Israel, powerful among his people (Is 45:14). It would also be incorrect to describe Jewish religion without qualifications as a hard and fast rule of the law. The law or Torah is no doubt an essential constituent of Jewish religion, but it is not the be-all and the end-all and must not be isolated from its many contacts. Along with pious exposition and observance of the law, important roles are also played by messianic hopes and mystical trends such as the Kabbala, the Chasidim and the Mitnagedim. The Jewish religion may indeed be called the great "religion of reason" (Herman Cohen, after Moses Mendelssohn and others), on account of the supreme importance attached to the law. But since it is so closely connected with what has sometimes been described as the "mystery" of the people of Israel, it cannot simply be contrasted with religions which appeal to mystery, though it remains resolutely opposed to all religions of myth and Gnosis.

Since the Judaistic religion is the forum of endless, comprehensive, subtle and often unsolved discussions about OT law and its practical implementation, there is every reason for designating it as a religion of law. But one must always bear in mind the evident truth that to the Jewish mind the demands of the God who chose Israel are behind the law. Beyond the nomocracy there is the theocracy. Finally, it may be remarked that according to the Jewish mentality, the question of Jesus Christ is only incidental to Jewish religion. Christians who assign to Jesus Christ a role in Jewish religion, either as the "cornerstone" or as a permanent reproach, are possibly misinterpreting the almost total silence of Jewish literature in his regard. It should also be considered that the Jewish attitude to Jesus Christ is not always simply total rejection and that there is a sense in which even a positive acceptance of Jesus need not mean rejection of Judaism.

The Jewish religion is an ethical monotheism connected with the historical destinies of the Jews. The diverse individual features of this monotheism are displayed in the religious history of the Jews (see bibliography on *Judaism* II).

2. *Sources.* Judaism relies on the divinely-revealed Torah ("proclaimed by the Holy Spirit") for the justification of its creed and its existence. The Torah has been transmitted orally and in writing. The written Torah is identical with the Tanach (OT) which according to the shorter canon used in Jewish reckoning consists of twenty-four books. The oral Torah has the same divine origin as the written law (bShab 31a; bNed 35b–37b). It is to be found above all in rabbinical literature, especially the Mishnah (compiled *c.* A.D. 220 by R. Jehuda Hanasi) and the Babylonian Talmud (finished in the 6th or 7th century A.D.). The Mishnah (literally, tradition, repetition) is the official commentary on the OT law and the traditions. It is chiefly due to the efforts of the Tannaites (transmitters, the five generations of rabbis from A.D. 70–220), whose interests were mainly legal. It contains 694 commands and prohibitions. Since the Mishnah left many applications open, the need was soon felt to collect the rabbinical discussions about the Mishnah. The commentaries of the Babylonian sages (Amoraim, the speakers) were compiled as the Babylonian Talmud, the last official expression of the oral law. The rabbis looked on their work of preserving traditions and expounding the law — which included the safeguarding of the text of the Bible — as the "rediscovery" of what was revealed by God on Sinai. It was all "already revealed to Moses on Sinai" (bNed 37b).

The rest of the rabbinical literature also exercised a lasting influence on Judaism. This is true above all of the Jerusalem or Palestinian Talmud, which comprised the discussion of the Mishnah carried on in Palestine and was finished in the 5th or 6th century A.D. Other important items are the Midrashim and the prayers used in the synagogues. The Midrashim are homiletic ("haggadic") or juridical ("halakic") reflections on biblical texts, of which the hidden meaning is sought in order to re-interpret it for the present time and for practical action. The process and the end-product are comprised under the term Midrash (searching). The halakic Midrash on the normative parts of the Torah is of far greater importance in the religious life of Jews than the haggadic Midrash which is mostly legend.

Among the prayers of early rabbinical times the Shemone Esre ("Eighteen Prayer") holds pride of place. It was compiled at the end of the 1st century A.D. It contains praises of God und the prayers and hopes of the oppressed Jewish communities. Pious Jews recite it three times a day, facing in the direction of Jerusalem.

The possession of the written *and* the oral Torah is a "nota" of Jewish religion, to the mind of the Jews, which distinguishes it from all others. Even the Tanach (OT) is said to indicate the divinely-willed function of the oral Torah, and hence of the Mishnah, Talmud and other main Jewish traditions. Texts such as Deut 17:8–11 and Haggai 2:11–14 are invoked.

3. *Religious outlook and practice.* Doctrines have not the same place or meaning in the Jewish religion as dogmas in Christianity. They are norms and inspirations for the practical life of the Jews. From this point of view, the Jewish religion is a system of conduct which directly affects the Jewish people, of which it is the mainspring and the formative element: "Our people is not a people, except in its doctrine" (Saadia Gaon, A.D. 882–942). Systematic expositions of Jewish religious teaching are mostly wrongly interpreted by Christian readers whose approach is that of dogmatic theology. The Jewish doctrine of God, for instance, can only be said to be identical with that of the dogmatic treatise *De Deo Uno* if one remembers that Judaism does not aim at producing consistent formulas — except those already given in the Bible — and is rather intent on the concrete "hallowing of the Name" *(Qiddush ha-Shem)* as outlined in the law. There is a contrast to Christian teaching in anthropological principle, where Judaism rejects the notion of original sin, instead of which it has the doctrine of the good and the evil urge in man. The evil urge can be mastered by effort, with the help of God; for this view Ps 8, Zech 1:3; Mal 3:7 are invoked in particular. This favourable view of human potentialities goes hand in hand with a strong emphasis on this life in general. The other life has little place in religious discourse, as compared to Christianity. This neglect of the other world is due to some extent to the unhappy experiences of the Jews with over-excited groups intent on eschatological and messianic hopes, or on esoteric speculations about the beyond.

Thus the religious Jew is a man who feels himself bound in all his actions to the God of Israel with his claims and promises, and to the people of Israel with its privileges and expectations (cf. Deut 6, the OT missionary precept). A visible symbol of this centring of the life of Jewish men and boys on God, tradition and community is circumcision (cf. Gen 17; Deut 10:16; 30:6; Jer 4:4; Ezek 44:7–9). For religious Jews in general the observation of the sabbath and feast-days, the recital of prayers, the keeping of the purity laws, the maintenance of ancient Jewish tradition, the hope of eschatological salvation and so on mean that they are bearing the yoke of God for the sake of the kingdom of heaven, that is, that they are being true to the obligations of the covenant.

See also *Christianity* I, II, *Islam*, *Law* I, *Monotheism*.

BIBLIOGRAPHY. W. Bousset, *Religion des Judentums,* ed. by H. Gressmann (3rd ed., 1926); H. L. Strack, *Introduction to the Talmud and Midrash* (reprint, 1930); C. F. Moore, *Judaism in the First Centuries of the Christian Era,* 3 vols. (1927–30); L. Baeck, *The Essence of Judaism* (E.T., 1936); G. Jasper-Bethel, *Stimmen aus dem neureligiösen Judentum in seiner Stellung zum Christentum und zu Jesus* (1958); A. A. Cohen, *The Natural and Supernatural Jew: A Historical and Theological Introduction* (1962); R. Bultmann, *Primitive Christianity in its Contemporary Setting* (reprint, 1960); R. Le Déaut, *Introduction à la littérature Targumique,* I (1966). See also: *The Jewish Encyclopedia,* 12 vols. (1901–6); H. Cohen, *Basic Jewish Encyclopedia* (1965).

Clemens Thoma

IV. The Philosophy

1. *Introduction.* There is no Jewish philosophy as such. There are only Jewish philosophies. All of the emphases and modulations of Western philosophy — Greek, Hellenistic, Christian scholasticism and Moslem rationalism and skepticism, German idealism, and contemporary existentialism have been registered within Jewish thought.

The Jewish people did not begin to philosophize because of an irresistible inner compulsion to do so. Rather it may be argued that the history of Jewish philosophy reflects the effort of successive generations of Jewish thinkers to come to terms with the challenges and assaults of foreign ideas and traditions, to apprehend their methods and principles, to assess their relevance to Jewish concerns, and — where possible — to accommodate them by rethinking and transforming

inherited and traditional categories of Jewish thought. Judaism has been singularly capacious and latitudinarian, therefore, in its response to foreign philosophies, primarily because its concern, after A.D. 135, was no longer to maintain an apologetic or missionary stance before the non-Jewish world, but to endure within an essentially hostile environment. Where Philo of Alexandria and Josephus were prepared to make use of the intuitions of Hellenistic philosophy and culture to establish Judaism as a religion in which reason and the holy spirit were conformed and the canards and blasphemies of paganism overcome, the speculations of the rabbis of the Talmudic Age were more concerned with the definition of the practical theology of Jewish life, the setting forth of the limits and bounds of permissible experience, and the provision of differentia by which Jewish life might remain secure in a politically, intellectually, and religiously inhospitable world. When Judaism ceased to be religiously aggressive before the pagan world, the uses of philosophy as missionary apologetics languished. It was only later when Judaism once more came under the attacks of its own dissenters, the Karaites, and received the glancing blows launched by the Mu'takallimun against the orthodox of Islam that it began to philosophize once more.

2. *The biblical origins of Jewish philosophy.* There are many philosophies of Judaism because there is but one revelation of God which Jews accept as authentic, preserve, and transmit. Judaism and Jewish philosophy begin therefore with the presumption of the biblical absolute: God covenanted his person to Israel, revealed to it his way, and instructed it that it might become a holy community. All of the formulations by which later Jewish thought sought to interpret, rationalize, and accommodate the biblical reality to the demands of non-Jewish traditions must reckon with the primacy of revelation. Indeed, it may be argued that the very multiplicity of authentic styles and emphases in Jewish philosophy — the absence of any normative Jewish philosophy or authoritative philosophical school — arises from the fact that the biblical datum is in no wise theoretically challenging. The God of the Patriarchs, of Moses, and of the prophetic and Wisdom literature is one who discloses himself under the aspect of nature, society, and

history. The biblical writ is thus a refracted and refracting document. It is never fully open, for God is never wholly present. It is proper then to describe the Bible as a document, eminently anthropomorphic (in that man always sees in God that which God has already given to man) and theomorphic (in that God always offers to man that which man has already sought from God). Such anthropomorphism (or as it has been more vividly called by the contemporary thinker, Abraham Joshua Heschel, "anthropopathetism") presents the image of God as a translation of his mystery into the accessible arena of human passions and actions. What is crucial is not the biblical translation of the revealed God into man apotheosized. The Bible is rather, as Heschel has observed, God's anthropology. God reads man in God's terms in precisely the same sense in which man reads God in his own.

What is decisive, therefore, in the biblical account of the relations of God and man, of God and world, and especially of God and Israel, is that the person of God and the corporate life of Israel are marked by a continuous dialectic tension of the holy and the unredeemed. Indeed, if one were to formulate the essential intuition of Israel about the character of God, it would emerge in the form of a theology of the holy. All other theological virtues and all other theological *realia* would turn upon one's understanding the nature of the holy.

Rabbinic Judaism (135 B.C. – A.D. 1035) is founded upon the characteristic emphases of biblical faith. Where it differs from biblical Judaism is not in the substance of its thought but in the attitudes and approaches by which the rabbinic mind sought to rationalize the biblical encounter with the holy. Rabbinic theology (for it was not properly philosophy) begins with certain "givens", with experienced realities about which the rabbis had no questions — the creation of the world, the gift of the Torah to Israel, the giving of the Land to the wanderers of the desert that they might inhabit it and fashion there "a kingdom of priests and a holy nation". These are the urgent data of Jewish faith. Beyond these, the God who created, revealed, and bequeathed is a God of mercy and justice, who is concerned with his creatures, gives them instruction and reproof, delivers to their keeping and transmission a regimen of conduct that channels intention, inspires

right action, and inhibits their impulse to infidelity. The theology of the rabbinic world was pragmatic; however, its pragmatism was dependent upon a cluster of primary realities available only to faith.

3. *Religious philosophy of Hellenistic Judaism.* If we leave aside the influence of Greek ideas upon Ecclesiastes and the Apocryphal literature (which were at best slight and marginal), it may be said that the first significant meeting of Judaism and external philosophy occurred and would continue to occur only within a diaspora where contact and communication between Jews and non-Jews, even if not free and unrestricted, were at least possible. Jewish philosophy did not flourish within the confined precincts of the Academies of Palestine and Babylonia nor within the ghettoes of Europe. It flourished only in cosmopolitan centres where an aristocracy of learning was permitted to mature, indifferent to the anti-intellectual bias of the narrowly orthodox. The Jews who lived in Alexandria and within the diaspora accessible to Greek culture regarded their religion as a philosophy and developed an apologetics which sought to unfold the philosophical character of the Jewish idea of God and the humanity of Jewish ethics. Hellenistic Jewish thought was characterized therefore by the attempt to supply a philosophical form for the intellectual substance of Judaism. In some Greek modes of expression only a superficial patina for Jewish ideas was provided, but in others — most extremely in the case of Philo of Alexandria — Jewish ideas were transformed by Greek ideas into what Julius Guttmann has called "a radical philosophical sublimation". Sincerely believing that he was in no wise misrepresenting the intention of Scripture, Philo extracted from the Bible a complete philosophy. Unlike the pantheism characteristic of the Stoics, Philo's God was absolute in his transcendence and utterly immaterial. In divesting God of every trace of anthropomorphism — exalting him above all knowledge and virtue, indeed, above all perfections conceivable to the mind — he laid the foundations for what would become in later times the distinctive emphases of negative theology. However, not content with defining a radical incommensurability between God and man, Philo developed a doctrine of mystical ascent whereby the knower might

come to union with God. In seeking, by allegorical interpretation of Scripture, to bring together human knowledge and divine revelation, to effect a reconciliation of mystical wisdom with *scientia,* Philo posed for the first time the problem which was to remain basic to the philosophy and theology of monotheistic religions.

4. *Medieval Jewish religious philosophy.* Jewish philosophy in the Middle Ages arose within the cultural world of Islam and was profoundly influenced by Islamic thought. Its original stamp was defined by the religio-philosophic ideas of the Islamic Kalam, and even after it had come under the influence of neo-Platonism and Aristotelianism, its connection with Islamic thought was maintained. Jewish neo-Platonists were dependent upon sources made available to them by Moslem translators and Jewish Aristotelians took up interpretations of Aristotle advanced by Alfarabi, Avicenna, and Averroes. Even later, when Jewish philosophy had spread to Christian lands, notably Spain, Provence, and Italy, the influence of Islam remained dominant, Christian scholasticism remaining a negligible and subordinate factor in its development.

The rise of Jewish philosophy within Islam is due to the fact that Judaism was obliged to defend itself, both by the heretic denial of the rabbinic tradition advanced by Karaism within and the energetic refurbishment by Moslem enthusiasts of old attacks against Judaism from without. In their effort to counter a rising tide of criticism from non-monotheists in the East and skeptics and unbelievers within Islam, there arose a school of believing rationalists, the Mu'tazilites who sought to supply a conceptual framework for the Kalam. Less adventuresome than Islamic thinkers who willingly entertained all kinds of philosophical and scientific questions, Jewish philosophy was content to reply upon Islamic thinkers for considerations of general philosophical questions, undertaking for its own part to inquire primarily into more specifically limited religio-philosophic issues. The primary concern of Jewish philosophy was the justification of Judaism. As Islamic thought expanded with the appearance of Al-Kindi's and Alfarabi's Aristotelianism at the end of the 9th century, so too the neo-Platonism of Isaac Israeli, the first Jewish philosopher,

gave way to the thought of Saadia b. Joseph (882–942), a follower of the Kalam. Saadia's doctrine of the relation between reason and revelation affords him the foundation of his religious thought. Religious truth originates in revelation and becomes thereby a distinct form of truth. The conflict between reason and revelation does not emerge for Saadia as a specific problem of human consciousness, but is posed rather in terms of the relation of reason to a specific religion claiming to speak the absolute truth. Jewish religion, in such a view, is radically different from others which are human creations, speaking erroneously of God and his nature. Saadia's view had the positive advantage of enabling reason to apprehend, through its own powers, the content of revelation as being without contradiction with the findings of reason. To be sure, it will be asked what need there is for revelation if reason, unaided, can achieve the presumably superior knowledge provided by revelation. Saadia's answer — one that became commonplace among later thinkers — was that revelation is an expeditious and efficient pedagogue of man, who is liable by the limits of his creatureliness, to inconstancy, confusion, and misapprehensions.

The followers of the Kalam, extending and embroidering the insights of Saadia, gave way a century later to an impressive period of Jewish neo-Platonism, the most notable representatives of which were Solomon ibn Gabirol (1026–*c.* 1050), Bahya ibn Pakuda (*c.* 1080–*c.* 1156), and that unique and only tangentially neo-Platonic thinker, Jehudah Halevi (1085–1140). Jehudah Halevi's *Kuzari* (The Book of Argument and Proof in Defence of a Despised Faith) does not, like earlier efforts, seek to identify Judaism with rational truth. Denying rational certainty in metaphysics, Halevi argues that philosophical doctrine is as arbitrary and dogmatic as it claims assertions of revelation to be. His concern, however, is not to destroy philosophy as such, but rather to undermine its pretentions. God, world, and man, as separate and uncorrelated facts are demonstrable by reason, but their connection, their intimate relation, is not available to reason, but to revelation alone. Halevi refutes the supposed opposition of reason to revelation by exposing the casuistry of the claims of reason. His method of argument is dialectical, rather than expository, for Halevi is not asserting the autonomy of religion as regards reason but a supernatural conception of revelation.

It was in the middle of the 12th century that Aristotelianism displaced neo-Platonism as the dominant style of Jewish philosophy. Abraham ibn Daud of Toledo (d. *c.* 1180), whose work *The Exalted Faith (Emunah Ramah)* exhibits the apparent harmony of Judaism and Aristotelian doctrine, is actually a commonplace presentation of the major characteristics of Avicenna's reconciliation of religion and philosophy. It was only when Maimonides (Moses ben Maimon of Cordova, 1135–1204) published his classic *The Guide of the Perplexed* (Arabic: *Dalalat al-Hairin;* Hebrew: *Moreh Nebukhim*) about 1190, that the issue between philosophy and revelation was squarely put. Although Maimonides sought to reconcile the apparent contradiction between philosophy and revelation and hence reassure those who might come to doubt either the truth of faith or the propriety and significance of philosophic inquiry, Maimonides did not conceive his task as the reunion of irreconcilables, but rather the demonstration of their essential conformance and identity. Unlike his predecessors, who held similar views to his own, Maimonides did not seek *only* to prove that the content of philosophy and revelation was the same, but that philosophy was the only proper means for the apprehension of revealed truths. For Maimonides, religious faith was a form of knowledge. Whereas it is the task of tradition and the continuity of historical faith to provide an external, and therefore indirect, form of knowledge, the internal apprehension of truth — an apprehension which is direct and unmediated by external forms and customs — is made possible by philosophical knowledge. Such an intellectualist concept of faith aims at making the inwardness of the believer dependent upon the deepening of philosophical understanding. The philosophical enterprise is essentially religious; and the pathos of religious rationalism is given an articulate and definite form in Western philosophy.

It can well be imagined that such a thorough-going intellectualism in religion, conjoined, as it was in both Jewish and Christian minds, with Averroist Aristotelianism, produced a considerable reaction within the exposed and vulnerable Jewish communities of Southern European Chris-tendom. The 13th century witnessed in consequence a violent controversy, not only about Maimonidean rationalism, but about the right of philosophy to exist at all. The controversey itself eventually acquired a philosophic form, with anti-Maimonideans either opposing philosophy as such, or else defending Averroes against Maimonides's strictures, or, as did Levi ben Gerson (1288–1344), undertaking to recapitulate and strengthen Maimonides's criticisms of extreme Averroism. The response of the 14th century, as evidenced by Moses ben Nahman of Gerona (1184–c. 1270) and Hasdai Crescas (*c.* 1340–*c.* 1410) was to undertake, in the case of Nahmanides, a supernaturalist critique similar to that of Jehudah Halevi against theistic rationalism, or, as did Crescas in his *The Light of the Lord* (*Or Adonai*, 1410), the construction of an anti-Aristotelian dogmatics in which ultimate religious values were preserved beyond the precincts of reason.

5. *The emergence of modern Jewish philosophy.* The cleavage of Jewish life from the intellectual currents which bathed Christian Europe was not bridged until the middle of the 18th century. Although the course which 18th and 19th century Jewish philosophy was to take cannot really be discussed independently of the movements of secular humanism and Enlightenment, the rise of extra-ecclesiastical culture, and the political struggle for civil emancipation in Europe, it may be said that the issues which had once defined the ambit of Jewish (and Christian) scholasticism were to wane in importance as the challenge and promise of secularization materialized. Moses Mendelssohn (1729–1786) most conspicuously set the tone which was later to find particularly meaningful expression in the work of *Wissenschaft des Judentums.* Although Mendelssohn preserved many of the distinctions developed by medieval Jewish philosophy, he established in common with the optimistic rationalism of the Enlightenment a view of Judaism in which reason became the sufficient arbiter of faith; in which both pure and practical reason might judge the relevance and universality of intellectual and moral truths. Judaism became a religious polity which might within a messianism of reason provide salvation (liberation from error) for all mankind.

It should not be surprising that the legacy

of Mendelssohn (although surely not Mendelssohn alone) was one of dissolution within Jewish intellectual life. Although Nahman Krochmal's (1785–1840) *Guide for the Perplexed of Our Time* (published posthumously in 1851) undertook to provide an internal historico-philosophic justification of Judaism on the grounds of idealist (but anti-Hegelian) impulses and Samson Raphael Hirsch (1808–1888) was to defend Judaism in his *Nineteen Letters* by utilizing Hegelian models to elevate and incorporate Judaism into the rhythm of the unfolding logos, it was not really until Solomon Formstecher (1808–1889) published his *The Religion of the Spirit* (1841) and Solomon Ludwig Steinheim (1789–1866) his eccentric *Revelation according to the Doctrine of the Synagogue* (published between 1835 and 1865) that Judaism found two more or less congenial philosophers, Formstecher offered a rationalism with which Judaism (albeit one reformed) could survive and Steinheim, in almost violent opposition, a Judaism in which religious truth was once more grounded in revelation.

It is with Hermann Cohen (1842–1918) that Judaism is set forth in a manner compatible with the putatively best in European culture — German idealism and liberal religion. Cohen's works, *The Concept of Religion in the System of Philosophy* (1915) and *The Religion of Reason drawn from the Sources of Judaism* (1919) expound a consistent and plodding rationalism in which no other religion than that of reason is to be considered; moreover, he finds that Judaism, notably prophetic Judaism, is that religion in which reason, the moral direction of man, and a God of ethics and humanity are united. In the present century, Franz Rosenzweig (1886–1929) and Martin Buber (born 1878) proclaimed an opposition to the rationalism dominant within Judaism as well as within Western religious philosophy generally. For Rosenzweig, the existential particularity of the living subject addresses the facts which are God, world and man and defines through them and before them the relations by which they are bound to one another; while Buber has formulated the dialogal principle of I—Thou in such a manner as to disqualify intermediating and objectifying discriminations which depersonalize the relations of man with man and silence the ultimate Thou of which all human beings are particularizations. Rosenzweig and Buber

reopened the question of being within Judaism on grounds of existence in the world, rather than from the more conventional epistemological perspective. The train of thought which Rosenzweig and Buber have developed within Judaism is at present finding expression in Israel and the United States among thinkers for whom the reality of Jewish existence is being sought in a renewal of the connection between the existential-historical situation of the Jew and the problematic reality of a God who lives, but speaks not. It is not surprising, given the events of recent decades, that for Jewish thinkers such as Nathan Rotenstreich, Steven Schwarzschild, Will Herberg, Emil Fackenheim, Arthur A. Cohen, and others the relation of God, evil, and history is of particular importance.

BIBLIOGRAPHY. J. B. Agus, *Modern Philosophies of Judaism* (1941); G. Vaida, *Introduction à la pensée juive du moyen âge* (1947); A. Altmann, *Jewish Philosophy* (1953); H.-J. Schoeps, *Jüdische Geisteswelt* (1953); M. Buber, *Writings,* ed. by W. Herberg (1958); H. Cohen, *Religion der Vernunft* (2nd ed., 1959); J. Guttmann, *Philosophies of Judaism* (1960); N. N. Glatzer, ed., *Franz Rosenzweig: His Life and Thought* (1962); A. A. Cohen, *The Natural and Supernatural Jew* (1962); J. Blau, *Introduction to Modern Jewish Thought* (1962); I. Efros, *Ancient Jewish Philosophy* (1964); L. Baeck, *This People Israel: The Meaning of Jewish Existence* (1965); M. Buber, *On Judaism*, ed. by N. N. Glatzer (1967).

Arthur A. Cohen

JUDAISM AND CHRISTIANITY

A. General Observations

There are many points of contact and contrast between Judaism and Christianity, arising from the OT, the NT and from post-biblical Judaism. Hence the ideal and historical boundaries of Judaism and Christianity often cut across one another, and both latent and open conflicts as regards "marginal" relationships between the two faiths are hardly avoidable. Since it would be wrong to erect either the links or the contrasts into absolutes, it is well to consider the common origin of salvation, as claimed by both Christians and Jews, and the common eschatological hope in the light of the four notions of OT, NT, Judaism and Christianity. The key to the understanding of the relationships between Christianity and Judaism lies in a survey of the scripture of the OT and NT, and in the recognition and acceptance of the possible and actual developments from both Testaments. This can only be sketched in outline here. For particulars the reader is referred to the various relevant articles, especially *Old Testament Books, New Testament Books, Revelation* III, *Eschatology*.

1. Neither in its basic documents nor in its redactional strata does the OT provide a thoroughly consistent set of affirmations. This lack of unity means that many OT assertions cannot be related to the NT, at least without many qualifications. Further, the OT has a certain "plus-value" with regard to the NT, insofar as it deals more fully with profane and religious life, humanity, political power, law, liturgical worship, human love, etc. Then there are OT values which have lost their original meaning in the NT. Thus the observance of the law in the OT was definitely in the context of grace and reflects an attitude designed to protect religious life and mark it off from all that is outside (Ps 119).

The NT, especially the Pauline parts (see, for example, Gal 3) is fiercely hostile to the Jewish devotion to the law. These attacks, which do not affect the whole sphere of the law, must be explained above all in the light of the polemical situation then obtaining and the Christian view of its faith as an eschatological prophetic movement. When the essentials of the polemic are laid bare, it appears that the NT, by virtue of its summons to faith in Christ, includes a protest against a community which tries to cleave exclusively to the OT. This does not deny all legitimacy to Judaism, in the history of religion and even in theology. Its legitimacy is higher than that of the "law in the heart" (Rom 2:15). The law sacred to the Jews, even in its situation of disobedience now that Christianity has come, is covered by the OT. In the discussion of the relationship of OT and NT, Judaism and Christianity, it is better to omit entirely all notion of continuous or discontinuous progress in a sort of evolutionary schema. At each new historical situation the people of God actualized anew in principle its own past salvific history. No generation of Jews or Christians could have ever regarded mere

unthinking repetition as a way of responding to the covenant.

2. Christians are convinced, in the light of the NT, that the person and work of Christ was a unique concentration and summary of OT history and expectations. As Jesus delivered his message, he linked it with the beliefs, successes, failures and needs of his Jewish contemporaries. To separate Jesus from his times and his people, to say that his message was absolutely novel or mainly Hellenistic is only possible if one ignores completely the copious literature of the inter-testamental period. The NT authors interpreted the actual events of Christ's coming from the standpoint of the OT. This was to take up the affirmations and interests of the OT in a way which may be called inspired, but which was certainly not historical in the critical sense. It should also be noted that polemics in the NT is directed not only against the unbelief of the Jews, especially the Pharisees, but also against such Christians as allowed themselves to be dominated uncompromisingly by the idea and expectation of the imminent end, which was to intervene visibly in the form of a definitive cosmic salvation. The NT writers emphasized against such views that the salvation given by Christ was only embryonic and inward, that no one knew when the comprehensive messianic salvation ($\sigma \upsilon \nu \tau \acute{\epsilon} \lambda \epsilon \iota \alpha$) would be brought by the coming of Christ in power and glory. The delay of the parousia was to be borne in an attitude of faith and watchfulness (Mk 13:32–37; Rom 8–11; Rev 10–12, etc.).

3. Present-day Judaism is neither an OT that has stood still nor a fully representative OT. It cannot be identified with the OT without more ado, any more than Christianity with the NT. Both movements, which may be described rather as interpretative of than identical with either the OT or the OT and NT, have suffered from sin and shortcomings in the course of their post-biblical history, but both have also made real progress. From the point of view of tradition, Judaism is closer than Christianity to the OT. Christianity follows the risen Christ, through whom the definitive interpretations of the OT were observed into the significance of his person. But Judaism is not completely alien to the NT, since like all the OT

authors, many NT authors were Jews by origin. Judaism and Christianity are at different stages of the tension of the "Already and Not Yet" of, for example, Rom 8–11. But the expectation of the perfect eschatological salvation has its climax, in Christianity, in its relationship to the Christ who has already appeared and who has given all possible pledges of fulfilment. By contrast, Judaism affirms, with reference both to the salvific past and to the salvific future, the collective and material elements, in particular the people and the land. Nonetheless, the common nature of Judaism and Christianity is nowhere more apparent than in their perspectives of past and future salvation.

B. The Second Vatican Council and the Jews

The declaration of Vatican II on the Christian attitude to the Jews undoubtedly represents a happy synthesis of the best works on Israel by Catholic and Protestant writers in recent years. As such the *Declaratio de Judaeis* may be taken at once as representative of the proper Christian attitude towards the Jews. We shall here try to explain the text of the Council in the light of the characteristics of Judaism as worked out in *Judaism* II.

1. The partnership between Judaism and the God of Israel is not questioned in the decree of the Council. The Catholic Church, it may be thought, admits that the ancient covenants of God with the ancestors and tribes of Israel, with various individuals of the OT and with the primary heir, Judaism, have not been revoked. Nonetheless, the Church claims also to be partner in the covenant with the God of Israel. How the new people of the covenant, the second heir, the Church, stands to Judaism, is not said expressly in the declaration. In the framework of the discussion here possible, it may be that justice is done to the Christian faith if it is said that Christ is at the centre of the old and new people of God. Since the salvation of God already actual in the world as a structural factor — whose seed already put forth shoots in the OT — has not yet attained cosmic dimensions, but is still pressing on to full manifestation, it may perhaps be admitted theoretically as well as practically that the Jewish faith and law are possible and legitimate during the interval before the glorious day of the coming of the Lord. But the question remains as to whether this type of ecumenical thinking can bring about a just verdict on Judaism, in view of its long and independent development, externally so far from Christ, and in view of its actual concrete type of existence today and its diverse interests.

2. The land which was once called the "holy land" is not mentioned in the declaration. It would seem therefore that the question of the possession of Palestine is not a specifically Christian question at all. But for Judaism — at least in many of its forms — the land of Palestine is of central importance. To say the very least, Christianity and Judaism diverge widely in the question of Palestine, since they start from different principles and use different norms. Even in NT times Christianity was characterized by the tendency to dissociate itself from any religious and predestined link with the land (and language) of Israel. But some see a possibility of applying the ancient maxim that the body is the end of God's ways, that is, God's ways reach their ends within the horizon of the earth. These are inclined to raise once more the question of the land of "Israel" as one that is of interest in Christian thought.

3. The Church's thought is bent on past as well as future, as is that of Judaism, and it sees its own origin, like that of Judaism, in the election and faith of the OT patriarchs. As regards eschatology, we may perhaps risk the following formula: the Church professes the ancient doctrine of the Jews, that the union of mankind under God's kingship will only take place when all men in one way or another belong to the seed of the unrevoked covenant and thus are rightful heirs of the Spirit.

4. The way in which anti-Semitism is condemned by the Council may suggest that the Church recognizes the ancient covenants as unrevoked and demands that they be understood in the light of the dogma of universal redemption.

C. Convergent Viewpoints

Grave difficulties still remain in making a real comparison between the ideals and principles of Judaism and those of Christianity, even though many points of agreement have been pointed out. The efforts now being made in some Catholic circles to create a "theology of Isarel" must not be dismissed as syncretistic wheedling or as proselytizing with regard to the Jews. But they may also be considered efforts of the Church to understand and express its debt of gratitude to Judaism. Judaism is also capable of seeing lofty values in Christianity, as when it praises the providential role of Christianity in the world-wide spread of monotheism, when it includes Christianity as members of the Noachic covenant (cf. Gen 6–9) or when it praises Jesus as a "great witness of faith in Israel" (Shalom ben Chorim). In this way the foundations are laid for mutual esteem, co-operation and understanding between Judaism and Christianity, without the risk of confusion or underhand conversion campaigns. As M. Buber says, common traits are not to be invented. In any case, the precise nature of the common future salvation must be left to God's wisdom (cf. Rom 11:3–36).

Within the framework of Christian convictions as regards what is common and what can be done to further union, the following possibilities may be envisaged in the discussion of the election of the Jews and of the Church.

1. In the OT, the people of Israel was the people of God. Under the new covenant its place is taken by the fellowship of Christian believers who are the new people of God. From this point of view, the Jews have been provisionally left to one side, eliminated, in the matter of the election. Nonetheless, Judaism remains dear to God, on account of its past and on account of the eschatological future. It would be wrong to use this truth to draw up statistics, as it were, about God's works of mercy and to encourage pride (cf. 1 Cor 4:4 f.). God's fidelity remains unchanged (cf. Ezek 17:14).

2. Since the coming of Christ, there is only one people of God, within which it is de facto possible to belong to Judaism. But Judaism is not constitutive. What constitutes the people of God is faith in Christ. While this way of speaking often obscures the many permanent roots which Christianity has in Judaism, it still points to further possibilities of belonging to the people of God by virtue of the universality of Christ's redemption.

3. Hypothetically once more, it may perhaps be suggested that we may speak of two peoples of God — the people of God by virtue of the (presumedly continuing ancient) covenant, and the people of God consisting of those who believe in Christ. This formula is only acceptable to the Christian faith when it is clearly kept in mind that the old and the new people of God — or rather, the old in the new — is moving towards the Christ who is to be eschatologically revealed. Great obscurities undoubtedly remain, because the election by the God of Israel, externally and internally, and both as regards the past and as regards the future, cannot be clearly and definitely demarcated.

See also *Judaism* I–IV, *Ecumenism* V, *Zionism*.

BIBLIOGRAPHY. E. Meyer, *Ursprung und Anfänge des Christentums*, 3 vols. (1921–23); M. Simon, *Verus Israel* (in French, 1948); J. Isaak, *Jésus et Israel* (1948); A. A. van Ruler, *Die christliche Kirche und das Alte Testament* (1955); M. Buber, *Writings*, ed. by W. Herberg (1958); G. Baum, *Is the New Testament Anti-Semitic?* (1962); R. Bultmann, *Primitive Christianity in its Contemporary Setting* (reprint, 1960); H. Gollwitzer and others, *Das gespaltene Gottesvolk* (1965); Shalom ben Chorim, *Bruder Jesus, der Nazarener in jüdischer Sicht* (1969); C. Thoma, ed., *Auf den Trümmern des Tempels, Land und Bund Israels im Dialog zwischen Christen und Juden* (1968).

Clemens Thoma

JURISDICTION

In the legal terminology of the Church, jurisdiction is the authoritative power to govern (*potestas jurisdictionis seu regiminis, CIC*, can. 196), which was bestowed on the Church in the metaphor of the shepherd (cf. Jn 10:1–28; 21:15–17); hence it is sometimes called, in contrast to the power of teaching and sanctifying, the pastoral office. Jurisdiction is exercised in the external and internal forum, in the sacramental and the non-sacramental realm. In contrast to the power of orders, which comes from a consecration which is permanent in its effect, the power of jurisdiction is linked with an office in the Church and can be lost with it. Power of jurisdiction and power of order are complementary elements of the one sacred authority in the Church.

JURISDICTION

1. *History of the term.* Jurisdiction is a term from Roman law, and like the modern "law", chiefly designated the judiciary, and more precisely, civil law. In Roman law, the judiciary was not contrasted with the *imperium* or the legislature and administration, but was "a form of the *imperium, the imperium* itself as it took effect in the exercise of justice" (L. Wenger). In canon law, jurisdiction took on a wider sense which is already met with in Roman law, and means not only judicial powers but the whole system of ecclesiastical government. The technical term was gradually adopted by canonists in a process which lasted for many centuries. The first instances are to be found in the novellae of Justinian (Nov. 131, cap. 3; 120, cap. 6, § 2), in the *Liber Diurnus* and the *Exemptions* dependent on it and in the letters of Pope Gregory I. The power of jurisdiction was distinguished from the power of orders only subsequent to the *Decretum Gratiani,* and this conceptual distinction soon gave rise to an untoward distinction of the two powers in actual usage.

The distinction was considered by R. Sohm as the second stage of deformation in the constitutional development of the Church. In his view, the "Old Catholic" sacramental law, which had taken the place, about A.D. 100, of the supposedly original charismatic constitution of the Church, was then replaced by the "New Catholic" corporate law. He saw in the notion of jurisdiction a purely corporate governmental power derived from civil law. The Church, once the Body of Christ, became a Christian corporation. Government became distinct from sacrament. Only the liturgy of ordination remained unchanged, but was now in contradiction with the New Catholic law of ordination. The *hierarchia ordinis*, once the only regulatory power in the ministry of the Church, was now subordinated to the all-powerful rule of jurisdiction. The critique of Sohm, which has been taken up again recently by J. Klein, contains a kernel of truth, insofar as it signals the deformation implied in the real division between the two powers. The two-fold division of ecclesiastical power, which was in vogue till a three-fold distinction was introduced in the 19th century, always insisted that the power of orders was conferred by consecration, and the power of jurisdiction, apart from the supreme authority of the Pope, by canonical mission, with the result that

the former power was inalienable, but the latter not. However, this view was also combined with the notion that the power of order was ordained to the administration of the sacraments, while the power of jurisdiction was confined to external order in the Church. Until our own day it has been widely held that the power of jurisdiction is inherent in the Church as a *societas perfecta* and has nothing to do directly with the activity of the Church as mediator of salvation. In the doctrine of the three powers, developed from the notion of the three offices of Christ and of the Church, the three powers (sanctification, legislation, teaching) remain disconnected and the power of jurisdiction has no relationship to that of order. The doctrine of the one sacred authority upheld be Vatican II restored the ancient "unity in duality".

2. *Transmission and destitution.* Apart from the supreme authority of the Pope and the college of bishops, ecclesiastical jurisdiction is conferred by canonical mission (*CIC,* can. 109). This takes the form either of the conferring of an office in the Church or by delegation, that is, authoritative jurisdiction is transmitted to a person or corporate body without the mediation of an office (*CIC,* can. 197, § 1). Hence there is a distinction between ordinary and delegated jurisdiction (*potestas ordinaria* and *delegata*). All jurisdiction conferred by canonical mission can be withdrawn or be lost for other reasons. The supreme authority conferred by God on the Pope cannot be withdrawn, but can be lost, since the Pope can resign from his office or lose it for other reasons. The supreme authority belonging to the college of bishops cannot be lost or alienated, because the college always exists as a corporate body (*persona juridica*). But individual bishops who lose hierarchical fellowship with the head and members of the college cease thereby to be members of the college and lose their collegiate rights.

According to the nature of the office through which jurisdiction is conferred, a distinction is made between proper and vicarious ordinary jurisdiction (*potestas ordinaria propria* and *vicaria*). The distinction is not always clear. As a rule, both offices of divine institution and of ecclesiastical institution are regarded as conferring proper jurisdiction. If a valid criterion is to be found, it would seem that the distinction in question should be in accord with the new distinction now made between primary and subsidiary offices, prescinding from whether a primary office is of divine or ecclesiastical right.

3. *Functions.* Ever since the notion was taken over from Roman law, a distinction has been made between *jurisdictio contentiosa* and *voluntaria,* the law as applying to the unwilling *(in invitos)* and to the willing *(in volentes et petentes).* The principles for the exercise of both types of jurisdiction are maintained by the *CIC,* but with a change of terminology, distinguishing between judicial authority *(potestas iudicialis)* and voluntary or non-judicial authority *(potestas voluntaria seu non-iudicialis) (CIC,* can. 201, §§ 2, 3). All efforts to treat this as an adequate division of the functions of ecclesiastical jurisdiction are doomed to failure. It should rather be admitted that the distinction worked out in civil law between legislature, judiciary and executive also applies to ecclesiastical jurisdiction. In contrast to the State, however, where there is usually an actual division of powers, the constitutional law of the Church, where the notion of the unity of jurisdiction has been developed to the full, can basically envisage only a conceptual distinction. The Pope and the heads of local Churches possess all three functions, but for the exercise of their jurisdiction as a whole are obliged to follow the principles which apply to the exercise of each particular form of jurisdiction. Since they cannot exercise personally all the functions incumbent on their office, the historical development has been that the judiciary and the executive have been entrusted to organs distinct in principle, while legislation, if one prescinds from synods, has always remained in the hand of the authorities with full jurisdiction.

See also *Ecclesiastical Authority, Ecclesiastical Office, Ecclesiastical Law* II, III, *Forum.*

BIBLIOGRAPHY. ON 1: F. Leifer, *Die Einheit des Gewaltengedankens im römischen Staatsrecht* (1914); R. Sohm, *Das altkatholische Kirchenrecht und das Dekret Gratians* (1918); L. Wenger, *Institutionen des römischen Zivilprozessrechts* (1925), p. 28; M. de Van Kerchove, "De notione iurisdictionis in iure Romano", *Ius Pontificium* 16 (1936), pp. 49–65; id., "La notion de juridiction dans la doctrine des Décrétistes et des premiers Décrétalistes de Gratien (1140) à Bernard de Bottone (1250)", *Études franciscaines* 29 (1937), pp. 420–35; id., "De notione iurisdictionis apud Decretistas et priores Decreta-listas (1140–1250)", *Ius Pontificium* 18 (1938), pp. 10–14; L. M. De Bernardis, *Le due potestà e le due gerarchie della chiesa* (2nd ed., 1946); J. Klein, *Grundlegung und Grenzen des kanonischen Rechts* (1947). ON 2: V. Politi, *La giurisdizione ecclesiastica e la sua delegazione* (1937); E. Rösser, *Die gesetzliche Delegation* (1937); K. Mörsdorf, *Lehrbuch des Kirchenrechts,* I (11th ed., 1964). ON 3: K. Hofmann, *Die freiwillige Gerichtsbarkeit (iurisdictio voluntaria) im kanonischen Recht* (1929); C. Lefebvre, "Pouvoir judiciaire et pouvoir administratif en droit canonique", *Ephemerides Iuris Canonici* 5 (1949), pp. 339–53; K. Mörsdorff, *De relationibus inter potestatem administrativam et iudicialem in iure canonico (Questioni attuali di diritto canonico)* (1955); C. Lefebvre, "Pouvoirs de l'Église", *Dictionnaire du Droit Canonique,* VII, pp. 71–108.

Klaus Mörsdorf

JUSTICE

I. Scripture. II. Moral Theology.

I. Scripture

1. *The social sense of justice in the Old Testament.* The OT idea of צדקה (usually δικαιοσύνη in the LXX), unlike justice as conceived of in terms of objective theological principles, is not determined by permanent and immutable norms of human behaviour such that a man is accounted just when he acts in conformity with them. Throughout the whole of the OT in general, צדקה is a style of action, in a relation of fellowship between partners, which is the permanent constituent of this relationship and hence has its norm in the very existence of this relationship. Now since man is involved in various relations of fellowship there are various modes of justice which must be exercised between the parties as the basis of their partnership. Hence too there is no negative or punitive aspect in the OT idea of justice. The punishment of offenders is not numbered among the activities proper to the just man (with Cazelles and against Nötscher). The idea of the "justice of God" which appears especially in the apocalyptic writings and later in Paul (the corresponding idea in the OT is the just action of God conceived of as the deeds of salvation performed by him for Israel) suggests that in relationships between men justice can also be described as an act directed towards others and positive in its effects, by which one accords to them some advantage or opportunity which helps them and (thereby too the doer of justice) to preserve fellowship. Hence

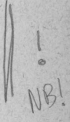

without justice to each other, fellowship between partners is impossible. This applies both to fellowship between men and fellowship between men and Yahweh. To be just, therefore, means to be free from any fault which would damage fellowship. To make just is to remove the obstacles set up by the other party (e.g., Is 53:11).

In the relationship of men to one another justice can denote a favourable attitude towards the innocent in judgment (thus in the series of "prohibitives" forbidding men to base their ethical conduct on their social rank in Exod 23:6–8; cf. Deut 25:1, where, accordingly, the hifil of צדק is used to signify: "to let the innocent have his due, to "justify him"). But the concept extends far beyond the forensic sphere. Especially at the beginning of the series dealing with the social order (e.g., משפט, Ezek 18:5) justice appears combined with משפט as an expression of the totality of the prescribed social attitudes towards those in a lowly walk of life. In relation to these groups the right, that is, the just attitude is one which extends beyond the basic requirements of mere giving and taking, and imports sympathy and compassion. The just man of the Wisdom literature is he who conducts himself so prudently in his dealings with his social equals and with those of lower station that he can obtain profit by it in the end. In antithetic proverbs he is often set in contrast to the "wicked", who is therefore also the foolish, for the comparison embraces both behaviour and its outcome. The just, however (in the course of the theological development this becomes clear), are rewarded with what is conceived to be true happiness. In later books this means that the just obtain not earthly riches (the unjust are requited with these) but eschatological or heavenly recompense. In Proverbs the just is the prudent man who bears in mind the outcome naturally to be expected of things. In passages influenced by the liturgy, however, the just man is one whose relationship with Yahweh is right, one who joins in his worship (Ps 15), one, therefore, who obtains from Yahweh the title of "righteous" and the promise of life (Ezek 18:9). Again the fact that faith is counted as justice (Gen 15:6) must represent an extension of the idea of ratification originally belonging to the sphere of worship (von Rad). Evidently those taking part in the liturgy were first subjected either collectively or individually to an examination as to their loyalty to the commands of the covenant bestowed by Yahweh (cf. Ps 24). Since one was either qualified to take part in worship or not, there was no intermediary position between justice and lack of justice.

In the psalms in particular we frequently find the צדיק described in quite general terms as one who takes joy in Yahweh's will and his precepts, with no mention of any concrete individual commandments. (We often encounter a similar phenomenon in parenetic discourses addressed to the just in later literature: cf. Ps 1 with the parenetic sections of Enoch.) The just man is pronounced blessed not by reason of what he does but in view of his life as a whole. Not until later, in the rabbinical literature, do we find a notably different concept of justice. Here it is the sum total of a man's acts of obedience to individual precepts (D. Rössler). In the apocalyptic literature, on the other hand, a sharp distinction is drawn between the just and the unjust (as in the Wisdom literature), and the just are consoled by parenetic discourses for their present unavoidable sufferings, and warned against apostasy.

While in the later literature it came increasingly to be doubted whether Israel could be just before Yahweh at all (Ps 143:1; Dan 9:18), Yahweh himself remains absolutely just towards Israel. The deeds of salvation which he has performed on its behalf are called the "manifestations of Yahweh's justice" as early as Jg 5:11 (cf. 1 Sam 12:7; Mic 6:5; Ps 103:6; Dan 9:16). This justice of Yahweh is not only often set side by side with the concept of חסד (faithfulness, love, "grace"), but also finds expression in the commandments which Yahweh gives to Israel, which are therefore considered to provide the possibility of salvation (Zeph 3:5; Ps 50:6). Even before the prophets, therefore, the justice of Yahweh is used as a synonym for the salvation bestowed by Yahweh (von Rad), and, furthermore, that salvation as applied to the individual.

Finally, a point to which so far too little attention has been paid is that justice is frequently spoken of in connection with the kingship (1 Sam 24:18; 26:33; 2 Sam 8:15; 1 Kg 3:6; 10:9). Justice is not only attributed to individual kings, but is actually the essential quality of the work proper to their state. The theology of the royalty may have been an important factor in the OT concept of justice. Hitherto the analysis of its cultic roots has often overlooked the fact that the texts in question (Ps 89:15; 97:2; 85:14; 89:17) have been applied to Yahweh only at a secondary stage, and analogously. In the context of sacred kingship justice is originally the proper attitude towards God, towards one's social equals and towards those of the humbler classes. In Is 11:1 ff. the accomplishment of justice is attributed particularly to the son of David who is to come. Hence Jesus too is called the "holy and righteous (just) one" in Acts 3:14.

2. *Justice in the theologies of the New Testament.* In the NT concepts of justice elements from the OT, Judaism and Greek popular philosophy are combined. For Paul and Matthew in particular "justice" has acquired a primary significance, and in both of them with reference to the end or judgment shortly to come. For both authors justice is required from men at this judgment. For both, man can obtain this justice by deciding to embrace the message of Jesus and the community belonging to him. For this is the community of the just. In concrete terms this is achieved through faith and baptism. By these means man ceases in principle to belong to the unjust, unless he proves himself by his conduct to be not yet just or unless he falls away. For at present the community possesses justice only in a "provisional" and veiled manner. For Matthew as for Paul, therefore, the fulfilment of the ethical commandments is not the *condition* of justice but rather an *expression* of the justice which has been obtained by baptism and must therefore be preserved until the judgment. Thus the norm of judgment is the fulfilment of the law (for Matthew as for Paul this consists in the fulfilment of the social commandments), but the just are those who in principle have entered into a state in which they are capable of such fulfilment. In Matthew this is because Jesus is the teacher of justice for his community (the Sermon on the Mount), and because the baptized possess the Spirit. In Paul it is because justice has been imparted through the Pneuma in such a way that by it love, precisely the fulfilment of the law, is bestowed as a charisma (1 Cor). Certainly Matthew too recognizes that justice does

have this character of a gift (18:23–35), but justice for him consists primarily in being free from sin, whereas in Paul the predominant idea is that of being in Christ as being in the justice of God (2 Cor 5:21, etc.). In particular Paul's thought is dominated by the idea of the indwelling Spirit, by which justice is affirmed as something present, as a gift and as a force.

For *Paul* the question of the relationship between the justice required of man and the justice of God is vital. Paul takes over the idea of the justice of God from the apocalyptic literature (cf. also Deut 33:21). For Paul too justice is not one of the attributes of God, but a gift manifested in God's actions towards man. God opens up a cosmic sphere of power in which the just are included. This sphere is somewhat like the Pneuma, for it signifies the sphere of the salvation bestowed by God. Hence the believers themselves become "the justice of God in Christ" (2 Cor 5:21). Here the new being is designated by the name of the power which constitutes and defines it (Stuhlmacher). This justice of God is revealed in Christ (Rom 1:17f.), in contrast to the injustice of Jews and Gentiles, which, when measured by the standard of the law, is shown to be such. This justice of God bestowed upon man in Christ is nothing else than the faithful execution of God's promises to the fathers (Rom 4:9–11). For this reason justice can only be obtained through a faith such as Abraham too possessed (Rom 4), and now, therefore, this must be faith in Jesus Christ. This connection between "justice" and "faith" was taken over by Paul from Gen 15:6 (elsewhere in the OT only Hab 2:4), and this is because on the one hand the justice of God for him consists in the fulfilment of the promises to the fathers, while on the other he feels compelled to connect this indissolubly with faith in Jesus Christ. Faith here as the way by which justice is to be obtained (according to Gen 15:6 the justice of Abraham, but for Paul God's own justice) is contrasted with the traditional way of the Jews, who seek to obtain justice by fulfilling the law. According to the Jewish notion, justice was obtained by fulfilling the commandments. As a possible way to salvation this law was linked with the Jewish people; as a gift of God bestowed in the course of the history of salvation it was a distinction. But in the light of the faith now required of man it represents a temptation to pursue one's "own" justice (Rom 10:3; Phil 3:9), that is, by the exclusively Jewish way of the law. But in the justice that comes by faith, the distinction between Jews and Gentiles is actually removed, and thus the universal way of salvation is revealed which alone can correspond to the universal, eschatological salvation in Christ. Hence the justice of God has now been revealed without the law (Rom 3:21). In concrete terms justification is achieved through the death of Jesus, the primary function of which is to take away sins. In the OT too justice did indeed mean to a large extent freedom from sin, but this was in the context of a relation of fellowship, and so signified that this relationship was still intact. Now in Paul over and above this the possession of justice is characterized in positive terms by the possession of the Spirit and the life which proceeds from it.

In the Gospel of Mark, the term justice is not found. But it appears in the Lucan writings, in Lk 1:75; Acts 10:35, where it is combined, in a manner characteristic of Hellenistic thought, with the fear of God (as the sum total of human duty), and elsewhere in Luke is used to designate the whole moral well-being of man, as the prior condition for the reception of the Spirit. In Matthew all the passages in which justice appears are of redactional origin. Here too justice is a collective concept, one namely which stands for all that constitutes the "religion" of the community henceforward separated from Judaism. The apocalyptic pattern of the division of mankind into just and unjust is adhered to. The Jews now become the types of the unjust, and among them the Pharisees in particular, by reason of their hypocrisy, will not survive the judgment, and will not obtain any heavenly reward (5:20; 6:1). Man becomes just through baptism, by which he already obtains the fullness of justice (Mt 3:15), although he still remains in danger of losing this by apostasy. According to the ideas of the apocalyptic tradition the just must necessarily endure persecution (Mt 5:10, etc.). This traditional principle also provides the background to earlier interpretations of the death of Jesus as that of the suffering just man (Ps 22 as cited in the Passion narrative; Mk 8). The justice of the community is contrasted with that of Judaism by being brought into relation with the βασιλεία (Mt 6:33), and by the fact that it will be revealed as justice in the judgment to come. As the parables of the weeds in the wheat etc. attest, the justice of the just is thought of solely from the aspect of the judgment. The sharp dualism between just and unjust is not to be understood in the sense of an available criterion, for both groups live together in the world. But the just are persecuted here, and thereby their difference from the unjust becomes ever more apparent and the reward they are to receive to compensate for their sufferings is prepared.

In the Letter of James justice is likewise brought into connection with the idea of retribution at the judgment. Justice before God (1:70) is bestowed as a fruit (3:18) growing out of men's actions (2:23). It was not by faith alone that Abraham obtained his justice. Rather he was called "friend of God" only after the sacrifice of Isaac, and hence it is only here that Gen 15:6 was fulfilled.

In the rest of the NT writings the idea of justice as a sphere of salvation as in Paul is to be found here and there. The saved are taken into this sphere. Thus according to 2 Pet 3:13 justice dwells in the new heaven and the new earth as a blessing of salvation which permeates the whole. According to 2 Pet 1:1 the justice of God is a sphere within which faith in God and Jesus Christ has been bestowed. In conformity with the special concept of miracles in Heb 11 the work of justice on earth belongs, according to 11:33, to the special deeds of the just which transcend this world and cause astonishment to men. Elsewhere too in the Letter to the Hebrews justice is orientated to the heavenly world. The "word of justice" is only for the perfect (5:13). The high priest Jesus is the completely just one who has loved justice (1:9), and to whom Melchizedek pointed by his name. As in Jas 3:18, so too in Heb 12:11 justice and peace are combined as mutually complementary blessings of the eschatological age. Thus for Hebrews justice is a power reaching into the world through Jesus and through faith in him, and it is also an eschatological gift. 1 Pet 2:24 clearly stands in the line of the Pauline tradition. The sacrifice of the body of Christ means for believers that they are separated from sin, and that it is possible to "live to righteousness". But this is not understood in the light of the

Pauline Θ of Justice since it does a bit unique... ground Justice for... in H of ∆.

justice of God as in Paul, but rather, as the context shows, is already (or perhaps still?) primarily ethical. Then in the Pastoral Letters we find a concept of justice which is still more remote from that of Paul, for here it is regarded as one virtue among others. Frequently emphasis is laid upon the doing of justice (1 Jn; Rev; Tit 3:5). Here what justice actually consists in is either left undecided or is defined as brotherly love and compassion. (This is connected with the usage of later Judaism, in which צדקה meant alms; cf. δικαιοσύνη in Josephus.) Thus in the non-Pauline writings the ideas which are most emphasized are: the doing of justice and the insertion of justice into the list of the virtues. There is little or no link with the justice of God, with the idea of justice as the heavenly reward (2 Tim 4:2) or with the person and work of Jesus (2 Pet; Eph 4:24).

See also *Society* II, *Faith* II, *Baptism*, *Law* I, *Law and Gospel*, *Apocalyptic*.

BIBLIOGRAPHY. T. Häring, Δικαιοσύνη θεοῦ *bei Paulus* (1895–96); C. Cremer, *Die paulinische Rechtfertigungslehre im Zusammenhang ihrer geschichtlichen Voraussetzungen* (2nd ed., 1900); F. Nötscher, *Die Gerechtigkeit Gottes bei den vorexilischen Propheten* (1915); K. Fahlgren, *Sedaka* (1932); A. Descamps, *Les justes et la justice dans les évangiles et le christianisme primitif* (1950); H. Cazelles, "A propos de quelques textes difficiles relatifs à la justice de Dieu dans l'Ancien Testament", *Revue Biblique* 58 (1951), pp. 169ff.; J. Pedersen, *Israel*, I–II ("Righteousness and Truth") (1959); G. Strecker, *Der Weg der Gerechtigkeit* (1962); P. Stuhlmacher, *Gerechtigkeit Gottes bei Paulus* (1965).

Klaus Berger

II. Moral Theology

The notion of justice is fundamental to the human spirit. All men have some sort of aspiration, at least obscurely, towards justice. From the beginning, the notion of justice has been attached to the sphere of religion, as may be seen in Plato's *Gorgias*, 507b, and *Republic*, I, 331a. In the most ancient texts of the Bible, the first monuments of supernatural revelation, there is also a bond between justice and religion (in the covenant by which Israel was bound to Yahweh). "Abraham believed the Lord; and he reckoned it to him as righteousness" (Gen 15:6). In the Book of Proverbs, the "just" is frequently contrasted with the "impious" (or the "wicked",

the "foolish", in a profound and complex religious sense). See Prov 10:11, 20f.; 11:10, 23, 31; 12:3–13; 5:13, 9, 21, 25, etc.

1. *Uncertainties and errors*. This undoubted sense of a salvific and transcendent justice, this demand for justice in the mutual relations of men and in the order of the city did not free men from profound uncertainties as to the nature and meaning of justice. In the dialogues of Plato, various speakers are criticized for concepts of justice based on a purely hedonistic, utilitarian or materialistic outlook — that, for instance, justice is merely the law of the stronger. There is the radical relativism of Protagoras and the theory of justice as a social compromise to avoid greater evils. Avoiding such errors and incertitudes, the profound humanism of Aristotle, in the *Nicomachean Ethics*, crowned a long process of secularization of the concept of justice. Medieval scholasticism took over the heritage of Aristotle and transformed its spirit, in the concrete and in the theory of ethics. The notion of justice came to be placed within the horizon of religious transcendence. For the ethical thought of Thomism, along with biblical and Augustinian influences, the impact of Stoicism, through the Latin writings of Cicero etc., was very important. Thomas Aquinas, while remaining faithful to the Aristotelian concept, was responsive to the strong social trends which are at the heart of the patristic tradition on justice and the proper use of goods.

Then once more, in the great process of the secularization of thought which came to a climax in the 18th century, the notion of justice was deprived of its transcendental roots. In much more profound and complex forms, in keeping with a much more highly evolved thinking for which the progress in the new positive methods of science was decisive, the errors and uncertainties of ancient Greek thought appeared once more. They are to be found in Hobbes, Nietzsche and the many forms of positivism and sociological theories of justice which multiplied at the end of the 19th and the beginning of the 20th century. Faced with the uncertainties as to the content of the notion of justice, some were tempted to accept a purely relative system of values. Hence came the tendency to take refuge in a purely formal concept of justice. On account of the value of "security at law" and the universal character of law

need 4 a transcndt base

itself, there was a tendency to reduce justice to the virtue of impartiality in the general application of the one law, leaving aside as insoluble the problem of "natural justice".

2. *The impact of the "spirit of capitalism".* This whole modern picture of deviations and uncertainties with regard to the ever-imperative ideal of justice was coloured throughout the 19th century by the "spirit of capitalism" (see the encyclical of Paul VI, *Populorum Progressio*, no. 26). Its influence on the ideals and concept of justice were deleterious. Economics attained the rank of ultimate and absolute values and claimed to be ruled by its intrinsic and wholly autonomous laws. *Homo economicus* was bound to aim, as the ultimate goal of his activity, at the maximum quantitative development of the economy. Economic ethics were rationalistic and individualist, like the political liberalism of the age. The central point in this concept of economic life was profit, which came to be radically separated from all demands deriving from the solidarity of an *ordo amoris* and from all metaphysical, ethical and religious bonds. Economics became a world with a law of its own independent of all other norms. The individual in the system followed only the dictates of his individual interests (gain), as rationalized by foresight and calculation, and thus inserted himself and his activity into the "natural order" of the world of economics.

The "classical" school of economics, drawing on a philosophy of a very special type and on historically-conditioned experiences, produced the new "economic science" and gave the "spirit of capitalism" its final perfection and consistency, consummating the breach with all moral norms transcending the internal laws of the economic system. What remained of the concept of justice in this outlook on the world and life? The whole notion of social justice was eliminated. Justice became commutative justice which obeyed no other law than the conventions of negotiated contracts within the framework of the law of supply and demand, with no restrictions on individualistic enterprise. The function of the State was to allow free play to the forces of individualism by enforcing public order and the fulfilment of contracts, while remaining rigorously neutral as regards their contents. This was the general notion of justice in liberal capitalism. The aberrations of the "spirit of capitalism", along with another

complex series of factors, produced the ideas of Marx and Engels and the movements which flowed from them. Marxism is a tragic contradiction between a messianic aspiration after justice — raised to its highest coefficient of secularization in the form of a systematic atheism — and the acceptance of an immanent natural determinism in economics. It substituted, no doubt, for the atomistic mechanisms on which classical economics were based a dialectic and historical materialism. But this was no less a renunciation of the whole transcendent ideal of justice. This is the historical context in which the Christian of today has to ask himself about the ideals and concept of justice.

3. *The comprehensive and religious sense of the idea of justice.* The Bible constantly uses the word "justice" in a sense which is at once ethical and religious. The OT already puts forward the idea that this justice cannot come to man through his own strength but is a gift of God. This order of ideas is developed more and more fully in the NT, the supreme revelation of the salvific grace ("justice") of God.

Though on an essentially different plane, since the supernatural revelation of the "justice of God" is lacking, the Platonic concept of justice has a comprehensive character and a religious colouring. It is immediately related to the supreme form, that of the good. The form of the good in Plato is the supreme principle, the initiative behind all initiatives (cf. *Republic*, VI, 508 b – 510 b). It is the *logos* of all things, not only in the sense of their explanation but as the inventive and efficient cause. Everything that exists is essentially ordained by it, according to Plato, to a function which derives directly from the form of the good. The functional purpose of the essence demands that things be intrinsically structured in such a way that they are apt to fulfil their function. This principle of functional structure applies both to individual things and to organic compositions. Any of them can pervert their structure and render themselves unable to perform their function. This deviation and decadence, when the realities affected are the soul and the State, is for Plato the constitutive element of injustice. Justice is the structural equilibrium (rectitude) of the soul (personal justice) and of the State (political justice), which has to secure their functioning in the best possible way, in accordance with an order of functions determined by the illuminating radiance of the supreme form of the good.

4. *Comprehensive (religious) justice and general justice*. This fundamental tendency to identify the ideal of justice with full religious and moral rectitude and — in a more genuine religious way of thinking — with a salvific realization of the good (justice) in man by a free intervention of God which justifies, has gone hand in hand from the beginning with the tendency to conceive justice as a characteristic virtue, qualitatively distinct from the other virtues. The Bible speaks of justice not only in the comprehensive sense mentioned above, but also with reference to a characteristic virtue distinct from the others. Sometimes justice has a juridical colouring and means conformity with a legal norm (Prov 11:4,19; 12:28; 16:8; Deut 1:16; 16:18; 25:15). In the historical and prophetic books, justice is often the equivalent of due rights (Hos 10:12; Is 9:6; 11:4f.; 16:5; 32:1; Jer 22:3f.; 23:5; Ezek 45:9f.; 2 Sam 8:15; 1 Kg 10:9; 1 Chr 18:14; 2 Chr 9:8). Jeremiah denounces the injustice of riches accumulated by paying starvation wages (Jer 22:13–15). In this context the prophets sometimes call the oppressed poor the "just" (Amos 2:6; 5:12; Is 1:17, 23; 3:4f.; Lam 4:13); Jas 5:6 speaks in the same way. The Wisdom literature teaches that justice demands rectitude in the mutual relationships of men (Job 35:8; Eccles 5:7) and in the concrete, rectitude in the exercise of judicial functions (Ecclus 45:26). Justice is used as a synonym of benevolence (ἐλεημοσύνη in the LXX) (Tob 7:6; 9:6; 12:9; 14:9–11; Ecclus 3:30). This identification of justice with beneficence (alms) is given great prominence in the patristic age (e.g., Basil, *Hom. in Lk*, 12:8, no. 7: *PG*, XXXI, cols. 276f.; Ambrose, *De Nabuthe*, 12, 53, *CSEL*, XLVI, p. 426, *PL*, XIV, col. 747; John Chrysostom, *Hom. 12 in 1 Tim*, 12, 4; *PG*, LXII, cols. 562f.; Augustine, *Sermo 50*, 2, 4; *PL*, XXXVIII, col. 327; id., *Epist. 153*, no. 26, *CSEL*, XLVI, p. 426, *PL*, XXXIII, col. 665). In the NT justice also appears as a virtue distinct from others (Act 24:25 along with self-control; 1 Tim 6:11 along with piety, faith, charity, constancy and mildness; 2 Cor 9:9f. a synonym of beneficence, almsgiving; Rev 19:11 the virtue of just judgment).

Can the comprehensive religious idea of justice and the idea of justice as a particular virtue be reduced to some type of unity? Aristotle introduced the concept of legal justice (an integral or general justice embracing all the virtues) and that of particular justice (equity in the attribution of ownership among individuals), cf. *Nicomachean Ethics*, V, 1129a–1131a. In both cases justice involves a relationship to others *(ad alterum)*, in the first to the common good, in the second to the good of an individual. Legal justice includes the exercise of all the virtues, insofar as they bear on the common good (integral justice) but maintains the character of relationship to others which is characteristic of the special idea of justice. No doubt, the Aristotelian concept of legal justice is completely secularized and purely political. It is the civic virtue of observing the positive law of the State (in the context of the strong community spirit characteristic of the Greeks). In Scholasticism, which based itself on the notion of the eternal law of God, in which all other laws participate, legal justice includes the civic virtue of observance of positive law but goes beyond it to become once more a comprehensive justice under the sign of religion.

But why is it called "justice"? The solution seems to lie along the line of an idea much favoured by the Fathers. Man does not belong to himself but to God. Hence all virtue is giving God his due. But God is Father, and his love binds us in solidarity. It is therefore a duty in justice to work for the common good, and especially — from the standpoint of the Fathers — to aid the neighbour in his needs and not to use one's goods as if they were absolutely and exclusively one's own. See, for instance, *Letter of Barnabas*, 19, 8; *Didache*, 4, 8; Clement of Alexandria, *Paedagogus*, 2, 12 (*GCS*, Stählin, I, p. 229); Tertullian, *De Paenitentia* 7 (*CSEL*, XLVII, p. 11, *PL*, I, col. 1261); Lactantius, *Epitome Institutionum Divinarum*, 5, 14; 6, 11–12 (*CSEL*, XIX, pp. 445ff. and 519ff., *PL*, VI, cols. 596ff. and 671ff.); Basil, *Hom. tempore famis*, 8 (*PG*, XXXI, cols. 324f.); Gregory of Nyssa, *De Pauperibus Amandis*, 1 (*PG*, XLVI, col. 466); Ambrose, *De Officiis Ministri*, 3, 3, 19 (*PL*, XVI, col. 150); Jerome, *Epist.*, 120, 1 (*CSEL*, LV, pp. 476f., *PL*, XXII, col. 984); John Chrysostom, *Hom. 10 in 1 Cor*, 3 (*PG*, LXI, col. 86); Augustine, *De Trinitate*, 14, 9, 12 (*PL*,

JUSTICE

XLII, col. 1046); Leo I, *Sermo 10,* 1 (*PL,* LIV, col. 164).

5. *General and particular justice.* We may now attempt a synthesis. Justice is always fidelity in giving (*reddere,* rendering) to another what is his due (cf. St. Thomas, *Summa Theologica,* II, II, q. 58, a. 1). There is a radical and comprehensive justice, of a religious character, which consists in man's "sur-rendering" himself to God. Hence every sin is really an injustice (*injuria*) to God. On this level justice and love are inseparable. In a general way, the NT sets up an existential dialectic between love (supernaturally "open" to God and to the neighbour, and inseparably so, cf. 1 Jn *passim*) and justice, though love alone is capable in fact of accomplishing adequately all justice, in freedom of spirit. To justice in the religious sense general justice is intimately linked, its object being the general good in all its aspects and implications, with no other limit than the due proportion between one's own needs and those of others (cf. 2 Cor 8:13–15 and the patristic texts referred to above). For this general or social justice has as its immediate object a common human good which is transcendentally ordained to each man (Thomas Aquinas, *Summa Theologica,* II, II, q. 58, a. 5).

Hence social justice can take the form of obligations in justice towards certain persons in need of aid. But this grave obligation in justice does not entail (except in the case of extreme necessity) the right of the individual to claim directly for himself the good due to him, if it is due in virtue of social justice. Social justice involves particular justice — the accomplishment of which is always a social value — which is divided into distributive and commutative justice. The former is the proper distribution of the goods and offices of common life among the members of the community, which suffers unjustly in the goods proper to it if the distribution in question is not in keeping with the capacities, needs, functions, sacrifices and merits of the various subjects. The latter (so called by Thomas Aquinas, whereas Aristotle spoke of "corrective justice"—τὸ ἐπανορθωτικόν) governs exchange of goods between individuals and, in general, their mutual relations with regard to the goods belonging to or due to each, when the individuals are on a footing of equality (Aristotle, *Nicoma-*

chean Ethics, 1131 b ff.). The immediate object of particular justice is "the property of the individual" (*Summa Theologica,* II, II, q. 7; cf. q. 61, a. 1). Goods are the object of commutative justice insofar as they are related to the needs of the persons who enter into relationships. Justice demands mutual equilibrium in the satisfaction of their needs by each party concerned (*Nicomachean Ethics,* 1133 a–1133 b). On the other hand, commutative justice, which cannot be embodied in the concrete without its tending to social justice (cf. *ibid.,* 1159 b–1160 a) needs to be completed by aspects of distributive justice (*ibid.,* 1131 b).

These various types of justice must be considered to be aspects of one fundamental demand, which takes on various forms in concrete relationships. In the comprehensive sense, justice, in a given situation, is the concrete accomplishment of the fundamental imperative which calls for positive respect for the dignity and rights of others and contribution in solidarity to the meeting of human necessities. John XXIII (in *Mater et Magistra*) recalled repeatedly the demands of "justice and equity" and emphasized the comprehensive character of justice in the concrete, very much in keeping with the patristic notion. Vatican II spoke in the same sense (*Gaudium et Spes,* arts. 23–32; 63–72).

See also *Platonism* I, *Aristotelianism, Equity, Law* I, *Society* I, II, *Marxism, Moral Theology* I, *Old Testament Ethics, New Testament Ethics, Scholasticism* IV.

BIBLIOGRAPHY. Aristotle, *Ethics,* Oxford translation, ed. by J. Smith and W. Ross (1925); H. Robertson, *Aspects of the Rise of Economic Individualism* (1933); A. Brucculeri, *La giustizia sociale* (1941); E. Brunner, *Justice and the Social Order* (1945); E. Cahn, *The Sense of Injustice* (1949); A. Descamps, *Les justes et la justice dans les évangiles et le christianisme primitif hormis la doctrine proprement paulinienne* (1950); G. de Vecchio, *La giustizia* (4th ed., 1951), E. T.: *Justice: An Historical and Philosophical Essay* (1952); P. Lachièze-Rey, *Les idées morales, sociales et politiques de Platon* (2nd ed., 1951); J. Newman, *Foundations of Justice. A Historico-Critical Study in Thomism* (1954); P. Trude, *Der Begriff der Gerechtigkeit in der aristotelischen Rechts- und Staatsphilosophie* (1955); J. Fernández, *Justicia Social* (1955); P. Tillich, *Love, Peace, Justice* (1960); J. Pieper, *Four Cardinal Virtues* (1960); J. M. Díez-Alegría, *Il concetto di giustizia nell' Enciclica "Mater et Magistra"* (*L'Enciclica Mater et Magistra, Università Gregoriana*) (1963), pp. 105–19.

José María Díez-Alegría

JUSTIFICATION

The concept of justification is a relative one. To be justified is not merely to be just but also to be acknowledged as such. And so it implies a relation with a judgment rather than a mode of being. Use of the term to designate a new aspect of the new being that Christianity gives us, dates from St. Paul's controversies with the Judaizers. They held that a man is just if he observes the law by the minute keeping of particular commandments rather than by a general disposition to serve and love God (Mt 23:23). At the end of a man's life there is a judgment: his observances and transgressions of the law are weighed and his justification or condemnation pronounced accordingly. Justification here is eschatological and simply declares the antecedent existence of righteousness (Billerbeck, I, pp. 250f.). Not all Jews were of this mind; some admitted that mercy intervenes to justify those who cannot appeal to good works (4 Esdras 8:36). But the Pharisaism St. Paul combatted exists in every age as a religious attitude, so that his doctrine of gratuitous justification always has an immediate relevance for us. St. Paul is familiar with the purely juridical and eschatological idea of justification (Rom 2:13–16) and the term with him always has a certain forensic flavour which prevents its becoming a mere synonym of regeneration or re-creation.

In later theology, however, this sense is often lost, and justification comes to mean nothing more than the infusion of grace (D 799). Now when St. Paul applies the juridical terminology to the new Christian reality, it acquires an entirely new meaning. It refers now not to the future but to the past (Rom 5:9), not to the just man but the sinner (Rom 4:5). And so the basis of justification must also be different. It can no longer be observance of the law. It must be Christ, whom God has made our righteousness and sanctification and redemption (1 Cor 1:30), which is the same thing as saying that we are justified by faith in Christ (Rom 3:28). But if God's judgment can no longer be the mere acknowledgment of an antecedent and autonomous righteousness, neither can it be a mere legal fiction. It must be a judgment which creates a new bond between man and God, whereby man is not only destined for the possession of God but also orientated towards that possession. This new orientation presupposes a transformation in man himself.

So justification can be regarded as an act of God and as an effect in man. As an act of God we have said that it is mainly judicial in character. Other terms that refer to the same Christian reality primarily connote other aspects of it: a new nature, a principle of new acts of knowledge and love. By a paradox, what the term justification primarily connotes is the gratuitous nature of the process (the justification of the sinner). God's initiative is absolute. Only God justifies, and any self-justification is radically excluded (Gal 2:16). And yet this expression does not plainly set forth the whole role of Christ in justification. Nor does the Council of Trent, in declaring Christ's death the meritorious cause, claim thereby to have said the last word about his causality in justification. The Council says that the justified are personally united with Christ by faith, but that the union remains imperfect unless faith be joined with hope and love (D 800). That is, it presupposes an incorporation in Christ which cannot be reduced to merely meritorious causality. God's righteousness in Christ (2 Cor 5:19–21) is subjectively appropriated by faith (Rom 3:28), understood as the antithesis of the works of the law — as the acknowledgment of our absolute inability to justify ourselves before God by our own powers, and our unconditional surrender to God justifying us in Christ. Yet faith is not identical with justification, not even with its subjective aspect; rather it is a disposition prerequisite for justification (Rom 10:10), the foundation and root of all justification (D 801) — that is to say, of its acquisition, its growth, and its recovery. This total faith as distinct from the merely intellectual, is not simply acceptance of an abstract or purely historical truth; it means accepting the personal intervention of God in history and, with respect to justification, absolutely ceasing to rely on oneself in order to attain it (Rom 9:30f.; 10:3). Accordingly faith is also a sacrificial offering (Phil 2:17), obedience and subjection (Rom 1:5; 10:16; 16:19), and in this sense also, to be justified by faith is exactly equivalent to being gratuitously justified.

As to whether any given individual is in fact justified, this is not a matter of faith, in the sense of absolute certainty, but of confident hope (D 802, 822). True, while treating of justification by faith and the gratuitous nature of justification in the same chapter, the Council of Trent does not explicitly connect the two (*D* 801). This is because of the different point of view adopted by the Council in the Lutheran controversy. Not content with the absolutely gratuitous character of the faith which must dispose us to justification, the Council goes on to deny that even this faith merits justification *(de condigno)*. And yet St. Paul's language (by faith, through faith, etc.) does imply that faith in some way causes justification. But if we regard the process of justification as a whole — including the first call to the faith, the more or less lengthy preparation, and justification itself with its sacramental symbol, baptism — then being justified by faith and being justified gratuitously are one and the same thing.

It would not do to conclude that a man remains passive because justification is gratuitous. Indeed he cannot consent to it unless prompted by the interior grace of a vocation to the faith (*D* 178). But God's gifts to man are not bestowed as upon wood and stones; they are bestowed as upon a free, responsible being. And therefore the faith which justifies a man is obedience, submission, a free acceptance of God's creative word.

If justification as proceeding from God is creative judgment, we must then ask what it is as realized in man. Justification in this latter sense has a negative aspect and a positive one: the forgiveness of sins, and a transformation. In order to see how justification forgives sins we must first determine the general nature of the sin from which we are delivered. One reason why the average Catholic is uninterested in justification is that he lacks a sense of sin. When people have received baptism in infancy, the state which St. Paul calls being in the sign of the wrath of God (Rom 1:18–3:20) seems something remote and unreal to them, not a reality from which they have been delivered (and are at every moment delivered). And then a humanistic reaction hardly compatible with Catholic tradition (*D* 130, 200b, 789, 793, etc.) has tended to minimize the reality of original sin, reducing it to a sort of neutral state. On the other hand, a certain atomistic view of morality leads to a shallow estimation both of personal sin and of conversion. Nevertheless sacred Scripture (Rom 1:18–3:20) and Catholic tradition (*D* 793) consider sin to be not merely an act that happened in the past but a permanent state under the sign of the wrath of God. Here two contrasting exaggerations must be avoided: one which minimizes sin, making it a mere overstepping of moral bounds that has no effect on the being of man (divorcing being from freedom); the other, which identifies sin with concupiscence, and concupiscence with man's elemental need to seek himself. In the latter case sin is not given its true dimensions, it is identified with the inevitable limitations of human nature, and so with the existential fault that is affirmed by the dualist conceptions of man.

So on the one hand sin affects the very being of man, depriving him of his orientation to intimate communion with God (the beatific vision) and leaving him helpless to return by his own powers to the state he enjoyed before the Fall. On the other hand sin does not rob man of his essential nature — that of a responsible being — nor change the fact that his appointed end is the possession of God. Now this discrepancy between man's appointed end and his orientation the Church has always held to be literally sinful (*D* 174, 175, 788, 789); and it constitutes the tragic situation of the sinner. Whether we judge that this situation leaves human nature maimed (*D* 130, 174, 200b, 788) or not (*D* 1055) depends on whether we think of that nature historically or in the abstract. Let us set aside the conjecture that God might eliminate man's supernatural end and leave him on a purely natural plane. Certainly the discrepancy between man's appointed end and his orientation would then cease, but what this change would do to the intrinsic structure of man is quite unimaginable.

In fact, God has chosen to leave our appointed end undisturbed and gratuitously restore our orientation. But concretely, there are various stages in the forgiveness of sins: 1. God sends his Son to reconcile the world to himself (2 Cor 5:18). 2. He applies this reconciliation to those who accept his call by believing in Christ, forgiving their sins. This pardon likewise has two aspects.

a) The sins a man has committed God no longer imputes to him. Obviously the only way God can pardon a sinful act itself is by non-imputation, by forgetting it. Scripture says so in eloquent metaphors (Ps 103:12; Is 38:17; Mic 7:19). Yet for all that eloquence, we must ask how far sin has ceased to be a reality for the justified man — in other words, to what extent sin and justification co-exist;

to what extent the justified man can be called *simul iustus et peccator*. We cannot say that sin and pardon co-exist in a dialectical sense. Such a thing can only be affirmed if one identifies sin with mere human limitations and justification with a purely eschatological judgment. Nonetheless a certain co-existence is undeniable. Man being a historical creature, his past is not simply annulled; in some sense it lives on in his present. Furthermore, that present is the new aeon which began with the death and resurrection of Christ but has not yet achieved its fullness, is still in germ on earth (Rom 8:24; 13:11; 1 Ju 3:2; 1 Pet 1:5, 20). And so, though freed from sin, the just man is always in jeopardy from it (Gal 5:7). At the same time we must remember that the main theme in the NT is not the threat to the just from sin (Rom 7 is disputable), but joy in our Christian freedom and confidence in final victory (Eph 5:8; Gal 5:22ff.).

b) But God's pardon is not a purely negative thing. Above all it is the restoration of a lost friendship, recovery of the status of adoption. This is the positive aspect of forgiveness and justification, and it emerges more clearly from other terms which describe the same Christian reality from other points of view (indwelling, the adoption of sons, rebirth, new creation). The juridical and the mystical are not two heterogeneous conceptions (Jewish and Hellenistic) but rather two complementary views of the same thing. There is no real forgiveness of sins unless love be restored, and for love to be restored the lover must be present. What is altogether new is that presence of God which by its own weight *(causa quasi-formalis)* transforms a man (created grace) and once more gives him the capacity to possess God. This trinitarian presence is not undifferentiated: we are incorporated in the Son (in Christ) by the presence of the Spirit, and in virtue of this incorporation in the Son we can call God our Father. Thus we are not called to a mere contemplation from without of the supreme beauty, the supreme goodness; we are swept away in the very torrent of divine life.

Without going to the excesses of certain mystics (*D* 510 ff.; 1225 f.), Scripture itself uses the boldest language to adumbrate the ineffable reality God calls us to by his reconciliation (1 Cor 6:17; 2 Pet 1:4; 1 Jn 3:9). Still it is well that each word in the Christian message should keep its own particular shade of meaning. That of "justification" is the absolutely gratuitous and paradoxical character of God's judgment upon sinful man.

See also *Law* I, *Justice* I, *Judaism* I, *Grace* I, II, *Faith* II, *New Testament Theology* II.

BIBLIOGRAPHY. See bibliography on *Justice* I; also: J. H. Newman, *Lectures on the Doctrine of Justification* (1838; 3rd ed., 1878); E. Tobac, *Le problème de la justification dans S. Paul* (1908); J. Hefner, *Die Entstehungsgeschichte des Trienter Rechtfertigungsdekretes* (1909); S. Lyonnet, "De justitia Dei in epistola ad Romanos", *Verbum Domini* 25 (1947), pp. 23–34, 118–21, 129–44, 193–203, 257–63; H. Rondet, *Gratia Christi* (1948); A. Descamps, "Justice et justification", *DBS,* IV, cols. 1417–71, 1496–1510; L. Cerfaux, "St. Paul", *DBS,* IV, cols. 1471–96; J. Dupont, "La réconciliation dans la théologie de St. Paul", *Estudios Biblicos* 11 (1952), pp. 255–302; J. Alfaro, "Persona y Gracia", *Gregorianum* 41 (1960), pp. 5–29; S. Lyonnet, *Exegesis Epistulae ad Romanos* (cap. I ad IV), excursus de iustitia Dei, pp. 80–107; R. Hermann, *Luthers These "Gerecht und Sünder zugleich"* (2nd ed., 1960); R. Franco, *El Hombre Nuevo* (1962).

Ricardo Franco

K

KANTIANISM

1. By Kantianism we understand all philosophical systems dependent on the transcendental philosophy of Immanuel Kant (1724–1804). Kant's philosophical development is generally divided into two periods. In the pre-critical period (1755–81), Kant remained on the traditional ground of the metaphysics of Leibniz and Wolff. But his dissertation of 1770 already contained elements which anticipated the structures of his *Critique of Pure Reason* (first published 1781, and then in a revised edition in 1787). Kant also expressed doubts as to the validity of *metaphysica specialis* in his polemical *Träume eines Geistersehers* ("Dreams of a man who sees ghosts"). The second period, that of his critiques, begins with the publication of the first in 1781.

In the philosophy of the late Middle Ages a cleavage had been made between sensible experience and thought by which the problem of human knowledge gradually became insoluble in philosophy. There was an empiricism which could affirm no essential or universal properties, but confined itself to the study of the associations between sense impressions. It was therefore chiefly Hume's criticism of the notions of substance and causality which awakened Kant from his "dogmatic slumbers". Then there was an intellectualism which spoke in terms of the essential and the universal, but based itself on innate concepts and hence was also alienated from experience, as in Descartes and Leibniz. Faced with this cleavage in the unity of human knowledge, Kant sought to restore the primordial unity of senses and intellect. Unlike Hume, however, Kant tried to revive classical metaphysics, though determined to do away with its existing "dogmatism", or traditional forms. His critical philosophy turns metaphysics into logic, but gives logical determinations an essentially subjective meaning. His philosophy is transcendental, not a philosophy of transcendence, whereas the ancient metaphysics claimed, according to Kant, to attain things "in themselves", that is, in what they "really" were — their transcendence. Kant affirmed that all knowledge was through *a priori* forms. He thus identified the conditions of possibility of being and of knowledge, since "the conditions of possibility of experience in general are likewise conditions of the possibility of the objects of experience". The "subjectivity" of Kant's philosophy is not, of course, that of individual subjective reactions. It is that of the logically transcendental, a law which is absolutely binding on every human mind. Hence the transcendental philosophy of Kant is an epistemology as well as a "metaphysics".

2. The central question of the *Critique of Pure Reason* is: How are synthetic *a priori* judgments possible? This is to pose the question of the possibility of metaphysics as a science, since "metaphysical knowledge must contain pure judgments *a priori*". If *a priori* knowledge was merely analytical, that is, merely meant that the predicate was contained in the subject, metaphysics could not extend knowledge in a way that would be both necessary and universal. Against the

empiricism of Hume and Locke, who interpreted the universal and necessary elements in scientific judgments as accidental habits of thought, Kant wishes to show that human knowledge contains elements which derive from that knowledge itself, which are equally valid for every thinking mind and hence are strictly necessary. This is the "Copernican revolution" in thought: knowledge is not directed by objects, but objects have to be directed by our knowledge. This is the only way in which to have *a priori* knowledge from metaphysics.

In the *Critique of Pure Reason,* Kant explains in the first part (the transcendental aesthetic) that though things appear with the forms of space and time, this does not imply any "absolute reality" of time and space, i.e., they are not concerned with the thing in itself. Space and time are *a priori* forms, that is, preceding all experience, which make up the constitution of our sense perception, insofar as our sensible perception makes intuition possible. The subjectivity of these forms of the intuition is, however, a "transcendental ideal", since it holds good for all human minds. From sensible intuition, human knowledge finally progresses to concepts and judgments. But for Kant, knowledge is intuition and concept, intuition plus thought. Thus, for Kant, the intellect achieves knowledge of the object within the realm of possible experience, by means of the concepts or categories. Sensible intuition is ordained to the categories for its fulfilment, so that the categories can constitute the objects in keeping with them, and produce knowledge of the objects. These are not objects "in themselves" but objects "for us" or "phenomena". Just as space and time are the *a priori* forms of all sensibility, to be used when this rises above a state to objective content, so too the categories are the principles of order in every finite mind, when it achieves objective experience. As the conditions for all finite objective experience, the categories are arrived at by a "transcendental deduction" (by having recourse to the constitutive elements preceding consciousness). Thus, in the Analytics, the second part of the *Critique,* Kant starts from the "I think" of the transcendental apperception to determine twelve categories, whose presence he also demonstrates from the analysis of the forms of judgment. But empirical and transcendental consciousness are not distinguished as consciousness and object. The empirical consciousness is of itself transcendental, insofar as it has knowledge and makes correct judgments.

For Kant, the categories and the objects are in the intellect. Its knowledge seems to be experience of the world. Its categories extend to and are valid for the sensible only and tell us nothing of a transcendental world, of the metaphysical, of the thing in itself. Kant sees all knowledge as beginning with the senses, continuing into the intellect and ending with the reason. Hence the third part of the *Critique,* the Dialectic, is devoted to the activity of the reason. The special activity of the reason, the drawing of conclusions, the discovery of the conditions whereby something is conditioned, leads Kant to assume the existence of "ideas". The Idea, (not to be confused with the Platonic form or idea) is a purely *a priori* concept, which transcends the possibility of experience. The ideas could be given content only by intellectual intuition, but this is beyond man. Hence the ideas cannot constitute the objects proper to them or give knowledge of such objects. They are left with only a regulative function, in as much as they orientate the objective knowledge of phenomena to the ultimate unities. Thus reason is the effort to think out the totality of the conditions for things, and the ideas are regulative, heuristic principles. The ideas of the I, the world and God function in this way, as the sum total of all conditions, and thus Kant returns to the great themes of the ancient metaphysics — the soul, God, the world, immortality, etc. Kant finds that the endeavour to think out such ideas inevitably ends in fallacies and antinomies. This transcendental point of view is developed in his doctrine of the four antinomies. In the same line of thought, he reduces all the traditional proofs for the existence of God to the ontological argument — an illegitimate transition from the logical to the ontological order. But this is not to deny the existence of God. It is just that for Kant the way to God by proofs of his existence is impassable.

3. The great questions of philosophy, according to Kant, are: What can I know? What must I do? What is man? He is not content with providing a new foundation for knowledge. In the *Critique of Practical Reason* (1788) in particular, he also defines the

nature of morality as an unconditional "must" against eudaemonism and utilitarianism. Ethical action, for Kant, is the free action of reason which is only free when it takes place independently of the senses, which constitute a foreign element. But reason, as a spontaneous spiritual faculty, is necessarily left without content by this division of receptivity from spontaneity, and can of itself perceive or receive no such content. The practical reason is only free when it determines itself by reason of itself, independently of sense. Thus the free self-determination of the practical reason must be purely formal. The moral will must be the will to pure will, to pure reason. But the pure practical reason is the purely empty form of necessity and universal validity. Only the will is morally good, insofar as it is determined by this form. From this transcendental consideration comes the notion of the "categorical imperative" and the formalism of Kant's ethics. It is a renunciation of all material goals and notions of value and order with specific content. Reason is its own sole law-giver.

It is through the moral action alone that Kant then opens up last the field of metaphysics. Because of its unconditional nature, the moral imperative is independent of the sensible world and goes beyond phenomena to the thing in itself or reality. At the same time, the endlessness of the moral task demands survival after death, the immortality of the soul. A further postulate of the practical reason is given by Kant as "freedom", which is disclosed as the pre-condition of obligation and demonstrates that we belong to the "intelligible world". Then there is the postulate of the existence of God. Though Kant rejects (eternal) happiness as a moral motive, he nonetheless recognizes it as the consequence of morality. Thus moral endeavour comprises, along with perfected morality, a proportional happiness. But for the provision of such happiness only God can be the "adequate cause". Kant sees in this argument from morality the only possible proof of the existence of God. But from beginning to end, theoretical knowledge remains without access to the intelligible order of what is "in itself". The metaphysical reality remains at the mercy of a faith in postulates which is not rationally explicable. Kant's narrow conception of knowledge, which was formed in the light of the exact sciences, places a cleavage between the theoretical and the practical reason. Their ultimate common root remains unexplored.

4. According to Kant, religion can only function within the bounds of pure reason. It is nothing else than morality. The universally valid *a priori* of revealed religion is the rational faith of morality, for which religion is merely a pedagogical preamble. The moral imperative and not a divine revelation is the real word of God within us. The question of the nature of Christianity becomes the question of a purely human, non-historical idea, a Christianity without Jesus or Church, and also without a history of salvation. In Kant's eyes, all religious and ecclesiastical life, beyond the purely ethical service of God, is a "spurious service of God in a statutory religion". Christianity is then reduced to a religion teaching good behaviour, in which Jesus appears as the "man whose mind is set on God" and thus the model of moral perfection. Those who strive to imitate this ethical example will have a "common ethical being" in the Church, though this is not at all a necessary consequence.

5. Though the substitution of the subject for the object in the transcendental philosophy of Kant was of immense importance for all subsequent philosophy, he was not the initiator of a "school" of philosophy in the strict sense. But without the question posed by Kant German idealism would be inconceivable (Fichte, Schelling, Hegel). The neo-Kantianism which was prevalent in Germany from 1870–1920 devoted its attention chiefly to working out a theory of science in the sense of Kant (the Marburg School). A methodology of the historical sciences was developed by W. Windelband. History was seen as the result of specific methods of constituting the object of science (a notion which influenced M. Weber, E. Troeltsch, G. Simmel). In social philosophy and the philosophy of law the influence of Kant can be traced in many ways, from the neo-Kantian socialism of Cohen to the "pure theory of law" of H. Kelsen. The thought of Kant attained great importance in Catholic scholasticism through J. Maréchal and his followers. Maréchal sought for a synthesis between the transcendental philosophy of Kant and the metaphysics of Thomas Aquinas. His effort has been of great significance in modern theology.

See also *Empiricism, Knowledge, Experience, Metaphysics, Transcendental Philosophy, Time, Concept, Idea, Categories, God* III, *Freedom, Scholasticism* II.

BIBLIOGRAPHY. H. Cohen, *Kants Begründung der Ethik nebst ihren Anwendungen auf das Recht, Religion und Geschichte* (1877); E. Cassirer, *Kant's First Critique* (from the German of 1918) (1955); G. Simmel, *Kant* (5th ed., 1921); N. Kemp Smith, *Commentary on Kant's Critique of Pure Reason* (2nd revised and enlarged ed., 1923, reprint 1963); J. Maréchal, *Le point de départ de la métaphysique,* 5 vols. (1923–26); M. Heidegger, *Kant und das Problem der Metaphysik* (1929); K. Rahner, *Geist in Welt* (1939); R. Daval, *La métaphysique de Kant* (1951); M. Scheler, *Der Formalismus in der Ethik und die materiale Wertethik* (4th ed., 1964); J. B. Lotz, ed., *Kant und die Scholastik heute* (1955); W. D. Ross, *Kant's Ethical Theory* (1954); G. Martin, *Kant's Metaphysics and Theory of Science* (1955); M. Heidegger, *Kants These über das Sein* (1963); id., *Die Frage nach dem Ding. Zu Kant's Lehre von den transzendentalen Grundsätzen* (1963); G. Rabel, *Kant, A Study* (1963); H. Paton, *Categorical Imperative: A Study in Kant's Moral Philosophy* (5th ed., 1965).

Kurt Krenn

KERYGMA

1. Concept. The Greek term κηρύσσω was adopted by the NT writers (mostly in the form of the noun κήρυγμα) and used to signify in a specifically biblical way a central reality of Christianity. It can indeed be regarded as one of the key concepts for the description of revelation. Neither the OT (where the most frequent corresponding term was קרא) nor the NT explain the term explicitly, but the usage is clear enough. The word, as a substantive, denotes both the act and the message, and ranges in meaning from "address" and "call out" to "summons"; in English the word is either transliterated or rendered as "preaching", though for this latter, which has in general the implication of a doctrinal and moral exposition, the word "proclamation" is often used.

2. Scripture. In a remarkable departure from the ordinary approach to reality and from the traditions of classical philosophy, the NT writers are profoundly inspired by the conviction that "salvation" is essentially linked with the "word". And there the "word" is not just information about a salvation which might be in itself and in its manifesta-

tions "wordless". Salvation is understood as the reality of the word: God himself in his epiphany is word and expresses himself as such. In this sense, kerygma is the word of salvation, understood as the word which is constitutive for the coming of salvation. The challenge of the OT prophets and finally and supremely that of Jesus of Nazareth and his envoys was not merely that they spoke of God's name or in God's name, but that God himself spoke in their words – in such a way that all, speakers and hearers, understood that salvation or loss depended on responsive self-commitment to the word of God. This coming of the word, understood as coming of salvation, is given more or less prominence and expressed in various ways in the NT writings. But in general it may be said that kerygma is the proclamation of salvation *as* the real coming of the kingdom of God (Mt 4:23; Lk 9:12). It is deliverance (Acts 8:5; 9:20), grace (Acts 20:32), reconciliation (2 Cor 5:19) and truth (Col 1:5; Eph 1:13) for men. Whatever forms the kerygma takes, it is always the expression of one thing only: the "word of Christ" (Rom 10:17), which is the origin and medium and object of the whole kerygma (as event). Since the Lord himself presents himself in the kerygma, it judges and justifies and is bringer of salvation. Hence as it affirms itself as true and life-giving, it can also summon to confident faith and then empower those who are convinced of and filled by this word of the Lord to speak in turn in the same way, so that their mission is summed up in the words: "He who hears you hears me" (Lk 10:16). In this way the kerygma is constitutive of the Church as the fellowship of those who hear and follow the word of God (Mt 8:12). Hence the kerygma, as an event which takes place in and through the "word of Christ" is at once historical and suprahistorical. It is the presence of the past and the future, of the temporal and the eternal. It is the one Lord who did his work as Jesus of Nazareth, who dwells as Spirit in his own and is to come as the Lord of glory. In this threefold way the Lord is the living and present though hidden Lord in the kerygma.

3. Theological reflection. These basic characteristics of the NT understanding of the kerygma at once throw light on the comprehensive nature of the kerygma as a dialogal and dialectical reality. The Lord is the subject and object and medium — in an analogous way: in one way as Jesus of Nazareth "obedient in the flesh" and in another way as the risen Lord. So too those who preach in Christ are themselves in their own way subject and object and medium of the kerygmatic event. Paul, for instance, is the subject who preaches, the medium of the preaching and also, in an analogous way, the object of his preaching, inasmuch as he has recourse to his experiences with the Lord. In this twofold mediation, already of itself analogous, which not merely takes place in the kerygma but is itself actually the kerygma, there takes place the free act of God and the free act of man as a totality interwoven in each other. Thus the twofold mediation proves to be once more mediated. This dialectic of mediation, which is personal as well as instrumental, and which may be termed dialogal, is a kerygmatic event both in the sphere of metaphysical principles and of the concrete historical.

Hence, qua historical, and thus involved in the contradictions of history by virtue of original sin and guilt, the kerygma is submitted to a new dialectic: the tension — in terms of glory as well as of logic — between true mediation of salvation and culpable barring of salvation. The primordial salvific and kerygmatic mediation through the cross and resurrection of Jesus, when historically mediated as kerygma, is once more crucified by history and must rise again in this dimension, if the message of salvation is to be fully unfolded. Resurrection and cross, as dialogue and dialectic, combine once more on the plane of history to give at last the fullness of the dimensions — dialogal and dialectical — of the kerygma. They are the dimensions of a dialogal and dialectical historical mediation where there is an interplay of the eschatological and the linear, the doxological and the objective, the personal and the material, the socially public and the pneumatically charismatic, the officially determined and the creatively free. All these elements of the kerygmatic event act and react on each other and are finally to "sublimate" all contradictions in a genuine harmony. Hence the kerygma is a reality which is at once its own subject and object in the medium which it itself is. It forms — in the metaphysical and in the historical and dialogal dimensions described above — a reality which mediates salvation and which under-stands itself as such. It sees its origin and its goal, its being and its purpose and thus its subject, object and medium — its whole nature as mediation — as given in the "word of Christ", its only possible ground.

It is understandable that the many dimensions of this dialogal and dialectical reality should have been approached on many levels and in different ways by the NT writers. And it is still more readily understood that the subsequent practical exercise of preaching in the history of the Church should always have been and be in danger of a one-sided self-understanding, not merely theologically, but with reference to its own life and origin. There is a tendency to simplify a gift and a task which is multi-dimensional. The act of preaching may be misunderstood. A one-sided emphasis may be laid on the act of preaching as merely the work of God. Its dimension of personal dialogue and pneumatic dynamism may be obscured by that of its merely factual occurrence. On the Protestant side, there is a tendency, on the public level, to an altruism centred on God in the preaching which may occasion a non-dialogical dualism. On the Catholic side, in modern times, there is a strong tendency towards an institutional and factual historicism. Such erroneous trends are numerous and could be verified in the history of the kerygma in the Church (and the Churches). Fundamentally, they coincide with the great public or cryptogram heresies or reflect them on the kerygmatic level.

The question of the nature and the reality of the kerygma has become much more acute today, when the preaching is faced with a situation which is becoming more and more difficult. And there are philosophical complications. Some are the heritage of German idealism, with its understanding of the constitutive contribution of consciousness to reality in general, which raised still more sharply the whole question of the possibility of revelation. Others arise from existentialism, with its view of the constitutive nature of concrete historical self-understanding for the understanding of reality in general. Finally, there are the questions raised by the historical criticism and exegetical discussion of a relentless biblical research. But all this has helped in fact to show the problem of the kerygma in its true light, since it now appears as the question of revelation in general, its historical mediation and its self-understanding in ecclesiastical, biblical and dogmatic contexts.

In this situation, where the Protestant preaching of the faith seemed to have reached an impasse, R. Bultmann sought to find an answer with the aid of existential philosophy, in an effort to do justice to the understanding of man and the world conditioned by present-day science and technology, and also to the demands of historical exegesis. His "existential interpretation" which undertook a systematic "demythologizing" of the NT, succeeded in fact in depriving revelation of its historical content. Revelation, as mediation of salvation, became essentially the summons given here and now in the actual preaching, the summons itself being the "Christ-event" which calls the hearer to decide in the act of faith. The consequences of this principle are not taken to their logical conclusion by Bultmann, and it is hard to say what precise theological meaning he attached to this "Christ-event" as the act of preaching. But it is certain that the kerygma is now given a very definitely central place, which involves a very definite theology of the kerygma. However, the complexity of the notion of kerygma, as propounded in the NT, is certainly deprived of its full dimension when the kerygma, as in Bultmann, is viewed merely as the event of the summons in the here and now of the preaching, since its mediated character, historical both dialogically and dialectically, is not sufficiently taken into account, and the material content of its traditional character also suffers.

But this theology of the kerygma has the merit of excluding an objectivating misunderstanding of the kerygma which would reduce the word of God and its mediation to a mere report supplying information about the past. The kerygma ceases to be the abstraction of mere narrative of the past as such, and appears emphatically as the event of the word of God, a salvific event of personal attestation, pneumatic dynamism and eschatological presence. But to arrive at this it was not necessary to exclude *a priori* the historical content of the NT and its transmission in the Church as unimportant or not part of the data. No doubt there is a dialectic in the public, social, official and institutional mediation of the kerygma-event, as there is in the apostolically authorized ecclesiastical form of its legitimation. In spite of authorization and legitimation from the official Church, the

kerygma can be distorted and diminished by the preachers, not so much in the letter as in the spirit. But such possible tension cannot be obviated beforehand by simply excluding the historically objective and hence also official and institutional dimension of the kerygma. This dialectic is not set up for the first time by Church preaching in the wider sense. It has its origin in the initial commitment of the word of God to writing as sacred Scripture. This is a clear proof that the full understanding of the kerygma is ultimately dependent on the understanding of the incarnation and of revelation in general.

The discussion launched by Bultmann still goes on, even among Catholics. But if theological thinking is to make an advance in this sphere, it must first leave behind the ill-considered and inadequate contrast between "act and content" in the kerygma. To counter the revival of the "subject-object-transcendence" schema in existential philosophy, it must develop a dialogal theory of history of salvation which will throw more light on the historically objective as the medium of intersubjectivity and hence as medium of the history of salvation. Such a theory, embracing all the dimensions of the kerygmatic event, will at last be able to throw light on the glorified body as medium of the historical coming of salvation, and hence the significance of the glorified body for the kerygma. This would lead to a better understanding of the relationship of word and sacrament in the mediation of salvation and kerygma. Whatever form this dialectical theology of the history of salvation may take, Catholics will see the kerygma in the actual life of the Church as a mediation of salvation which takes place essentially in a sacramental event which is also the action of the word. Its supreme form is the liturgy, especially the celebration of the Eucharist in its framework of prayer, Scripture reading, exhortation and homily: the most real presence possible, in the "time of the Church", of the crucified and risen Lord and of the salvation of all in him.

See also *Revelation, Word, Redemption* I, IV, *History* I, *Resurrection, Idealism, Existence* II, III, *Demythologization, Eucharist, Liturgy.*

BIBLIOGRAPHY. G. Friedrich, "κηρύσσω", *TWNT,* III, pp. 683–718; G. Goldammer, "Der Kerygma-Begriff in der ältesten christlichen Literatur", *Zeitschrift für die neutestamentliche Wissenschaft* 48 (1957), pp. 77–101; O. Kuss, *Auslegung und Verkündigung* (1963); H. Schürmann and K. Rahner, "Kerygma", *LTK,* VI, cols. 122–6; G. Ebeling, *Word and Faith* (1963); A. Vögtle, *Werden und Wesen der Evangelien* (2nd ed., 1964); O. Semmelroth, *Preaching Word* (1965); H. Ott, *Theology and Preaching* (1965); G. Ebeling, *Theology and Proclamation* (1966); E. Simons, "Die Bedeutung der Hermeneutik für die katholische Theologie", *Grenzfragen des Glaubens* (1967), pp. 277–302.

Eberhard Simons

KINGDOM OF GOD

See *Reign of God.*

KNOWLEDGE

A. KNOWLEDGE AS A PROBLEM

1. *The self-acceptance of knowledge and of scepticism.* The question of the "nature" of knowledge, as posed in philosophy, is itself aimed at knowledge, that is, at knowledge about knowledge. If it is posed as a meaningful and rational question, it positively anticipates the possibility of knowledge, and accepts itself as knowledge and has thereby begun to give concrete reality to the nature of knowledge. To put the problem and solve it by denying that knowledge is possible in any identifiable sense is to pretend to know and understand what knowledge is, and at the same time use it to maintain that it does not exist, concluding that the problem of knowledge is not merely insoluble but non-existent. Hence absolute scepticism cancels itself out. Its intrinsic contradiction has been constantly proved against it in the course of the history of philosophy, in classical form by Augustine (*Contra Academicos; Soliloquium,* II, 1, no. 1; *De vera religione,* 39, no. 73; *De Civitate Dei,* XI, 26; *De Trinitate,* X, 10, no. 14; cf. Descartes, *Meditationes de Prima Philosophia;* Kant, *Logik,* Introduction, X). The decision of the spirit to evade all effort to attain knowledge of reality does not lead to the concentrated repose of self-possession. It is the abdication and self-dissolution of the spirit. For the spirit would be unreal and futile if it did not know what really is and could not know its own existence and nature in such knowledge of reality.

But it is legitimate to be (relatively) sceptical with regard to particular forms of knowledge which claim in fact to be valid, and with regard to the self-analyses of these particular forms. Even in such analyses there is always

the danger of not getting behind the naive claim to validity and testing it against its valid foundation. One could remain at the stage of naive reflection, where the theory of the validity of such acts of knowledge would be merely dogmatism. Hence it is legitimate to enquire into the particular structure of the various forms of knowledge, their relevant fields and the sources from which they derive their effectiveness. But all such questions are combined in the basic question as to the extent, nature and unifying origin of all knowledge qua knowledge.

2. *Epistemology as the logic of ontology.* Hence it would be just as absurd as absolute scepticism to seek even a positive solution from a standpoint outside knowledge, that is, "to try to know ... before one knows". "The examination of knowledge can only take place in acts of knowledge", as Hegel said, trenchantly underlining the fact that all questions about knowledge are themselves knowledge (*Enzyklopädie,* § 10, in the course of an objection, too severely framed to be sustainable, against the critical philosophy inaugurated by Kant). "Total absence of presuppositions" in the investigation of knowledge can only mean that the process presupposes nothing but knowledge itself (*ibid.,* § 78). It must admit such presuppositions as stem intrinsically from knowledge as such and its individual forms, and hence must be accepted by it as its own presuppositions. With this, Hegel has only said in his own way what Western philosophy has been aware of from the beginning: that the question of "what is" always included the question as to what knowledge itself was and what the spirit itself was in such knowledge of "what is".

It is true, however, that the question only became fully explicit and of primary interest when philosophy took its transcendental turn in modern times. The "ignorance" which Socrates and Plato put at the beginning of all knowledge, including philosophy and epistemology, does not mean that the mind is totally sundered from the reality which is to come to it in knowledge. It is the initial stage of this coming, as knowledge, the veiled but irrecusable presence of what is to be known: a dawning knowlege which is still ignorant, or an ignorance which is dawning knowledge. Later efforts of theories of knowledge to get behind all knowledge and try to see whether and how the "subject" supposed to be closed in on itself can emerge from the immanence of its "consciousness" and attain knowledge of an "object" transcending it (reality, being), are mistaken from the start. For spirit is by its very nature a thinking relationship (intentionality) to beings, the gathering-in *(logos)*, the co-ordination *(cogitatio)*, that which "takes in" beings

3. *Formal logic and the real logic of epistemology.* If the philosophy of knowledge is basically the "logic" of ontology, it is a "material" or "real" logic in contradistinction to "formal" logic, which merely investigates the "formal rules" of all thought couched in propositions. Formal logic analyses the laws of "how" articulate thought connects its possible content — in the formation of concepts, judgments and conclusions — in order to be in harmony with itself, logically "true" or rather, "correct". It prescinds from the concrete content of its thought,

from the relationship of the proposition to "what" (elements of reality) should be comprehended. Thus a proposition may be correct in formal logic but not necessarily in accord with reality and hence not necessarily knowledge, for which it displays the indispensable conditions without being the adequate cause. Such logic considers the thought of the knower "one-sidedly", from its formal aspect, though with its own stringency.

Epistemology as material or real logic investigates the "conditions" for knowledge from the point of view of its concrete content, by which it is grasp of a real "something" if it is knowledge, and hence also comes under the conditions of the object known. But epistemology also obeys the laws of formal logic, not just spontaneously, but with the most rigorous attention. For the basic principles of propositions, which are abstracted by formal logic, are now interpreted in the sense in which they are "also" principles of being in things themselves. This identity is investigated as the ultimate source of the possibility of knowledge — the source which as formal is also real. And the logic which confines itself to the abstract, formal aspect of thought, is likewise not merely logically accurate. It is knowledge, the real grasp of formal rules, the abstract aspect of all comprehension. As conscious reflection on itself, this logic is more than the thought on which it reflects. When formal logic is made to reflect comprehensively on itself, it must also explain the sense in which its rules are "given it", in what sense these formal laws "are there". In such reflection it ceases to be merely formal logic and becomes real, it is epistemology as metaphysical and ontological philosophy of knowledge. When formal logic, in the legitimate pursuit of assurance of accuracy, merely reflects one-sidedly on itself, that is, when it restricts itself once more to the formal and abstract aspect of the knowledge which it actually is, it begins a regressive process of self-formalizing and becomes a meta-logic etc. of itself.

4. *The primordial nature of epistemology and its link with historical tradition.* Epistemology, intent though it is on taking cognizance of its present object, is likewise orientated to its own historical past. Like all philosophy, it must always begin anew, and still be mediated by tradition, since there are no

fresh starts and new perspectives simply in immediate contact with the object. They must also be won through the critical examination and the transformative reception of the history of philosophy. Epistemology too has a general understanding of itself and its object, knowledge, from history, an understanding which it must accept or transform critically, but cannot simply skip. The supposedly fresh start from a zero unaffected by history is merely the naive concentration on a conceptual knowledge of which the traditional character is not recognized, and to which it remains willy-nilly tributary, merely by speaking of "knowledge", "philosophy of knowledge", "principles and methods of knowledge", or by contrasting abstract and concrete, subject and object, consciousness and reality and so on. Hence insight into the historical character of the philosophy of knowledge, of philosophy and of knowledge as such in all forms is part of epistemology today.

B. NATURE AND FORMS OF KNOWLEDGE

The basic self-understanding of knowledge, as investigated and explained in the metaphysics of knowledge and as maintained peremptorily throughout its history and its various interpretations, is the understanding of being and spirit as identical: τὸ γὰρ αὐτὸ νοεῖν ἐστίν τε καὶ εἶναι (Parmenides, Fr. 3; Diels-Kranz, *Fragmente der Vorsokratiker*, I [11th ed., 1964], p. 231); "cognoscens ens in actu est ipsum cognitum in actu" (Thomas Aquinas, *In Aristotelis librum de anima*, II, lect. XII; cf. Aristotle, *De anima*, III, 5; 430a, 20, τὸ δ᾽ αὐτό ἐστιν ἡ κατ᾽ ἐνέργειαν ἐπιστήμη τῷ πράγματι; "the conditions of the possibility of experience of objects are the conditions of the possibility of the objects of experience" (Kant, *Critique of Pure Reason*, B 137); "the real is the rational" (Hegel, *Philosophie des Rechts*, E. T.: *Philosophy of Right* [1942], preface).

It is the same with the basic divisions of the forms and degrees of knowledge. The particular historical forms of epistemology can be given their proper place in the history of metaphysics when we see what forms and degrees of knowledge obtained some predominance through them, or became patterns for the interpretation of knowledge in general. In the light of history, the antimetaphysical epistemologies appear as fixations of a type of knowledge or of a partial moment of it, and sometimes as epistemologies which deny that knowledge can be meaningful in itself. Thus they deny that knowledge is simply the presence of the thing known to the knower and vice versa, that it consists of this common, reciprocal presence and is truth in, of and for itself. They try to have all possible knowledge, that is, actuation of presence and truth, referred to an end outside itself and measured by its adaptability to this end (as, for example, in pragmatism).

1. *Sensible knowledge, perception or experience in the strict sense.* Knowledge begins with its most obvious and everyday form, man endowed with sense-perception encountering consciously a concrete object, a being perceptible to the senses which is "outside" as something else. This is the perception of external data, or, since it is in a certain manner man himself, as a bodily being in his interiority, it is the perception of his "inner" state. This perception, the "external" and "inner experience" or sensible knowledge, is not simply bombardment by a disordered multiplicity of stimuli and hence the structureless reception of a chaotic mass of sensible data. Nor does such a process of reception of a mere multiplicity of elementary data precede temporally and objectively the perception as such and condition it, as the atomizing psychology of the 19th century supposed. If so, perception would only be the aggregate of such elements combined according to certain laws which again would need repeated perceptions and the comparison of their similarities and dissimilarities before they could be recognized (associative psychology). But the multiplicity of sensible elements and the mere mass perception corresponding to it are in fact secondary abstractions from the one concrete act of perception and its object, which is immediately perceived as this or that in such and such a determined form. It is perceived as a "sensible thing" comprised by a unifying "spiritual" meaning; it is perceived *as* some thing (identical with this meaning).

No doubt such perceptions "as" this or that have different degrees of definiteness, attentiveness or "consciousness" in various acts in the course of human life. Particular objects of perception can stand out or recede among the field of perceptible things. But an isolated process of "mere" sense-perception is not an independent primary element of human perception. If it did occur, it would be a radical destruction of the human character of sense perception. Even in infra-human, animal "perception" we must not suppose such feelings as primary processes to be taken in isolation. They must be supposed to be comprised and permeated by a prior "instinctive meaning" which is a factor of their constitution, given in the sense-structure of each different animal. In human perception too the encounters by which it is affected are mostly taken in their significance for the "sensual", instinctive life of man — as helpful or not towards a particular end serving the general maintenance and promotion of "vital" (biological) existence. But first of all, human perception can detach itself from the bond of this "vital structure" and concentrate its attention solely on the aspects of the thing perceived which are independent of its possible relationship to any particular sensual and instinctive complex. And secondly, in human intercourse with reality, even the "vital" relevance of what is encountered is based on a self-disclosure of what is encountered. It displays what it means in itself, prior to any vital relevance, which is, therefore, based on perception in the strict sense, as acceptance of the arrival itself as presence. For the setting-up of vital relationships in man is not an automatic and instinctive process. It is mediated and determined by this acceptance, which is the perception of a sensible arrival, but also of some thing significant in itself. ("Because the arrival is this and that and does such and such, it is suitable or useless for this or that purpose which I undertake.")

Perception as acceptance is not a merely "sensible" passivity, receptivity to impressions. It is also actuated by an active anticipation (spontaneity) with regard to this possibly significant something, by an out-going expectation of a possible "nature" proper to the arrival itself. It is only by reason of this factor of expectation that the arrival can display itself as the presence of a determinate being in perception. If this active expectation of essential significance is understood and characterized as a moment of the spirit, then, in the one act of perception, the sensible and the spiritual are not to be considered as two ingredients which were once realities in themselves. They are such

that they are what they are only in this reciprocal reference and their common and indivisible actuation. Just as that which is met with in perception is never totally indeterminate matter to which later a certain meaningful form can be imparted (εἶδος, μορφή, forma, significant content), but of itself is an informed and structured material thing; so too human sensibility is never a "pure" sensibility (only conceivable in the abstract and as a limit-concept) and never a purely instinctive and biologically determined sensibility. Of itself it is always "more" than instinctive or pure sensibility; it is "spiritual" sensibility. Hence men's instincts cannot be analysed merely by comparison with those of the brutes, but must further be seen in the setting of the "spiritualized" sense-perception of man, which likewise runs through his instinctive effort to survive and expand. In the same way, man as spirit is intrinsically and indissolubly a sensible being.

Hence the first act of his "spiritual sensibility" (or spirit in sense), perception, is at once the identification of "this" which arrives with its essential meaning ("what this is"), an identification which combines "in the consciousness" what is understood as occurring together in the thing perceived, in its "being", and which can be expressed in the perceptive apprehension. Hence too the process of knowledge always begins with perception, with this identification explicit in the apprehension, the σύνθεσις which claims to correspond to the σύνθεσις in the thing perceived itself and indeed to be "identical" with it. Hence reflection on knowledge implies ontological theses from the start (with regard to the structure of beings insofar as they are met with in perception and "as what" they are so met). And there are also anthropological theses (with regard to the structure of man as sense-spirit, insofar as he knows beings in perception and in what guise). When Gestalt-psychology, in opposition to the atomistic and associative (and their repercussions on epistemology) stressed the character of wholeness, form and significant content in human perception, and the meaningfulness of the objects of perception, it was really enriching once more the psychology of perception with an insight traditional in metaphysics from the start and which had always had to defend itself against similar objections and distortions, such as those of the atomist theories of antiquity and of later sensism.

The first traits of beings present to perception are their temporal and spatial ones. In view of what has been said, the spatial and temporal characteristics of the thing perceived are not just extrinsic properties adhering to a merely material aggregate object, or forms applied by a disparate, "abstract" sensibility in the subject, but constituent notes of the beings perceived and known, and modes of presence of the rational-sensible beings, men, who perceive and know. The critique of Kant distinguishes sharply between the faculties of receptive sensibility and spontaneous spirit (intellect, reason), though they only bring about perceptional knowledge in co-operation. For Kant, space and time are not significant forms of the spirit or understanding, but primarily only forms of the "mindless" receptive sensibility. Their "common root" with the spiritual must be divined, but remains unfathomable. In spite of this isolation and the obscurity of the supposed common ground, Kant considers the (spatio-temporal) combination (σύνθεσις) in sensibility as the effect of spirit (intellect) on sensibility (cf. *Critique of Pure Reason*, B 152).

Anthropologically, this separation and inexplicable relationship of spirit and sense in Kant means that man is treated as a spiritual and also sensible entity, while knowledge strictly speaking is only perceptive knowledge or is restricted to the reality of perception and to reflection on and explanation of the perception of reality (i.e., to theory). But the reality in question is not really the homeland of man, and the knowledge is not really a human act. And again, the essentials of man are confined to the spirit, which is an entirely non-sensible realm above and beyond sensibility. Indeed, the truly human act is spiritual representation devoid of sensible elements, and this realm of presence is man's true homeland. But it is a realm which is apart from the reality of things, and what comes to be present there is not knowledge in the strict ("theoretical") sense, but "only" in a practical sense.

Ontologically it follows that the beings met with in perception are not beings as they are in themselves ("the thing in itself"), but only as they are for the sentient subject: not that that makes them different beings, since they are the beings themselves, but only in their appearances (as phenomena). The phenomenon-reality of perception is not the essential reality, but the reality amenable to physics and mathematical sciences in spatio-temporal relationships. And the phenomenal (and hence knowable) spatial and temporal relationships of a being are not significant elements of its (unknowable) essence. Pre-critical (and likewise post-Kantian) metaphysical philosophy interpreted sensibility as a mode of being of spirit itself in the oneness of man, the perceptible appearance of a being as something belonging to what it was in itself spatio-temporal relationships as proprieties of its essence. They were "qualities" of the thing perceived which combined with other qualities to make up "what" it was and show how it was partly of the same nature as other beings and partly different. Hence the qualities, as moments and consequences of the essence, are "concepts" which, in perception, are attributed to what is met with as specific proprieties, constitutive of and consequent to its substantial nature, in which it coincides with other beings of the same nature. And they are also attributed to it as individual and changeable, and hence as "unessential" characteristics of its nature, differentiations by which it stands out from its class.

Hence perception is always the identification of what is met with with generalities already understood and known "in concepts". Nominalism and conceptualism treat these generalities as "mere" names and "pure" concepts. They are just convenient labels, individual or collective, to help one to master the multiplicity of things. But the concept is not something that appertains merely to the ("subjective") mind in a wrongly understood immanence, and the common essence is not something that appertains only to things in their wrongly understood transcendence. And hence if the concept is the "there-ness" of subject and object combined, the "presence in essence" of the knower and the known, the question now is how the essence is actuated in the concept and the concept in its essence. It is not only a matter of individual acts of perception, in which an arrival is perceived "as" this or that, identified with some generality already known. It is a matter of how this universal essence can become known, how this grasping of the essence is itself possible. The answer of empiricism (positivism) is that the so-called essence only exists through perception itself, that conceptual knowledge of essence only comes about as a consequence of perception and as perception in the comparison of perceptions. But all comparison of perceptions ultimately presupposes something that cannot be simply explained as perception.

2. *Experience in the wider sense and scientific experience*. Experience in the strict sense, individual perception or sensible knowledge, is the estimation of something that shows itself directly here and now, to the effect that it is and is thus and thus behaves. The estimation, which may be formulated in the percipient judgment, has the character of immediate certainty and validity, momentary and localized (in the individual subject) though it be. Hence it cannot be directly affected by another judgment, but only contradicted, modified or confirmed by further perceptions. The comparison of similarities and differences in a number of perceptions, the memory of past perceptions and the expectation of perceptions only now taking place or still to come, constitute experience in the wider sense. It is not the knowledge that something met with is there, is just so and behaves just so, but knowledge of natures and rules of behaviour as they are interconnected in a whole realm of possible objects of the same or similar type. It can be formulated in a "judgment based on long experience". It has the character of a certainty transmitted by such a process of experience, of an assurance of consistency in significant relationships, results and patterns of behaviour. It provides a "pragmatically" adequate insight, since it alone guarantees realism and hence success in adapting to various ends what may and usually does happen in a given sphere. And this insight can be transmitted as a set of propositions, and even to a certain extent be taught to others, discussed and enlarged. In this sense we speak of practical professional knowledge, especially in handicrafts, of knowledge of men, experience of life and so on.

Based on experience in the strict and wider sense, but on a higher plane, there is the knowledge of scientific experience. It is not the immediate grasp of something "there" by grasping "how" it presents itself. It is not the necessarily somewhat naive acquaintanceship with the significant relationships and regular

laws of a given field of possible objects of experience. It means knowing "why" these possible objects must so appear and behave, "how" they may be met with in individual perception and also referred to each other in general experience. Scientific knowledge is objective knowledge of causes and effects in their necessary links. Hence it is not merely possible and useful to formulate it as a judgment, but it presents itself expressly as a self-explaining judgment which is the justification of its strict scientific certainty and intersubjective validity. This justification is twofold. It is the appeal to facts and ostensible causal connections which can be verified by repeated experiment. It is also — since even these experiences are comprehended in the judgment — an appeal to further judgment on which a scientific judgment is based. Just as the matter considered is in co-ordination with other matters, so too the scientific judgment is subsumed into a co-ordinated group of judgments, that is, into a "system" of scientific knowledge, the science of the subject in question. The facts of experience are not ascertained in the more or less random way of individual occurrences, and then linked together as in general experience. They are traced and arranged according to a planned perspective of research and expressly ascertained rules. Scientific knowledge is knowledge methodically gained. In the judgments of immediate perception and general experience, the concepts used for the characteristics considered are derived from the sense mainly expressed in ordinary language, and hence there is a wide variation in the meaning of the words used for them, because this vocabulary has to be able to meet all possible situations. But the meaning of scientific concepts and terms is strictly confined to the limited possibilities of the scientific field in question. The scientific judgment aims at the greatest possible clearness (univocity) of its concepts.

Even individual perception does not apprehend the whole nature of the beings it encounters with the same intensity as regards all their significant elements. It emphasizes this or that trait of the thing. So too in general experience in a given field. There is no comprehensive grasp of the common nature of possible occurrences in this field, but certain characteristic structural essentials are more strongly grasped than others. Scientific knowledge, on the other hand, confines itself from the start to a possible field of experience (the "material object"), which it envisages only in the perspective of a chosen set of characteristic notes and relationships. And this choice is strictly defined and unified from a certain aspect (the "formal object"). The scientist prescinds from all other possible traits of the material object, though such traits can be then taken as the formal objects of other sciences of the same material object. Thus the formal object of a science does not coincide with the "concrete" fullness of meaning in its object; and this means that even in the hypothesis of a completed science we should not have exhaustive knowledge of the "whole" essential meaning of its object. The self-restriction of a science to a definite section of the totality of meaning is what provides it with a clear set of concepts to work with, and with its specific method. Even if we suppose that all experimental knowledge has the same material object, the objects of possible perception, and that a plurality of material objects (scientific fields like "nature" and "history") only comes from a preliminary singling out of aspects ("formalizing") when, for instance, the object of perception is taken "as" having come about naturally or "as" having been produced by men in history: even then the sciences are fundamentally distinct, at least according to their formal objects (their basic interest) and hence in method and conceptual framework. Hence no method or mental frame can claim "universal validity": we cannot speak of *the* scientific method or mind. The effort to reduce all scientific method and concepts to one single type (the so-called monism of method and concept) would not be helpful. It would be the pruning away of possible knowledge to leave only one possibility, which would be to renounce the multiple access offered by knowledge to the richness of meaning of beings.

On the other hand, the fact that each science is restricted by its sectional formal intention to being "partial knowledge" does not mean that the mere sum of the findings of particular sciences or a subsequent systematic effort to combine them provides at once "total knowledge" of a field of scientific reality. An attempt, for instance, to integrate all historical disciplines into one general history does not furnish knowledge of "all" history and historical reality as a whole. So too with the natural sciences. This is not merely because,

as in the case of history, the object of knowledge is not (yet) finally there, or because, in general, scientific findings can and must be expanded and are never rounded off. It is primarily because the aggregate and systematic combination of the formal objects, of natural science and history, for instance, never gives the full essence of nature and history, much less of "beings in their totality". Conscious experience, in the strict and wider sense, of nature and history, in spite of the different emphasis resulting from more or less accidental occurrences, in spite of its dependence on the various individual qualities of the multiplicity of reality and on the individual personal interests of the observers, is always "more" than scientific knowledge can present to the "inter-subjective" consciousness, even through an organized division of labour and its co-ordinated and definite acquisitions.

3. *Knowledge of essence and a priori knowledge.* Empirical knowledge, as it appears in the judgment, is the conceptual, generalized and permanent mode of presence of possible individual items (of the knower and the known) which enter and disappear from this presence. Empirical scientific knowledge gains its definite validity by doing its utmost to restrict its concepts to such significant moments as occur in strictly the same way in each experience, and hence can be verified by repetition of the experience. Hence this knowledge consists of the formation of concepts, insofar as it is the demarcation and clarification of concepts against the background of less restricted, more comprehensive, "more general" concepts. But it is not the pure and simple production of concepts. Empirical knowledge, especially in scientific experience, has also presuppositions which it recognizes but cannot work at with the concepts and methods of its own discipline — because knowledge of the suppositions cannot come in the same way as what is known on the basis of these presuppositions. These are "subjective" and "logical" as well as "objective" and "ontological". The more comprehensive concepts presupposed in all the restrictive judgments of scientific knowledge, especially the notion of a field of experience such as "nature" or "history", represent the mental horizon within which scientific knowledge works to form and combine concepts. But this mental horizon

as such is not explained and interpreted in its totality by the science in question. The natural sciences, for instance, investigate what can be found in "nature" under various restricted aspects. But they do not investigate the more comprehensive notion of "nature" here presupposed. So too history of art is preoccupied with the events of the "history", but not with the notion of "artistic happening" as such. And all such self-limiting scientific knowledge proceeds with an inkling, a proleptic notion of what "knowledge" in general means, but is unable to explain the concept of "knowledge" in its full significance. On the contrary, it restricts it to certain determined processes of registering knowledge.

The self-understanding of conceptual knowledge includes the insight that the concepts do not merely mean themselves, but that they bring the beings referred to into the presence of knowledge, with regard to certain of their essential characteristics. So too the more general concepts in the presuppositions include, as present in consciousness, the integrating totality of the "essence" of the being in question (e.g., the "essence" of nature, of inanimate beings, of plants and animals, the "essence" of art, history and so on). This knowledge of essences and the formation of such "essential concepts" as are always presupposed in the conceptual knowledge of scientific experience, do not proceed in the same way as the formation of concepts within a science. And the general, necessary essence of a field of reality cannot be "objectively" ascertained in the same way as certain notes and proprieties comprised in the essence.

For Plato, the essence, the truly universal, was the noetic prototype (ἰδέα) which was represented in sensible beings by participation (μέθεξις) in the "form". But this essence ("form") was already contemplated by the knower's mind. Knowledge of the beings of sense-perception was therefore being reminded (ἀνάμνησις) of the original knowledge of their essence. Their encounter in perception was primarily only the occasion of re-possessing the already (we should say *a priori*) known and contemplated essence. In contrast to the Platonic tradition which presented knowledge of essence as "intuition", the Aristotelian and Thomistic tradition interprets it as "abstraction". The general essence is inserted into the individual things themselves and is really there. It can only be

derived from them, by means of the encounter with concrete beings. Hence knowledge of essence is not *a priori* but completely *a posteriori*, a knowledge to be gained empirically, though it can only become explicit in an empirical approach which does not concentrate on this or that essential element in the beings in question, but remains perceptive and open for the essential unity of all the moments there encountered. A similar "experience of essence" is taught by Husserl in his *Phenomenology*, which, however, does not attribute the formation of the concept of the essence to abstraction, but, more in the Platonic tradition, to intuition, contemplation of essence and description of the essence contemplated. Husserl also developed the fundamental notion of a multiplicity of ontologies for various fields ("regional ontologies"). He spoke of sciences of the essence in contrast to the individual sciences at work within each realm of essence. But implicitly, in the experience of beings in everyday life and in the individual sciences, the experience of the essence common to such and such beings is included, being communicated in the experience of concrete beings, which is a factor in its genesis. And implicitly too, in all detailed conceptual knowledge of beings, the general essence which demarcates the realm of similar beings is included as a "horizon", which one may intend at least to turn into a concept, by means of an explicit "science of essence". This will not be in the nature of a particular science, but will be philosophical in type, method and concepts.

The essence is the "more general", in relation to beings in their individuality, and to this or that typical characteristic; and according to Aristotelian and Thomistic epistemology it is grasped by abstraction. But this does not mean that it is in all respects more meagre in content than beings in their real individuality, and that the concept of the essence is more "abstract" in the sense of being more one-sided than the concepts formed within the given horizon. On the contrary, the concept of the essence is more comprehensive, because less limited and less selective, and the essence is richer than any portion of the elements which it comprises.

Thus in all experimental and scientific knowledge essence and concept of essence of similar beings are present factors. They demarcate the "objective" field of knowledge and provide the "subjective" horizon of knowledge. But there is a further presupposition. Knowledge of essence is only possible and practicable by virtue of a "premonition" which reaches out beforehand to the highest modes of mutually exclusive being (self-sufficient being and contingent being; categories), and also to the highest modes of mutually inclusive being. These latter are aspects of what is one and the same, and import no differences, no division, into the multiplicity of beings (i.e., anything that is, any being, is one, something, good and valuable, etc., according to its degree of being; transcendentals). And in all this there is also the consciousness that the possible composition (σύνθεσις) of the moments of knowledge will be in accord with the composition of the moments of being in beings themselves. The "logical" laws of knowledge are at one with the law of being of beings, of the "ontic", in ontological identity.

The traditional metaphysics of knowledge understood the categories (and the concepts of essence within the categories) as univocal concepts, distinguished, however, from the concepts of essence ("empirical categories") by their character of being *a priori*. And only the (likewise *a priori*) transcendentals were regarded as analogous concepts, which did not apply to all beings in the same sense, but in keeping with their similarity which was also dissimilarity, spoke of them in various senses which were still not wholly distinct from one another. Now modern science consists of a number of disciplines, in which the individual science remains separate by virtue of its univocal set of concepts. But in spite of such differences, they are not entirely dissimilar in their categories of concepts and they remain connected. Indeed, it is only through what is common in the variety of their concepts that the common "marginal problems" as such can be investigated from different angles. Hence we have to ask whether and how the categorical concepts themselves are to be considered analogous: in an analogousness not simply of a uniform type, but "analogous" to that of the transcendentals. For instance, time and space mean different things for physics and for biology (here living-space and time lived), but still not something radically different. "Final causes" do not mean the same thing in biology and in scientific history, but they are not entirely unconnected.

Further, the traditional epistemology has accepted the number of *a priori,* though not empirical categories as fixed once and for all — though the number and enumeration of the categories has not in fact been entirely consistent throughout the history of the doctrine. Here too we must ask whether and how, in the course of human knowledge, new approaches may be opened (as for instance, undeniably, in the foundation of new independent scientific disciplines), and how new *a priori* concepts may be formed there. This is not irrational when one remembers that the *a priori* categorical concepts do not derive "from experience" — by abstraction — in the same way as the concepts of essence. And they are not formed in the same way as the empirical concepts of science within a horizon of essence, where their bearing is strictly limited, and where they can be repeatedly confirmed by (verifiable) "experience". From the point of view of their justification, the *a priori* categories, on the contrary, precede experience of essence and experience of concrete beings "as" this essence. They are, to use the terms of Kant (who, however, denied the experience of essence as a constitutive of concrete sensible-spiritual knowledge) "*a priori* conditions of possibility" of ordinary and scientifically verifiable experience. Nonetheless, just as we may speak of an "experience of essence" in contrast to experience of concrete perceptible beings, so too we may speak of "basic experiences of categories". Modern interpretations and developments of Aristotelian and Thomistic metaphysics and epistemology reject a rationalist view of being which takes it merely as the "primary concept", and hold that the *conceptus entis* only becomes possible and actual through a primordial experience *(conceptio)* of being and its self-deployment in the transcendental analogies. Hence we should look to an experience of the basic modes of being of the categories which gives rise to a conceptual knowledge of the *a priori* categories. The concept of "experience" itself proves to be not merely univocal but analogous, like that of knowledge, of method and of the concept itself in all "analogous concepts". Hence no one mode of knowledge, no one method or world of concepts, no science or type of science can claim to be exclusively valid.

In all knowledge that which is encountered is at once transcended to reach its essential notes, its essence which links it with similar beings, its *a priori* categorical structure and the truth that it is in fact a being in the variegated unity of its transcendental modes of being. Each degree of knowledge points of itself to the other gradated basic forms of knowledge and to the analogous unity of all forms of knowledge, though this unity cannot be expressed in a single act of knowledge, through any one method and in a concept of "higher" univocity which would comprise all analogy. (This in fact is what the "identity philosophy" of Hegel tried to carry out, treating knowledge, method [dialectic] and concept as the same, and identifying them with absolute "science", which had nothing but itself to bring into the presence of its knowledge — no "other", no beings and being prior to itself; science was both being and beings).

And at every degree of conceptual knowledge in the judgment it is also recognized that the σύνθεσις ("composition") in the judgment seeks to be the equivalence, the representation, that is, the presence of the σύνθεσις in the object of judgment itself. Knowledge is *adaequatio rei et intellectus* in the judgment, and the judgment is the true seat od knowledge because it is the "logical" concretion of the truth. But logical or mental truth is based on the truth given in experience. This is ontic truth since it is the disclosure of the beings met with and their general essence. It is ontological truth as the categories and transcendentals in which being is disclosed to the spirit, which knows because it experiences.

4. *The historicity of knowledge.* All knowledge is based on experience, *a posteriori,* ontic knowledge on the sensible perception of this or that individual being, *a priori,* ontological knowledge on the categorial and transcendental experience of essence and being. This raises a number of problems.

a) What being and its most primordial explicitation signify, the "meaning" of being and of its essential articulation is not on principle at once in the possession of the spirit in the act of knowledge. Knowledge of being and of essences in general is not simply the *de facto* explicitation of an implicit body of knowledge, of an immutable though mostly unarticulated deposit of consciousness — as in the metaphysics of consciousness in modern rationalism. The essential

significance of being is something imparted to the spirit, and spirit is a participant in being. But this again does not imply a disclosure of being and a constitution of spirit which has taken place once and for all. Ontological knowledge is not just the more or less accurate re-enactment of a permanently identical (because always already actuated) grasp of being on the part of the human spirit — as in the participation theory of the classical metaphysics. The primordial event of truth, the illumination of spirit by being and the acceptance of being by spirit, is always a new "encounter", ontological "experience". But this means that ontological experience, like all experience, is temporal and historical in character, and indeed is so in a more primordial sense than any ontic experience. There is something more, therefore, than the ontic history of changeable beings and their various relationships, of the *de facto* and *a posteriori* and its "empirical" experience. This ontic history is itself based on an ontological history of the changing meaning of being and its most essential order, the history of the *de jure* and *a priori* and its "transempirical" experience. The fundamental history is that of the epochal changes of meaning of the "being" of beings in the totality, the world, and of the being of man in his changing world, his "time".

The unity of being and time was first considered by Hegel, who, however, could only treat the historical present as a necessary grade of being in an immanent dialectical system of development through which the Absolute became for itself what it had already always been in itself in an absolute past. This view ignored the precisely characteristic element of historical time — its non-deducibility from past moments and its vulnerability to incalculable future happenings. The historico-temporal character of world-disclosing being and of world-knowing spirit then began to come to the fore in reflection on the basic elements of (narrative) history in the late 19th century (Ranke, Droysen) and in the theory of the human sciences (Dilthey), to receive its strictly philosophical emphasis from M. Heidegger. Since then the notion of the history and historicity of being and its truth, of the spirit and its knowledge, is unavoidable. It does not solve the problem, but it sets the terms of reference. The effort must now be to explain conceptually the experience of the historical consciousness which has come to the fore in a way which can no longer be ignored. It is now a matter of trying to understand the unconditional claim of being and truth on the spirit, and at the same time the historico-temporal conditioning and ever new and unique concrete form of this claim. It is a matter of seeing the connection between the tradition of the past and each new historical task set for the future. We cannot take up the historicist position which makes all bonds merely relative or indifferent and reduces history to a set of disconnected items. But neither can we relapse into a non-historical substance-and-accidents schema of nature and cosmos, where history can only be the accidental and indifferent recurrence of the realization of an inviolable and immutable substantial order.

b) All knowledge, including the ontologically conceptual, is based on experience, and first and last on the ontological experience of the truth of being and essence. But conceptual knowledge does not exist on its own. It is interwoven into a complex of basic acts, the living totality of the experience of truth. Conceptual knowledge, the "logical" crystallization of truth, is not the sole crystallization. Truth is also concrete in the moral act, in personal love, in the works of art, in the action of religious faith. The question then arises as to whether conceptual logical knowledge — in its scientific and philosophical as well as in its ordinary form — is not only not the sole form of knowledge, but not even the most perfect crystallization of knowledge. The perspective of this living historical experience which unifies the many modes of personal and interpersonal consciousness may lead one to reject the priority of conceptual knowledge which has been maintained more or less explicitly since philosophy first took shape in the West. But the new perspective is not irrational or anti-intellectual and does not set up an opposition between conceptual "knowledge" and "life". It is an effort to do justice to the free and there-fore more than conceptual decision of conscience in personal responsibility, to the work of art, to the word of the poet, to the symbol of religious faith. For none of these may be totally submitted to the norm of the concept and its crystallization of truth, as if ethics, the conceptual theory of moral action, was "truer" than this action itself, as if aesthetics and theology were "truer" than art and faith. This is the proper modesty of the concept, which is not master of truth and time but can be the servant of these fundamental modes of truth in their self-elucidation, and has constantly to renew its structures in their light. No doubt, the traditional priority of conceptual knowledge has reasserted its claims in modern times. The sciences are concentrated forms of it, and man's attitude to the world is predominantly an effort to master it by the concepts and weapons of scientific technology. The steady growth of the power of this knowledge to manipulate the individual elements of the world is as obvious as its bewilderment when trying to cope with existence as a whole.

See also *Scepticism, Dogmatism, Transcendental Philosophy, Experience, Being, Logic, Ontology, Spirit, Nominalism, Universals, Essence, Concept, Existence* II.

BIBLIOGRAPHY. E. Husserl, *Logische Untersuchungen*, 2 vols. (1900–01), French tr.: *Recherches Logiques*, 3 vols. (1958–63); M. Heidegger, *Sein und Zeit* (1927), E. T.: *Being and Time* (1962); M. Müller, *Sein und Geist* (1940); J. Maréchal, *Le point de départ de la métaphysique*, V (1947); N. Hartmann, *Grundzüge einer Metaphysik der Erkenntnis* (4th ed., 1949); E. Cassirer, *The Problem of Knowledge: Philosophy, Science and History since Hegel* (1950); A. Marc, *La dialectique de l'affirmation* (1952); J. B. Lotz, *Das Urteil und das Sein* (1957); M. Heidegger, *Introduction to Metaphysics* (1959); id., *Kant and the Problem of Metaphysics* (1962); M. Merleau-Ponty, *The Phenomenology of Perception* (1964); M. Heidegger, *What is a Thing?* (1966); E. Coreth, *Metaphysics* (1968); K. Rahner, *Spirit in the World* (1968); O. Muck, *The Transcendental Method* (1968).

Alois Halder

L

LAITY

I. The Layman in the Church: A. Historical
Survey. B. The Second Vatican Council. II.
Clergy and Laity. III. Catholic Action: A.
Organization. B. Objectives. C. Importance.

I. The Layman in the Church

Since it is impossible to discuss here all the
possible aspects of the word "laity", this
article will confine itself in the first part to a
survey of the mind of the Church on the
subject, as it developed in the course of
history. The second part will be an attempt to
assess systematically the declarations of
Vatican II on the laity. If the laity is to play
its proper role in the Church, this will not be
the result of pastoral encouragement and
organizational measures. It depends above
all on the mind of the Church, which again
depends primarily on the theological self-
understanding and self-realization of the
Church.

A. Historical Survey

1. The NT speaks of the Church as a fellowship which is contrasted with the world by
its special relationship to God through Jesus
Christ. The members of this fellowship —
called κλητοί, ἅγιοι, μαθηταί, ἀδελφοί —
are singled out from the world and formed
into a special "people" by the call which
went forth in Christ (cf. 1 Pet 1:10). This
people and all its members are given the
epithets which were used in the OT to
describe the special standing and holiness of
the OT worship and its ministers: holy
priesthood, priestly kingship, spiritual tem-

ple (cf. 1 Pet 2:9f.; 1 Cor 3:16f.; 2 Cor
6:16f.; Eph 2:19-22; Heb 10:21f.). The
special character does not mean separation
from the world, but holiness on behalf of the
world and testimony to the world. The NT
notes that there are differences within this
people. They differ according to charisms
(1 Cor 12:7; 14:26) and again according to
authority: there are ministers (1 Cor 4:1;
2 Cor 3:6; 6:4), presidents (Rom 12:8;
1 Thess 5:12; Heb 13:7, 17, 24; Acts 13:1;
20:28), pastors (Eph 4:11), elders (Tit 1:5)
and teachers (Acts 13:1; 1 Cor 12:28). Stress
is laid on the fact that these special gifts and
ministries serve to build up the community
and are tributary to the community (cf.
1 Cor 12).

2. The primitive Church knew what it was
to be a "little flock". Christians were the object
of persecution, and individuals suffered
martyrdom. The sense of being singled out
and of being a closely-knit fellowship grew.
Parallel to this came the sense of the special
role of the hierarchy of the community as the
reflection of divine order and as the representation of the authority of God and
Christ. In the letter of Clement of Rome
(c. 95) we meet then for the first time the
term λαικός, applied to the ordinary faithful
in contrast to the officials. The Latin translation *plebeius* then led to the notion of the
laity as the mass of the people with no
special competence. This was due in part to
the profane usage of the word, and chiefly to
a change in mentality (Congar).

3. The further development in the Middle
Ages was determined in the main by the

various circumstances which brought about a gradual interweaving of the Church and civil society. The tension and opposition between the Church and the world was transferred to within the Church itself. The *spiritual* man, such as the monk, is contrasted with the man who is occupied with the things of this *world*. The contrast is not so much historical and eschatological as moral. The world of the Spirit finds itself opposed to the world of the flesh, which appears as a menace. Thus true Christianity appears above all as detachment from the world. The Church, the one stable factor in the upheavals of the barbarian invasions, has to take upon itself the burden of upholding the earthly and political order among the young nations. The mission of the Church is combined with political action in a very special way which had been hitherto foreign to Christian experience.

For the holders of office in the Church, this development brought with it an approximation to the monastic form of life, as in the matter of celibacy, while the Church hierarchy became a distinct sociological entity, with special dress and the tonsure, which had certain effects in civil law. The contrast of the wordly and the spiritual became an element distinguishing the ordinary faithful from the clergy.

Pastoral work in the Middle Ages paid special attention to the layman. The duties of his state in life were kept before his eyes, to help him to lead a Christian life within the world, though always in terms of a Christian ideal which was monastic in flavour. He was ἅγιος only in a metaphorical sense, by having a religious element in an otherwise neutral life. The great representative of the laity was the prince and the ruler, whose formation was taken very seriously, and whose work was regarded as real service of the Church, as may be seen from the rite of the consecration of kings. This dualism within the Church is clearly reflected in the changes which took place in the liturgy during the transition from antiquity to the Middle Ages. The action is carried on by the clergy, while the ordinary faithful are reduced to a community of "hearers". A veil is drawn between them and the mystery — as by the liturgical language, the canon of the Mass pronounced inaudibly, the rood-screen across the chancel, the decrease in the frequency of Holy Communion.

4. Humanism, the Reformation, and the French Revolution which ended the Middle Ages and brought in a new organization of the political world, the broadening of horizons in the ages of discoveries and the transition beyond the borders of the Christian West — these were the factors which produced the epoch of emancipation, when the world was set free from Church tutelage and became conscious of its own intrinsic value and autonomy. For the first time in the course of its history, the Church was confronted with the world in the full sense of the word: a world of incalculable dimensions, fully self-conscious, in which Christians were once more a little flock. The first reaction of the Church in this encounter was an intensification of its effort to assert and defend itself. The pastoral work of the 19th century was mainly organized with a view to maintaining little islands of the older Christendom within this new profane world. Relations between Church and State were envisaged from the point of view of defending the regions of freedom allotted to the Church, as in the Concordats. The layman, being regarded as an expert in this matter of dominating a more and more complicated world, was sought out and welcomed as a helper in these efforts. But his services to the Church had still to be distinguished — in keeping with a still medieval mentality — from the level of the ordinary Christian life. Solutions were found to explain his special relationship to the Church, but they were all clearly tentative: a mandate from the episcopacy, a combination of a worldly form of life with certain monastic ideals, Catholic Action and so on.

B. The Second Vatican Council

These transitional forms were, however, unavoidable stages in the development of an understanding of the Church which took the autonomy of the world more and more seriously and could not but have consequences in the ecclesiastical sphere. The tension Church—World begins to regain its eschatological component in the climate of historical thought, and loses its one-sided moral quality. The defensive mentality yields to a sense of the mission of the Church in the world. At the same time, the tension Church—World ceases to work so strongly within the Church: there is less sense of hard and fast lines being drawn between hierarchy and faithful, and less danger from clericalism and anti-clericalism — which had not been without effects even within the Church. The laity have a new sense of their proper role in Church life. These new stirrings — which had not of course been equally marked in all parts of the Church — were recognized and ratified by the Second Vatican Council, which saw there the "unmistakable work of the Holy Spirit" and gave it expression in its teaching. The doctrine of Vatican II as a whole, and not merely in the sections which dealt expressly with the laity, provides a large number of important elements for the further development of a notion of the Church which gives the laity its due place.

1. Chapter ii of the Constitution on the Church develops, on the basis of 1 Pet 2:9–10, the doctrine of the unity of all members of the Church. This unity is founded on the common baptism, confirmation and call of all, and on their participation in the triple office of Christ. This unity is prior to all distinctions, as may be seen at once from the place allotted to this chapter in the constitution in the course of the discussion in the Council.

This people of God exists, however, in historical fact, as an articulated fellowship. There is the "common priesthood" of all the faithful — a clear allusion to the doctrine of the universal priesthood formulated in the Reformation, which had been constantly invoked as an argument against it in preconciliar discussions among Catholics. Then there is the "ministerial or hierarchical priesthood", distinct from the former in essence and not only in degree (Lumen Gentium, art. 10). This ecclesiastical ministry is "divinely established" (ibid., art. 28).

Other distinctive elements are the special gifts of the Spirit, the charisms, which are distributed throughout the Church. They are signs that the people of God is animated by the one Spirit, but they differ in their concrete historical forms. Common also to these different gifts and offices is their function of service in the Church, by virtue of which the ordination of these various services to each other can be emphasized (as in arts. 7 and 10).

2. Chapter iv of the same constitution discusses the special place of the laity in the Church as a whole. This is the basis of the Decree on the Apostolate of the Laity. The layman is distinguished from the hierarchy and the religious state not by a lesser degree of participation in the Christian life, but by his position in the world, as is clear, for instance, from the description of the "layman" in Lumen Gentium, art. 31, and from the repeated stress on the calling and dignity common to all. But the Christian call is always a summons to a "participation in the saving mission of the Church itself" (art. 33); the "right and duty to exercise the apostolate is common to all the faithful, both clergy and laity" (Apostolicam Actuositatem, art. 25). The call to the "apostolate" is given in baptism and confirmation, and not by a special mandate of the hierarchy which singles out some of the faithful from others. One may contrast the ironical notion of the "professional Catholic" or the unhelpful notion of the "militant Catholic" as occurring in certain countries. To describe this activity of the laity, the texts of the Council use the traditional expression "lay apostolate", though in a sense which departs so much from the original usage that it needs to be carefully explained, if the danger of restricting it to "spiritual co-operation" is to be avoided.

In view of these texts, the role of the laity cannot be based on a dualism of priests and faithful, or an opposition between the spiritual and the worldly. The Church as a whole is in the world, and not the laity exclusively. The laity is only "of the world" in a special way (Lumen Gentium, art. 33). The primary element must always be the one Christian quality which is common to all and the mission given to all. This is the framework within which the differences between the various services must be discussed.

Clergy and laity must rely on each other for help, if the common goal is to be attained. Hence the Council exhorts the pastors to humility, since they must remember that "they themselves were not meant by Christ to shoulder alone the entire saving mission of the Church toward the world" (Lumen Gentium, art. 30). The prerequisite for the fruitfulness of the work of the laity is their "living union with Christ", which means that they must go to the pastors who are the servants of the word and the ministers of the sacraments (Apostolicam Actuositatem, arts. 4, 28, 29). The laity must be receptive to the testimony of the religious state "that the world cannot be transfigured . . . without the spirit of the beatitudes" (*Lumen Gentium*, art. 31). In the light of this unity and mutual dependence, in the spirit of brotherhood (*ibid.*, art. 32), respecting each other's special gifts and talents and the freedom resulting therefrom (cf. *ibid.*, arts. 25, 37, where the duty of obedience incumbent on the laity is carefully circumscribed), Christians are to work out the various forms of organization in which the laity co-operate in the life and mission of the Church. The Council alludes to such forms in several places (cf. *Lumen Gentium*, art. 33; *Apostolicam Actuositatem*, arts. 15–27; *Christus Dominus* [on the bishops], arts. 10, 27; *Ad Gentes* [on the missions], art. 21). But it refrains from giving detailed precepts and thus leaves Christians free to find solutions which can be adapted to varying circumstances. This does not mean of course that the line of least resistance should be taken, or that there should be uncritical efforts to follow out political models and slogans. Whatever the form of organization, it must do justice to the special constitution of the Church.

The sense of the unity of the people of God will depend to a great extent on the success of the reform of the liturgy. It envisages the "full, conscious and active participation of all the faithful", and its various stages — simplicity and intelligibility of the rites; use of the vernacular; sharing of the liturgical functions — are both spurs to development and a way of measuring how much has been attained or missed.

3. Another important element in forming the ecclesiastical consciousness of the laity is the delineation of their own proper mission. This was attempted by the Council on several occasions, though in the line of a description rather than that of a precise definition. The Council speaks, for instance, of "the effective presence of the Church in the world"; of "testimony in faith, hope and love" — either through the laity's own words or through the preaching of the word of God in the work of evangelization; of the "ordering of temporal things"; of the "sanctification of the world". These indications are to be understood in the light of the relationship of the order of creation to the order of salvation. The missionary character of the Church is emphasized in the definition of the Church given at the beginning of *Lumen Gentium*, where it is described as the sacrament, that is, the sign and instrument for intimate union with God, and for the unity of all mankind (cf. art. 1). This definition is then elaborated according to its historical and eschatological aspects (art. 48) and in its cosmic dimensions (*Gaudium et Spes* [on the Church in the Modern world], art. 45; cf. also art. 39). This incarnational recapitulation of human effort and world history in Christ (in the light of Eph 1:10) rules out any dualism which would divide the two orders, juxtapose Church and world as if indifferent to each other, or blur the newly won vision of the unity of the Church. The Church cannot be divided into specialists for nature (the laity) and specialists for supernatural matters (the clergy). There is an implicit rejection of the "two-storey" theory of nature and grace which makes it clear that the activity of the laity in the world, as described above, is to be understood in the light of the history of salvation. The "ordering of temporal things" and the "testimony" or evangelization are not two distinct activities, but must take place at one and the same time in the same human effort. Only the rejection of such dualism will make it possible to give full effect to what the Council says about the laity's task in shaping the world (*Gaudium et Spes*, arts. 35, 43).

The unity of the two orders, however, is that of a common end and that of the divine plan of salvation. It is not an actual fact of the present time. Further, the convergence of the historical dynamism of mankind upon Christ is endangered by sin (*Gaudium et Spes*, arts. 37, 45). Hence the Council affirms the "rightful autonomy of earthly realities" (cf. *Gaudium et Spes*, art. 36). For Church and world are not identical, but penetrate one another in a mutual dialogue (*Gaudium et Spes*, art. 36). This imposes on the layman the special task of recognizing the true and peculiar nature of the world and of working together with the rest of men at its development (*ibid.*, art. 43). He is in conscience bound to bear the burden of the conflicts which are imposed upon him by his membership of both civil and ecclesiastical society. (*Lumen Gentium*, art. 36; *Gaudium et Spes,* art. 43.) He can expect help from his pastors, but not concrete solutions. For the Church is not tied to any particular form of civil society, and hence cannot allow itself to prescribe any models of political, economic or social order, just as it may not betray its mission by giving it the form of earthly sovereignty (*Gaudium et Spes*, art. 43). When Christians, in their judgment of a given earthly situation and the line of action to be adopted, reach their own independent solutions, "as happens frequently, and quite legitimately" (cf. *Gaudium et Spes*, art. 43), they are free to do so as far as the Church is concerned (*Lumen Gentium*, art. 37). Hence such terms as "the ordering of earthly things" and the "sanctification of the world", as used by the Council, need to be properly interpreted in the light of the normative force of revelation and the forces of salvation at work in the history of the worldly world. But they may not be interpreted in terms of any particular "Christian political programme" or "Christian social order" in the popular sense of such terms.

See also *Ecclesiastical Authority, Charisms, Ecclesiastical Office* II, *Religious Orders, Church and State, Church and World*.

BIBLIOGRAPHY. P. Dabin, *Le sacerdoce royal des fidèles dans la tradition ancienne et moderne* (1950); O. Semmelroth and L. Hofmann, *Der Laie in der Kirche. Seine Sendung, seine Rechte* (1955); I. de la Potterie, "L'origine et le sens primitif du mot 'laïc'", *NRT* 80 (1958), pp. 840–53; L. R. Ward, *Catholic Life in the U.S.A. Contemporary Lay Movements* (1959); Y. Congar, *Laity, Church and World* (1960); P. Glorieux, *Le laïc dans l'Église* (1960); A. Auer, *Weltoffener Christ. Grundsätzliches und Geschichtliches zur Laienfrömmigkeit* (1960); J. Ratzinger, *Die christliche Brüderlichkeit* (1960); *Laici in Ecclesia. An Ecumenical Bibliography on the Role of the Laity in the Life and Mission of the Church* (1961); C. Colombo and others, *Laïcs et vie chrétienne parfaite* (1963); D. Callahan, *The Mind of the Catholic Layman* (1963); J. Cadet, *Le Laïcat et le droit de l'Église* (1963); K. Rahner, *Mission and Grace*, I (1963); F. X. Arnold, *Le laïc dans la liturgie* (1964); Y. Congar, *Lay People in the Church* (revised ed., 1965); E. Schillebeeckx, *The Real Achievement of Vatican II* (1967); G. Philips, *Achieving Christian Maturity* (1967); Léon Cardinal Suenens, *Co-Responsibility in the Church* (1968); Y. Congar, *Christians Active in the World* (1968).

Ernst Niermann

II. Clergy and Laity

1. The relationship between clergy and laity in the life and work of the Church is determined by the unity of its mission — the salvation of men, which they lay hold on by faith in Christ and by his grace. Clergy and laity are therefore one as members by baptism of the one people of God, members of the same body which all are called on to build up. Nevertheless the individual members of the Church carry out its mission in different ways.

2. If the clergy carry out the Church's mission (apostolate) by formally proclaiming the good news and bestowing Christ's grace on the world through the sacraments, the laity work in the self-same mission by imbuing the order of temporal things with the spirit of the gospel. A layman carries out the Church's mission "in the manner of a leaven" (Decree on the Apostolate of the Laity, chs. i, ii) on the basis of his position in the midst of the world and his secular tasks. His witness before the world is a living witness — he represents the virtues of faith, hope, and love — but also a witness of the word: he is a "fellow-worker in the truth" (3 Jn 8) which he announces to his environment. Precisely this witness of the word relates his apostolate to that of the clergy, so that in much of their mission we can hardly draw a sharp distinction between the respective roles of cleric and layman. For his part the layman shares in Christ's office as priest, prophet, and teacher, while the cleric remains a citizen of earthly society and in his special apostolate may not overlook the earthly conditions in which the word of God must be heard and done.

Thus the two competences overlap in a wide range of well-defined functions and are distinguished by emphasis rather than by two different natures. The layman's share in the Church's mission does not derive from emergencies of the moment (such as a shortage of priests) or a special authorization by the hierarchy; it is given him "by the Lord himself" (Decree on the Apostolate of the Laity, chs. i, iii) in baptism and confirmation. Each equipped with his special gifts from the Holy Spirit ("charismata", *ibid.*), laymen carry out their apostolate as individuals or as members of various associations. So it is not some ecclesiastical ordinance that gives laymen the right and duty to be apostles as individuals and to found and direct apostolic associations; they have that of themselves. What the ecclesiastical hierarchy has to do is to acknowledge the layman's native right and train him in the faith in view of his apostolate; make him realize that he must play an active part in the Church; provide him with spiritual help, not with ready-made models of Christian living in this world but the power of Christ's word and grace, to endure his terrestrial situation in faith, hope, and love; and order the activities and aims of individuals and groups to the common good of the Church. Apostolic associations of lay people are variously ordered, or subordinated, to the hierarchy in law according as the proper aim of each association relates it to the hierarchical apostolate. Here those associations commonly called Catholic Action, whose characteristics are precisely set forth by the Second Vatican Council (cf. Decree on the Apostolate of the Laity, ch. iv, art. 20), find themselves in a special position; but in view of other statements of the Council they must renew their conception of themselves and bring it into sharper focus.

3. If clergy and laity are to co-operate each must have confidence in the other — no small task, considering the wrong attitudes of the past (clericalism, anti-clericalism). Theological insight is as necessary to this end as a sound psychological approach. The fact that there is but one mission, though there are different ministries, should move each to respect the proper function of the other and its contribution to his own. It should prevent the cleric reducing the Church's mission to the proportions of his particular role, and expecting any would-be lay collaborator to give proofs first of a clerical spirituality. It should make the layman realize that his own work in the world requires the priestly function, that constant renewal by Christ's word and sacramental grace which is the task of clerics, for its full saving efficacy. Only in close association with the priestly ministry does that lay work become truly Christian and Catholic.

But modern man, so given to secularization, so engrossed in this world, must be admonished that all human activity is ordered to an eschatological event, so that he may see the import of what he does and see his need of God's word and grace. On the other hand, the cleric's knowledge that the temporal order has to be consummated eschatologically, not from within, should restrain him from infringing on the autonomy of this world and the layman's competence in its affairs.

See also *Clergy, Baptism, Confirmation, Hierarchy, Charisms, Laity* III, *Secularization.*

BIBLIOGRAPHY. J. R. Mott, *Liberating the Lay Forces of Christianity* (1932); J.-H. Oldham, *The Function of the Church in Society,* ed. by W. A. Visser 't Hooft (1937); G. Philips, *The Role of the Laity in the Church* (1955); O. Semmelroth and L. Hofmann, *Der Laie in der Kirche. Seine Sendung, seine Rechte* (1955); Y. Congar, *Lay People in the Church* (1957; revised ed., 1965); H. Kraemer, *A Theology of the Laity* (1958); Y. Congar, *Laity, Church and World* (1960); *Laici in Ecclesia,* published by the Department on the Laity, World Council of Churches (1961); A. Auer, *Open to the World* (1962).

Miguel Benzo and *Ernst Niermann*

III. Catholic Action

A. ORGANIZATION

1. *Origins.* Catholic Action grew out of the Catholic movements of the 18th and 19th centuries, the main aims of which had been the defence of the Church against the free-thinking, revolutionary, Erastian and absolutist trends of the time, and the solution of the social problems which had become increasingly urgent since the Industrial Revolution. Catholic congresses were held in many European countries to further these aims and Catholic organizations and associations founded; often very concrete political ends were pursued, such as Catholic emancipation in Britain, so that there was a mixture of temporal, worldly, spiritual and ecclesiastical aims. Nevertheless the Church authorities claimed, without much discrimination, the right to control all Catholic associations, including economic, social and political ones, appealing to the duty of obedience, to the unity of the body of Christ and of the apostolate, and to the necessity of combining all forces. This attitude is particularly understandable in Italy, in view of the Roman question. Gradually a more selective point of view gained ground — Leo XIII recognized the intrinsic independence of the temporal realm — and two trends emerged within Catholic popular movements, one towards Christian democracy, Catholic social movements and Christian political parties, the other towards Catholic Action. But there still remained (and there are to this day) organizations with mixed aims, nor was the nomenclature clear for a long time. Thus Pius X said in his encyclical, *Il fermo proposito,* of 11 June 1905 that Catholic Action included not only "anything pertaining to the mission proper of the Church, to lead souls to God, but also anything that derives naturally from that divine mission", such as cultural, economic, social, civic and political activities. However, a clear distinction is made between the two kinds of association, regarding their

relationship with the hierarchy. The first, those who "help directly with the spiritual and pastoral work of the Church", the encyclical goes on, "must be subordinate to the Church down to the smallest detail"; the second type should accept "the advice and general guidance of ecclesiastical authority", but mention is also made of "the reasonable freedom due to them" and of their own responsibility, "especially in temporal and economic affairs".

When Pius XI called the whole world to Catholic Action in his first encyclical of 23 December 1922 and more and more urgently thereafter, he had the Italian model and its development immediately before his eyes. Its beginnings can already be seen in the *Amicizie Cristiane* which had come from France in 1775. As a result of the International Catholic Congress in Malines, an association was formed in 1865 "for the defence of the freedom of the Church in Italy"; this was followed in 1867 by the "Catholic Youth Association" and in 1876 by the "Association of Catholic Congresses and Committees", to which the combined Catholic Students' Societies became affiliated in 1892; about the same time an association was formed for social studies, and then workers' associations. Pius X, because of the desire for autonomy in the *Democrazia Cristiana*, dissolved the Congress Association in 1904 and confirmed four associations, independent of each other, in 1906: the *Unione Popolare*, based on the model of the *Volksverein für das katholische Deutschland* of 1890, with the object of defending the social order, creating a Christian culture and forming the popular conscience; an "economic-social association" which was to include relief and vocational organizations; a "Catholic Electors' Association" which was to rally and provide political training for Catholics with the local and provincial elections in mind; and a "Catholic Youth Association". The leaders of these organizations combined in a body in 1908 for "the general co-ordination of Italian Catholic Action". An organization, similar to the "German Catholic Women's Association" was founded in Italy in 1908 (the "Catholic Women's Association of Italy") which was followed in 1918 by an "Association for Italian Catholic Girls"; these two combined in 1919 and were joined in 1922 by a third section, the "Italian Catholic Women Students". In 1926 a children's

movement was started. The *Unione Popolare* co-ordinated activities from the beginning, although this arrangement only became official with Benedict XV's reform of 1915 which set up a "directing committee of Catholic Action" under the presidency of the *Unione Popolare*.

This concentration of Catholic forces under the hierarchy was followed after the First World War by grants of independence to Catholic organizations with mainly worldly objectives; but an "economic-social secretariat" was set up under the "directing committee" to study the social problem in the light of Christian principles. Thus the situation necessitated a re-thinking of the real function of Catholic Action. In 1920 the statutes of the *Unione Popolare* were altered, to be followed in 1922 by the re-organization of Catholic Action by Pius XI: in November the new "Central Committee of Catholic Action" took over the directing, co-ordinating functions of the *Unione Popolare,* the members of which were to be absorbed by the various organizations of Catholic Action; an organization for men, which had still been lacking, was created in December. On 2 October 1923, that is, after the general call to Catholic Action, the new statutes were confirmed.

It is quite wrong then to assert that Catholic Action is an exclusively Roman or Italian creation; its roots are to be found in France, Belgium and to a great extent in Germany. Nor was it created from above but, like its associated organizations, it has a long history. It is not even organized solely according to the four "natural pillars", as the students' and workers' organizations are among the oldest and the men's and children's among the most recent. Nor had it been envisaged from the beginning as a purely internal aid to pastoral work: even after the organizations with mainly temporal aims had become independent, Catholic Action continued to claim the right to study, in the light of Christian principles, individual, family, vocational and cultural-social problems, and to form the consciences of Catholics accordingly; in fact Pius XI speaks of the links of Catholic Action with the world-wide kingdom of Christ and the Church's work within society. This also disposes of the assertion that Catholic Action had only been intended for the difficult times of Fascist oppression, but never for normal times. Its history is far older than Fascism; the decisive turning points were reached in 1915 and 1919, while Fascism only came to power on 28 October 1922.

2. *Forms*. Pius XI repeatedly defined Catholic Action as the "participation and co-operation of the laity in the hierarchical apostolate of the Church". Pius XII preferred the word co-operation, in order to avoid any misunderstanding as to participation in the hierarchy itself.

The Catholic Action of Pius XI did not imply any particular method or structure, but adjusted itself to the circumstances of time and place as far as such adjustments were compatible with its essence and objectives. This is shown by the development in Italy and other countries, even if the Italian model was sometimes too slavishly imitated, or the relationship of Catholic Action to other organizations misunderstood in a monopolistic, uniformist sense, an error against which Pius XII warned. New and old organizations were integrated with Catholic Action, some on an international level like the *Jeunesse Ouvrière Catholique,* or on a national basis, like the Legion of Mary. Pius XII said in his Apostolic Constitution *Bis Saeculari* of 27 September 1948 that the Sodalities of the Blessed Virgin had "every right to be called Catholic Action, led and inspired by the Blessed Virgin Mary".

Gradually the following types of Catholic Action emerged, though they were sometimes only partly concerned with the proper objects of Catholic Action and did not always fall entirely into one category:

a) Catholic Action simply as an idea which can be embodied in various degrees in various organizations; sometimes co-ordinating committees are formed, ranging from the parochial to the national level.

b) Catholic Action as a collective name for various organizations, which retain their own names and independence, but form a federal union as Catholic Action; at the second Congress for the Lay Apostolate an attempt was made to have this system adopted everywhere.

c) Catholic Action as a name for certain apostolic organizations, connected with each other in one way or another: it might be a federal arrangement, often under a very vague umbrella, or else centralized, perhaps with several sections, which would be entirely independent.

d) Catholic Action with the character of an élite such as the Marian Sodalities, or a vocational organization which would however be animated by an élite group, as in the *Jeunesse Ouvrière Catholique.*

e) Catholic Action to deal with problems common to people of various ages, backgrounds or spheres of work, or else specialized for a certain age-group, vocation or milieu; these may supplement each other.

f) Catholic Action organized down to parochial or supra-parochial level within a town, a deanery, a diocese or a country, such as academic or artists' organizations; these types also are not mutually exclusive.

g) Catholic Action which confines itself in advance to a certain limited field of activity, such as help with pastoral work.

Vatican II rejected all attempts to adopt any particular system on a world-wide basis, but also pointed out the elements essential to genuine Catholic Action, whatever the method, form, or name, which would be adjusted to fit time and place: thus the problems of organization are secondary to the basic objectives.

3. *Relationship with other organizations*. At first any association with personal sanctification as the primary objective was regarded as auxiliary to Catholic Action; co-operation with associations with primarily temporal objectives was recommended; apostolic organizations proper were envisaged as in some way integrated with Catholic Action, or at least affiliated. The Decree of Vatican II on the Apostolate of the Laity recognizes the right of the laity to free association and the advantages of such a system, while at the same time warning against fragmentation, and recommending the creation of co-ordinating committees. Contact with the hierarchy, which will of course vary in degree with the type of organization, must be maintained; where temporal objectives are concerned, it is only necessary to take care that they accord with Christian principles (arts. 19, 24, 26).

B. Objectives

There are four characteristics evident in true Catholic Action, as is clearly shown by its development and by the Decree on the Apostolate of the Laity (art. 20), even when the name itself is not used because other names were there first or because it might lead to — possibly political — misunderstandings, as in Anglo-Saxon countries.

a) The immediate aim is the apostolic aim of the Church, the evangelization and sanctification of man, in which the laity have a specific task, as well as the Christian formation of conscience, so that laymen can pursue their task in the world in a Christian spirit, but on their own responsibility. In this sense Catholic Action is working towards the Christianization of the world. In the temporal sphere it is of course merely concerned with the application of Christian principles, in the light of which human problems are studied and consciences formed. Anything beyond that is either a service of love, helping men in their many troubles, or else it is simply a kind of stimulant. The actual process of building the world is not part of its task. Although it is of course part of the Church's task to influence the world at every point, it can only do so through those who are entrusted with the construction of the temporal order. The Church — and Catholic Action — must help men to recognize the general principles of revelation, but it is not its task to transmit the equally necessary knowledge of affairs. Therefore members of Catholic Action must "make a clear distinction between what a Christian conscience leads them to do in their own name as citizens, whether as individuals or in association, and what they do in the name of the Church and in union with its shepherds" (Pastoral Constitution on the Church in the Modern World, art. 76).

b) The laity contribute their specifically lay experience and take responsibility for leadership, planning and action. They must enjoy freedom and trust, and be allowed to work together with the hierarchy, so that responsible laymen can find scope to use their knowledge and initiative and can undertake work proper to a layman within the ecclesiastical sphere.

c) Laymen are united in collegiate and corporate action.

d) The laity act under the supreme guidance of the hierarchy itself who thus in a way take the ultimate responsibility, which in turn implies the right (and the restriction) to lay down general guidance, to confirm office-holders and the most important decisions and statutes; but they must also judge whether or not the four characteristics

are present. This special relationship to the hierarchy is called a mandate, which does not confer any new competence, but does provide a certain official standing. The theological implications of the mandate were deliberately left open by the Council. Supreme control by the hierarchy and the lay character of Catholic Action must not cancel each other out; they should supplement, not contradict each other. After all, responsibility in the world too is divided in varying degrees; furthermore, within the community of Christ there applies the principle of a universal, collegiate responsibility of all for all.

All this means that the classical definition of Catholic Action is now outmoded. The laity is no longer seen as an extension of the hierarchy, its instrument and executive organ. The old definition is echoed, no doubt, in the Decree on the Apostolate of the Laity, art. 20, but only in the historical introduction. And in fact only a minor section of Catholic Action can be regarded as co-operation with or participation in the functions of the hierarchy. This view of it would not do justice to the specifically lay or secular Christian character of the apostolate in question, nor to the true and proper co-responsibility of laymen in the Church. Catholic Action cannot, of course, go beyond its ecclesiastical mandate, but even here the laity should not be regarded as merely collaborators with the hierarchy. They remain responsible themselves in part for the apostolate of the whole Church. Even their apostolate can only be properly seen when contrasted with the hierarchical apostolate; otherwise they would have no specific contribution to make to the Church. Under modern conditions, the best way to describe Catholic Action is to say that it is "the official participation of the laity in the apostolate of the Church".

When these four characteristics and their inherent tensions are studied seriously, many controversies of recent years become clearer: the connection between the kingdom of God and the building of the temporal world, the evangelization, sanctification and Christian penetration of the temporal order, a Church structure into which the Christian can be fully integrated, including his worldly interests; they are in fact controversies about a new, Christian, comprehensive, integrated concept, or in concrete terms, about the temporal, possibly political function of

Catholic Action, the part its lay members should play in internal Church reform, their place in the confrontation with an atheist world, and their role in general in the work of building the world.

Since Vatican II the Christian's work in the world must be seen as part of the Church's mission and, therefore, of the apostolate, if he approaches it in the spirit of the gospels; but he must do this on his own responsibility and not in the name of the Church. On the other hand, although Catholic Action is a true lay apostolate and not merely a help with pastoral work, it is not a means of giving the Church control of the world, in the sense of a new integralism.

C. Importance

The importance of a Catholic Action which is true to itself seems to lie in its mediating function: because of its truly secular and lay character it can directly provide the Church with the world's own vision and contribution, and even help the Church work out and proclaim religious moral principles; conversely it can, because of its official ecclesiastical standing, show the world a vision of the Church and transmit to the Christians of the world the help of the Church through theoretical and methodical apostolic training, to help them cope in a Christian spirit with their work in the world. Thus it combines the power and the worldly wisdom and knowledge of the layman with the work of the pastor (Constitution on the Church, art. 37). This type of apostolate has, it is true, always existed in the Church in some form or other, but it is specially important in a society and Church which needs a planned, global strategy more than ever. Although any apostolic initiative must be recognized as valuable in principle, it is only natural that the Decree on the Apostolate of the Laity should recommend with particular emphasis those organizations which have the four characteristics of true Catholic Action, whether they bear that name or not. This certainly does not imply any claim to a monopoly, but it does pledge them to service of a special, brotherly kind.

See also *Church and World, Laity* I, II.

BIBLIOGRAPHY. J. M. V. Pollet, "De Actione Catholica principiis theologiae thomisticae dilucidata", *Angelicum* 13 (1936), pp. 442–83; A. Alonso, *Catholic Action and the Laity* (1936); S. Tromp, "Actio Catholica et Hierarchia", *Periodica* 25 (1936), pp. 105–18; F. Magri, *L'Azione Cattolica in Italia*, 2 vols. (1953); Y. Congar, *The Layman in the Church* (1957); J. Verscheure, "Katholische Aktion", *LTK*, VI, cols. 74–77; F. Klostermann, *Das Christliche Apostolat* (1962); M. Quigley and E. Connors, *Catholic Action in Practice* (1963); K. Rahner, "Notes on the Lay Apostolate", *Theological Investigations,* II (1963), pp. 319–52; *De Laicorum apostolatu organizato hodie toto in orbe terrarum diffuso. Commissio permanens conventuum internationalium apostolatui laicorum provehendo. Documenta collecta et systematice exposita pro Patribus Concilii Oecumenici Vaticani II* (1963); G. Poggi, *Catholic Action in Italy* (1967).

Ferdinand Klostermann

LANGUAGE

A. Anthropological Pre-Understanding

As a rule, language is distinguished from thought and both thought and language from the thing thought about or spoken of. This distinction is already found in Plato and Aristotle, who countered the Sophists' abuse of language by offering a valid critique of language. Their aim was to restore responsible discussion within the city-state to its rightful place as relevant and objective. This use of language in the service of the community has as its comprehensive goal the good of the State, but is grounded in the household and family which primarily consist of man and wife. In this family fellowship of male and female man starts to practise that "giving and accepting an account or *logos*" (δοῦναι καὶ δέξασθαι λόγον) by which the Greeks described the active potentiality of the whole man in his scope and limitations. It is from this fellowship of love (χάρις) between husband and wife, with its *logos* which is given and received reciprocally, that other modes of the *logos* stem, immediately or subsequently. There is then the giving and accepting of rights, giving account of a thing (in dispute), the dialectical didactic talk of philosophers, talk of death, discussion between men enmeshed in guilt (in Attic tragedy) and even a sense of the gods' speaking to men (διάλεκτος, Plato, *Symposium,* 203a). Hence Hegel could describe the natural constitution of the sexes as the immediacy of the spirit-mediated dialectic of the particular and universal, substance and subject, divine and human law (*Werke*, II, p. 351; see also *Philosophy of Right* [E. T.,

1942], para. 166; *Werke*, X, p. 556). But this dialectical to and fro of the spirit takes place through the medium of διαλέγεσθαι, human language. The life and work of the family and other groups (as K. Marx pointed out most impressively) starts with the natural, cultural and conventional differentiation between male and female existence, and the division of labour which this entails. It then proceeds to develop a polarity in the experience of reality which is reflected in a corresponding polarity and progression in dialectically pondered language.

Heraclitus was fully aware of the dialectical relationship of φύσις and λόγος, which he brought into connection with the contrast of male and female, according to tradition (Frg. 10). But Parmenides denied absolutely that the language of mortals which is no more than *mere* names (ὀνόματα) (Frg. 8, 38) could have precedence over pure thought (νοεῖν) or that the reality of becoming in φύσις could have precedence over pure being (εἶναι). Thus for the philosophical tradition of the Occident the definitive priority of "being" before "becoming", "thought" before "language", was established – and based on the anthropological priority of a specifically male interpretation of reality over a female experience of reality. While then the "concept" remains an essential reality (still retaining in Aristotle its primordial relationship to the historical *logos* of language) post-Aristotelian tradition debases the "word" to an audibly perceptible sign, to the total neglect of the mediation of concept-word, sense-sound which is given at once in the totality of language. As a consequence of the distinction between being (root: [e]s, cf. Latin *sum*) and becoming (root: bhu-, Greek φύσις, cf. Latin *fui*) — a distinction only possible in the Indo-European languages and occurring in fact only in Greek — Greek philosophy could make explicit the world-view which was latent in the Greek language, and declare that being was prior to becoming.

Hence too the duality of the pre-philosophical experiences of reality, in religion and myth — "matriarchal" and "patriarchal" according to J. J. Bachofen, "Dionysiac" and "Apolline" according to F. Nietzsche's philosophical analysis — could be interpreted in terms of the ἀρχαί (principles) which were understood by Greek metaphysics to be the principles of being and becoming — εἶδος

(ἐνέργεια) as contrasted with ὕλη (δύναμις). (The same interpretation of being was then used for the much richer primordiality of the Hebrew-biblical experience of God.) In this process the real *logos,* conceived of as thought, is absorbed into the unchangeable divine "being", while the other aspect of the same *logos,* which is addressed to and indicates the individual and particular, the historical becoming of things, their involvement in situations ("Materia prima est principium individuationis") is identified with the imperfect αἴσθησις — imperfect, because not attaining "being in general" or the universal, and always directed, "a-logically", to some particular thing. A theology embedded in the city-state, culminating in the "Nous" — God of metaphysics, is then no more than an objectivation (ἐπιστήμη θεολογική) of the metaphysical concept of language, according to which the manifold *logos* of historical language must be transformed into the speculative notion of the "essence" (εἶδος, τὸ τί ἦν εἶναι) which is also one, even in its universality. The cleavage between language and thought in Greek culture was continued in Latin, where *verbum (oratio)* was distinguished from *ratio,* and so continued till modern times. In the 17th and 18th centuries philosophy itself could be understood as the science of the intellect and reason (Kant). More recently, with the revival of interest in popular speech and native languages, it could at last be seen that only a relative value could be attributed to the sediment of world-images which had settled in the Greek and Latin languages. Nonetheless, the Greek view of language remained predominant. And the anthropology which it implied, culminating in the primacy of the male over the female, was given fitting expression in the growing tendency to equate specifically "male" experience of and reflection upon reality (in philosophy and science) with the thinking "subjectivity". Thus, for instance, Hegel "sublimates" all the immediately substantial into the mediation of the (absolute) subject. Nietzsche proclaims the "will to power" as the will to the unity and eternity of being. We are only beginning today, it seems, to find our way back critically to the metaphysical origins of Western culture in Hellenism, and to use the comparison with cultures of non-Greek origin (through comparative religion, linguistics, history of cultures, etc.) to gain new insight into the necessary link between all thought and language. This will pave the way for a revision of the undue isolation of language from thought.

B. The Problem and its Historical Origin

The "concern for language" which is so characteristic of present-day philosophy and many sciences reveals two different basic tendencies. There is general agreement on the fact that man and language are fundamentally related to one another, but not on the nature of this relationship. The conflict which here ensues is, however, an echo of a more basic disagreement as to the nature of man. The point at issue might be put paradoxically as follows: Has man language at his disposal or is man at the disposal of language? If one accepts the first alternative, language is seen primarily as a means by which man masters life, an instrument and expression of his effort to master the future in thought and plan. In the second case, language will be understood primarily as the mediator between human tradition of the past and a present (and future) which is to be read in the light of this tradition. On closer inspection, however, it soon appears that in such alternatives and their various contrasting formulas (analytic or synthetic, prospective or retrospective, etc.) we are meeting once more the ancient alternatives put forward in the Western metaphysics of being and language which have been described above. For in the first case, where language is man's instrument, the proponents are chiefly concerned with "neopositivism" and "linguistic analysis" and see themselves as carrying on the torch of the Western scientific claim to explain and master the world rationally. And the upholders of the second alternative are concerned with "hermeneutics", that is, with thought as it reaches back to the historicity of language's genesis. Here language is looked on as a "message" (ἑρμηνεία ἑρμηνεύειν, in the double sense of receiving a message, understanding, expounding a message, Latin interpretari, cf. Hermes, the "messenger" of the gods). It is a message addressed to man, the discussion developing in history between man and his equals, between man and the world and between man and divine powers. But in the first alternative, language functions as an instrument for the rational knowledge and domination of

the world — an instrument which must be constantly improved and constantly purged of its native failures of vagueness and incorrectness, by means of logical analysis.

The main representatives of "logical positivism" (R. Carnap, F. Waismann and O. Neurath) belonged to the "Viennese Group" of the thirties, founded by M. Schlick. It had a profound influence before and after World War II in the English-speaking world, and was gradually transformed into the linguistic analysis of the present day partly by its own followers and partly through the original contributions of B. Russell, A. N. Whitehead, G. Frege, A. Tarski, J. Ludasiewicz and L. Wittgenstein to basic thinking on mathematics and logic (logistics).

Linguistic philosophy is represented chiefly by such authors as A. J. Ayer, W. V. Quine, C. W. Morris and G. Ryle, through whom it has influenced the treatment of ethics (C. D. Broad, C. L. Stevenson, R. M. Hare, J. L. Austin, G. H. v. Wright), to which the process of linguistic analysis had been tentatively applied by G. E. Moore. It has also been used in the fields of sociology and psychology (G. Ryle, H. Feigl, P. Winch and others).

Logical positivism and linguistic analysis share the view that language functions as a system of signs ("syntax" being the relation of the signs to each other, "semantics" the relation of the signs to the thing signified, the *designatum*, the meaning). In this way it remains tied to the metaphysical notion of language in all its historical forms, beginning with Aristotle, going on to Stoic logic with its distinction between λόγος and λεκτόν as the utterable "meaning", then to Boethius (d. 525) and medieval logic (signification and supposition as the *proprietates terminorum*), with the problem of "universals" (realism and nominalism), to modern empiricism (F. Bacon, T. Hobbes, J. Locke) and rationalism (Descartes to Leibniz and the Enlightenment), with their ideal of language based on mathematics and science — the *mathesis universalis,* and so finally to the modern concept of language as "calculus" and "information". Dominant throughout was the separation between "thought" (the *idea clara et distincta* of the rationalists, the images of the outward and inner senses for the empiricists) and "language", the defects of which as an instrument of social intercourse were to be eliminated in the construction of an ideal language. The tendency to logic, formalism and mathematics already present in the Greek *logos* of speech may be illustrated by Plato's description of the supreme form of the good as μέγιστον μάθημα (*logos* in Greek also meant "mathematical proportion"). And Aristotle could compare the names used in speech with the *calculi* used to reckon with (see *Sophistici Elenchi*, 165a). This formalizing tendency reaches its climax in the modern scientific and technical concept of language, as does also the concept of being orientated on the εἶδος - οὐσία -being of things and grown constantly more "essentialist".

The most modern types of logic distinguish between the "language of objects" used to speak of things, and "meta-language" used to speak of the language of objects. This enables us to avoid certain logical paradoxes since, for instance, the predicate "true" cannot be used both in object-language and meta-language (cf. the ancient antinomy of "I am a liar" — true or false?). But the distinction also shows that a "hierarchy of meta-languages" (B. Russell), that is, of skilfully thought out languages, always supposes the natural, non-formalized language of everyday intercourse. This means that the precisions and formalities introduced into everyday language by thought (δια - νοεῖν — the "eidetic" determinations) form only one mode — justifiable within its proper limits — of the *logos* of language which articulates human encounter and action but cannot be fully and adequately formalized. (It must be remembered that the "hyletic" looseness of form of everyday speech with its manifold and nuanced acceptations is not a disadvantage there, as in philosophy and science, but rather an advantage.) This principle, that prior to conscious distinction between "thinking" (concept) and "speaking" (word) language exists in a number of "language-games", that is, in various different "forms of life" each with its own usage, we owe to the later thought of L. Wittgenstein (1899–1951).

Previously Wittgenstein had been to a great extent an upholder of the sign-theory of language — each word has a "meaning", which meaning is ordained to the word — but in his *Philosophical Investigations* (E. T., 2nd ed., 1958) he puts forward the idea which runs contrary to the traditional theory of language since Plato — that the "meaning" of a word or phrase is to a great extent its "use". By learning to use a word — in various situations — one learns its "meaning".

Thus Wittgenstein abandons the one-sidedness of the εἶδος- approach to language and re-affirms the ὕλη-character of language, its connection with the various situations and actions in which it occurs. It is to affirm that the language and the activities into which it is woven make up a whole (cf. *Philosophical Investigations,* para. 7). By separating "concepts" (meanings) from "words", the Western notion of language committed the error of treating "meanings", concepts and so on as structures of "thought" independent of languages, as "meta-things", so to speak (cf. Platonism, universals as independent realities).

As against this approach, Wittgenstein notes how thought, like all "meta-languages" is tied to (historical) everyday language, which is a "form of life". Men, he notes, are at one upon language. This is not a consensus of opinions, but a union in a form of life (cf. *Philosophical Investigations,* paras. 23, 241). Thus Wittgenstein goes back to the dialogal (διαλέγεσθαι) character of language which the Greeks recognized in the fundamental "form of life" of the family, and then in the city-state and in Hellenistic times, in the cosmopolitan human fellowship. (It is instructive that Wittgenstein calls the differentiated likeness between the various fields of speech "family likeness" [*op. cit.,* para. 67], which is an application of the traditional notion of analogy in linguistic philosophy.) Here we have, then, by implication — not voiced expressly by Wittgenstein — a criticism of the onesidedly metaphysical notion of being and language favoured by Western culture — where the main concern was the correspondence between εἶδος and νοῦς, form and thought. This is replaced by a notion of language which is more "operative", more orientated to action — as in other languages and cultures — which, however, does not itself escape the charge of onesidedness, inasmuch as it pays too little heed to the creativeness of language in religion and poetry, in philosophy and science. For such activities cannot be simply reduced to that of everyday language.

Thus with Wittgenstein the school of linguistic analysis, which had considered language simply as the syntax and semantics of a system of signs, performed its dialectial "reversal" by returning to the *logos* of language in its historical immediacy, adopting, therefore, an "operative", "pragmatic"

271

view of language which saw it as linked with life. And similarly since the publication of *Sein und Zeit* in 1927 (E. T.: *Being and Time* [1962]), M. Heidegger has gone back to the beginnings of Western metaphysics in Greece (and, derivatively, to science as ἐπιστήμη in contrast to the ordinary scientific opinion or δόξα), where he has re-discovered the "hermeneutic" and historical dimension of language. In this view of matters, the Greeks did not originally see language as the tool of man. Man himself was understood in the light of the *logos* of language. Prior to the metaphysical distinction between "thought" (meaning) and "speaking" (expression), prior also to the modern distinction between subject and object, this is the historical total unity of the *logos* which discloses "being" (φύσις) to man. The primordial endowment of man's existence with *logos*, which belongs *a priori* to his historicity, is where man has a primordial experience of "being", implicitly, before he consciously articulates the manifold "beings" into categories. This primal sense of "being" is not that of "being" in the substantial but in the verbal sense — the historical affirmation of "is". And this is the primordial message received and expounded (ἑρμηνεύειν) — symbolized by the Greek god Hermes. Here man finds himself the "messenger" of a "message" already gone forth (in the historical utterances of poets, thinkers and so on) and still to be taken over in a new and different way each time. "Everywhere there is the play of the hidden relationship between message and messenger" (M. Heidegger, *Unterwegs zur Sprache,* p. 153). Hence one can only start *from* the message (ἑρμηνεία), as disclosed in the actual context of language, to speak *of* the message, that is, the content and utterance of the various groups of speakers, consciously affirming relations. This is the "hermeneutic circle" between "understanding" and "interpreting" (already indicated in *Sein und Zeit,* para. 32) — and interpretation which then fixed more and more one-sidedly upon the logical structure of subject and predicate in the judgment (affirmation) and a precise distinction between "meaning" and "word", ever since the *logos* was taken in a metaphysical sense. The affirmation then disguised other modes of the *logos* such as request, wish, command and so on – what may be called with the commentators of Aristotle, the concrete historical λόγος ἔνυλος.

Thus even before Wittgenstein, Heidegger could treat the affirmation (and its verbal expression in "meanings") as "derivative modes of interpretation" which were in fact based on "understanding". Since man is not primarily a "thinking subject" (in the sense prevalent in modern times from Descartes and Kant to Husserl) but a historical "to-be-in-the-world" all "thought" is based on world and language. "Words accrue to meanings. It is not a matter of providing word-things with meanings" (cf. *Sein und Zeit,* para. 34).

There are also parallels to Wittgenstein's critique of the one-sided "meaning-theory" of language when Heidegger, anticipating this approach and criticizing the one-sided "judgment(affirmation)-theory" points to the manifold nature of usage in human discourse. "Speaking is the 'meaningful' articulation of the intelligibility of the in-the-world, to which being-along-with appertains, and which has definite ways of interested being-with-one-another. This latter is speech, which is granting and denying, summoning, warning; utterance, response and intercession; the making of affirmations and speaking in the sense of making speeches . . . That which speech is about has not necessarily the character of a definite affirmation; indeed, more often than not there is no assertion. A command is given 'about' something; a wish points to something about which it speaks. An intercession does not lack something about which it intercedes. Speech inevitably has such a structure, since it helps to constitute the awareness of the in-the-world, and the structure of speech is prefigured in this basic constitution of existence. That which is spoken of in speech is always to a certain extent and within certain limits itself 'spoken to'" (*Sein und Zeit,* para. 34). This mode of "address" of human speech seems to show that even the most formal "categorical" attribution of a "predicate" (κατηγορούμενον) to a "subject" (ὑποκείμενον) only reflects the essentially "dialogal" (διαλέγεσθαι) structure of human existence, which is given its first articulation by the in-the-world (compare the dialogal notion of language put forward by F. Ebner, M. Buber, F. Rosenzweig and G. Marcel).

The metaphysical notion of language, which culminates in the supreme formalizing of everyday language, in the scientific and technical usage of "terminologies" is undoubtedly one-sided. Is this not due to the over-emphasis on the "logos of definition", λόγος ὁρισμός de-finitio, determinatio (symbolized by the male attitude) which in the form of the logical predication of every "subject" (the ὑποκείμενον, symbolized similarly as the female attitude), ultimately tries to determine totally the "being" which evades such domination (φύσις κρύπτεσθαι φιλεῖ: Heraclitus). One might compare the ambit of the "speculative statement" in Hegel. This suggests that in men's basic "dialogue" (διαλέγεσθαι) with each other, since the Greeks, "the male spirit has triumphed over the female" (M.Scheler, *Die Wissensformen und die Gesellschaft,* p.443). It would explain the fact that the creative emancipation of man from nature, which went on under the banner of a specifically male ("patriarchal") attitude, was able to leave logical, rational "thinking" unduly foot-loose as regards historical "language". This process of language, beginning with Greek metaphysics, was then powerful enough to give the biblical and Christian notion of God (which still integrated the matriarchal, female moment in the name "Father") a theologically one-sided exposition. Thomas Aquinas, for instance, using the framework of act (ἐνέργεια and potency (δύναμις), could only assign an analogous origin in the immanent trinitarian life of God to the male and paternal, but not to the female and maternal. "In generatione Verbi Dei non competit ratio matris, sed solum patris" (*Summa contra Gentiles,* IV, c. 11). The anthropology behind this (*Summa Theologica,* II, II, q. 26, a. 10) is Greek, not biblical. Nonetheless, it was the Logos mysticism of Christianity which paved the way, as K. O. Apel has shown, for the major linguistic thinkers of modern times. (This mysticism had its historical presuppositions and its "efficacious history [H.-G. Gadamer]: the prologue of the Gospel of St. John, Augustine, Denis the Areopagite [the "unutterable" God in the depths of the soul], Master Eckhart [Logos-birth in the 'worded' soul], Nicholas of Cusa and J. Böhme. It was reinforced by a stream of tradition going back to the Rhetorics of antiquity [Cicero, Dante as the discoverer of the history-centred "mother-tongue", the Italian humanists and G. B. Vico with his re-discovery of the historicity of language — "ens et factum covertuntur".)

In the 18th and 19th centuries there were thinkers who are only now influencing the science of language, "research into the content of language" as carried on by such writers as J. Trier, L. Weisgerber and H. Gipper. In his *Metakritik* of 1784, J. G. Hamann based himself on the historical nature of language as the "one first and last organ and criterion of reason" to attack Kant's transcendental philosophy of "pure reason" and to maintain the *a priori* obligation laid on "thinking" by language. G. Hegel (1770–1831), in spite of his dialectical understanding of language as evidenced in his famous review of Hamann, could not liberate himself from the established metaphysical distinction between "language" and "thought" (reason). Hence, though in the "world of morality" Hegel assigned language the function of law and command, he treated it in the "Phenomenology of Mind" under the heading "The alienated spirit; culture" and explained it simply as an expression of the consciousness as it unfolded to "universality" (cf. the introduction to the second edition of the *Logik*). J. G. Herder (17744–1803) opposed the Cartesian rationalism which in the wake of a critique of language in F. Bacon (denouncing the *idola fori,* like Plato on the "weakness" of the *logoi* in the Cratylus) had finally sundered language and thought, to safeguard the "true", attainable only in *cogitatio,* from the deceptiveness of language. It may therefore be taken as a just comment on the Cartesianism envisaged by Herder when a modern writer says: "In Plato, the action and reaction of language and thought on each other was still undecided, but nonetheless undeniable. With Descartes, it was transformed definitively into an aloof indifference or into a dialectic of domination and slavery. The assumption that all *praeiudicata* had either to be justified by recourse to the judgment of the *cogitatio* or rejected as *praeiudicia* ultimately reduced language to a mere tool or even hindrance as regards true knowledge" (J. Pleines, *Das Problem der Sprache* [1967], p. 41).

The reciprocal causality between mind and language had been pointed out in particular by W. von Humboldt (1767–1835), with his distinction between "work" and "act". His view, that men are offered a "world-image" in the living language of ordinary life, prior to all reflective judgment seems to be confirmed today by the comparative study of linguistics (cf. the school of L. Weisberger and the researches of E. Sapir and B. Whorf into the Indian languages of the U.S.A.), partly inspired by the depth psychology of S. Freud and C. Jung). Humboldt says that language is not a "work" (ἔργον) but an "act" (ἐνέργεια), the perpetual dialectic of the individual and the universal: "For language cannot be regarded as a ready-made material which can be measured out and gradually divided up as a whole. It is perpetually self-generating, according to determinate laws of reproduction, but the amount and to some extent the type of the product remain entirely unforeseeable" (*Schriften*, VI [1903], p. 177; see M. Heidegger, *Unterwegs zur Sprache*, p. 246). The approach of Humboldt has given considerable impulses to the science and psychology of language in the 20th century, and indeed also to the philosophy of language (see, for instance, the investigations of W. Wundt, K. Bühler, E. Cassirer, F. de Saussure, the "Platonizing" linguistics of E. Husserl and the more Aristotelian approach, orientated to the psychology of Brentano, of A. Marty, the linguistic analyses of F. Mauthner as an anticipation of modern linguistic philosophy). Humboldt's view would also provide a valuable corrective in many ways to the recent concept of language known as "structuralism", which considers language from the quantifiable aspects (syntax, structure), to the disregard of problems of "meaning" (American structuralism, the "glossematics" of L. Hjelmslev, H. J. Ulldal and others).

It should be noted finally that the specifically Western notion of language, which distinguishes between language and "thought", "word" and "concept", is seen today as having been historically conditioned by a certain anthropological principle. And hence the pluralism of past and present worlds of language is accepted. In spite of the consensus of all men in the κοινὸς λόγος — which does not imply identity and uniformity — the plurality of all that is human is recognized as a creative power to be and not merely a static entity. For the Christian "theology of the word" this means that there is a necessary task to be accomplished in time to come. The message of the gospel which was given in the past must be made accessible to the various "universes of discourse" in terms of the world-image available to their various languages. It cannot be confined to the particular world-image of Western metaphysics.

See also *Spirit, Pre-Socratics, Concept, Being* I, *Tradition, Science* II, *Hermeneutics, Positivism, Logic, Universals, Existence* II, *Metaphysics*.

BIBLIOGRAPHY. B. Croce, *Aesthetic as a Science of Expression and General Linguistics* (1922); H. Delacroix, *Le Langage et la pensée* (1924); F. de Saussure, *Grundfragen der allgemeinen Sprach-Wissenschaft* (1931); L. Bloomfield, *Language* (1933); E. Cassirer, *Language and Myth* (1946); A. Gardiner, *The Theory of Speech and Language* (1951); E. Cassirer, *Philosophy of Symbolic Forms,* I: *Language* (1953); D. Pole, *Later Philosophy of Wittgenstein* (1958); L. Wittgenstein, *Philosophical Investigations,* German text with E.T. by G. Anscombe (2nd ed., 1957); R. Carnap, *Introduction to Semantics* (2nd ed., 1958); S. Ullmann, *Principles of Semantics; Formalization of Logic* (1959); A. Ayer, *Logical Positivism* (1958); M. Heidegger, *Unterwegs zur Sprache* (1959); J. Herder, *Sprachphilosophische Schriften,* selected and annotated by E. Heintel (1960); K.O. Apel, *Analytical Philosophy of Language and the Geisteswissenschaften;* L. Cohen, *Diversity of Meaning* (1963); L. Wittgenstein, *Tractatus Logico-Philosophicus,* German text with a new translation by D. Pears and B. McGuinness (1961); F. Copleston, *Contemporary Philosophy* (1963); K. O. Apel, *Die Idee der Sprache in der Tradition des Humanismus von Dante bis Vico* (1963); W. Christian, *Meaning and Truth in Religion* (1964); F. Mayr, "Prolegomena zur Philosophie und Theologie der Sprache", *Gott in Welt,* I (Festschrift K. Rahner) (1964), pp. 39–84; W. Alston, *Philosophy of Language* (1964); J. Mohanty, *E. Husserl's Theory of Meaning* (1964); J. Bochenski, *Logic of Religion* (1965); G. Hallett, *Wittgenstein's Definition of Meaning as Use* (1966); K. Rahner, *Theological Investigations,* IV (1966), pp. 221–52; F. Smith and G. A. Miller, *The Genesis of Language: A Psychological Approach* (1966); C. Osgood and others, *Measurement of Meaning* (1967); R. Rorty, ed., *Linguistic Turn: Recent Essays in Philosophic Method* (1967); R. Brown, *Wilhelm von Humboldt's Conception of Linguistic Relativity,* in preparation (as of 1967).

Franz Mayr

LAST THINGS

1. In religious language, especially in catechetical instruction, we find the term "the last things" *(novissima)* used to designate the realities which form the limit — or lie beyond the limit — separating time, history of salvation or loss and free acts from their definitive and eternal fulfilment. Hence the last things are the various partial aspects of the one total definitive state of man, as individual before God, as member of humanity and as mankind entire. This total, definitive state of history can be in the form of positive fulfilment or radical, final and permanent disaster. There

are the personal aspects of death, particular judgment, beatific vision or hell (*D* 175, 530, 693, 983), as the final destiny of the individual. And there are the general aspects of the return of Christ in the parousia, the resurrection of the flesh, general judgment and kingdom of God, as the cosmic fulfilment of mankind. As the limit of history and as the fulfilment, there is a formal element common to these realities, in spite of their being so radically diverse as loss and salvation, so that they can be called the "last things". The term does not merely embrace disparate realities under the one formal concept of an abstract finality or fulfilment. For if the whole reality of creation forms a real unity in which each element has a relation to the whole and depends on the whole, this is also true of the fulfilment of this one totality.

2. The hermeneutical principles for the understanding of eschatological assertions, as the doctrine of the last things, are dealt with under the headings of *Eschatology, Afterlife, Millenarianism, Apocatastasis, Eschatologism.*

3. If man is really a manifold reality — as for instance in the body-soul relationship — and is thus a unity in which each element of this manifold reality is determined by all the others, without being simply identical with them, the multiple ways in which tradition speaks of the last things cannot be simply and on principle reduced to one and the same "de-mythologized" meaning. Nonetheless, they cannot be clearly distinguished from one another. No assertion can be understood except in connection with the others, and even in their content they cannot be fully and neatly distinguished from each other. This becomes even more evident when one recalls that very great prudence is needed when speaking of the "time" of the "intermediate state", "between" particular and general judgment, beatific vision and resurrection of the flesh, beginning and end of purgatory. It is certain that this "interval" cannot be regarded as a continuation of time as we know it. This makes the definition of the relationships between the last things all the more difficult to attain. Is it right, for instance, to imagine that the particular judgment on a person who dies today is separated from the general judgment by a length of time which runs in this world from now to the end of history? If this is unthinkable, the relation between particular and general judgment is hardly capable of positive definition. It may be said that the particular or personal judgment is primarily concerned with the destiny of the individual insofar as he is not just an element in the collectivity of mankind. The general judgment speaks of the fact that mankind and its history, as a collective unity, comes under God's judgment. But one should not try to dove-tail the two statements by attaching a positive definition of their meaning to two given points of the one system of temporal co-ordinates.

4. Since man already lives through Christ in an eschatological situation, the last things should not be regarded merely as future events which are only anticipated in thought. They are not just events to which man moves. They are already proleptically real in grace, in the yes or no to grace, in faith and hope. In faith and hope the future judgment and salvation are already realized (Jn 5:24; 12:31; 16:8; contrast, for example, Heb 9:27; Rom 8:24, etc.). The Pneuma which transforms the lowliness of our fleshly existence is already given (Phil 3:21; Rom 8:23) and with him the resurrection has already taken place (Jn 5:25, 28, though not simply empirically, 2 Tim 2:18). The doctrine of the last things thus appears as the doctrine of an eschatological presence of the last things in the life of man. This is not to deny that the present does not exist except in the tension in which it aims at a future different from itself.

The doctrine of the last things has, therefore, relevance to society as well as to the individual and his private "interior" life. For Christians must seek to implant their eschatological hope (which can only bear ultimately on the last things) into the social structures of the world (Vatican II, *Lumen Gentium*, art. 35). This means that even in the social order the Christian cannot merely be "conservative", since his eschatological hope means that any given condition of things must be only of relative value in his eyes, and the same hope which gives the present its true proportions tries to manifest itself in the structures of human society. By his hope of the last things which God himself will bring about, the Christian is set free from the principalities and powers of this aeon (Rom 8:35–39). For he knows that even though he must feel their impact, they cannot, in the last resort, do him harm. And further, he knows that he can and must actively and creatively criticize them and try to transform them, even at the cost of his life.

5. As a rule, the description of the last things can easily appear rather pallid, giving the impression of a purely philosophical discussion. Unwittingly, they are presented as deductions from a philosophical doctrine of the immortality of the soul and of the freedom of man to make definitive decisions. The further elaborations added to this philosophical kernel then give the impression of merely embellishing it with elements of biblical imagery, in terms of the parousia, Antichrist, the resurrection of the flesh understood as that of the body. This can only be avoided by bringing the doctrine of the last things into connection with the relevant dogmatic treatises, more explicitly than is usually done. Thus death is or should be participation in the death of Christ. Judgment is the visible manifestation of the judgment – primarily acquittal – which took place in the cross of Christ (Jn 12:31 f.; Rom 8:3; Gal 3:13, etc.). The consummation of the world is the disclosure of God's acceptance of the world in the incarnation of the Son of God. The doctrine of purgatory can only be made understandable by a profounder analysis of concupiscence and the punishment of sin. The parousia of Christ must be seen more clearly as the final stage of the one coming of Christ which began with the incarnation of the Word of God, continued with the descent of Christ into death (cf. Mt 12:40) and initiated in the resurrection and in the outpouring of the Spirit the transformation of the world. Hence the "return" of Christ is the arrival of all things at their destination in Christ.

See also *Eschatology, Afterlife, Millenarianism, Apocatastasis, Eschatologism, Death, Purgatory, Limbo, Hell, Resurrection* II, *Beatific Vision, Parousia, Concupiscence, Sin* II.

BIBLIOGRAPHY. See bibliography on *Immortality;* also: F. von Hügel, *Eternal Life: A Study of Its Implications and Applications* (1929); H. Thielicke, *Tod und Leben* (1946); M. Lods, *L'espérance chrétienne d'Origène à St. Augustin* (1952); A. Winklhofer, *Das Kommen seines Reiches* (1959); K. Barth, *Church Dogmatics,* III/2 (1960); A.-M. Henry, "Die Wiederkunft Christi", *Die katholische Glaubenswelt,* III (1961); E. Brunner, *Dogmatics,* III (1962) (Church, faith and the consummation); R. Bultmann, *History and Eschatology* (reprint, 1962); P. Schütz, *Charisma Hoffnung* (1962); J. P. Martin, *The Last Judgment in Protestant Theology from Orthodoxy to Ritschl* (1963); C. S. Callian, *The Significance of Eschatology in the Thoughts of N. Berdyaew* (1965); W. Pannenberg, *Offenbarung als Geschichte* (3rd ed., 1965); H. U. von Balthasar, *Zuerst Gottes Reich* (1966); R. Guardini, *The Last Things* (1966); H. Kimmerle, *Die Zukunftsbedeutung der Hoffnung. Auseinandersetzung mit dem Hauptwerk Ernst Blochs* (1966); P. Lain-Entralgo, *L'attente et l'espérance* (1966); C. Kegley, ed., *The Theology of Rudolf Bultmann* (esp. P. Minear, "Interpretation of New Testament Eschatology"; H. Ott, "Philosophy of History") (1966); H. Dolch, "Zukunftsvision und Parusie", in L. Scheffczyk and others, eds., *Wahrheit und Verkündigung,* I, *Festschrift M. Schmaus* (1967), pp. 327–39; H. Fries, "Spero ut Intelligam", *ibid.,* pp. 353–75; J. Pieper, *Hoffnung und Geschichte* (1967); F. Mussner, *Christ and the End of the World* (1968).

Karl Rahner

LAW

I. Biblical: A. Old Testament. B. New Testament. II. Theology and Moral Theology. III. Rule of Law. IV. Philosophy of Law: A. Concept and Technical Definitions. B. Systems. C. Historical Development.

I. Biblical

A. OLD TESTAMENT

1. *The character of the Old Testament collections of laws.* As used to designate certain sections of the OT the term "law" is derived from the rendering of תורה by νόμος in the LXX and NT. Originally *torah* means direction and instruction in general. Thus it is found in the Wisdom literature in the sense of instruction given by elders (Prov 1:8; 6:20) and sages. In the earlier strata of the Pentateuch the word occurs only in Exod 13:9; 16:4, passages which O. Eissfeldt assigns to the "Lay source" (Yahwist). This is already the *torah* of Yahweh. Hos 4:6; Jer 2:8; 18:18 are early passages which bear witness to the fact that this *torah* of God was entrusted to the lips of the priests, and thus contrasted with the knowledge bestowed by God, the counsel of the wise and the word of the prophets. According to Is 8:16, 20; 30:9 (cf. 1:10), on the other hand, the *torah* is the message of the prophets by which Israel must guide its actions. In Hos 8:12 *torah* already stands for written "commandments". But it is only in Deut that the designation becomes frequent, and here in fact it is used alike of individual precepts (Deut 17:11) and of Deut itself, which is referred to as the "book of the *torah*" (Deut 17:18f.; Jos 8:32).

In the Deuteronomist writings it is chiefly Deuteronomy itself which is designated by this term, but it can also be used quite generally of all that God has commanded. In the work of the Chronicler, the entire Pentateuch is designated as *torah* ("*torah* of God, *torah* of Moses, *torah*"). This usage is reflected in the division of Scripture into "law and prophets" found in the writings of later Judaism and in the NT. Thus *torah* originally signified an individual precept, then Deuteronomy, and finally all the writings attributed to Moses. Since over and above Deuteronomy the rest of the "collections of laws" in the OT were also regarded as binding and valid norms of behaviour, *torah* came to designate the totality of all the divine precepts in the Pentateuch (thus in 2 Chr, Neh, and certain of the psalms, cf. Ps 1). In particular the fact that this word is translated by νόμος in the LXX makes it clear that at this period the emphasis was laid upon the aspect of norm. These norms are to be found in the Pentateuch in the Book of the Covenant (Exod 21–23), Deut, the Holiness Code (Lev 17–26) and the ritual laws in P. These sections consist of collections of individual clauses of extremely varied origin incorporated in the narratives of Moses.

The distinction between apodictic and casuistic law was introduced by A. Alt, who maintained that there was a fundamental difference between the two. According to Alt apodictic clauses are those which contain a bare directive formulated for the most part in the negative and without any punitive sanctions attached (e.g., "Thou shalt not steal"). Casuistic clauses, however, are formulated as hypothetical cases with "if . . ." and with concrete legal decisions attached to them. According to Alt the apodictic clauses are typically divine law in Israel, for behind the phrase "Thou shalt . . ." stands the authority of Yahweh. By contrast the content of the casuistic clauses is to a large extent common to Israel and the surrounding peoples, and is derived from legal decisions. The distinction drawn here by Alt has on the whole proved too inflexible to fit the facts, and with regard to the origin of the apodictic clauses it has been shown to be questionable. The works of Rabast, Reventlow, Kilian and Feucht threw light upon the problems of literary criticism, and then Gerstenberger solved in a new way the problem of how the apodictic clauses originated. Taking as his starting-point the observation that these clauses are handed down in lists (sometimes as decalogues and duodecalogues), he found that the content of these clauses suggested they once comprised sage rules such as the fathers of the tribe handed down to their sons by way of instruction in the context of the clan (Lev 18:20 may be an allusion to this). The attribution of these to Yahweh would have been secondary.

A more far-reaching solution to this problem has been proposed by W. Richter: he suggests that the designation "apodictic", which is derived from the content, should be abandoned, and that in its place the designations "prohibitive" (negation with לֹא), "vetitive" (negation with אַל) and "imperative" should be introduced. Richter has established parallels, often of considerable extent, between the content of the lists of "prohibitives" in the collections of laws and the "vetitives" contained in the Wisdom literature. From the aspect of the history of forms the "vetitives" belong to the sapiential exhortatory proverbs *(Mahnsprüche)* which are always accompanied by a motivating clause. In "prohibitives" such motivating clauses are always secondary. Both forms are expressions of an educational system in which those belonging to the upper classes, especially officials, were brought up. (This is to be deduced both from the content and from Egyptian parallels.) The prohibitives are collected into series on the basis of a common theme (persons who are sexually *taboo*, judges and judgment, commerce). This ethos would have applied to priests also. It is not law or justice that is in question here but an ethos which in the "prohibitives" is "applied to public and professional life" and "is intended to regulate behaviour in a circumscribed sphere of life". By contrast the "vetitives" of the Wisdom literature are more concerned with interior motivation and the formation of disposition and character. Thus the "prohibitives" of the classic decalogue also embody an ethos pertaining to a particular class. It is the free, male and property-owning Israelites that are envisaged.

Furthermore, we can plainly recognize how law and ethos are related in the decalogue: for the "prohibitives" of the decalogue precisely as "prohibitives" are not concerned with juridical practice. The crimes listed here are rather of a kind which cannot be brought home to the offender in the law-court, so that in order to prevent them the ethos has to be appealed to. Thus the ethos of the "prohibitives" blocks up a loophole at this point in the maintenance of social order which the juridical case-law is unable to cover.

The cultic procedures prescribed for individual crimes in the Priestly laws (6th–8th commandments) represent secondary developments. Secondary and subsequent also is the process by which the ethos of these decalogue "prohibitives" is made subordinate to the worship of Yahweh by the "prohibitives" which have been placed before the third commandment: in this way a new basis could be provided for the ethos. In later strata the earlier "prohibitives" are further developed by the addition of positive clauses (cf. the commandment to love one's neighbour in Lev 19:18 in the light of its context), and in the "imperatives" thus formed special value is attached to man's interior disposition and attitude. But even the casuistic clauses were not simply law from the start. If we take, for instance, the group of "if-thou" clauses established by Feucht, we can say with certainty that they are not intended to prescribe for particular cases, but were rather the expression of reform movements of a social and humanitarian kind. The special interest apparent in these clauses is also to be found in the prescriptions of the so-called "social" lists. What we have here are lists of exhortations to the upper classes and property-owners in order to make them treat the humbler classes (widows, orphans, strangers, day-labourers) justly, and to accord them due respect as members of society.

In terms of content exhortations of this kind are also to be found in the "collections of laws". But it is not until the preaching of the prophets that we find actual lists. (Here, therefore, is an important area in which the preaching of the prophets overlaps with the "legal" tradition contained in the Pentateuch.) This category is especially developed and extended from Ezra on. The opening and closing clauses contain, as a rule, general formulations concerning justice and judgment and the relationship to Yahweh. Each of these enumerations of rules of social conduct is a summary of what is demanded by Yahweh. A series of double catalogues in the Priestly tradition contain in the first section a list of social crimes, in the second a list of cultic ones. The fact that this category

appears so frequently is due to the necessity of summing up ethical exhortations concerning social behaviour, which as such are often incapable of being enforced by law.

A special kind of legal clause is that characterized by the so-called מות יומת formulation ("Shall be put to death"), which probably did not intend to impose the death penalty, but merely constituted a special kind of curse. The death which is to overtake the perpetrator of the crime consists in the withdrawal of life by God. The criminal has fundamentally transgressed the rules of communal life and thereby has set himself outside the sphere of life bestowed and protected by Yahweh (cf. Lev 20:10 with the 6th commandment of the decalogue). It is not until post-exilic times that formal excommunication from the community in the form of the "ban" is found in the practice of the synagogue, at Qumran and in Christian circles.

In reality, therefore, only a minor part of what we describe as "law" really deserves to be called so. It is chiefly concerned with crimes against property, which are always formulated casuistically, and such crimes as are requited by fines or corporal punishment. The Priestly prescriptions regulate sacred matters in particular, which are envisaged as the decisive instruction delivered to Moses by Yahweh; for the dwelling of God in Israel and the manifestation of his glory commenced with the revelation at Sinai: "Thereby Yahweh drew near to Israel in a manner which made necessary the comprehensive cultic rules and safeguards" (von Rad, *Old Testament Theology*, I, p. 180).

Little light has yet been thrown on the manner in which these various clauses came to be combined, formed as they were from exhortations based on ethos in general, or on the ethos pertaining to a particular class, or deriving from writings envisaging particular occasions and circumstances, laws of property and cultic laws. The procedure is similar in all the collections and is often based on "catch-words", which have broken up older groupings. The two versions of the decalogue have a role of their own.

2. The theological function of law in the Old Testament. Probably none of the individual forms which have been mentioned bore originally any theological implications (although in particular cases they may have been theological in content). The theological element is located in the motivations and the framework of such clauses. Thus, for instance, the reference to the slavery in Egypt ("For you were a slave in the land of Egypt") is a motivation for clauses designed to protect slaves. This was the model for the motivations which contain references to the "stranger" (cf. Lev 19:34 with Lev 19:18 and Deut 12:12–15). The concluding formula, "I am Yahweh" set at the end of a list, which is probably intended to bear a meaning similar to that of Exod 20:2 (". . . who brought you out of the land of Egypt") is also an instance of the process of theologizing. Other motivations are, for instance, Deut 14:21: "For you are a people holy to Yahweh", or the classification as "an abomination to Yahweh". Deut imparts a deeper meaning to these motivations by the demand it lays upon men to love Yahweh with their whole hearts. But the most comprehensive way of subsuming the prescriptions under the Yahwistic faith was to bring them into connection with the event of Sinai and the person of Moses. Everything which could be described as a norm of behaviour is firmly anchored here in the revelation of Sinai (in contrast to the prophets, who represent such demands as proceeding immediately from God in the present).

Appealing to Exod 20:2 von Rad offers the following interpretation of the process by which the laws were anchored in the Sinai revelation: "The proclamation of the divine will in law" is "like a net thrown over Israel", "the process by which it is made over to Yahweh as his own". This event the OT itself already interpreted as the establishment of the covenant (with the constituent elements: proclamation of the covenant prescriptions, establishment of the covenant, blessing and cursing). Israel understood these commandments as life-giving (Ezek 18:5–9), as a guarantee of the election, which is for Israel's own good (Deut 10:13), but not as a sort of ukase where all that mattered was the work of obedience as a human achievement. This view of the law, according to von Rad, is not found before the post-exilic development in which the law lost its function of service. As against this view, we may point to the parenetic elements, especially in Deut and the Holiness Code, which make the possession of land in particular dependent upon the fulfilment of the commandments.

From Ezra on the concept of ṭorah or nomos undergoes a development in which it becomes the sum total of what the external onlooker might describe as the "Jewish religion". Nomos becomes identified with the Jewish way of life as a whole, which man abandons the moment he ceases to observe "the laws". D. Rössler showed that in the language of apocalyptic "law" is used in a comprehensive sense, and seldom defined in more concrete detail. The "law" does not merely regulate religious conduct, but is actually identical with it. This led at the start to a universalization of the law. It is seen as the order which is eternal, and which alone brings salvation, which was given to Israel as its light, and which gives it a central place among the peoples of the earth. And if this is true, then it was also contained in the basic plan of the world. It must already have been known to the patriarchs, and, in its minimum demands, even to the Gentiles. Thus the OT law becomes the eternal law written upon heavenly tables, which is identical with the natural law, and according to which even the course of the stars is directed. Another process, likewise arising from the universal meaning attached to nomos, results in a reduction of the contents of OT law, and it becomes identified to a large extent with social commandments in general (the writings of later Judaism, and, so far as Jewish, the *Testament of the Twelve Patriarchs*. This process by which the law becomes detached from the actual contents of the ṭorah of Moses is also presupposed in the synoptic tradition, and wherever it is found possible to sum up the "law" in the "love of neighbour" or the "golden rule" (Mt 7:12), disregarding the cultic and legal elements of the OT. What is presupposed here is a concept of the law which includes only the worship of the one God, the social commandments and the combined Jewish and Greek catalogues of vices from Hellenistic Judaism.

B. New Testament

1. *The position of Jesus in regard to the law.* None of the gospels attributes Jesus' death to his attitude to the law. (According to Mark the causes of Jesus' death are the envy of the leaders of the people and the blasphemies attributed to Jesus.) Citations of the law are attributed to Jesus by the Synoptics: the two chief commandments, the social

commandments of the decalogue in the pericope concerning the rich young man, the commandment to honour parents in Mk 7, Moses's commandment concerning divorce and the sixth commandment in the pericope on divorce, and the fifth and sixth commandments of the decalogue and a series of formulations similar to commandments in the "antitheses" of the Sermon on the Mount. But they cannot be attributed to Jesus in this form. The first area which these interpretative citations are to be found in Mark is the secondary and anti-Jewish stratum of the Marcan controversies, which contains other citations from Scripture also directed against the Jews. Secondly it should be noticed that the formulation of the social commandments of the decalogue, together with the two commandments of love, is common to the Marcan tradition and to the popular theology of Hellenistic Judaism which precisely regarded this combination of decalogue and chief commandments as the most important part of the law (Philo).

In the formulation of the antitheses in the Sermon on the Mount this tension between the community and Judaism, which appears in the Marcan controversies, is intensified. The remnant of OT law which is regarded as still in force, and which is defended as Christian in the community against the Jews, is nothing else than the conservation of specific Jewish-Hellenistic or Jewish-apocalyptic positions of the 1st century. This finds expression in Mark and Luke in the fact that only the commandment of love and the social commandments of the decalogue have been retained, and in Matthew over and above this, in a concept of law which includes only social duties towards one's neighbour so that the law can actually be summed up in the golden rule. Again for Mark the reason for restricting the law to the commandment of love and the decalogue (for him no other commandments are in force) was the same peculiar concept of law characteristic of later Judaism, which only included duties towards one's neighbour. When this concept of law came into contact with apocalyptic traditions, these invariably had the effect of establishing a relationship between the duty of fulfilling the law and the judgment according to works: either the law must be fulfilled in such a way that a heavenly reward is obtained (antitheses 1,5 and 6), or a special act must be performed which went beyond

mere fulfilment of the law, so that it was through this act that the heavenly reward would be obtained (Mk 10:17–21).

Apart from this conclusions are to be drawn concerning the attitude of Jesus: a) from the clauses concerning the preservation of purity which constitute the basis of the three earliest antitheses in the Sermon on the Mount. Of these Mt 5:28–32 constitutes an interpretation of the sixth commandment inserted into the actual clause itself, while Mt 5:34–37 constitutes a remote interpretation of the second commandment. Since these clauses can hardly have had their origin in Jewish or Hellenistic circles, they may be taken to approximate most closely, relatively speaking, to the actual message of Jesus himself. The clauses in Mt 5:28–32 are cast in the form of Wisdom teaching, and lay down that the impurity entailed in looking lustfully at a married woman or in marrying a divorced woman is so great that it constitutes a transgression of the sixth commandment. The ancient tradition of the purification of the temple might be adduced as evidence of the fact that an interiorized conception of purity of this sort is not strange or unprecedented in the preaching of Jesus. b) Conclusions can be drawn concerning the attitude of Jesus to the law on the basis of a series of individual logia which constitute the basis of the Marcan controversies (Mk 2:17a, 19, 27; 3:4b; 7:15; 10:9). The structure of these clauses is that of the Wisdom literature. Their mode of thought is clearly different from that of the cultic tradition, and they display a definite "realism". In the pericopes under consideration there are two elements: the actual maxims laid down and the questions which prompt them, and which are introduced and "framed" by references to some practice of the community. Now this practice of the community always reflects a considerably lower moral standard of behaviour than that prescribed in the maxim, so that the question as to what is permitted by the law envisages customs which are only slightly different from the practice of the Pharisees. But the reply to this question contained in the key clause of the pericope concerned is more universal in character, and goes far beyond what was initially envisaged. These pericopes, therefore, have to some extent been supplemented by secondary interpretations of the law. The basic maxims, however, which may be ascribed to Jesus himself, are distinguished by the fact that they convince the hearer by their compelling intrinsic logic, and not initially by reason of the authority of the Lord who utters them. Just as in the case of the Sabbath healings, it is not so much the law as such that is being called in question and re-evaluated. Rather, questions concerning the practice of religion in daily life are being answered with a definite measure of liberalism and an evaluation, which is emphatically unritual in character, of what is right for man. On the whole it was probably only because of the death of Jesus that a cleavage arose between the community and the Jews on the question of the law. The circle of the "Hellenists" in the primitive community upheld positions on the question of the law which must have been quite similar to those of Jewish Hellenism. These positions only became anti-Jewish when Judaism itself, in the course of the 1st century, withdrew more and more from these positions as the rabbinical view prevailed.

2. *The law in Paul.* In his conception of the law Paul shows close connections with the thought of later Judaism in two respects: where he has occasion to speak of the content of the law (Rom 13:8–10; Gal 5:14) he points to love of the neighbour as its essence and designates social commandments of the decalogue as its expression. Other commandments too could only be regarded as relevant here in that they are concerned with one's attitude to one's neighbour. Then, both Paul and Judaism see the law as an independent theological entity: according to the claim of those who submit to it, it is an independent way of salvation, in competition with faith in Jesus Christ. While Paul leaves untouched the social conception of the law upheld in Judaism, the salvific function of the law becomes a problem for his theology. It is axiomatic for him that salvation can be obtained only through faith in Jesus Christ, and this applies to Jews and Gentiles alike. Although the demands of the law (as understood by Paul) remain in force, and although man will one day be judged according to the works of love for his neighbour which he has performed, the law as a way of salvation must be excluded. Salvation consists in the justice of God, i.e., in the fulfilment of the promises made to the patriarchs. Whereas in Judaism justice is achieved by the fulfilment of the law, Paul goes back to the close connection

of justice with faith in Gen 15:6 (Abraham) and, with the help of scriptural proofs, is able to show that the promises, and therefore their fulfilment also, are linked to this justification by faith. The law, therefore, as a way of salvation is excluded because those who observe it hope thereby to achieve righteousness, whereas Scripture demonstrates that righteousness is linked with faith. Law and faith (faith here being understood as faith in Jesus Christ) are made exclusive alternatives. Paul goes on to demonstrate that man could never have obtained righteousness by the way of the law, for no one (as Paul postulates) can fulfil it completely (Gal 3:10; 5:3; cf. 6:13). Hence all men come under the curse which is the penalty threatened in Deut 27:26. But Jesus alone can free man from this curse, for in him is promised the opposite of the curse, the blessing for all peoples already promised to Abraham. Man attains this blessing, however, only by faith and baptism, since it is by these that he puts on Jesus and is so identified with him, the seed of Abraham, that the promises given to this seed now apply also to all believers.

In order to safeguard the universality of redemption, Paul shows in Romans that the Gentiles like the Jews had sinned against the law, which must therefore have been known to them (Rom 1:18f.). Paul probably regards the law by which the Gentiles are to be judged as an interior norm which corresponds to the Mosaic law, and which, if actually expressed in words, would coincide with the Mosaic law. By the acts which they have committed against the law men have fallen into the realm of the *sarx,* sin and death. So long as they remain in this realm they will never be able to fulfil the law, for this belongs to the opposite realm of the Pneuma (Rom 7:14). It is only when man has been raised into the realm of the Pneuma that he can conform his actions to this "spiritual" law. Now man attains to this Pneuma through Jesus Christ, as the fulfilment of the promise. From the time of Adam until Christ the power of sin prevailed, activating the sphere of the *sarx,* and bringing the sinful works of the flesh to light (von Dülmen), so that the power of sin signified both the sinful act itself and also the state of bondage to sin, while law assisted sin to gain power and life (1 Cor 15:56). For with the advent of the law all became guilty of transgression. In contrast to sin, however, law is only destructive in its effects and function, not by nature. Sin avails itself of the law in order to kill. The law is the catalyst which reveals the ruinous and hopeless state of man. But when the curse of the law is concentrated upon Jesus he endures the penalty of death, and thereby sets aside the demand of the law. For this reason, and also because the law is no longer used to demonstrate the presence of sin, Christ is the end of the law. Henceforward by the gift of the Pneuma Christ makes possible a life in which the law is fulfilled. Christ, therefore, does not put an end to works of every kind, but only to those works which are the result of accepting the law as the way of salvation, instead of faith in himself. The ἐν Χριστῷ brings the ἐν νόμῳ to an end. For just as the law was the decisive factor in the old dispensation, so Christ now becomes the decisive factor in the new aeon (von Dülmen). Paul regards love of the neighbour as summing up the whole of the law, yet at the same time includes it among the charismata. For him, therefore, the fulfilment of the law is a gift of the Pneuma.

At present the law only has a part to play in bringing out the obstinacy of the unbelieving section of Israel, which opens the way for the Gentiles to be taken into the community (Rom 9:11). Thus the law of Israel was bestowed for such a purpose and in such a manner so that its function in the history of salvation might contribute to the attainment of the promise by all.

3. The law in the other New Testament writings. In the Gospel of John, in contrast to Paul and the synoptics, the law is no longer regarded as a norm of action for the community. The requirement that men shall love one another, the new commandment (Jn 13:34f.), does in fact originally stem from Jewish tradition, but it is no longer connected with the authority of the law. Its sole basis is the work of Jesus. The possession of the law is confined to the Jews ("your law"). The law of Moses (which does not mean merely the Pentateuch: Jn 10:34) finds its most positive function in the fact that it bears witness to and promises Christ. Jn 1:17 presents the overall pattern: the law and Moses are contrasted with grace and truth and Jesus Christ, and thereby the imperfect revelation in the Jewish religion is contrasted with the revelation which comes through Jesus (Grässer) (cf. 9:28). According to 19:7 Jesus has to die because of the law against blasphemy. Thus the law itself derives from an imperfect stage in revelation. The fact that it pointed to Jesus went unrecognized by the Jews, and it was used as an instrument against him.

The Letter of James presupposes the same late Jewish concept of the law as the synoptics and Paul. According to Jas 2:8–16 the command to love one's neighbour sums up the content of the law. It is the word of salvation which can save souls and is the royal and perfect law of liberty (1:21, 25; 2:8). The question may be left open as to whether the law has these characteristics because it is not merely an OT summary of individual prescriptions, and is to be applied by the individual freely according to the standard of love (Gutbrod), or whether it is simply a law which does not impose Judaism and circumcision. Ch. 2 is concerned not with the contrast between faith and law, but only with the manner in which faith and works are related to one another, which is also a problem for Paul.

The concept of law in the Letter to the Hebrews is similar to that in the Pauline letters inasmuch as the law, as a way of salvation, is set aside by the death of Jesus. Here, however, the law does not regulate the moral conduct of men, but is chiefly concerned with cultic and priestly precepts. The concept of law in Hebrews, therefore, has its origin in the Priestly tradition. The priesthood of Jesus is based not upon a law consisting of earthly commandment, but on the power of eternal life (7:16). Because it is only the high priest Jesus Christ who has brought true purification, the law of the OT was not able to achieve this; for the priests instituted by it were only mortal. It is not because man cannot fulfil it (Paul) that the law is incapable of causing salvation, but because only mortal men fulfil it (cf. Gutbrod). The priesthood of Christ in the form of the priesthood of Melchizedek had always been in competition with the Levitical priesthood according to the law (Heb 7).

See also *Old Testament Books* I, *Commandments (the Ten), Covenant, Judaism* I, III, *Apocalyptic, Sermon on the Mount, Apostolic Church, Justice* I, *Salvation* I, *New Testament Theology* II, III, *Charity* I.

BIBLIOGRAPHY. OLD TESTAMENT: R. Marcus, *Law in the Apocrypha* (1927); A. Jirku, *Das weltliche Recht im Alten Testament* (1928); M. Noth, *Die Gesetze im Pentateuch* (1940); D. Daube, *Studies in Biblical Law* (1947); K. Rabast, *Das apodiktische Recht im Dt und im Heiligkeitsgesetz* (1949); A. Alt, "Die Ursprünge des israelitischen Rechts", *Kleine Schriften*, I (1953), pp. 278–332; R. Rendtorff, *Die Gesetze in der Priesterschrift* (1954); D. Rössler, *Gesetz und Geschichte* (1960); P. Renaud, "La loi et les lois dans les livres de Maccabées", *Revue Biblique* 68 (1961), pp. 39–67; H. Graf Reventlow, *Das Heiligkeitsgesetz formgeschichtlich untersucht* (1961); N. Lohfink, *Das Hauptgebot* (1963); R. Kilian, *Literarkritische und formgeschichtliche Untersuchung des Heiligkeitsgesetzes* (1963); J. Hempel, *Das Ethos des AT* (2nd ed., 1964); C. Feucht, *Untersuchungen zum Heiligkeitsgesetz* (1964); E. Nielsen, *Die Zehn Gebote* (1965); E. Gerstenberger, *Wesen und Herkunft des sogenannten apodiktischen Rechtes im Alten Testament* (1965); H. Graf Reventlow, *Gebot und Predigt im Dekalog* (1965). NEW TESTAMENT: H. H. Huber, *Die Bergpredigt* (1932); W. G. Kümmel, "Jesus und der jüdische Traditionsgedanke", *Zeitschrift für die neutestamentliche Wissenschaft* 33 (1934), pp. 105–30; W. Gutbrod, "νόμος", *TWNT*, IV, pp. 1029–84; G. Bornkamm, *Das Ende des Gesetzes. Paulusstudien* (1952); W. D. Davies, *Torah in the Messianic Age and in the Age to Come* (1952); C. H. Dodd, *Gospel and Law* (1953); E. Percy, *Die Botschaft Jesu* (1953); H. Ljungmann, *Das Gesetz erfüllen (Mt 5:17ff. und 3:15)* (1954); E. Lohmeyer, *Probleme paulinischer Theologie (Gesetzeswerke)* (1954); H. Braun, *Spätjüdisch-häretischer und frühchristlicher Radikalismus*, 2 vols. (1957); P. G. Verweijs, *Evangelium und neues Gesetz in der ältesten Christenheit bis auf Marcion* (1960); H. Schürmann, "Wer daher eines dieser geringsten Gebote auflöst . . .", *Biblische Zeitschrift* (new series) 4 (1960), pp. 238–50; G. Eichholz, *Glaube und Werke bei Paulus und Jakobus* (1961); W. Schrage, *Die konkreten Einzelgebote in der paulinischen Paränese* (1961); G. Strecker, *Der Weg der Gerechtigkeit* (1962); R. Bultmann, "Christ the End of the Law", *Essays Philosophical and Theological* (1963) (= *Glauben und Verstehen*, II, pp. 32–58); G. Bornkamm, G. Barth and J. Held, *Tradition and Interpretation in Matthew* (1963); R. Hummel, *Die Auseinandersetzung zwischen Kirche und Judentum im Mt* (1963); W. D. Davies, *The Setting of the Sermon on the Mount* (1964); W. Trilling, *Das wahre Israel* (3rd ed., 1964); A. von Dülmen, *Die Theologie des Gesetzes bei Paulus* (1967).

Klaus Berger

II. Theology and Moral Theology

On the theology of law, see *Old Testament Theology*, *Salvation* IV A, *Freedom*, *Law and Gospel*, *New Testament Theology* II, *Sin* I, *Works*.

1. A consideration of the notion of law in moral theology must start with the moral law

and then proceed to the other types of law. The laws of nature and positive laws then appear as deficient modes of the moral law. By laws of nature we understand a rule for what must be, which those subject to it must follow by an intrinsic necessity. By positive laws, those which are imposed on man from outside, we understand a rule for what ought to be, to which those subject to it freely adhere, according to the will of the law-giver. The free will of those who are bound in such a way is not subject to the law by intrinsic necessity but by reason of their own free decision or external compulsion. The moral law, on the other hand, is both a rule for what must be, which man obeys by an intrinsic necessity and also a rule for what ought to be, to which he freely adheres – though from a different aspect. Hence the moral law combines the perfections of the two types of law: accord with nature and free self-determination. For when he acts morally, man is subject to the claims of the moral law by an intrinsic necessity, since moral action is only possible on the supposition that something is recognized in one way or another as what absolutely ought to be, that is, as something to which he must freely take up an attitude. Thus, through the moral law, man is obliged to follow an order of things which alone makes free individual and social life possible and whose claim forces itself on the reason. On the other hand, he must freely take up an attitude to this necessarily recognized obligation, since he must himself freely decide whether he will bind his freedom to the claim of what ought to be, or act contrary to what he recognizes as imperative. Thus he must himself decide on the order of things to which he is bound, and thus freely acknowledge it. The refusal of this acknowledgement is seen by theologians as the sin against the Holy Spirit (Mt 12:31ff. and parr.; Acts 7:51).

The moral law, however, points to the divine law-giver who establishes it, since the life endowed with reason and freedom according to the image and likeness of his orderly perfection *(lex aeterna)* is produced by him *(lex naturae rationalis)* and enriched with the dynamism of his free self-communication *(lex gratiae)*.

Accordingly, the moral law is formally a necessary rule of free moral action, whose claim that man ought to do this or that is absolutely binding, but to whose content man can freely take up an attitude. The obligation imposed on the moral subject by an absolute ought is always an obligation imposed by God himself, whether it is recognized explicitly or only implicitly, since absolute obligation can come only through God, who binds men by granting an external and internal participation in his absolute perfection — the former by creation, the latter by grace — and hence concretely imparts himself. Man may only bind himself in the moral law to this communication of the divine law, insofar as he recognizes it explicitly or implicitly as the radiation of the divine "ought". This means that subjectively and in the concrete the content of the moral law is that which the moral subject recognizes in one way or another as what absolutely ought to be and hence implicitly or explicitly as the obligatory will of God, so that the subject is guilty of a moral failure if he does not respond to the known claim.

2. As regards the content of the moral law, it does not follow from what has been said that the content of what has been recognized by the moral subject as divine law is definitely willed by God, independently of the subjective decision and hence in this sense objectively. For what appears to man as obligatory moral law is infallibly at one with the divine order only from the formal aspect of absolute obligation to God. As regards the content, the contingence of man is such that under the appearance of accord with divine order there may in reality be a link with mortal disorder, by reason of error or sin. Hence, as regards content, there is only accord with the divine law when what appears to man subjectively as divinely established order is also such independently of his subjective opinion and thus corresponds objectively to the divinely established order of nature and grace.

This order of divine law, as Christians hold, consists of the self-realization of man by his living for his fellow-men and so for God. This involves observation of the known laws of nature and civilization which make the development of man possible, and which he must apply in such a way as to serve the development of the person as such, that is, the realization of love of God and of the neighbour. What this precisely means man may learn from the revelation proposed and interpreted by the Church and from the laws of nature and civilization as formulated by the philosophy and the sciences according

to their various stages. In this way, reason enlightened by faith has objective knowledge insofar as it measures the contribution of various actions to the perfection of the moral subject by using norms independent of the subject.

However, the channels through which revelation comes expresses the content of the divine law in a limited and conditioned way, imperfectly therefore, though sufficiently. Further, the laws of nature and of civilization can be influenced by men's free decisions and are also imperfectly known. Thus the content of the divine law which is incorporated in the natural and supernatural order is only accessible to men in a limited way. But though we may therefore speak of development and corrections in the knowledge and formulation of the content of the divine law, the content itself cannot change. But the subjective obligation towards this content can change, which means that there is a development of the moral law. For the moral law only exists insofar as it is known concretely and subjectively as binding, for freedom is only effectively under an obligation where it has to react existentially to an obligation imposed on it. But knowledge of these obligations is subject to constant change on account of our being involved in historical change and differs in the case of each individual according to the formation of his conscience.

3. As regards obligation, the following is to be noted. Since law always has two aspects which influence each other, the formal attitude of the person involved and the material content of the ordination of the moral subject to his fulfilment, it must be affirmed, both from the existential and the essential point of view, that the divine law obliges in analogous ways.

a) If the fulfilment of a concrete law is so necessary for the realization of the content of divine law, subjectively or objectively, that without it the order seen as the content of the divine law is essentially disturbed, then one is obliged *sub grave* to keep this law. If man offends in such a case, he takes, by the very fact of doing so, a fundamental decision against God, because he deliberately violates God's will which is recognized as essential.

b) If without the observance of a given concrete law the integral maintenance of the order in question is disturbed, one is obliged *sub leve.* An offence in such a case does not affect essentials and hence is not a fundamental decision against God.

c) If the observance of a given concrete law makes possible a more perfect fulfilment of the order of love, while the neglect of such a law (which in such cases is called a counsel or a work of supererogation does not positively disturb the order of love, one is obliged only *sub perfectione.* One knows that to follow the counsel is to avail of an opportunity offered by God, but to fail to use the chance does not mean that one turns away from God.

Hence, contrary to the opinion of some modern theologians, it can scarcely be said that the notion of counsel or work of supererogation is confined to the order of essences, while in the concrete order one either sins or acts meritoriously. For it is impossible to consider the absolute claim of the "ought" apart from the content of the law. A prescribed action is formally God's law and existentially of obligation because and insofar as it is seen, from the point of view of its content, as divine law. But that which subjectively or objectively, *sub grave, sub leve* or *sub perfectione* appears formally as divine law, is only analogously divine law according to its content.

To sum up: God desires man to be freely his partner. He only judges him insofar as man judges himself by turning away from the one source of life or by turning towards it imperfectly. Once Christian existence has been established, it will to a considerable extent work out in a region where only a greater or less perfection is at stake, and not salvation or loss. The divine law *(lex aeterna)* consists of all that corresponds objectively to man's perfection. This obliges man insofar as it is recognized by him as the moral law. Hence the will of God is materially the divine law and formally the moral law. The communication of the divine law in the moral law takes place in the *lex divina supernaturalis (lex gratiae)* and the *lex naturalis* (the *lex naturae humanae rationalis*). The law of grace and the law of rational nature are formulated in concrete terms in the organs of revelation *(lex positiva divina)* and the rules of ethics (the *lex naturalis* formulated in the moral law). The divine law, as grasped existentially, is only rendered imperfectly here because apart from the reasons given above they also comprise it in a way which is independent of the subject, while, however, the existential dependence on the subject is essential to the *lex gratiae* and *naturae rationalis* in the concrete. It must be maintained, nevertheless, that at least the positive divine law interpreted by the Church by virtue of the assistance of the Holy Spirit always renders sufficiently the will of God. The moral law is inscribed subjectively in the conscience, which alone binds absolutely, because in it alone there ensues a direct confrontation with the will of God as grasped in the concrete.

4. It is only in this context that the question of the moral justification and the possible extent of positive human law can be asked, with regard both to ecclesiastical and civil law. The answer must be based on the truth that a human law obliges to obedience insofar as the human law-giver partakes of divine authority and represents it. How far this is true depends on the function to be exercised by the authority in question with regard to the persons entrusted to its charge when this function is exercised in the service of the good which it upholds by virtue of divine mandate. This means that human law is only morally justified insofar as the human law-givers exercise their specific function of service. Thus, for instance, the civil power may only make laws insofar as this is demanded by the common good of the citizens. This is also true, *mutatis mutandis,* of the Church, parents and so on. To determine whether there is justification for making a given law, and whether it is to be obeyed for moral reasons, it follows that objective criteria must be applied to the material contents of the law, to see whether it corresponds to the demands of the limited values to be upheld by the human authority. If this is the case, the law also binds morally.

Hence the theory of purely penal laws needs a certain modification. According to this theory, if the lawgiver does not wish to bind in conscience, in the case of laws which are not absolutely necessary, the subject need only be ready to pay the penalty attached to a breach of the law. This theory does not take into account the fact that the human lawgiver can never directly bind in conscience and that the indirect obligation in conscience stems exclusively from the intrinsic aptness of the law to attain its end — for the good reason that the moral obligation always derives formally from God and always derives, as regards the material content, from the objective aptness of the law with regard to its end. But the theory sees correctly the intrinsic importance of authority as such, in cases where respect for the law is not called for by intrinsic material reasons. And thus it affirms the obligation of being ready to suffer the penalties for breaches of the law, since the just dignity of authority cannot be preserved otherwise. For it is the objective intrinsic end and goal of human authority as such that has been opposed. This means that the human lawgiver, if he is exercising his charge justly, always binds morally, indirectly, because he either makes apt regulations or exercises his office aptly. Only when the law is inept is the punishment of the justifiable violation of a legitimate but incorrect law unjust.

5. It is impossible to judge the aptness of human law merely on ethical principles. But from the point of view of morality (or politics) it is possible to decide, with the help of prudence, a) what value the law ought to serve in the concrete situation; b) what formal principles ought to be observed if a law is to be just, i.e., to serve the value in question with due regard for other relevant values; c) whether an order can justly claim the character of a law. The canonical directives for the interpretation of the law (*CIC, normae generales,* especially can. 8–24) and the rules of jurisprudence, comprise the detailed principles which are to be observed in judging universal laws.

The following points are to be noted with regard to all laws, whether universal laws or personal precepts: a) whether the lawgiver is entitled and empowered by virtue of office and authority (jurisdiction) to make a given law, who precisely are affected by it, where and how long it is valid; b) what precisely is the content of the law, whether it has been regularly promulgated and how it is to be interpreted; c) whether the dispositions of the law correspond to the just end which the lawgiver ought to serve, or whether it is dishonourable, unjust, superfluous, or impossible to fulfil; d) how important the commands of the law in question are for the maintenance and furthering of the order of things in question and hence how far it binds morally, by permission or prohibition, or again, how far there are grounds for exceptions, impediments, excusation or rejection, or how far a law ceases to exist or

is invalidated. The objective criteria which are to be observed in the drafting of apt and hence morally justifiable laws are derived from experience. They correspond to the intrinsic demands of the matter in question as studied by the relevant scientific disciplines and are therefore unaffected by moral values. Neglect of these objective demands for aptness in practice must *eo ipso* be detrimental to the moral value which a law should promote, since a law is objectively just only by being of proper service to the value in question. Thus if a just law is to be drawn up, there is need both of a well-ordered moral or political will to serve the value in question, and also of expert experimental knowledge of the matter under legislative treatment. The synthesis of these two conditions always remains imperfect on account of our human imperfection.

6. It must therefore be noted that the moral law must always appear as in a state of tension and in a certain aloofness with regard to positive human law. This recognition of the "relativity" of human law, whose moral aims should often only be indirect, prevents its being overhastily charged with moral values and perhaps being transformed into something alian to its proper nature. It also makes it impossible to identify morality too hastily with positive law, which can never do more than reflect imperfectly the demands of morality. This clear distinction between morality and positive law opens up the possibility of showing the faithful that the claims of the divine law are not adequately met if one restricts onself to positive laws. In this way the divine law appears as a force which is always working for the reform of human law. Thus the formulation of the moral law can be freed from the suspicion of being abused as moral coercion to help to establish or confirm earthly interests in power to which their claim is unjustifiable.

See also *Morality* II, *Natural Law, Equity, Obedience, Necessity* II, *Human Act, Ethics* I, *Creation* I, *Conscience, Person, Charity* I, II, *Supernatural Order, Evangelical Counsels, Vow, Authority, Society* II.

BIBLIOGRAPHY. See the handbooks of moral theology and canon law; also: K. Barth, *Evangelium und Gesetz* (1935); E. Brunner, *The Divine Imperative: A Study in Christian Ethics* (1937); P. Althaus, *Gebot und Gesetz* (1952); J. Heckel,

Lex Caritatis (in German) (1953); J. Pieper, *Prudence* (1960); M. Herron, *The Binding Force of Laws* (1958); B. Häring, *The Law of Christ,* I (1961), pp. 260–365 (with bibliography); E. Hamel, *Loi naturelle et loi du Christ* (1964); J. Fuchs, *The Natural Law* (1965); P. Benenson, "Natural Law and Statute Law", *Concilium* 5 (1967), pp. 24–29; H. H. Schrey, "Beyond Natural Law and Positivism", *ibid.*, pp. 30–36; P. Althaus, *Divine Command* (1966); B. Häring, *Towards a Christian Moral Theology* (1966).

Waldemar Molinski

III. Rule of Law

1. *The fact of law*. The term "law" refers to a historical and cultural reality that is found to exist in human society. Law in this sense is positive law. The Latin word *ius* is a homonym, designating a number of different things (rules of public authority that are in force at a given moment, the place where justice is administered, private juridical acts of binding force, ownership which is juridically protected — what we now call subjective rights). All these things are closely akin. In each case the word *ius* means some kind of bond in force within a public, organized society furnished with public powers. Law efficaciously imposes a public obligation on society: it is *positive*.

2. *Historical origin of law*. In the last analysis the historical origin of law is to be sought in that of the phenomenon which is human society. But in primitive societies, religious rules, social custom, and law are hardly distinguished; and this lack of differentiation entails a certain confusion between social conscience and the individual conscience. Originally, law probably tended to find expression in custom that was mandatory and in religious rules that bound society. The code of Hammurabi (Babylonia, before 1700 B.C.), which belongs to a very advanced civilization, from the point of view of economics and legal structure, seems to be a compilation of earlier customary laws. The legal texts preserved in the Pentateuch reflect the idea that crime is a sin which more or less directly affects society, and which society must rid itself of by condemning the offender to death (Exod 21:12–14; Lev 18:24–30; 20:1–5, 8, 14f., 17; 24:14; Deut 7:1–16; 17:2–7; 19:1–13; 21:1–9; 22:22; cf. Ezek 14:12–23; 18; 33:10–20). Quite possibly law came to be distinguished from morals, religion, and social custom because the function of judges gradually became secularized. The Law of the Twelve Tables, in ancient Rome, seems to have been in part the result of a popular demand for equality before the law, in protest against a customary law worked by the powerful to their own advantage. Greek influence can be detected in the abstract nature of the Law of the Twelve Tables. The later development of Roman law is bound up with the role of the Praetor, whose power is supreme because it is a share in the *imperium* (separation of powers in the modern sense was unknown to the constitution of the Roman Republic). Society was notably advanced and rejuvenated by the law which the Praetors created. That renewal of the *ius civile*, however, was not effected through legislation but through a jurisprudence devised to cope with unusual cases. Parallel with this achievement of the *Praetor urbanus*, the *Praetor peregrinus* created the *Ius gentium*, a private international law with rules of its own.

A similar transition from a variety of local customs to a single jurisprudence took place in medieval England (12th century). This "Common Law", consisting of decisions in particular cases, was created by judges reasoning on the basis of local custom and Roman law. Thus, paradoxically, the only country in Europe where there was no "reception" of Roman law, created a jurisprudence quite in the spirit of Roman law (pretorian law, or *ius honorarium*); whereas the Roman law received on the Continent derives from a theoretical system worked out by the post-glossators of the later Middle Ages on the basis of Justinian's Romano-Byzantine *Corpus Iuris*. This is an orderly, abstract kind of law, gradually deduced from general principles by academic lawyers and judges; it forms the basis of the numerous codes that were drawn up in the 19th century.

Thus two contrasting systems largely govern modern juridical life: the *legal* system of Continental Europe (also including Latin America, some African countries, the Middle East, and Japan) and the Anglo-American system of *jurisprudence* (to which most English-speaking countries more or less adhere). In those countries where Marxist Socialism prevails (Russia, China, etc.), juridical institutions have been greatly influenced by doctrinal assumptions and by the social and economic situation under the new regime. The resulting juridical system is something new, that cannot be simply identified with the classic legal system and yet, for all its special features, remains a legal rather than a jurisprudential system.

3. *Law as a norm.* Anyone reflecting philosophically on the fact of positive law is inevitably confronted with a problem. On the one hand, law is a cultural and a historical fact. Positive law, organizing the life of society, does exist and must do so. A law that is not enforced (is not effectively observed by the community) has no existence as positive law. On the other hand, law is an authoritative standard of behaviour: it declares what "ought to be". It is not a mere description of facts, dependent for its existence on them, but a command that addresses itself to men — a norm for their actions. Now what makes it a norm?

Because law is something factual and positive, many jurists are loath to bring "metaphysics" into their conception of it. This attitude led in the 19th century to juridical positivism (the jurist works from the bare fact of a rule in force, without inquiring behind it at all), and later on in that century to sociologism (which reduces the norm of law to the sum of social forces brought to bear on individuals). In both views, law is valid only insofar as it is enforced (not necessarily enforced in every single case but at any rate imposed on society in general). But that idea conflicts with our basic meta-empirical experience of the "value" which is law. Law as law calls for respect, and obedience to law is a "value" in itself (an "absolute" value), not merely something of utility. Hence it is that thoroughly unjust demands on the part of the State, though they may be enforced in society and appear in juridical trappings, can have no claim to be considered law. Ultimately law is a norm because it is something ethical. The necessity to obey it, which all law essentially entails, is a moral necessity. Positive law is coercive of its nature, but sheer coercion does not make it a norm. Force is legitimately used to uphold law but force alone cannot create law.

4. *Foundations of law.* Modern constitutional lawyers — where the "rule of law" prevails, not in those regimes, whether Leftist or Rightist, which regard the juridical system as a mere instrument for furthering the ends of the State — tend to see a hopeless antinomy between the supremacy of the State and the supremacy of law. On the one hand law makes the State (the rule of law, constitutional law); and on the other hand law is made *(positum)* by the State (positive law). The theory of law, therefore, cannot be something absolutely self-contained. Here we must apply the Aristotelian dictum that the principles of a given science lie outside the scope of that science. It can be said that only the juridical establishment of a constitution brings the State into being. But beforehand (at least by a priority of logic) there exists a constituent community and a State *in fieri* that represents it. Here we are sent back to natural law, the Catholic doctrine on the origin of authority. Man's social nature requires that he shall be able to set up a polity furnished with juridical power. From the moment that a civic community resolves to set up a State, it is *ipso facto* clothed with an authority that comes from God and that is prerequisite to the juridical validity of the positive constitutional measure whereby the State itself is instituted. All real positive law, therefore, is endowed with a formal legitimacy because it has been enacted in accordance with the Constitution. And the Constitution derives its formal legitimacy in the first place from the consent of the community which set it up. The validity of this constituent consent derives from the very order of creation. Thus authority comes from God.

5. *Material and formal legitimacy.* Law properly exists as law when it is laid down by legitimate authority (formal legitimacy) and when what it requires conforms to the general principles of justice, which conformity gives law its material legitimacy.

Both kinds of legitimacy must be verified before positive law can come into existence. Here we face a crucial problem in law. Material and formal legitimacy are both ultimately based on the order of creation, and therefore neither one can be isolated from the other. But the question then arises whether a genuine positive law is really possible, since the cultural and historical forms taken by human life (one of which is law) always fall considerably short of ideal justice (cf. 2 Pet 3:13).

6. *Law and morality.* Protestant thinkers have felt this problem most keenly. Justice as known in the juridical order, among men, cannot be identified with divine justice. And

yet neither can we abandon juridical institutions to the diabolic energy which possesses itself of them when the contingent is made absolute (unquestioning obedience to any command a government may care to issue). Whereas Catholics think in terms of natural law, Protestants have recourse to revelation (the order of creation as known by faith: E. Brunner; the wisdom of Scripture: E. Wolf). Both Catholic and Protestant thinkers substantially agree in their view of the problem posed by the dialectic between positive law and justice — juridical security and justice. Wolf holds that so far as a jurist is concerned the Bible does not teach "juridical theses" but "juridical principles", in the light of which we must study legal history and attempt to create a juridical system that can truly be called law. Wolf's distinction between juridical "principles" and juridical "theses" fits admirably into a view of things which accepts natural law but at the same time tries to deepen the concept of the latter. On the other hand we must not place too much reliance on a purely natural knowledge of the order of justice. For a Catholic, natural law and "scriptural wisdom" are not mutually exclusive. Besides, the Catholic theologian admits as readily as his Protestant counterpart that among fallen mankind only that love which comes from God and is the goal of our faith (1 Jo 4:16) provides a strong enough motive for seeing that justice is done (Rom 11:32; 13:8–10). Wolf is right when he says that the only law we can really establish is "the law of our neighbour's rights".

7. *Legality and morals.* A final problem: What attitude should a person take towards the "theses" of positive law if he wishes to respect the "principles" of justice? He should be neither abject nor hypercritical. In principle he ought to work within the juridical order to remedy its injustices. But cases arise where the subject has a duty to offer active resistance — which may be non-violent — to an unjust law imposed by established authority. The two terms of this dialectic are found in St. Paul's *positive* doctrine on sovereignty in the historical State (Rom 13:1–7) and in the *negative* doctrine of the Apocalypse on the diabolic State (Rev 13 and 17).

See also *Old Testament Books* I, *Natural Law, Society* I, *State, Authority, Justice.*

BIBLIOGRAPHY. See bibliography on *Justice, Natural Law;* also: R. Pound, *The Spirit of the Common Law* (1931); F. Geny, *Méthode d'interprétation et sources en droit privé positif,* 2 vols. (2nd ed., 1932); E. Wolf, *Rechtsgedanke und biblische Weisung* (1948); E. Käsemann, "Römer 13, 1–7 in unserer Generation", *Zeitschrift für Theologie und Kirche* 56 (1959), pp. 316–76; J. C. H. Wu, *Fountain of Justice* (1959); L. Legaz Lecambra, *Filosofía del Derecho* (2nd ed., 1962); W. Buckland and A. McNair, *Roman Law and Common Law* (1962); P. Zampetti, *Il problema della giustizia del Protestantismo tedesco contemporaneo* (1962); A. Hogue, *Origins of the Common Law* (1966); H. Schlier, *Relevance of the New Testament* (1967); P. Vinogradoff, *Roman Law in Medieval Europe* (1967).

José-María Díez Alegría

IV. Philosophy of Law

A. Concept and Technical Definitions

1. The "philosophy of law" is one of the main pillars of philosophy (Anaximander, Pythagoras, Heraclitus, Democritus, and the tragedians), not a mere off-shoot, though the term has been in use only since the 18th century. But every new start in philosophy is preceded or followed by reflection on the nature of law. Each region of philosophy has a corresponding position in the philosophy of law, and every philosophical system provides a specific place for it (from Plato, Aristotle and Thomas Aquinas down to Leibniz, Wolff, Thomasius, Kant, Fichte, Schelling, Hegel, Cohen and so on). It is the basis and presupposition of political and legal theory, and of jurisprudence. Today, the philosophy of law is classified either as a "branch of philosophy in general" or as a "branch of legal science" which exposes "the foundations of law". It is a basic and comprehensive view of law which will provide "a profounder understanding of the great and mysterious phenomenon of law" in general (E. Fechner). The philosophy of law includes political theory, for even where State and law do not form a systematic unity under the rule of law, the theme of the State inevitably comes up in discussion of law. Political theory is a philosophy of law which investigates one aspect of law, the State.

2. The philosophy of law is intrinsically based on the spontaneous, inarticulate knowledge of law which prevents the spurious from being taken as rightful law. Law presupposes a basic knowledge of the reality of being (Heraclitus Frg. 23). The objective truth of things, which imposes a distinction between

spurious and rightful law, i.e., "the normative structure of reality", goes with the natural subjective ability to distinguish spurious from real or rightful law (cf. Aristotle, *Nicomachean Ethics,* V, 6; 1134a [κρίσις]; Thomas Aquinas, *Summa Theologica,* I, II, q. 91, a. 12 — the *synderesis* which is known by the *lumen naturale*).

All philosophy of law is based on two things: the validity of law independent of the subjective attitude as the objective ground, and the possibility of knowledge of the law, which is conditioned by the state and approach of the subject. If either is denied — and above all, if both are denied, as in agnosticism, nominalism or "absolute" relativism — no philosophy of law is possible. It begins as reflection on a knowledge of law which is prior to all conscious perception of it (J. Fuchs) and is then analysed as deliberate and articulate investigation from a given theoretical standpoint: objectivism, subjectivism, idealism, realism, nominalism, voluntarism, positivism, objective transcendental metaphysics or relativism. It ends with an effort to state a solution. a) Christian philosophy implies some form of philosophy of law. b) The philosophy of law put forward by Aristotle and Thomas Aquinas, culminating in the objectivism of values in late scholastic (especially Spanish) philosophy of law (G. Vasquez) is the classical theory of law on which modern ontology of law is built (J. Messner, G. Manser, J. Maritain, H. Rommen, J. Van der Ven, A. Verdross, E. Fechner, M. Reale, L. Recaséns Siches, J. Dabin, R. Marcic, etc.). c) Akin to this are the theories of the "nature of things" (G. Radbruch, N. Bobbio, H. Coing, H. Schambeck), to which the existentialism of G. Cohn's legal philosophy may be attached. d) The theory of the historicity of law discusses the relative validity of law against the background of the absolute (E. Husserl, J. Fuchs, A. Auer, R. Marcic). e) The core of all philosophy of law is a theory of natural law, even when the latter is only implicitly presupposed, e.g., the "general theory of law". f) The general or "pure" theory of law takes as its subject positive law, works on the results of comparative law, with the help of transcendental methods, to arrive at universal basic concepts, examines in particular the logical *a priori* of positive law and displays juridical structures as structures of thought. In contrast to b) it does not suppose any prior ontological norm (J. Austin,

H. Kelsen, J. von Kempski). g) The logic and methodology of law are concerned with formal logic and methods of interpretation (K. Engisch, I. Tammelo, U. Klug); h) This logic is now being completed by "rhetorics" and "topics" (T. Viehweg). i) The phenomenology of law (A. Reinach, G. Husserl) and the existentialist approach (W. Maihofer, C. Donius, U. Hommes, E. Fechner) have a certain amount in common with b). k) An ethics of law in the strict sense is to be found in the authors who establish tables of values which put law at the disposition of its user. This whole approach is taken a step further where the philosophy of law is treated as a doctrine of values with specific contents (G. del Vecchio, J. Dabin, H. Coing, E. Fechner; cf. also G. Radbruch and J. Moor and — ambiguously — A. Verdross). This latter approach is inclined to treat standards other than those positively created as "metajuridical" or "ethical". l) The psychology of law (T. Erismann) and the sociology of law (E. Fechner, Roscoe Pound) are now appearing as subsidiary or independent disciplines in the study of law. m) Similarly, a Christian philosophy of law is making itself heard as an independent field of knowledge at present. Among Catholics there are K. Rahner, J. Fuchs, R. Guardini, G. Söhngen, J. van der Ven, and A. Geck; among Protestants, K. Barth, E. Brunner, R. Niebuhr. The initial stages of a Jewish philosophy of law may be found in M. Buber.

B. Systems

There are a number of formal problems to be dealt with in the philosophy of law: grounds of validity, basic proprieties, purpose, scope of law as limit to the power of the State, historicity, knowability (principles by which law is known, as distinct from the principles by which it is valid), the connection between positive and pre-positive law. The concrete, material questions include the dignity of man, the common good, right of resistance, justice, law and ethics.

1. *Validity of law.* The classical explanation of the binding force of law is three-fold: God, world (being, nature), man. Where God is taken as the foundation, the essence of God is regarded as the *lex aeterna* (so Augustine, Anselm, Thomas Aquinas) or the divine intellect as determinant ("theonomous rationalism" — so Greek and Roman Stoicism and

under certain conditions, Cicero, Augustine, Aquinas) or the divine will ("theonomous positivism"). By this last is meant the voluntarism or nominalism according to which the lawgiver is eternal, but not the law. God's will is arbitrary, law is no more than a precept which is a sheer decision of the will (so Duns Scotus, Occam, Biel, Calvin, Gerson, Descartes, and Pufendorf).

The foundation is likewise in transcendent being *(esse)* and beings in their totality *(ens)*. Here exist fundamentally the relationships which appear as the primary precepts or prohibitions, the sum of which is "pre-positive" natural law or law of being in the strict sense (φύσει δίκαιον, *jus naturae;* cf. Anaximander, Heraclitus, Aristotle [*Rhetorics,* I, 13, 1373b; *Nicomachean Ethics,* II, 1107a], Cicero, Horace [*Satires,* I, 1, 106f.], Anselm of Canterbury [*Cur Deus Homo,* I, 12], Thomas Aquinas [*Summa Theologica,* II, II, q. 57, a. 2 ad 3; *Contra Gentiles,* III, 129; *De Veritate,* XXIII, 6], Vitoria, Molina, G. Vasquez, Suarez, Leibniz [with restrictions]; more recently, A. Utz [*Die Deutsche Thomas-Ausgabe,* XVIII (1953), pp. 403f.], B. Thum, R. Marcic). Before any decision of the will *(positio, decisio, institutio),* before any discernment *(judicium),* "ante omnem prohibitionem, non solum imperantem sed etiam indicantem, non solum creatam sed etiam divinam" (Vasquez), values and standards with the quality of law exist in things themselves, "indeque se diffundit in praeceptum" (Molina). The norms subsequent to decisions of divine or human will are called positive law, divine or human, which is contingent, because it corresponds to the laws of being *(derivatur, oritur,* Thomas Aquinas, *Summa Theologica,* I, II, q. 95, a. 2; cf. Cicero, *Rhetorica,* II). Without exception, all determination of law *(iuris positio)* is the implementation of a higher law *(iuris executio).* The immediate ground of validity of the law (its formal object) is an "ontonomous" (τὸ ὄν, νόμος) one, "pre-positive". Essential and real in law is what is at the basis of law beyond all experience, active behind the law, though not *ante rem* (Plato) but *in re* (Aristotle, Aquinas, Vasquez) — much less *post rem* (nominalism). This presupposes that reality has a normative structure (Aristotle, *Physics,* B, I, 1), according to which perfected being is what ought to be and every deviation from the way thither is a flaw or lack in the form. The principle of the being of beings is the

form (norm), not the indeterminate. (Revelation may be said to be on the side of Aristotle, if the primordial meaning of Logos, Jn 1:1, is noted).

Then there is the nature of man. As part of the order of being or nature, it is a ground of the validity of law. This is the objective doctrine of the "natural law". Or it may be seen as validating law of itself, as subject, whether as individual or collective. In the latter case it may be a rationalism based on man ("anthroponomous") or a voluntarism ("anthroponomous positivism", "biologism"), according to which law is only human command, the (instinctive) decision of the will) or a totality of unity (as in existence-philosophy).

2. *Basic proprieties.* Law is permanent. It is basically unchangeable, but it contains an element of change, so that it is valid till it is duly amended, i.e., by prescribed procedures. It cannot be arbitrarily modified (whence the certainty and force of law under the rule of law), though this is denied by voluntarism (positivism), which sees sheer will as the basis of law. Law is promulgated *a priori* in the sense of truth, and is knowable, so that the addressee finds it familiar at once (γνώριμον, *norma*).

Since it is grounded on being, law extends basically to gods, men, beasts, plants and all beings (Anaximander, Heraclitus, Exod 21:28f.). But law in the strict and univocal sense is confined to man, whose relationship to being is the highest, and whose dignity it guarantees institutionally — as freedom, equality, responsibility.

Because of the dignity of man, man can never be treated as a mere object. He is always also subject (Plato, Gregory of Nyssa). He is not only the static and passive possessor of inviolability, he is also the active and dynamic participant in the establishment of law and order.

The other side of the coin is the common good, which ceases to have a claim where human dignity is essentially interfered with (Verdross, Pius XII, John XXIII, J. C. Murray). It should not be confused with *raison d'état,* or political purposes.

Human dignity and common good limit legally the power of the state. Hence the right of resistance comes into force, or the duty of resistance, if authority transgresses its limits. Obedience is determined by the lawfulness of the act of the giver of the command. "Law is not simply identical with the command of the powers that be" (Hans Welzel). Since positive law is part of the *ordo transcendentalis* (H. Meyer, A. Auer, A. Kaufmann, R. Marcic), all concrete, historical positive legal institutions *(ordo accidentalis)* go back formally and materially to the law of being. The right of resistance is one of the sanctions provided for the natural law. Ethical duties can be added to legal relationships, but not reduced to them, since the two regions are ontologically independent (O. von Gierke, J. Fuchs, A. Auer, R. Marcic).

Law is objective. It is an order of things which prevails independently of the persons addressed *(norma agendi)*. Justice is the corresponding attitude of the subject, by virtue of and within the framework of the *facultas agendi* ("subjective rights") constituted by the *norma agendi* (objective law). The ontological disposition by which the addressee is ready to listen to the norms which come to him as "musts" is called "respect for the law" (a sense of justice). This is not the binding force of law, as individual or collective subjectivism holds. A conviction of legality can be a criterion or indication, but not the ground of validity.

3. *Positive law.* Positive law is related to the law of being, the natural ("pre-positive") law in the strict sense, as the conditional or contingent is to the unconditional or absolute, the changeable to the unchangeable. But the latter is also linked with the former, if it is to become manifest in the world of actual experience. All positive law presupposes the pre-positive basic norm, which is not applied to positive law as an alien standard, but is intrinsically and systematically prior to it. Even the final steps are pre-eminently juridical and not "metajuridical", i.e., not "merely" ethical etc. This is brought out very clearly by Thomas Aquinas, *Summa Theologica,* I, II, q. 95, a. 2; *Ethics,* V, lectio 12 — with an appeal to Cicero. Law can only proceed from law (cf. Kelsen, Merkl), either directly by way of logical deduction, or indirectly by way of derivation ("delegation"), when the law-giver within his powers (of free discretion) determines more particularly the general principle (Thomas Aquinas, *loc. cit.*).

In the visible world of experience, the subject meets only a mixture of natural and positive law. "Nulla enim est nec potest esse lex civilis, quae non aliquid naturalis aequitatis immutabilis habeat admixtum" (J. Althusius). Even Kelsen, the author of the "Pure Theory of Law", the main spokesman of positivism, has to concede that his theory tries to be a pure theory of law, but cannot be a theory of pure law. And A. J. Merkl, another spokesman of the Vienna school, maintains: "No order of law, however constructed, is without a sort of root in the natural law. And no doubt all positive law has passed through the stage of the norm of natural law." So too a third spokesman of the Vienna school, A. Verdross-Drossberg, discusses how every lawgiver is subject to law.

The distinction between the two elements in the mixture and observance of the difference are necessary, because the only elements of positive law which have the validity of law are those covered by the natural law (in one of the ways indicated by Aquinas in the *Summa Theologica,* I, II, q. 95, c. 2.). Otherwise it is a spurious law which is neither valid nor binding and hence cannot call for obedience. Indeed, to obey could be actually against the law (as in such cases as commands to kill unlawfully or inflict torture).

It remains true that positive law is inevitable from another aspect, since the faculty of knowledge in man, to whom law is addressed, is deficient as regards the natural law. All the time, the great thing is to observe and preserve the due limits, and it is the task of the philosophy of law to help to make this investigation fruitful.

C. HISTORICAL DEVELOPMENT

The basic outlines of all philosophy of law may be traced in Greek antiquity, which in a way foreshadows subsequent history. It is a tension between a law with essential foundations and a positivism which identifies law and legislation. Positivism, which formed a cross-current against the main stream from the very beginning (Glaucon, Thrasymachus, Callicles and Gorgias and many of the Sophists, later Hobbes, Spinoza Rousseau, Nietzsche) only gained the upper hand in the 19th century, remaining more or less predominant till the middle of the 20th. This relatively short reign of positivism was preceded by another stage in the history of human thought and legal philosophy. Till the 18th century, law, above all the natural law, was never identifie substantially with ethics. "No one doubted that the principles by which earthly powers were subjected to natural and divine law . . . were really principles of law; that there was a law prior to, independent of and above the State" (O. von Gierke). The ethical obligations which set limits to the sovereignty of the will of the prince or the State, were superadded. C. Thomasius was the first to blur the ontological distinction between law, ethics and morality. Since then the principle has been that the sovereign will of prince or State is "only" bound in conscience, ethically or morally *(obligatio interna)* but not by virtue of law *(obligatio externa)*, as has been shown in particular by H. Welzel.

1. We may distinguish the following stages in Greek and Roman antiquity.

a) In the archaic period, the law was seen as a mythic and theomorphous element. Divine law cut across human (Homer, Hesiod, Pindar, Solon). Then came a rational and matter of fact type of thinking, which did not, however, lose sight of the primordial image of law. Law is the main attribute and most intrinsic structure of the cosmos (Anaximander, Heraclitus, Aeschylus, Sophocles, Euripides, Xenophanes, Anaxagoras, Pythagoras).

b) The Sophistic "Enlightenment" (Hippias, Antiphon, Lycophron, Alcidamas) tried to eliminate both the mythic world image and the thinking which examined the rational foundations of law, calling in question the derivation of positive from natural law and equating law and legislation. But at the same time nature (φύσις) and law (νόμος) were seen by the Sophists as in radical opposition to one another, while natural law was in fact regarded as the principle of the unity of the human race (national obscurantism and slavery being rejected on this ground). The critical relativists (such as Protagoras) and the theoretical materialists (such as Democritus and Antiphon) were two groups of Sophists who upheld the rights of man in the framework of the theory of human dignity, equality and freedom, thus helping to lay the foundations of the doctrine of democracy. These are not really positivists, as are, however, the radical sceptics — such Sophists as Gorgias, Thrasymachus, and later Carneades and Epicurus. For these, legitimacy and morality are exclusively based on legality,

i.e., legislation as positive law. Lawfulness is no more than conformity with legal measures. The first theory of biologism is developed by Callicles: the strong have the (natural) "law" on their side; so too Glaucon, Gorgias, Thrasymachus (might is right). Individualism then begins to withdraw from political responsibilities; theories of social contract with no really social obligations appear. These were to come to fruition in the modern Enlightenment.

c) In the midst of this confusion the classical ontological, cosmological and teleological statement intervenes, with Socrates, Plato and Aristotle. Here we have a consistent theory of natural law. Aristotle looks for the ground of law in the perspective of the ontological question, "What is the being of beings?" rather than in the theological one, "What is the supreme being?" Thus a distinction is made between the ontonomous and the theonomous, and the problem of law is treated only in the light of the ontonomous. Just as the beings which are such by nature (φύσει ὄντα) rank prior to and prevail over all human production (ποιούμενον, τέχνη ὄν), so too all positive (man-made, "engendered") law (νόμῳ δίκαιον) without exception depends on the natural law, the law of being (φύσει δίκαιον).

d) Greek Stoicism obscured the difference, in order to ease the tension between nature and law, which had been exaggerated almost to breaking-point by the Sophists. The Stoics made the law of being part of the positive divine law, and natural law became the law of God. There was a tendency to adopt the contradictory notion of God as the lawgiver, who as such "produced" the natural law; or at least, the terminological basis for the fine distinction in formal objects between the law of being and the law willed by the legislator was eliminated. Attention was called instead to the dignity of man, the rights of man which belong by nature and therefore by divine right to all who bear the visage of man, the unity of the human race and the cosmopolitan future of the State.

The Roman Stoics such as Cicero, and classical Roman jurisprudence preserved the heritage so successfully built up by the Greeks, and carried it westwards and eastwards (to the Byzantine empire) in the wake of Hellenism. The word for νόμος is *lex,* which may be called one of the most distracting transformations in the history of the human spirit. The law which is of itself prior to all positive determination is now suggested to be positive — *lex naturae, lex naturalis,* and on the highest level, *lex aeterna.* Cicero avoids an anthropocentric positivism of moral law and all sort of scepticism, but comes very near a theonomous positivism. Roman jurisprudence in the East and in the West, especially the Corpus and Codex of Justinian, still retains, however, unmistakable traces of its ancient basis in the ontological self-subsistence of law.

The principle by virtue of which the ἴδιος νόμος of the Romans, the *ius civile proprium,* became the *ius gentium* and thus came into the perspectives of the natural law, was the *bona fides romana,* loyalty and good faith, which placed not only Roman citizens but aliens and enemies, people and humanity, under the protection of law: *pacta sunt servanda.* The principle of freedom, in the sheer autonomy allowed to private contracts which is a feature of Roman law, is only intelligible in the light of a voluntaristic metaphysics which was unknown to the Greeks.

2. Along with Athens and Rome, Jerusalem had a basic contribution to make to the philosophy of law. Israel's thinking was strictly theonomous, but with its concept of the creator God as person, to whom man was in the personal I-You relationship, human rights could be given an initial contour. Law is understood as the setting up of an order which binds both ruler and ruled: "et Deus ex promissione obligatur" — the notion of the covenant.

3. The decisive step was taken in Christianity. The ideal of the cosmopolitan man, citizenship of the world, which had been launched by the Sophists, Euripides and the Stoa, was taken up as a notion and an institution by Christianity, in the biblical imagery of man as the image of God, and in the establishment of the Church. Christianity "opposed to the multiplicity of States the unity of the world Church . . . And the individual ceased to be simply a citizen of the State, to become likewise a subject of the kingdom of God in its pilgrimage on earth" (Verdross). Once man is seen as belonging not only to this or that earthly State but to the *Civitas Dei* as well, the inviolability and inalienability of human rights become obvious. The rights by which man extends into the kingdom of God cannot be withheld from him by any political power.

4. In late antiquity, the patristic age and early scholasticism, the question of law was treated solely from the theological point of view, to the neglect of the ontological. But the doctrine of the dignity of man was underlined, especially by Gregory of Nyssa, who coined the expression "the royal dignity of man" and rejected slavery unconditionally. The doctrine that all political power was limited *(potestas ordinata, imperium limitatum)* became clearer and clearer (from Augustine to Bonaventure); so too the doctrine of the right of resistance, which had been provided with proofs by Ambrosius.

5. Anselm of Canterbury (*Cur Deus Homo,* I, 12) Alexander of Hales, Albertus Magnus and classical scholasticism, especially Thomas Aquinas (*Summa Theologica,* II, II, q. 57, a. 2 ad 3; *Contra Gentiles,* III, 129; *De Veritate,* XXIII, 6), strive to disentangle the syncretism into which the various themes had been combined, and put the question of the basis of law once more on an ontological footing, which was a new effort to prevent the philosophy of law degenerating into subjectivism. Where natural law appears as contrasted with positive divine law, the theological point of view is of course maintained, insofar as God the creator of nature, establishes, indirectly as it were, the law of nature. In other words, "Vult tamen facere mediante natura ut servetur ordo in rebus (id est: ius naturae)", as Aquinas says (*De Potentia Dei,* VII, 9). God can be compared to a constitutional monarch who is himself bound to the constitution which he has established. Even the *potestas absoluta* of God is a *potestas ordinata,* to some extent an *imperium limitatum.* Right sets up authority, and in this way all political authority is dependent on the force of law. Slavery is against the natural law. Man has a basic right to follow his conscience even when it is in error, and hence his freedom is also a freedom of conscience. The well-tempered democracy, under the rule of law, over which the constitution presides, is what suits man best as a rational being. Rebellion can be legitimate and even desirable. Positive law, if contrary to the common good, can be shown to be a spurious law. At critical moments, the judiciary which supervises the legitimacy of the exercise of authority

intervenes to hold the balance (independence of the judiciary).

Thus we find in Thomas Aquinas all the elements which are precious to the upholders of the rule of law. Aquinas, and his predecessor Aristotle, then became the fathers of the constitutionalism which is typical of the Anglo-Saxon and Anglo-American societies, upholding the rule of law based on natural law as a political principle. These were principles which were to be lost sight of for centuries on the continent.

6. This way of seeing even God, as it were, bound by law was opposed then by the theonomous positivism of the concept of law in such thinkers as Duns Scotus and Occam. God does not will something because it is right, but it is right, and therefore law, because God wills it. This was the attitude passed on to Luther by his teacher Gabriel Biel, and also adopted by Calvin. But this orientation brought individualism to the fore, and contributed a new element to the building up of liberalism as the doctrine of the rule of law in the State.

7. A reaction set in with late and baroque scholasticism, chiefly represented by the Spanish school of legal and moral philosophy (Las Casas, Vitoria, Soto). De Vitoria extended the notion of the dignity of man to take in the existence of peoples, and laid down the principles of modern international law. The doctrine of ontonomous, objective values was given its full expression in the writings of Gabriel Vasquez (d. 1604) and was echoed by Francisco Suarez, Molina, Covarruvias, Laynez, Bellarmine and Althusius. Here we find developed the theory of democracy as political liberty under the rule of law and the doctrine of the sovereignty of the people as a *potestas suprema ordinata*.

8. In the individualistic and subjectivistic rationalism of the modern Enlightenment, which was to degenerate into the despairing voluntarism represented by Nietzsche for instance, the philosophy of law ceased to be orientated on an objective order. "Right" in the subjective sense, as the claim of the subject in his *facultas agendi* comes to the fore, without any back-reference to the *norma agendi*. Hitherto law in the objective sense had been prior, and both rights and duties had been seen as derivative in its regard. Now "rights" become the basic

interest. Natural law continued no doubt to hold pride of place, but this was really only in terminology. For what is prior to the State, and in this sense has the character of natural law, is attributed to man, his reason and *his* subjective rights, which no longer presuppose "the right" in the sense of an objective order of natural law: so Locke, Grotius, Pufendorf, Wolff, Thomasius. The historic achievement of this type of legal philosophy was that it could start from its subjectivist standpoint to construct a system of rights which were both personal and public — the "rights of man" — promoting such basic rights as freedom and other civil rights and providing for them institutional and constitutional safeguards. "The notion of human freedom and the consequent rights of the person form the major contribution of modern times to the development of the philosophy of law" (Verdross). The thinkers of the Enlightenment regard man fundamentally as an isolated individual who lives in a non-social state of nature and has to be brought into a tolerable order by means of a contract among individuals. This is, for instance, the contract of submission envisaged by Hobbes, the contract to form a society envisaged by Rousseau – both at the nadir of the philosophy of law in the West. Spinoza salvaged at least inner freedom. But law is no longer the foundation of the State. The State is considered the ultimate source and force of law, even where the terminology conceals this shift. The philosophy of law becomes political theory, a process for which Hegel is typical. Though Kant had taken up the old Germanic notion of the State as entirely a matter of law, existing only in, through, by and for law, he failed to re-establish it, since no philosophy of law is possible without a minimum of objectivism.

Neo-Kantianism, as typified by H. Cohen, showed itself equally powerless to save the notion of law, and for the same reasons: law is totally dissolved into the process of its production, the methods of its engendering. The Vienna school of the theory of law arose under the spiritual dominance of Kantianism. The historical school (Savigny) threw light on the historicity (mutability) of law, took it as its main theme and explained change as the principle of law. This was only an apparent progress on individualism, since the "spirit of the nation" as here understood was no more than a macro-individual conceived along subjectivist lines. In collectivism, this philosophy of law is equated with Marxism, or dialectical and historical materialism in general, and the philosophy of law degrades law to a mere instrument (*orudye, sredstvo*) of the power of the party, the class, the State. Such a notion means the end of law. A certain renaissance can be seen in the works of the Marxist Ernst Bloch. Where there is nothing objective at work, either through a theonomous or an ontonomous theory, and the isolated autonomy of the human subject is left to hold the field alone, reason is too weak to resist and it yields the ground to the arbitrary rule of purely human legislation. Once the doctrines of the natural law as put forward by the Enlightenment had broken down, the excessively anthroponomous profane positivism of modern legal theory took over (D. Hume, J. Bentham, J. Austin, K. Bergbohm, T. Heck).

9. It is characteristic of the philosophy of law in the English-speaking world that it has held out to the present day against the positivism of modern thought on the continent. Among English thinkers the Aristotelian and Thomist tradition has been maintained, thanks chiefly to the great theologian and jurist Richard Hooker (1553–1600), Sir Thomas Smith, the judge Sir Edward Coke. The constitution of the U.S.A. contains clearly recognizable traces of the classical doctrine of the natural law. The more recent (1937) constitution of the Republic of Ireland is designed to reflect as fully as possible in a pluralistic society the great classical principles. But in the present day, sociology, psychology and positivism threaten to swamp the ancient tradition in many parts of the English-speaking world, while in Europe the philosophy of law seems to be regaining some of its classical traits.

10. The incredibly base phenomena in Europe during World War II show how the appeal to a general conviction of legality or the "spirit of the nation" is merely an arbitrary individualism which disguises itself in collective terms, unless the prior rule of an objective kernel of law is assumed which is both common to and beyond the reach of rulers and ruled. The philosophy of values in the objective sense, personalism, ontology and phenomenology are bringing about a return to an objectivist approach and a sense of the validity of law prior to all determinations of it. The encounter of the transcendental philosophy of Kant and the fundamental ontology of Heidegger in J. Maréchal led to the effort to build bridges between structural analyses of positive law and an ontology of law with an outline of a pure theory of natural law. The famous Vienna school of the theory of law, which was at first positivist and orientated towards a purely logical and transcendental analysis (Kelsen, Verdross, Merkl, Pitamic), and which has dominated the philosophy of law for many years in Latin America, Spain, South-east Asia, the Far East, Scandinavia and North America, has received strong new impulses from the new attention to the ontology of law. Its main achievement in the institutional sphere is the ideal of judicial inspection of law which leads from constitutional jurisdiction to obligatory international jurisdiction. This corresponds to the demands made in John XXIII's encyclical *Pacem in Terris* (part IV) for an international State which will assure world peace as the *opus justitiae* for the sake of the dignity of man and of the individual. Never have the Aristotelian-Thomistic principles of legal philosophy been so near to realization on a worldwide scale as at the present day.

See also *State, Agnosticism, Nominalism, Positivism, Relativism, Law* I, III, *Justice, Existence* II, *Collectivism* II, *Marxism, Resistance, Rights of Man, Ethics, Natural Law, Society* II, III.

BIBLIOGRAPHY. HISTORY: O. von Gierke, *Johannes Althusius und die Entwicklung der naturrechtlichen Staatstheorien* (1880; 5th ed., 1958); id., *Political Theories of the Middle Ages* (1900); L. E. le Fur, *La théorie du droit naturel depuis le XIIe siècle et la doctrine moderne* (1927); W. Seagle, *The Question of Law* (1941); H. Cairns, *Legal Philosophy from Plato to Hegel* (1949); L. Strauss, *Natural Right and History* (1953); A. Truyol y Serra, *Historia de la filosofia del derecho* (1954); E. Voegelin, *Order and History*, 3 vols. (1956); R. Marcic, *Vom Gesetzesstaat zum Richterstaat* (1957); T. Gilby, *Principality and Polity, Aquinas and the Rise of State Theory* (1958); P. Stanlis, *E. Burke and the Natural Law* (1958); E. Bloch, *Naturrecht und menschliche Würde* (1961); H. Welzel, *Naturrecht und materiale Gerechtigkeit* (4th ed., 1962). SYSTEMATIC: N. Korkunov, *General Theory of Law* (2nd ed., 1914); M. Hauriou, *Précis de Droit Constitutionel* (1923); B. Cardozo, *The Growth of the Law* (1924); H. Roscoe Pound, *An Introduction to the Phi-*

losophy of Law (1930); L. E. le Fur, Les grands problèmes du droit (1937); L. Recaséns Siches, Vida Humana (1939); A. de Bustamente y Montoro, Teoria General del Derecho (2nd ed., 1940); P. Dabin, Théorie générale du Droit (1944); H. Kelsen, General Theory of Law and State (1945); A. Ross, Towards a Realistic Jurisprudence (1946); G. del Vecchio, Lezioni di filosofia del diritto (5th ed., 1946), E. T.: Philosophy of Law (1954); C. Coing, Grundzüge der Rechtsphilosophie (1950); E. T. K. Wilk, Legal Philosophies of Lask, Radbruch and Dabin (1950); C. K. Allen, Law in the Making (1951); A. Utz, Recht und Gerechtigkeit (1953); G. Cohn, Existenzialismus und Rechtswissenschaft (1955); H. Kelsen, The Communist Theory of Law (1955); J. Fuchs, Lex Naturae. Theologie des Naturrechts (1955); F. Castberg, Problems of Legal Philosophy (1957); F. Cohen, Ethical Systems and Legal Ideals (1959); S. Shuman, Legal Positivism (1963); S. Engel and Rudolph Métall, eds., Law, State and International Legal Order. Essays in honour of Hans Kelsen (1964); D. Lloyd, Idea of Law (1964); R. Marcic, Mensch, Recht, Kosmos (1965); M. Golding, ed., Nature of Law (1966); H. Kelsen, Pure Theory of Law (1967).

René Marcic

LAW AND GOSPEL

A. State of the Question

1. *The practical problem.* The distinction between law and gospel helps us to define Christianity: it is regarded as the distinctive feature of the Christian faith as contrasted not only with Judaism but also with all pagan religions, with philosophy, ethics, and the like. Today, as in St. Paul's time, that distinction is still an important matter for the Church's mission and its relationship with the world; on it depends the Christian character of canon law, dogma, and moral teaching, which must hold a middle course between the opposite extremes of an antinomian spiritualism on the one hand and legalism on the other. In short, it prevents Christianity becoming either secularism or Churchmanship.

2. *The historical problem.* The distinction between law and gospel derives from Jesus' denunciations of legalism in the Judaism of his day, his criticism of the pious people of his time, and St. Paul's struggles with Judaizing tendencies in the early Church which seem to him little different from the legalism of pagan (Gnostic) religion. Nevertheless the Church presently had to set its face against the dualism of Marcion, so that a

synthesis emerged (a dialectical one, to be sure). Luther made the distinction between law and gospel the main theme of his theology, emphasizing the difference but never himself misinterpreting it in an antinomian sense. Calvin, on the other hand, stressed the facet of law in the gospel. Unfortunately the theme of law and gospel never became a major one in Catholic thought. The Council of Trent dealt only marginally with the doctrine of the Reformers on this point, emphasizing once more the harmony between the two elements. A reconsideration of the matter in the light of Scripture and tradition is greatly needed.

B. The Doctrine

1. Law in this context does not mean human law, designed to secure the common good, but the disclosure of God's will by the natural law he has written in the hearts of the gentiles (Rom 2:15f.) and by the word of revelation in the history of salvation. In the OT this law, regarded as a token of election, is seen in the context of God's promised salvation. Christ himself acknowledges the law (Mt 5:17), restores it (Mt 5:31–42; 19:8), indeed radicalizes it (Mt 5:20); and Paul says that it is just, good, and holy (Rom 7:12, 16). Law, then, does not necessarily mean human regulations. Only in Judaism did it harden into a self-assertive, legalistic human system, interposing itself between God and man and leading to the idea of righteousness by the law.

This attitude, which may be found in any age, takes God's will not too much but too little to heart, confining it to set commandments in which casuistry then finds convenient loopholes. Above all, such righteousness wholly mistakes man's position before God, assuming that it is possible to "reckon" with the Almighty (Greek νομίζειν θεούς). This is how the law provides an opportunity for sin, which kills (Rom 7:10ff.). Under a law that he cannot observe, sinful man becomes aware of his impotence. So the task-master law is pointing on to Christ (Gal 3:24).

Natural law, as well as the law of the OT, can be thus misinterpreted, in which case it turns into "principalities and powers" that hold men in bondage. We find this kind of law where people are enslaved under abstract laws by institutions, principles, or ossified traditions instead of responding to the personal will of God. From the theological point of view, law can only be rightly understood in relation to the promise of grace as fellowship with God. Of its nature, then, law is ordered to the gospel.

2. For Scripture, the gospel is not primarily a doctrine to be believed, much less a new law, nor again a purely inward law of grace as contrasted with external law. Rather it is the proclamation of God's kingship which has dawned eschatologically in Christ and demands men's radical obedience. Since the gospel is essentially a personal summons, the antithesis of "law and grace" does not quite express our theme. It is from this point of view, too, that we must understand Jesus' criticism of the law: a man's salvation does not depend on his attitude towards the law but on his attitude towards the person and word of Christ. Accordingly, St. Paul does not contrast law with grace, but the works of the law with hearing in faith (Rom 10:17). Such faith has nothing to do with a desire to excel in observance of the law; it is an unconditional surrender of self to the dominion of God in Christ, who has fulfilled the law for us once and for all. That is why the law is not a means to human salvation.

Scripture itself, however, condemns misinterpretation of the gospel in an antinomian sense. Far from annulling God's will, the gospel makes it more peremptory; only now that will no longer addresses men from without, it is written upon their hearts (Jer 31:31ff.); the imperative follows from the indicative, from our status as sons of God. Faith works through love (Gal 5:6). Thus we are no longer under the law, but in the law: we are ἔννομοι Χριστοῦ (1 Cor 9:21). Only in this analogous sense can we speak of the law of Christ, of Christ as a lawgiver (D 1571). Accordingly, the dictum that the gospel abolishes the ceremonial and judicial law of the OT but not its moral law, is an inadequate attempt to express the fact that under the Christian dispensation law (even the moral law) retains only an analogous validity.

If the gospel reveals a God who always transcends any idea we have of him, then he must also be more demanding than we can ever imagine; man is always an unprofitable servant (Lk 17:10), in concrete reality always both just and a sinner. God's will,

then, cannot be objectified and defined: dogma is not "the" word of God, canon law is not justice itself, office is not the Spirit. Law no longer sets a fixed goal of achievement which can be attained by fulfilling it. It is a summons (paraenesis) towards a point which always lies beyond our grasp, a call to perfect love with our whole heart and soul, as in the Sermon on the Mount. The function of law is to show how serious a matter is faith, to embody faith in concrete form as a safeguard against sentimental enthusiasms.

3. Within history, as we have seen, law and gospel are permanently balanced against each other in a tension that is not to be resolved in any higher synthesis.

a) We must not conceive of law and the gospel primarily as two eras of the history of salvation, nor as two different kinds of divine revelation (sometimes a temptation for Protestants). In the OT as in the NT, law and gospel are always elements of the one word of God, though their mutual relation is always a dialectical one: "Lex data est ut gratia quaeretur, gratia data est ut lex impleretur" (St. Augustine). Grace fulfills the law in such a way as to deprive it of its legal character.

b) The *primum in intentione* is the gospel of grace, as Karl Barth in particular has forcefully reminded us. This means that not only the OT but also creation itself is ordained to Christ; that the foundations of the State and of human culture are Christological. On the other hand the gospel remains transcendent: by showing us that law is "mere" law the gospel strips the world of its numinous character, of its pretensions to divinity. Thus it comes about that the distinction between law and gospel preserves the specific nature of both Christianity and the world and their ordination to each other.

c) Law and the gospel, however, also stand in historical relation to each other; the history of salvation advances from the law to the gospel.

No doubt the OT too is gospel, but its promise may mean either judgment or grace. No doubt the NT too is law (analogously) but it is a law that has yielded to grace — a verdict of death and condemnation that has been quashed. Thus the distinction between law and gospel points on to the ever greater mystery of God and the full revelation of God's kingdom, one only to be looked for at the last day, when there will no longer be any need of an external law (Rev 21:23; 22:5).

See also *Spiritualism, Liberalism and Liberal Theology, Modernism, Traditionalism, Ecumenism* VI B, *Judaism* I, *Law* IV, *Salvation* III, *Natural Law, Works, Sermon on the Mount.*

BIBLIOGRAPHY. F. X. Linsemann, *Untersuchungen über die Lehre von Gesetz und Freiheit* (1912); M. C. Darcy, *Christian Morals* (1937); C. H. Dodd, *Gospel and Law* (1952); V. Hasler, *Gesetz und Evangelium in der alten Kirche bis Origenes* (1953); S. Lyonnet, "Liberté chrétienne et loi de l'Esprit selon S. Paul", *Christus* 4 (1954), pp. 6–27; K. Barth, *Evangelium und Gesetz* (2nd ed., 1956); id., "Election and Command of God", *Church Dogmatics*, II/2 (1957); H. Schlier, *Principalities and Powers in the New Testament* (1961); G. Friedrich, "εὐαγγελίζομαι...", *TWNT*, II, pp. 705–35; "νόμος", *ibid.*, IV (1967), pp. 1016–77; R. Schnackenburg, *The Moral Teaching of the New Testament* (1965); B. Häring, *The Law of Christ*, III (1966); H. Kleinknecht and W. Gutbrod, "νόμος", *TWNT*, IV, pp. 1016–77.

Walter Kasper

LEISURE

I. Leisure: A. The Notion. B. The Basis of Leisure. C. The Various Ways of Spending Free Time. D. Problems of Leisure Occupations. II. Tourism. III. Sport.

I. Leisure

A. THE NOTION

The notion of leisure, with its counterpart of work, will naturally depend on the notion one has of man in anthropology. If work and achievement are taken to be the purpose of life, leisure will be held in low esteem and man at leisure will be considered as something less than he ought to be (Guardini). But if amusement is held to be the important thing in life, work is regarded as a "negotium", and the frustration felt in work will be compensated for by an exaggerated esteem for leisure. Hence a balanced view of work and leisure presupposes a view of man which sees life as a whole.

Man is a being endowed with mind and will, with freedom and grace, striving to give himself his perfect fulfilment in personal and social activity. This is composed of work and leisure, at times more productively, at times more receptively. Beyond these varying emphases in life, it is the total integration of work and leisure which makes possible the harmonious development of man.

If the matter is to be properly understood, it may be helpful to distinguish certain aspects. Leisure may be understood as ease — the time free from professional and gainful occupations. It may also be understood as rest — the time for physiological and psychological re-building through sleep and hygiene. Finally there is the aspect of amusement — but taken in the sense of the time when the claims of man to be free for the liberal arts — the "Muses" — are satisfied, a time of "musing" which culminates in the religious act. Leisure in the widest sense includes ease, rest and amusement. In the strict sense, man is at leisure when he is a-mused in the (possibly etymological) sense of the term — an activity for which ease, rest and recreation are prerequisites.

B. THE BASIS OF LEISURE

In practice, the possibility of true leisure (more extensive than the feast-days of feudal society) is based on the economics of modern society, where increasing productivity (through industrialization, technology, rationalization and automation) has made it possible to shorten working hours. This made it possible to meet the general demand for an eight-hour day, a five-day week and guaranteed annual holidays of an adequate nature. The forty-hour week, though achieved only in varying degrees in different countries, the amount of industrialization being decisive, and varying in each country according to the type of employment — small farmers and shopkeepers, mothers of large families and social workers still have the longest hours — has become the ideal of the leisure society. The character of life in these conditions is determined by leisure rather than by work, since only some 24% of the time is spent at work, 33% at rest, while some 43% is available for real leisure.

From the point of view of sociology, it may be noted that the level of society which had free time at its disposal took on a new structure in the industrialized society. Leisure is no longer confined to the propertied classes, since the free time now available makes real leisure accessible to all. But leisure is no longer "conditioned by the environment". It is a matter of the "subjective potentialities of the individual" (A. Mann), who is free to choose his own way and to educate himself. The danger here, especially for the "other-directed", is that leisure activities may be dominated by notions of prestige, an effort to copy the "leisure class" (T. Veblen).

Philosophically speaking, it must be conceded that the regenerative notion of leisure, as stressed above all by K. Marx in his analysis of work as alienation, has been superseded today by the attribution to it of a compensatory and liberatory (or "suspensive") function (cf. J. Habermas). On the basis, then, of an integral anthropology, seeking a common denominator to which all the claims of life may be reduced, leisure might be described as follows. It is the activity in which man implements the sketch-plan given him in his nature, sketches the plan for his own person and develops in growing receptivity and creative outgoing. While man exercises his powers of domination at productive work, he grows to maturity when he is definitely in a receptive attitude, when physically at rest, when at play, when giving free rein to his mind and feelings through the fine arts, or through his own handicrafts or hobbies. He thus grows ripe for the encounter with the world and God which answers his question about the meaning of life. In this view, the purpose of all leisure is the *humanum,* the whole man as a moral and religious being. He is the contrary of the one-sided character whose development is confined to certain sectors, who is merely a "worker", a manager or an intellectual, the man without a genuine culture or true basic education. "Ripeness is all", but it is the ripeness of man *capax universi,* able to "see life steadily and see it whole". But mere humanism is not enough to ensure true leisure. Leisure, to be real and meaningful, must be based on religious worship. It starts with the time in which man belongs in a special way to God — with the Sunday liturgy.

In this anthropological context it can be seen that leisure makes certain demands on human nature. A one-sided view of man and of his work and of the relation between work and leisure can only be harmful. In the physical and psychological sphere it leads to illnesses and neuroses. The development of character is stunted. In the religious sphere, the Christian is unconvincing, since he refuses the challenge of the world.

A historical note may be in place here. The struggle for proper hours and conditions of leisure began almost simultaneously with the age of industrialization. Workers' movements began at the end of the 18th century. The slogan of the national congress of trade unions in the U.S.A. in 1866 was: "Eight hours work, eight hours sleep and eight hours to do what we like." Now that this objective has been gained to a great extent, the second phase is concerned with the proper use of free time, the achievement of true leisure. The challenge has been recognized explicitly in the U.S.A. since the beginning of the century. Since 1925 the "National Recreation Association" has been one form of the movement, and there are similar organized efforts in Belgium, France, Great Britain and Germany.

C. The Various Ways of Spending Free Time

Aristotle points out in his *Politics* that the main question concerning human activity is what man ought to do in his leisure hours (cf. *Politics,* VIII, 3; 1337b). Idleness, "killing time", is one possibility, and this situation is not basically altered if the boredom of idleness is exchanged for the busy-ness of overwork. As J. Pieper points out, sloth and restlessness correspond, while leisure is contrary to both. This boredom (the accidie of the scholastics, cf. Thomas Aquinas, *Summa Theologica,* II, II, q. 35, a. 3 ad 1), in which man runs away from himself and violates the repose of the spirit in God, is at the basis of juvenile delinquency and of the de-humanization of the entertainment industry — its "relapse into barbarism" (M. Weber). If idleness is merely a form of rest, however, it can have a positive value as recreation, as a preparative for true leisure.

Leisure occupations can be very passive when concerned only with the pre-packaged culture offered to the masses by the cinema, radio, television and press. So too in certain forms of tourism and sporting interests. This "consumers' culture" arouses misgivings, since it renders creative effort superfluous and thus blocks the one way to self-discovery, all the more so since the entertainment industry has found the way to penetrate all domains of private and family life, with television and so on. This widespread passivity and this submission to the "hidden persuaders" is to be attributed in the last resort to an ethos of work which is meaningless and frustrating, to an unscrupulous readiness to conform in the "other-directed" man and to a sort of compulsive response to the instinct of "keeping up with the Jones's", on which advertizing plays so much.

Active leisure occupations can vary widely. They include entertaining or instructive reading, games, hobbies such as painting or gardening, family amusements, amateur theatre or choral groups, adult education and charitable works. Such active leisure leads to self-discovery, self-development, the re-integration of man who is so often tied to "secondary systems". The more fully a man is committed, the greater his joy and contentment. The aim is not just pleasure but real re-creation. There must also be room for religious activity, for celebrations and quiet prayer, for the individual and for the community, as the close link between leisure and worship demands.

D. PROBLEMS OF LEISURE OCCUPATIONS

1. *Organization*. The unhappy experiences of the "Kraft durch Freude" in National-Socialist Germany, of the "Opera Nazionale Dopolavoro" in Italy and of the holiday systems of the Communist bloc are enough to make one wary of State-controlled leisure. Leisure activities sponsored by industry must also be viewed with reserve, since the presence of "big brother" everywhere is undesirable. The provision of leisure activities by commercial interests is of highly doubtful value, since their main interest is profit-making, to which truly human interests will be for the most part sacrificed. Since the important thing is to find a style of leisure remote from the commercialized, it should primarily be a matter for the social groups, including the Churches, which are the mainstay of human fellowship. With a proper application of the principle of subsidiarity it should be possible to set up community centres, youth hostels, camping sites, clubs, institutes for adult education and so on, in which the town and county councils also take part of the responsibility. In this way the conditions can be provided in which each one can freely enjoy the benefits of well-directed leisure. An important part can also be played by the family, the primary and the technical schools in educating the individual to a morally responsible use of leisure. This is a sphere in which the Churches also must be more purposefully committed, in their works of charity, youth movements and catechesis.

2. *Restrictions on the use of free time*. A sense of responsibility for society as a whole will set the proper limits to the forms in which leisure is enjoyed. The need for the protection of youth must be kept in mind and the necessary measures taken. By developing a genuine asceticism of leisure and forming consciences in this regard, practical theology could contribute to the proper and responsible enjoyment of leisure.

See also *Man, Person* II, *Work, Education* I, *Worship, Sunday, Leisure* II, III.

BIBLIOGRAPHY. T. Veblen, *Theory of the Leisure Class* (1899); H. Viscount Samuel, *Leisure in a Democracy* (1949); W. Schöllgen, "Soziologie und Ethik der Unterhaltung", *Aktuelle Moralprobleme* (1955); A. Mann, *Arbeit und Muse* (1957); R. Denney, *Astonished Muse* (1957); J. Habermas, "Soziologische Notizen zum Verhältnis von Arbeit und Freizeit", *Konkrete Vernunft (Festschrift E. Rothacker)* (1958); E. Larrabee and R. Meyersohn, *Mass Leisure* (1958); *Leisure and the Schools,* 1961 yearbook, pub. by the American Association for Health, Physical Education and Recreation; N. Miller and D. Robinson, *The Leisure Age, its Challenge to Recreation* (1963); J. Pieper, *Leisure, the Basis of Culture* (revised ed., 1964); R. Guardini, *The World and the Person* (1965); K. Rahner, *Theological Investigations,* IV (1966), pp. 368–90.

Roman Bleistein

II. Tourism

1. *History*. In every age of the world man has been a traveller, as nomad, warrior, discoverer, pilgrim, refugee, adventurer or seeker of culture. But these travels or wanderings were confined to certain types or classes. Mass tourism is a phenomenon of the present century. But it had its precursors. There was the "grand tour" of the young nobles of the 17th and 18th centuries and the visits to the watering-places, a type of travel which was linked to the traditions and privileges of a certain class. In the early 19th century the richer middle classes who were making their way upwards in the social scale also yielded

to the call of the far countries. Organized tourism soon followed, "invented" in England by Thomas Cook in 1841. Continental Europe followed the lead of England. The first German travel agency was founded in Breslau by Louis Stangen in 1863 and was offering world tours in 1878. The first volume of the *Baedekers* which were to cater for this desire to see the world had appeared in 1827. Romantic enthusiasm for nature also played its part. Alpine and tourist clubs were founded, the first Alpine club likewise in London, in 1865, with Germany and Austria soon following. The German "Friends of Nature" formed a proletarian appendix to these middle-class clubs from 1895 on. When finally young people combined to form bicycling clubs and found youth hostels and go camping, society as a whole was drawn into the pattern of tourism. A history of tourism would show how social and cultural developments such as changes in class-consciousness were paralleled by the development of the tourist business, and how this again was connected with technological progress and social legislation, such as paid holidays. The end result of all the various factors is the present-day phenomenon of mass tourism, characterized by fixed programmes, attractions and group travel — travels made to measure for all.

2. *Statistics.* Europe, which is still by far the most important region of the world for foreign travel, registered some 95,500,000 arrivals in 1966. (Travellers who used Heathrow Airport, London, in 1967 amounted to over twelve million.) This is nearly 75 per cent of all travellers registered over the whole world. The "Union Internationale des Organismes Officiels du Tourisme" estimated receipts from tourism at $ 8,120,000,000. Compared with 1965, the number of arrivals was up by 11% and receipts by 12%. According to a study published by the "Union Internationale" in 1964, the Swiss are the keenest on foreign travel. Out of each 1000 Swiss, 390 travelled abroad. Next come Canada (326), Benelux (312), France (239), Western Germany (215) and U.S.A. (112). The most frequently visited countries are still Switzerland, Austria, Italy, Spain and Germany. But the Near East, Africa and Asia are now being discovered by tourists, and more and more Europeans are going to the U.S.A.

3. *Sociology.* The holiday-making group, which is quite a modern phenomenon, has been little investigated. Preliminary investigations suggest that the choice of holiday resort is largely determined by the effort to escape one's milieu, calling, everyday life, with all their obligations and stresses. In comparison, the desire for culture, pleasure, new contacts or prestige plays very little role. The background of mass tourism is the industrial society with its hectic pressures and centralization, its division of labour and only partial actualization of men's capacities, its planning and standards, its social pressures and sanctions. The tourist is the mirror of the society of which he rids himself. The effective continuity between industrialism and tourism must be noted, whether it be explained as transference of everyday working-life to the free time of holidays, or as consumption which is "a continuation of production by other means" (Habermas). Even where people think that they have freed themselves from the world of work, they orientate themselves to it. In consequence, the decision about the meaning and priority of holidays and leisure is already taken in work and everyday life, or rather, in an overriding comprehension of both, in the notion of an ordered life which goes beyond itself both in work and in leisure, because it is aimed at a goal.

The centrifugal tendenies — and the distortions — of tourism can only be overcome when its largely irrational and yet real motives are recognized. Tourism is a symptom of an industrialized society and a form of life conditioned by it, which still needs to be "humanized".

4. *Church and tourism.* The Church has come to recognize the tasks and opportunities provided by tourism. In tourist resorts, special pastoral attention has been paid to tourists, in the form of masses and sermons, in some cases adapted to the needs of those searching repose. Pastoral work of a missionary nature on behalf of tourists was discussed at international congresses (Munich 1960, Rome 1963, Lugano 1964, Monaco 1965, Rome 1966). Pope Paul VI set up a "commissio de re pastorali peregrinatorum in ambitu internationali" (which has since been attached to the "Sacra Congregatio pro Clericis") and spoke of tourism as a "passport of peace" (as a means of international under-

standing), when addressing the international congress on "The Spiritual Values of Tourism" (18–21 April 1967). This congress was preoccupied with international co-operation of Church authorities and new pastoral methods. But the real problem of tourism seems rather to lie in the lack of a Christian sense of calling in one's work which would lead to a more truly human type of industrial society. To create this is the first task of moral theology and Christian preaching. Then there must also be a discreet presence of the Church at the various touristic centres — from camping sites to chapels at airports and railway-stations — so that the Christian community or the individual Christian may serve by their testimony the welfare of those who seek in recreation the well-being of the whole man, "body and soul".

See also *Industrialism, Profession, Work.*

BIBLIOGRAPHY. H. Habermas, "Notizen zum Missverhältnis von Kultur und Konsum", *Merkur* 10 (1956); E. Larrabee and R. Meyerson, eds., *Mass Leisure* (1958); J. Knebel, *Soziologische Strukturwandlungen im modernen Tourismus* (1960); M. Gunther, *Weekenders* (1964); C. Brightbill, *Educating for Leisure-Centred Living* (1966); R. Bleistein, "Kirche und Tourismus", *Stimmen der Zeit* 180 (1967), pp. 154–66; "Vacances et Tourisme" (by various authors), *Communicationes* 10 (1967).

Roman Bleistein

III. Sport

Sport is a kind of play. Play is one of the components of human activity, like work and contemplation. A concrete activity is mostly composed of several elements, but receives its name from the predominant component which determines its sense. Sport is therefore play, though there are considerable elements of work in it, as we see best of all in professionalism.

Play is not a matter of producing certain goods or of performing certain services (as in work), and it is not a matter of letting ourselves be captivated by reality (as in contemplation). The reason for play is the joy we find in the experience of our own or a group activity. Like the liturgy, play creates a world of its own which is different from the difficult world of work. Play has a time of its own, play-time; space of its own which can be a stadium or a chess-board; it has rules of its own which are meaningless when seen from outside: the silly decision to propel a

ball only by the feet. This shows the complementary role of play with regard to work. One leaves the world of work for that of play in order to relax. Technological developments have left more room for free time, of which there is also more need since work has become more exacting. For many people, their free time is the only time when they really live. The world of leisure is beginning to be at least as important as the world of work. Sport is a major element of this free time.

Sport is a kind of play which is completely suited to men of the present day.

1. Sport is practised regularly and systematically. Every game is a test of man's powers. Children try to throw a ball as high as they can. This is the element of "performance" or achievement which can develop into competition in games played in common. Efforts are made to raise the standard of performance in sport by training and regular practice, and sometimes use is made of the means provided by science and technology. Particular pleasure is taken in bettering a given performance. It is a way of experiencing the possibilities of the human body, and it counter-balances the one-sidedness of work or study. It can make man aware of his own powers when he is threatened by self-alienation in the highly complicated process of life in common.

2. Through technical developments men and peoples have become more accessible to each other and have begun to share a common lot. This has made it necessary to know and understand other men from different races and countries. This can be done happily and spontaneously in the sphere of sport. Men at play regain a certain spontaneity which can free them from inhibitions which make it difficult to make contacts with strangers. Further, the special world of play is something apart from the world of work and economics and politics and so is free to some extent from the estrangements and conflicts which may prevail elsewhere. In sport, play has developed into a means of making contacts, which is one of the reasons for the official and even international character of sport. The rules of the game are usually established officially and ratified by international organizations. The basis of competition is being constantly broadened. De Coubertin did well to make the brotherhood of man the ideal of the Olympic Games.

Apart from active participation in sport, sport is also important for the relaxation it offers to large numbers of spectators. Spectators really join in the game in a certain way. They identify themselves with a given club or player, so that after the game they feel they can say: *we* have won or lost. They also experience the special form of community spirit which is brought about by games. As play goes on, a group of strangers becomes a community with mutual sympathies and the same spontaneous reactions.

What enthralls the spectators above all is to see how the lot is cast: they are not certain how it will turn out. Just as the ancient Greeks sat in breathless excitement in the theatre to see the workings of fate which comes upon gods and men alike, so the destiny of the ball going into the net or skimming over it now holds thousands of men in suspense. The tension of the game lifts men out of the tensions of ordinary life and so provides real relaxation. The strong spectator interest of sport makes it tend to develop into professionalism. Professionals are players, not workers. Just as the professional musician is constantly gripped by the beauty of his music, the good professional player is constantly absorbed by the joy of the game. His rough or foul play may infuriate the spectators, but his task is to set up the perfect pattern for the game by his technical and tactical skill. What matters is not how sensational the effort is, but the sight of destiny at work in a game of a certain beauty.

Sport has its own, intrinsic ethical norms. These follow from the nature of sport, inasmuch as it is a form of play. Players and spectators are bound to do all they can to keep the sphere of sport "clean". Anything that falls short of this ideal, the desire to win at all costs, for instance, or the demand for sensation, is unsporting.

The Church must be equal to a task which also includes the upholding of earthly values. Just as it is engaged on problems connected with work and world peace, it is also its duty to reinforce the ethical character of sport. Working with all men of good will, the Church must try to inspire all participants to keep the sphere of sport "clean" and so contribute to the realization of a human existence of true dignity.

See also *Play, Work, Leisure* I.

BIBLIOGRAPHY. R. Caillois, *Man, Play and Games* (1961); P. McIntosh, *Sport in Society* (1963); R. Moore, *Sports and Mental Health* (1966); R. Slovenko and J. Knight, *Motivations in Play, Games and Sports* (1967).

B. Möller

LIBERALISM AND LIBERAL THEOLOGY

A. ORIGINS AND SOCIAL MEANING OF LIBERALISM (19TH CENTURY)

Liberalism, which dominated much of the thought and social endeavour of European middle-class life in the 19th century, stemmed in the main from the great spiritual impulses of the 17th century which are only partly comprised by the Enlightenment and the French Revolution. There was the broader, more general recognition that freedom gave man the chance and the task of self-determination, while this responsible "self" on which so much depended was chiefly if not exclusively "reason". The dominant note was the rational, analytical insight into all factors of life from the laws of nature to morality. This epoch-making view of freedom and reason was really first developed by Spinoza and Leibniz, who took up the thought of Descartes. Philosophy became basically an experience of the self which prescinded from all material reality. The self was a sort of other-worldly *a priori* reality which was to be regained from the world of objects and then be set free to follow its own autonomous laws of thought. In this way it was to re-discover all reality for itself and re-build it anew. This "egological" principle set social philosophy the task of explaining the possibility and the norms of intersubjective unity in the light of the same immanent laws and needs of the Ego. The political and legal theorists of the epoch started from here to set up a liberalistic individualism which could only see society as a secondary contract entered into freely and all social authority as strictly subordinated to the rational autonomy of the individual. This notion of freedom did not remain confined to the professional philosophers. It was already at work in the "Declaration of Rights" of 1689 and the growing influence of the Whigs in England, in the American constitution of 1787 and very decisively in the French Revolution. It may be said to have been one of the main factors in social history and must be presupposed in all analysis of modern social thinking.

The new wave of humanism and the Romantic Movement of the beginning of the 19th century saw things differently. They recognized that where "reason" was set up as the only valid judge, it readily degenerated into an alien and stifling domination of a really much more complex individual. The ideal of freedom was retained, of course, as inviolable, but less stress was laid on finding the truth of the authentic self in the reason. It was replaced by the notion that life should be lived to the full. The many sides of personality, now seen to be highly complicated, were to be freely developed, almost to the limits of anarchy. There was a "pre-established harmony" which would enable men who gave their individualities free rein in this way to do justice to their real selves and hence be free. It was this notion of "liberty" which dominated all realms of social life as the ideal in the liberalism of the 19th century.

An important consequence of this notion of liberty as regards social practice was the separation which now ensued between State and society. In the new relationships now set up, civil society was regarded as the more or less mechanical coupling between self-centred individuals who lived only for themselves. In this marvellous play of forces of a totally unrestricted *laissez faire* which automatically ensured fair shares for all, the State had merely to be a sort of "night watchman", ready to intervene if the process of social development was menaced. The State was regarded merely as a secondary function of social aggregation and was to regard itself as such, not claiming legitimacy from a higher authority of a questionable nature, but relying on the automatic conjunction of the wills of the individuals in a freely elected parliament. This upheaval in social thinking, and consequently, in political and economic practice (the latter based on the theories of Adam Smith and similar liberals) eventually brought to light the intrinsic tensions of the liberal notion of freedom. How could the claim to be free from State interference be reconciled with equal freedom for all? The older liberalism found itself in conflict with the democratic theory which it had itself to some extent fathered. This democratic theory sought for the benefits of social order not from the very dubious workings of spontaneous free wills, in harmony without a tuner, but from the State. Social organization was to be assured through political institutions on an egalitarian electoral basis. But the real conflict came with socialism, which extended the egalitarian system of democracy to take economic life as well.

The relationship between the Church and a society which was gradually "liberalizing" itself in the sense described above took on various forms. In Protestantism especially, but also in the Catholic lands, movements arose within the Churches to shake off all tutelage of believers by the State or by a quasi-statutory hierarchy. This was a corollary of the general political reaction against the omnipresence of civil authority. There were a number of emancipation movements, mostly in connection with liberalism in theology (see below). In France at the beginning of the century there was the mostly lay movement grouped around the periodical *L'avenir*, and at the end of the century *Le Sillon*. In German-speaking countries there were the "Eos" group in Munich, the "Protestant Union" of 1863, the Swiss "Union for Free Christianity", and also the "Protestant Friends" who had been forced out of their Church by disciplinary measures. In Italy there was the "Democrazia Cristiana" of Romolo Murri.

But then, in the second place, since the Churches often identified themselves with the reactionary forces in politics, the opposition of liberalism to alien authorities was also and indeed above all directed against the political and social potentiality of the Christian Churches. Liberalism became the demand for the total restriction of religious life to the private sphere. Finally, the State itself, especially in the Catholic countries where liberalism had come to power against clerical conservative opposition, took forcible or even violent measures to restrict the social influence of the Church. So, for instance, in Latin America, especially Mexico, in southern Europe and in another way in Germany, in the *Kulturkampf* of Bismarck.

Within the Catholic Church, all demands for liberalization, for the separation, for instance, of Church and State and for a withdrawal of the Church from political life were met by sharp opposition from Rome. Gregory XVI in the encyclical *Mirari*

Vos (1832), Pius IX in the *Syllabus* (1864), Leo XIII above all in *Libertas Praestantissimum* (1888) and Pius X in *Lamentabili* (1907) condemned liberalism as the effort of civil society to set itself free of the authority of God which was embodied in the Church. It is only in the present day that the *de facto* development of society has brought about a change in the attitude of authority. The Church is gradually beginning to re-consider its role in society, and to see its specific task less as a doctrinaire guidance of society, either inside or outside of the Church. Here there seem to be the beginnings of a tangible liberalization of Church life.

B. LIBERAL THEOLOGY

With the coming of liberalism, then, a notion of liberty which was basically individualistic penetrated all civil society in the 19th century. Theologians were inevitably confronted with the problems arising from this liberalistic individualism. How could Christianity be justified, not just rationally, as on the whole intellectually satisfying and useful to the common good, but in face of the Ego of freedom which saw itself as absolutely free and comprehensively responsible?

1. In Protestantism, Schleiermacher (d. 1834) worked out what was to be the decisive way of seeing the problem for a whole century of liberalism. He placed the Christian faith within the framework of the transcendental philosophy which understood reality as primordially "spiritual" or determined by the consciousness – and hence as the reality of freedom. Applied to theology this new philosophical approach meant that it too should not seek understanding in an effort to rationalize subsequently a rigid positive fact. All understanding must be "genetic", a dissolution of facts back to their transcendental conditions of possibility and constitutive elements. These include the concrete and historical as well as the *a priori*, and aim at the primary origin of consciousness and reality. From this point of view, Schleiermacher investigates the Christian faith, not primarily as it appears historically and objectively in its contents *(fides quae creditur)* but as the *fides qua creditur* which contains the former as its objective counterpart. The question now is: What is the real situation of the *fides qua?* How can it be genetically exhibited in the light of freedom as the primordial and normative disclosure of meaning?

The origin of "faith" — in the verbal sense — appears to Schleiermacher as the wholly personal "feeling of absolute dependence". Feeling here is not taken psychologically as a mere mental state. It is the immediate and irrefutable self-presentation of existence, with the claim of transcendental experience involved. On these principles, the articulation of faith as doctrine can only be the conceptual self-interpretation of the subject in the light of his truth-disclosing "feeling". And hence theology must take the same view of the faith of the Church as presented in Scripture and doctrinal tradition. When then dogmatic theology still normally speaks of the believing Ego, the world as seen in the light of faith and the "divine attributes" as apparently distinct realities, this can only be legitimate when Christian faith is re-absorbed into the act of self-consciousness as consciousness of God. But then we have the acute problem of how to reconcile this luminous inwardness with the historical person of Jesus as the Christ "outside" us. (The orthodox viewpoint is that it is only in and through Jesus that the relationship to God is possible which Schleiermacher affirms is directly realized in the "pious consciousness" itself.) It is the problem of what Lessing called the "troublesome gap" between eternal truths of reason and contingent truths of history. Schleiermacher's solution was to give the theological significance of Jesus a drastically new interpretation. "The redeemer . . . is like all other men, by virtue of the identity of human nature, but differs from all others by the persistent force of his consciousness of God, which was a true existence of God in him" *(The Christian Faith,* para. 94). For this reason, the "ecclesiastical formulations" concerning the person of Christ are to be constantly revised in a critical spirit. Jesus is redeemer and mediator insofar as he is the supreme model who stimulates, impels and guides men, in repentance and conversion, to self-knowledge as knowledge of God. "The redeemer imparts to believers the force of his own consciousness of God. This is his redemptive activity" *(ibid.,* para. 100).

2. With this interpretation of Christianity, the 19th century was faced with the systematic

problem, at its most acute, of reconciling self-understanding (as self-justificatory) with the mediatorship of Jesus. And the way was also paved for the effort which liberal theology then saw to be its real task, and where in fact it was to make its most important contributions: the critical investigation of the historical sources of the Christian faith. This effort took three forms.

First there was the critical research into the texts, for which the way had been prepared by the similar projects of rationalism (J. S. Semler, d. 1791). Text-criticism was inspired now by the transcendental approach, which sought to reduce the whole of Christian revelation to the perspicuousness of the "pious consciousness". Thus it had a theological function, inasmuch as it broke down the resistance of the texts to the proper grasp of them, and so prepared the statement for its integration into the act of faith. Then, the principle of liberalism was also a justification of the critical sense in historical research, not merely, as in rationalism, to help out when exegesis broke down, but as in principle the true and adequate method of theological exegesis in general. In consequence namely of the fundamental sameness of Christ and Christian, the self-communication of Jesus which is the awakener of faith cannot by its very nature proceed otherwise than does the self-communication of historic personalities in general. Hence the method by which their history is investigated must likewise be the means of encounter with Christ. Finally, the liberal principle did not merely allow critical historical research to be generalized and made the exclusive principle of theological exegesis. It actually demanded such research if its "pious consciousness" was to continue at all to understand itself as specifically Christian. For since all that the Christian preaching has to say is absorbed and transformed into intrinsic evidence, the function of Jesus is restricted to his stimulating example. But this can only make an impact when his person is known, and this can only be through critical historical research. Hence the "quest for the historical Jesus" became the most burning question of liberal theology in the 19th century and its real theological interest.

With this re-valuation of historical criticism, the historical conscience of the exegete was now endowed with a really independent criterion of theological truth. The sense of the truth of history freed itself from its roots in a set of principles which also underlay to some extent, as a philosophy of religion, the classical dogmatic theology. Historical research could then become a court of appeal against all concrete pre-sentiments about the true content of Bible and dogma, whether these attitudes came from religious experience or from orthodox tradition. And in fact the whole history of liberal theology is dominated and stimulated by the action and re-action between an intrinsically evident religious *a priori* (however derived) and the content of the sources proved most reliable historically. The main interest was always the image they presented of Jesus.

3. The first phase of liberal theology was characterized by the effort to link up with the "lived theology" (*Erfahrungstheologie*) of Schleiermacher and the historical speculation of Hegel. It was always an endeavour to master the problem of uniting the concrete content of faith and the positive historical material of faith. In Switzerland, A. Biedermann (d. 1885) was for long the dominant figure in theology, following to some extent the subjective principles of Schleiermacher's experiential spirituality. German Protestantism, however, was in the main under the influence of the so-called "Younger Tübingen School". Its founder, Ferdinand Christian Baur (d. 1860), sought to reconcile the dogmatic content of Christology (and hence theology as a whole) with history by means of a philosophy of history which was derived from Hegel. The genesis of the truth of the absolute in the consciousness was considered to be both historically mediated and to include Jesus as a decisive moment in this historical genesis. This was a view which was to be maintained above all as a hermeneutical principle in the historiography of dogma and of Church life. But Baur's disciple, D. F. Strauss (d. 1874), abandoned entirely the historical figure of Jesus, as non-essential for Christianity. In his epoch-making *Life of Jesus* he described the figure of Jesus as totally overgrown by myths, and buried so deeply under secondary theological and mythic interpretations that even in the Bible it was no longer historically attainable. Baur and Strauss for the first time used the method of historical criticism not merely to rationalize away the miraculous elements in biblical narratives but as a theologically decisive criterion. They thus

became the founders of the exegetical tradition of liberal theology.

The problem of modern mediation was also taken up on the Catholic side, chiefly at Tübingen, by Catholic professors such as J. A. Möhler and J. E. Kuhn. An effort was made to solve it in terms which would do justice to the Catholic notion of dogma — and may still perhaps be used as directives today. It was an effort to grasp dialectically and dynamically the findings of positive, historical theology as moments in the universal dialectic of perceptible "immediacy" and conceptual "universality". This dialectic was seen as moving towards Jesus Christ by an intrinsic necessity, since he is the Idea in the concrete. And thus the dialectic moves towards the synthesis of self-understanding and understanding of history in the Christian faith in the history of salvation.

4. At the middle of the century, liberal theology in Germany received a major new impulse from A. Ritschl (d. 1889) and his disciples. He declared that practical love of the neighbour, realized very concretely in social life and in one's calling, was the true and only meaning of the love of God. Hence it was the heart of Christianity, and when given adequate extension, could be the reality of the "kingdom of God", in the form of a cultured and ethical society. Jesus Christ was seen as the original bringer of this very worldly kingdom of God, since his life was exemplary as regards the love of God now seen as requisite. His example enables the moral life to be lived by those who trust in him in spite of all their consciousness of guilt and all their despair of fulfilling this precept of love. Thus God is understood as the reality of this love which has become manifest and efficacious in Jesus. With this theological conception, Ritschl and his extensive and influential school abandoned all philosophical speculation on religion in history or the consciousness and placed their dogmatics squarely on an ethical foundation. They claimed to have derived the criteria for this ethics from historical biblical criticism and the resulting scientific picture of Jesus. The same criteria were then widely used as hermeneutical keys in exegesis and history of dogma.

This broad mainstream of liberal theology, of whom the most important representatives include W. Hermann, A. von Harnack, Holtzmann, Wellhausen, Duhm, Weizsäcker, Jülicher and Schmiedel, had its strongest repercussions among the middle-class Protestants of Germany, but also had parallels and effects outside. In France, for instance, there was the "(Symbolo-)Fideism" of A. Sabatier and E. Ménégoz. Then there was the "Social Gospel" movement on the non-theological level (in America and England), which stressed the ethical example of Jesus and the optimistic view of society as embodying the kingdom of God, with a view to social reform. It was one of the factors in the rise of Christian socialism. In France in particular liberal theology penetrated Catholicism, especially through its exegetical findings, and so contributed essentially to the rise of modernism.

5. But there was also persistent criticism of liberal theology itself from the "left". Taking its principles to their radical and logical conclusions, critics like the later D. F. Strauss, Gottfried Keller, Jacob Burckhardt, E. von Hartmann and Franz Overbeck denounced a lack of honesty and consistency in the liberal spirituality which remained centred on Jesus while destroying Bible and dogma by its historical criticism. New approaches, partly inspired by liberalism itself, brought about a major crisis in the classical liberal theology at the turn of the century. The exegetical studies of younger scholars, especially those of the "school of history of religions", itself a product of the Ritschlian school, demonstrated the close connection between the biblical affirmations and their ancient religious environment. This was the work of such scholars as Eichhorn, Gunkel, Bousset, Wrede, Weiss, Wernle, Heitzmüller and Troeltsch, with the support of A. Schweitzer. It was evident that there was an immense distance between the Scriptures, and especially the biblical picture of Jesus, and the optimistic social ethics of liberal theology and its notion of humanity. The Scriptures and their Jesus seemed to lose their claim to absoluteness and even any claim to special force of obligation. But there was also a trend in the opposite direction, inspired by the controversy with the school of historicism. The need was felt once more of a philosophy of religion which while allowing for the many-sided relativity of Christianity, would still demonstrate clearly the proper nature of

religion and the uniqueness of what was specifically Christian. Hence Otto, Bousset and Troeltsch in particular introduced once more into theology the questions raised by metaphysics, epistemology and religious psychology. What was finally fatal to the old liberal theology was the collapse of a bourgeois historical optimism and its ethics with the First World War. This crisis found its exponents in the school of dialectical theology, which reproached the liberals with having merely projected their own humanistic ideals, no matter how valuable, into the Bible and their image of Jesus. By contrast, these theologians stressed the "otherness" of God and the uncompromising verdict on the world through his paradoxical manifestation in Jesus Christ. This did not fall within the bounds of any human certainty or *a priori*, of a speculative, religious or ethical philosophy. Under National Socialism in Germany, the "Confessing Church" of Protestantism was impervious to the old liberal theology, and so its last defendants could survive only in Switzerland (where it is represented in a certain way by M. Werner, F. Buri and U. Neuenschwander).

6. Liberal theology was right in seeking to disclose a way to the Christian faith which would be justifiable in the eyes of modern men, once they had been led by modern philosophy to recognize explicitly and consciously their fully personal responsibility to their conscience in the matter of the truth. Its legitimate interests are recognized on the Catholic side as well as the Protestant (there especially in the school of Bultmann), in the effort inspired to some extent by existence-philosophy to base exegesis on a concept of history and of understanding which is philosophically alert and no longer the naivety of historicism. There is an effort to develop a corresponding theological hermeneutics which will demonstrate the point of contact and unity between the historical person of Jesus and the "pious consciousness" of the modern man whose existence is wholly responsible to itself and thus — and only thus — given a religious dimension. Only such a philosophy of historical existence, as (logically) the theology of the history of salvation, can bridge — if anything can — the distance between a liberalism which has ceased to be Christian and an ideological "Orthodoxy".

See also *Enlightenment, Rationalism, Individualism, Humanism, Romanticism, State, Society, Socialism, Church and World, Church and State, Modernism, Transcendental Philosophy, Jesus Christ* II, *Tübingen School, Historicism, Existence* II.

BIBLIOGRAPHY. See bibliography on *Enlightenment, Church and State, Rationalism;* also: E. Barbier, *Histoire du catholicisme libéral et du catholicisme social en France*, 5 vols. (1923); J. Schapiro, *Liberalism. Its Meaning and History* (1958); G. de Ruggiero, *History of European Liberalism* (1959); E. Hughes, *The Church and the Liberal Society* (1961); G. Cherry, *Early English Liberalism* (1962); L. Feuer, *Spinoza and the Rise of Liberalism* (1965); L. Dunbar, *The Republic of Equals* (1966). On C see bibliography on *Idealism, Romanticism, Form Criticism, Dialectical Theology;* also: A. Schweitzer, *The Quest of the Historical Jesus* (E. T., 1910; 3rd ed., 1963); C. Jenkins, *Frederick Denis Maurice and the New Reformation* (1938); P. Tillich, *The Protestant Era* (1957); K. Barth, *From Rousseau to Ritschl* (1959); A. M. Ramsey, *From Gore to Temple* (1960); J. Carpenter, *Gore: A Study in Liberal Catholic Thought* (1960); R. Bultmann, *Existence and Faith* (Selections from *Glauben und Verstehen,* I and III) (1961); K. Cauthen, *The Impact of American Religious Liberalism* (1962); C. Welch, ed., *God and Incarnation in Mid-Nineteenth-Century German Theology* (1965); M. Werner, *The Formation of Christian Dogma* (1965); W. Philipp, ed., *Der Protestantismus im 19. und 20. Jahrhundert* (1965); F. Buri, *Christian Faith in our Time* (1966); P. Tillich, *Perspectives on 19th and 20th Century Protestant Theology* (1967).

Konrad Hecker

LIFE

I. Natural Science. II. Moral Theology.

I. Natural Science

1. Scientifically speaking, no valid answer can yet be given on the question of life. But its characteristics can be described in great detail. Life is linked to protoplasm, the substance, which is the highest known form of organized matter. The protoplasm is basically a system of structures and functions in which nucleic acids, carbohydrates, fats, hormones, vitamins, and enzymes occur. This living matter never occurs, even in its simplest forms, except in a cellular organization. The cellular schema means that life is only present in an individualized form. We can distinguish in the cell, which can range from .001 mm to 500 mm in size, a membrane, a nucleus and the body of the cell with its

organelles or suspended granules. The most important elements of the composition of the cell are the basic substance (hyaloplasm) with its inclusions, which are of great importance for the chemical processes, and the nuclear matter (caryoplasm). Along with water and the ions of inorganic compounds, the hyaloplasm is chiefly composed of organic compounds, mostly in the form of proteins. These proteins result from the immense number of combinations possible for the twenty or so amino acids, whose number and sequence constitute the various macromolecular structures and can thus bring about the various specific proteins. The caryoplasm, which occurs in the form of effector and transport structures, is composed of proteins and the typical nucleic acids DNA and RNA (desoxyribonucleic and ribonucleic acid). The basic units of the nucleic acids are the nucleotides, which consist of a purine or pyramidine base, phosphoric acid and a pentose sugar. Over 100,000 such nucleotides are here polymerized to polynucleotides, and offer innumerable possibilities of combinations.

The precise structure of these polynucleotides has been visualized by the Watson-Crick model, which shows that they have the form of two helices wound round a common axis. Each of them fits the other like key and lock, according to the given possibilities of pairing off determined by the bases. These polynucleotides of the nucleus undergo a change of form when passing from their steady or working state to that of division. Under the light microscope they can be seen at various stages of the division of the cell as chromosomes. The number and form of the chromosomes is constant in each species. The vital processes take place in and through these structures of the cell (of which only a selection has been given). The basis of the vital processes is the metabolism of the cell, an interchange of materials which may again be divided into a metabolism of nutrients and energy. Building materials external to the cell are assimilated from the environment and become matter proper to the cell.

The metabolism brings about as a rule a synthesis of simpler materials in more complicated forms. From one half to two-thirds of these synthesized products are enzyme proteins. The rest of the synthesized protein serves as building materials or nutrients, and continues to undergo constant trans-

formations and finally dissolution (katabolism; the formation process is called anabolism). The anabolism is an energy-consuming process, which is fed by a metabolism of energy-producing factors, in which the furnisher and storehouse for the necessary energy is ATP (adenosine triphosphate). The most important source of energy is the respiratory function of the cell, the biological oxydation, through which the nutrients absorbed — autotrophically by plants, heterotrophically by animals — are turned into the requisite energy, insofar as they do not enter into the anabolism. The metabolism of the cell means that the organism is in a constant relationship to its environment and that it is in a position to develop and preserve the capacities for the maintenance of life. These may be briefly characterized as follows. Living matter forms a continuous system in time, both as regards the individual and the species. The anabolism means among other things that growth takes place which remains true to the original pattern. This is the basis of the formation of new cells by division (mitosis). The living matter also remains continuously homogeneous throughout the reproductive cycle, which makes it potentially "immortal". The DNA is the main bearer of the hereditary information which preserves the identity (of the organism). It can transmit (this information as) identical copies by means of replication in the mitosis and the reproductive process. But the constancy of the hereditary information in the DNA is not absolute. It is subject to "mutations" by which the information is suddenly altered at a statistically measurable rate, but mostly by small stages. This is the basis of evolution in living things.

The metabolism of the cell means that the living thing is in active movement, that is, it is empowered to bring about the contractions of its macromolecular elements which are the basis of all active movement of the organism. The mobility is specified by the differentiation of the cells and the resulting tasks allotted them. The fundamental process is the transmutation of the chemical energy supplied by the ATP into mechanical energy. A further property of life is its specific irritability or response to stimuli This enables the organism to maintain itself (within limits) as individual or species against its environment. In living systems there is no opposition or juxtaposition of structure and function. The living thing is always a constant flow of activity. Living forms cannot be said to be: they rather take place. They form a perpetual flow of matter, energy and information. This flow is kept in harmony in a regulated "flowing equilibrium", sometimes called a steady state of non-equilibrium. This steady state makes the living organism an open system which is involved in a constant interchange of matter, energy and information with its environment, a process in which it remains constant over long periods. Possibly analogically open systems are also to be found outside the typically living thing. This steady state with its input and output holds good of all levels of living things, even up to the level of "psychic" behaviour. This equilibrium enables the organism to adapt itself and hence safeguard its continued existence and its individual and specific development. The process which takes place in this open living system is irreversible. The second law of thermodynamics is not applicable in its usual form, since it constantly receives and must receive an input of energy, which enables it to continue to work. In the more highly organized individuals a number of causes which are still not fully explained lead to the dissolution of the system in death. Meanwhile the steady state can only be maintained by a complicated system of regulation which follows essentially cybernetic laws, as modern research sees more and more clearly. The enzymes (and the nervous system, where it exists) play a role in this regulation. A rigid machine-like regulation occurs relatively seldom. What is preponderant in directing the systems are the feed-back mechanisms which are often intermeshed. It seems that life is inconceivable without regulation by such feed-back mechanisms as a basic principle.

2. The question of life in natural philosophy has been, as a matter of history, restricted to the specific aspect of one question of being. Do organisms, in contrast to non-living structures of matter and functions, form a special level of being which cannot be derived from the lower degrees of being, or is the special treatment of organisms ultimately a convention which allows a line of demarcation in research between the disciplines? Has life, qua life, special laws of its own or is

it subject exclusively to laws outside itself? Are the ultimate presuppositions of the theory of the inorganic sufficient to explain the typical characteristics of the organic (metabolism, reproduction), or must there be special presuppositions, not required by general physical and chemical theory?

In the course of a controversy extending over the centuries, this question of the degree of being of living things has been intrinsically linked with more general problems of philosophy such as the body-soul relationship, monism, dualism, teleology and ethics. It seems in the process to have been given a special importance which it hardly has of itself. The wide range of answers given to the question may best be illustrated by the theses of mechanism and vitalism. Mechanism views the laws of physics and chemistry as the effective laws of life and also often holds that the genesis of the first living beings can be explained on the basis of a continuous transition from the non-living. Vitalism attributes to life a principle of operation which is wholly its own, and which cannot be identified with the laws of the non-living. Hence it refuses to allow the origin of life from the non-living. Neither of these schools has been able to prove its thesis either by empirical or logical analyses. The sometimes passionate discussion was often confused by a lack of adequate methodological distinction between what is the criterion of life and what is the explanation of it. Mechanism is inclined to deny the experiential traits of order in the vital processes or to disregard them and leave them outside the boundaries of research. Vitalism is inclined to hold that it has demonstrated the irreducibility of life when it has registered its typical characteristics. The strongest argument against the whole controversy and against the extreme positions taken up by some debaters is probably the fact that the standard of comparison for the organic order, the physico-chemical theory with its notion of matter, has undergone a profound change, so that its significance as regards reality of being or degree of being is not now definable.

The controversy between mechanism and vitalism is today an anachronism, though the psychological situation which has all along been to some extent characteristic of research means that continual vigilance is called for. Otherwise the importance of causal and analytical research may be underestimated, and the way thrown open to fantasies and speculation such as the natural philosophy of Romanticism indulged in. Or again, exclusive attention to physico-chemical analysis may overlook what is typical in the process of life.

In view of these facts, modern theoretical biology tries to find a way which will eliminate the blind spots of the problem-makers. Its research is characterized rather by heuristic principles or working hypotheses rather than by "statements about reality". It avoids any metaphysical interpretation of experimental science in the direction of any given form of philosophy. What were formerly seen as "ontological" assertions about "degrees of being" are now merely provisional characterizations of various regions of being, while the problem of explanation is left open. The task of natural philosophy today in its consideration of life is not so much to take up a more or less well founded attitude towards the various classical explanations of life, as to keep the question open. For this is undoubtedly the only way in which even in biology due attention can be paid to man, whose existence represents a life which ranges from what are certainly inorganic natural processes to an ethical behaviour which is determined by values and by the consciousness of responsibility.

See also *Matter*.

BIBLIOGRAPHY. A. Baker and others, *New Dynamic Biology* (1957); American Institute of Biological Sciences, *Cell Biology* (1961); D. Reid, *Introduction to Biology* (1962); R. Schubert-Soldner, *Mechanism and Vitalism: Philosophical Aspects of Biology* (1962); M. Sirks and C. Zirkle, *The Evolution of Biology* (1964); I. Baker and G. Allen, *Matter, Energy and Life* (1965); G. E. Nelson and others, *Fundamental Concepts of Biology* (1967).

Werner Bröker

II. Moral Theology

1. *The right and duty to live.* When moral theology considers the right to life and the duty to live, the necessity and value of preserving life, it has to examine how life can best and adequately serve the love of God, the neighbour and oneself. Its starting-point must be that the Bible and theology consider life to be a participation of man in the life of God, in such a way that earthly life makes

possible and prepares for participation in eternal life. Since the definitive attainment of salvation presupposes the maturation of earthly life, the latter is an intrinsic moment of the development of the religious and moral personality. Hence fundamentally all men have the same right to life and the duty to preserve life as long as it can be reasonably thought to serve the development of the person. This right to life is limited by the rights of other men and above all by the right of God, to whom alone it belongs to dispose freely of life. Hence life must be preserved as long as it can be reasonably put at the service of love. Since the necessity of placing life at the disposition of love admits of various degrees of urgency, there are also various degrees of obligation to preserve life. Hence earthly life has not an absolute value but merely a relative one, since it is there to serve the religious and moral personality (cf. Mk 8:35).

Hence it follows that all men have fundamentally the same right to as much medical care and protection of health as society at a given state of development can reasonably supply. In addition to this, each one has the right to use all the means within his power to protect his health, insofar as this can be done without detriment to his social obligations. But he is only obliged to do so within the bounds of what is possible and reasonable.

The justification of the artificial prolongation of life in its terminal stages must therefore always be judged in the light of how far the prolongation of life, in the service of the person in question, is compatible with his links and duties to society. Thus artificial prolongation of life, where it may be imposed on the dying person, may be appropriate as a service to science. But it would not be fitting to prolong life artificially at the cost of necessary efforts on behalf of others who are urgently in need of help.

Experiments to produce human life in test-tubes and artificial insemination are forbidden insofar as according to human estimation life so engendered opens up no proper possibilities of a development in keeping with human dignity.

But just as responsible parenthood in marriage cannot be considered as a violation of the sovereignty of God, so too the responsible efforts of science to trace the biological laws of living organisms cannot be considered as an unlawful effort to intervene in a field reserved to the authority of God. Man is merely trying to learn the structural laws implanted into life by God, in order to use them in the service of life. Such efforts are only forbidden when they lead to a manipulation of life which is no longer in the service of the worthy development of the human person.

2. *The crime of murder*. It follows that man may only dispose of earthly life when its preservation cannot reasonably be compatible with love. Hence the fifth commandment (Deut 5:17), as understood by the Church and its theologians, forbids all killing on one's own authority which cannot be reconciled with the demands of love. This is the grave sin of murder or suicide because it is interference in the sovereign decision of God on one's own authority.

If no relationship between human life and eternal life is acknowledged, the wrongness of murder can only be based on the equal right of all men to life, without respect of persons. The prohibition of euthanasia and suicide can then only be based on possible duties towards others and on the consideration that it is irrational to throw away incalculable chances of self-realization.

Such merely immanent justifications of the prohibition of murder, euthanasia and suicide lack the stringency given by the theological proof. Hence it is difficult, if not impossible, to reach a consensus between believers and non-believers in difficult marginal cases, where it is a matter of the morality of killing men whose lives, according to human estimation, are no longer worth preserving (or worth living). It will be impossible to persuade non-believers that in extreme cases suicide is forbidden or euthanasia, if the person in question assents.

3. *Indirect killing*. All voluntary homicide is not necessarily murder. If one defends one's own life or that of another against arbitrary attack, even by killing the arbitrary aggressor (when there is no other effective means), one is not arbitrarily preferring one life to another but deciding in this case for the life of the innocent to the detriment of that of the arbitrary aggressor. This may be called indirect killing, because the intention is the preservation of (innocent) life and it directly serves this preservation. It is

allowed by theological tradition, because love will seek to protect life against irrational destruction, if necessary at the cost of the life of the aggressor.

This argument is all the more stringent, the more people there are who can be protected from arbitrary death in this way. Thus in the case of a heavily-armed killer who is running amok, there is an obligation to kill him rather than to allow unresistingly many others to be killed by him. But this argument does not prove that there is an obligation to kill an arbitrary aggressor rather than to allow oneself to be killed, since well-ordered love does not need to prefer one's own life to that of another. We are rather invited to follow the example of Christ and surrender our own life rather than take that of another (Jn 15:13; cf. Mt 16:25; Jn 12:25). But one still has the right to prefer one's own life to that of an arbitrary aggressor. However, it is already questionable that the killing of an innocent should be permitted, if it can be prevented by the killing of the arbitrary aggressor.

From this point of view, it is doubtful whether the death of two innocents may be permitted, where neither of them is an aggressor against the other and where the killing of one could save the life of the other. The Holy Office declared (*D* 1889, 1890 a–c; cf. Pius XI, *Casti Connubii: D* 2242–44; Pius XII, *AAS* 43 [1951], pp. 838 f., 857 ff.) that the permissibility of killing the child in the womb, and in particular craniotomy, could not be safely taught even where it could be foreseen with certainty that both mother and child would die ("tuto doceri non potest"). But the ruling also made it clear indirectly that in this case the prohibition of craniotomy cannot be regarded as certain. Similar problems about the inviolability of human life have been recently presented to moral theology by the fact that it is impossible to say with absolute certainty when life has ceased, while vital and viable organs can be transplanted from dead or dying people and effectively used to sustain the life of others.

Rational consideration seems to suggest that it is part of the rational service of life that where death is directly and inevitably supervening, life should be allowed to perish, where, according to human estimation, it can no longer be the vehicle of a worthy human existence, and where it can save

313

another life which cannot be saved otherwise. The difficulty is that man seems here to arrogate to himself the decision about life and death. In such extreme marginal cases, it is practically impossible to decide when exactly the independent, responsible application of reason swings over to the arbitrary disposition of human life. The limit between the direct killing of the innocent, which is always forbidden, and indirect killing, which may be permitted in the service of life, is clear in theory but cannot be neatly drawn in practice. In any case, killing is only justified insofar as it serves the optimum expansion of life and does not arbitrarily sustain one life at the expense of another. It is scarcely possible to say definitely that this is so in the case of craniotomy and the transplantation of certain organs.

Since man's right to life is not given him by man, and man has the duty of placing himself as fully as possible in the service of life, the killing of men when forced to defend oneself can only be done within the limits of the absolutely necessary, that is, insofar as it serves the optimum preservation of life. Hence even a defensive war is unjust where the protection of the lives of the attacked is out of all proportion to the destruction let loose by the war. For the same reason, passive resistance is to be preferred in the first place to violent revolution. But even revolution may be permissible when it is the means of averting a worse reign of terror. Under normal circumstances the death penalty is likewise to be rejected as unjustifiable.

4. *Protection of embryonic life.* The protection of human life raises special problems in the case of the embryo. From the scientific point of view, it must be assumed that human life begins with the fertilization of the ovum. Hence means of birth control which allow the ovum to be fertilized but not to be implanted in the womb cannot be regarded as means of avoiding conception but only as causing abortion.

From the anthropological point of view, it is still possible to ask whether such a fertilized egg is already a human person, since a successive animation — as taught by Aristotle and medieval theologians and more and more widely once again today — seems to correspond better to the evolutionary mode of thought (J. Feiner in *Mysterium Salutis,* II, p. 581). The question as to the exact moment of the animation of the human embryo has not been decided by the magisterium of the Church (cf. G. Siegmund, "Beseelung der Leibesfrucht", *LTK,* II, col. 294). In 1679, Pope Innocent XI condemned the opinion that animation took place only at the moment of birth (*D* 1185). In 1887, Leo XIII condemned the view of Rosmini, who held that animation only took place with the first intellectual act of the child (*D* 1910). The opinion is sometimes heard today that personal life need only be assumed to begin when the brain has developed enough to serve as the substratum for specifically human activities. The persistance of personal life on earth is said to be amenable to the same criteria.

But it would be wrong to derive from such arguments the practical consequence that abortion may be more widely permitted in certain cases (cf. *CIC,* can. 2350, § 1). On account of the inviolability of the human person, one must be certain in practice that there is no human person in the embryo, when it is not to be allowed its full rights to personal integrity. Otherwise the killing of the embryo would imply the readiness to sacrifice the life of a person if necessary for the sake of values not vital to life. But it is not at all certain that the embryo, at the moment of fertilization, is not a human person.

Nonetheless, the circumstances are different in the killing of unborn and born life, since in the case of unborn life, the dependence on the mother is qualitatively different, as compared with the child once born. Hence in general abortion is not as grave a sin as murder. Hence too the State for the most part provides much more definite and comprehensive legal protection to born than to unborn life. The neglect of the State to proceed against those who arbitrarily kill embryonic life can hardly be justified either on juridical or on moral grounds.

Nonetheless, civil law and moral theology must allow for the possibility of intervention to bring about indirectly an interruption of pregnancy, if this is the direct means of preserving life. First, it is a debatable question, whether abortion is ruled out if there is danger of both mother and child dying. Then, the Church is not in a position to give a clear and definite answer to the question of how far the exercise of the right to self-preservation, e.g., by the use of medicines with abortive side-effects, justifies an indirect interruption of pregnancy. Here a grave task is imposed on the responsible conscience. But it may be affirmed as a principle that the right to life of either cannot be sacrificed merely to the well-being of the other. Economic and social needs must be catered for by economic and social measures. They do not justify the elimination of existing life, even if it is in a state of dependence. Even the life which results from a rape comes from God and has its own right to free development. To destroy it irresponsibly is sinful.

5. *Principles for the estimation of values.* Since life is the presupposition of all salutary action of man, it must ultimately take precedence of the preservation of all other values whose immediate acquisition is not necessary for the attainment of salvation. This means that the preservation and development of life, if it is to be morally justified, always implies an estimation of values. Consequently, man must renounce life if its preservation would bring him into direct opposition to the attainment of salvation. This would be the case if one had to turn away from God or commit any other formal offence against charity and so sin directly in order to preserve life. In such a situation man should be prepared for martyrdom, since it is irrational to try to preserve earthly life at the cost of turning away from eternal life.

On the other hand, even high moral values whose realization is not immediately called for, must be renounced if they can only be attained at the cost of life. Hence duelling, which endangers life, cannot be regarded as a legitimate means of defending honour, though personal honour is a higher good than earthly life. The redress of insults must be sought within the provisions of law.

So too what is useful and pleasant in life may not be sought and developed at the expense of what is necessary to life. Life must be protected even at the cost of very great material values, provided that the loss of these goods does not mean indirectly the loss of the necessities of life for a large number of men. Above all, luxuries must be renounced to provide the necessities of life for others. It must, however, be remembered that a certain standard of living may well serve the optimum development of life.

The optimum preservation and develop-

ment of life are only possible if one is prepared to take calculated risks with regard to the loss and the maximum development of life. This must be allowed for in the estimation of values. Hence, for instance, sports such as motor-racing can be regarded as in the service of life, even though such activities cannot be carried on without more or less danger to life and health. Consequently, their effects on life and health must be assessed, as far as is reasonably possible, and then risks more or less dangerous to life may be undertaken, insofar as they are seen as on the whole of service to the optimum development of life. Accordingly, one must be neither too light-hearted nor too timid about the preservation of life, since either attitude would be detrimental to the optimum development of life. Relatively little consideration has yet been given to the rules to be observed in the calculations of such risks.

See also *Rights of Man, Health, Person, War, Punishment (Capital), Property, Leisure* III, *Situation Ethics, Moral Theology* III.

BIBLIOGRAPHY. Apart from the recent standard moral theologies see: G. Clément, *Le droit de l'enfant à naître* (1931); E. Grassi, *Verteidigung des individuellen Lebens* (1946); O. Vannini, *Delitto contro la vita* (1946); A. Mitterer, *Die Zeugung der Organismen nach dem Weltbild des hl. Thomas und dem der Gegenwart* (1947); M. A. Ricaud, *La vie est sacrée* (1948); K. Fecht, *Das Recht der Ungeborenen* (1949); J. A. Sullivan, *Catholic Teaching on the Morality of Euthanasia* (1949); P. Lorson, *Défense de tuer* (1953); G. Debacke, *L'euthanasie devant la morale chrétienne* (1956); E. F. Healy, *Medical Ethics* (1956); G. Williams, *The Sanctity of Life and the Criminal Law* (1957); "Suicide et euthanasie", *Lumière et Vie*, Cahier 32 (1957); T. J. O'Donnell, *Morals in Medicine* (1959); E. Quay, *Justifiable Abortion – Medical and Legal Foundations* (1961); G. Perico, *A difesa della vita. Problemi morali di vita moderna* (1964); W. Ruff, "Das embryonale Werden des Individuums", *Stimmen der Zeit* 177 (1968), pp. 107–19.

Waldemar Molinski

LIFE-PHILOSOPHY ("BERGSONISM")

It is a matter of history that philosophies lose their freshness and that their concepts and systems become inadequate to the reality of nature, world and history and men's consciousness of them. Their theoretical and moral doctrines grow stale and appear as empty formulae. Reality seems to escape their grasp and to demand spontaneously, as it were, a new effort to comprehend it. The thinking that claims to answer this demand must contradict existing systems, because it must begin by renouncing normal concepts, to give free rein to a living dynamism. Hence it brands the others as insufficient, empty and dead. Such new thinking presents itself as irrationalism and declares that mystical intuition, vital experience, is the only possible way of attaining an adequate knowledge of reality. This is the situation and self-understanding of the philosophical current which came into modern thinking under the name of "life-philosophy". It spans some sixty years, having reached its zenith about the beginning of the 20th century. Its chief representatives were Dilthey, Nietzsche, Simmel, Klages and Spengler in Germany, Guyau and Bergson in France, Unamuno and Ortega y Gasset in Spain. In spite of differences in detail, they are at one in a common feeling for the self-explanatory nature of self-sufficient, self-creative life, and they radically reject all positivist explanations of the world and all professedly rationalist and intellectualist metaphysics.

They had precursors in Friedrich Schlegel, for instance, with his *Philosophy of Life* (1828), put forward in opposition to Kant and Hegel as a transcendental philosophy of full consciousness, not merely that of the intellect. There was also reaction against the Enlightenment, against an artificiality of social life, intellectualism, philosophies of immanent self-reflection and pedantic scholarship. This reaction, reinforced by Rousseau's theory of "natural" man, was one of the factors in the "tempestuous urges" *(Sturm und Drang)* voiced by Herder, Jacobi and Goethe, in the Romantic Revival and in German Idealism (Fichte, Schelling), all of which display traits akin to those of "life-philosophy". Then, under the influence of the Historical School and Christian mysticism, as well as the anti-bourgeois criticism of culture and the Dionysiac understanding of life proclaimed by Nietzsche, Dilthey and Bergson developed the anti-rationalist conception of reality as a perpetual flux of becoming, a lived experience directly apprehended, not through abstract thought. This was "life-philosophy" in the strict sense. In its reduction of knowledge and all objective spiritual phenomena

to their function in life and its preservation and enrichment, it was akin to the pragmatism of Dewey. It was chiefly influential through the stress it laid on intuition (Bergson) and insight (Dilthey), and through its corresponding understanding of the object, in which reality became an expression of creative life in the flux and reflux of its changing forms. Thus it affected the literature (D'Annunzio, Gide, Proust, George, Hofmannsthal, Rilke, Hesse), art (expressionsism) and politico-social movements of its times (youth movements, educational reforms). In philosophy it was responsible for the posing of new problems. The phenomenology of Scheler and the existence philosophy of Heidegger would be unthinkable without it, as would be many modern forms of the philosophy of education (Nohl, Litt, Spranger). And it would seem that the problem of "historicity" which dominates the present situation of philosophy, is part of the heritage of the life-philosophy with its way of amalgamating life, history and metaphysics. Needless to say, a number of sciences (such as graphology, characterology, certain branches of psychology) have received some of their main impulses from it, as it has also influenced methodological reflection on the foundations of psychology (Rothacker, Gadamer), literary criticism, the science of language and history of art.

In its origin, development and interests, life-philosophy, historically speaking, belongs to a definite type of literary and spiritual reaction. It stands for the utopian protest enunciated in philosophical reflection against the attempt to fix life in conventional schemes of thought which men reject and find too abstract, and inadequate and extrinsic to their new experiences. But since any attempt to reflect philosophically on a new experience must be made in concepts, the impulse embodied in the philosophy of life is never itself philosophy (cf. Rickert), but at the most an occasion for developing an adequate philosophy. It is a phenomenon of transition, though a necessary one, in the history of thought. If one confuses its negative character of protest and its call to new horizons with the positive utterances of a deliberately considered statement on reality as a whole, one arrives at such self-contradictory positions as historicism and irrationalism, of which the corollaries in theology are known as traditionalism (fideism) and modernism. But the destructive effort is justified insofar as it unmasks the undue self-satisfaction of a conceptual thinking which disregards the difference between concept and life, and thinks that with the concept it possesses reality in full.

The operative word "life" already displays an ambivalence. It has a meaning as an expression of protest, a war-cry (cf. Bollnow), but as a basic concept of reality it fails for indeterminateness. In contrast to an outlook that sees only rigid objects, to a static philosophy of being and mind, it proclaims the lived reality of creative movement, of Heraclitean becoming. Against a one-sided intellectualism it stands for the fullness of the soul's powers: for feeling, mood, passion, and longing. Thus it is lent conviction or evidence by its alternatives (Lersch), while of itself it is devoid of structure and content. It offers a number of opposites to choose between: the closed and the open, intuition and intellect (Bergson); history and nature, understanding and explanation (Dilthey); the organic and the mechanical, destiny and causality, depth and surface, wisdom and science (Spengler), soul-principle and spirit-principle (Klages), time and space, continuity and discontinuity, life and form (Simmel). But as they stand these have the character of phenomena and are problems which must first be philosophically explained, and not proclaimed as philosophical. They need first to be exploited in view of a total interpretation of reality. Steps in this direction were taken above all by Bergson, Dilthey and Simmel, though the critical question of the meaning of life, even when conceived of as the self-transcendence of life (Simmel) is reduced once more to the incomprehensibility of all-creative life.

But since "life"-philosophy exists only through its alternatives and is itself structureless and vague, it is open to all sorts of interpolations, which is the occupational hazard of all philosophy which negates the concept. Some content gleaned at random from history, or novelty itself, merely for the sake of its promising dynamism, are substituted for life as the "really true". All the more so, because the latent pantheistic component compensates for distrust of reflective intellect by producing an uncritical optimism in face of all living being, as though it must be the acceptable expression of the ground of life. All historical becoming is thus reduced to the same level, and this is finally accompanied by a purely contemplative attitude to history. Present and future can only be thought of in the guise of the past, and the most vital thing in life is denied: the critically justified act which detaches itself from the past or decides for it.

Historically speaking, the philosophy of life failed because of the inner contradiction of a philosophy without concepts and the intrinsic indeterminateness of its basic term, but its aim, seen as the task incumbent on the concept of distinguishing itself from life, remains significant for all philosophical thought.

See also *Irrationalism, Transcendental Philosophy, Enlightenment, Pragmatism, Phenomenology, Existence* II, *Historicism, Traditionalism, Fideism, Modernism.*

BIBLIOGRAPHY. H. Rickert, *Die Philosophie des Lebens* (2nd ed., 1922); V. Jankélévitch, "Deux philosophes de la vie, Guyau et Bergson", *Revue philosophique de la France et l'Étranger* (1924), pp. 402–49; F. Heinemann, *Neue Wege der Philosophie. Geist – Leben – Existenz* (1929) ; A. Poggi, *La filosofia come scienza del vivere* (1948); G. Boas, *Dominant Themes in Modern Philosophy* (1957); O. F. Bollnow, *Die Lebensphilosophie* (1958); H. Thomas, *Bergsonian Heritage* (1962); P. Gardiner, *Schopenhauer* (1963); F. Copleston, *History of Philosophy,* VII: *Fichte to Nietzsche* (1963); VIII: *Bentham to Russell* (1965); K. Jaspers, *Nietzsche* (1965); E. Gilson and others, *Recent Philosophy. Hegel to the Present* (1966).

Hans Michael Baumgartner

LIMBO

1. *Notion.* Limbo (Latin: hem, edge, etc.) is a technical theological term for the place and state of the dead who are neither in heaven nor in hell nor in purgatory. A distinction is drawn between the *limbus patrum,* i.e., the place and state of the pre-Christian just, who could not enter into eternal happiness before Christ's descent into hell and his ascension, and the *limbus infantium,* i.e., of the human beings who on earth never attained the use of reason, and to whom the sacrament of baptism was never administered, although the gospel was sufficiently proclaimed in their countries for the possibility of their sacramental incorpora-

tion into the Church not of itself to have been excluded.

2. *History*. Neither revelation nor the oldest Christian tradition deals expressly with the eternal lot of unbaptized children in general, or with their limbo in particular, though they both particularly stress that our salvation in Christ depends on belonging to the Church, and that this depends on baptism. It was only when Pelagianism denied these fundamental Christian truths, and asserted in proof of its views that God does not deny access to the kingdom of heaven to unbaptized children, that this specific problem was envisaged. Augustine put forward the doctrine, which went uncontested for centuries, that these children are condemned to the real (though mitigated) pains of hell. Anselm of Canterbury and after him the great Scholastics firmly held with Augustine that these human beings remain excluded from eternal beatitude, but they also postulated for them the existence of a place and final state of their own, that is, limbo. The nature of this limbo, however, was differently conceived in the course of the centuries and in general was interpreted more and more benignly (intellectual sadness — unawareness of the loss of the beatific vision — purely natural happiness).

3. *The modern discussion*. In present-day theology the existence of limbo is questioned by many, including some distinguished theologians and historians of dogma, and there is much discussion whether the assumption behind all teaching on limbo, namely that the persons in question are excluded from the beatific vision, is in fact a theologically irreformable, established doctrine. Representatives of the new and so-called liberal tendency appeal in particular to the dogma of God's universal salvific will, to the unity and solidarity of the human race which as such was called to the supernatural and redeemed by Christ, as well as to the possibility of a special kind of baptism of desire, which would make it possible for those persons sufficiently to enter into relation to Christ and his Church. Within this school of thought, however, opinions diverge at many points, especially the following: a) the degree of certainty with which the concrete possibility of salvation for children who have died without baptism is maintained (extend-

ing from tentative hypothesis to the affirmation that this doctrine is implicitly revealed); b) the range of its application (all such persons — children of Christian parents — unborn children, etc.); c) the actual concrete mode in which the baptism of desire, universally considered necessary, is regarded as realized (by the intermediary of the Church, or the parents, or through those persons' attaining the use of reason at the moment of death and being made capable of a supernatural act of love for God through special actual graces); d) the theological methods employed (more speculative considerations — critical, historical research into the contrary and supposedly theologically binding "tradition"). In view of the fact that theology, as the science of faith, not only takes its starting-point in the content of revelation, but also finds the norm and limit of its endeavour in authentic tradition and the binding interpretation of the Church's magisterium, it is evident that the elucidation of the last question ("tradition") is of the very greatest, and indeed decisive, importance for the problem of children dying without baptism and consequently for the question of limbo. It is not in accordance with the spirit of genuine theology to hold fast uncritically to inherited doctrines and opinions, but it is equally untheological to set aside a doctrine that for many centuries has been held practically universally in the Church to be a binding one, and which as such has been taught to the very widest extent in the Church's catechesis.

As regards the present state of the relevant and extremely complex learned researches, it must be noted that a) opinions still differ very widely among specialists; b) those who hold the liberal view have been able to establish many important items in their favour; c) conclusive proof of the theological tenability of their views has not even yet, however, been provided. The Church's magisterium has so far not favoured the liberal opinions but allows inquiry to continue without hindrance. This being so, in preaching the faith any categorical or even polemical pronouncement must of course be avoided and caution must be observed in every respect. It remains obvious that the persons in question are to be baptized without delay if this is at all possible. (Suprema Sacra Congregatio S. Officii, 18 February 1958: *AAS* 50 [1958], p. 114.)

4. *Pastoral theology*. The pastor can and should tell the Christian parents of children who have died without baptism that there is no definite doctrine of faith regarding the fate of such children, and that consequently they can entrust the final lot of their child to the mysterious but infinitely kind and powerful love of God, to whose grace no limit is set by the earthly circumstances which he in his providence has allowed to come about.

See also *Beatific Vision, Hell, Purgatory, Baptism, Pelagianism, Salvation* I.

BIBLIOGRAPHY. W. A. Van Roo, "Infants Dying without Baptism: A Survey of Recent Literature and Determination of the State of the Question", *Gregorianum* 35 (1954), pp. 406–73 (critical review in *Downside Review* 73 [1955], pp. 328–33); P. Gumpel, "Unbaptized Infants: May They be Saved?", *Downside Review* 72 (1954), pp. 342–458; *ibid.* 73 (1955), pp. 317–46; P. De Letter, "The Question of Limbo", *The Clergy Monthly* 18 (1954), pp. 321–34, 361–72; *ibid.* 19 (1955), pp. 3–18; M. Labourdette, "Problèmes d'Eschatologie", *Revue Thomiste* 54 (1954), pp. 658–75 ("Enfants morts sans baptême", pp. 662–75); G. J. Dyer, *The Denial of Limbo and the Jansenist Controversy* (1955); id., "Limbo: A Theological Evaluation", *TS* 19 (1958), pp. 32–49; L. Renwart, "Le baptême des enfants et les limbes — A propos d'un document pontifical récent", *NRT* 80 (1958), pp. 459–67; H. de Lavalette, "Autour de la question des enfants morts sans baptême", *ibid.* 82 (1960), pp. 56–69; V. Wilkin, *From Limbo to Heaven: An Essay on the Economy of the Redemption* (1961); G. J. Dyer, "The Unbaptized Infant in Eternity", *Chicago Studies* 2 (1963), pp. 141–53.

Peter Gumpel

LITURGICAL MOVEMENT

The liturgical movement is the effort, now highly successful in the Church, to bring our largely ossified liturgy back to life as the corporate worship of the people of God. The reforms of the Council of Trent made the Roman liturgy, practically as it stood, a definitive standard, consciously halting a process of growth whose main features had emerged by the 6th century but which also continued throughout the Middle Ages, though not always organically. Bishops were no longer allowed to adapt the liturgy in any way and Rome concentrated on preserving the traditional inheritance intact (the Congregation of Rites was set up in 1588 to supervise the liturgy). Meantime, however, the world had greatly changed, and in matters of religion too a new cast of thought began to prevail. Even in Romance countries the Latin of the Mass had become a foreign language, the liturgy a clerical preserve, a set of mysterious actions which the Christian people could only follow from afar. It grew increasingly difficult to ignore the incongruity of this situation as the faith of the people was progressively threatened and Christian scholarship rediscovered the living liturgical piety of the ancient Church.

Publication by the Maurist Benedictines of their laborious research into the sources marked a turning-point. A number of new breviaries and missals appeared in France, beginning in 1680, quite different from the old, which were soon displaced. These changes had no sanction from Rome but neither, at first, did Rome protest against them. Certain responses in the Mass were to be made by the people. The Enlightenment brought in its wake a series of attempts at liturgical reform in Germany. Vernacular hymns, reintroduced even during Mass, ensured that the people took some active part in public worship, but the other aims of the movement — to simplify the liturgy and make it meaningful to the people — came to nothing because of the liturgical revival that occurred in the mid-19th century. In France that restoration, brought about almost single-handed by Abbot Guéranger (1805–75), swept away the neo-Gallican reforms we have mentioned in favour of the purely Roman liturgy. On the other hand the Second Spring of monasticism — also the work of Dom Guéranger — with its devotion to the liturgy and Gregorian chant, contained in germ the liturgical movement of the 20th century.

This movement was launched as such by Père Lambert Beauduin (1873–1960), originally a diocesan priest but a monk of Mont-César from 1906, on the occasion of the Catholic Congress at Malines (23 September 1909). It insisted that in a world increasingly threatened with dechristianization the prayer of the Church must be thrown open to the people, but for the time being it contented itself with disseminating vernacular translations of the Sunday Masses and Vespers. The Abbey of Maria-Laach, which notably supported these efforts by means of its scholarship, tended to become the centre of the movement from 1918 onwards. A keen sense that it was anomalous for an essentially congregational liturgy to be merely read in silence by the people along with the priest, led to the introduction of a congregational Mass, using the vernacular (among others, Romano Guardini, 1920). When consulted about this innovation in 1922 the Congregation of Rites replied in cautious terms, but stated that it was permissible "per se" for the congregation to give the responses at Mass. The movement now made great strides in German-speaking areas, especially among students (Catholic youth movement). By 1930 parish life began to be affected. Here the leading spirits were Pius Parsch, with his popular books and pocket editions of liturgical texts, and Ludwig Wolker, leader of the powerful Catholic youth groups. Opposition, some of it in literary form, was overcome when the bishops themselves took over leadership of the movement in 1940, setting up machinery for reports on the liturgy and a Liturgical Commission, a step sanctioned by a Roman decree of 1943. Pius XII's encyclical *Mediator Dei* (1947) intimated the Church's definitive approbation of the liturgical movement.

Meantime the movement had rapidly spread through France. A very active "Centre de Pastorale Liturgique", established in Paris in 1943, had its German counterpart in the "Liturgisches Institut" at Trier (1947). Other countries quickly followed suit. Major international liturgical conferences, made possible by co-operation between Paris and Trier, have been held since 1951. An International Congress of the Liturgical Apostolate, held at Assisi in 1956 with the encouragement of Rome, was another obvious milestone. The movement has borne fruit in directives on the form of parish worship that the bishops of many countries have issued, in the Roman instruction (1958) consolidating these directives, in the vernacular rituals that may now be used everywhere, and particularly in the restored Vigil of Easter Eve (1951) and the reformed liturgy of Holy Week (1955) for which we are indebted to Rome. But the general reform decreed by the Second Vatican Council, 4 December 1963, crowns all the efforts of the liturgical movement.

Complete success, of course, will depend on whether the liturgical forms now to be created for the whole Church and for individual countries will be in keeping with the high ideals prescribed and find a congenial soil in a reinvigorated sense of the faith among clergy and people alike.

See also *Liturgy, Enlightenment, Eucharist* II.

BIBLIOGRAPHY. W. Trapp, *Vorgeschichte und Ursprung der Liturgischen Bewegung* (1940); E. B. Koenker, *The Liturgical Renaissance in the Roman Catholic Church* (1954); J. Hofinger and others, *Worship: The Life of the Missions* (1958); H. Schmidt, *Introductio in Liturgiam occidentalem* (1960), pp. 164–208, 742–85; L. Sheppard, *The People Worship: A History of the Liturgical Movement* (1966); W. Birnbaum, *Das Kultusproblem und die liturgischen Bewegungen des 20. Jahrhunderts,* I (1966) (on Germany).

Joseph Andreas Jungmann

LITURGY

I. The Liturgies: A. Definition. B. Historical Survey. C. Structural Laws. II. Liturgical Language. III. Liturgical Year: A. Principles. B. Description. IV. Study of Liturgy.

I. The Liturgies

A. DEFINITION.

The word λειτουργία in classical Greek means a function (ἔργον) undertaken on behalf of the people (λαός): fitting out a ship, preparing a feast or doing any public service.

In the Greek Bible, the word is regularly used of divine worship, to speak of the sacred ministry with which the priests and levites of the OT were charged. In Heb 8:2 Christ himself is designated as λειτουργός. The word remained current among Greek-speaking Christians, first to indicate the ministry of Church officials in general (for instance, *Didache*, ch. 15), and then divine worship in particular. As early as the 4th century it was restricted to meaning the Mass. This is the sense in which it is used at present by the Greeks and the Eastern Slavs. The word went out of use in the West till it was revived by the Humanists of the 16th century. In the official terminology of the Church it re-appears only in the 19th century.

No complete agreement has been reached about the definition of the liturgy. This is because different elements may be stressed in the group of ecclesiastical institutions which are generally classed as liturgical. Some have proposed to understand by liturgy simply the outward forms of divine worship, or the sum total of regulations which govern the Church's worship. This would be to restrict the concept to an aesthetical or juridical approach. In contrast to such views it has been maintained, especially since the beginning of the liturgical movement, that by liturgy we are to understand the worship offered to God by the Church itself (L. Beauduin). This view is also presupposed in the encyclical *Mediator Dei* (1947), when the liturgy is taken to be the "whole public worship of the mystical body of Christ, head and members".

Within this worship, however, it is still possible to emphasize in particular the priesthood of Christ which underlies the action of the Church (R. Stapper) or again, the trinitarian structure of Church worship (H. Schmidt); or emphasis may be laid on the redemptive act which becomes a present reality in it (as in the mystery-theology of O. Casel). Or one can stress in particular the sanctifying work of God which accompanies the worship of the Church (J. Vagaggini).

It should not, however, be necessary to stress such particular aspects when merely giving a definition. It should be enough to say that the liturgy is the worship offered to God by the Church, provided that we give their full force to the concepts used in the definition.

But we must also note an important difference in the usage of the word, as it occurs in canon law.

According to *CIC*, can. 1057, the regulation of the "liturgy" is a matter reserved exclusively to the Holy See. Vatican II affirmed the rights of the bishops in this matter. By a declaration in the *Instructio de Musica Sacra et de Sacra Liturgia* of 3 September 1958, it has been established that according to the terminology of Church law, only such acts of worship are to be regarded as "liturgical", as are performed according to books approved of by the Holy See. These alone are subject to Roman regulations, while the bishop is put in charge of all other devotions, holy hours, processions, etc., which are regarded as *pia exercitia*. Thus the concept was restricted to a narrower usage in the terminology of Church legislation. Historically speaking, so narrow a concept would be applicable to the liturgy only from 1568–70 on, since it was only after this time that books approved by the Holy See were pre-scribed for use in the whole Latin Church. A more general view of the liturgy, which must take in all ages since the foundation of the Church, and all areas, including those of Eastern Christianity, would find the canonical concept inadequate. We hold therefore that the liturgy is the worship offered to God by the Church: "cultus Deo ab Ecclesia praestitutus".

This definition calls for a closer explanation. Not all divine worship is liturgical, but only such as is offered publicly by the Church as such. Beside it there exists the worship offered privately by the individual faithful. The NT itself speaks of personal prayer, for which the individual goes "into his room" (Mt 6:6), as well as the public worship of God in the Temple and then the celebration of the Eucharist as enjoined by Christ (cf. Vatican II, *Sacrosanctum Concilium*, art. 9).

The Church is only at worship, that is, we only have liturgy, when divine service is held by a legitimately assembled group of the faithful (from parish, religious order or ecclesiastical institute), under the leadership of someone holding office in the Church. Here the Church becomes visible, here it is "Event". When the Church is gathered to pray and celebrate, its prayer will necessarily take on a form which is not only worthy of such an assembly — whence the liturgy makes use of noble art — but is also a very faithful mirror of the nature of the Church. This Church is the people of God, because it is the community of those who are redeemed by Christ and sanctified in the Holy Spirit. In the liturgy, therefore, the word "we" will predominate, not the "I" of the individual, and the Christological and trinitarian character of its basic attitude will come to the fore.

These essential traits must find expression in every actual liturgical institution. It belongs to the Church authorities to lay down the rules for such institutions: the Pope for the whole Church, and the bishop for the sphere assigned to him by law. Juridically there is a difference between a liturgical action prescribed by the bishop and one prescribed by the supreme authority of the Church. But it does not alter the religious and theological value of the worship offered. In the first case the liturgy exists by episcopal right ("Sacra exercitia", according to Vatican II, *Sacrosanctum Concilium*, art. 13), in the second by papal right, a liturgy universally valid.

321

Liturgy is in the last resort always a sacred ministry directed to God. A prayer, rite or devotional gesture can in fact be addressed immediately to a saint or Mary or Christ, but ultimately its object is always the Father of our Lord Jesus Christ.

The worship of the Church is accomplished most perfectly in the celebration of the Eucharist, because the Church is "gathered" most intensively in the one bread of the Eucharist and so is most truly itself. There the Church fulfils the inmost law of its being and thus God is supremely glorified through Christ and in Christ.

The concept of liturgy is also verified in another way in the sacraments.

The celebration of the Eucharist is only possible on the basis of the other sacraments, which form its substructure to a certain extent. They prepare the holy people in baptism and confirmation, they purify it in penance and extreme unction, they sanctify the means whereby it is perpetuated from generation to generation, and equip the ministers of the altar for their sacred service (matrimony, orders). Further, the sacraments are accompanied by various forms of the prayer which pervades all liturgy.

But Eucharist and sacraments do not cover the whole field of the liturgy. Prayer is also asked of the Church outside the Eucharist, if the Church, and not just the individual is to "pray always and not lose heart" (Lk 18:1). Such prayer has in fact been offered in the Church since the earliest times. It accompanied the reading and preaching of Scripture, or it stood more or less on its own in the form of psalm-singing, or it was offered for various necessities and wants.

The most important manifestation of the Church at prayer is the canonical hours or office, by which certain hours of the day, especially morning and evening, are sanctified. The contrast of one time of day with another was enough to suggest that the form and content of prayer should vary with the hour of the day. A similar change extending over longer periods was found desirable for another reason. Since the worship of the Church is based on the divine dispensation of salvation, it was necessary to recall continually in the Eucharist not only the climax of redemption, but also the stages of its development as given in the Scriptures.

The recollection of the most important events in the history of salvation was then spread over certain dates in the year, given further development and finally combined with the anniversaries of the great heroes of the faith. Thus the liturgical year took shape.

B. Historical Survey

The liturgy is necessarily as old as the Church. But only the innermost nucleus of Christian worship was enacted by Christ himself and thus not left subject to alteration. All other developments were to be the work of the Church and of the forces within it which change from age to age, always fertile in new forms and always seeking still more. On the other hand, the liturgy is of its nature conservative, since it is a sacred ministry. Forms once laid down appear to be somehow sacred, and hence are preserved and transmitted unchanged as far as possible. Thus no understanding of Christian liturgy is possible unless it is considered in its historical development. In the primitive Church, divine worship was restricted to the celebration of the Eucharist, which being the memorial of the Lord took place every week on Sunday, the day on which Christians recalled the completion of redemption through the resurrection, called the Lord's Day as early as Rev 20:7 ($\varkappa\upsilon\rho\iota\alpha\varkappa\grave{\eta}$ $\dot{\eta}\mu\acute{\epsilon}\rho\alpha$). On certain occasions there was also the evening *Agape,* when food was distributed to the poor, a function accompanied by psalm-singing and prayer at which the clergy presided. Traditions from the way of life of pious Jews (such as Qumran) are seen to be at work here. The heritage of the synagogue also makes itself felt in the stylization of prayer: the introduction with the greeting "Dominus vobiscum" and "let us pray"; the conclusion with the affirmative "Amen" of the people.

At least from the 2nd century onwards, the Church celebrated Easter every year. It was a nocturnal celebration, in which the transition ("passover") was made from the memory of Jesus' passion to the joy of the resurrection. The baptism of converts also took place on the night of Easter, a procedure which gave apt expression to the truth that the baptized shared the resurrection of Christ and became partakers of his divine life. Further, Easter was considered to be the continuation as well as the fulfilment of the OT Pasch. Hence efforts were made to keep to the Jewish lunar calendar in fixing the date of Easter. However, after some wavering on the point, the rule prevailed, from about A.D. 200 on, that Easter was to be celebrated on a Sunday.

Thus the thought of Easter pervaded the life of early Christianity and strengthened it in the tribulations of persecution.

Fixed liturgical texts did not yet exist. A typical formula for the celebration of the Eucharist, which was recorded by Hippolytus of Rome about 215, the text of which has been preserved, states expressly that any bishop who might wish to use it is not bound to follow it word for word. Some centuries later, in the manuscript tradition of this work, the "not" was eliminated from the remark, and thus the set form of words was made into the norm. From the 4th century on, fixed texts became more and more the rule, as indeed they probably also became a necessity with the continued expansion of the Church and the waning of inspiration. It was the same with the places where the liturgy was held. The primitive Church displays no interest in special places of worship, least of all in the type of temple which the pagans had and the Jewish people once possessed. These were majestic buildings enshrining only a tiny inaccessible sanctuary. In complete contrast to this, the community of the faithful knew that it formed a living temple. All the congregation needed for divine worship was a room large enough to hold it, which it found at first in the dwelling-houses of the well-to-do members of the community.

With the freedom granted by Constantine, and under his generous patronage, came buildings designed for worship. The basic structure was that of the "Basilica" (Palace, hall) as developed by Roman architecture. About this time the Hellenistic culture of the surrounding world also began to exercise other notable influences on the shape taken by the Christian liturgy. Indeed, the liturgy has preserved since then many features which belonged to the culture of that age. This is true of liturgical vestments. These are, not only in the Roman liturgy but also in the Oriental rites, a slightly elaborated form of the dress worn on festive occasions in late Roman antiquity (a tunic with a girdle; a *paenula*, cloak, which became the chasuble). Further, some insignia belonging to the higher state officials of the time were taken over for the bishop's dress in particular (the maniple, stole, pallium and episcopal shoes).

Forms of court ceremony were also adopted by the liturgy. It was, for instance, the privilege of the highest officials to be preceded by torches and cressets on solemn occasions. From this arose the custom of carrying candles and incense before the bishop, and later before any celebrant of solemn High Mass: two elements of liturgical solemnity which were later used to advantage mainly as marks of adoration offered directly to God.

The religious rites of antiquity on the other hand supplied only marginal items to the Christian liturgy, when indeed they did not give rise to counterparts which were rather in the nature of protests. The origin of Christmas is a case in point. Towards the end of the 4th century the feast in honour of *Sol Invictus* had been raised to the status of an imperial holiday. In opposition to this the feast of the Nativity was introduced, to celebrate the birth of him who rose upon the world as its true sun. In the cult of the dead, however, the choice of certain days had become deeply embedded in popular paganism, and these dates managed to survive into Christianity. It was the custom to pay honours to the dead and to try to help them by sacrifices and funeral banquets, not only on the day of burial, but also on the third, seventh (or eighth) and thirtieth (or fortieth) days. Of these dates, the third, seventh and thirtieth days are still regarded as privileged days for Requiem Masses in the regions of the Roman rite; in the East they are the third, ninth and fortieth days.

The years of the 4th to the 5th centuries were also the time in which what had hitherto been a fundamentally uniform liturgy, though with some local differences, split up into the sharply distinct liturgies which survive to the present day. A variety of languages had of course been used from the very start. Divine service had invariably been held in the vernacular of each region. It was, however, supposed, if for no other reason than that the liturgy necessarily included sacred Scripture, that the language in question had reached a certain stage of development and could be put to literary uses. This principle was not indeed always observed later, as, for instance, at the beginning of the Chinese missions. During the early days of Christianity the three languages used in the inscription on the Cross, "Hebrew" (Syriac), Greek and Latin, were of primary importance. With these one could make oneself understood in any part of the world of the time.

In the East, beyond the Roman frontiers, Syriac became fundamental. This is the liturgy which still survives today as the Eastern Syrian, which comprises what is known as the Chaldaean inside the Catholic Church, as well as the Nestorian, and the Syro-malabar of India.

Greek predominated in the eastern part of the Roman empire. Latin prevailed in the West after the strengthening of the Latin element in the Christian communities from the 3rd century on. Within the Greek-speaking area, however, from the 4th century on, various centres stood out which proceeded independently of each other in establishing their liturgical institutions. One was Alexandria, which held the leadership in the Egyptian area and developed a liturgy known as the liturgy of St. Mark. Another was Antioch, which dominated the Hellenized area of western Syria, though in liturgical matters it soon had to abdicate its leadership in favour of Jerusalem, which had been flourishing again since the days of Constantine. The liturgy here developed is known as that of St. James.

The third centre, which made itself felt at once, was the new imperial city on the Bosphorus. It took up and developed further the liturgy of Antioch, forming from it the Byzantine liturgy. Favoured by the political authorities, the Byzantine liturgy spread in the course of the Middle Ages over the whole remaining territory of the Greek empire, took in Antioch as well as Alexandria and finally covered the whole eastern Slavonic area, following the Byzantine missionary effort. Among the Russians, Serbs and Bulgarians it is celebrated in old Slavonic (Church Slavonic), among other peoples of this area in the language proper to each. The originally Greek-speaking population of the regions of Antioch and Alexandria, who had remained within the sphere of the Byzantine Empire and Catholic Church — known by the Syrians as Melchites ("royalists") on account of their close connections with the imperial court — also went over to the Arab language in their (Byzantine) liturgy after the triumph of the Arabian peoples. The western Syrians, however, in the hinterland of Antioch, who had liberated themselves more and more from Byzantine influences after the Council of Chalcedon (451), and had developed a national consciousness of their own, gradually went over to Syriac in their liturgy. This is the liturgy of St. James, still used by the Jacobites and Maronites.

The same thing happened in Egypt, where a Coptic and an Ethiopian liturgy, each in the native language, grew out of the Greek liturgy of St. Mark. And then the Armenians, exposed to Byzantine and Syrian influences, drew on both sources to build up a liturgy of their own, which has been celebrated in Armenian since the 5th century, by which time it had become a literary language. All these rites survive to the present day and are grouped under the heading of Oriental liturgies. They have many typical features in common, which are most strongly marked in the Byzantine rite. Characteristic is the lengthening of the preparatory part of the Mass, which is composed of a number of preludes, and above all, the great solemnity of the rite, which comes from the thought of its being a participation in the heavenly liturgy of the angels. Several forms of Byzantine court ceremonial are used, such as the προσκύνησις. The two processions of the eucharistic liturgy are notable features. In solemn train, first the sacred book and then the offerings are carried into the sanctuary (the little and the great entry). Where a number of priests are present, a Mass read in silence by each priest is unknown in the East. In such cases the rite is performed by all together (concelebration), though the words of consecration need not be pronounced by each individual, except among the Russians and in the Uniate Churches. An attitude of profound submission and humble adoration in face of the divine majesty was further reinforced by the fact that during the long defensive struggle against Arianism, the thought of Christ as mediator was forced into the background. His role of mediator remains undoubtedly an aspect of his historical work as Saviour, but for fear of misinterpretation, it is no longer considered as part of the function exercised by Christ in his humanity at the right hand of the Father. So prayer is no longer regularly addressed to God "through Christ", which was the style of liturgical prayer in the preceding centuries and still characterizes the Roman liturgy. Prayer is directed to Christ himself or to the triune God, whose praise resounds in the doxologies with which each prayer is concluded. A strong Marian note, which is heard above all in many hymns (*theotokiae*), provides a certain substitute for the recessive mediatorship of Christ. The Epiclesis after the words of consecration, a solemn invocation asking for the descent of the Holy Spirit upon the offerings, also stems from a line of thought which is predominantly centred on the Trinity. A sense of holy awe in face of the divine mysteries is expressed in the veiling of the sacred species, and especially in the marked distinction made between the sanctuary and the nave of the Church. The original barriers have been extended upwards in course of time to form a lofty partition covered with images (iconostasis). This cuts off the view of the altar, and only the voice of the celebrant maintains the connection with the faithful.

All Oriental liturgies, on the other hand, make provision for the ministry of the deacon. He assists beside the celebrant at various points of the liturgy, and also intones the litanies in non-eucharistic services, where each invocation is answered by the people. The *Kyrie eleison* which is common to all rites is one of the oldest forms of such acclamations by the people. This ensured an intensive participation of the people in the liturgy, even though at a certain distance from the heart of the process, and did much to link it to the life of the people and sustain Christianity under a hostile pressure lasting a thousand years. Much as was done for the vernacular, no general effort was made to grasp the exact meaning of the words in the various elements of the liturgy or to understand objectively the real and original meaning of each rite. As early as the 5th century, an allegorical interpretation took its place (ἄλλα ἀγορεύειν, that is, reading something else into the actual rites). The liturgy is taken as the earthly projection of the heavenly liturgy, or as a representation of the decisive events in the work of salvation: the incarnation, passion, burial and resurrection of Christ.

In contrast to Western usage, it is characteristic of all Oriental liturgies that in the Mass and the Office the prayers of the priest remain unaffected by the liturgical year. Only lessons and chants follow the cycle of the year and the festive seasons. However, some changes were provided for in another direction. For the principal part of the Mass, the Anaphora ("Oblation"), which followed the introductory Scripture readings, a number of formulas are provided in which the Canon and its immediate setting are treated differently. Only two such formulas exist, however, in the Byzantine liturgy, the "liturgy" of St. John Chrysostom and the "liturgy" of St. Basil.

There are three in the East Syrian liturgy, three in the Coptic, and only a few more in the Armenian, while seventeen have been traced in the Ethiopian. In the West Syrian liturgy, the number of formulas for the Anaphora rises to around eighty, though only some of these are still in use today.

Towards the end of Christian antiquity, several liturgies had also been evolved in the West, on the basis of a common structure which originated no doubt in Rome. It is due to this common structure that, Latin being retained of course everywhere, the prayers of the priest in these liturgies changed with the feasts and seasons of the year, as well as other parts of the Mass. Beside the Roman liturgy, with which the North African was closely akin (as far as we can tell: it is mainly known through St. Augustine), we have to distinguish a Gallic type of liturgy, from which stem further the old Spanish, Milanese (Ambrosian), Gallican and Celtic liturgies. Of this group, the last two are merely ways of classifying texts from the British Isles and Gaul in which some kinship can be descried. They have been preserved only very haphazardly. But complete liturgical books have been preserved from the old Spanish liturgy, while the Ambrosian survives to the present day, though strongly penetrated by later Roman elements. The Roman liturgy finally prevailed all over the West in the course of the Middle Ages, and on the whole, without any particular pressure from the part of Rome, apart perhaps from the intervention of Gregory VII in Spain.

The Roman liturgy came into the British Isles along with the Roman missionaries sent to the Anglo-Saxons by Gregory the Great. But it was only centuries later that it succeeded in penetrating Celtic Christianity also. In Gaul, the native forms of the liturgy had lost the esteem of their own clergy, since liturgies varied from place to place, were open to every outside influence, especially from the East, and hence presented a very disordered picture. The Carolingian rulers Pepin and Charlemagne, who wanted a uniform Church order throughout their dominions, were thus able to suppress them completely without much trouble and introduce the well-ordered Roman liturgy as part of their reforms. The ancient Spanish Church on the other hand had evolved in the 6th to the 7th century a rich and fully elaborated liturgy, when the Moorish invasion arrived, to destroy the kingdom of the Visigoths and arrest the flowering of the Spanish Church. As the country was reconquered from the north, the Roman liturgy was also introduced here. The old Spanish liturgy survived till the end of the Middle Ages, but only in the parts still subject to the Arabs. This is the origin of the name "Mozarabic" given to the liturgy, meaning the liturgy used by the "Arab" Catholics of Spain.

Finally, the old Spanish liturgy is characterized by a peculiar trait. It was coming to full flower at the time when the Spanish Church was engaged in sharp controversy with the Arianism of its Visigoth neighbours. Hence reaction to the denial of the true Godhead of Christ led to similar results in the liturgy as we have noted in the East. And the powerful influence of the flourishing Spanish Church spread through Ireland to the Anglo-Saxons and ultimately into the Carolingian Empire, to make this anti-Arian strain of Christian piety one of the essential elements in the religious culture of the Middle Ages.

We may now concentrate our attention on the Roman liturgy. In the Eternal City, Christianity was at first predominantly Greek-speaking. Only when the Latin elements had grown strong enough to compete with the Greek could a Roman liturgy in the Latin language take shape. It is only in the 6th to the 7th century, however, that the Latin liturgy of Rome appears in its full development, enshrined in complete liturgical books. The manuscript witnesses date only from the 8th to the 9th century, the time when many scribes were hard at work in the Frankish scriptoria, naturalizing the Roman liturgy in their own country. The form fixed in Rome during the last centuries of antiquity was preserved almost without exception in the Roman liturgy till modern times, only partially embroidered with additions that came in later on Frankish soil.

The most ancient books of the Roman liturgy were not divided, as they are today, into Missal, Ritual and Breviary, according to the sphere of worship in which they were to be used: the division followed the character of the officiant. The Sacramentary contained the prayers to be said by the Pope and the bishop, at Mass, at the administration of the sacraments and at the Office. The *Liber antiphonarius* contained the chants for the choir during Mass, the *Liber responsorialis* the chants for the Office. Lectionaries provided Scripture readings, though a Capitulary, or list of chapters to be read on each occasion, was enough for the gospel readings, which were mostly taken from a complete codex of the gospels. Finally, the cleric who was a sort of Master of Ceremonies in charge of the general arrangements was provided with an *Ordo*.

At the start, before these books had been filled out in each case to meet the requirements of the annual cycle, help was provided in the form of single libelli, small books of texts containing some suitable formularies for each occasion. This is still to be seen quite clearly in the sacramentaries, of which three Roman ones are known. The oldest of them, the *Sacramentarium Leonianum,* is in fact merely a loosely-assembled series of such libelli, from the 5th to the 6th century, covering the whole year. One of these libelli, for instance, offered a choice of several sets of prayers formulated to suit the feast of the Princes of the Apostles; another gave texts for Paschal time or for a certain group of functions such as the conferring of major orders.

Another sacramentary is the so-called *Gelasianum,* which already displays an arrangement worked out to suit the whole liturgical year. It was likewise composed in Rome in the 6th century, but was later expanded in France, where it was given a strong Frankish tinge, which is the form in which it has been preserved.

The third is the *Sacramentarium Gregorianum,* which is attributed to Gregory the Great (d. 604), and on which the texts of the prayers in our present-day Missal are based for the most part. A little later than the sacramentaries, the books giving the chants and order of lessons in the Roman liturgy were composed, each book providing for the whole annual cycle. The 7th century also saw the appearance of the oldest Roman Ordines, which describe the outward procedure in the more complicated rites of the liturgy, such as the "Stations", the liturgies of Lent and Easter, the rites of baptism and of ordination.

These were the books which the Frankish clerics and bishops sought after with ever increasing zeal from the 8th century on, and which they took as the basis of the new order of their worship. As was to be expected, it was not the pure Roman rite which was observed in the Churches of the Carolingian Empire, but one which had been interpreted in the spirit of their own tradition interspersed with existing native customs of many kinds, and even misunderstood at certain points. This was almost inevitable, as the directions given by the books were often vague, and the rare traveller to Rome could only report what he thought he saw, which was a very meagre help. Furthermore, the directions on which the Franks had to rely catered almost exclusively, especially in the Ordines, for the solemn liturgies of the major feasts and it was very difficult to apply them to the ordinary occasions of popular worship. A shift in meaning was also imposed by the fact that many of the piously preserved rites of antiquity no longer suited the new circumstances. And the Latin of the books was no longer understood in its new environment, either by the Romanic or the Germanic populations. The liturgy became the preserve of the clergy. The long series of rites by which the adult catechumen had been prepared during Lent for baptism at Easter were now condensed into one single act, and finally combined with baptism itself, though they no longer had much meaning, since baptism was now administered only to children. The people continued indeed to frequent the daily services in which they had once taken part, morning prayer and evening Vespers (the former, Matins, corresponds to our Lauds; daily Mass was not yet the custom). But the prayers were offered by the clergy alone, and then expanded to form the full diurnal cycle of the canonical hours (Breviary). Under the growing influence of monasticism, the clergy of the great ecclesiastical centres, since Chrodegang of Metz (d. 766) and Benedict of Aniane (d. 821) in particular, had adopted not only common life but also the monastic form of the office, which was said in common and distributed over seven canonical hours. It became thereby all the more remote from the ordinary world of the faithful. So in many places in the later Middle Ages, the logical step was finally taken, and the choir where the office was chanted was completely divided from the nave of the Church, by means of a choir-screen, where it was not simply transferred to the "Chapter-house".

Since it was almost impossible for the people to follow the words of the Mass, its visual possibilities were at once exploited in Frankish lands, enriched by dramatic elements and interpreted allegorically. Solemn High Mass in which all the clergy participated was long predominant. At the beginning of Mass and at the beginning of the Offertory the altar was incensed from all sides. Differences of rank as between the lessons were stressed, epistle side was distinguished from gospel side, and the gospel surrounded by a number of marks of honour. Every movement of the congregation or of the priest was now given a special meaning in the allegorical explanation of the liturgy, which was worked out systematically by Amalar of Metz. The great acts of the history of salvation were re-discovered in the ceremonies of the Mass, from the cry of the OT patriarchs in the Introit and Kyrie to the birth of the Saviour in the Gloria and so on to the last blessing, which represented the blessing given by our Lord to the apostles before his ascension. Thus the congregation was relegated to the role of reverent onlookers. The weakening of the bond between altar and people is also exemplified by the fact that prayers to be said only by the priest, on his own behalf, were now introduced at all parts of the liturgy where the action or process had hitherto been performed in silence: at the beginning and end of Mass, during the preparation of the gifts, before and during the Communion. In the eucharistic prayer, the Canon was explained as the sanctuary which the priest alone could enter; its words were therefore to be pronounced softly.

The meaning of the word *Praefatio* was misunderstood, and so it was taken to be a mere preface to the Canon, instead of the first section of the great prayer which should have been uttered out loud "before" the people and before God: *praefatio* is the same as *praedicatio*.

This is the form in which the Roman liturgy, transformed in fact into a Franco-Roman liturgy, made its way back to Rome from the 10th century on. During the "dark ages", traditional Church order and liturgy had fallen into decay and disintegration in

Rome and Italy. So when the German kings, starting with Otto I, appeared in Rome in the company of numerous prelates, and undertook in their role of Roman emperor to set up a new order, it was also the liturgical books and institutions of the north which regulated divine worship henceforth, even in the centre of Christianity. The monks from Cluny, the starting-point of the inward renewal of Church life in the 11th century, also worked in the same direction. The Cluniac reform, however, did not result in a set of strictly uniform institutions. All through the Middle Ages the principle was indeed maintained that each Church should conform to the Metropolitan of the province to which it belonged. But very often not only the various provinces but even the individual Churches of bishop or monastery observed their own particular customs. The liturgical books, which had of course to be copied out by hand in each case, were subjected to a constant process of expansion and transformation, which affected especially their later parts, dating from Carolingian times. Only some leading centres, and the religious orders then beginning to flourish, tried to establish firm and obligatory institutions on their own behalf.

This epoch also gave rise to the special forms of the Franco-Roman rite which still survive today among the Carthusians and Premonstratensians, in the ecclesiastical provinces of Lyons in France and of Braga in Portugal. The special forms then established for the Cistercians, various Benedictine abbeys, the Churches of Cologne, Trier, Mainz, Liège and elsewhere, were abandoned in favour of the post-Tridentine reform after the Council of Trent.

Only one important change has come into general use since the 13th century, the elevation of the host and chalice at the consecration of the Mass. This provided an unmistakable climax in the Canon which met medieval man's longing for contemplation, and the sight of the sacred host also furnished him with a certain substitute for sacramental Communion, then rarely permitted and even more rarely practised. Otherwise, the end of the Middle Ages was not only a time of liturgical variations; it was also a time of many abuses and superstitions. The violent assault of the Reformation, which with its principle of "the Bible alone" rejected not only obvious abuses but even the Canon of

the Mass, was the occasion for the "Catholic Reform" of the liturgy, which was demanded by the Council of Trent and carried through by the succeeding Popes, beginning with Pius V and his editions of the Breviary and Missal (1568 and 1570).

At the same time the principle was laid down which was expressly formulated later on, in CIC, can. 1257: that in matters liturgical the Roman See was the only competent instance in the Latin Church. A strictly uniform liturgical practice now became possible with the introduction of printed books. It was further supervised by the Congregation of Rites set up by Sixtus V in 1588 and was maintained successfully from then on, down to the 20th century. The first notable changes in this somewhat rigid liturgical order were instituted by Pius X. He led the way back to the early Christian practice of frequent Communion by his decree on Holy Communion. He also made new regulations for Church music and introduced a new arrangement of the psalms for the Breviary. Another factor of change was the liturgical movement, which strove hard to bridge the gap, grown wider with the years, between the altar and the people in the liturgy. A radical reform was started under Pius XII with the new liturgy for the Easter vigil (1951) and for Holy Week (1955). The Second Vatican Council has provided for the extension of the reform over the whole field of the liturgy (decree *Sacrosanctum Concilium*). As the sub-divisions of the liturgy are treated in special articles, we have now only to speak of the structural laws and the most important constitutive elements of the liturgy.

C. Structural Laws

Sacramental actions form the heart of the liturgy, and their climax is the celebration of the Eucharist. Obviously, the liturgical setting of each sacrament can only take the form of an extension of the sacramental sign. It will prepare for its enactment, aid its understanding and ensure the disposition of the recipient. Prayers will be offered for the efficacy and persistance of the sacramental effect. The various blessings in the liturgy will follow more or less similar rules. But no such obviously obligatory norms exist to direct worship when it consists merely of prayer. It can only follow out the laws of its own being.

Every time Christians meet to pray, their assembly should reflect the relationship in which the Church stands to God, by virtue of the Christian order of salvation. If full expression is to be given to this relationship, the word of God will come at the beginning, either in the form of Scripture reading, or in the form of a sermon which proclaims the word. For it is God who calls the Church together. And we can only answer when we are called by God's grace.

The word of God must then resound in our hearts. This could be in silent meditation. But in the assembly of the Church the echo in the hearts of the faithful will mostly try to express itself in some outward form. It will manifest itself in song. Only then comes the prayer. And since it is precisely a community which has gathered for prayer, the community will now speak, either in silence for the prayer of each one's heart, or in a common invocation, and above all in alternating prayer. Prayer, however, will culminate in the formal *Oratio,* the "Collect", in which the representative of the hierarchy "brings together" the prayer of all and puts it before God.

This sequence is in fact presented more or less clearly by all the liturgies, but above all by the Roman. Here it determines the structure of the second part of each canonical hour: a *capitulum* or short reading from Scripture to begin with, followed by a hymn or a responsory. The *oratio* of the officiant forms the conclusion, which on certain occasions is still introduced by the alternating prayer of the congregation, as was formerly always the case.

The same sequence could be repeated several times if a longer period was to be filled out with prayer, as was the case in the ancient Christian vigils lasting all the night. So we find it repeated six times in the first part of the Mass for the Saturday of Ember Days, and twelve times in the liturgy of Holy Saturday, the former Easter vigil, as it was conducted up to 1955. In both these cases each *oratio* is introduced by silent prayer, to which the individual is summoned by the *flectamus genua.*

The word of God in the form of Scripture reading has its most honourable place in the Mass: but lengthier readings from Scripture could find a place only in the Office.

In many medieval monasteries, the whole of Scripture was read each year. But under the regulations in force since then, the Bible is read through every year in selected portions. The reading does not follow automatically the order of the books, but is so adjusted that certain books with relevant themes are arranged around the two cycles of feasts.

For the Church's song, after a first brief period when the hymn flourished, the psalter has always been favoured, ever since Christian antiquity, and it has remained the primary song-book of the Church. The psalter is the inspired word of God and as such superior to any human creation. Its OT matter may not always have corresponded to the language of the people of God under the new covenant. But there did not seem to be any difficulty in reading its obscure allusions in the light of fulfilment. The words of the psalmist were taken to be the voice of Christ or of the Church redeemed, where they were not used as an invocation to Christ himself.

The recitation of the psalms took two forms in the Church. In early times, the responsorial method was predominant, where a precentor recited the psalm and the congregation answered each verse or section of the psalm with a refrain, a verse given out at the beginning of the psalm. The so-called responsories used today, where the former text has been shortened and the melody enriched, are a remnant of this method. But ever since the early Middle Ages, the antiphonal method of recitation has prevailed. Here the two halves of the choir alternate verse by verse, and the verse used as a framework, the antiphon, melodically more richly developed, is sung only at the beginning and the end.

The early history of this type of chant, which begins in the 4th century, and even the original meaning of the word "antiphon", are, however, still a matter for controversy among the historians of music.

In the canonical hours of the Byzantine rite, the chanting of psalms was again almost entirely eliminated at an early date by a rich flow of hymns. But in the West the hymn could only succeed in establishing itself after strong opposition. It was adopted into the liturgy of the city of Rome only about the 12th century, under northern influences. Needless to say, the ordinary hymn-book must in principle be allotted the same role as the Latin hymn, especially in vernacular worship. It must, however, be noted that in a large number of the compositions which we have inherited from the last few centuries, the richness of religious thought has been far too much restricted to narrow fields where subjective feelings held sway. Hence severity must be exercised in their choice.

As regards the type of music used and the executants, the widest possible choice is offered: from simple unison to the riches of polyphony, accompanied or unaccompanied. The principle, however, should be that except on very special occasions which suggest or necessitate a display of artistic brilliancy, community hymn-singing is what corresponds best to the nature of the Church.

As already suggested, alternating prayer, where the congregation responds with short invocations to the words of a spokesman, seems the most suitable form for the prayer of the people. The typical example of such prayer is to be found in the litanies. We might take as a model the form given in the oldest section of the Litany of the Saints, where the people respond to the petition mentioned by the officiant with: "We beseech thee to hear us." Still older tradition was used to the same effect by the *Kyrie eleison*.

Other forms of prayer suitable for congregational use have been evolved in the so-called *preces,* which now precede the *Oratio* in the Office when "prayers" are indicated, and which regularly preceded the *Oratio* in former times. The intention is expressed within a summons to prayer addressed to the community: "Let us pray for our absent brothers." In response, the verse of a psalm is used for preference: "Save thy servants, O Lord, who trust in thee" (Ps 85:2). The communities of long ago, well-versed in the Scriptures, rightly felt that texts from Scripture were particularly apt, even though their intention was only imperfectly expressed in the verses used. This procedure supposes a certain knowledge of the Bible which we can of course no longer count on in the average faithful of today.

This form of prayer can be seen in a further stage of development in the various litanies, where, however, the principal thing is to recite with reverence a list of holy names and titles of honour. These have now become independent prayers, with ecclesiastical approbation.

The prayer of the Church comes to a conclusion, and is also given its most perfect expression, in the prayer uttered by the priest (or, as the case may be, by the leader of the liturgical assembly). It begins, according to primitive Christian tradition, with a greeting to which the congregation responds, followed by a summons to prayer. Two basic forms of this prayer exist, corresponding to the occasion on which it is offered: the Preface for the prayer of thanksgiving, the *Oratio* for the prayer of petition. In thanksgiving, the summons to prayer is: "Gratias agamus Domino, Deo nostro." The supreme expression of all thanksgiving is the "Eucharist" itself, the Canon of the Mass with its Preface. But the structure found in the Preface is also used at other important acts of consecration: for the consecration of persons (deacon, priest, bishop, abbot, abbess), and of objects (chrism, baptismal water, paschal candle, church, altar, cemetery).

It begins by praising the salvific action of God and then passes on as a rule with an *igitur* or *quapropter* to the petition, in which God's blessing is asked for the occasion in question.

In a petition, the summons to prayer is usually short: *Oremus.* But in many cases, as for instance in the *Orationes* of Good Friday, the particular object of the petition is also indicated. In our Roman liturgy the prayer itself is usually very distinctive. It is in fact absolutely characteristic, especially where the intention has already been mentioned in the summons to prayer or in the preliminary supplications, that the prayer with which the priest appears before God as the appointed spokesman of the people, does not lose itself in fluent rhetoric or indeed in poetry. The prayer pronounces the essential in a few well-ordered words, as is in fact the case in the Roman *orationes* as they have come down to us. Clearly, these are laws to be observed also when new prayers are composed, which may well be called for in a vernacular service. The important thing is not to give a copious exposition of our human needs, but to make sure that our prayer is in conformity with the great ordinances of God. Hence the prayer is directed, not to any of the heavenly powers, such as the saint whose feast we may be celebrating, but to God himself. And it ends as a rule by looking to Christ "through whom we have obtained access" (Rom 5:2) to the Father. The "amen" of the people responds to it and confirms it.

Part of the constitutive elements of all liturgies, along with the words, are the external rites, the gestures, the well-ordered movements. One remains standing before a superior; hence well into the Middle Ages, standing was the predominant posture at prayer. This was also explained, especially in early times, by saying: We rise to our feet, because we have risen with Christ. For the same reason it was emphasized that standing was the only possible posture for prayer on days connected with Easter: Sundays and Paschal time. In antiquity it was also thought important that prayer should be made facing the East, the direction of the rising sun. This was again in memory of Christ, in whose resurrection the sun rose upon us. The easterly direction is still favoured today as far as possible in the orientation of Church buildings. Later on, kneeling became more and more prevalent for prayer, a posture expressive of submission. It had always been in use for the prayer of petition from the earliest times, as the "Flectamus genua" shows. Where the element of adoration is emphasized, it has also been the practice, from ancient times, to fall on one's knees before the divine majesty. This is particularly true of the awesome moments when God comes so close to us in the mystery of the Incarnation. Till the recent reforms, it was usual to kneel at the words "Et verbum caro factum est", at the "Et incarnatus est", and also before the Blessed Sacrament.

The reposeful attitude of being seated seems indicated whenever it is a matter of listening receptively. So we sit down for the lessons, except when they are taken from the gospel, and for the sermon. Sitting is also normal during pauses in the liturgical action; such moments of rest are in fact provided by the longer chants. It has also become usual to sit down for the chanting of the psalms, so that the lengthy service may not prove too tiring. Prayer also demands that the hands should be held properly. In Christian antiquity, the usual practice at prayer was to spread out the hands, pointing upwards, ready to offer and to receive. This is the attitude of the *Orantes,* familiar to us from the paintings of the catacombs, and still taken by the priest at the present day for all the prayers of the Mass which come from ancient tradition. Germanic usage favoured bringing the hands together. In the feudal system, the vassal placed his joined hands in the hands of his liege lord, as a sign of submission and obedience. The gesture is still used today by newly-ordained priests as they make their promise of obedience to the bishop. This way of holding the hands also gained prevalence in the liturgy from A.D. 1000 on, under the influence of the northern countries. The hands are either intertwined, or laid palm to palm, as is done by the priest at the altar.

The laying on of hands is an important liturgical symbol, whose use extends to the administration of the sacraments. It serves above all to signify the transmission of authority, at the conferring of major orders; but it also signifies the bestowal of grace (when the priest raises his hand in the sacrament of penance) and blessing.

In recent times, however, the sign of the cross has become the chief symbol of blessing. The priest makes the sign of the cross over persons and objects, and one signs oneself with the cross when receiving a blessing and beginning a prayer or a sacred action.

See also *Liturgical Movement, Sacraments* II, *Eucharist* II, *Breviary, Sunday, Passover, Qumran, Constantinian Era, Missions* II, *Arianism, Reform* II A, B, *Reconquista, Reformation, Word of God, Prayer.*

BIBLIOGRAPHY. F. E. Brightman, ed., *Liturgies Eastern and Western,* I: *Eastern Liturgies* (all published) (1896); E. Bishop, *Liturgica Historica* (1918; reprint 1962); R. Guardini, *Spirit of the Liturgy* (1940); J. Jungmann, *Public Worship* (1957); J. Jungmann, *The Early Liturgy to the Time of Gregory the Great* (1959); I.-H. Dalmais, *Eastern Liturgies* (1960); H. Schmidt, *Introductio in liturgiam occidentalem* (1960); A.-G. Martimort, *L'Église en prière* (1961); T. Klauser, *Kleine abendländische Liturgiegeschichte* (5th ed., 1965); C. Vagaggini, *The Canon of the Mass and Liturgical Reform* (1967).

Joseph Andreas Jungmann

II. Liturgical Language

1. *The data of comparative religion.* Most religions hand down their sacred teachings and hold their sacred rites in sacred, cultic languages. Sometimes these are merely severely classical or literary forms of the ordinary language, from which they can be sharply distinguished. Where a strictly cultic language is used in worship it is usually an earlier form of the living tongue (as among the Romans); often it is the language of a

former culture, since displaced by "more modern" languages (as Hebrew was by Aramaic among the post-exilic Jews); often it is no longer intelligible even to the priests (in Rome, for example). Cultic languages exist because of a belief that the gods can be reached only through "their own language" (thus the ancient Germans), a fear that speaking of holy things in ordinary language is a profanation which will incur the divine wrath, a sense that the numinous and awesome may only be approached by means of extraordinary words; because of the solemnity with which cultic language invests an occasion, or because of reverence for and a desire to preserve the linguistic form in which a saving event has taken place (Hebrew as the language of the OT). These sacred languages are static in character; apparently beyond the reach of historical change, they express the timelessness of revelation and prayer, at once protecting and bringing home to men the unfathomable mystery of the divine, the *arrheton,* the ineffable. They spring from a conviction that the divinity can only be addressed "divinely", that compared with the otherness of God and his holiness human words are blasphemous (cf. "holy silence"). Since the very existence of cultic languages, then, betokens a definite idea of God, the problem they pose is more than a rubrical one; it is theological.

2. *Christian liturgical languages.* The liturgy of the Church uses cultic languages at the present day: Latin in the West, various "ecclesiastical languages" in the Eastern rites (hardly any of which use the current vernacular). In the course of four centuries the English of the *Book of Common Prayer* and the German of Luther's Bible have also hardened into sacred languages. The Roman Church in particular has cherished Latin as "the language of the Church" and stoutly defended it down to our own day, almost as if it were part of the Church's nature. But liturgical Latin was never a completely foreign language: the Church has always been concerned that liturgists, at least, should understand it. (Thus in 1949 Mandarin Chinese — not the vernacular — was again sanctioned for use in the Missal, as had been done in 1615.)

3. *Theological analysis.* Any critical discussion of the language of Christian worship must start from the following premises: Jesus Christ is God's unsurpassable, definitive Word to mankind, which, though prepared and uttered in a particular historical setting, so far transcends it — given God's universal salvific will and the consecration of all that is human by Christ's incarnation and resurrection — that the historical forms of the Jewish-Hellenistic world have no abiding validity. Much less, then, need we cling to the forms of any other culture: man is constantly summoned anew to final decision. Since Christ is God's definitive Word to us, a valid answer is possible only in Christ and according to Christ (that is, we must now speak to God in human words, not "divine" ones): so that in Christ every possible form of worship has been superseded. Until the end of time the only appointed temple of God's Word and man's answer is now the Church formed by the new people of God who are called out of every tongue, in permanent diversity (cf. Acts 2:4–11). The people of God adore him in the spirit and the truth that are Christ himself, by accepting the salvation he has wrought and praising him for it. Here, in this Church, each in his own mother tongue, every human being is entitled to hear God and respond to him. What this means is that there are no longer any strictly cultic languages, nor even any specifically "sacred languages" which ought to be the vehicle of God's Word and man's response. Now every human language is potentially a liturgical language once it is used to proclaim the gospel and to embody the decision of faith. The seriousness of the content will, however, give the language of liturgy a special style (for example "Christian Latin") that sets it apart from ordinary speech, just as the utterances and decisions of poets and philosophers go beyond the language of business and practical needs.

4. *History of Christian liturgical language.* Ancient Christianity, unlike other religions, made free use of the vernacular in its worship: Aramaic, Greek (at Rome as late as the 4th century and even in Gaul [Lyons]), Latin (first in Africa). The extemporaneous character of the ancient liturgy, whether charismatic glossolalia or the "official" anaphora, necessarily presupposed use of the mother tongue. The witness of faith at Christian worship is "sine monitore, quia de

pectore" (Tertullian, *Apologia*, 30). But just as the gospels, confessing the way of salvation that history has established, bore traces of their origins ("Abba", Mk 14:36; "Eloi, Eloi, lamma sabacthani", Mk 15:34; cf. Mt 27:46 and other texts), so too the worship of the Church: "Amen", "Hosanna", "Alleluia" from the temple liturgy, "maranatha" (Aramaic) from the primitive Christian community of Palestine (1 Cor 16:22; *Didache*, 10, 6), Greek "Kyrie eleison" (and at one time, perhaps, Latin formulae). If special liturgical and ecclesiastical languages nevertheless came into being, the reason is to be sought outside the liturgy. The barbarians who invaded the Empire adopted the culture of nations who saw in Old or New Rome the model of all civilized practice, even where religion was concerned: it was only natural to adhere to those centres of worship and missionary activity. While the Greek of Byzantium, however, did not spread as an ecclesiastical language, the Latin of Rome became the liturgical language of the new medieval Church. No doubt the Roman liturgy if not "understanded of the people", did endow the West with a noble example of the solemn worship of God, for which we must be grateful, and the problem of having the liturgy in a foreign language only emerged in modern times, when Latin had ceased to be familiar to the learned world. Those who early perceived the "latina miseria" of the Christian people (an expression used by the Italian Camaldolese Giustiniani and Quirini, addressing Leo X in 1513) were doomed to remain isolated, since Latin had acquired an almost dogmatic importance in reaction against the principle of worship in the vernacular upheld by dissidents from the 13th to the 16th century (Catharists, Waldensians, Hussites, Reformers). Yet the Council of Trent made no positive statement on the value of Latin in Catholic services: its use must simply be recognized as legitimate, even though one function of the liturgy is to proclaim God's word (*D* 946, 956; the actual decrees are a good deal more cautious in tone than the texts originally submitted to the Fathers). The arguments advanced in favour of liturgical Latin by apologetics and on occasion by the magisterium itself (those cited in section 1, above, are found in a letter of 1080 from Gregory VII to Vratislav, king of Bohemia;

Mansi, XX, 296 f.), are either inadequate ("Latin is the vinculum unitatis Ecclesiae" — contrast Acts 2:4–11), or unsound ("changeless Latin safeguards the purity of doctrine" — compare the Latin of the Roman Missal with that of the 13th century Scholastics): they fail to carry conviction. Taking its cue from Trent, the Second Vatican Council did not merely grant that the mother tongue was a handmaid of, or a poor substitute for, Latin (thus the instruction of the Congregation of Rites as recently as 3 September 1958), but recognized its complete suitability for liturgical use (Constitution on the Liturgy, arts. 36, 63 and 14, 26, among others). This means more than permission to use accurate vernacular translations of the liturgy to which we have been accustomed: in effect the Council said that the vernacular would be meaningful — as Latin once was — only in the setting of a liturgy that was modern in the best sense of the word, one that for the people of God today was eloquent of his saving deeds, and in which it was natural for them to declare the obedience of their faith. To work out such a liturgy will be a task requiring great patience and constant meditation on the nature of Christian salvation. And its language will always be a task calling for new effort.

See also *Liturgy* I.

BIBLIOGRAPHY. *Maison-Dieu* 11 (1947); 53 (1958); C. Korolevsky, Liturgie en langue vivante (1955); C. Mohrmann, "Die Rolle des Lateins in der Kirche des Westens", *Theologische Revue* 52 (1956), pp. 1–18; K. Rahner, "Latin as a Church Language", *Theological Investigations,* V (1966), pp. 366–418.

Angelus Häussling

III. Liturgical Year

A. Principles

1. The most essential statement of revelation, and the very nature of revelation, is that God addresses mankind in a history which progresses beyond creation and the covenant with Israel (to mention only the most decisive stages) to the supreme and definitive salvation which is Jesus Christ, whose revelation in glory will bring both the goal and the end of all history. Hence to each generation as it enters the flux of time, salvation is present when the

memorial of the historic saving acts of God is celebrated with reference to the end still to come. Hence salvation is transmitted through the celebration in faith of the mystery of Jesus Christ, the memory of which is perpetually recalled by the Church, that is, mankind called to salvation.

2. The definitiveness and universality of salvation gives to the Church the task of renewing this anamnesis in every dimension of human life and hence at all appropriate places and times. Accordingly, the material world through the sacraments (and sacramentals) attests salvation and is filled with it. The time, however, which is allotted to and at the disposal of man, is arranged in phases of the presence of salvation through the celebration of days and hours: in the cosmic unity of the day, the Church sees the representation of salvation in the order of the hours of the Office. The cycle of the year through the calendar of feasts and seasons is the time of salvation which we call the "liturgical year".

3. It would be artificial to contrast the celebration of salvation in the sacraments with its celebration in feasts, since the sacrament, as a cultic act inserted into time, always establishes and structures a time of salvation. The feast, however, signifies the presence of salvation of itself, not only through the celebration of a sacrament — the latter normally has its time and place within the feast.

4. The various memorial celebrations can establish the presence of salvation in different ways and in different degrees of intensity. The content of the anamnesis can, indeed, now only be the salvation of Christ in its entirety and definitiveness, and is therefore the paschal mystery (so the Constitution on the Liturgy, arts. 5 f., 106), i.e., the passing of the God-man through the death imposed by sin into the life of divine glory which could only be entered this way (cf., for instance, Lk 24:46). This theme is propounded specifically in the Eucharist and the Easter celebration (Sundays and the feast of Easter). However, a valid commemoration of events which prefigure or form part of the definitive salvation is also possible. For the salvific work of Christ is the fulfil-

ment of the history of salvation which God began with the people of the Old Covenant. According to the normative understanding of the early Church, it was not accidental that the passing-over of the Lord from this world to the Father occurred in the context of the great redemptive feast of the Old Covenant; the new fulfils the deepest meaning of the old (cf. 1 Cor 6:7: Christ — "our Paschal Lamb"). Hence, the great feasts of the New Covenant (Easter and Pentecost) actually grew out of the institutions of the old period of salvation (Passover and Harvest feast).

5. Sunday is pre-eminently the model of the Christian anamnesis in the course of history. The (first) creation-narrative (Gen 1:1–2:3) considers the time of the world as parcelled out among the first salvific acts of God, and proclaims it a time of salvation by the repeated observance of the seven-day week (with the Sabbath as the goal). So too the first feast of the Church is the Sunday, or the "Lord's Day" (cf. the Constitution on the Liturgy, arts. 102, 106), because on the first day of the old week the Lord, completing his Passover, made the memorial of the original age of salvation the measure of time in the new age, as the permanent beginning of the new work of salvation. While the external observance, that of the week, remains the same, the celebration of different deeds of God now re-enacts the definitive salvation — the fulfilment of creation, a salvation that was, moreover, the beginning of the new creation.

6. Something similar is true of the hope of salvation in the non-biblical religions among which the Church was founded. Their feasts are also fulfilled in the salvific work of Christ and can provide the date and occasion for feasts of the Church (as happened no doubt with Christmas and Epiphany), though their content is something new.

7. This is all the more possible because the celebration of the mystery in the fullness of time (Gal 4:9 ff.) is not concerned with an exact historical date (which is in any case mostly impossible to establish in the majority of cases). It is the commemorative act of the Church through which it shows itself to

be the repository of salvation and the primordial sacrament of all the signs of salvation (Constitution on the Liturgy, art. 2). The Church is therefore the author of the commemoration and can determine the particulars of its celebration within the temporal sphere of the world. The Church is, however, all the more involved and is bound to unity in its celebration, the more salvation as a whole is the object of its *anamnesis*. For this reason there could be no Church without the eucharistic celebration and the Easter memorial, and hence *one* Sunday celebration and *one* Easter date are of great importance to Christianity (cf. the ancient dispute concerning the date of Easter; and now the Decree on Eastern Catholic Churches, art. 20; Constitution on the Liturgy, appendix). For feasts that represent, so to speak, a "partial" phase of salvation (as feasts of saints, or feasts of local Churches), the actual calendar date is of more significance.

8. The salvation of Christ in its entirety is also represented when it is celebrated in concrete form in the exemplary history of an individual, a "saint" (Constitution on the Church, art. 50), either a figure of the old period of salvation (as is done in the Eastern Church) or of the new. Such feasts can remain entirely limited to the Church which was directly concerned with the salvific action of Christ in the saint. This took place in a concrete historical situation; this is most clearly shown in the dedication-feasts of the local Churches within the ecclesiastical cycle of feasts.

9. Since, therefore, only a genuinely salvific event, affecting those celebrating it, can mark divisions of time (as a whole or that of a certain area) in the history of salvation, it alone can establish a feast. A "pious theme" may give food for meditation but it is never a feast properly speaking. Although the entire human existence of Christ is significant for salvation, all the events within it do not have an equal importance for us; and so it is not necessary for the liturgical year to present us with a spiritual drama that would be a complete "life of Jesus". Its purpose is to effect the presence of the mystery of salvation in Christ within our time, arranged in its yearly cycles.

B. DESCRIPTION

1. The source and focus of the liturgical year is the celebration of the paschal mystery of Christ, our salvation, (on Sunday and) at Easter. The Easter celebration, which is most probably of apostolic origin and borrows from the Easter feast of the Synagogue in its content and form, includes the commemoration of all the salvific events of the "departure" of Jesus Christ which took place "in Jerusalem" (Lk 9:31), namely, his suffering and death, his resurrection and his transition to the Father (ascension), the sending of his Spirit and his promised return. It is *the* great feast, "the cultic expression of the essence of Christianity" (Odo Casel).

2. Its celebration unfolds as it were in concentric circles. On the hallowed eve of Easter which is the "mother of all vigils" (Augustine), the Church watches and waits, listening to sacred history in the word of God and the singing of psalms. It makes its profession of faith, gives thanks and prays, greets the light which is the Lord. The number of the elect is increased by the conferring of the sacrament of baptism, and with the coming of the Lord in the early morning celebration of the Eucharist. The Church rejoices in the "day which the Lord has made" (Ps 117:24: long understood as referring to Easter).

3. The Easter feast in the narrower sense of the word is the triduum of Good Friday (with Maundy Thursday evening) with the suffering and death of Christ, Holy Saturday with the rest in the tomb and descent into the realm of the dead, and Sunday (following the Easter Vigil) with the Resurrection. The seriousness of Good Friday sets the tone for the week preceding Easter (Holy Week), and the joy of the Easter feast that of the week after Easter ("Octave of Easter").

4. The celebration of Easter ("paschal time") lasts for seven weeks (50 days of "Pentecost"). It ends with Pentecost, when the sending of the Spirit of Christ upon the Church is especially commemorated. What the Lord accomplished for himself, as it were, at Easter, he applies to the Church through the abiding gift of his Spirit (cf. Jn 7:39; Tit 3:5). Within the celebration of

Easter occurs the feast of the Ascension of Christ (on the 40th day after Easter, corresponding to Acts 1:3): the Risen Lord took possession of his share in the glory of God in which he created, for himself and for his own, the "heavens" (Heb 1:3 f.; Eph 2:6 f.).

5. The continuance of the feast of Easter for 50 days after, corresponds to its introductory period of the "40 days" (cf. Mt 4:2), a time of fruitful penance as a fitting preparation for salvation (cf. Mt 3:8; Acts 26:20), not only for the neophytes of the Easter vigil and public penitents, but for all the members of the Church, since their life is to be constantly renewed through the Easter celebration. The practice of Lent is extremely ancient. In the Eastern Church, as early as the 5th century, it was a period of 8 weeks; in the liturgy of the Roman Church, the development of the present order (6 Sundays of Lent, beginning of Lent on Ash Wednesday, 3 Sundays in the "pre-Lenten" period) was completed in the 7th century.

6. In the theology of the NT, the Easter glorification of the Lord already influenced the understanding of the life of the God-man in his conception and birth (Acts 13:33; cf. Rom 1:3 f.), and (especially in Jn) the general understanding of his existence prior to Easter: the Son came as the salvation of the world and is that at every moment of his existence. His first coming is at the same time the pledge and the witness to his second. And so there arose within the liturgical year, under the influence of the Easter celebration, a second but minor climax: the feasts of Christmas and Epiphany. Their contents concern the salvific events of the appearance of Jesus Christ, but not as mere recollection of the stories of his conception and birth. They celebrate rather the investiture of Christ as Saviour, as sacrifice and priest for all the world (Heb 10:5–10). Christmas (which was first celebrated in the Church of the West) announces not only the birth from Mary, but the mission, for our salvation, of the Son who was begotten from the Father before all time. The Western liturgy of Epiphany (a feast which originated in the East) celebrates in the homage of the Magi the enthronement of the Saviour of the world; in the baptism by John, his consecration as Messias; in the "beginning of the signs" which lead to faith (Jn 2:11), his

espousal to a mankind destined to salvation, to his Church at the marriage feast of Cana. The feasts of Christmas and Epiphany were not at first distinct in content from each other.

7. Christmas also has its "Lent", the time of "Advent". Its length varied in the different Western liturgies; the Roman custom of the four Sundays of Advent was only definitively adopted in 1570, though the first Sunday of Advent does not take up a theme distinct from the previous Sunday in the present liturgy. This time is a preparation for the Lord who will come in the mystery of his birth and again at the end of time. The place that is given to the Parousia in the Western liturgy within the liturgical year (and in general) might seem rather scanty. However, the content of the liturgical year is the Lord: he can only be thought of as the Lord who must and will come. Hence, each feast and especially the Easter (and its vigil) is a celebration that looks to his return.

8. Because the liturgical year is a year of the Lord, the content of all other feasts is also the mystery of Christ, especially the feasts of Mary "who is joined by an inseparable bond to the saving work of her Son" (Constitution on the Liturgy, art. 103). In the commemoration of the saints, the Church proclaims the paschal mystery as achieved in the saints who have suffered and been glorified with Christ (ibid., art. 104). These feasts also have their place in the liturgical year, because they are part of the whole mystery of Christ.

9. According to what has already been said, it would be a misunderstanding to seek in the liturgical year an exact end or beginning. The first Sunday of Advent has often been taken as the beginning of a new annual cycle, although the break at the beginning of the Easter cycle (Septuagesima Sunday) is much more significant and clear.

10. But this misunderstanding is only one of the many that have obscured the structure of the liturgical year. Quite early (first verified in the 4th century) the octave of Pentecost disturbed the 50-day Easter celebration (and led to the interpretation of Pentecost as the "feast of the Holy Spirit"), and the feast of the Ascension was given the questionable interpretation of a departure

(which again disturbed the unity of paschal time). In general, the liturgical year was seen too much as the story of the life of Jesus. This went hand in hand with the development which in the West made Christmas rather than Easter the central point of piety, to the detriment of the fullness of Christian life. Also, the multiplication of feasts of the saints and the exaggerated rubrical importance accorded them often obscured their relation to the glorified Lord. This is even truer of the many modern feasts celebrating an idea or theme, even though they were often intended to perpetuate the memory of some event given exaggerated importance in the course of the Church's history. Thus the feast of the "Seven Dolours of Mary" on 15 September was introduced by Pius VII in 1814 in thanksgiving for his return to Rome from captivity. So too feasts commemorating victories over the enemies of Christendom, jubilees, holy years, consecrations of the world, private revelations, occasions of reparation, etc. It is to be hoped that with the reform of the liturgy the liturgical year will more clearly be shown to be the celebration of that mystery which is the Lord himself, even if ancient customs (or abuses) have to be abandoned (see the Constitution on the Liturgy, art. 102 ff.).

11. The liturgical year certainly proclaims "the riches of the power and the merits" of the Lord, "so that these are in some way made present at all times and the faithful are enabled to lay hold of them and become filled with saving grace" (Constitution on the Liturgy, art. 102). But as the celebration of the liturgy is only complete when those taking part "carry out in their lives what they have received in faith" (Easter liturgy; cf. Constitution on the Liturgy, art. 10), the liturgical year needs a basically clear structure to present the offer of salvation in a convincing way and as an invitation to testimony in daily life.

See also *Breviary, Sunday.*

BIBLIOGRAPHY. N. Denis-Boulet, *The Christian Calendar* (1960); O. Casel, *The Mystery of Christian Worship* (1962); J. Pascher, *Das liturgische Jahr* (1963); G. Courtois, *Les temps liturgiques* (1964); K. Rahner, *The Eternal Year* (1965).

Angelus Häussling

IV. Study of Liturgy

Liturgical science might be taken to mean a purely theoretical study of the many different forms of worship that Christians have used in the course of two millenia — a branch, in other words, of cultural history and archaeology. But such a view would fail to do justice to liturgies as an ecclesiastical science, which for all its interest in historical forms is ultimately concerned with interpreting the contemporary liturgy.

This task is of considerable importance for the reason that liturgy is naturally conservative: it tends to cling to established forms even after these have grown unintelligible to a changed world. Non-Christian rites, as comparative religion shows, often deliberately renounce intelligibility; but Christians may not be content to persist with the unintelligible, because they must adore God "in spirit and in truth".

First of all, the existing liturgy must be made as comprehensible as possible; then its original form and basic principles must be rediscovered, so that it can be suitably restored or adapted.

There was no need for a science of liturgy in the early Church. The forms of Christian worship were drawn from contemporary culture and the people shared in a service that was held in their own language.

As early as the 4th century, however, we find explanations of the liturgy, forms of catechesis on baptism, confirmation, and the Eucharist, which the bishop gave neophytes in Easter week — only, however, after their reception of the sacraments on Easter Eve. It was taken for granted that the direct sense of word and rite would be grasped without difficulty; only afterwards came a deeper religious interpretation. Among such catecheses — which contain important data on the liturgy — we should mention those of St. Ambrose, St. Cyril (or John) of Jerusalem, and Theodore of Mopsuestia.

By the early Middle Ages, however, the need was felt for an explanation of many traditional forms. But recourse was had to allegory, instead of the original sense: that is, a sense different from the original was read into the liturgy. These allegorical interpretations, beginning with St. Isodore and reaching a climax in Amalarius of Metz, prevailed throughout the Middle Ages. St. Albert attacked them in vain. Some few attempts at sober interpretation date from this period: we should mention Florus of Lyons, the opponent of Amalarius; Strabo, Abbot of Reichenau (d. 849), whose book bears the striking title *De exordiis et incrementis quarumdam in observationibus ecclesiasticis rerum;* and Berold of Constance, who wrote his *Micrologus* about 1085.

Only when the Humanists had awakened a sense of history and the Reformers had made the liturgy a subject of controversy can we speak of a strictly scientific treatment of the matter.

First some important source material was printed by Catholics in defence of their liturgical inheritance. In 1565 Jacobus Pamelius, Archdeacon of Bruges, published two quarto volumes of ancient liturgical texts (antiphonary, sacramentary, lectionary). Three years later Melchior Hittorp, a canon of Cologne, published a selection of early medieval liturgical commentaries, together with a collection of Roman Ordines and a Pontifical which, as M. Andrieu has shown (1931), dates from about 950 and subsequently became the standard Roman Pontifical for Germany.

The second period of liturgical scholarship is dominated by the "Maurists" (French Benedictines of the Congregation of St. Maur), who methodically collected and published liturgical manuscripts together with the results of their exhaustive research. Specially notable among the Maurists are Hugo Ménard (d. 1644; edition of a Gregorian Sacramentary); Jean Morin (d. 1639; studies and liturgical texts relating to the sacraments of penance and holy orders); Jean Mabillon (d. 1707; Roman Ordines and early Gallican liturgy); and above all Edmond Martène (d. 1739), whose four volumes *De antiquis Ecclesiae ritibus* are still a mine of information on the wealth of liturgical forms that existed north of the Alps during the Middle Ages. We are indebted for similar labours to the Cistercian Abbot John Bona, the polymath Muratori, and Martin Gerbert (d. 1793), Abbot of St. Blasien; in the case of the Eastern rites, to Eusèbe Renaudot (d. 1720) and the Assemani brothers.

With its lack of interest in history, the Enlightenment was not an age favourable to liturgics. About the middle of the 19th century commenced the period in which we still find ourselves, thanks to the renewal of theology that was by then under way and especially to the revival of patristic studies and Christian archaeology. Impressive general surveys now appeared, histories of the liturgy as a whole, like those of Ferdinand Probst of Breslau (d. 1899) and the ecclesiastical historian Louis Duchesne (d. 1922), or studies of special subjects — of the Breviary, like that of Dom Suitbert Bäumer O.S.B., of the medieval Mass or Benediction, like that of Adolf Franz (d. 1916). E. Bishop's *Liturgica Historica* (1918) was reprinted in 1962.

The sources too were being methodically collected, in Italy by Adalbert Ebner (d. 1898), in France by Victor Leroquais (d. 1946). On the Protestant side the Henry Bradshaw Society in England began publishing liturgical source material, British and Continental, on a large scale. Of F. E. Brightman's projected *Liturgies Eastern and Western* only the first volume was published (*Eastern Liturgies,* 1895). Anton Baumstark (d. 1948) also did much for the advancement of Oriental liturgical studies; and much light was shed on the transition from antiquity to Christendom, so crucial for the liturgy, by the research of Joseph Dölger (d. 1940) and his school.

Over the past century or so there has been a series of discoveries of basic liturgical source material from Christian antiquity (the *Didache,* the *Euchologium* of Serapion, the *Pilgrimage* of Aetheria, the *Testamentum Domini*). Analysis of Church ordinances for the ancient East has made it possible to reconstruct one of their sources, Hippolytus's *Apostolic Tradition,* which dates from about the year 215 and gives us a general picture of liturgical practice in the Roman Church at that time.

The research carried on by the monks of Maria Laach and the Abbot, Ildefons Herwegen (d. 1946), is of great importance — the two collections (afterwards merged) of *Liturgiegeschichtliche Quellen* (1918 ff.); the *Liturgiegeschichtliche Forschungen* (1918 ff.); and the *Jahrbuch für Liturgiewissenschaft,* largely directed by Dom Odo Casel (d. 1948), begun in 1921 and reappearing since 1950 as the *Archiv für Liturgiewissenschaft.*

It was Odo Casel who first gave deliberate consideration to theological questions in the light of liturgical history. He put forward a "mystery-theology", which was afterwards much disputed. In Christian worship, he held, more precisely in the sacraments, the saving act of Christ that happened only once in history is made present, so that the faithful may enact it with Christ and share the fruits of the redemption. Although this thesis has had a persistent influence on the theology of the sacraments, complete synthesis does not appear to have been reached.

But there is now general agreement that the liturgy demands more than mere historical consideration and that it must be studied from a theological point of view. Theology had already begun to include such study, especially under the stimulus of the liturgical movement. But the liturgical movement itself only became possible because the investigation of the nature of the Church as the community of the faithful in contrast to a purely hierarchical conception was pursued in particular by German theologians, after the first studies of J. A. Möhler (d. 1838) at Tübingen.

It was left, however, to a Roman Benedictine, Cipriano Vagaggini, to treat the matter comprehensively in his book *Il senso teologico della liturgia*. Here the liturgy is seen as the continuation of saving history: the Church, sanctified by God through Christ in the Holy Spirit, responds by offering its worship through Christ.

Other major theological problems bearing on the liturgy are: the nature of Christian worship, Christ as high priest, worship and Church fellowship, the explicitation of the sacramental sign. The communal character of the liturgy is a central issue. Here there arises the further theological question of how far the liturgy coincides or can coincide with the life of piety in the Church, and how far the personal religious life of the individual is demanded by it or even indispensable to it. Then there is the question of how the communal character of the Church can or ought to be developed within the liturgy. This last question calls for a close scrutiny of the various pastoral and liturgical interests to which more and more study has been devoted in the literature of recent years. They are such matters as the active participation of the people in worship, the position of the laity, the language of the liturgy, the role of Church music and ecclesiastical art, popular devotions and their connection with liturgy, the rights of the bishop and the episcopate within the liturgical framework laid down by Rome.

All these, obviously, are important practical problems that must be clarified at least in principle. Light will only be thrown on some of these questions by the course of history itself. Where the liturgy is concerned history and theology must always go hand in hand.

As to the future, the liturgical sources must be brought to light with the aid of the appropriate sciences (paleography, philology, and the like) and modern techniques (such as the photography of palimpsests), and important texts published in critical editions.

For the West as a whole this task is fairly complete; but in particular areas, not least in Germany, the sources have by no means been exhausted. For the East, outside the Byzantine area, little has been made available in European languages except the eucharistic liturgies. Research based on these will require help from the biblical sciences and comparative religion, patristics and Christian archaeology; the cultural history of antiquity, and Oriental philosophy and literature; the history of the kerygma, dogma, and spirituality; the history of art, iconography and musicology. If these studies are to be fruitful for the liturgical life of the Church, surveys must be produced summing up and interpreting the findings of the scholars. Thus too the way will be opened to further reforms. Such books will practically always raise theological questions.

It is hardly necessary to point out that the reforms we have already seen in this century — from the revival of Gregorian chant by Pius X, on the basis of the research done at Solesmes, to the restoration of the Easter Vigil — were only possible thanks to labours undertaken in liturgical science. So too the reforms launched by Vatican II.

The new appreciation of the Oriental rites, and the abandonment of efforts to reduce them to uniformity along Latinized lines, are due to the relevant studies in liturgics. Sound developments in the worship of the Church will only be possible if liturgical science continues to fulfil its tasks. Prospects that it will do so have brightened in the past few years with the foundation of liturgical institutes (one at the Institut Catholique in Paris and one at Sant' Anselmo in Rome) and the decision of the Second Vatican Council to include liturgics among the *disciplinae principales* in faculties of theology.

See also *Religion* II A, E, *Sacraments* II, *Archaeology* II.

BIBLIOGRAPHY. For bibliographical details of the texts mentioned above, see the text-books and dictionaries of liturgics. PERIODICALS, COLLECTIONS, etc.: *Ephemerides Liturgicae* (1887 ff.); Henry Bradshaw Society (1891 ff.) (90 publications so far); Alcuin Club (1899 ff.) (44 publications so far); *Les Questions liturgiques et paroissiales* (1911 ff.); *Jahrbuch für Liturgiewissenschaft* (1921 ff.), since 1951 *Archiv für Liturgiewissenschaft*; *Liturgiegeschichtliche Quellen und Forschungen* (1909–40; 1957 ff.); F. Cabrol and H. Leclercq eds., *Dictionnaire d'archéologie chrétienne et de liturgie*, I–XV (1924–53). BOOKS: G. Dix, *The Shape of the Liturgy* (1945); G. Ellard, *Christian Life and Worship* (revised ed., 1956); C. Vagaggini, *Il senso teologico della liturgia* (1957); L. Fendt, *Einführung in die Liturgie* (1958); A.-G. Martimore, ed., *L'Église en prière. Introduction à la liturgie* (1961); O. Casel, *Faites ceci en mémoire de Moi* (1963).

Joseph Andreas Jungmann

LOGIC

1. *Notion and purpose of logic.* The word logic has been used for several different kinds of mental activity throughout the history of Western thought. It covers matters as diverse as the syllogistic of Aristotle, the technique of Scholastic disputation, the transcendental logic of Kant's *Critique of Pure Reason,* the dialectical logic of Hegel and the mathematical logic of our own days. The wide use of the word may be justified by understanding logic as the most characteristic element of a theory of rational discourse — that element which in its various branches can be shown to have a rational structure by means of a general reflection on rational discourse.

The universal purpose of discourse is to be intelligible. Hence in principle, if we prescind from accidental difficulties in the individual or group, rational discourse is speech whose meaning can be verified and whose justification may be made clear to all. On principle, it is clearly assimilable by all. If discourse is to attain this general perspicuousness, that is, if it is to be on principle followed by all, the vagueness of usage in everyday speech must be eliminated by the application of sufficiently clear and expressly applied norms for the use of language. This can be achieved in three stages. The first is agreement upon the usage of individual words, which may need to be clarified by examples and counter-examples. The second is a set of rules for the combination of words into sentences, according to the purpose of the discourse, e.g., question, affirmation, command. The third is the elaboration of procedures by which one can decide whether a given sentence is rightly asserted or not — prescinding for the moment from its content.

Since it was the sciences above all which demanded precisely regulated discourse, this type of regulation has been mainly confined hitherto to sentences of the type of "Peter is a man", "If the temperature is lowered, the thermometer falls", and so on, that is, to propositions. At any rate, up to the present, little progress has been made in the study of sentences, such as commands, which are not propositions. There is also lack of agreement in the study of modal propositions, those namely which are characterized by such qualifying words as "possibly", "necessarily" and "really". This article treats only of investigations concerning non-modal propositions.

Presupposing the functions of a) grammar and definition, b) syntax and composition, the proper task of logic in the strict sense is c) to provide processes of decision for the justification of propositions independently of their content: that is, independently of the field of application of the words used on the basis of the examples and counter-examples which establish the usage. Hence logic is the science of the justification of normal statements (propositions) insofar as this justification can be established independently of the content.

2. *Formal and non-formal (transcendental) logic.* In regulated language we can distinguish two types of words: words which can signify only one particular person, thing or event, that is, one object, and words which are so used that they can be affirmed of some objects and denied of others, and hence serve, so to speak, to "divide up the world". The first class includes proper names, and such combinations of words as "the capital of France", that is, identifications, descriptions, etc. The second class are the predicates or predicators (predicating words). The simple propositions are those in which one predicate is affirmed or denied of an object or objects represented by a proper name or names, identifications, etc. If the predicate is affirmed or denied of only one object, it is said to be uni-referent (singulary, unary, monadic), as "to be man"

in "Andrew is a man". If it is affirmed or denied of several objects (expresses several relations), it is said to be multi-referent (n — ary, polyadic). Thus "promise" in "Andrew promises John the book" is tri-referent (ternary, triadic). Elementary propositions are those in which only one predicate is affirmed or denied.

Since logic is not concerned with the content of the propositions, the words which designate various objects or are denied or affirmed of them, are replaceable by symbols. The symbols in turn can be replaced by any other words or expressions, provided only that symbols for proper names are replaced by proper names, and symbols for predicates are replaced by predicates of the same referent power. Symbols are also used for the copula and to distinguish denial from affirmation, for instance: ε (epsilon) for affirmation and ~ (the tilde) for denial, a statement of negation. With the aid of such symbols a proposition is replaced by a propositional form, e.g., "Andrew is a man" is represented by the propositional form (formula) "$S \varepsilon P$"; "Andrew promises John this book" (Andrew, this book, John; affirmation; promise) is replaced by "$S_1 S_2 S_3 \varepsilon P$". In the latter, the indices (subscripts) attached to the symbol S for the proper names indicate that the objects represented by them have three different relations to the predicate — no matter how these are to be determined in each particular case.

Since S and P indicate that they can be replaced by various proper names or predicates, they are also termed variables. The copula, however, the symbol for the attribution or denial of the predicate, does not indicate that it can be replaced by any other word at choice. It represents the linguistic "operation" of making a statement or proposition. Another kind of linguistic operation connects propositions or propositional forms. It cannot be carried out within a single elementary (or unanalysed) proposition. It is expressed by the connectives "both — and —", "either — or —", "if — then —", "neither — nor —" and so on. Yet another kind of linguistic operation treats of the range of objects for which a predication (affirmation or negation) is made. It can be expressed by the quantifiers "for all —", "for at least one —" or other formulas. The connectives and the quantifiers are called the logical particles.

Since logic tries to determine when a proposition is correctly asserted or not, without reference to the type of object about which the assertion is made, it examines the propositional form: either the elementary propositions or propositions composed of elementary propositions. In the first case logic is the theory of the affirmation or denial of a predicate insofar as the predicate need not itself be known. It is the theory of the copula, that is, of the correct use of the copula. This could be called "transcendental logic". At any rate, Kant's theory of the *a priori* conditions of the constitution of the object would fall under this head: an "object" is constituted, according to Kant, by the fact that at least one predicate is affirmed or denied of an object in the sense given above. This "constitution of the object" can be treated of *a priori* when the investigation does not depend on knowledge of the predicates in question. In the second case, logic would be the theory of how the transition may be made from one propositional form to another, that is, how one propositional form implies another. For since this logic supposes that the elementary propositional forms as such are already justified, it investigates the justification of a propositional form not by virtue of the affirmation or denial of a predicate, but by virtue of the justification of another propositional form. It is the theory of the implications of propositional forms, or, since the transition from one proposition to another is regulated by the logical particles, it is the theory of the logical particles, that is, of their correct use. Since it prescinds entirely from the content (matter) of the propositions, and does not even investigate, like non-formal or "transcendental logic", the affirmation or denial of predicates in general, it is called "formal logic". Not only the contents but also the copula aspects of the propositions are left aside, and only the inferential properties, the implication aspects are considered.

Since all propositions can be constructed from elementary propositions and the logical particles, the two logics, non-formal and formal, investigate the justification of all regulated propositions, insofar as this can be done without knowing how particular propositions are justified — hence, *a priori*. The task of logical analysis is so to regulate the form of propositions in science, philosophy, theology and, as the case may be, in ordinary language, that their structure from elementary propositions and logical particles can be clearly seen.

3. *The standard examples of logical inference* are still the Aristotelian syllogisms. Aristotle considered the propositions: All S are P; Some S are P; No S are P; Not all S are P, in order to draw conclusions from them. But none of these are elementary propositions. They use the logical particles without having introduced them explicitly. They call for an intuitive understanding of the logical particles. But it is precisely the recourse to intuition which is to be avoided by the clear regulation of discourse. All such recourse would bring back the danger of vague modes of language not subject to methodical control. Hence the proper procedure is to introduce the logical particles first and on this basis to draw conclusions or make inferences.

The commonest way of introducing the logical particles today is to make use of "truth-tables". The elementary propositions are considered merely in terms of their "truth-value", that is, all elementary propositions are divided between "true" and "false", though no understanding of "true" and "false" is called for. (Instead of "true" and "false" — symbolized by T and F — one could use other symbols such as 0 and 1 for the two different [opposite] values of propositions). If we take, for instance, two elementary propositions p and q, they can be connected, according to the distributions of their truth-values, in sixteen different ways, distinguished by their sixteen "truth-functions". Two of these are given in the table:

p	q	p · q	p ∨ q
T	T	T	T
T	F	F	T
F	T	F	T
F	F	F	F

These combinations are characterized by their two truth-functions TFFF and TTTF. (Once the series are determined in which the truth-values T and F are applicable, the indication of the truth-function is enough to characterize a combination.) The combinations are made by "and" and "or", symbolized by · and v. The particles "and" and "or"

have been given a precise meaning by being introduced in this way: "p and q" is true only when p is true and q is true, "p or q" is only false when p is false and q is false. In the other three cases it is true.

This method of truth-tables allows us to bring in all the connectives, but the quantifiers cause difficulties. Where the universal quantifier "for all' ("it is the case for all objects that . . .") is used of a finite sphere of objects, it might be explained by saying that when one is speaking of n objects one forms n elementary propositions which are linked by "and". Then the universal quantifier would be short for the repeated use of the conjunction "and" in a given number of cases. So too the particular quantifier — also known as the existential operator (quantifier) — ("it is the case that at least one object . . ."), when used of a finite sphere of objects, could be short for the repeated use of the alternation "or" in a given number of cases. But where there are an indefinite number of objects, as in the natural numbers in arithmetic, the quantifiers could not be defined as the repetition of the connectives "and" or "or". For such a definition would assert the existence of an infinitely long expression. But there is no such thing as an infinitely long expression.

To overcome this difficulty, P. Lorenzen has proposed a solution for the logical particles in the light of the "dialogal" situation of our discourse, which tries to reach a decision on correctness by weighing it in terms of statement and counter-statement. He suggests that the logical particles should be taken as operations practicable in regulated dialogues, independent of the content of the statements. The conjunction "and" is explained as follows. A "proponent" affirms the combination "p * q". The * receives the meaning "and" by virtue of the dialogue demanded by this assertion. The "opponent" can question either the left-hand side of the assertion, "p", or the right-hand side "q". If the proponent can maintain both sides, he has won the debate and can rightly affirm "p · q". The alternation "or" means that the opponent can only question the assertion "p x q" as a whole. The proponent is free to defend whichever part he will. If he can defend one part at choice of his assertion, he may rightly assert "p v q". The two dialogues may be represented as follows:

Proponent	Opponent
p · q	
p	left?
q	right?
p v q	?
p , q	

(In sum: "p x q" — p is true — q is true — "p · q" "p x q" — p is true [alternatively] q is true — "p v q")

This "operative-dialogal" way of introducing the logical particles avoids the difficulty of affirming the existence of an infinitely long expression. The particular quantifier is defined by the fact that the proponent has the choice of the object for which he defends his assertion. The universal quantifier is defined by the fact that the choice of object to be defended by the proponent is incumbent on the opponent.

Both the tabular method and the dialogal method define the logical particles by certain schematic operations. They are schematic because their execution does not demand that any "meaning" should be attached to the symbols used in the operation. A "meaning" is only demanded to introduce the operations clearly as these particular operations — by means of symbols. Once the logical particles have been introduced by certain operations, these operations can be used for establishing formulas. Certain basic figures or axioms result, which are composed for elementary propositions and which are the starting-points for these operations. The procedure for establishing such formulas is called a calculus. By using the definition of the logical particles to define a calculus, one has a schematic procedure which enables one, in keeping with the definition of the logical particles, to test whether propositional forms are correctly made, or even to establish correct forms.

The calculus which has only operations defined by quantifiers as the rules for its formulas may be called the quantification calculus, in contrast to the connective calculus, correspondingly defined. But it appears that there is no procedure to decide whether all propositional forms made with quantifiers can be established or not in the calculus (— the principle of undecidability of A. Church, 1956).

4. *The copula.* According to the theory proposed above, it is the task of transcendental logic to establish the justification of the affirmation or denial of a predicate, or to regulate the use of the copula, without needing to know what the predicate is. But if there is any point at all in establishing whether or not a predicate is justified, it means that one accepts the principle that affirmations cannot be arbitrarily made, as instances reflecting the inclinations of the individual. The justification of a statement involves the neutralization of one's own wishes, individual or social, though of course these wishes may also appear justifiable after a critical investigation or argument. In traditional terms, this may be called the postulate of the "neutralization of subjectivity". Positively, it is the demand that the justification of all assertions should be made clear, either on the basis of appropriate investigation or discussion. This postulate is the starting-point of all logic, and means that logic itself has an "ethical" foundation — being modal in its foundations — or, as Kant might say, is under the primacy of the practical reason.

See also *Aristotelianism, Stoicism, Scholasticism II C, Transcendental Philosophy.*

BIBLIOGRAPHY. A. N. Whitehead and B. Russell, *Principia Mathematica,* I (2nd ed., 1925); A. Tarski, *Introduction to Logic* (2nd revised ed., 1946); W. Quine, *Mathematical Logic* (1951); S. Kleene, *Introduction to Metamathematics* (1952); A. Church, *Introduction to Mathematical Logic,* I (1956); id., "Logic" (in part), *Encyclopaedia Britannica* (1957); A. N. Prior, *Formal Logic* (2nd ed., 1962); W. C. Kneale and M. Kneale, *The Development of Logic* (1962); J. M. Bochenski, *Précis of Mathematical Logic* (1963); H. Krings, *Transzendentale Logik* (1964); V. Richter, "Logik und Geheimnis", *Gott in Welt, Festschrift K. Rahner,* I (1964), pp. 188–206; P Lorenzen, *Formal Logic* (1965) (3rd German ed., 1967); W. Kamlah and P. Lorenzen, *Logische Propädeutik. Vorschule des vernünftigen Redens* (1967).

Oswald Schwemmer

LORD'S PRAYER

The "Our Father" is found in the NT in two different traditions, in Mt 6:9–13 (with a commentary in vv. 14–15) and in Lk 11:2–4. The two versions reflect not merely two traditions but two different attitudes towards the expected end. On the whole, Mt seems to have preserved the prayer in its most original form. If so, the theological problem of the

Our Father is really that it is meant to be the prayer of the community (or a model for such prayer; cf. οὕτως Mt 6:9) but that it contains no originally Christian elements. There is no mention of the person of Jesus nor of the redemption effected by him. Salvation is expected only in the future, when the reign of God is established. For the present time, the disciple asks to be preserved from (the eschatological) distress and from sin (in view of the coming judgment).

This type of prayer is also found in the Shemone Esre ("Eighteen-Prayer") of contemporary Judaism (no. 3: "You are holy, and terrible is your name"; no. 4: Our Father, give us in your mercy knowledge of yourself; no. 2: "You care for the living; no. 6: Forgive us, our Father, we have sinned against you. Blot out our misdeeds; no. 7: Deliver us for the sake of your name; no. 9: Bless ... this year with bounty in all the harvest-crops ... Fill the world with good things; no. 11: Rule over us, you alone; no. 18: Establish your peace over Israel; no. 13: Give us the rich reward of those who only do your will).

It would be an unsound apologetic approach to maintain that the Jewish prayer was merely nationalist while the Our Father is purely religious. The lack of specifically Christian content also explains the lack of an assured place for the Our Father in the Christian liturgies.

The Matthaean version forms part of a paranaetic section running from 6:2 to 18, composed of a set of rules for the community in the form of ὅταν with the second person, dealing with alms, prayer and fasting. Mt already provides a commentary on the Our Father in the introduction to it. The Our Father can be distinguished from the "many words" of the heathens. The just are well aware that God knows their cares before they put them in the form of prayer (v. 8). Mt does not regard the Our Father as a prayer for one's needs, but an appeal to God to guard the community of the just in the last days and hence glorify his name, that is, himself. The two parts of the Our Father — an invocation with three imperatives in the third person, three imperatives joined by "and" in the second person, which latter are concerned with "us" — are therefore intrinsically connected. If God is to show his power — which is the meaning that runs through all the appeals of the first part — this

can only be, according to traditions as old as Deut, Ezek and Dan, by God's preserving Israel, or rather, the community of the end of days, in very real safety throughout all the trial of the last days. The community of the just is the means whereby God manifests the holiness of his name and through which alone he can show that he is Lord. This is achieved when his community, for whom he is a Father, survives triumphantly the last days and the judgment.

The invocation is probably in the original form in Mt rather than in Lk (cf. Lk 6:35 and Mt 5:45; Lk 11:13 and Mt 7:11; also in Mt at 5:45, 48; 6:1, 9, 2, 26). The invocation "Our Father" is not specific here for the relationship of Jesus or the disciples to God, since it is found in many formulas of Jewish prayer. In the OT (at least in LXX) there are models at Is 63:16 (ἡμῶν εἶ πατήρ); 64:7 (πατὴρ ἡμῶν σύ), and 1 Chr 29:10 is noteworthy, ὁ πατὴρ ἡμῶν (but TM, "God of our father Israel"). In "early Judaism" the invocation is found in Wis 14:3 (πάτερ), the apocryphal Ezekiel (= 1 Clement 8:3, πάτερ), 3 Mac 6:3,8 (πατερ at the end of the prayer). In rabbinical prayer it is found in the Shemone Esre (b Rez. 5; p Rez. 4.6, אבינו) and in the New Year prayer, Abinu Malkenu, "Our Father, our King". (Another example may be in the Testament of Isaac [Test XII Patriarch], 8, 10 — again, if pre-Christian).

Also in rabbinical writings, the invocation "Our Father in heaven" is found in the Seder Eliyahu 7(33) and in Tama debe Eliyahu 21. The localization "in heaven" does not signify the transcendence of God but is an initial glimpse of the principle to be applied in the following prayers — that what exists in heaven should also be established on earth. Hence heaven is here the special region of God's sovereignty, where his power is already assured (cf. 1 QM, 12, 1f., 7). The notion of the correspondence between heaven and earth is by no means confined to future eschatology but is in line with apocalyptic thinking and is expressly formulated in the Testament of Solomon, 20, 15 (what happens in heaven also happens on earth), and in the Ascensio Isaiae, 7, 10 ("Quia sicut est in terra ita est et in firmamento").

The prayer for the hallowing of the name is found in the traditions based on Ezekiel (20:41; 28:22; 36:23): God manifests his name as holy by making Israel triumph over the nations at the end (i. e., in the judgment).

Here the coming βασιλεία is not a kingdom, but the fact that God will reign (see the Targum on Micah 4:7, "The royal lordship of God will be manifest" instead of TM, "Yahweh will rule as king"). The coming of the reign of God is also spoken of at Mk 9:1; Lk 22:18; cf. Mt 12:28; Lk 11:20.

The actual meaning of God's reigning is that his will is enforced. There is a parallel not often noticed in *Liber Antiquitatum,* 6, 11, where Abraham asking for the coming of a just judgment says, "Fiat voluntas Dei". At 26:42b, Mt departed from the Marcan text to give the prayer of Jesus on the Mount of Olives in a form closer to that of the Our Father: γενηθήτω τὸ θέλημά σου. Jesus thus becomes the model for the community at prayer. He sees his sufferings as a necessary part of the series of events which bring about at the end the triumph of God. Mt also underlines elsewhere the sufferings of the just, who are then rewarded as they deserve. Hence Mt takes this phrase not only to mean the establishment of God's glory, as was the original intention in the Our Father, but also puts it into the context of his theology of suffering. The suffering necessary to the attainment of the reward is understood to be part of the accomplishment of this will. Indirectly, the original meaning of this petition brought out the contrast to the perverted will opposed to God in the apostate creatures who choose their own will (cf. *Slavonic Enoch,* 7, 3; *Liber Antiquitatum,* 44, 1).

The prayers in the second part envisage the community. They begin with the prayer for "tomorrow's" bread (or the "regular" bread, as מחר is translated here in the *Gospel of the Nazarenes;* or the "necessary" or "for the world to come": the meaning of ἐπιού- σιος is uncertain because of lack of parallels). God is to provide for the community, for which there are clear parallels in the Shemone Esre (see above). Hence the petition probably asked originally for the necessities of life, putting the prayer in such a way that God was represented as nourishing the community day by day. This notion is derived from that of the providential care of God for his creatures in the Wisdom literature (cf. Ps 104) and hence gives rise to such sapiential and not primarily eschatological expressions (cf. Mt 6:34; so too the prayer for bread in Prov 30:8 TM). The petition has a special sense in an eschatological framework, when a general collapse of the order

of things is envisaged. But in any case, God takes care of the just in a very concrete way, renewing his attentions every day.

The next petition, for the forgiveness of sin, is characterized by the fact that God's treatment of the just is compared with their treatment of their debtors. Behind this comparison there is, no doubt, the notion of how each of the two acts of forgiveness of sin is the condition for the existence of the other. The thought occurs elsewhere in Mt (5:21–26; 18:23–35) and is found in Mk 11:25 which is formally akin to Mt 6. There are traces of it in Judaism, cf. Ecclus 16:14; *Letter of Aristeas,* 208; *Testament of Zebulon,* 8, 1. Mt gives a commentary on this petition in vv. 14 and 15, in the form of a unilateral condition which makes God's pardon dependent on that of man — contrast 18:23ff., where it is assumed that God has forgiven the just.

The prayer to be preserved from temptation can be interpreted more definitely than the two preceding petitions in an eschatological sense. The notion corresponds to the older parts of the OT (J), according to which Yahweh himself submits men to tests and leads them into temptation, while in the later parts fallen angels (demons, devils) take over this function. In the Our Father we are not dealing with a temptation or trial which approximates to education, as in the Wisdom literature. The apocalyptic traditions of the NT (e.g., Mk 13; Lk 22:31f.; Rev 3:10) reckon precisely with the just being tempted in the last days.

The final petition, which is not in Lk, is probably a Matthaean addition. Mt uses the stem πονηρός to describe all the phenomena of the last days which appear as the counterpart of the Christian community, opposed to it and to God (cf. Mt 13:19 and Mk 4:15; Mt 5:37, 39; 13:38). But this final petition corresponds exactly to the first three of the Our Father.

As regards the Lucan version of the Our Father, we must reckon with the possibility that the original text of the second petition may have been: "Let your Holy Spirit come upon us and cleanse us", followed at once by the petition for bread. This reading is attested in the minuscules 162 and 170, Gregory of Nyssa (*PG,* XXII, col. 1157c), Maximus the Confessor (*PG,* XC, col. 840) and Marcion (according to Tertullian, *Adversus Marcionem,* IV, 26, 3). Lk would have replaced the petition for the kingdom by this formula because in his theology the imminent expectation of the end is much less to the fore than the notion of the certain and sudden irruption of the end — which is why one must always pray, Lk 18:1–8. Further, the prayer of the community is primarily for the Spirit, whose coming has replaced for the present the manifestation of the kingdom (cf. Acts 4:31 and especially Lk 11:13 in contrast to Mt 7:9–11; Acts 1:6ff.). The petition for bread is modified in Lk by the addition τὸ καθ᾽ ἡμέραν. Since this phrase is found also in Acts 2:46 and also appears in Lk 9:23 as a sign of theological reflection, the question has been raised as to whether the petition for bread is already understood here as related to the Eucharist. But it is certain, at any rate, though not hitherto considered, that the sequence of prayer for the Spirit and prayer for bread in the original Lucan version is connected with the origin of the epiclesis. This is already suggested by the formal consideration that a number of epicleses begin with ἐλθάτω or *Veniat,* introducing the prayer for the coming of the Spirit to change the bread. It seems certain, therefore, that the Lucan petition for bread must be given a eucharistic meaning. In the next stages of tradition, the Our Father was primarily the prayer of the individual. According to the *Didache,* 8, 3 — where the doxology of the *Textus Receptus* appears — it is to be said three times a day. Ambrose suggests on rising and on going to sleep (*De Virginitate,* III, 4, 19), so too Augustine, Niceta of Remesiana and Theodolf of Orleans. Here the Our Father took the place of the Jewish *Shema,* which could not be used by Christians on account of the opening words, "Hear, O Israel". The Our Father had already become very important by the time of Tertullian and of Cyprian, who call it the "legitima oratio" and the "publica et communis oratio" respectively. Tertullian was the first to give it an explicitly eucharistic interpretation (*De Oratione,* 6). It is then found as a Communion prayer at the end of the 4th century (Cyril of Jerusalem, Jerome, Ambrose), but the petition for the Spirit and for bread, in part of the Lucan text, had been influential much earlier in the initial stages of the epiclesis (cf. the *Veni sanctificator* of the Mass). But the petition for forgiveness was also influential. Combined with the petition for bread before Communion, it gave rise to the confession of sins and prayers for forgiveness in the rites of Mass and Communion. In the baptismal liturgy, when the *disciplina arcani* was in force, the Our Father was confided to the candidates shortly before baptism. In the Middle Ages, the Our Father was sometimes inserted at the end of the "Bidding Prayers" and sometimes joined to the sermon. The lack of fixed place in the liturgy was due to the difficulty of harmonizing Jewish notions of the Kingdom of God with the sacramental notions of popular Paulinism. Early signs of this effort at harmonization are the insertion of the prayer for the Spirit (Lk) and the resulting eucharistic interpretation of the bread. The expectancy of the Kingdom of God recedes.

When the Our Father is used as part of the preparation for Communion, the eucharistic interpretation should be linked with the notion of the future heavenly banquet in the Kingdom, for whose coming the Christian prays. In this way the three first petitions could help to bring about a more biblical and eschatological understanding of the Eucharist, which is an anticipation of the heavenly fellowship with the Son of man.

See also *Apocalyptic, Apocrypha, Reign of God.*

BIBLIOGRAPHY. T. W. Manson, "The Lord's Prayer", *Bulletin of the John Ryland Library* 38 (1955), pp. 99–113, 436–48; R. Leaney, "The Lucan Text of the Lord's Prayer", *Novum Testamentum* 1 (1956), pp. 103–11; J. Jeremias, "The Lord's Prayer in Modern Research", *Expository Times* 71 (1959/60), cols. 141–6; E. Lohmeyer, *Das Vater Unser* (4th ed., 1960), E. T.: *The Our Father* (1966); J. Jeremias, *The Lord's Prayer* (1964); H. Schürmann, *Praying with Christ* (1964); J. Jeremias, *Prayers of Jesus* (1967); P. Bonnard, J. Dupont and F. Refoulé, *Notre père qui es aux cieux,* Cahiers de la Traduction Œcuménique de la Bible 3 (1968).

Klaus Berger

LUTHERAN CHURCHES

1. *Nature and history.* Luther did not intend to found a new Church. His reforming views led him to an understanding of Christianity which was in contrast with the medieval world and centred on the saving and sanctifying gospel of Christ. The movement thus set afoot originally sought to reform the existing Church, not to establish another one. Only when the Curia precipitately declared the movement heretical and frustrated its activities within Catholicism, was it forced

to introduce the ecclesiastical reforms called for by Scripture in such territories as were opened to it, without reference to the authority of the old Church. But even then there was no thought of founding a "new" Church. The evangelical movement that Luther began solemnly acknowledged — and still acknowledges — "*one,* holy, Catholic and Apostolic Church" which has existed since Christ and will continue to exist as one until the end of time (Confession of Augsburg, VII). But it holds that the structure which the Church had developed in the course of history was not necessarily legitimate. At the time of the Reformation it maintained that this structure had become so distorted as to extrude the gospel from the centre of the Church's life. By calling for a deliberate return to the gospel, the Reformers hoped to restore the Church to the true and abiding law of its own being. The changes they made in certain territories were to be only the beginning, which would lead the whole Church eventually to submit itself anew to the power of the gospel. This hope was not fulfilled, and so, contrary to its original intention, the Lutheran movement came to set up a Church of its own among other Churches. The Lutheran Church repudiated not only the papacy but also Zwinglianism and in particular the "spiritualist" Anabaptists and other visionary sects. Hence we must distinguish between the real idea behind the Lutheran Reformation — a summons to restore the gospel to its central place in the *one* Church of Christ, an appeal to the real "must" of all Christendom — and the actual historical result it achieved (apart from side-effects), the establishment of one particular Church among others. That is why the "Lutheran Church" cannot and may not regard itself as something absolute. It will never deny that other Churches preserve elements, at least, of the true Church. What really matters is the authentic "must" of the Church, which the gospel alone determines and which the Lutheran Church feels it understands peculiarly well in the light of the Reformation, even though it exists in the improper form of a particular Church.

As the Lutheran Reformation (that is, the one that Luther set in motion) actually worked out, friendly princes or magistrates of imperial cities set up a new Church along Lutheran lines in their territories. There was no attempt to derive an ideal Church order from the NT, as the Calvinists and most radical Protestants aimed at; traditional forms were preserved except where they plainly conflicted with the gospel, and the remainder were given a new evangelical orientation. The chief care was for the preaching of the gospel, to which all else was to be subordinated. To take such steps was in effect to remove these territories from papal jurisdiction and the control of Roman canon law. There was no objection to recognizing the jurisdiction and sacramental powers of the historical episcopate provided the bishops would tolerate the gospel. But when they tried to suppress the movement by force — the bishops in Germany were also princes of the Empire — the Reformers were compelled to abjure them and break the apostolic succession. Only the Scandinavian countries (and for the time being the Prussian and Baltic territories of the former Teutonic Knights, now become a secular duchy) retained the historic episcopate, separated from Rome, of course, and subordinate to the crown which had introduced the Lutheran reformation there.

Elsewhere the gap in Church government left by the disappearance of the bishops was patched by various expedients. Since the structures of the Church were to be essentially determined by the preaching of the gospel and the administration of the sacraments, the "means of grace" by which according to the will of the founder of the Church the word of God was to be proclaimed in it and reach it, the Lutheran Church was on principle opposed to "Congregationalism", with its claim to rule the Church by "democratic" structures.

In practice, superintendents and consistories appointed by the secular ruler generally replaced the bishops. And presently these rulers themselves began to exercise "Crown government of the Church". This practice was based on a 15th-century theory that the secular authority has a *ius reformandi* should an emergency arise in the Church, reinforced by the opinion of the Reformers that if ecclesiastical superiors do not acquit themselves well of their duties, the Christian congregation must look after itself, appointing others in their stead by authority of the "priesthood of all believers". Obviously secular rulers, as *praecipua membra ecclesiae,* were in the best position to make such changes. It was not *as* secular rulers, then, but as responsible members of the Christian congregation that territorial princes and the magistrates of imperial cities were to reform the Church and provisionally (as "bishops for the purposes of an emergency") make arrangements for the government of the Church until a new Protestant episcopate had established itself. Nor were signs lacking in the period of the Reformation that such an episcopate would develop, but these were overtaken by events. More and more the territorial princes came to regard the ordering and government of the Church, which in practice had fallen to their lot, as their proper right, and in the end they ruled as "supreme bishops" *(Summepiskopat)* over a State Church. This was a pernicious development as is recognized today. If Luther acquiesced in its beginnings, despite his strong personal objections, this was partly due to the fact that matters of Church organization held little interest for him. Trusting in the creative power of the gospel, he was sure it would assert itself if only given scope. But on principle, he was indifferent to the discipline and organization it would make use of. His passionate concern was the gospel alone. Thus it happened that reformed Christianity of the Lutheran type took the shape of established national or regional Churches *(Landeskirchen)*. Juridically speaking *the* "Lutheran Church" has never existed; there have always been a number of independent ecclesiastical bodies calling themselves "Lutheran", meaning thereby that in accordance with the gospel they affirm the Reformation of the Church which Luther set in motion and acknowledge its principles.

2. *Characteristics*. The term "Lutheran" is misleading. It seems to refer to a Church founded by Luther and committed to the person and views of Luther. Originally it was used by the opponents of the Reformers as a derogatory term for heretics; for from time immemorial it has been the mark of a sect to adhere to a single person as the only true interpreter of revelation. Luther strongly objected to Christ's Church being called by his name; and the apologia for the Confession of Augsburg, 1530, complains that opponents "defame (!) the doctrines of the dear, holy gospel by calling them Lutheran" *(Bekenntnisschriften,* p. 305). Throughout the 16th century and even into the 17th, the unwillingness to be called "Lutheran" persisted. But in time the term became an accepted one, and eventually was even adopted in a positive sense by those who clung to the original doctrine of Luther (Primitive Lutherans) after the divisions within Protestantism. Yet the Church as such was not to be called "Lutheran": it was "evangelical", or it "adhered to the Confession of Augsburg". "Catholic evangelical" is also a term met with, just as the Reformers long clung to the word "Catholic", to show that according to the gospel they believed in one universal Church. Only after the Treaty of Westphalia, 1648, did the expression "Evangelical Lutheran *Church*" (and "Evangelical Reformed Church") become general, diffused by the legal parlance of the Empire. The misleading term "Lutheran", which has now become established, simply indicates the connection with the confessions of evangelical faith produced by the Reformation that Luther began. The term "Evangelical" would be more appropriate. But since that term has meantime faded into a general designation for Protestants in general, there seems to be no way round saying "Evangelical Lutheran" when what we have in mind is the connection with the aforesaid confessions of faith.

It is the common confessions of faith that bind together the Lutheran Churches, which are independent organizations; so that for all their historical and juridical pluralism we can still speak (in the singular) of *the* Evangelical Lutheran Church. Its existence and nature are best seen in the content of its confessions of faith. While they reaffirm the ancient creeds of the Church, they are understood as a confession of the central and decisive elements of "the Gospel" — the salvific core of Sacred Scripture. They invoke Scripture as the canonical and original attestation of the gospel and submit to its final judgment *(norma normans)*. In this sense the confessions of faith are the standard of preaching and doctrine in the Lutheran Churches. Sound doctrine is considered of such importance because it is doctrine bearing on *salvation,* the conscientious preaching of which is the Church's first duty. Therefore Lutherans believe that agreement on scriptural doctrine is necessary to, and sufficient for, the unity of the Church, which is manifested in Church fellowship. In all other matters — Church organization, form of worship, types of piety, and so forth — they are free to adapt to the demands of the times. Church unity is not thereby prejudiced. In all such matters, Lutherans ought to try to agree, for the sake of charity and peace, so far as truth and conscience allow; but agreement is not absolutely necessary. Since the Lutheran Churches hold in common to the crucial points of the doctrine of Salvation, they display a family resemblance: they are characterized by an anti-spiritualist piety that stresses the bodily and the concrete and esteems the sacraments very highly, the same type of worship with a high esteem for the liturgy, a reverence for ecclesiastical office regarded as a means of grace ordained to and distinct from the congregation, a respect for historical tradition rather than an abstract biblicism, and accordingly a certain conservatism.

3. *Expansion.* During the 16th century national or regional Lutheran Churches were set up in various parts of Germany, in Scandinavia, Finland, Latvia, and Esthonia — in which territories the bulk of the population joined them — and in parts of Hungary, Slovakia, and Transylvania. Substantial Lutheran bodies in South Germany, Austria, Bohemia, and Poland reverted to Catholicism following the Counter-Reformation, leaving behind mere remnants of themselves. Thus besides national Lutheran Churches there are also minority Lutheran Churches in Europe. A good many areas of Germany and Western Europe that were originally Lutheran later adopted the Calvinist "Reform". In the first three decades of the 19th century unions were brought about in parts of Germany (notably what was then Prussia, the Palatinate, Baden, Hesse, and Anhalt) between the Lutheran and Reformed ("Calvinist") national Churches. Here, then, Lutheranism ceased to have an independent existence and was only an element along with Calvinism within the united Church, which became simply a "Protestant Church". The reaction against these unions, and the positive inspiration from the revivalist movements of the 19th century, led to a restoration ("neo-Lutheranism") in the remaining Lutheran Churches in Germany (especially in Bavaria, Hanover, Saxony, Mecklenburg, and Schleswig-Holstein) and henceforward there were efforts to form a single Lutheran Church for all Germany. Some of the Lutheran ministers and congregations in the States where the union was effected protested against the change and organized themselves as a Lutheran Free Church. From this time, accordingly, non-national Lutheran Churches exist in Germany, voluntary bodies no longer organized on the territorial principle but simply adhering to the Lutheran confessions of faith. This type of Lutheran Church had in the meantime spread widely overseas, especially in North America, where emigrants from the national Churches of Europe formed a number of Lutheran "synods" that are now uniting in one great American Lutheran Church. After Germany and Scandinavia, North America is the leading centre of world Lutheranism. Independent Lutheran Churches have recently sprung up in Australia, and lately even in Latin America, where of course they are very much minority affairs. Owing to the displacements of population in recent years there are now Free Lutheran Churches in practically every part of the world. Thanks in particular to missionary work in the 19th and 20th centuries minority Lutheran Free Churches have been established in many parts of Africa (notably Tanganyika and South Africa) and Asia (especially India). In North Sumatra and parts of New Guinea there is even a tribal Lutheran Church, the Batak Church.

4. *Constitution.* The constitutions of these Churches vary, though something of a common framework is discernible. Everywhere Church order is based not on the religious quality of the Church's members but on the ("objective") "means of grace", which must operate in accordance with the profession of faith; and everywhere the "means of grace" (the office of preaching and administering the sacraments) are adjoined to the responsible congregation. But there are differences of emphasis. The synodal element figures more prominently in the government of the Free Churches, whereas the episcopate and the synod are co-ordinated in the Lutheran regional Churches. With the definitive end in 1918 of "Church government by the crown", the Lutheran (and other) State Churches (henceforth regional Churches) were able to organize themselves independent of the State. On the whole, the

constitutions they devised struck a balance between bishop and synod. In 1948 the great majority of the German Lutheran regional Churches joined together to form the "United Evangelical Lutheran Church of Germany" (VELKD: *Vereinigte Evangelisch-Lutherische Kirche Deutschlands*), within which there is full communion in preaching and sacrament. A common liturgy, common canon law, and common Church action are gradually coming into being. At the head of the VELKD are the Conference of Lutheran Bishops, the Lutheran General Synod, and an executive composed of the presiding bishop — elected by the General Synod — and representatives of the Bishops' Conference and the General Synod. At the same time all the Lutheran regional Churches of Germany united in the federation called the "Evangelical Church in Germany" (EKD: *Evangelische Kirche Deutschlands*), likewise founded in 1948, which embraces all the Protestant regional Churches of Germany. In Scandinavia the principle of the separation of Church and State has been proclaimed, so that one can no longer properly speak of State Churches there. Scandinavian Church constitutions give more prominence to the bishop and his cathedral chapter than to the synod.

In 1923 the great majority of Lutheran Churches throughout the world joined the "Lutheran World Convention" and in 1947 the more tightly organized "Lutheran World Federation". This body has no ambitions to become a Lutheran world Church. It allows its members complete autonomy and only seeks to foster co-operation among them and a common policy. But it does express the Christian fellowship that exists among the Lutheran Churches of the world, encouraging a steady exchange of views that is certainly fruitful, and a growing spiritual solidarity. Some Lutheran Churches with a more strictly denominational outlook, like the Evangelical Lutheran Synod of Missouri" (U.S.A.), have not yet made up their minds to join the Lutheran World Federation. The Churches which are members of the Federation have also joined the "World Council of Churches", so as to make an active and specifically Lutheran contribution to the world-wide effort to make the essential unity of Christ's Church more visible, for the Lutheran Churches have had an ecumenical outlook since the Reformation.

See also *Protestantism, Reformation, Reform II D.*

BIBLIOGRAPHY. A. Drummond, *German Protestantism since Luther* (1951); T. G. Tappert, *Book of Concord* (Augsburg Confession, Apology, Small and Large Catechism, Smalcald Articles, Formula of Concord) (1951); E. Kinder, *Der evangelische Glaube und die Kirche. Grundzüge der evangelisch-lutherischen Kirchenverständnisse* (2nd ed., 1960); E. Schlink, *Theology of the Lutheran Church* (1960); *Die Bekenntnisschriften der evangelisch-lutherischen Kirche* (5th ed., 1963); W. Elert, *Structure of Lutheranism* (1963); C. Bergendorf, *The Church of the Lutheran Reformation* (1967).

Ernst Kinder

M

MAGISTERIUM

A. HISTORY OF THE DOCTRINE

The history of the doctrine concerning the magisterium is in the concrete almost identical with the history of the self-understanding of the Church itself, which cannot but understand itself essentially except as the bearer of the gospel message. To ask about the bearers of the message in the Church and their right to demand faith is always a question about the essence of the Church, and vice versa. Hence as regards the history of dogma and of theology in this connection, it will suffice to a great extent to refer to the articles *Church* II, III, *Word of God, Bible* I, *Tradition, Ecclesiastical Authority, Apostolic Succession, Hierarchy, Pope* I, *Bishop*.

At the end of the apostolic age, the monarchical episcopate was firmly established as the decisive court of appeal in the Church, in contrast to a class of enthusiastic prophets. And the doctrinal authority thus reserved to these bishops was understood as the mandate of handing on the doctrine of the apostles. Hence there are two elements in tradition. One is the material element, the doctrine of the apostles about the Christ-event (in the broadest sense of the word) which is handed on and given the expression corresponding to the needs of the times. The other is the formal or active element, the claim of the bishops to demand faith as they testify in the name of Christ and with the assistance of the Holy Spirit. Tradition is both something transmitted and the action of transmitting it. This tradition involves

a number of moments which act and react upon each other in a relationship which cannot be reduced to any one single element. The Christ-event attests itself and demands faith, and in doing so also establishes the "authority" of the witnesses. But it attests itself on the lips of the qualified witnesses and envoys themselves, in the authority which is thereby given them, and which is handed on from witness to witness in a historical continuity of a juridical type. If one also considers that the Church of Christ understands itself to be the community of faith in its Lord, the pillar and the ground of truth (1 Tim 3:15), against which the gates of hell cannot prevail (Mt 16:18; cf. also Gal 1:8), one must undoubtedly acknowledge with the ancient Church that the episcopate as a whole possesses an "infallible" doctrinal authority, in all cases where the whole episcopate teaches a doctrine as part of its actual testimony to Christ, to be accepted with an absolute assent of faith (cf., e.g., Rouët de Journel, *Enchiridion Patristicum*, nos. 204, 209 ff., 242, 296, 298; C. Kirch and L. Ueding, *Enchiridion fontium historiae*, nos. 124 ff.). This is also attested by the early efforts — as in Ignatius of Antioch, Hegesippus, Irenaeus and Tertullian — to register the consensus of the ancient episcopal Churches and to use lists of bishops to establish the formal aspect of the apostolic succession and the authority of the bishops. Hence too the unquestionable authority of general councils in the early Church is at once understandable. In spite of the denial of the infallibility of general councils by the Reformers (and by some few precursors such

351

as Wycliffe and Huss), the only point that can be open to debate within the Catholic consciousness of the Church is how this universal episcopate is to be understood as a unity, since it cannot be merely the sum of the individual — fallible — bishops. From this point of view, the history of the doctrine concerning the magisterium of the Church coincides with the history of the doctrine concerning the primacy of the Pope, as the concrete centre of unity and head of the whole episcopate. The development of the doctrine concerning the inner structure of the magisterium, against Conciliarism, Episcopalism, Gallicanism and Febronianism, reached a high-point in the dogma of Vatican I on the infallible doctrinal magisterium of the Pope. This was completed by the doctrine of Vatican II on the infallible doctrinal authority of the episcopate as a whole with and under the Pope. But this does not mean that all the questions as to how the primacy of the Pope is related precisely to his function as head of the whole episcopate have been given a generally accepted solution.

B. On the Basic Notion of the Magisterium

1. In a theology of the ecclesiastical magisterium, it will not do to start at once with the simple notion of a transference of formal authority from God, imparted to a man in such a way that he is clothed with this authority as he confronts other men "from outside". In such a pattern of thought, which is very common in fundamental theology, it is inexplicable, for instance, that a doctrinal authority such as is found in the Church of the new covenant should not have existed under the old covenant, though the need for certainty as regards the truth of revelation was then equally desirable. For a proper theological understanding of the (infallible) magisterium of the Church, one must begin with the eschatological triumph of the Christ-event as such. Part of its intrinsic composition is the word in which it testifies to itself. It can only remain eschatologically triumphant and present in the world if it does not falter and fail in the word of its self-attestation. This word of testimony, by which the Christ-event becomes historically present to all ages, is uttered primarily by the whole community of Chris-

tian believers, by the Church as such and as a whole. Hence the action of the Spirit is from beginning to end directed to this Church as a whole, which is preserved in the truth of Christ by the Spirit (cf. *D* 1821, 1839). But this Church which is the historical presence of Christ preserved in the truth of Christ, through which the truth of God is offered to the world, accepted in faith and manifested in historical confession, is essentially something more than the mere sum of individual believers, totted up as it were from below. It is not just a meta-historical fellowship, but a historically-structured society with a confession of faith and a doctrinal authority. Hence in the last resort, the precise nature of this authority is only to be explained in terms of the eschatological nature of the Church. While the actual teachers do not receive their authority by being appointed by the members of this community as the sum of the individuals, still, their authority and its "infallibility" is only conceivable within this eschatological community of belief. It is a moment of the implementation of the decree of God in Jesus Christ, by which he willed that the salutary truth of the Christ-event should remain historically present in the world. The Church would not be the eschatological community of salvation if it were not in "infallible" possession of the truth of Christ. For the Church proclaims that the grace of God — hence also the grace of truth and faith — is not merely constantly offered anew, but that this grace of truth in the Church always remains in fact triumphant there, and that this triumph remains tangible and manifest in the historically concrete Church, and hence also in its confession of faith.

2. When we speak of the magisterium of the Church, we should not forget the inner unity of the offices of the Church. Vatican II speaks frequently, especially in *Lumen Gentium*, of the three offices of Christ and of the hierarchy, though this three-fold division is comparatively recent in the history of theology, and cannot be easily harmonized with the classical teaching of canonists on the two powers in the Church, the power of sanctification *(potestas ordinis)* and the power of government *(potestas iurisdictionis)*. All these offices *(munera)* and powers *(potestates)* can be comprised within the one authority

of the "creative" word of God, which does not merely notify what is said, but actually brings into play *(verbum exhibitivum)* the grace, presence and power of God. It is the word which judges and sanctifies as it is uttered into the concrete presence of man and of the Church. As anamnesis, it re-presents perpetually the one, single past event of Christ's salvific deed, and as prognosis anticipates the promised future in hope. In keeping with the nature of man and the diversity of his history, this one word has necessarily various degrees of intensity. It ranges from the seemingly merely doctrinal proclamations of the magisterium, and the directives which define a Christian task in a given situation of the Church and the individual, to the word which is the "form" in the sacrament and makes the grace of God historically present and effective *ex opere operato*. This is the basis of the unity of offices and powers in the Church, and it must be carefully considered, if the magisterium of the Church is to be rightly understood. Thus the magisterium is not strictly speaking the authority to teach abstract doctrines for their own sake. It is the guarantee that the salvific word of Christ will be really addressed to the concrete situation of a given age, in view of Christian life. And this forms the history of dogma, not just the history of theology. The magisterium as thus understood does not replace the work and rule of the Spirit, through whom it lives and to whose guidance it is always subject. But the magisterium is the concrete form in which the guidance of the Spirit, as the Spirit of Christ who gives the Christ-event historical presence, maintains historical continuity with Jesus Christ.

3. In spite of the individualism of later days, which is still very much the prevailing temper of the West, a new understanding for the magisterium of the Church must surely now be possible, in view of our knowledge of the man of today and tomorrow. Man cannot possess his truth as an isolated individual, since he is no such thing. Hence there can be truth for the individual only in inter-communication with other men — especially if the truth is that of the one and total existence of man. And such fellowship can only be realized in a society with concrete institutions. The truth of man would be dissipated into the hazard of private opinions

which the self-doubting man of today would not take particularly seriously if in free and inevitable resolve he did not allow himself to be corrected by the truth which is not *a priori* his own but which comes to him as that of a socially instituted fellowship. Truth of its very nature has to do with fellowship, society and institution, even though the precise relationship of an individual and his truth to the truth of a fellowship and society differs essentially according to the nature of the society in question. But in a post-individualistic epoch new possibilities of understanding may be opened up, even for the understanding of the magisterium in the Church.

C. The Magisterium on the Magisterium

1. The doctrine proposed by the magisterium about itself is to be found in its fullest and most authentic form in the third chapter of Vatican II's Dogmatic Constitution on the Church (*Lumen Gentium,* especially arts. 24–25). This whole chapter must be kept in mind throughout, though there will be no need to refer to it constantly for the points of doctrine now to be proposed. Most of the references in the following will be to earlier pronouncements of the Church on its magisterium.

2. We need not go into detail here about the concrete manner of the origin of the Church from the historical Jesus (for which see *Church* I–III). We may refer to the biblical justification of the magisterium given by Vatican II, which needs, however, some further nuances from the point of view of historical criticism, since it deals with the connection of the Church with the pre-Easter Jesus. Otherwise the teaching of the magisterium is as follows. In the college of the apostles (*D* 1787, 1793, 1798, 1828, 1836, 2204) Jesus Christ endowed the Church which he founded with a permanent magisterium (*D* 1821, 1837, 1957). This magisterium is authentic, that is, demands assent by virtue of the formal authority confided to it and not merely by virtue of the contents of the message (*D* 1800, 1839), and is also essentially infallible (*D* 1800, 1839). This magisterium has authority with regard to the rest of the faithful, in keeping with the constitution of the Church (*D* 1958, 2313), without prejudice to the infallibility of the believing

Church as a whole (cf., for example, Mansi, LI, 542, 552, 1214; *Lumen Gentium,* art. 25: "charisma infallibilitatis ipsius ecclesiae". This doctrine is already implicit in the doctrine of the Church on tradition, the apostolic succession and dogma. It was also propounded against the Reformation (*D* 765 ff., 769 f., 783, 786, 1788), defined in substance by Vatican I (cf. also *D* 1957 f.), and re-asserted by Vatican II.

3. As has already been remarked, there is still no absolutely clear and unanimous doctrine in Catholic theology about the ultimate essence of the possessors of authentic and finally infallible doctrinal authority in the Church. The point at question is the precise nature of the relationship between the whole episcopate with and under the Pope, without whom it is not a college, and the Pope as wielder of the same supreme doctrinal authority such as is proper to the whole episcopate. Two wielders of the supreme doctrinal authority in one and the same society is inconceivable, and the usual solution of text-book theology, that in this case there is only partial non-identity, while correct, does not really solve the problem. The question was also finally left open by Vatican II. With this reservation in mind, it may still be affirmed that the wielder of the supreme doctrinal authority in the Church is the college of bishops, as the legitimate succession to the college of the apostles, with and under the Pope as its head. This college can act through the ordinary magisterium, which can be quite well considered as a collegial act, though it may not be a *new* collegial act, and accordingly may be referred to an explicit act of the whole episcopate or to an act of the Pope as head of the whole episcopate. This college of bishops can also act when it assembles as such in one place in a Council or when it is represented by the Pope. For the Pope, in the exercise of doctrinal primacy, acts as head of the whole episcopate, though the juridical validity of his act does not thereby depend on the previous assent of the other members of the episcopal college. But this again does not mean that the Pope is independent of the college in the discovery of the doctrine taught and for the moral justification of his act. On the ordinary magisterium, see *D* 1683, 1792; *CIC,* can. 1323; *Lumen Gentium,* art. 25. For the authority of a Council, see

D 54, 212, 349, 691, 792a, 810, 873a, 882, 910, 929a, 1000, 1781, 1821; *Lumen Gentium,* art. 25. For the doctrinal authority of the Pope, see the articles *Pope* I, *Infallibility; D* 1839; *Lumen Gentium,* art. 25.

4. The object of the magisterium is the content of Christian revelation and all that is necessary or useful for the preaching and the defence of this revelation. In determining the content of revelation and demarcating it off from matters on which the magisterium is not competent, the magisterium is itself the judge of its own authority. That the magisterium does not go beyond its powers when demanding the absolute assent of faith (at any rate), is guaranteed, according to the Catholic faith, by the assistance given to the Church by the Spirit. This is the one ultimate guarantee, but it is sufficient.

a) Hence the primary and direct object of the magisterium are the truths of Christian revelation which are revealed *per se* (for their own sakes, and not for the sake of revealing something else). This is the *depositum fidei,* the doctrine on faith and morals (*D* 1792, 1800, 1836, 1839; *Lumen Gentium,* art. 25). This principle does not solve at once the question of the precise explanation of the divine revelation itself as to its origin, unity and essence. Hence the principle must not be taken to mean that the deposit of faith contains divine revelation in the form of a number of individual propositions (no matter how numerous) which are to be authoritatively taught by the magisterium as purely doctrinal propositions.

b) The secondary or indirect object of the magisterium are other truths which, though not revealed *per se* or explicitly, touch matters of faith and morals directly or indirectly. This may be by their logical connection with revealed truths, of which they may be the presupposition or the imperative consequence — and thus "virtually revealed". Or they may be "dogmatic facts", e.g., the legitimate authority of a given Council. Or they may be propositions of purely "ecclesiastical faith", in contrast to the truths of "divine faith" which are revealed *per se.* They would be doctrines taught with absolute binding force by the Church, when the Church does not claim that they are implicitly or explicitly revealed by God, but finds them necessary for the safeguard and the effective and relevant preaching of the faith strictly speaking (*D* 783, 1098 f., 1350, 1674 ff., 1710 ff., 1798, 1817, 1930a, 2005, 2024, 2311 f.). This affirmation of a secondary or indirect object of the magisterium is put forward rather as a matter of principle. Whether and where such statements of the magisterium occur, and how they share in the magisterium and the quality of propositions of faith strictly speaking, is, it seems, to a great extent an open question.

5. The source of the magisterium of the Church and its ultimate norm is the divine revelation in Jesus Christ, which on account of its eschatological fullness was closed with the apostles (*D* 2021). It is not augmented by the magisterium, but transmitted, given relevant expression in each age and in this sense, developed (for which see *Dogma* II; also *D* 783, 1800, 1836, 2020 f., 2145, 2313; Vatican II, Dogmatic Constitution on Divine Revelation, *Verbum Dei*, arts. 1–10). Revelation is given in the apostolic tradition, which again crystallizes in Scripture and "oral tradition" (*D* 783, 1787, 1792, 2313 f.; *Dei Verbum*, arts. 7–10; see the article *Scripture and Tradition*). The content of this divine revelation, as preserved by the magisterium of the Church and the faith of the Church, can be seen — primarily by the magisterium itself, secondarily by individual believers and theologians — by referring back to the expression of this revelation at any period of the Church's history. Recourse is had for this to the consensus of the Church Fathers and theologians. In this recourse to the *loci theologici*, however, careful note must be taken of the exact degree of insistence with which the Fathers and theologians proclaim that the doctrine in question is really an attestation of the divine revelation in Jesus Christ.

6. The magisterium can propound its doctrine as obligatory in various degrees. Even where it does not demand an absolute and irreformable assent of divine faith (or of purely ecclesiastical faith, if there is such a thing), it can of itself and normally demand interior assent (*D* 1350, 1683 f., 1698, 1722, 1820, 2007 f., 2113, 2313; *Lumen Gentium*, art. 25). The degrees of obligation towards the doctrine of the magisterium is expressed by means of the "theological notes". See further under E below.

D. THE SCRIPTURAL DOCTRINE

Against the background of the biblical doctrine of the magisterium, as propounded by Vatican II in *Lumen Gentium* and *Dei Verbum*, we may confine ourselves here to some general indications of texts which affirm substantially, though often relatively implicitly, what the ecclesiastical magisterium teaches about its own nature. The Church, the community necessary to salvation, knows that it is the fellowship of the one faith (Eph 4:5) and the one confession, and hence in touch with the salvific reality of Christ. As was said above under A, the real nature of the magisterium derives from the Christ-event, which is eschatological triumph and possesses in the Church and its confession of faith its permanent presence. If the Church is the pillar and ground of truth (1 Tim 3:15), and if it has a social constitution and hence sacred offices, among which, primary and fundamental, must be the authority to preach salvation in Christ and demand belief, then this office is to be explained by the very nature of the Church. Its doctrine is not an innovation to be discovered by the office or the community. It is that which has been received and handed on, the tradition which is defined by its necessary relation to the one and unique salvific event (1 Cor 11:2, 23; 15:3; 2 Pet 2:21). This teaching is handed on (1 Tim 6:20; 2 Tim 1:14) by envoys who are sent by Christ as witnesses, with authoritative power (Mk 16:20; Lk 24:48; 2 Tim 1:13; 2:2, 15; see the article *Apostle*) to all nations. In Peter and the college of the apostles, and, since the Church is to endure to the end of time, in the primacy of the Pope and in the college of bishops, this Church has an authoritative government by mandate and mission from above (Lk 10:16; Jn 20:21; Rom 10:15). This mandate is handed on in the apostolic succession. And since the Church finds its being in the doctrine of the apostles (Acts 2:42; 2 Jn 1:9), the college of bishops with the Pope at its head has the mission and authority to hand on the doctrine of the apostles. This is a mission with an authority which cannot be overwhelmed by the gates of hell (Mt 16:18), since the Church is eschatological in nature. Its mission and authority is exercised with a sense of absolute claim (Mk 16:16; Mt 10:14 ff.; 16:19; 18:18; Gal 1:18), because it knows itself sustained by the permanent assistance of Christ (Mt 28:20; Lk 24:47ff.; Acts 1:8; Jn 14:16) and of the Spirit (Jn 14:16, 26; 15:26; 16:13). This absolute claim would be irrational and immoral if the Church could fall away from the truth of Christ and hence destroy itself as the historically tangible community which confesses Christ, at the very moment when it commits itself with all its might to its doctrine and demands an absolute assent of faith.

E. VARIOUS QUESTIONS

1. As regards the definitive decisions of the magisterium, while they are "irreformable", they are also subject to the created dimensions of human statements and the historicity of human knowledge of the truth — into which too, however, the Word of God became incarnate, without ceasing to be the Word of God. When we say that a doctrine is irreformable, we mean that in its true and proper meaning it can never be rejected as erroneous: it is not revocable as regards the past. The creatureliness and the historicity of dogma mean that it can and must be interrogated age by age and confronted with the mental horizons and the knowledge of each age. The various dogmatic expressions must be constantly related to each other in new ways, which is one way by which marvellous insight may be gained into them and their knowledge renewed (see *D* 1796). In this sense a dogma is always "reformable" in the forward direction — though in "eodem sensu eademque sententia", *D* 1800 — and indeed it can be a real duty for the Church not simply to repeat monotonously its ancient dogma but to re-phrase it in such a way that earlier and possibly misleading overtones or outdated forms of thought may be excluded, and that it may cause no more difficulty to faith than is intrinsic to the mystery contained in revelation. The permanent identity in the varying utterances of the history of dogma can and must be investigated historically. But ultimately the presence of this identity is an element of the faith of the Church in its identity throughout history, which cannot be adequately grasped in conscious reflection.

When a dogma is to be taught by the ordinary magisterium of the whole episcopate, without conciliary or papal definition — as is quite possible — it is not enough that

a doctrine be propounded with moral unanimity by the whole episcopate. It is further required that the doctrine be explicitly propounded "tamquam definitive tenenda" (*Lumen Gentium,* art. 25). Hence mere *de facto* universality of Church doctrine related to the faith is not enough. It has often been assumed in the past, with practical effects, that a doctrine is irreformable in the Church simply because it has been generally taught without clearly notable contradiction over a considerable period of time. This view runs counter to the facts, because many doctrines which were once universally held have proved to be problematic or erroneous, and is fundamentally unsound. It follows that though the notion of authentic doctrine as opposed to definitive is not to be rejected or made light of, we may expect a greater "reformability" in Church doctrine than was counted on in modern times, before Vatican II.

2. Unquestionably, the attitude of Catholics, even of non-theologians, to the *per se* authentic pronouncements of the magisterium, the non-defined statements, has become more critical. This is due to the experiences of the last hundred years. It cannot be denied that the practical preaching of Church doctrine often unduly blurred the basic and acknowledged differences between doctrinal utterances, as regards their binding force. In the preaching of doctrine in the Church today this distinction must be clearly brought out. The normal duty of inner assent to non-defined doctrinal pronouncements of the magisterium (*Lumen Gentium,* art. 25) is not to be propounded in such a way that in practice an absolute assent is still demanded, or as if there were no instance in which one of the faithful might withhold his assent. Reference may be made to the pastoral letter of the German bishops of 22 September 1967, where this difficult question is frankly and soberly treated. The pastoral says:

"At this point we must soberly discuss a difficult question, which in the case of many Catholics today, much more than in the past, either menaces their faith or their spontaneous confidence in the doctrinal authority of the Church. We are thinking of the fact that in the exercise of its office, the doctrinal authority of the Church can be subject to error and has in fact erred. The Church has always known that something of the sort was possible. It has stated it in its theology and developed rules for such situations. This possibility of error does not affect doctrines which are proclaimed to be held with absolute assent, by a solemn definition of the Pope or of a General Council or by the ordinary magisterium. It is also historically wrong to affirm that errors of the Church have subsequently been discovered in such dogmas. This of course is not to deny that in the case of a dogma growth in understanding is always possible and always necessary, the original sense being maintained while previous possible misunderstandings are eliminated. And of course the problem in question must not be confused with the obvious fact that there is changeable human law in the Church as well as divine and unalterable law. Changes in such human law have nothing to do with error, but simply raise the question of the opportuneness of legal dispositions at different times. As regards error and the possibility of error in non-defined doctrinal pronouncements of the Church, where in fact the degree of obligation can vary very widely, we must begin by accepting soberly and resolutely the fact that the whole of our human life in general has also to be lived simply 'according to the best of our knowledge'. We have to follow our conscience according to our lights, which cannot be justified with absolute intellectual certainty but still remain 'here and now' the valid norms to be respected in thought and action, because for the present there is nothing better. This is something which everyone knows from his own experience. It is a truth accepted by every doctor in his diagnosis and by every statesman in his judgment of a political situation and the decisions to be taken in view of it. The Church too, in its doctrine and practice, cannot always allow itself to be faced by the dilemma of either giving an absolutely binding doctrinal decision or simply remaining silent and leaving everything to the personal opinion of the individual. To safeguard the real substance of the faith, the Church must give doctrinal instructions, which have a certain degree of obligation but not being definitions of the faith, have a certain provisional character, even to the extent of possible error. This is a risk which must be taken, since otherwise the Church would find it quite impossible to preach its faith as the decisive reality of life, to expound it and to apply it to each new situation of man.

In such a case, the situation of the individual with regard to the Church is somewhat like that of a man who knows that he is bound to accept the decision of an expert, even though he knows that this is not infallible.

"There is no place, at any rate, in sermons and religious instruction for opinions contrary to such provisional doctrinal pronouncements of the Church, even though in certain circumstances the faithful should have the nature and the limited scope of such provisional pronouncements explained to them . . . The Christian who believes he has a right to his private opinion, that he already knows what the Church will only come to grasp later, must ask himself in sober self-criticism before God and his conscience, whether he has the necessary depth and breadth of theological expertise to allow his private theory and practice to depart from the present doctrine of the ecclesiastical authorities. The case is in principle admissible. But conceit and presumption will have to answer for their wilfulness before the judgment-seat of God."

F. Present-Day Problems

The development of Western theology with regard to the magisterium was influenced by the formal juridical thinking of the Latins. This led to very precise and juridical formulas in answering the question: by whom and how is a doctrinal pronouncement to be made in the Church, so that there can be no doubt of its legal validity and hence of its binding force? The question of the formal juridical structures of a doctrinal pronouncement completely overshadowed the question of its nature and of its concrete historical and sociological (ecclesiological) characteristics. Even in Vatican II, little attention was devoted to such non-juridical questions of doctrine. There is a brief statement, for instance, to the effect that the Pope and the college of bishops, when considering how their doctrine is contained in revelation and tradition, must be zealous in using the necessary means to answering this question. But theologians gave little thought to how this is to be done in general and how in particular it is to be done in the social and spiritual situation of the present day. In this matter, Vatican II hardly went beyond what Bishop Gasser had already said in Vatican I. Nonetheless, there are very many problems behind these simple questions. It is quite possible, for instance, to think that the magisterium would no longer be morally justified today, when trying to fulfill its duty of informing itself before making a doctrinal pronouncement, if it simply followed the procedures which were formerly the best available and also adequate. One reason for this is that the magisterium must not aim simply at material accuracy, but also at the greatest possible efficacy in its declarations. Hence, in face of the *ecclesia discens*, the Church to which instruction and enlightenment is due, the magisterium cannot just appeal to its formal authority. The faithful must also be able to see clearly in any given step taken by the magisterium that the magisterium sees itself as organ and function of the Church as a whole, that it not merely offers men doctrine true in itself but tries to bring them into contact with the very reality of salvation and its salutary force. And since the magisterium receives no new revelation when making its pronouncements, it must make every effort to explain intelligibly to the educated faithful *how* it arrived at its decision in the light of the totality of the one revelation which is the life of the Church.

The question of the "opportuneness" of a doctrinal decision, especially in the case of a definition, must not be lightly dismissed by saying that the question is already solved if the decision in question is correct in itself. Even when a doctrine is true (in the ultimate sense and when properly interpreted), it can be uttered too hastily, couched too harshly, be of too little use for the real life of Christians or formulated against certain backgrounds of thought which make the obedience of faith unjustifiably difficult. Even in the Church too much reliance must not be placed on formal authority. In an atheistical age, when the faith is being radically threatened, important decisions of the Church, including definitions — and new ones may be given in the Church of the future — will have to be less a matter of the further material explicitation of revelation and rather aim at safeguarding the basic substance of the Christian faith and seeing that it is presented in new ways in the living preaching of the Church. Finally, the theology of the magisterium should reconsider the fact that beyond studying the eternal truth of gospel revelation, the magisterium may have the task of addressing a prophetic word of directive to the Church for its inner life, and also to profane society, as the Church discharges its

task in the world. These are tasks which need to be precisely envisaged today, and are difficult to bring within the competence of the magisterium as it is normally conceived, or within the pastoral office, as it is commonly understood.

BIBLIOGRAPHY. D. Palmiere, *Tractatus de romano pontifice* (2nd ed., 1891); E. Dublanchy, in *DTC*, IV, cols. 2175–2200; id., *ibid.*, VII, cols. 1638–1717; J. Filograssi, "Tradizione divino-apostolico e Magisterio della Chiesa", *Gregorianum* 33 (1952), pp. 168–72; C. Journet, *The Church of the Word Incarnate*, I (1953); I. Salaverri, "De Ecclesiae, Magisterio", *Sacrae Theologiae Summa*, I (1955); M. Schmaus, *Katholische Dogmatik*, III/1 (5th ed., 1958), pp. 704–820; H. Schauf, *De corpore Christi mystico* (1959); M. Nédoncelle, R. Aubert and others, *L'ecclésiologie au XIXe siècle* (1960); S. Tromp, *De Christo capite mystici corporis* (1960); U. Betti, *La costituzione dommatica "Pastor Aeternus" del Concilio Vaticano*, I (1961); K. Rahner and J. Ratzinger, *The Episcopate and the Primacy*, Quaestiones Disputatae 4 (1962); H. Küng, *Structures of the Church* (1965); J. M. Todd, ed., *Problems of Authority* (1962); J. Hamer, *L'église et une communion* (1962); W. Bertrams, *De relatione inter episcopatum et primatum* (1963); K. G. Steck, *Das römische Lehramt und die Hl. Schrift* (1963); G. d'Ercole, *Communio — Collegialità — Primato* (1964); K. Rahner, *Theological Investigations*, V (1965) (On General Councils); O. de la Brosse, *Le pape et le concile* (1965); Y. Congar, ed., *La collégialité épiscopale* (1965); K. Rahner's commentary on chapter III of the Dogmatic Constitution on the Church in H. Vorgrimler, ed., *Commentary on the Documents of Vatican II*, vol. I (1967), especially pp. 205–16; H. Bacht, "Primat und Episkopat im Spannungsfeld der beiden Vatikanischen Konzile", in L. Scheffczyk and others, eds., *Wahrheit und Verkündigung (Festschrift M. Schmaus)*, II (1967); H. Fries, "'Ex sese' non 'ex consensu ecclesiae'", *Volk Gottes (Festschrift J. Höfer*, ed. by R. Bäumer and H. Dolch) (1967); K. Rahner, *Schriften zur Theologie*, VIII (1968).

Karl Rahner

MAN (ANTHROPOLOGY)

I. Philosophical. II. Biblical. III. Theological: A. History. B. Attempt at a Systematic Outline.

I. Philosophical

Anthropology is man's explanation of himself, the reflection of his own being, a being that is never simply at hand as a given datum, but has always presented itself as a question, and (whether this is explicitly realized or not) has always had its existence merely as its own answer at any given time to that question. Here is not a matter of the content of this answer, or of the "object" of question and answer; the point of concern is rather the theoretical, scientific reflection on the different ways in which this question and answer have found historical expression.

1. *History*. Man has always been a source of enquiry to himself. The earliest answers are contained in the pre-historic myths and legends of origin of the so-called primitive peoples and of the early civilizations. It seems likely that, in the beginning, man was explicitly conscious neither of the question nor of the answer; both take shape in the rites, the place and the instruments of religion: they come to verbal expression in myth, in which religion seeks to explain itself — until such time as this way no longer suffices. Then the question is seen to be a rational and philosophical one seeking for a consciously theoretical answer.

In the West, after the early beginnings in the pre-Socratic period, attention was first focussed on man in a decisive way in the time of Socrates. While the Sophistic Enlightenment declared man to be the measure of all things, tragedy (Sophocles) and metaphysics (Plato, Aristotle and the Stoa) place him, precisely as a rational being, under the universal law of the cosmos. Judaeo-Christian thought, meeting with this tradition, regards man as one called in an absolute, personal way into a unique historical process of salvation *(Heilsgeschichte)*. Not the nature of man but his salvation, that of the people as of the individual, is sought for here (prophets, Paul, Augustine). While Greek thought in general dominates scholasticism (but, besides other incipient manifestations, note especially the teaching on the absolute binding force of conscience from the time of St. Thomas), the special place of the person as an individual comes to the fore in Eckhart and especially in Nicholas of Cusa. In contrast to the Renaissance cult of the hero and the genius, the question of the special place of man was felt in the Reformation period (and in a similar way by B. Pascal) as an urgent problem. The theoretical correlative to this desire for certainty is provided by the philosophy of Descartes, laying the foundation for the modern distinction between subject and object, between man and the world and, in its distinction of *res extensa* from *res cogitans* in man, setting the course for the future development of anthropology.

The term anthropology first appears at the beginning of the 16th century in a work on physiology by the Leipzig scholar M. Hundt. In 1594–96 O. Casmann published in Hanover his two-volume *Psychologia anthropologica sive animae humanae doctrina. Secunda pars anthropologiae: hoc est Fabrica humani corporis*. Here, as subsequently, anthropology consists in a combination of physiology and psychology on the one hand and ethics (especially theory of the emotions) on the other. This is true of the English as well as the French and German Enlightenment, up to Kant who distinguishes a pragmatic and a physiological anthropology. More comprehensive is the picture of man given in German classical literature, in the pedagogy of humanism and in the philosophy of German idealism according to which man is the seat par excellence of the general reason *(allgemeine Vernunft)* and of the absolute spirit.

Kant's reference to research into races and peoples was taken up by Blumenbach, thus giving modern anthropology a decisive turn in this direction in the second half of the 18th century. As well as this research which concerns itself with the earliest archaeological discoveries, modern anthropology devotes its attention to the doctrine of evolution and today in the Anglo-Saxon countries consists for the most part of ethnology and the morphology of culture.

In Germany in particular, especially through M. Scheler, anthropology freed itself after World War I from its limitations to the biological and developed into philosophical anthropology. Here the opposition, different in each case, of Feuerbach, Marx, Kierkegaard and Nietzsche to German idealism, takes its effect in the study of man as he is, real and historical. This study starts from the phenomenon of culture and history (Dilthey, Rothacker), from biology (Plessner, Gehlen) and medicine (Weizsäcker, Binswanger, Frankl) and takes distinctive shape from existential philosophy. In this sense Heidegger's *Sein und Zeit* (1927) has been of decisive importance (even though is was by way of a one-sided interpretation of his intention) even for modern theology both Protestant and Catholic.

2. *Questions and tasks*. More than anything else, the impossibility of giving a final answer to the question about man — and this was

already apparent in antiquity (Heraclitus Fr., 78, 101, 115) — has once again become evident. For here it is not a matter of making a statement about a given object the nature of which is clearly outlined; the statement is itself an element in the self-articulation, the free self-shaping of the "as yet undetermined animal" (Nietzsche), so that only on looking back at the objectivations of his freedom, at his history, can man say what and who he is, and even this answer is not definitive, since his history is not ended and besides, his statement is itself always a free act of this history.

From the point of view of the theory of the sciences the problem here is to find an adequate dividing line between anthropology and the other philosophical disciplines. On the one hand anthropology is a necessary aspect of ontology, cosmology, natural theology and ethics, and these are on the other hand necessary aspects of a philosophical anthropology. Yet all philosophy cannot and should not be reduced to anthropology. So too it is hard to determine the relation of philosophical anthropology to the individual sciences (anthropology, biology, history, medicine, psychology, sociology, linguistics, etc.). It cannot simply build on them "inductively" by interpretation and synthesis, nor can it attempt to plan and structure them in an *a priori,* deductive way.

The same question arises in the relation of anthropology to the culture and life of an epoch. On the one hand it is conditioned by its times just as conversely it conditions them. From this point of view a historical review remains always questionable, since anthropology in itself, not only in the content of its answer but even in the nature and meaning of the question itself, does not always mean the same thing (and therefore it is not without significance that the name anthropology — and the discipline itself, as a defined science — came only so recently into use). On the other hand it must rise above its times to a validity which neither derives merely from the point of view of the particular period nor is able *a priori* to limit and relativize it using a concrete, supra-historical knowledge. Anthropology must therefore avoid a rationalistic and unhistorical notion of the nature and existence of man no less than an ideological fixation in a particular concrete historical or social view of man (an ideology). Yet it must not restrict itself to recording man's self-interpretation in a relativistic and positivist presentation of facts (as in historicism). It cannot — turning the temporal, historical aspect into that of material content — present an abstract notion of man nor a collection of the results of the individual sciences. It must rather be built up as a unity, which being itself independent and irreducible, must be accepted as historical, although the acceptance of this historicity does not imply the renunciation of critical reflection on it, nor of knowledge and truth. Here we find, in fact, the same form of analogy that we have in being where the attempt to extract a univocal nucleus misses the transcendental unity just as completely as does the assumption that being is merely equivocal. (See the articles *Spirit* and *Being; anima quodammodo omnia.*) Justice is not done to this unity of man — whether considered as genus or as individual (against the Cartesian body-soul dualism) — merely by distinguishing it from the brute and its proper environment. And the theory of the degrees of being does not grasp the unity of man except as something statically objectivated. It does not encompass it as the operative process of living of a being that becomes itself only in the other and has its existence only in this process of self-deprivation and self-acquisition *(red-itio)*: in an indefinable "between" — between the basis of freedom (little more than a point) in the person and the pluralism of the relations in which he lives and realizes his existence.

Thus by a variety of approaches philosophical anthropology has to secure an understanding of man: from the point of view of a philosophy of the spirit and of freedom, in the light of culture, history, religion, ethics, aesthetics, economics and technology, politics and biology; and in these his "eccentricity" and transcendence are to be demonstrated. This is done by interpreting (through hermeneutics) man's epochal condition (and, at least for Western man, Christianity is an essential element in it), because it is the context in which absolute meaning is conferred on man, the apprehension of which is what makes him human in the first place. Thus man's questionableness is revealed and his answer sought for, in the entire process of his living (especially in the religious act) as well as in theoretical reflection, in anthropology.

See also *Man* III, *Myth*, *Worship*, *Person* II, *World*, *History* I, *Historicism*, *Existence* II, *Hermeneutics*, *Religious Act*.

BIBLIOGRAPHY. M. Heidegger, *Sein und Zeit* (1927), E. T.: *Being and Time* (1962); M. Scheler, *Die Stellung des Menschen im Kosmos* (1927); W. Brüning, *Philosophische Anthropologie* (1960); M. Landmann, *Der Mensch als Schöpfer und Geschöpf der Kultur* (1961); D. Browning, *Act and Agent: An Essay in Philosophical Anthropology* (1964); J. Platt, *New Views on the Nature of Man* (1965); J. Endres, *Man as the Ontological Mean* (1965); M. Buber, *Knowledge of Man*, ed. by M. Friedmann (1966); G. de Laguna, *On Existence and the Human World* (1966); P. Le Fevre, *Understandings of Man* (1966); N. Rotenstreich, *On the Human Subject* (1966); J. Donceel, *Philosophical Anthropology* (1967).

Jörg Splett

II. Biblical

1. *Preliminary questions of hermeneutics.* None of the writings of the Old or New Testament represents a conscious attempt to produce a systematic anthropology either from the scientific, the philosophical or the theological points of view. In view of the complexity of the material covered by anthropology, which embraces the most disparate periods and branches of tradition, it is especially important to determine the line of approach of the interpreter who is looking for a self-consistent anthropology in the Bible. The nature of the evidence in Scripture, primarily religious in intention as it is, makes it futile to put questions to it which properly belong to the realm of metaphysical psychology, or still more to those of scientifically or bio-psychologically orientated phenomenology. The analysis of existence *(Dasein)* inaugurated by "existence" (existentialist) philosophy can be considered more fruitful to the extent that it is based upon the following correct position. Every historical *(geschichtlich)* understanding of "the world" has prior to, but inseparably connected with it a corresponding self-understanding of man. Thus this understanding of self acquires a central importance as the stand-point from which all anthropologically relevant statements must be understood. Admittedly in the case of the Bible the question of its anthropology must be understood as essentially a theological one, and must be investigated on that basis. But since in the case of the biblical evidence theological and anthropological lines of investigation can be shown to be one and the same, it seems possible to fulfil this requirement. For statements about God and Jesus Christ, creation and redemptive history, life and death, sin and justification, salvation and judgment all involve in the last analysis an understanding of man and his situation (which in the Bible is never considered in itself but always in relation to God) as a factor most intimately connected with them. To the extent then that this "explicitation" of man's understanding of himself (as existing by and for God, or else as having fallen away from him) has the character of revelation in the Bible, its statements about man are made "with absolute binding force". It is because of this too that "they claim to be first and alone in bringing man to an experiential knowledge of his proper (concrete historical) nature, which would otherwise remain hidden from him" (K. Rahner in *LTK,* I, col. 619).

2. *Old Testament.* The hermeneutical presuppositions of our investigation having been indicated, we must consider first the various statements of an anthropological nature to be found in the OT. The importance to be attached to these varies considerably. *Fundamental themes* are: man's wholeness as person, his relationship with God as covenant partner and as member of a community, his creatureliness, his responsibility, his consciousness of sin and his hope of salvation.

a) Regarded in his relationship with God and the world, man, the creature who has historical *(geschichtlich)* existence is essentially a creature of God subject to earthly limitations (Gen 2:7). As such he is seen as a *living personal whole.* In this view man is considered under various of his principal aspects as "flesh", as "soul" or as "spirit" (בָּשָׂר — נֶפֶשׁ — רוּחַ) but not as a compositum with these as his parts. The theological significance of this integral view of man is shown by the fact that well-being or calamity affect the entire man as an indivisible whole. As "whole person" in this sense (represented especially by the heart, לֵב as the seat of the faculties of feeling, understanding and willing), with "will" as his definitive aspect, man does not "have" a soul and body, he "is" soul and body. Thus in the later OT period the hope of salvation is expressed in terms of hope of the resurrection of the body (Is 26:19; Dan 12:2ff.; 2 Macc 7:14), a conception which is taken up and developed in the NT (Mk 12:18f.; Jn 6:39ff.; Acts 24:15; 1 Cor 15). The idea of the immortality of the soul (Wis 2:22f.; 3:4) is derived from a way of thinking which is of Greek provenance and which is anthropologically speaking completely different. It is not developed in the writings of the later OT period or in the NT.

b) OT anthropology is concerned not with the concept of man "in himself" but with man as *a creature of flesh and blood,* that is, as socially involved in family, tribal and national relationships; with the solidarity of men under blessing and curse. As a member of the community man feels himself related to God as gracious Lord of history, as covenant partner and as guide. Involved by his very nature in the community, man is also committed to his fellow man by his relationship with God. For by the terms of this relationship his fellow-man is not only equally powerless in the face of God's transcendence, but also possesses equal value as himself. He is presented as a brother who, in virtue of a right deriving from God must be protected, and in virtue of a love of neighbour commanded by God must be cherished (Lev 19:9–18, 34; 25:35–38). The responsibility of man for man is especially inculcated by the prophets (cf., for example, Is 3:13ff.; Amos 8:4ff.), and the *Torah* becomes in a certain measure the form in which the dialogue between God and men is crystallized" (V. Warnach in *Handbuch theologischer Grundbegriffe,* II, pp. 149f.).

c) In addition to the aspects of covenant partnership and dialogue, the portrayal of man in his relationship with God is dominated by an awareness of his *creaturehood.* While as derived from dust (Gen 3:19) he is absolutely impotent and dependent, this does not exclude his dignity as image of God (Gen 1:26f.) and the position of dominance which he occupies in the world (Ps 8). The two creation narratives (Gen 1–2) convey the idea of man's nature by describing how he came to be. Pre-eminent among creatures (Gen 1:26ff.; 2:7), he is endowed with the godlike faculty of speech (Gen 2:19f.). He is God's representative in the world below, and as person, in spite of all his defectibility, he is the "thou", the partner in relation to God. Created male and female (Gen 1:27; 2:18, 21ff.), man is most deeply "himself" as the "thou" in a relationship of personal love.

d) Called into life by a word ("by his name", Gen 35:10; Exod 31:2f.; Is 45:3f.) which occurs once and for all in history, but which once uttered is irrevocable, man has an *inalienable responsibility for his own acts* (Gen 2:16f.), and finds himself summoned to a decision and a response or "counter-word" (*Ant-Wort*). By his basic involvement in (salvation) history and covenant partnership, no less than by his relationship as creature and his openness to dialogue, man is the being confronted with a decision, the being who refuses, repents and finally proves himself in virtue of a saving pardon. Responsibility is intensified too in view of death, which is set before him as the strange and inexorable boundary to life, and also in view of the fact that time is bestowed upon man as *kairos,* opportunity. But in spite of all menaces and shadows (and so far as the OT is concerned, death is the ultimate shadow), a life lived responsibly, that is, in obedience to God, will in its innermost depths be joyful (1 Kg 4:20; Ps 43:4). (In the NT this joy is based upon the "joyful tidings" of definitive salvation.)

e) In his state of freedom and responsibility man has decided to refuse and to set himself in "contradiction" to himself (because — and in consequence — in contradiction to God). The OT sees *man as sinner.* Although it has not developed the idea of original sin, it designates all men as sinners (Gen 8:21; Ps 143, 2, etc.), because their hearts are filled with pride and disobedience and they refuse the claims of God and of their neighbour. Gen 3–11 depicts the outbreak and the swift spreading of sin (man's "refusal") in the world as a prelude to the vicissitudes of Israel's covenant history. Yet so far as the Bible is concerned the advent of sin is "not so much a temporal event as an ontic one, having significance for the theology of salvation" (H. Haag, *Biblische Schöpfungslehre und kirchliche Erbsündenlehre* [1966], p. 57). The guilt and liability to punishment which all men have in common is not thought of as transmitted through the medium of biological descent.

f) Suffering and death are regarded in the OT as conditions of nature rather than as punishments for sin. It is by the ordinance of God that birth is followed by death, a state in which life is reduced to a minimal, shadowy and enfeebled form of existence (Is 14:10; Ps 88:5). Indeed this can no longer be considered as life in the true sense, in which the praise of God is an essential element (Is 38:18f.). The *hope of man* is orientated towards a joyful, "replete", "worldly" life on this earth, graciously made possible for him by God, who is faithful to his promises of favour. Hopes for a saviour and a time of salvation, for resurrection and new life are only very gradually explicitated from the covenant promises of Yahweh. They develop concomitantly with a deepening of the consciousness of sin (Jer 13:23), which looks for a renewal of the heart only from God (Jer 31:31–34), for he alone could "change the human heart and so bring about perfect obedience" (G. von Rad, II, p. 217).

3. *New Testament.* In the NT "man" stands commandingly at the centre of things in the person of Jesus Christ. In him the "new man" of the promises is present, mankind constituting the new body and he the head. For the rest, NT anthropology (only the essential outlines of which can be sketched in here) is based upon the ideas of the OT. The problem of man is presented as essentially concomitant with the question of sin and redemption, and is treated of chiefly by Paul and John.

a) The vision of *Jesus* points in the same direction as that indicated in the message of the prophets but goes beyond it. He regards all men as sinners, and subjects them all to God's demand for a radical conversion (Mk 1:15), which is also, for the moment, the salvation which he himself offers. Man now stands irrevocably "between" salvation and perdition. Thus Jesus discloses the paradox of man's existence before God as judge and as gracious father (cf. R. Bultmann, I, pp. 23ff.). He does not describe the "nature" of man in abstract terms (so no superiority of the soul as opposed to the body can be deduced from Jesus' preaching), but brings man to the crisis of decision, and thereby (through the medium of his own offering of salvation) to his authentic existence. Jesus does not paint any picture of the ideal man (nor does he present himself as such an example). True to the tenor of OT thought he finds reality in the true sense in history. It is with man as he exists in concrete history that Jesus is concerned, and it is to him that his claims are addressed. This emphasis on man as he exists in concrete history is most clearly exemplified in Jesus' radical interpretation of the command to love one's neighbour, in which even enemies are regarded as neighbours (Mt 5:43ff.). The claim of God summoning him to a decision reaches him in and through the concrete demand represented by the continuous presence of his neighbour to him in the world (Mt 25), and it is by his response to this that he stands acquitted or condemned. With Jesus' preaching, salvation as well as the possibility of perdition are in the world and among men. The position of man "between" salvation and loss is reduced to its basic anthropological dimensions. In Jesus himself — as preached by the Church after his death and resurrection — the character of absolute salvation in this intermediate position is revealed. The new man belongs entirely to God: he is Son of God and child of God.

b) *Paul,* in the perspective of the death and resurrection of Christ, makes more explicit the theological anthropology latent in the preaching of Jesus. He is able to sustain the dialectical tension involved in statements about man, in spite of his dualistic and Gnostic environment, precisely because of the perspective of redemption in Jesus Christ. Just as his Christology is at the same time soteriology, teaching about the redemption of man, so "Paul's theology is, at the same time, anthropology" because "every assertion about God is simultaneously an assertion about man" (R. Bultmann, II, p. 191). It is in a soteriological sense that Paul develops (although unsystematically) his anthropology in statements about the condition of man as he was before the coming of Christ, unredeemed, and man as he is in Christ, redeemed, about man as he was, under the law, and man as he is, in faith, man as he was, subject to the dominion of sin, and man as he is, enjoying the freedom of a child of God. In the light of the gospel of grace all individual, social and national distinctions lose their ultimate significance. The Christian message is concerned with a new man in a new community, the Church. Although Paul takes over concepts from Greek tradition (νοῦς, διάνοια, συνείδησις, etc.), he adheres to the line of thought the OT in refraining from speculations about the nature, elements and properties of man. Hellenistic dualism, which had infiltrated into Hellenistic Judaism, is no less foreign to his thought, as is attested by his statements concerning the body. For him the hoped-for resurrection is to involve a transformation of the body (1 Cor 15).

Among Paul's anthropological concepts (σῶμα, ψυχή, πνεῦμα, ζωή, νοῦς, συνείδησις, καρδία, σάρξ) is the broadest in extension and the most complex, while *sarx* is the most important and the most difficult. These therefore deserve special attention.

The body (σῶμα) for Paul is intrinsically necessary to the being of man (1 Cor 15:15 ff.). "Body" is not just how man appears: it is often used to describe the person as a whole. Man is body (Rom 12:1; 1 Cor 7:4; Phil 1:20). As such he can view himself objectively in his active and passive roles, be at one with himself or divided against himself, this relationship with himself always ensuing from, and being an expression of his relationship with God. For the unavoidable necessity of taking a decision before God (laid upon him as creature) affects man as a whole. Man finds himself a sinner in this world, in the power (σάρξ) of alien forces, in the domain of the flesh considered as human self-sufficency and self-seeking, which is rebellion against God (Rom 8:6 f.; 10:3; 2 Cor 10:5). When he is considering man as alienated from himself and in opposition to God, Paul calls him flesh, the sinner. Flesh is "put off" at baptism (Rom 8:9 f.), while body, man as a physical whole, is transformed at the resurrection (1 Cor 15:44; Phil 3:21). The "old man", man as he was prior to Christ's coming to him, whether he is under the "law" (which does not prevent sin) or "without the law", is in a state of radical division which prevents him from achieving a free and integral existence (Rom 2:12 ff.). Only when he believes in Christ and so turns his attention from his own righteousness (always presumed in his "glorification of self") to the mercy of God, is he set free with the freedom of authentic existence, at peace with God and thereby free too for a life in which he is united to his fellows in fraternal love. But man continues in the state of eschatological tension, awaiting the completion of salvation; for although this has already "taken place" and "been appropriated", it is for all that not yet fully accomplished and bestowed. The freedom of the children of God is either achieved in its fullness or else lost once more to the power of sin, which works through man's self-seeking. The position of man is characterized by the imperative no less than by the indicative of salvation (cf. Gal 3:27; Rom 3:14; Col 2:12, 20). But in faith in

Jesus Christ the possibility of fully personal (eschatological) existence is given; that is, of an existence in the midst of this world which has still been emancipated from this world. In this faith there is no more fear of death, but rather hope for the "appearance in glory" (Col 3:4) and the love that is man's response to this (Col 3:14).

c) The statements concerning man in *the Johannine writings* are couched in terms which are still more explicitly Christological in import. The existence of man is determined by his origin: man is "of this world" considered as the domain of Satan, of evil, darkness and the lie. Man is closed in on himself in the darkness of self-assertion manifested in disobedience, unbelief and hatred towards his brothers. For John as for Paul the cosmos is above all the world of men who, by reason of their wickedness, would be lost, were it not for the coming of the revealer, the Son. By sending his Son the Father does indeed bring the world to a crisis, but from the motive of love (Jn 3:16 f.). He sends him not to judge the world but to save it (1 Jn 4:9, 14). For man in his self-assurance and in his desire to confine himself to the sphere of the self-evident (in which the peculiar "extravagance" of man stands revealed) is imprisoned within the domain of evil; and he can be freed from this only by the "birth from above" (Jn 3), of God. By believing in the sending of the Son man receives a fresh possibility of life starting from a fresh source. This implies a withdrawal from the world amounting to the "shattering . . . of all human norms and evaluations" (R. Bultmann, II, p. 67). This new life is the eschatological existence in which the believer becomes a stranger in the world, yet finds a new home in the community of the faithful by his freedom from sin as well as by the love of his brothers, in which he proves his sinlessness (1 Jn 3:14–18; 4:19 ff.). It is not for man actively to decide whether he will be born again or not. This is achieved rather by his "submission" (by submitting himself to be "drawn" by the Father, Jn 6:44) in the act of faith as an act of radical "self-surrender". With regard to the Christ-event, the claim which the revealer makes upon men introduces a crisis into their lives and by the immediate decision which he educes from them to believe or to disbelieve reveals them for what they are, either children of Satan "from below" or children of God "from above". Human existence does not thereby cease to be a time for decision. Rather this aspect of its significance is brought to the fore. As believer man must abide in Jesus' word and act according to Jesus' command (1 Jn 1:6f.; 2:3ff.). Naturally man is anxious to find out about future salvation, but in John the strong emphasis upon eschatology as a present fact finally draws man away from all speculations concerning the "when" and "how", and concentrates his mind on the "that" of future glory. Though this is a truly "future" reality, man finds it in the unity of life with Son and Father which he achieves by faith in the here and now (cf. 1 Jn 1:2f.; Jn 17:3). The message of the Bible is that to be a man means in its deepest sense to live by grace.

See also *Existence* II, *Creation* II.

BIBLIOGRAPHY. See the articles καρδία, νοῦς, πνεῦμα, συνείδησις, σῶμα, ψυχή in *TWNT;* H. W. Robinson, *The Christian Doctrine of Man* (1911); E. D. Burton, *Spirit, Soul and Flesh* (1918); W. G. Kümmel, *Das Bild des Menschen in dem Neuen Testament* (1944); K. Galling, *Das Bild vom Menschen in biblischer Sicht* (1947); A. R. Johnson, *The Vitality of the Individual in the Thought of Ancient Israel* (1949); R. Tournay, "L'Eschatologie individuelle dans les psaumes", *Revue Biblique* 56 (1949), pp. 481–506; F. C. Grant, *An Introduction to New Testament Thought* (1950); H. van Meyenfeldt, *Het Hart in het Oude Testament* (1950); S. V. McCasland, "The Image of God in Paul", *JBL* 69 (1950), pp. 85–100; C. Ryder Smith, *The Biblical Doctrine of Man* (1951); H. Mehl-Koehnlein, *L'homme selon l' Apôtre Paul* (1951); W. Zimmerli, *Das Menschenbild des Alten Testaments* (2nd ed., 1951); J. A. T. Robinson, *The Body* (1952); R. Bultmann, *Theology of the New Testament*, 2 vols. (1952–55); D. Cairns, *The Image of God in Man* (1953); G. Pidoux, *L'homme dans l' Ancient Testament* (1953); G. E. Wright, *The Biblical Doctrine of Man in Society* (1954); W. D. Stacey, *The Pauline View of Man* (1956); S. Laeuchli, "Monism and Dualism in the Pauline Anthropology", *Biblical Research* 3 (1958), pp. 15–27; D. Lys, *Nephesch. Histoire de l'âme dans la révélation d'Israel* (1959); G. Bornkamm, "Gott und Mensch im der Antike", *Gesammelte Aufsätze*, II (1959); G. von Rad, *Old Testament Theology*, 2 vols. (1962–65); P. van Imschoot, *Theology of the Old Testament* (1965).

Rudolf Pesch

III. Theological

Among the things directly spoken of by the word of God is man's knowledge (e.g., Rom 1:19ff.; *D* 1806); it follows that

methodological reflection by theology on its own activity is itself theology. What is intended here is, therefore, a *theological* reflection on theological anthropology, not on the secular sciences which in their various ways deal with man *a posteriori* and not on the basis of the revealed word of God. How a theological anthropology is distinguished from an *a priori,* transcendental understanding of man by metaphysics, cannot be laid down beforehand by definition. That is a question which belongs to theological anthropology itself. In this perspective a glance at the history of theological anthropology shows that it has not yet been worked out in Catholic theology as a coherent, comprehensive unity and that for that reason what is said here inevitably consists chiefly of preliminary reflections.

A. History

In these historical notes it is not a question of the history of dogma regarding the various propositions which theology expressly lays down as theses concerning man: the creation of the first human beings, the spirituality, individuality and immortality of the soul, its relation to the body, original sin, redemption, grace, justification and all that is said of man in moral theology and eschatology (for which the relevant articles may be consulted). Here it can only be a matter of indicating the questions which orientate these various branches of knowledge towards an originally unified anthropology.

1. *Scripture.* Divine revelation in the Old and New Testaments contains of course statements about man and these assume absolutely binding force and claim alone to bring man to an experiential knowledge of his own real (concrete, historical) nature which otherwise would remain hidden from him or be his only in a repressed way — "suppressed" (Rom 1:18). Man is the being who is without parallel in his world, so much a personal subject that he is God's partner, in comparison with whom everything else is by its nature only man's environment. Man's subjectivity as mind, freedom, eternal individual significance and value before God, constitutes his capacity for partnership with God in an authentic dialogue, which makes possible a "covenant" (a genuine, responsible re-action to God despite his universal causality), and

extends even to the absolute intimacy of "face to face" in inaccessible light and the "sharing in the divine nature", in knowing as we are known. It even constitutes the possibility of God's expression of himself in the incarnation. And it makes man truly a being who, ultimately, is not a mere part of a greater whole, the world, but who is himself the whole in a unique way in each individual, in other words, a person, a personal subject, authentically "existent" as opposed to merely "there". As a consequence the genuinely historical, i.e., unrepeatable, non-cyclical history of the cosmos is, in its ultimate significance, from beginning to end a component of the history which takes place between God and man; the history of man is not an element in a comprehensive cosmogony. The world is, therefore, only the preparatory basis which renders possible the history of man (and of the angels) and has the ultimate ground of its own possibility in that history; the goal of the cosmos is determined before God by the history of man. From these and other reasons it follows that the statement of what man is, when theologically made, is not a proposition in one branch of study alongside others, but the statement of everything that has to be said. For there is no domain of reality (at least since the Incarnation of the Logos) which does not formally (and not merely indirectly and by reduction) enter into theological anthropology. This is what constitutes the special character of such an anthropology: it is also the whole of theology.

Nevertheless this revealed affirmation of radical personal subjectivity as fundamentally expressed in Scripture, is not itself an anthropology such as is meant here, and this in two respects. In the first place, Scripture does not attempt explicitly and systematically to organize the data on the basis of a conscious principle. Secondly, the categories used in the statement of this direct anthropology are to a large extent those of the world of things, of mere objects, and of the ontology that can be derived from it, and so the danger remains of mistaking the special theological character of man and of regarding him as an item in a world of objects having only the reality of things.

2. *The Fathers*. Patristic theology represents an advance to the extent that it makes the first attempts at systematization (Tertullian's *De Anima* is the beginning) and seeks more clearly for unifying principles, for example, the idea of man as image and likeness of God, that of the history of the universe and of mankind as the history of divinization, that of the spiritualization of the universe, etc. In all this, however, essentially the same state of development remains. In fact the persistent latent danger continues that the distinction and union between man and the God who is communicating himself to man are either reduced to an opposition and union of spirit and matter (so that with one part of his nature man from the start stands on God's side: Greek theology) or of the sinner and the merciful God (Western theology: Augustine). In that way the beginning (the Garden of Eden) and the end (eternal life) are deprived of their profound unity-in-opposition, because the history of the world is only the history of its restoration, not the free history of God himself in the world.

3. *The Middle Ages*. As regards medieval theology, an indication that no decisive advance towards an independent anthropology had yet been made can be seen in the fact that the various components remained dispersed among very disparate treatises, despite all the systematization of the Summas. The reason is that man, overlooking his own subjectivity, in which alone he possesses and knows everything else, saw himself as one creature among others about which he "naively" made his statements one by one, without recognizing that in doing so he always implicitly affirms and strives towards himself and his own mystery (that is, God himself). Consequently in these medieval treatises the various creatures are simply listed one after another (angels, corporeal world, man). This "objective" view could not do full justice to the special character of man. The Garden of Eden was taken as the starting-point from which to speak of man, but not on the principle that such teaching about man's original condition is based on aetiological retrospect, and is ultimately intended to say something about our own situation. That is also evident in other features, of which a few may be mentioned as examples: to a large extent reflection was lacking on the history of salvation; the necessary categories were scarcely developed beyond the data already

expressly contained in the original revelation. An analysis of faith and in general an existential description of the process of justification were still largely lacking; what was found interesting about the latter was what could be comprised within the categories of the various causes. The doctrine of grievous sin as essentially distinct from venial sin had not yet inspired an existential analysis of human action in general. There was not yet really any theological analysis of fundamental human experiences: anguish, joy, death, etc. The individual human being was still too much a mere "instance" of the universal idea of man. The world as such (in contradistinction to the Church) and as much more than simply the scene of concern for human necessities, as a condition of attaining salvation, scarcely really existed yet. The world was something ready-made by God, in which man works out his salvation; and it was not yet explicitly something which by God's command had still to be brought about.

Yet there are already signs that the mind of man was moving towards a genuine anthropology. The question of the history of individual salvation was propounded and answered in more individual terms: beatific vision even before the general judgment; the doctrine of the *votum sacramenti* and, therefore, of a non-sacramental possibility of salvation; the inviolability of the conscience. The profound difference in nature and consequences between original and personal sin became plain. Through a clear grasp of the really supernatural character of grace and of the last end even in relation to the spiritual creature in the state of innocence, the Greek and Western danger (to which we have already referred), of misconceiving the fundamental relation between God and man, was in principle eliminated. The growing recognition of the relative independence of philosophy in relation to theology, of the State in relation to the Church, of the domains of culture in relation to religious life, did not simply produce a dangerous impression that religion is a partial section of human reality, but (in the long run at least) compelled reflection on the reason why that is not the case: the transcendental subjectivity of religion, which can be merely a sector in its predicamental zone without thereby ceasing to imply the whole and to penetrate and determine it. Scholastic ontology, as a doctrine of being and mind, provided what was in fact a true basis for the recognition of genuine subjectivity, for it noted that anything is or has being, in proportion to the degree in which it is subjectivity in possession of itself, *reditio completa*.

4. *Modern times* are the centuries-long process of man's understanding himself as subject, even when he will not admit this. From the standpoint of the theology of history the process is something that had to be (δεῖ) — and from the start a "fall of man". We mean that the process never in fact took place except as a fall, though it "could" have been otherwise. It was a fall in which a very radical religious subjectivity before God was isolated in abstraction against Incarnation, Church and universal essence; a fall in which an individualistic subjectivity closed in upon itself and set itself up as independent, without transcending itself towards God. But the same process is also found, even if more hesitant and anxious, in the development of the Church and its awareness of its faith. It shows itself for instance in the factors to which we have already referred, in the course of Church life and orthodox theology. The *analysis fidei* becomes a problem. Historical theology is founded. Recognition of the wide possibility of salvation increases. Nature and supernatural grace are more sharply distinguished. World, culture and State are more clearly left free as the scene and objects of independent responsible lay action not directly and in the concrete subject to the Church. The question of God's mercy "to me personally" is raised just as radically within the Church as with Luther (Ignatius Loyola, Francis of Sales). A logic of concrete individual knowledge of the particular will of God here and now precisely for me personally is developed (the *Spiritual Exercises* of St. Ignatius). But there is no actual construction of an anthropology. Teaching about man is still divided between the various treatises and the systematic basis of anthropology as a whole is not explicitly worked out. Anthropology in the sense intended here is, therefore, a task which theology has still not fulfilled. It is not, of course, the case that the various propositions that such an anthropology would contain have still to be found, for of course they are the statements

of revelation concerning man. Nevertheless Catholic theology has not yet developed a systematic anthropology corresponding to the knowledge man has attained of himself as a "subject".

B. Attempt at a Systematic Outline

1. *Basis.* Only a theological affirmation can enter into consideration for this fundamental principle, for one of any other kind would make theology intrinsically dependent on other doctrines of man. Consequently what man knows about himself "naturally", i.e., independently of the historical revelation of God's word, must be drawn from this fundamental starting-point, otherwise it would be without importance for a theological anthropology as such, even though theology itself leaves man free to take seriously such secular knowledge of his own nature. A possible fundamental theological anthropology is subject to the same conditions as fundamental theology in relation to revelation and theology generally. The presupposition on which it is based is one laid down for theology by theology itself as a comprehensive whole, not an *a priori* foreign to it. The light of faith is the comprehensive factor which, from the moment theology is pursued at all, "supersedes" the light of reason while preserving this as a component of itself. The basis which we are seeking, since it is a theological one, and therefore implies a believer who has heard it, can certainly be regarded as *a posteriori,* i.e., as contained in what is heard in the historical message of faith. That message, being from God himself, presents itself by the very nature of its source (and despite its historically *a posteriori* character) as comprehensive and regulative. How that is possible despite the fact that what is heard *a posteriori* seems to fall under the measure of man's *a priori* self-understanding, is a question which it is precisely the task of a genuine theological anthropology to elucidate and one which is decisive for its own very existence. It is the question why an interpretation of man which comes from outside, in a historically contingent way, must not by that very fact always come too late to figure as a fundamental interpretation of man (which, as a theological one, it tries to be and must be). For man is a being primordially in possession of himself,

a personal subject. Ultimately the solution is that man's adequate *a priori* knowledge of himself includes the light of faith as a "supernatural existential". Man, therefore, does not approach the *a posteriori* revealed doctrine of man with an *a priori* norm alien to theology. Morever, by his very nature man is necessarily orientated towards what is historically *a posteriori* and cannot simply reject this in a rationalistic way as non-essential. As, however, in all his reflection man always finds himself historically conditioned, he can never fully and explicitly formulate this concrete historical situation by any process of reflection (called science). It remains part of himself as he accepts himself confidently and spontaneously, though understandingly. For that reason it is quite legitimate to begin with the factual self-knowledge obtained from faith heard and historically exercised, provided that this starting-point stands up to explicit reflection.

The Christian man knows that despite his being a creature and despite his sinfulness — and in fact in it — he is a person spoken to by God in history, in the word of God's absolute, free self-disclosure in grace. This affirmation is directly intelligible for the Christian as a summary of what he hears in faith about himself, and is also suitable as a fundamental principle of theological anthropology. (That of course is not intended to deny the possibility of a more clearly defined and simpler approach. It merely indicates the basic self-understanding of the Christian.)

2. *The development* of this basic principle into a Christian theological anthropology can only be sketched in rough outline here. For we are merely trying to indicate the nature and method of a theological anthropology which does not yet exist; we are not trying to construct one.

On the basis of this fundamental idea the most comprehensive definition of man would have to be worked out: the fact that he is a creature, a determining characteristic which comprises the distinction between nature and grace. It is true that what primarily would have to be envisaged would be man's character as a created personal subject. (The created character of mere things is a deficient mode of such personal existence.) It would be the limitless receptivity to God in one who is not God, a determination both positive and negative, both aspects of which increase in the same proportion before the incommensurable God.

It might then be shown that, despite the possibility — which need not be further defined here — of recognizing by natural reason the fact of revelation, its true hearer is he who accepts it in the absolute (and therefore loving) obedience of faith in such a way that the quality of the word of God as God's revelation of himself is not lost or, through the (necessary) *a priori* of a finite human being's capacity to hear it, reduced to a human utterance on the merely created level. From this theological starting-point, it would be possible to establish the root distinction between nature and grace without having antecedently to assume the purely natural concept of "pure nature" as a fixed philosophical norm — instead of as a concept regulated by theology. Grace is the condition of the possibility of the capacity for connatural reception of God's self-manifestation in word (faith — love) and in the beatific vision; nature is the constitution of man which is presupposed by, and persists in, this capacity to hear. That nature persists in such a way that the sinner and unbeliever can shut themselves to this self-manifestation of God without thereby implicitly affirming what they are overtly denying (as in a man's culpable refusal of his metaphysical nature). Nature also persists in such a way that this self-communication, in relation to man as already created, can still appear as the gratuitous marvel of personal love which of "himself" (= nature) man cannot demand, although he is essentially open to it (nature as positive *potentialis obedientalis* for supernatural grace). On the basis of this nature one could seek a theological understanding of all that man implies as "spirit": absolute transcendence, freedom, eternal validity (immortality), personality.

On the basis of the historicity of the hearing of the word of God, it would be possible to bring out the theological thesis of the historicity of man himself with its full content and significance: his intrinsic situation in the world as his environment, his corporeality, the racial unity of humanity of which he is a part, his sexuality, his social orientation (family, State and Church), the character of his existence as a test, as historically conditioned and incalculable. And there is the incalculable pluralism of his nature, which means that though he is primordially one and not a subsequent sum total, he cannot dominate this unity in the concrete, but must constantly strive anew to attain the obligatory form of his existence.

It would in itself be possible to bring the whole of dogmatic theology into theological anthropology, in view of the fact that man is endowed by grace not only with something created but with God himself. This, however, is not advisable for various reasons, ultimately based on the inescapable dualism in spiritual creatures between what belongs to their "essence" and what to their "concrete existence". Hence theological anthropology will only include statements which characterize man in every situation of his history, whether these characteristics are natural or supernatural existentials. It will therefore be appropriate to assign separate treatises to the history of salvation (or perdition), moral theology and the prospective aetiology of the *eschata* on the basis of the eschatological situation as it is "now". And separate treatment will certainly be reserved for doctrines directly concerning God. Not as though God (one and triune), of whom theology speaks, could be spoken of without something being said about man on whom by grace that God is bestowed. But because man is the being who by his very nature has his centre outside himself, in God (and only in that way is truly at home in himself), his statements about God should be made outside theological anthropology, in a theology which must never forget the actual concrete situation of man.

3. Special attention must finally be given to the *relation between Christology and theological anthropology*. In earlier times this problem was not perceived as a problem in the methodology of theology. People already knew what "man" was when they set about saying that Christ is a true man. It was, therefore, at most a question of considering in Christology what this statement did not include in the case of Christ. In addition they were clear that Christ is man in an "ideal way" and so is an example to men and the ideal model for a theological doctrine of man, but a model which, strictly speaking, was not required by anthropology. At the present time, since K. Barth and K. Heim, the problem of the relation between

the two treatises must be given serious attention. In the first place Catholic theology must reflect on the fact that a good number of its statements about man (resurrection of the body, divinizing grace) are only possible since the existence of Christology. This at least suggests that such statements were not merely contemporaneous, and that this part of theological anthropology which gives every other part its deep significance and measure, should be considered objectively as an effect of Christ's reality (and not merely "by way of merit"), and subjectively as a consequence of Christology. If furthermore the Logos himself became man, that statement is not understood if all that is seen in it is the affirmation of the "assumption" of a reality which has no intrinsic relation to the person assuming it and which could just as well have been replaced by something else. On the contrary, the Incarnation is only rightly envisaged if Christ's humanity is not only, ultimately speaking, a merely extrinsic instrument by which a God who remains invisible makes himself known, but is rather precisely what God himself becomes (though remaining God) when he exteriorizes himself into the dimension of what is other than himself, of the non-divine. Even if it is obvious that God could create the world without the Incarnation, it is nevertheless compatible with that statement that the possibility of creation has its ground in the radical possibility of God's self-exteriorization (for in the divine simplicity different possibilities cannot simply be juxtaposed without connection). In that case, however, the ultimate definition of man is that he is the possible mode of existence of God if God exteriorizes himself to what is other than himself; man is the potential brother of Christ. Precisely if the *potentia obedientalis* for the hypostatic union and for grace (that of Christ) are not merely capacities among others but human nature itself, and if the latter (nature = *potentia obedientalis*), which is not something self-evident, is known from its actuation, then it will appear most clearly and reveal its true mystery only in its highest actuation: that of being the other mode of existence of God himself. As viewed both in relation to God and to man, Christology therefore appears as the most radical recapitulation and transcendent culmination of theological anthropology. Consequently though theological anthropology would need at least at some point to have Christology as its criterion and guide, it is nevertheless not appropriate to sketch out theological anthropology solely on the basis of Christology. It is true that we never find man outside of a situation of partnership with the word of God, and this partnership does in fact only disclose its ultimate meaning in the God-man, in whom speaker and hearer, word expressed and total attention are one and the same person. Nevertheless we encounter this unsurpassable culmination of the history of that partnership within our human history as a whole in which we come to know man. And we already know something of man — partly by revelation — when we meet Christ and understand that he is a man. It would therefore lead to a limitation of theological anthropology if we tried to pursue it solely on the basis of its goal, Christology, for the ultimate experience does not annul the earlier.

See also *Metaphysics, Existence* II, III, *Essence, Person* II, *Dualism, Augustinianism, Creation* II, *World, Spirituality* III D, *Nature* I, *Jesus Christ* III, *Incarnation.*

BIBLIOGRAPHY. E. Brunner, *Dogmatics,* 3 vols. (1949–62); K. Barth, *Church Dogmatics,* 5 vols. (1949–65); R. Bultmann, *Theology of the New Testament,* 2 vols. (1952–55); M. Schmaus, *Katholische Dogmatik,* 5 vols. (5th ed., 1958 ff.); A. von Harnack, *History of Dogma,* 4 vols. (reprint 1958); K. Rahner, *Theological Investigations,* I–V (1961–66); G. von Rad, *Old Testament Theology,* 2 vols. (1962–65); B. Welte, *Heilsverständnis* (1966); H. Urs von Balthasar, *A Theological Anthropology* (1967); K. Rahner, *Hearers of the Word* (1968); H. Schlier, *The Relevance of the New Testament* (1968).

Karl Rahner

MANDAEISM

1. *Introduction.* Mandaeism is the religion of the Mandaeans, a Gnostic baptist sect which still survives in Southern Iraq and Southwestern Iran (Chusistan) with perhaps 5000 members. The name which they use of themselves, *mandāiā,* from *manda,* "knowledge", means "Gnostics", while the older term by which they described themselves, *naṣorāiā* (Nasoraeans) means "Observants". The ambiguous term *Sabeans* (baptists) which is found in Moslem literature from the Koran on (*Sura,* 2, 59; 5, 73; 22, 17) may possibly

refer to the Mandaeans (among others), who are known at the present day as *subba* (baptists) by the Arabs around them.

The main books of the Mandaeans are: *Ginzā* ("The Treasure"), ed. by H. Petermann (1867), tr. by M. Lidzbarski (1925); the *Book of John,* ed. and tr. by M. Lidzbarski (1908–15); *Qolastā* ("Selection"; prayers and hymns for baptism and for the ceremony of the ascent of the soul), ed. and tr. by M. Lidzbarski (1920) and E. S. Drower (1959). Important books by Lady Drower include: *Diwan Abatur* (1950); *The Haran Gawaita and the Baptism of Hibil-Ziwa* (1953), *The Thousand and Twelve Questions* (1960), and *A Pair of Nasoraean Commentaries* (1963).

The Mandaean magical texts from Mesopotamia are important because of their great age (bowls of the 6th century, ed. by H. Pognon [1898/9]; lead tablets of the 4th century, ed. by M. Lidzbarski [1909]). The *Ginzā,* the *Book of John* and the *Qolastā* were compiled in the 7th–8th centuries from texts which were in part very much older. Mandaean literature was written in an East Aramaic dialect, now understood only by the priests. The closest parallel to the Mandaean script is in the Elymaen inscriptions of Tang-i-Sarwak in Chusistan (2nd century A.D.). In Southern Babylonia, the existence of the Mandaeans at least in the 6th century is attested by Theodore bar Konai (8th century), and by the Acts of the Persian martyrs by Simon bar Sabba for the 5th century. The references to the Muġtasilah ("Washers") in An-Nadin (10th century) could indicate the Mandaeans. The Muġtasilah were also known as the Sabeans of the Marshes. The attempts to identify the Mandaeans with the Hemerobaptists, Masbothaeans und Sebuaeans of the Christian heresiologues rest on insecure foundations. The *Psalms of Thomas* from a collection of Coptic Manichaean psalms, ed. and tr. by C. Allberry (1938), show close affinities with the hymns of the *Ginzā* (the "Left" *Ginzā*) — which may therefore be placed in the 3rd century. Affinities with the Sethians, the Baruch-Gnostics of Justin, the Naassenes and especially the Marcosians indicate some connection with early Gnosis (cf. also the *Odes of Solomon*). The hypothesis that Mandaeism as a whole is a late phenomenon, as defended, e.g., by H. Lietzmann, is untenable.

2. *Doctrine, worship, ethics.* The myths of Mandaeism hardly allow of a systematic presentation, since the various strands of tradition are often intermingled without any attempt at harmonization and at times are left in open contradiction. Hence only a few of the main lines will be noted here. The world of light and its ruler, the "Great Life" or the Great Mānā (Mānā = vessel, soul), with his Uthras ("Beings of Light") is in absolute opposition to the world of darkness (black or muddy water) which is ruled by such demons as Ur and Krun and the queen of demons, Rūhā. The "Fall" from the kingdom of light begins with the emanations of the "Second Life" (Jōshamīn) and goes on through the "Third Life" (Abathur, "Holder of the Scales", the judge of souls) down to his "Son", the demiurge Ptahil, who creates the earth (Tibil) from the black water, without the consent of the supreme God. Rūhā and Ur engender the twelve signs of the zodiac and the seven planets, who then, with the aid of Ptahil, create the body of Adam. The soul coming from the realm of light, "Adakas-Zīwā" (the Secret Adam of Brightness) is enclosed in the bodies of men. Saviours and messengers (summed up under the designation of the "Strange Man"), especially Mandā d'Hayye ("Gnosis of Life") and Hibil-Zīwā (The Bright Abel), along with Shitil (Seth) and Anosh-Uthra (Enosh) reveal to men the Gnosis of salvation and the rites necessary to salvation. Meanwhile Rūhā and her powers strive to entangle the human race in the bonds of error and ignorance. They found the false religions (Judaism, Zoroastrianism, Christianity [Jesus being regarded as a false prophet] and Islam), who persecute the community of the Mandaeans. But the souls of those who keep the strict commandments of the Mandaean ethics and perform the prescribed rites ascend after death through the "guard-houses" of the planetary demons and reach the judge of souls, Abathur, who weighs their deeds. Then they return to their homeland in the realm of light. But most of the eschatological doctrine is obscure. There is an end of the world or worlds and a final judgment ("the great day of the end"), which is undergone by the demons and the souls which had not been purified even by then in the purgatories of the planetary spheres. But Jōshamīn, Abathur and Ptahil are rehabilitated as beings of light and return to the realm of light.

There is a general intrinsic consistency in the Mandaean religion in the realm of the liturgy, which is the basis of the religious life of the Mandaeans. The two fundamental rites are the *maṣbūtā* (baptism) in running water ("Jordan"), which is necessary to salvation and is constantly repeated, and the *massiqtā* (ascent), the ceremony of the ascent of the soul. Both rites include a meal of bread and water. There are also a number of ordinary lustral rites. The Mandaean ethics differs from that of the other Gnostic sects by its positive attitude to life, which is obviously due to the Jewish factors in Mandaeism. The Mandaeans actually view marriage with favour, and make it a precept.

3. *The Mandaean problem.* What is of importance here is the origin of Mandaeism and its relationship to Judaism and Christianity. Though the Mandaeans are early attested in Babylon and south-west Iran, their original settlements were in the West, as Lidzbarski already maintained, in the general direction of Jewish or semi-Jewish baptist sects of the eastern boundaries of Syria and Palestine. This is suggested strongly by the Mandaean word for baptize, *ṣb'*, which is West Aramaic (for East Aramaic *'md*); by the sometimes exaggeratedly strict Jewish ethics, such as the precept to marry, which admitted of no exceptions; by the amount of Jewish elements in their mythology and its connections with the western and northern Semites. The sagas of Miryai and of Haran-Gawaita, according to which the (proto)-Mandaeans emigrated to Haran under the Parthian King Artabanos (1st to 3rd century A. D.) may point in the same direction. Haran would have been a stage on their way to Southern Mesopotamia. A break with Judaism at one stage is also suggested by the anti-Jewish polemic which is mostly very fierce. The Mandaean baptism is fundamentally no doubt a Gnostic re-interpretation of Jewish ablutions, which was only later further developed, under Nestorian influences. Nestorian and other Christian influences such as the observance of Sunday are secondary. The Mandaeans' attitude to Christianity is hostile, probably as a result of persecutions. The figure of John the Baptist occurs only in late traditions in Mandaean literature, and the name sometimes given to the Mandaeans, the "Christians of John", is misleading. Some scholars assume that there is a connection between the proto-Mandaeans and the Gnostic traditions which are supposed to be echoed in the NT, especially in Jn (so, for example, R. Bultmann).

See also *Manichaeism, Gnosis, Gnosticism.*

BIBLIOGRAPHY. R. Bultmann, "Die Bedeutung der neuerschlossenen mandäischen und manichäischen Quellen für das Verständnis des Johannes-Evangeliums", *Zeitschrift für die neutestamentliche Wissenschaft* 24 (1925), pp. 100–47; H. Lietzmann, *Ein Beitrag zur Mandäerfrage* (1930); H. Jonas, *Gnosis und spätantiker Geist,* I (1934; 3rd ed., 1964); id., *The Gnostic Religion* (1958; 2nd revised ed., 1963); J. Thomas, *Le mouvement baptiste en Palestine et Syrie* (1935); E. S. Drower, *The Mandaeans of Iraq and Iran* (1937; reprinted 1962); R. Bultmann, *Das Johannes-Evangelium* (1942); C. H. Dodd, *The Interpretation of the Fourth Gospel* (1953), ch. IV: "Mandaeism"; C. Colpe, in *RGG,* IV, cols. 709–12; E. S. Drower, *The Secret Adam* (1960); K. Rudolph, *Die Mandäer,* 2 vols. (1960, 1961); G. Widengren, *Die Mandäer* (1961); R. Macuch, "Zur Frühgeschichte der Mandäer", *Theologische Literaturzeitung* 90 (1965), pp. 649–60; id., *Handbook of Classical and Modern Mandaic* (1965); R. Haardt, *Die Gnosis — Wesen und Zeugnisse* (1967) (selected texts).

Robert Haardt

MANICHAEISM

1. *Introduction.* Manichaeism is the religion founded by Mani (Manes, Manichaeus; Μάνης, Μανιχαῖος; Syriac, Persian and Arabic: *Mani*). Mani was of the higher Parthian nobility, born in A. D. 216 in Babylon, where his father, Patik, joined a baptist sect (called in Syriac the *menaqqedē,* in Arabic *al muġtasilah,* "the washers", possibly akin to the Mandaeans). Mani also adhered to the sect in his early youth. Inspired by divine revelation, which he received according to the legend at the ages of twelve and twenty-four, he began to preach in 240 as the envoy of God. He proclaimed his revelations in a missionary journey in the "land of the Indians", the Iranian provinces of Turan, Maqran and north-west India. Here he apparently came into contact with Buddhism. On his return he received permission for his missionary work and protection for his religion from King Shapur I (*c.* 242–273). He travelled widely on his missions throughout the Sassanid kingdom, and continued his work successfully under Ormuzd I (273–274). But under Bahram I (274–277), he was arrested at the instigation

of the Zoroastrian priests *(magi)* and after a trial before Bahram in Gunde-Shapur (Beth Lapat) was thrown into prison, where he died after twenty-six days in chains (14 February 276 or 26 February 277). Conflicting reports say that he was crucified or flayed alive. The sources speak of Mani's death as crucifixion, a borrowing from the passion of Jesus. Crucifixion is the Manichaean term for martyrdom in general.

Mani's authorship is well attested for the following writings, in which, in the hope of preventing schism, he deliberately committed to writing his revelations: (I) *Shapurakan,* "The Book dedicated to Shapur"; (II) *The Great* or *Living Gospel* — possibly with a volume of illustrations annexed, the "eikon"; (III) *The Treasure of Life;* (IV) *The Pragmateia* ("Treatise"); (V) *The Book of the Mysteries;* (VI) *The Book of the Giants;* (VII) a collection of letters. The *Shapurakan* is in middle Persian, the rest are in Eastern Aramaic. Fragments of most of the writings are preserved in various languages (the *Epistula Fundamenti* which is frequently cited by Augustine is possibly identical with the *Letter on the Two Principles* mentioned by An-Nadim). This canon is followed by a copious post-canonical literature in the languages of the missionary territories of Manichaeism. There are historical and didactic texts, psalms or hymns, letters, rules for a good confession, etc.

The primary sources (on which see bibliography) only came to light at and after the end of the 19th century, when the Turfan Expeditions in the region of Turfan in Chinese Turkestan discovered the remains of original Manichaean literature in three Iranian dialects (Middle Persian, Parthian and Soghdian) and also in Uigur (ancient Turkish). Several Manichaean writings were also found in Tuan-Huang, in the province of Kan-Su, in Chinese. All these texts, most of which have been published, are known for the sake of brevity as the Turfan Texts. A Latin writing, which has been published, was found in 1918 in Tebessa, Algeria, and a Coptic Manichaean library, which has been published in part, was found in 1930 in Medinet Madi (Fayum, Middle Egypt). The Manichaeans also used Jewish and Christian apocrypha and Gnostic texts, though in their own revised versions. Secondary sources include the Church Fathers, neo-Platonist and Moslem authors, Zoroastrian refutations, oaths of abjuration and imperial edicts.

2. *Origin and nature.* Research into Manichaeism is of great importance for the knowledge of Gnosis, of which it is the concluding phase. At first confined to the secondary Latin and Greek sources, the discovery of the secondary Syriac and Arabic sources gave research new impulses, till finally in the 20th century a considerable number of primary sources became avaible. This, along with examination of the original literature of Mandaeism, opened up a new phase in the study of Gnosis.

As regards the origin and nature of Manichaeism, various hypotheses have been put forward. It was associated with Hellenism by H.-H. Schaeder and others, with early Christian Gnosticism by P. Alfaric, F. C. Burkitt, etc., with Oriental religion by K. Kessler, R. Reitzenstein, G. Widengren, etc. H. Jonas, on the assumption that Manichaeism is basically Oriental, puts Manichaean Gnosis along with Mandaeism at the heart of his analysis of the existentialist character of Gnosis. Manichaeism is said to contain the purest Gnostic tradition, so that Gnosis is sometimes described to a great extent in terms of Manichaeism, for example by R. Reitzenstein and R. Bultmann, who find there the paradigm of the myth of the *Urmensch* (primordial Man) as saviour. The elements of truth in the main lines of the general history of the themes involved have been carefully assessed by H. J. Polotsky, H.-C. Puech and C. Colpe in particular.

3. *Definition and typology.* Manichaeism is the final and logical systematization of the Gnosis of late antiquity as a universal religion of revelation with a missionary character. Deliberately syncretist in character, Manichaeism drew on the religions of its missionary fields (Zoroastrianism, Buddhism, Christianity) in an attempt to decipher the elements of truth in other faiths and give them their valid consequences in its own revelation. Manichaeism, as the main representative of the "Iranian" type of Gnosis, contains, unlike the "Syro-Egyptian" type, two originally independent principles. Above there is the kingdom of light, with the Father of Greatness and his powers or beings, below the kingdom of darkness with the king of darkness, his archons and demons. These two principles or natures, light and darkness, good and evil, God and matter, are envisaged in the perspective of the "three

ages". In the first, the two kingdoms existed independently of each other. The second (middle or present) time is a period of mingling. In the third, future age, the two natures will be definitively separated.

When the kingdom of light is assailed by darkness, God sends an emanation, the primordial Man, to overcome evil by fighting it (or by self-sacrifice). But he is defeated and his soul, his five lightsome elements, is swallowed by darkness. A hypostasis of the kingdom of light, however, the Living Spirit, saves the Man and brings him back to the kingdom of light. But the elements of light from the Man remain in the power of darkness, and the Living Spirit, along with his emanations, creates the cosmos as an apparatus for sifting out this light. He makes heaven and earth from the bodies of the Archons who have been killed, and the "Light-ships" (the sun and moon), the stars, and the "three wheels" of fire, water and wind from the light filtered out in various degrees of purity. (The stars are therefore good, while in Gnosticism in general they are "wicked elemental spirits"). Finally, the Third Envoy summoned by God sets this cosmic apparatus in motion, to filter out the rest of the light from the world and bring it to the paradise of light by way of the moon and the sun. He shows himself in male and female form to the surviving archons imprisoned in the firmament, to entice them to surrender their light. Purified light escapes on high from the seed of the male archons, while other light falls on the earth and springs up in the form of plant-life. Abortions which fall to earth from the self-impregnated female archons give rise to demons, who produce animal life. Matter opposes itself to this cosmic process of purification which threatens its existence. To bind the light definitively to darkness, the master devil Ashaqlun and his female partner Nebroel (who can appear under various names), having devoured the other demons and thus assimilated all the light they contained, engender Adam and Eve in the image of the Third Envoy. The latter sends a messenger (the Lightsome Jesus) with Gnosis, to awaken Adam, from the "sleep of death" in which he has sunk (since mingling with matter robs the soul of consciousness). But Adam and his descendants are misled by the demons to commit the crime of procreation whereby the enslavement of the light to the world is

perpetuated. Hence the Lightsome Jesus invokes the Light-Nous, who sends a succession of apostles to man — Seth, Enosh, Enoch, Noah and so on, including Buddha, Zarathustra and Jesus, down to Mani — who renew and complete the divine call. Mani sees himself as the "Seal of the Prophets", the Paraclete promised by Jesus Christ (Jn 14:16, 26; 15:26; 16:7), the spokesman of the final, universal divine revelation of redemptive Gnosis which awakens the human soul and thus enables it to become conscious of its divine nature by means of the *Nous*.

Mani's Church, the manifestation of the *Nous,* plays a decisive role in the purification of the elements of light. After apocalyptic persecutions, it triumphs at the end of time, whereupon the last judgment is held and a world conflagration lasting 1468 years begins which is to sift out the last remaining elements of light. Then the demons, matter, and the souls of men (all men have an element of light in Manichaeism, the soul) which have obstinately resisted knowledge in spite of constant incorporation, will be shut up for ever in a prison of cosmic dimensions. With this, the final separation of the two principles has been achieved.

4. *Ethics.* The redemptive mission of the Manichaean Church is its co-operation with the general process of separation of light from darkness. This work at the liberation of the light mixed with matter in nature (especially the plants), above all in man, demands of the Manichaean a rigorous abstinence, which avoids the contamination of the soul by matter (particularly active in fleshly desire) and prohibits damage to the light embedded in nature, which could be brought about by work, war, agriculture, hunting and so on. This duty of abstinence is summed up chiefly in the *Tria Signacula* (the seal on the lips — avoidance of meat, wine and curses, strict fasting laws; the seal on the hands — abstention form work, possessions and other things which damage the light; the seal of the bosom — abstention from sexual intercourse). Such rigorous demands could, of course, be imposed only on an élite. Hence the Manichaean Church was composed of two classes of men, the Elect or perfect (*electi,* ἐκλεκτοί), who were absolutely bound to follow out the three seals, and the Hearers (*auditores,* κατηχούμενοι), who were allowed to marry, beget children, work, hold prop-

erty, drink wine and eat meat — though the slaughtering of the animals could not be done by Manichaeans. Their main duty was to provide for the sustenance of the Elect, but they also had ten commandments (including prohibition of lies, fraud, witchcraft, theft, fornication and idolatry). The Hearers could hope that their souls would be purified in the course of transmigration and so enter the bodies of the Elect, whose souls enter the kingdom of light immediately after death.

5. *Organization and liturgy.* The ecclesiastical hierarchy was divided into five classes, under the supreme head (ἀρχηγός) who was the successor to Mani. The first three degrees were accessible only to the male Elect — the twelve apostles (teachers), the seventy-two bishops and the three hundred and sixty priests. Then there were the male and female Elect, and the male and female Hearers. Some of the Elect were active as wandering missionaries.

Our information about the liturgy of the Manichaeans is meagre, but it seems to have consisted chiefly of prayers. The Elect were obliged to pray seven times a day, the Hearers four. Hymns were chanted, fasts of varying length observed, and feasts celebrated. The great feast-day was the Bema, which recalled the death of Mani and his ascent to the kingdom of light. The Bema, which occurred each year about Easter-time, was preceded by a thirty days' fast and confession, the confession of the Elect being kept separate from that of the Hearers. No type of baptism was allowed. The Manichaeans had sacred meals — the Elect took their single daily meal in common, consisting of particularly "lightsome" food such as gherkins, melons and wheaten bread, from which the imprisoned light was thereby released — but their meals cannot be regarded as strictly sacramental.

6. *Expansion.* One of the fundamental principles of Manichaeism was the world-wide preaching of its universal revelation. Manichaeism soon spread from the Sassanid kingdom to the Roman part of Mesopotamia, then to Syria and from there to Palestine (A.D. 274), Asia Minor and finally Armenia, to northern Arabia and Egypt (refutation by Alexander of Lycopolis, A.D. 300; Edict of Diocletian, 297), to North Africa, Italy (Rome under Pope Miltiades, 311–314), Dalmatia, Gaul and Spain. The changing destinies of Manichaeism in the West can be re-constructed from the writings of its opponents and the imperial edicts of persecution. In the western parts of the Roman Empire, Manichaeism underwent a persistent decline from the 6th century on. It was still being opposed in the 9th century in the eastern part of the Empire, along with the Paulicians. The influence of Manichaean thought can be traced in the Bogomiles, Albigenses and Catharists, and also in the Priscillianists.

In the East, in consequence of Sassanid oppression, the Manichaeans turned mostly to the provinces of Chorasan and Trans-Ochsus. After the Moslem conquest of Iran (640–644) some of them returned to Mesopotamia, where they experienced a golden age under the tolerant Omayads, till bloody persecutions set in under the Abbassids, causing the Manichaeans to emigrate once more towards the East. From the end of the 7th century on, Manichaeism spread from its eastern settlements along the silk routes into East Turkestan and into central China (by 694). An Uigur ruler adopted Manichaeism in 763 and made it the State religion, the only instance of this kind.

Though the Uigur kingdom was destroyed in 840 by the Kirghiz, Manichaeism survived in Turkestan till the Mongolian invasions of the 13th century. After being tolerated initially in China, it later became the object of severely repressive measures (especially in 843), so that it survived only in the form of secret societies. Small pockets of Manichaeism seem to have persisted down to the 14th century.

See also *Gnosis, Gnosticism, Mandaeism, Dualism, Catharists.*

BIBLIOGRAPHY. SELECTED PRIMARY AND SECONDARY SOURCES: A. Adam, *Texte zum Manichaeismus* (1954); R. Haardt, *Die Gnosis — Wesen und Zeugnisse* (1967), pp. 211–62; St. Augustine, *The Catholic and Manichaean Way of Life,* E. T. by D. and I. Gallagher (1966); cf. *CSEL,* XXV (1891; reprint 1966); M. Boyce, *The Manichaean Hymn Cycles in Parthian* (1954). — LITERATURE: K. Kessler, *Forschungen über die manichäische Religion,* I (1889); F. Cumont, *Recherches sur le manichéisme* (1912); P. Alfaric, *Les écritures manichéennes,* 2 vols. (1918–19); R. Reitzenstein, *Das iranische Erlösungsmysterium* (1921); O. von Wesendonk, *Die Lehre des Mani* (1922); F. C. Burkitt, *The Religion of the Manichees* (1925); H.-H. Schaeder, "Urform und Fortbildung des Manichäischen Systems", *Vorträge der Bibliothek Warburg,* IV (1927), pp. 65–157; A. V. W. Jackson, *Researches in Manichaeism* (1932);

H.-J. Polotsky, *Abriss des manichäischen Systems* (1934); G. Widengren, *The Great Vohu Manah and the Apostle of God* (1945); H.-Ch. Puech, *Le Manichéisme* (1949); T. Säve-Söderbergh, *Studies in the Coptic Manichaean Psalmbook* (1949); H. Jonas, *Gnosis und Spätantiker Geist*, I (2nd ed., 1954); P. J. de Menasce, "Augustin manichéen", *Festschrift E. R. Curtius* (1956), pp. 79–93; W. Lentz, "Fünfzig Jahre Arbeit an den iranischen Handschriften der deutschen Turfan-Sammlung", *Zeitschrift der deutschen morgenländischen Gesellschaft*, 106, new series 31 (1956), pp. 5–22; R. Ibscher, C. Colpe and A. Böhlig, "Der Mani-Fund", *Akten des 24. internationalen Orientalistenkongresses München 1957* (1959), pp. 226–30; J. Ries, "Introduction aux études manichéennes", *ETL* 33 (1957), pp. 453–82; 35 (1959), pp. 362–409; M. Boyce, *Catalogue of the Iranian Manuscripts in Manichaean Script in the German Turfan Collection* (1960); C. Colpe, "Manichaeismus", in B. Spuler, ed., *Handbuch der Orientalistik* (1961); id., *Die religionsgeschichtliche Schule* (1961); A. Böhlig, "Die Arbeit an den koptischen Manichaica", *Wissenschaftliche Zeitschrift der Universität Halle-Wittenberg* 10 (1961), pp. 157–61; H.-Ch. Puech, "Mani", *LTK*, VI, cols. 1351 f.; id., "Manichaeismus", ibid., cols. 1352–5; W. Widengren, *Mani and Manichaeism* (1965); K. Rudolph, "Gnosis und Manichaeismus nach den koptischen Quellen", *Koptologische Studien in der DDR* (1965), pp. 156–90; L. J. R. Ort, *Mani, A Religio-Historical Description of His Personality* (1967).

Robert Haardt

MARIOLOGY

I. Biblical. II. Theological: A. The Problem. B. The Answer. III. Marian Devotions.

I. Biblical

Mary, the "mother of Jesus" (Mk 6:8; Mt 13:55; Acts 1:4), does not figure largely in the NT writings. The testimonies of faith in her regard take on greater extent and depth with the growing interest in the life of Jesus, the death and resurrection of Jesus being the event first and primarily proclaimed in Scripture. In the letters of Paul, which are earlier than the gospels, Mary is mentioned only in Gal 4:4. But the important truth is already uttered here. Paul speaks of the Messiah by speaking of Mary, though without mentioning her name. "But when the time had fully come, God sent forth his Son, born of a woman, born under the law." According to this text, Mary is the place in which the Son of God entered human history. The birth from a woman guarantees the true humanity and historicity of the crucified and risen Lord whom Paul preaches,

and excludes all "spiritualizing" tendencies. When Christians began to have recourse to the life and actions of Jesus before his death and resurrection, the mother of Jesus who was part of his life began to play a greater role. This new interest was satisfied most fully in the gospels of Matthew and Luke (about A.D. 80), which narrate the conception and birth of Jesus and do not confine themselves like Mark to scenes from the public life of Jesus. According to the gospel of Mark (3:20f.; 3:31–35), Jesus' relatives, and also his mother — whose participation, however, was merely that of a silent bystander — sought to fetch Jesus back home, since his activity was arousing the crowds and drawing attention. Mt (12:46–50) and Lk (8:19f.) present this text in such a way as to lessen the awkwardness for Christian readers. Lk gives another scene from the public life of Jesus. He relates that when a woman praised his mother, he responded by saying, "Yes, blessed indeed are they who hear the word of God and follow it" (this translation is more correct than "No, blessed rather ..."). Interest in the beginning of the life of the Messiah led to the composition of the infancy narratives in Mt 1 and 2 and Lk 1 and 2. They diverge from each other in many points, especially the genealogies, so that the stories cannot be fully harmonized. The two evangelists were obviously drawing on different streams of tradition. Further, each evangelist had a theological purpose, which meant that the traditions were placed in a theological perspective. Both infancy narratives have OT and Jewish traits. The influence of the story of Moses is recognizable in Mt. His text is interwoven with OT quotations and composed as the fulfilment of OT promises. The Aramaic background is also perceptible in Lk. Both narratives are in the line of popular traditions, recounting, for instance, many apparitions of angels, in contrast to the other parts of the gospels. But the historical kernel remains. We learn that Mary came from Nazareth and that she was espoused to Joseph, of the house of David (Mt 1:18; Lk 1:26f.). Whether Mary herself was of the house of David is not clear from the text. Joseph's ancestry was enough to make Jesus legally son of David. Before Mary had been brought to Joseph's house as his married wife, the angel Gabriel announced to her (Lk 1:26ff.) that she was most highly favoured and that the Lord was with her. She was to conceive and bring forth a son whom she was to call Jesus. Her motherhood was not to come about through human intervention but through the action of the Holy Spirit (Mt 1:18; Lk 1:35). The heavenly message telling her that she was to be the mother of the Messiah prompted her to pay a visit to her cousin Elizabeth. The evangelist attributes to Elizabeth, to Mary herself and to Simeon, as he greets the Messiah in the temple, hymns of praise and thanks which are mosaics of OT elements. The birth takes place in Bethlehem (Mt 1:23; 2:1; Lk 1:27; 2:4). Shepherds come to pay homage to the child, and wise men from the East. Herod's murderous intentions force Mary to take refuge in Egypt. When the family returns, Mary lives at Nazareth with Jesus and Joseph (Mt 2:23; Lk 2:39). Jesus was circumcised and presented in the temple according to the prescriptions of the law (Lk 2:21–40). Only one other scene from the childhood of Jesus is narrated, the visit to the temple in Jerusalem (Lk 2:41–52). It is a striking scene, because instead of joining the returning pilgrims and without warning his parents, Jesus stayed behind. And when his parents found him after an anxious search, he gave them the astonishing answer, "How is it that you sought me? Did you not know that I must be about my Father's business?" As the evangelist says, Mary and Joseph did not understand, but Mary kept all these things in her heart, to meditate on them in faith.

One particular question forces itself upon our attention in the story of the infancy. It is that of the virginal conception and birth. Since Augustine (*De Sacra Virginitate*, 4, 4), theologians in general were convinced that Lk 1:34 meant that Mary must have made a vow of virginity. But this traditional view has been criticized in recent years. Why should Mary have let herself be espoused if she had no intention of leading a married life? Hence many theologians now assume that Mary resolved on a life of virginity only at the moment of the annunciation. She then dedicated herself exclusively and without reserve to the service of the divine plan of salvation. Through this dedication, she conceived the Son of God in her spirit as well as in her body. The Holy Spirit is here represented not as the father who begets Jesus, but as the active force which brings about the conception. The notion of a procreation

without a father is foreign to the OT. It also differs essentially from pagan mythology, according to which a god unites himself to an earthly woman and begets a child like an earthly father. Hence the virginal conception and birth of Jesus must be considered as a revelation proper to the NT. Nonetheless, this revelation was prepared for in the OT narratives in which great men were born of mothers who were humanly speaking doomed to sterility (Gen 18; 1 Sam 1). The promise of the Messiah in Is 7:14, which speaks of the bringer of salvation and his birth from a woman *(almah)* was probably already understood by the Greek translators of the Septuagint as a prophecy of the virginal birth. This, at any rate, is the meaning given to the text of Isaiah in Mt. The view that the texts of the infancy narratives deal only with the hearing of prayer does not do justice to the actual words and overlooks the decisive elements. If one asks why Jesus should have been virginally conceived, the answer is not that an earthly father would have been a sort of unwelcome rival to the heavenly Father of the pre-existent Logos. Nor is it that conception in the course of marriage would have been unworthy of the eternal Son of God. The reason is the transparency with which the virginal conception and birth lets the creative power of God and his sole initiative in the work of salvation shine through. It is occasioned by no human deed. It is part of the most ancient faith of the Church that after the birth of Jesus, her first-begotten (Lk 1:7; cf. Mt 1:25), Mary renounced married intercourse with Joseph, in consequence of her total dedication to the charge given her by God and hence to God himself. The "brothers of Jesus" who are mentioned several times in Scripture (Mk 3:31; 6:3 par.; Jn 2:12; Acts 1:14; 1 Cor 9:5; Gal 1:19) could be the actual brothers of Jesus as far as the literal sense of the texts is concerned, but according to biblical Greek they need only have been cousins of Jesus (Gen 13:8; 14:14). The latter meaning is taken by Catholic exegetes. Then, according to Mk 6:3; 15:40, Mary, the mother of the brothers of Jesus, is different from the mother of Jesus himself.

Further information is provided by the Acts and the Gospel of St. John. According to Acts, Mary was with the disciples of Jesus at Jerusalem as they awaited the coming of the Holy Spirit promised by Jesus (Acts 1:14). According to John, Mary took part in the marriage feast of Cana (Jn 2:1–11). She asks Jesus to come to the aid of the hosts, whose wine has run out. Jesus first refuses his mother's request and then grants it. Mary appears here as the lady of the house. It is obvious that at the time when the fourth gospel was composed, Mary's place was fully recognized in the Church (Bultmann). Under the cross (Jn 19:25ff.) she is told by her dying Son that she is now to consider the beloved disciple as her son. The disciple is told by Jesus that he must consider Mary as his mother. The transparently symbolic character of the fourth gospel allows us to conclude that the words of Jesus go beyond the purely historical and point to the relationship between Mary and the Church. It is difficult to say whether Mary is meant by the woman of the Book of Revelation. The woman probably stands primarily for Israel and then for the Church itself.

In post-apostolic times the indications of Scripture are developed more and more fully. The basic notion throughout is that of Mary's motherhood. The actual title of Deipara, the bringer-forth of God, seems to be found for the first time in Hippolytus of Rome, at the beginning of the 3rd century. The sense of the term became clearer and clearer in the Christological controversies of the 3rd and 4th centuries and became so well established that the Council of Ephesus could use it as the hall-mark of orthodox Christology in contrast to Nestorianism, which endangered the unity of the structure of Jesus. The term expresses the personal unity of Jesus, and represents a confession of faith in the true humanity of Jesus against Gnostic spiritualizations, and in the true Godhead of Jesus against Judaism. The method of the communication of idioms was employed in the use of the term Deipara. By reason of the personal unity, the personal self of Jesus is possessor both of the divine nature and of the human nature born from Mary through the action of the Holy Spirit. When the term Deipara, bringer-forth of God, was used in a heretical sense by the Monophysites, it was displaced by the term Mother of God, which had been coming into use over a long period. It was a term which brought out better than Deipara the fact that Mary's function was not merely physiological but also spiritual and personal. It paved the way for the concept of Mary as the spiritual Mother of all the faithful.

Patristic theology understood Mary as the virgin mother of the Lord. The virginity was primarily regarded as *virginitas ante partum* (Ignatius of Antioch, Justin). As regards the perpetual virginity of Mary there was no fully general consensus before the Council of Ephesus. It was not taught by Tertullian, Origen or Jerome. But it was upheld by Irenaeus, the apocryphal writings of Clement of Alexandria, the *Consultationes Zacchaei et Apollonii*, and Gregory of Nyssa. The virginity of Mary *in partu*, after the birth of Jesus her first-begotten, was taught by Origen, Peter I of Alexandria, Gregory of Nyssa, Hilary and Jerome. Basil held that the contrary opinion was not against the faith. The most powerful defenders of the virginity of Mary in and after the birth were John Chrysostom, Ephraem, Ambrose and Augustine. The conviction of the virginity of Mary soon grew into belief in her perpetual virginity. From the 4th century on, her perpetual virginity is often mentioned. After the 7th century (Lateran Synod of 649), the formula of "virginity before, in and after giving birth" came into use.

The antithesis "Eve — Mary", stemming from the proto-evangelium and developed by Justin and still more by Irenaeus, proved very fruitful. It was for a long time the keynote of Mariological thinking on the faith. The unbelief and disobedience of Eve brought ruin, the faith and obedience of Mary brought salvation. Another theme, also developed by Irenaeus and then by Hippolytus and Tertullian but above all by Augustine, was the comparison of Mary's role in the history of salvation with that of the Church. The Church here appears as the mother of the faithful by reason of its preaching of the word and also by reason of baptism. Mary brought forth the head of the Church. This identification suggested that many traits of the personified Church should be transferred to Mary. After some uncertainty about the holiness of Mary, inspired by Lk 2:48, and indeed some negative pronouncements (Cyril of Alexandria), the absolute sinlessness of Mary was taught for the first time by Pelagius and Augustine. This thesis was soon expanded into the freedom from original sin which was then attributed to Mary. In the East, something similar was taught by Andrew of Crete and John of Damascus. No express testimony to Mary's freedom from original sin is found in the

West before about A.D. 1000. Bernard of Clairvaux, a fervent admirer of Mary, and Thomas Aquinas remained doubtful. Theologians could not harmonize the universal necessity of redemption with the thesis being developed of Mary's freedom from original sin. In the course of the controversy William of Ware (c. 1300) and Duns Scotus developed the notion that Mary remained free from original sin by virtue of Jesus' redemption, while the rest of mankind was freed from it. This view makes Mary a subject of the law of original sin, but it did not actually take effect in her, simply by reason of a special divine decree. Mary too was redeemed, but in a more excellent way. Pope Sixtus V recognized the general conviction of Catholics in this matter and forbade the opponents and the upholders of this mystery to brand each other as heretics. The doctrinal declaration of the fifth session of the Council of Trent on original sin stated that it was not the intention of the Council to include Mary in its teaching on the universality of original sin. In the 19th century, faith in the freedom of Mary from original sin had matured so widely that Pius IX could teach it as a dogma in 1854. The freedom from original sin had wide bearings on the whole spiritual life of Mary. According to the doctrine of tradition, Mary was also granted the gift of preternatural integrity which was man's before the fall. This meant that she could integrate into the wholeness of her dedication to God even the spontaneous emotions which precede every human decision. This was also true of the sufferings which she had to undergo, and of her death. Her death was very often regarded as the pure absorption of her life into the love of God. But this does not mean that her death was not as a consequence of illness or old age.

In the development of the faith after the patristic age the thought of the divine motherhood of Mary was completed by that of her participation in the cross of Jesus. Her salvific function is considered here. As mother of the Redeemer Mary herself is called Redemptrix, from the 9th century on. This term was changed into Co-Redemptrix in the 15th century. In the 17th and 18th centuries Mariology was strongly determined by feelings and polemics — "no praises too great". A Mariology founded on the patristic data was introduced by J. H. Newman and M. J. Scheeben. The main questions centred on Mary's share in the redemption. The problem crystallized in the question of Mary's relationship to the Church and vice versa. In 1950 Pius XII defined the doctrine of Mary's bodily assumption into heaven.

If we sum up the gradual development which was accepted as authoritative in the Church and leave aside the far-reaching speculations and theologies which sometimes overshot the mark, the doctrine of the Church emerges as follows: Mary conceived Jesus the Messiah through the Holy Spirit and is therefore truly bringer-forth and mother of God. In and after the birth of Jesus she remained a virgin. From the 3rd century on, the general doctrine of the Fathers of the Church and the theologians was that the birth took place without pangs and without bodily lesions in Mary. But this cannot be regarded as dogma. In recent years theologians have been discussing the question, on which the Church has made no pronouncement, as to whether a birth in the ordinary sense necessarily involves a lesion of virginity and whether virginity is not adequately preserved if one accepts that Mary's giving birth to the child is not a sign of previous sexual intercourse as in the case of ordinary births. It may be affirmed that Mary's giving birth was a fully human and personal act and that even as a bodily process it was entirely determined by the grace of her motherhood, though it is impossible to indicate precisely the nature of the virginity in the birth. To sum up, it may be said that Mary conceived Jesus of the Holy Spirit without a male principle of generation. It is the constant teaching of the Church from the beginning that she gave birth to Jesus without violation of her integrity and that she remained ever virgin. Though there has been no formal definition on the subject, but only non-infallible declarations of the Church in the course of Christological assertions (Lateran Synod of 694: DS 504; Constitution of Pius IV, Cum quorundam, 7 August 1555: DS 1888), the perpetual virginity of Mary is certainly part of the faith and preaching of the Church.

Mary's election as mother of Jesus brought with it so high a degree of union with God that she was preserved from original sin. Her closeness to Christ brought with it according to God's eternal plan of salvation her assumption, body and soul, into heaven

NB two extremes   center 'you   Jas Redeemer

(Constitution of Pius XII, 1 November 1950: *DS* 3900–4), that is, this union with Christ worked out as the transfiguration of her body. There is no formal testimony to this effect in Scripture. Patristic testimony begins only in the 6th century. But the picture of Mary in Scripture indicates that she is most intimately united to the risen Lord. Her bodily transfiguration is the supreme degree of that "conformity" with her Son Jesus which grew steadily closer during her life. The similarity linked her to God in love and penetrated the whole of her existence. Thus she became, as Pius XII said (Constitution *Ad caeli reginam,* 11 October 1954: *DS* 3913–17), "Queen of Heaven". This title, which comes from mythology but is used in a non-mythological sense, indicates the lofty position of Mary in the divine economy and in the historical course of salvation. A number of important theological questions such as the body-soul relationship, the beatific vision and the resurrection of the dead are involved in the dogma of the transfiguration of Mary.

A general survey of the main points which emerged in the course of the historical development might take the following form. The fundamental truth is the virginal motherhood of Mary. All the other Mariological assertions can be derived from this, not with logical necessity but as a well-founded development. The fundamental grace given to Mary was embodied in each of her actions in the history of salvation. When discussing the greatness of Mary's role in the history of salvation, theologians have brought to bear on the doctrine of the divine motherhood of Mary many considerations which have led to too widely divergent views. The question can only be satisfactorily solved by a sober theological exposition of the testimony of Scripture as laid before us by the Church. It would be most inappropriate to judge the various opinions from the point of view of maximizing or minimizing assessments. The question of Mary's participation in the work of salvation may be divided into two parts. The first is: what share had Mary in the redemptive work of Jesus Christ? Was her participation a constitutive or an integrating element in the work of salvation? The second is: what share has Mary in the appropriation of Christ's salvation by the men to whom it is ordained? Is Mary the "mediatrix of all graces"? Nothing has been proposed as of faith in this matter by the Church, though Mary is several times described as co-redemptrix in the doctrinal pronouncements of the Popes. Pius XII was reserved with regard to requests to have the function of co-redemptrix defined. Those who maintain this doctrine must explain it in such a way that the clear doctrine of Scripture on the unique mediatorship of Christ is neither denied nor obscured, so that any salvific function which may be ascribed to Mary can only be understood as a derivative one, depending on the saving action of Christ. Mary's task is in any case a subordinate one (Vatican II, *Lumen Gentium,* art. 62).

Vatican II declared that it had not the intention of giving a complete doctrine with regard to Mary or of deciding questions which were not yet fully clarified by the work of the theologians (*ibid.,* art. 54). As regards the texts which were issued, it is important to note Paul VI's comment on the theological notes of the conciliar decrees, in his speech at the last public assembly on 7 December 1965. The Council, he said, has propounded no new dogma and did not aim at any such (except on the sacramental character of episcopal ordination). This does not mean, however, that the Council confined itself to pastoral exhortation. "Its texts, according to their literary form, have serious claims upon the conscience of Catholics; their pastoral dispositions are based on doctrine, and their doctrinal passages are suffused in concern for men and for a Christianity of flesh and blood in the world of today. This Council is 'pastoral' in its fusion of truth and love, 'doctrine' and pastoral solicitude: it wished to reach beyond the dichotomy between pragmatism and doctrinalism, back to the biblical unity in which practice and doctrine are one, a unity grounded in Christ, who is both the *Logos* and the Shepherd: as the *Logos* he is our Shepherd, and as the Shepherd he is the *Logos*" (Joseph Ratzinger's commentary on the Dogmatic Constitution on the Church in H. Vorgrimler, ed., *Commentary on the Documents of Vatican II,* vol. I [1967], p. 299).

Mary entered into the process of salvation through her faith. As the Fathers frequently affirmed, she first conceived the Son of God and saviour in her heart through faith, and then in her body. By her Fiat to the divine message Mary contributed to salvation, just as Eve had done to man's ruin (*Lumen Gentium*, art. 56). This does not mean that God made his plan of salvation dependent on Mary's consent but that according to the eternal plan of salvation man for his part was to assent to his salvation, through divine grace. Humanity's Yes to God and to Christ the saviour is summed up in Mary. In her Fiat of faith, she received salvation for all. "She embraced the salvific will of God with her whole heart, unhindered by sin, and gave herself wholly as handmaid of the Lord to the person and work of her Son. Thus she was united with him and under him, and with him in the grace of the most high God, to the mystery of redemption" (*Lumen Gentium*, art. 54). Mary's participation is founded on the fact that she gave life to the historical bringer of salvation and followed his work in faith and love to the death of the cross. But this was not all. The salvation brought by Christ is ordained to man by its very constitution. It calls for acceptance and assimilation. This is where its essential purpose is fulfilled. Mary was the primary recipient of this salvation, which she took to herself in the most excellent way, not only for herself in individualistic isolation but with a willingness and an openness which were orientated to all men. Her personal appropriation of salvation has ecclesial significance. The salvation of Christ is concretely embodied in the sacrament of the Church, as *Lumen Gentium* affirms (art. 59). Salvation is present and accessible in the Church, and Mary is the first and most privileged member of the Church.

This notion of the ecclesial significance of Mary's appropriation of salvation is based on a definite interpretation of the notion of the Church, as given by St. Paul. The Church is the body of which Christ is the head, and the Church is the bride of whom Christ is the bridegroom. The first image is not meant to point to a natural but to a personal relationship, and the second is even more explicitly personal. They both mean that the Church, the fellowship of the faithful, is called to bring about and maintain the saving bond with the saviour, and that this is its responsibility. But Mary was the type or model of all in pronouncing her Fiat, both of those who already belong to the Church and of all others insofar as all are called to the Church, that is, to Christ. But it would be wrong to see Mary's role in such a way that the im-

mediate relationship to Christ and in him to God would be obscured. The function of Mary means that dedication to Christ in faith has a Marian colouring but not that it loses any of its directness. Mary is where the salvation of Christ came to man in the world, not just as an objective entity but as the movement of Christ towards man. That this is involved in the relationship of Mary to Christ is particularly clear from the fact that she was with the disciples in Jerusalem awaiting the descent of the Holy Spirit (Acts 1:14). She was not invited to the Last Supper, but her presence is noted with some emphasis as the Holy Spirit was awaited. She knew from her own experience since the annunciation the power of the Spirit. In the Spirit Jesus himself remained present, in the fellowship of the Church. That Mary was there when the Church was constituted in the Holy Spirit, in the Spirit of Christ, is significant for the whole course of its history. When she died, and above all when her body was glorified, her heavenly existence was stamped for ever by her earthly role in the work of salvation. Her "assumption into heaven" did not mean that she left mankind far behind, but that she came all the more personally close to them. Her loving gaze is fixed for ever on her risen Son and on his brothers and sisters. But her whole glorified existence is also praise, thanks and intercession before God. What she is, she is through Christ. What she does, she does through Christ. Vatican II avoided speaking of her universal "mediation of grace". But the truth behind such terms is taught with reserve, while the mediatorship of Christ is strongly stressed and all Mary's activity is seen exclusively in the perspective of Christ. If, nonetheless, the mediatorship of Mary is affirmed, this is in order to bring out a fundamental thought from the Bible, the solidarity of all men. Men do not receive salvation as individuals or monads in isolation from each other, but as social beings. Each one who receives the gift of salvation becomes himself a source of salvation. The good of one is fertile in good things for the other. This general principle holds good for Mary in a special and comprehensive way. Hence Mary's mediatorship is to be understood on the level of the solidarity of all mankind which is in need of redemption, to which she herself belongs, and not on that of the one and only saviour (O. Semmelroth). In the light of the thesis that Mary's glorified existence is that of intercession, and that this is essential for her, the much discussed question of whether Mary's function is sacramental or petitionary seems to be given too much superficial prominence. Mary's heavenly life of dedication to Christ is marked by her care for the brothers and sisters of her Son who are still on their pilgrim way to the Father. Her existence is perfect exchange of love and also hopeful concern.

The function of Mary in salvation determines her relation to the Church. At a very early date, though the doctrine was first propounded explicitly by Ambrose, Mary was regarded as the type or model of the Church, and the Church as the image of Mary (*Lumen Gentium,* arts. 60–65). Mary is type or model in her motherly fruitfulness and virginal integrity. In the tradition of the Church, especially in Augustine, Mary's motherhood of Jesus expands to the spiritual motherhood of all the faithful. Her virginity is displayed in her total dedication to God. The Church in turn mediates the salvation of Christ through its preaching and the sacrament of baptism. It thus brings forth the Son of God by grace in men, as is affirmed with especial emphasis by the medieval mystics. The Church is virginal because it remains true in faith, that is, in the loving acceptance of God mediated by Christ. Hence the Church has a Marian life inasmuch as it contemplates, grasps and proclaims the salvation of Christ realized in Mary.

In a work attributed to Ambrosius but actually written by Berengarius of Tours in the 12th century, Mary is termed mother of the Church itself as well as mother of the faithful united in the Church. In an anonymous work from the beginning of the 13th century the mother-child relationship between Mary and the Church takes on a twofold aspect. From one aspect, Mary is mother of the Church, from another the Church is mother of Mary. Vatican II avoided the title of "Mother of the Church". But the term was used by the Pope in his speech at the end of the third session. The formula had not a prominent place in theology before the Council, but was often used in preaching and even in theology without any exact definition. The term is in any case a metaphor. It can be understood in two ways, according to two ways of looking at the Church. The Church may be understood as a community which is prior to any individual member of it. Here Mary's relationship is that of mother, because she gave birth to the head from whom flows the existence and life of the community, and also because she accompanies the life of the community by her fruitful intercession. The Church can also be regarded, though less aptly, as the hierarchically constituted multitude of all the individual faithful. Mary is mother of the Church under this more individualistic aspect, since she is effectively concerned for the salvation of each individual (O. Semmelroth, *loc. cit.,* pp. 292 ff.).

See also *Church* II, III, *Communion of Saints, New Testament Theology* III, *Dogma* II, *Jesus Christ* III, *Mediatorship, Resurrection* I A, D, II.

BIBLIOGRAPHY. BIBLICAL: F. Ceuppens, *De mariologia biblica* (2nd ed., 1951); F. Braun, *La mère des fidèles. Essai de théologie johannique* (1953); E. T.: *Mary Mother of God's People* (1965); M. Dibelius, "Jungfrauensohn und Krippenkind", *Botschaft und Geschichte,* I (1953); G. Delling, "παρθένος", *TWNT,* V, pp. 324–35; P. Gaechter, *Maria im Erdenleben* (3rd ed., 1955); R. Laurentin, *Structure et théologie de Luc,* I–II (1957); A. Kassing, *Die Kirche und Maria. Ihr Verhältnis im 12. Kapitel der Apokalypse* (1958); O. Michel and O. Betz, "Von Gott gezeugt", *Festschrift J. Jeremias* (1960); A. Vögtle, "Kindheitsgeschichte Jesu", *LTK,* VI, cols. 162 ff.; A. Feuillet, "La vierge Maria dans le Nouveau Testament", *Maria. Études sur la Sainte Vierge,* VI (1961); id., "Les adieux du Christ à sa mère (Jn 19:25–27) et la maternité spirituelle de Marie", *NRT* 86 (1964), pp. 469–89; id., "L'heure de la femme (Jn 16:21) et l'heure de la mère de Jésus", *Biblica* 47 (1966), pp. 169–84, 361–80, 557–73; J. Galot, *Mary in the Gospel* (1964); J. Cantinat, *Mary in the Bible* (1965); F. Mussner, "Der Glaube Mariens im Lichte des Römerbriefes", *Praesentia Salutis. Gesammelte Studien* (1967); A. Dauer, "Das Wort des Gekreuzigten an seine Mutter und den 'Jünger, den er liebte'", *Biblische Zeitschrift* 11 (1967), pp. 222–39, 12 (1968), pp. 80–93. DOGMA AND THEOLOGY: H. Du Manoir, *Maria,* I–III (1949 ff.); K. Rahner, *Mary, Mother of the Lord* (1958); *Maria et Ecclesia. Acta Congressus Lourdensis,* 16 vols. (1959–62); M. Schmaus, *Katholische Dogmatik,* V (2nd ed., 1961); H. Holstein, "Le développement du dogme marial", *Maria. Études sur la Sainte Vierge* VI (1961); H. von Campenhausen, "Die Jungfrauengeburt in der Theologie der alten Kirche", *Kerygma und Dogma 8* (1962); W. Tappolet and A. Ebneter, *Das Marienlob der Reformatoren* (1962); *De Mariologia et Oecumenismo,* pub. by Pontificia Academia Mariana Internationalis

(1962); J. Alfaro, "Maria salvada por Cristo", *Revista Española de Teologia* 22 (1962), pp. 37–56; C. Neumann, *The Virgin Mary in the Works of St. Ambrose* (1962); J.-H. Nicolas, *La virginité de Marie* (1962); "Mariologie et Œcumenisme", Études Mariales. *Bulletin de la Société Française d'Études Mariales* 19 (1962) and 20 (1963); E. L. Mascall, ed., *The Blessed Virgin Mary: Essays by Anglicans* (1963); G. M. Roschini, *La médiatrice universale* (1963); E. Schillebeeckx, *Mary, Mother of the Redemption* (1964); M. Thurian, *Mary, Mother of the Lord, Figure of the Church* (1964); O. Semmelroth, *Mary, Archetype of the Church* (1964); J. Galot, "Mère de l'Eglise", *NRT* 86 (1964), pp. 1163–85; H. C. Graef, *Mary. A History of Doctrine and Devotion,* I (1963), II (1966); G. Philips, "Marie et l'Église", in H. du Manoir, ed., *Maria,* VII (1964); M.-J. Nicolas, *Theotokos — Le Mystère de Marie* (1965); C. Vollert, *A Theology of Mary* (1965); A. Brandenburg, *Maria in der evangelischen Theologie der Gegenwart* (1965); R. Laurentin, *Mary's Place in the Church* (1965); id., *The Question of Mary* (1965); T. A. O'Meara, *Mary in Protestant and Catholic Theology* (1966); H. Volk, "Maria, Mutter der Gläubigen", *Gesammelte Schriften,* II (1966); K. Rahner, "Virginitas in partu", *Theological Investigations,* IV (1966), pp. 134–63; K. Barth, "Ein Brief in Sachen Mariologie", *Ad Limina Apostolorum* (1967), pp. 61–66; J. F. Craghan, *Mary. The Virginal Wife and the Married Virgin. The Problematic of Mary's Vow of Virginity* (1967); M.-J. Nicolas, *Marie, mère du sauveur* (1967); O. Semmelroth, *Commentary on the Documents of Vatican II,* "Lumen Gentium", ch. VIII (1967); O. Semmelroth's commentary on ch. VIII of the Dogmatic Constitution on the Church in H. Vorgrimler, ed., *Commentary on the Documents of Vatican II,* vol. I (1967), pp. 285–96.

Michael Schmaus

II. Theological

A. THE PROBLEM

Mariology concerns us here not in the sense of theological reflection on the person and character of Mary, her role in the history of salvation and the orderly presentation of the results, but as reflection on these primary theological truths. Hence our primary interest is not the content of Mariology, but the ranging of this content in its place in theology as a whole. But the two elements cannot be kept totally separate, since the place of Mariology in theology is determined by the nature of its assertions. The solution of this theoretical task is only now taking definite shape. Up to the present, theologians have been content in general with working out the contents of Mariology in systematic form. But they thereby prepared the way for the general theological assessment of Mariological treatises. The problem falls into three parts:

1. Should there be a special Mariological treatise at all, drawn up on the same lines as the other treatises of dogmatic theology such as Grace, the Last Things or Christology? No one can doubt that Mary played a role of her own in the history of salvation. But the question is whether the perspectives and aspects which it implies should not be inserted into the conventional treatises which have prevailed almost universally since Peter Lombard. Or should they be combined into an independent presentation of the whole of Mariology? The first method is that of the Fathers and also of medieval theologians on the whole, though particular questions such as the virginity, assumption and immaculate conception of Mary were sometimes treated separately. They were dealt with at times in special works like sermons, allocutions, homilies and monographs or discussed in the course of other works such as commentaries on Scripture. The advantage of this method is that it avoids isolating Mariology from the rest of theology and hence eliminates all distinctions between theology and Mariology. Further, the matter of the other treatises such as Grace or Eschatology can then be illustrated by the supreme example of its realization. The theologian can demonstrate all that Mary has in common with the rest of the redeemed and also the special nature of the redemption as imparted to Mary. The disadvantage is that then Mary is not seen as a whole in the fullness of her role and her person, and the intrinsic connections between the various Mariological assertions are not brought to light. The second method avoids these disadvantages but loses the advantages of the former. And it can easily fall victim to an isolated Mariology, which mistakes its allotted theological boundaries and can give the whole of theology a lop-sided appearance. If, however, one opts for the second method, its inherent dangers can be avoided if reference is made to Mary in the usual treatises and if the Mariological treatise shows how Mary is inserted in each case into the process of salvation — redemption, justification, consummation — as it affects all men. In

this way, the treatises can be integrated with one another, without making too much or too little of the treatise on Mariology.

2. The second part of the problem is the legitimate place to be assigned to any such Mariological treatise within the whole framework of theology. Since Mary and her work are entirely dependent on Christ, the Mariological treatise can be an appendix to Christology. But since Mary is the spiritual mother of the faithful, the most excellent member of the Church and indeed the beginning and the archetype of the Church (cf. Rev 12), the Mariological treatise can also be prefixed to ecclesiology or appended to it. When medieval theologians made Mariological assertions within the framework of systematic theology, such assertions were inserted into Christology. See, for instance, Thomas Aquinas, *Summa Theologica*, III, q. 27–30, or the *Commentaries on the Sentences*, where Mariological questions are dealt with in the third book. The plan of Thomas Aquinas is to discuss the hypostatic union and its salvific consequences and then to deal with the life and actions of Jesus. The Mariological assertions are meant to throw light on part of Jesus' life, his entry into the world. The doctrine of his conception and birth as well as that of his work demanded some knowledge of the woman in whose bosom the conception took place. It was necessary to know the special nature of her place in the spiritual and religious world, and also the consequences which her function with regard to Christ had for herself.

3. The third part of the problem is concerned with the basic principle of Mariology. To be precise, one should here distinguish between the basic reality of salvation as applied to Mary and the basic perspective of a Mariological treatise. Though the basic reality of Mary must be reflected in the basic notion of the Mariological treatise, the latter need not coincide fully with the former. In consequence of Mary's place in the whole plan of salvation, the basic notion can be prior at least to the basic reality and be its theoretical presupposition.

B. The Answer

1. The general possibility of Mariological assertions is based on Scripture. It is particularly clear from Gal 4:4 and from the gospel texts which deal with Mary. Mary is included in the testimony of Scripture to the Son of God made man, not accidentally, so to speak, in the way in which the Lake of Genesaret is mentioned, but in the essential sense in which the assertions about the historicity of Jesus are linked indissolubly to the assertions about his mother. Everything, no doubt, which is said of Mary occurs in a Christological context. But one cannot reasonably speak of the Son of God made man, of his belonging to the human race, of his situation in human history, without thinking of how he was inserted into history, of his continuity and his discontinuity in its regard. This is particularly clear from Matthew and Luke. Truths of faith with regard to Mary form part of the truths of faith with regard to Christ, as may be seen from the articles of the creeds of the Church which speak of Jesus Christ as "born of the Virgin Mary". Here the assertions of the faith of the Church with regard to Mary are clearly linked with Christology. That Mariological assertions should occur in theology from the earliest times is quite understandable. Such assertions are concerned with particular questions and are often not the result of scientific thinking of the faith but the expression of pious veneration. Hence they often have the character of poetic intuition and enthusiastic exuberance, which means that they must be interpreted by a method appropriate to such literary forms. Even Albertus Magnus, who was formerly considered the greatest Mariologist of the Middle Ages, is not a Mariologist in the modern sense. The *Mariale* represents in fact the first systematic effort at a theology of Mary, inasmuch as all assertions about Mary are reduced to one single principle, that of the all-embracing fullness of grace. The principle, however, cannot be sustained and is not without dangers. And the *Mariale* itself is not a work of Albertus. Mariological reflection did not go beyond particular questions and the effort to introduce some order into them, till after the Reformation. Independent treatises were then drawn up, by Peter Canisius, Francis Suarez, Charles Vega and others. Very soon, however, individual problems came once more to the fore (mediation of all graces, co-redemption). These brought with them the danger of isolating Mariological assertions from their

basis. Having first appeared only as intrinsically connected with Christology, there was a tendency to make of them a Mariology equal in rank with Christology and ecclesiology. At present, the dialectical law of thesis and antithesis seems to have brought about a synthesis, the main principles of which are to be found above all in the Mariological texts of Vatican II. The development of dogma seems to have shown that the revelation in Mary implicit in the self-disclosure of God allows us to state a number of truths of faith as regards Mary. These may then be built up into an organic whole or rather combined to form a part complete in its kind within theology as a whole. This is the ground of possibility of a Mariological treatise or at least of a presentation of Mary on the lines of a treatise.

2. The second question is concerned with the place of the Mariological treatise within theology as a whole. Medieval theology, when it took up Mariological problems from a systematic viewpoint, always dealt with them within Christology. But this is not a decisive argument for a Mariological treatise which would be exclusively Christocentric. It was impossible in the Middle Ages to give Mariology an ecclesial stamp, since there were no fully developed treatises on ecclesiology in existence. But in any case, a Mariology inserted into or appended to Christology should never be treated simply as an element or annexe of Christology. Mariology is more than a developed Christology, just as ecclesiology is more than a developed Christology. The opposite approach would lead to an identification of Christ and Mary or to a volatilization of the Mariological element. After long discussions, the Second Vatican Council adopted an intermediate position. It declined to answer all problems of Mariology, but gave a coherent presentation of it on the lines of a brief theological treatise, which it then inserted into the Constitution on the Church (*Lumen Gentium*, ch. viii). Thus the ecclesial perspective of Mariology appears at once in a clear light, while the Christocentric quality is given due attention. The two aspects appear as indissolubly linked, though the ecclesial is the more immediately prominent. The Church is considered only in the light of Christ. Hence, though it is described as the people of God, its special characteristic as

people of God is that it is the body of Christ, of which Christ is the head. The liturgy of the Church, which is an expression of the faith of the Church, brings out the unity of the ecclesial and Christological aspects in the canon of the Mass: "Communicantes, et memoriam venerantes, in primis gloriosae semper Virginis Mariae, Genitricis Dei et Domini nostri Jesu Christi." The difficulties inherent in the ecclesial approach will have to be accepted. They arise from the fact that not all Mariological assertions fit in logically with this arrangement (as, for instance, Mary's share in the objective redemption).

3. The third problem posed by the treatise on Mariology is that of its basic principle. By this we mean the basic notions or perspectives from which all the assertions of the treatise on Mariology can be derived — not by logical necessity, but with some sort of reasonable coherence through which their unity is assured. The answer will of course be determined and coloured by the basic principle of theology as a whole. The particular solution applied to Mariology will vary according to whether one takes as the basic principle of theology "God as God" or God as self-communicating, or again, if one takes the Church or the consummation of the world and man in the glorified body as basic principle. In the course of history the following notions have come to the fore as characteristic of the basic principle of Mariology: Mary as the second Eve, Mary as the most fully redeemed, Mary as archetype of the Church, Mary as mother of the Church, Mary as bridal mother of God or Mary simply as mother of the Son of God made man. What is most in keeping with the Marian tradition is the notion of the maternity of Mary and of Mary as archetype of the Church. But it would seem that the notion of the divine motherhood is what answers best the demands which must be made on the basic principle. It seems also the notion which represents most fully the perpetual mind of the Church in its faith and theology. It contains within itself the theological elements comprised within the other proposals, but also lays the emphasis in the proper place, according to the role of Mary in the history of salvation, while remaining closest to a sober and concrete assessment of reality. The other proposals come, no doubt, to the

same thing ultimately, but need more copious explanations and contain many more abstract elements. When we speak of motherhood here, we mean it in a comprehensive, personal and existential sense. It is not considered merely as a biological process in which both human dignity and dedication to God in faith are reflected. Motherhood here includes the loving, obedient acceptance of the divine charge. It includes readiness for commitment to God's plan of salvation and to the life-work of Jesus. This readiness is an intrinsic and indissoluble element of Mary's motherhood. In Mary's assent, which was predefined by God, humanity itself accepts the grace of redemption. When Mary's motherhood is understood in this way, the other Mariological assertions can be derived from it — freedom from sin, bodily glorification, participation in the event of salvation — according to the various methods of logical explicitation, the theological analogy of reference to Christ, the due and fitting, etc. This notion of motherhood lends significance to the other assertions in the order of salvation. It gives them their proper co-ordinates in Mariology and indeed in theology as a whole. It also contains the principles of Marian devotion, for which it provides both legitimate grounds and boundaries.

See also *Mariology* I, III.

BIBLIOGRAPHY. K. Rahner, "Le principe fondamental de la théologie mariale", *RSR* 42 (1954), pp. 481–522; C. Dillenschneider, *Le Principe premier d'une théologie mariale organique* (1956); E. Gössmann, *Der Verkündigungstext in der dogmatischen Erklärung des Mittelalters* (1956); T. M. Bartolomei in *Divus Thomas* (Piacenza) 60 (1957); pp. 160–93; C. Oggioni, *Problemi e orientamenti di teologia dommatica,* II (1957), pp. 407–76; G. Philips, "De fundering van de Mariologie", *Revue Ecclésiastique de Liège* 44 (1957), pp. 193–242; D. Flanagan in *Irish Theological Quarterly* 25 (1958), pp. 367–81; J. L. Murphy, "The Development of Mariology", *American Ecclesiastical Record* 138 (1958), pp. 89–103, 158–72; A. Fries, *Die Gedanken des hl. Albertus Magnus über die Gottesmutter* (1958); L. Scheffczyk, *Das Mariengeheimnis in Frömmigkeit und Lehre der Karolingerzeit* (1959); A. Müller, "Maria et Ecclesia", *Acta Congressus mariologici-mariani* I (1958), II (1959), pp. 343–66; M. Schmaus, *Katholische Dogmatik,* V (2nd ed., 1961); P. Rusch, "Mariologische Wertungen", *Zeitschrift für Katholische Theologie* 85 (1963), pp. 129–61; R. Lack, "Mariologie et christocentrisme", *Études Mariales* 21 (1964), pp. 17–49; T. M. Bartholomei, "Esame critico-costruttivo delle varie sentenze sul primo principio mariologico", *Divus Thomas* (Piacenza) 68 (1965), pp. 321–68; O. Semmelroth's commentary on ch. VIII of the Dogmatic Constitution on the Church, in H. Vorgrimler, ed., *Commentary on the Documents of Vatican II,* vol. I (1967), pp. 285–96; H. Mühlen, "Neuorientierung und Krise der Mariologie in den Aussagen des Vaticanum II", *Catholica* 20 (1966), pp. 19–53; E. O'Connor, "The Virgin Mary in the Perspective of Salvation History", *Oikonomia. Heilsgeschichte als Thema der Theologie (Festschrift O. Cullmann)* (1967), pp. 273–83.

Michael Schmaus

III. Marian Devotions

1. There are many reasons why the eyes of faith should be fixed with special attention on Mary and why special reverence is due to her: her relationship to Christ, her role in the history of salvation, her perfect mode of redemption and the special nature of her membership of the Church. But the reverence paid to her is always distinguished in the faith of the Church and in theological thought from the adoration due to God alone. Mary is never worshipped as a divine figure of the type of the heathen mother-goddesses. And no causal connections can be traced between such pagan myths and the honours paid to Mary. Similarities provide no proof, because they can be adequately explained by the forms in which the human urge to pay homage expresses itself. In the act of adoration, man acknowledges God as the ultimate unfathomable ground of the world and of his salvation and as his last and absolute end. In the concrete, it is unquestioning confidence in God, total dedication to him and absolute hope in him. But when honour is paid to a creature, it is on account of the dignity which he possesses by virtue of his origin from God and his ordination to God. The "saints", who have reached their goal in God through Christ, even though not yet transfigured in the body, are paid higher honour (δουλία) than other men. This dulia is primarily honour paid to God himself. Every act of reverence paid to man has overtones of the adoration of God. But it is still something more than adoration of God occasioned by a creature. Being the encounter of the respectful I with the respected You, it is a response to the intrinsic value of the You. But this again is a facet of the God-

wardness of the creature revered. Thus reverence implies two things: the absolute reverence paid to God, adoration, and reverence paid to the creature because of his dignity as coming from God and as ordained to God.

The honour due to Mary far surpasses the response to the excellence of the other saints (ὑπερδουλία). Nonetheless, devotion to Mary is not a sort of intermediate entity between adoration of God and reverence for the saints. It is not a sort of mixture of the two. It is in the line of the reverence due to the creature and is essentially different from the reverence due to God. Popular forms of devotion may at times transgress these bounds, but if so, in formal contradiction to the doctrine of the Church. But in any case, such expressions of enthusiasm are not meant as theological assertions. In a number of prayers in official use in the Church, such as the "Hail, Holy Queen", titles are applied to Mary which in their original sense were predicated of Christ ("our life, our hope"); the normal rules of hermeneutics are to be observed in interpreting them. Very often we are dealing with pieces of poetry, and the literary genre of poetry calls for an interpretation which is not that of dogmatic texts. And then, since human activity is included in the process of salvation, epithets which in their full and primary sense apply only to Christ can also be predicated of the redeemed in a derivative (analogous) sense, since the holiness of one can be salutary for another. Thus while Christ may be called the primordial sacrament, the Church may be called the sacrament which stems from the primordial sacrament — the basic sacrament or the secondary prime sacrament. But in any case the principle of the *lex orandi, lex credendi* cannot be applied everywhere without distinctions and conditions. It is for the praying Church to explain how it understands the prayers which it offers (see the encyclical *Mediator Dei* of Pius XII).

One special form of the reverence paid to the saints is the appeal for their intercession. This pious faith is not easy to explain, but may be justified in the following manner. Invocation and intercession are based on the bond of loving concern for one another in the order of salvation, and on the solidarity in Christ which manifests itself therein. When he invokes a saint, the Christian turns to one who is united to him in the love of God as his brother, asking him to take him to his heart in a special way. The love at work in the man in the state of fulfilment is a love bestowed on him by God. Like all love, it is creative. It penetrates the human brother whom it embraces and makes him still more open to love. Since the love of the saint is enkindled by the love of God and can only exist in its creative power, the Christian loved by the saint is ultimately irradiated by the love of God himself. It is an instance of the principle that God does everything, even though he does not do everything alone. The effect of his love is that man loves. When a saint is invoked, the purpose of the invocation is not that God should be moved by the greater creative power of the saint to a salvific decree which the human petitioner himself would have been unable to obtain from him. Such an attitude would be an attempt to place God at the disposition of man. The prayer of petition, with or without the invocation of a saint, has the function of making man receptive to God and his gifts and of giving expression to one's readiness for God's will. God never imposes himself on anyone. The prayer of petition is a means whereby God can impart himself without doing violence to man. Since it stems from grace, because only he who is drawn by God can come to him (Jn 6:43), it is a means used by God to act on man, not a means used by man to act on God. Hence, when we invoke the intercession of a saint, we express the wish that the saint, with his love of God, should also embrace us and through the activating power of his own God-given love stimulate our own capacity to love and make our hearts ready and open for God. The content or object of prayer is primarily fellowship with God, secondarily all that serves such fellowship. Mary's intercession has the same meaning and purpose as that of all the saints. The profound difference lies in its intensity and universality. The glow of Mary's love embraces all men in its concern. Her loving care is inspired by her union with Jesus Christ, whose work of salvation she has of course at heart. This is what is meant when she is said to be "mediatrix of all graces". But for the sake of clearness, it should be added that it would be a theologically indefensible exaggeration to hold that the invocation of Mary was necessary to salvation and that to omit such invocation would be to be deprived of salvation.

2. In view of Mary's role in the history of salvation, it is easy to understand that the attention of the faithful was already directed towards her in apostolic times (Gal 4:4; Mt 1; 2; Lk 1; 2; Jn 2:1–11; 19:25–28), and that devotion to Mary developed quickly, mostly combined in a special way with the development of the Church's understanding of Christ. Inevitably, the true image of Mary was overlaid by a number of exuberant fancies, which could go so far as to compose the rhetorical phrase, "Christ judges, Mary saves". In the Council of Trent the Church laid down the theological norms for correcting the exaggerations which appeared in the Middle Ages and even more prominently in modern times. The first invocation of Mary is recorded in the 3rd century or at the beginning of the 4th. In the 4th century traces of Marian feast-days begin to appear. They had crystallized into definite form in the East by the 5th century at the latest. The same period saw the first dedication of churches to Mary — such as the church in Ephesus, Maria antiqua, Maria Trastevere and Maria Maggiore in Rome. From the time of Athanasius and Ambrose on, Mary was held up as model. The Eastern liturgies gave a large place to Mary, demonstrating thereby both the legitimacy of devotion to Mary and its proper place in the whole. The liturgy of St. Basil, for instance, offers prayers "through the intercession and help of our most illustrious Lady, the mother of God and ever virgin Mary, and of all the saints".

The fierce reaction against Nestorianism shows how strongly rooted was devotion to Mary in the life of the faithful. And conversely, the dogmatic declaration of the Council of Ephesus (431) stimulated in turn and intensified devotion to Mary. From Severian of Gabala on (d. after 408), the lauds of Mary were part of the "daily" customs. According to Sozomenos (5th century) there was a church in Constantinople where a "divine power" bestowed graces on those suffering from sickness and distress. Sozomenos adds that the general conviction was that this was the mother of God. Even apparitions of Mary seem to have been known in the 4th century, as appears from a discourse of Gregory of Nyssa. The first poetic greeting

was addressed to Mary by Ephraem the Syrian, in the 4th century. His mentality, however, was far from that of a critical theologian. Hymns to Mary were composed in the 5th century by Sedulius Scotus and Ennodius of Pavia. In the West, the first invocations of Mary appear in the writings of Augustine. In the 6th century, the name of Mary can be found in the *Communicantes* of the Roman Mass. This point is of particular importance, since it shows the setting of Marian devotion in the life of the Church and hence lays down the norm for all such devotion. The framework is the celebration commemorating the death and resurrection of Christ. Other saints, the apostles and the early Popes, are also mentioned at the celebration of Mass. Mary is one of the figures whose importance is stressed when the death and resurrection of Christ are celebrated. But Mary is at the head of all and is praised with special emphasis. From the 7th century on the number of Mary's feast-days multiplied in the Western Church. In the late Middle Ages and in post-Reformation times devotion to Mary grew and flourished to an extraordinary extent. It took many forms and was practised with great frequency, while its content was also very varied. We may mention the Hail Mary, the rosary, the scapulars, the *Angelus,* consecration to the Heart of Mary, consecration of towns, countries and communities, Mary as Queen of the Rosary, the feast of Mary the Queen, the sodalities of the Blessed Virgin, Marian movements such as the Legion of Mary, Marian and Mariological congresses on national and international levels, Mariological working parties, the foundation of the Pontificia Academia Mariana Internationalis, May and October devotions, Marian pilgrimages, Lady chapels in most churches, apparitions in various places, the most notable of which were at La Salette, Lourdes and Fatima. Confidence in Mary's "omnipotent intercession", in the "refuge of sinners", in the "consoler of the afflicted", the "Queen of Heaven" who can free her suppliants from all fear, distress and need, was expressed in such prayers as the *Memorare,* the *Sub tuum praesidium* and the *Salve Regina.*

After the Second Vatican Council, by virtue in particular of the Constitution on the Sacred Liturgy and also as a result of a more Christocentric theology and the biblical movement, Marian devotion fits more and more clearly today into the general pattern of the spirituality of the Church. Thus, for instance, the recitation of the rosary during Mass in October, a practice common since Leo XIII, has now disappeared. In spite of the wishes of a number of the Council fathers, the Decree on the Ministry and Life of Priests does not mention the rosary among the aids to the priestly life, the reason being that the rosary was not a universal practice in the Church. But on the other hand, the Council gives a word of advice to priests which is important for all Christians. "Priests have before their eyes an admirable example of such receptivity (to the working of the Holy Spirit) in the Blessed Virgin Mary who, under the guidance of the Holy Spirit, consecrated herself wholly to the mystery of man's redemption. Since Mary is the mother of the supreme and eternal priest, the queen and protector of men's priestly service, priests must honour and love her with childlike devotion and reverence."

3. As regards the apparitions of Mary, the great question is their authenticity. In view of the uncanny and incalculable powers of the subconscious and of mass suggestion, it is not easy to distinguish a supposed apparition of Mary from an illusion. Since the divine revelation given for the benefit of all men ended with the apostolic age, no apparition of Mary which may ultimately be verified can bring any universally binding revelation, beyond that already given in Christ. The claim to do so would be proof of its inauthenticity. If it strives to have any standing in the Church outside the purely private realm, it can only summon to faith in Christ and conversion. Though an individual may be free to interpret a phenomenon as an apparition of Mary, the Church is involved and thus competent to pronounce a verdict, when the process affects the community of the faithful, as when pilgrimages are started and new forms of devotion are practised within the fellowship of the Church. The intensity of the experience is not of itself a fully reliable proof of genuinity. The ultimate criterion can only be a miracle which accredits the apparition. With the present-day scientific progress in psychology, anthropology and sociology, the discernment of such a miracle calls for the greatest prudence, animated by faith and expertise.

But there should be no *a priori* prejudice which excludes all divine intervention from its view of the world. Recognition by the Church does not bring with it any obligation in faith, but is simply confirmation of the absence of superstition when a phenomenon is interpreted as an apparition of the mother of God. If the Church accepts an apparition into its common life of prayer, one would not be "thinking with the Church" if one were led by pride to opt out. Nonetheless, it is important to note that the conscience of the individual is the authoritative subjective court of appeal. On the other hand, it would be an inversion of the order of things if one sought to appeal to an apparition of the mother of God of which one was convinced, to defy the magisterium of the Church.

Even if there is a real revelation of Mary, this can only take place according to the divine plan of salvation. God is always the first cause. Even in the apparitions of Mary, God acts through Christ in the Holy Spirit in accordance with the whole structure of his salvific work. In the "apparitions", Mary is included in this activity, on the principle that God does everything, but does not do it alone; he does it through the activity of the creature. He who receives such a divine favour senses and experiences the Marian component. The recipient of the apparition is also active, insofar as he must strive to understand and interpret the divine action. The extent of the human operation in such an apparition is a matter for debate. Is the figure perceived produced directly by God in the recipient? Or is the figure the result of man's interpretation of God's activity? Is man translating his experience of God in certain words and images? The latter explanation is to be preferred, in the light of the general laws of human knowledge. This would mean that religious patterns conditioned by the times and situation of the recipient would become elements of the apparition. But this does not answer the question as to how the interpreter recognizes that there is in fact an apparition of Mary, since her transfigured form is a profound and impenetrable mystery. In view of the increasing number of apparitions of Mary and their lack of confirmation from the Church, one is bound to feel that their very number arouses misgivings rather than confidence, since they are difficult to harmonize with the transcendence and hiddenness of God, as taught by Scripture, Church tradition and theology. Where neither the champions nor the opponents of such phenomena allow themselves to be carried away by a fanaticism foreign to the faith, the phenomena in question, insofar as they preach penance, fulfil at any rate an important function, no matter how their reality is to be judged theologically.

See also *Saints* II, *Prayer, Charity* I, *Nestorianism, Miracle*.

BIBLIOGRAPHY. See bibliography on *Mariology* I, II; also: S. Beissel, *Geschichte der Verehrung Mariens in Deutschland während des Mittelalters* (1909); id., *Geschichte der Verehrung Mariens im 16. und 17. Jahrhundert* (1910); E. Campana, *Maria nel culto cattolico*, 2 vols. (2nd ed., 1945); P. Hitz, *Maria und unser Heil* (1951); R. Laurentin, *Court traité de théologie Mariale* (1953); K. Rahner, *Mary, Mother of the Lord* (1963); K. Rahner and T. Baumann, *Visions and Prophecies,* Quaestiones Disputatae 10 (1963); art. "Theotocos", *Enciclopedia Mariana* (2nd ed., 1958); J. F. Murphy, "Origin and Nature of Marian Cult", in J. B. Carroll, ed., *Mariology,* III (1961); *Estudios Marianos* (1961); R. Laurentin, "La Vierge Marie au Concile", *Recherches des Sciences Philosophiques et Théologiques* 47 (1964), pp. 32–46; J. Auer, "Um die dogmatische Begründung des Marienkultes", *Maria im Kult,* Mariologische Studien 3 (1965), pp. 21–38; G. Baraúna, "Die heiligste Jungfrau im Dienste des Heilsplans", in G. Baraúna, ed., *De Ecclesia,* II, pp. 459–76; "Recherches sur l'intercession de Marie", *Études Mariales* 23 (1967).

Michael Schmaus

MARRIAGE

I. Institution and Sacrament: A. Sociology and History of Religion. B. Marriage in Historical Revelation. C. Marriage in the History of Theology. D. Systematic Theology of Matrimony. II. Parents: A. Parenthood. B. Parental Duties and Rights. C. Limits of Parental Duties and Rights. III. Family: A. The Family in the Order of Creation. B. The Theology of the Family.

I. Institution and Sacrament

A. Sociology and History of Religion

1. Sociologically speaking, marriage is a sexual fellowship, the structure of which varies considerably according to general social conditions. Modern fieldwork in anthropology rebuts 19th-century evolutionary theories (especially that of Morgan) to the effect that marriage gradually developed from primitive promiscuity through various stages of group marriage (sexual relations of all the men with all the women in a group) and polygamy to monogamy. On the other hand it cannot be denied that extraordinarily various forms of marriage in fact exist and that the Catholic definition of marriage as a life-long, indissoluble union between one man and one woman is recognized, in this strict form, only by Catholics themselves. Monogamous marriage however, though dissoluble in certain circumstances, is very widespread indeed and associated with no particular form of culture. Polygamous marriage is favoured by complex social conditions where there is a particular demand for female workers, or where prestige and the desire for numerous offspring is involved. Polyandry is very rare; it is favoured by a firm rule of primogeniture, whereby the younger sons acquire marital rights only in the marriage of their eldest brother, or else a shortage of women.

The factors which determine the concrete structures of marriage can never be sought merely in terms of sex-life and sexual hygiene, or merely in terms of the relationship between man and woman. They are above all the needs of the family and society — that is, the demands of education, economics, property, social security, public morals and the like; because in the long run general social conditions are decisively affected by married life and family life. So we can readily understand why marriage has never been regarded as the private business of the two partners, but has always been fitted into the supraindividual, general human contexts of morality and religion and always considered to exist in view of the family, law, morals, and ethical rules concerning themselves more with this ordination than with the exigencies of marriage as such.

2. Hence it is not surprising to find that marriage, in the history of religion, is an objective, prescribed order which involves the partners in cosmic relationships. It is often held to have been instituted by the Supreme Being as a special stage of life that can only be entered upon through ritual initiation. Wedding brings a new status; it is a turning-point in the life of man, like birth, puberty (admission among adults), and death, and determines whether we can speak of marriage or not. As a rule the marriage-rite

is celebrated only once between one man and one woman, although a wider range of sexual relations of one sort or another is often permitted. In any case the wedding makes marriage valid in the eyes of the community. There is really no personal relationship that can compare in importance with this state of marriage created by the wedding. When intercourse is allowed, for example, with the wife's handmaid because the wife is barren, so that she may be given children (Gen 16:1–6; 30:1–13), this is considered to happen within the existing marriage, not to constitute a new one. And so we see that the idea of marriage as something willed by God is more deeply rooted in men's religious consciousness than one might at first suppose, considering the wide range of sexual relationships permitted in various cultures. In order to gain as clear an insight as possible into marriage as the Church understands it, with all it involves in the fields of theology and natural law, we must realize what a multitude of forms marriage may take and at the same time bear in mind the features common to those many forms.

B. Marriage in Historical Revelation

1. *Old Testament.* a) *Creation narrative.* The Catholic view of marriage stands in direct relation to the OT, Hebrew view. Marriage was given its basic law in what the creation narrative says about the relationship between man and wife, but because of the hardness of men's hearts — according to the words of Jesus which have been handed down to us (Mt 19:6) — the principle was never fully developed during the history of the chosen people. The creation narrative, then, says that woman was created for man's sake, man being in need of help and completion. Woman is created as a suitable helper for Adam, as it were "opposite him". She is to be his lifelong companion. So a man leaves father and mother for his wife's sake and becomes one flesh with her, precisely because it is only in her that he finds all of himself — only with her can he enter a union which has no parallel in the human order, which is even closer than the bond of descent with his father and mother. And man, created male and female, is instructed to be fruitful and to fill the earth.

Then in the NT conception of marriage another feature of the creation narrative plays an important part: the affirmation that the sexes are "hierarchically" ordered one to another (Reidick) — that Adam's nature is the measure of Eve's nature. This primordial priority and subordination underly the whole relationship between the sexes, making their union possible. The priority therefore does not aim at favouring an individual but completion in oneness: and the difference in position as between man and woman is to be appreciated in terms of the oneness that is its goal and fruit. That difference gives each sex its own dignity and at the same time presupposes equality of value. Man's dignity consists in being woman's head, woman's dignity in being the brightness and the glory of man. This priority and subordination is part of the order of creation, and the judgment pronounced upon woman (Gen 3:16) does not turn it into a moral and juridical subordination but simply recognizes a fact — that as a consequence of sin woman will not only find many a burden in motherhood but will also be subjected to violence and exploitation at the hands of man. This is not a rule of conduct, implying that things ought to be so.

b) *Old Testament tradition.* Against this background marriage primarily figures in OT tradition as an institution for the preservation of the husband's clan. The idea is not to found a new family but to continue one that already exists. Hence children are a blessing and a gift from God; childlessness is a disgrace and a chastisement; unmarried people are a sign of national decadence; and virginity as a consecrated state of life is unknown. Mutual help and support, and joy in sexual life, are also regarded as the meaning and purpose of marriage. It is an institution pre-ordained by God, yet not really something sacred. Accordingly the structure of marriage is altogether determined by the needs of the clan, which quite overshadow the interests of the partners. For the sake of the race, and in view of social and economic conditions, certain forms of polygamy and of concubinage with slaves are allowed (cf. Exod 21:7–11 and Deut 21:10–15, for instance), and when a woman marries, her family hand her over to the husband to be his property, in return for payment of the bride-money or other services. Not that the bride becomes her husband's slave; he cannot do what he pleases with her; she remains a free person and must be respected as his wife.

But adultery with the woman is now considered a violation of the husband's proprietary rights. Even when intercourse with a virgin is forbidden, the reason given is that it lessens her value. So logically enough a man can only violate someone else's marriage, and a wife only her own. This of course involves a certain sexual freedom. Also because the needs of the clan are the main consideration, marriage can be dissolved, at least by the man, not only for childlessness but also for dislike, incompatibility, and adultery. But if the wife cannot reasonably be expected to continue the marriage, she can also demand release from it. Thus the Hebrew notion of marriage was "naturalistic", which looked with favour on marriage, children, and intercourse within the limitations set by the force of circumstance.

2. *New Testament.* a) *The Synoptics.* In the NT Jesus deepens the Hebrew conception of marriage in two respects: on the one hand he spiritualizes it, not only forbidding the dismissal of the wife as an offence against the basic law of marriage contained in the creation narrative and ingrained in human nature, which makes man and wife one flesh, but also teaching that divorce does not sever the marriage-bond, since he declares that the re-marriage of divorced persons is adultery. Thus he indicates that the deepest purpose of marriage in God's eyes is the oneness of man and wife. St Matthew's Gospel seems to interpret this doctrine practically, without weakening it, when it allows separation for adultery, but declares re-marriage adulterous because the marriage-bond is still there. (In this case Mt 5:32 is to be read in the light of Mt 19:9, so that Jesus is re-interpreting as a separation *a mensa et thoro* the dismissal which the Jews took to be a divorce giving the right to re-marry [Dupont]. This view is disputed. On the other hand Jesus consistently states that marriage is a kind of life proper to this age, which will pass away with it. In heaven there will be no marrying, and those who have risen from the dead will be as angels (Mk 12:25 and parallels). Compared with the kingdom of God and its demands, marriage becomes a matter of secondary importance, so that it is better for those to whom the mysteries of the kingdom have been revealed, not to marry. And the concerns of marriage must yield to the claims of the parousia (Lk 14:20; cf. also Mt 24:38f.;

Lk 17:27). Given his essentially eschatological outlook and expectation, Jesus doubtless had this relative conception of marriage (with respect to the end) in the foreground of his mind, yet not in such a way as to lose sight of the value which marriage represents in its own right. Rather that value, which God himself gave it, was set in a special light, and at the same time it became clear that the value of marriage is a limited one when we consider the kingdom of God.

b) This ambivalent view of marriage emerges even more forcefully from the *writings of St. Paul,* the next most important source we have for the NT doctrine on marriage. On the one hand he is intent on seeing the basic law governing the relations of the sexes, as contained in the creation narrative, in the light of NT anthropology. Significantly, 1 Cor 6:12–20 tells us that sexual union is not merely a marginal erotic function, but an act which by its very nature so absorbs and expresses the whole personality as to be an entirely unique kind of self-revelation and self-commitment. And then he stresses the spiritual equality of man and woman, and makes it clear that in Christ the differences between the sexes, with all that they entail, are relatively unimportant. It is significant that 1 Cor 11:3–15 discusses the disciplinary question of women's head-covering in church, which concerned Christians at the time, in the basically theological terms of relations between the sexes. Above all, Eph 5:21–33 interprets Christian marriage as mirroring Christ's marriage with the Church, which in turn is foreshadowed by Adam's relationship with his wife (Adam being a type of Christ). Now this means that in their marriage man and wife preserve the relationship between Christ and the Church and reflect it in their relationship, so that the union of man and wife is not only compared to Christ's union with the Church but actually based upon it. Thus when husbands love their wives as their own flesh they are only doing what Christ does with the Church. But this great mystery of the love of Christ for the Church is mysteriously prefigured, according to Eph, in the text of Gen 2:24 about the mutual relationship of the sexes, and goes to constitute Christian marriage. Accordingly the relationship between man and wife is theologically set apart from all other human relationships — that, for example, between children and parents — of

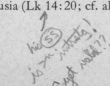

which it is only said, for instance, that they should be "in the Lord". And thus we are given a view of marriage which makes it possible and necessary to regard marriage as a sacrament in the dogmatic sense. According to the same text of Eph, conduct must agree with the relationship: wives are to be subject to their husbands "in all things". This subjection, however, is to the husband who for his wife's salvation must be lord like Christ. Only when he is lord unto her salvation does obedience become wholly possible. So the injunction to love one's wife is correlated with the injunction to obey one's husband (H. Schlier, *Der Brief an die Epheser* [2nd ed., 1958], pp. 252–80). Similarly Col 3:18f. warns wives to be subject to their husbands as to Christ, and men to love their wives in a Christ-like way. (1 Pet 3:1–7 says that by an exemplary fulfilment of the duties of their state in a Christian spirit, husbands and wives must win their partners over to the faith.)

Marital relations were bound to be affected by the fact that in the Churches founded by St. Paul women enjoyed a favoured position, considering the outlook and standards prevalent at the time. He asserts their equal dignity and equal rights as had never been done before, raising marriage from the all too material state in which he found it onto a spiritual and personal plane. His letters contain the definite beginnings of a specific Christian spirituality for married people, of which too little was made later.

On the other hand in 1 Cor 7 Paul wishes that the faithful would renounce marriage in favour of virginity because he thinks the Lord will soon return and fears that the hazards of this life may engross them to the neglect of the only things that really matter. True, not everyone has a vocation to virginity and there is no sin involved in marrying; but the married man is more tightly bound to the world by the nature of his life, less able to devote himself to Christ than is the unmarried man, who is not deceived by the appearance of this fleeting world and gives himself up altogether to the service of the Lord. Here Paul reduces marriage to something of secondary importance in view of the parousia, and stresses the dangers of married life. Whereas the creation narrative says that "it is not good that the man should be alone", St. Paul counters with "it is well for a man not to touch a woman". But he is not

carried away; he does not condemn marriage. His pastoral wisdom and theological insight make him affirm that marriage is necessary on account of the structure of man, and that to avoid disadvantages, married people should not abstain from intercourse except for a sound reason and a short time. Because husband and wife no longer belong to themselves, they may not refuse each other except by mutual agreement, and by Christ's command neither must leave the other. Only by the death of one of the partners is the marriage-bond dissolved. Thus Paul not only spiritualizes the "naturalistic" Jewish view of marriage but shows how fragile it is.

C. Marriage in the History of Theology

1. *The Fathers.* After the apostolic age this ambivalent attitude towards marriage grows more pronounced. Whereas the creation narrative had represented marriage as a glorious divine institution which fell into the realm of human distress because of the fall of man — whereas Jesus had shown marriage to be an indissoluble bond willed by God, and yet an ordinance of this aeon that will pass away with it and must be subordinated to the exigencies of the parousia — whereas St. Paul had laid the foundations for a specific spirituality of Christian married people, at the same time insisting on the dangers of the bonds between marriage and this world: now marriage is seen more and more as the justification of the use of sex which has been infected by original sin. And so marriage ethics, the doctrine on the subjective motive for the marriage act, comes to determine to a great extent the end of marriage and dogmatic teaching on marriage. The trend reaches a certain climax in St. Augustine, from whose theological views later ages found it hard to break away, as is well known.

Now Augustine assigns sexuality to the animal domain, seeing no specifically human aspect in it at all. The purpose of marriage is the begetting of offspring. Sexuality has been deeply wounded by original sin, which expresses itself in concupiscence. This truth is most evident from the fact that the sex organs move spontaneously, that the will cannot control orgasm, and that venereal pleasure is so intense. This means that sexuality can diminish and overwhelm the spirit, so that even an act of procreation good in itself must always involve a degree of "animal excitement". He went so far as largely to identify original sin, concupiscence, and venereal feelings; and then concluded that while marital intercourse is theoretically good, any concrete instance of it must be considered at least materially evil, so that one can say that every child is literally begotten in his parents' "sin", because procreation is only possible with the seductive aid of fleshly lust. Still, since God wills that children be born, it is a sort of permissible or tolerated sin; and so the marital act, subjectively directed to the begetting of children, is morally justified. The same is true of doing one's conjugal duty, because by marrying each partner has given the other a right to his body. Such conjugal embraces as are not motivated by either of these explicit intentions but do not interfere with the natural consequences of coitus, are "venial" sins, because one of the purposes of marriage is the abatement of sexual desire. Given the testimony of Scripture and the tradition that has been built upon it, Augustine will not deny — is not tempted to deny — that marriage is an honourable state, in some sense a sanctifying one; but this, in his view, is precisely because of the "goods" that excuse it, and especially the spiritual love between husband and wife. These goods — offspring, faithfulness, sacrament — he explains as follows: "Fidelity means that one does not have intercourse outside the marriage-bond with another man or woman. Offspring, that one lovingly accepts the child, and brings him up kindly in the fear of God. And the sacrament, that the partners shall not be divorced . . . This is the fundamental principle of marriage, since it ennobles the fruitfulness willed by nature and at the same time keeps perverse desire within its proper bounds" (*De Genesi ad litteram,* IX, 7, 12).

It may be that this altered view of marriage came in because the Fathers were influenced by Hellenistic dualism, which considered the essence of the good life to be ἀταραξία — the Stoic ideal of tranquillity, keeping oneself fully under control, especially in face of sensation, of which the keenest is sexual sensation. It was Encratist and Gnostic forms of this dualism in particular which could find allies in the Christian conception of marriage. While the perfectionist instinct of Encratism, with its over-emphasis on the ascetic principle of ἐγκράτεια, self-control, continence, was to over-exalt virginity and depreciate

marriage, the dualistic premise of Gnosticism that matter is evil provided Encratism with something like a dogmatic basis. Gnosticism maintained that marriage and sexual intercourse only served to imprison more souls in the flesh; and recommended continence in order to thwart this purpose of the demiurge and to subject the flesh to the spirit. Now this doctrine was an approach — though a heretical one — towards the Christian idea of the dangers of sex because of sin and the secondary position of marriage vis-à-vis the claims of God's kingdom. So it is understandable that the Fathers, with the emotional attitude they generally had towards marriage and intercourse, should have been much influenced by the spirit of the age in which Christian tradition took shape, especially as most of them lived in close touch with their environment. The limitations of their time became their own as well. Nevertheless they never went so far as to betray the substance of Christian tradition, and over the centuries they defended the basic value and sanctity of marriage in terms like those of 1 Tim 4:1–5. This is not to deny that the Fathers had a negative influence on the medieval theology of marriage and on preaching in general.

2. *Scholasticism.* Hence it is not surprising that marriage was readily accounted one of the seven sacraments when the idea of a sacrament in the present dogmatic sense was worked out in the 12th century, even though not all the Schoolmen agreed at first as to whether or how the sacrament of matrimony conferred grace. Thus Abelard (d. 1142) says of matrimony, which he groups with baptism, confirmation, Eucharist, and the anointing of the sick: "Among them (these sacraments) there is one that does not avail unto salvation and yet is the sacrament of a weighty matter, namely matrimony. For to bring a wife home is not meritorious for salvation, but it is allowed for salvation's sake because of incontinence" (*Epitome theologiae Christianae,* 28: *PL,* CLXXVIII, col. 1738).

But the sacramental character of marriage was soon embodied in pronouncements of the Church's magisterium: the decree for the Armenians (1439), of the Council of Florence, plainly teaches that this sacrament contains grace and communicates grace to those who receive it worthily (*D* 695, 698), and the Council of Trent expressly defines against the Protestants that matrimony is a sacrament.

D. Systematic Theology of Matrimony

1. *Dogmatic theology.* This doctrine that marriage is a sacrament affirms and guarantees that the married state is a lawful, and even salutary one; it ensures that it will not be wrongly seen in a profane light. The doctrine means that through marriage man must in some way share in redemption, since every sacrament conforms us after its own fashion to Christ and his saving deed — which neither man himself nor the sign of itself can do, but only God's grace bestowed on us through Christ. Now since that grace is henceforth attributed to marriage as such, it follows that only the marriage of baptized persons is a sacrament — that is, bestows *ex opere operato* the grace proper to marriage, provided no obstacle is placed in its way such as would destroy the disposition necessary in the recipient for the sacrament to take effect. Moreover, only marriage between baptized persons can be — at least in full measure — that sign and witness which conformation to Christ by grace enables marriage to be. Only such marriage, then, can so fully represent the bond between Christ and his Church that the mystery of God's incarnate love itself will become operative in it.

Accordingly the contracting of a marriage between Christians is a sacramental sign. That bond comes into being when the will to marry is made known *(matrimonium ratum)*, and reaches fulfilment in complete marital dedication *(matrimonium consummatum)*. The declaration of willingness to marry must, however, be made in the form prescribed by canon law, because marriage as a sacrament is also an ecclesiastical act and therefore the Church can and must regulate it according to the mind of the Church and the role of marriage in the Church. Canon law for its part must further the Church's work of vicarious sacramental sanctification.

Now according to Eph 5:21–23 marriage is a certain image of Christ's "great marriage" with the Church. So Christian married people are in duty bound to present an unmistakable image, for the world and above all for their own children, of the love between Christ and the Church, so that we can say the *res et sacramentum* of marriage consists in the visible bond of ultimate, indissoluble love between the partners till death do them part. That is why being in the state of Christian marriage gives one a "right" to the constant help of grace — grace to do one's duty as a Christian husband or wife and do it well — if we can call a right a claim upon God that he has freely given us apart from any deserts of our own. In this sense the marriage-bond can be compared to the other sacraments which found a state of redemption. By living their marriage, therefore, and so showing forth a mystery of redemption in their own way, Christian couples have a salvific function, which is why the Church has the right and duty to make suitable arrangements for the form in which marriage is contracted.

The grace bestowed by the sacrament *(res sacramenti)* consists in this: the mystery of God's incarnate love becomes so efficacious in the husband and wife who do not close themselves against it that they are supernaturally united with God and each other as Christ is united with the Church. True, baptism itself gives the whole Christian life a sacramental character; the grace of baptism has already put all our relations with God and man on an entirely new footing. But over and above this, marriage brings one into the mystery of redemption in a new, more perfect way. Now when the grace of marriage conforms one to Christ over and above the conformation wrought by the grace of baptism, one is of course linked in a new way with Christ's salvation and glory, to which the cross and death are a prelude. The grace of marriage too involves the cross. And so faith alone can look on this grace and the responsibility which it brings as ultimately a beatific gift. Since grace does not destroy our nature but fulfils it by transforming it on a nobler plane, the grace of marriage is not to be thought of as something that completes and perfects marriage as it were from without, but as a dynamism within marriage that penetrates and transforms its created nature, to make it not only a state of the redeemed but also a redeeming state. The created nature of marriage is not thereby abrogated or destroyed: it is fulfilled in Christ's way. This fulfilment means that Christian marriage is penetrated through and through, in a new and unique way, by the love that grace has shaped — the love that unites Christ and the Church (Volk).

Accordingly, husband and wife are rightly said to be *ministers* of the sacrament. We should of course remember that the Church's intervention — normally through an authorized priest — is essential for the contracting of marriage, even though the Church may participate more or less explicitly and though the manner of its participation has greatly varied in the course of history and still does so. Now there are certainly cases where bride and groom contract a marriage without thereby wishing to confer and receive a sacrament; and so the question arises whether Christians can marry without the conferring of the sacrament. This question was long and sometimes angrily debated in connection with the problem of who the minister of the sacrament is, especially after the Council of Trent, but was then settled in harmony with ancient Christian tradition by doctrinal pronouncements of Pius IX and by the Code of Canon Law (can. 1012), which says that among Christians the marriage contract as such has been raised to the dignity of a sacrament; so that by the very fact of marrying one receives the sacrament. Hence, according to whether one intends to contract a sacramental marriage or to exclude the sacrament, a marriage comes into being or fails to do so. Thus the sacrament is conferred by the giving and receiving of consent and a bond is created on terms which the partners to the contract cannot fix, because they are fixed in advance by the nature and purpose of marriage.

This nature and purpose subject the marriage contract to the requirements of natural law, Church, and State, in such a way that if a marriage does not duly satisfy these requirements it will be illicit or even invalid. We are dealing, then, with a contract *sui generis*. In particular, the continuance of the marriage does not depend on the continued will to be married, as Roman law supposed; for a marriage can only be contracted if one intends to bind oneself for life and regardless of what may happen in the future. Only such an intention accords with the nature of the marriage bond.

Such being the case, we can say that according to Gen 2:18 and Eph 5:21–33 the nature of marriage is a mutual completing and perfecting of the marriage partners through their union, which reaches its highpoint in its sacramental elevation and perfection, and finds its strongest expression in sexual encounter. But the immanent meaning of marriage points beyond itself to a transcendental purpose — personal and physical fruitfulness arising from the union and

therefore common service of the world, especially begetting and bringing up children — the family. This purpose, intrinsic to marriage and yet transcending it, flows from the way in which man and wife are ordered to each other in marriage, and necessarily follows from the nature of their union and of sexuality, which are ordained to fruitfulness. For being married perfects man and woman not only in their manhood and womanhood but also in the oneness that is proper to marriage. Now since any perfecting of the person makes him more open to God and neighbour, the personal union which is marriage must also order the partners more fully to God and neighbour. But that union, which embraces every dimension of the personality, has a sexual dimension and therefore includes the ordination of sex to fruitfulness. Marriage being thus intrinsically ordered to fatherhood and motherhood, sexual love exhibits fatherly and motherly characteristics from the very first, as sexual behaviour shows. By giving men a human share in God's creative power, consummated union orientates the partners to the human beings it brings forth. We must not, however, conclude, from the fact that marriage is ordered to the child, that marriage apart from children is meaningless or even non-existent. In that case all marriages which were known in advance to be childless, or which eventually proved to be such, would be invalid. This is admittedly wrong. On the other hand marriage is ordered not only to sexual encounter but also to procreation, and that so essentially that it is also agreed that no one can contract a valid marriage on the understanding that there shall be no sexual union or no children. Even where the partners *intend* to abstain, the *right* to sex is admitted; and the exclusion of children on principle invalidates matrimonial consent.

This interpretation of the nature and purpose of marriage seeks to avoid the widespread tendency to assert a "hierarchy" or a "dualism" in respect of the ends of marriage. The matter is a weighty one, considering the problems of moral theology that are involved. Whereas in the "hierarchical" view marriage exists primarily for the sake of procreation, only secondarily and derivatively for the sake of the marriage partners, the "dualist" view is always tempted to treat the child as an end that is really extrinsic to marriage. But in fact the procreation of children and the perfecting of the partners are not so much subordinated or diverse "ends" of marriage as co-ordinate structural principles of one total entity, marriage. This view of the nature and purpose of marriage is made possible, and indeed suggested, by certain utterances of Vatican II (Pastoral Constitution on the Church in the Modern World, arts. 47–52), which regard mutual love as the norm and meaning of marriage and at the same time affirm the ordination of marriage to the child who arises from the core of this love. Nor does this interpretation conflict with traditional doctrine as laid down in the Code of Canon Law (can. 1013) and other documents of the Church's magisterium, since that doctrine never divorces the purely biological ordination of sexuality to procreation from the total personal encounter of the sexes, much less subordinates the encounter to procreation. Indeed one is compelled to say that such a moral interpretation would falsify the purpose of sex by treating a personal value as a means to a biological end. Precisely to forestall such an interpretation Pius XII declared artificial insemination unlawful (*AAS* 41 [1949], pp. 557–61; 47 [1956], pp. 467–74).

The nature and purpose of marriage — especially as a sacrament — account for its necessary unity and indissolubility. By unity, we mean an exclusive and total union between one man and one woman. And indissolubility means that the union is lifelong. These characteristics derive from the natural ordination of the partners to one another, antecedent to the sacramental nature of marriage, for marriage is of itself a total surrender of each partner to the other for life. Given our frail, earth-bound, historical nature, a conditional dedication would be plausible, for when it comes to complex moral decisions we are our own masters subjectively but not objectively. For we can revoke our decisions, and we can neither foresee all that they imply for the future nor be fully aware of how past experiences shape our present motives. Nevertheless only an unconditional dedication quite befits the dignity of the human person, since it alone fully affirms and accepts the partner in a way appropriate to the total union and completion of body and soul in marriage. Polygamy and bigamy, therefore, reflect a shallow, actualistic attitude towards common life and sexual dedication.

Generally speaking they are more unfavourable to the woman, who finds it much more difficult — because she is more inclined to give herself wholly, because her maternal task ties her more closely to the family and because of her role in society — to break away from one set of social circumstances and adapt to another. Unity and indissolubility follow still more emphatically from the sacramental character of marriage, since marriage not only fully represents Christ's union with the Church but as a sacrament creates so intimate a supernatural bond that the partners are taken up into the mystery of redemption in a unique and specific way. When this sacramental marriage is consummated, the marriage bond acquires a new strength and perfection. Despite wearisome medieval discussions of the subject, however, the theological significance of the consummation of marriage has not been fully worked out even today.

For these reasons the Church teaches that marriage is intrinsically indissoluble — that is, that married people, whether Christian or not, can never abandon their own marriage and then lawfully contract a new one. Common life, however, can be given up for grave and just reasons (separation from bed and board — *separatio tori, mensae et habitationis: CIC,* can. 1128–32) so as to avoid a greater evil — that is, if continuing to live together as befits the nature and purpose of marriage as such, would in the actual circumstances be contrary to the dignity of either party or the good of the family or both. The right of the innocent party to a separation is limited by the duties of love, because marriage is a total dedication — which of course does not involve, but excludes, self-destruction.

The Church also teaches that sacramental marriage, once consummated, is indissoluble from without: that it can be ended by no power on earth, only by the death of the partners (*CIC,* can. 1118; cf. *DS* 1805–7). Apparently the reason is that in sacramental terms this marriage represents without restriction the union Christ has consummated with the Church. Further, "becoming one flesh" brings about a union in grace with God and each other, of divine origin, which no human intervention can affect. All other marriages can in certain circumstances be dissolved "extrinsically", that is, by human authority. Thus the unconsummated marriage of a baptized person can be dissolved by the solemn profession of religious vows. By the Pauline privilege even a consummated marriage between pagans can be dissolved if one partner is converted and the other will no longer live with him in the spirit of the natural moral law *(since contemptu creatoris)*. By the Petrine privilege the Pope sometimes dissolves a marriage between unbaptized persons or between baptized and unbaptized persons on other weighty grounds in the interests of the faith.

The Church has not always seen the problem of the extrinsic dissolubility of marriage in the same light, and has still not worked it out in every detail. We must say that the problem was an unimportant one for the Church in the first millennium. Originally, no doubt, stricter notions prevailed on the indissolubility of marriage, so that the permission given in Mt 5:32 and 19:9 to dismiss a spouse for unchastity at first applied to adultery alone, extending only by degrees to other offences against marriage. Even the Pauline privilege was not originally understood to allow a dissolution of marriage from without, but a separation from bed and board; only with the reforms of Gregory VII and the consequent recasting of canon law did the present interpretation win general acceptance. Doubts which arose before that time in some areas — notably in the Eastern Church, and then later among the Anglo-Saxons, Franks, and Germans — about how to treat people who, after a separation for some reason or another, entered upon a new union, were based on pastoral rather than dogmatic considerations, since re-marriage, though admittedly against the divine law, was held to be the lesser evil in some cases. Thus from the early 4th century down to the present time there have been certain differences between the Eastern and the Western Church in the disciplinary treatment of separation and remarriage.

If the matter of the extrinsic dissolubility of marriage was not much gone into in early times the reason probably was that the Church only recognized more clearly after A.D. 1000 its competence and duties with respect to marriage and then began to take more of an interest in the law of marriage. This development was fostered by the legalistic thought which so strongly marked the Middle Ages, and its desire to create an orderly society; and concretely by the Church's assumption of full jurisdiction as regards marriage. Whereas marriage had earlier been regarded as a more or less private concern of the two partners in which of course they were subject to God's laws, now much more was made of the Church's right and duty to control the institution of marriage. The development of our modern dogmatic concept of a sacrament also helped the process along a good deal. So laboriously and by degrees, with much fierce argument among theologians and canonists, it was finally established that the sacrament comes into being through the partners' matrimonial consent, but the external indissolubility only through consummation of the marriage. At the same time it was not only agreed that other marriages could be dissolved in the interests of the faith *(in favorem fidei),* but the validity of the contract was considerably restricted by legislation and the multiplication of impediments. Theological discussion of the Church's role in the contracting of marriage and in its external dissolubility continues. It is clear that the intervention of the Church in certain specific ways is essential for the contracting and continuation of sacramental marriage. It is also clear that the Church exercises jurisdiction over non-sacramental marriages only in relation to the faith. It is not quite clear how far non-Christian religious bodies and civil society have jurisdiction over non-sacramental marriages. And the precise explanation of the jurisdiction of the Church with regard to sacramental marriages is also obscure. How widely the *in favorem fidei* is to be interpreted is a matter that will need further study — not least in view of what the second Vatican Council says about the orientation of non-Catholics to salvation.

2. *Moral theology.* a) *The ends of marriage and matrimonial ethics.* Matrimonial ethics must be deduced from the nature and purpose of marriage and the basic structures of marriage which result therefrom. This point must be particularly stressed because, as we have seen, the Fathers and especially St. Augustine proceeded in the opposite direction; working from a negative kind of sexual ethics, they developed the idea of the *bona excusantia,* the goods of marriage which made it a respectable state. True, St. Thomas makes these the intrinsic structural principles of marriage, but he is still so dominated by Augustine's rigorist, pessimistic, narrowly sexual view of

marriage that he too places the problem of whether the sexual act is lawful in the foreground of his matrimonial ethics. For him too the basic thing in marriage is the procreation of offspring. This profound and fundamental element is constantly elevated to the higher planes of matrimonial common life and the sacrament, there acquiring an ever richer and more meaningful reality. But these levels still remain a "circumstance", a "superadditum", with regard to the more primary and "natural". Only in this context can we understand why the doctrine of the goods of marriage faded into the background from the 16th and 17th century onwards, leaving the *copula per se apta ad generationem* as the decisive standard of matrimonial ethics. This isolated stress on sex restricted considerably the perspective of matrimonial ethics. Even in the assessment of the marriage act, the accent was placed too one-sidedly on the formal structure of the physiological process. Thus a comprehensive matrimonial ethics, aiming at the intrinsic purpose of marriage, was not envisaged. Accordingly, neo-Scholastic matrimonial ethics — especially by introducing the notion of the *actus perfecti et imperfecti* — is largely a matter of analytical casuistry and prohibitions: nothing must be done contrary to the "natural" use of marriage. Now matrimonial ethics must not be reduced to mere sexual ethics; even though the latter is essential to the former, it is only a part of matrimonial ethics. And if matrimonial ethics is not to be mutilated, it must be related to matrimonial dogma with all the latter's anthropological implications. Only thus shall we find an ethics which does justice both to the dignity of this sacrament and to the reality of this state, since the various dimensions and levels of marriage can be brought into the closest possible harmony only if we order them all to the nature and purpose of marriage.

b) *The married state and the ideal of perfection.* We must start from the premise that marriage is a saving state through which those called to it are to reach their appropriate Christian perfection. That is, married people must regard the opportunities and tasks which marriage alone brings them as an essential part of their striving towards perfection; so that their perfection is to be achieved only through marriage, not outside it. All religious decisions taken by the partners must take their marriage into account, so that they

gain an entirely new perspective on their fully individual salvation, having to include the salvation of the partner in all their decisions. Hence it can rightly be said that marriage really becomes the saving state for the partners, the way to their perfection. It directly perfects a man who lives it according to its nature and purpose, and yet does not perfect him absolutely. For what grace does through sacramental marriage is to make a man more like Christ in one particular respect. Naturally this must not be understood to mean that marriage is the absolute way or even the most privileged way to human perfection. For perfection embraces every aspect of man's being and is therefore inexhaustible. We can attain it only to a limited extent, because our contingency, individuality, and particular circumstances mean that we never realize all our potentialities to the same degree and in perfect harmony. Thus marriage makes a man more perfectly human, but only in a way that is proper to marriage, not in every possible way. And so marriage as a state that leads to religious and moral perfection should not be contrasted with virginity. Each perfects man in its own way; and when all the concrete circumstances are right, virginity is better able to lead us to perfection as such, to total union with God. But virginity is not the best road for every individual to his own particular perfection; it is only best for those called to it. For the married, virginity should be a heartening example of self-denying love, just as the married should be a privileged example of self-sharing love. In this context marriage and virginity do not clash, but each sets off the other and makes it fruitful.

Though Scripture gives the principles of such a view, it is only in our day that theologians have become conscious of marriage as a state which actually leads those called to it to salvation and Christian perfection. Now we are witnessing the growth of an independent, positive spirituality for married people. We are shaking off the idea that marriage must be accepted because of the contingence and frailty of human nature but is rather a hindrance than a help to moral and religious perfection.

c) *Mutual completion.* If marriage is seen as a saving state which leads to religious and moral perfection, then its fundamental law must be the duty of the partners to do whatever will foster the love that completes and unites them, and avoid whatever will frustrate or destroy it; to orientate themselves as companions to the transcendent purpose of marriage which their complementing union makes possible — fruitfulness not merely biological but also moral and religious thanks to their new religious situation.

The final criterion of what concrete acts foster or frustrate marriage must always be what acts befit the partners as such. The specific possibility of union and completeness in marriage has a sexual component. But sexuality determines in various ways the totality of human nature. For men can only realize their nature in a sexual way, though on the other hand it is human nature that makes sexuality possible.

Completion means concretely that the husband helps his wife to be a woman, and the wife helps her husband to be a man. So the partners are to affirm each other in their difference, each thus helping the other to find selfhood. Now the specific completion which marriage offers is of a sexual nature, and must therefore also be sought in the realm of sex. But it must be remembered that while sexuality is directly biological, it is indirectly affected by sociological, economic, and psychical factors — and therefore also by spiritual and religious factors. And so completion is to be sought in all these domains, in the way appropriate to each; and the same with selfhood. However much it unites the partners, marriage must not impose uniformity but help each towards real manhood or womanhood — which are always intrinsically ordered to fatherhood or motherhood. One of the major problems in our modern spirituality of marriage is this: that for historical reasons access to the specific roles of man and woman, particularly that of woman, has become more difficult. Many marriages go through crises because the difference between the sexes is practically ignored, or is interpreted in an out-of-date way, and therefore it is most important for matrimonial ethics to ascertain how the sexes should complete each other today, so that marriage partners can act accordingly.

On the other hand completion presupposes a harmonious understanding, above all in matters that are specifically human, and therefore religious and moral harmony but also psychical, social and economic, and also biological harmony. Hence the choice of a partner must be made with care, taking everything into account, from religion to eugenics. In view of advances in medicine and the mounting scale of mutations it is all the more vital to consider eugenic factors; for the equilibrium between mutation and elimination in man now seems to be not far from the point where any further burdening of the inheritance might well jeopardize the continued existence of mankind.

d) *Mixed marriages.* Marriages between persons of different religions present a special problem in this respect. They are inevitably on the increase, because of the evolution of society and religion alike, and yet always make the common life of the partners considerably more difficult, the more so in proportion as the partners have firm religious convictions and are conscious of the religious dimension in marriage. The sacramental structure of marriage does not give it religious relevance, but simply makes that relevance crystal-clear. Marriage already has a religious character in that it embraces the total human being, including his moral and religious dimensions. On the other hand, marriage as a total claim and an intimate communion is particularly vulnerable to sin and its consequences. For that reason excluding the religious element, or relegating it to the background, must always prove detrimental to the whole marriage. As a rule one cannot simply say that difference of religion between the partners need not matter if only they are tolerant of each other; for tolerance makes co-existence possible but not oneness. By the nature of the case the disadvantages of a mixed marriage are even plainer when the marriage is blessed with children. For the child is not only the fruit of physical union; the development of his personality is decisively affected by the totality of the unity of his parents' marriage. So it is a mistake to look on mixed marriages as an admirable field for missionary work, for the attainment of each partner's special perfection pre-supposes common thinking and feeling to a very high degree. It will be all the more effective, the more the partners have humanly in common. The same ways of thinking and acting are more a foundation of marriage than a result of it. Thus 1 Cor 7:16 warns against false self-assurance as to the possibility of converting the unbelieving partner. On the other hand Paul stresses in the same context that the unbelieving partner, if he is prepared to live with the Christian one, will be sanctified by the believer (cf. also 1 Pet 3:1: wives must try to win over their unbelieving husbands to the faith by the silent example of their manner of life). Mixed marriages come nearest to being justified where there is no religious prejudice — a different thing from tolerance — and especially where the lack of prejudice is combined with a receptiveness to religion. So one must not hastily generalize about the difficulties involved in mixed marriages or make too much of them; not only because doing so makes the pastoral approach unjustifiably difficult and increases the danger of excluding religion from mixed marriages, but above all because given an unprejudiced outlook these marriages can prove sanctifying.

e) *The union of husband and wife* calls for a partnership so intimate that it is neither possible nor desirable outside marriage. It means strict solidarity and absolute faithfulness and the closest intimacy at every level including the bodily one. This is what makes adultery so grave at its various levels, just as it emphasizes the various degrees of "obligation" to conjugal dedication. A common house, table, and bed are as desirable in general for the sake of union as are common planning, finances, and action. Priority and subordination can be meaningful within this partnership only insofar as they contribute to union. Matrimonial modesty is to protect intimate union against misunderstandings arising from without, and against undue strain from within. And sexuality should be used in this encounter between partners to the extent that it will foster union, and subordinated to the extent that it would hinder it. That is the law of marital chastity. Of course this fellowship is only possible and desirable insofar as it fosters the dignity and personality of each partner, or at least does them no harm. Partnership and independence do not conflict in marriage; they nourish each other because love addresses the other person in his freedom and tries to persuade, not to coerce, when sacrifices are necessary for the sake of the partnership. It follows that partnership ceases at the point where either partner attempts to abuse the other for selfish ends. Any such attempt, and any readiness to let oneself become the slavish instrument of the other, is sinful, the more grievously so the more personal

judgment, freedom, and responsibility are violated. The duty of marriage partners to integrate all the many dimensions of marriage into their personality so far as possible often encounters great difficulties in the sexual sphere, for the management of this emotionally explosive force demands great personal maturity and is often made more difficult by the concrete conditions of civilization. All the same we should beware of trying to lay down in objective detail what befits the dignity of the human person and what does not, for that often depends on very individual factors; and we should be still more hesitant to say how far a person is responsible in a concrete situation and how far the situation arises from pre-personal factors. We must also remember that difficulties of adjustment in other aspects of marriage may result from differences of origin or upbringing, ingrained habits, crowded living conditions, insufficient acquaintance with one another and so on, and can only be overcome by a gradual growth in understanding and love. A matrimonial ethics that is no longer narrowly sexual has to call attention to the moral significance of all these factors in marriage; for the success of a marriage will often depend precisely on them.

f) *Marriage looks beyond itself,* and first of all requires the partners not to suppose that their exclusive, lifelong partnership shuts them off from God and all other people. Marriage must not be lived as a solitude for two, for the completion and union marriage brings tends of its own nature to make the partners more open to God and their neighbour. Since marriage of itself enables one to be more human in a specific way, and as a sacrament draws one deeper into the mystery of Christ, and therefore of God, it demands that one live in union with God and man and affirm both. But complete physical dedication to everyone cannot be what is meant by that greater capacity which we objectively receive and which should make us subjectively more disposed to love. For being bodily and temporal, we can make a complete and ultimate gift of ourselves only once, since, unlike spiritual values, spatio-temporal things can only be at the disposal of one person by being withdrawn from others. Spiritual values can be shared with others without thereby being divided or diminished, and in fact they count more by being thus shared. But a spatial object can be possessed only by one person at a time: no one can make use of it while it is in another's hands. Now in marriage a person gives himself completely and finally together with his bodiliness, so that to make himself available to a third person would be to withdraw the gift from his partner. Moreover, we can never realize our existence definitively in any given moment, but only step by step, so that the definitive gift of ourselves can only be made, in the concrete, by a lifetime of devotion. Being more open must therefore mean that because of the new and deeper self-discovery a person has made in marriage, in the union of man and wife, he is better able and more disposed to affirm all others in their otherness, to love them as they are, and also to accept himself with his limitations — even with his limited capacity for love.

Moral and religious fruitfulness, when the circumstances are right, should also take concrete shape in physical fruitfulness, marriage widening out into the family. The aim must not be to produce as many children as possible but to found a family which will be qualitatively the best possible. For personal responsibility must always be the proximate norm of specifically human, and therefore moral, acts. In the case of marriage, this means that the right number of children is the number which will best favour the personal development of all members of the family, at the same time taking account of the wider interests of society. Regulation of births will thus be necessary generally speaking. But it should always be inspired by a generous spirit of self-giving love in accordance with the purpose of marital fruitfulness. If marriage is divorced from its purpose — which of course transcends physical fruitfulness but includes it within the bounds of what is physically possible and morally responsible — its nature, "dualistically" split off from its purpose, will also be misunderstood and the result will be a group selfishness hostile to life. If the purpose of marriage is misinterpreted in "hierarchical" fashion, so that the greatest possible number of children actually becomes the ideal, then in sexual union one partner cannot "intend" the other for his own sake, as a person, but only "use" him as a means to a physiological end. Further, in such a case the right of the children already in the

family to live and develop — and perhaps the rights of society as well — would be irresponsibly infringed: marriage would become a mere institute for the breeding of children.

3. *Canon law*. Canon law as it relates to marriage must so dispose the faithful for the salvation to be communicated by marriage that the pastors of the Church can help them not to misunderstand or abuse marriage but to live fittingly in that state. Matrimonial law must therefore regulate for marriage, the social dimensions of which bear so directly on salvation, to further the common good of the people of God and the moral and religious advancement of individual Christians. Civil society attends to those aspects of marriage which affect the temporal common good.

a) *Marriage in the CIC*. The present law on marriage is substantially contained in can. 1012–1143 of the *CIC*. It codifies in a legally binding way the nature and effects of marriage, the rules of matrimonial consent, the impediments to marriage, the form for the celebration of the marriage and the laws on separation, so that the juridical norms for the regulation of sacramental marriage are ready at hand. For pastoral reasons a clearer and more compact arrangement would be better. These rules are not directly dogmatic but pastoral in nature. They were drawn up against the background of conceptions of marriage and the Church which have now in part been superseded by the findings of contemporary theologians and the declarations of the Second Vatican Council. As the expression of a mentality not abreast of the times, these juridical formulas often conflict with pastoral needs, causing real or psychological difficulties when there is no necessity to do so either by the nature of the case or for the sake of clarity. A comparison between can. 1013 and 1081, § 2, for example, and what the Pastoral Constitution on the Church in the Modern World has to say about marriage (art. 48), or between the canonical rules on mixed marriages and the present ecumenical spirit, will give some idea of the difference in point of view between the *CIC* and the Second Vatican Council. Considering the new understanding we have of the Church, and the needs of our time, the centralizing tendency in the regulation of matrimonial law seems questionable. A certain shift in emphasis from legislation to judicial rulings would seem more appropriate to our present idea of personal responsibility, and would make fairer decisions possible in cases that have not been, and could not be, foreseen, without any need for too frequent changes in the law. Again, various provisions are based on sociological and pastoral assumptions that have been overtaken by events. In this connection it would be well to reconsider without prejudice the civil laws of matrimony, which could not hitherto be done because of various obstacles (cf. can. 1016). It is therefore very important that we gain a deeper insight into the function of matrimonial law, so as to know how it can help solve pastoral problems, and be better able to judge the limitations of the present matrimonial law. This last is particularly desirable in view of the reform of matrimonial legislation which has been initiated by the Holy See.

b) The canons on the *nature and effects of marriage* set forth the differences between sacramental and non-sacramental, contracted *(ratum)* and consummated, valid and invalid marriage; they enumerate the "goods" of marriage and the effects of marriage as to unity and indissolubility, and the rights and duties of the partners. Can. 1111 affirms the wife's strict equality of rights as regards physical partnership. But as regards common life, can. 1112 provides that she shares the status of her husband, with regard to canonical effects, unless special provision has been made to the contrary. Thus the husband is given priority in the guidance of the family. The rights of the wife should also be expressly set down; suggestions of male domination should be eliminated.

c) The juridical implications of *matrimonial consent,* which constitutes marriage, are the subject of can. 1081–93. For a marriage to be validly contracted, they provide (i) that the matrimonial consent must be actually, present on both sides; (ii) that both parties must be able to marry; and (iii) that their consent must be expressed in the legally obligatory form. The consent itself must (i) relate to the nature of marriage, (ii) relate to a particular person, and (iii) be freely given. The law then determines in what circumstances these conditions for matrimonial consent are presumed to be verified; what minimum knowledge and acceptance of the nature of marriage are presupposed; it introduces the notion of error with regard to the person and "simple error"; and says when unjust external coercion, or grave fear induced within, makes the consent juridically invalid.

It is often difficult to apply these canons in a given case at law, because the criteria for the presence of an adequate consent are only adequate within limits, and because the purely legal presumption of a consent which is not actually present seems questionable in many respects when we consider how marriage bears on salvation. Perhaps the main difficulty is that nowadays the needful maturity for marriage cannot be so readily and so generally presumed as is done in the *CIC;* for on the one hand it has become extraordinarily difficult for many people to recognize and grasp personally that marriage is indissoluble, on account of the widespread errors touching the substance of marriage, and the *de facto* breakdown of marriage in so many cases; and on the other hand, the findings of modern psychology and sociology show that the personal moral maturity presupposed in the total obligation of marriage is more often and more seriously retarded than one was inclined to think in earlier times. Moreover, the conceptual difference between error with regard to the person and error with regard to the qualities of the person is perhaps too formal and not always very convincing. Serious vices, or circumstances altogether different from what the person represented them to be, and which, had they been known, would have precluded the marriage, do not seem to have been properly allowed for here.

d) The provisions on *impediments to marriage* recite factors which either because of natural law or because of a divine command exclude the possibility of marriage (diriment impediments of divine right are: an existing marriage, impotence, blood relationship in the direct line and probably in the first degree of the collateral line) or limit its lawfulness. Then come the impediments to marriage which the Church has laid down. These prohibitions of marriage are more or less obvious ones. Ecclesiastical prohibitions of marriage may restrict the natural right to marry, one of the fundamental human rights, only for weighty reasons. On the other hand the pastors of the Church have a duty to establish such impediments to marriage insofar as called for by the common good of the people of God and the good of individual Christians. Undoubtedly the scheme of impediments in force at the moment needs adaptation in the light of present-day pastoral needs, so that the natural right to marry may be limited as little as possible and only as far as necessary. Modest beginnings have already been made with the instruction of the Congregation for the Doctrine of the Faith dated 19 March 1966 (cf. Bibliography). It seems questionable whether the principle of the utmost possible legislative uniformity for the whole Church should apply to matrimonial impediments (cf. can. 1038–41), and one may hope that greater clarity and compactness will be attained in the diriment impediments. For example, why does the diriment impediment of abduction (can. 1074) appear again in quite another connection in can. 1087, where the Church declares that external coercion and grave fear invalidate matrimonial consent? Again it seems unnecessary to make impotence a separate impediment (can. 1068) when can. 1081, § 2, provides that there can be no matrimonial consent in such a case. There would appear to be more reason for making a special impediment of homosexuality in cases where the man is sexually potent but cannot take a sexual interest in a woman. Under certain circumstances eugenic considerations might make it necessary to limit the right to marry. At least in the more advanced countries people should be asked to provide a sufficient account of their heredity and genetic prospects.

The Church cannot dispense from the natural moral law or from divine positive law, but not every offence against these will invalidate a marriage. Thus a mixed marriage contracted in disregard of conscience is morally illicit, even if the Church dispenses from the canonical impediment, but not invalid. In principle all ecclesiastical impediments can be dispensed from; but the Church never dispenses from the impediment arising from episcopal consecration, and hardly ever from the impediment of public conjugal murder, affinity (by marriage) of the first degree in the direct line after consummation of the marriage, or priestly ordination. The practice of dispensing so as to regularize invalid marriages (ad convalidandum matrimonium) was established as early as the 6th century, but that of dispensing beforehand so that a marriage can be contracted (pro matrimonio contrahendo) dates only from the 11th or 12th century. To this day it is not usual in Greek Orthodox canon law to dispense from impediments to marriage. Dispensations are granted according to whether impediments are public or secret for the external or merely internal forum, by the appropriate authorities. Details of procedure are very complex. Where the diriment impediment ceases to exist in an invalid marriage, the marriage can be regularized by renewal of consent (can. 1133–7), or in the case of sanatio in radice (can. 1138–41), where the consent continues, even without explicit renewal of the consent.

The distinction between impedient and diriment impediments does not refer directly to dispensability but to the canonical validity or invalidity of marriage. It follows that matrimonial impediments may have the indirect function of dissolving marriages (from without) which for some reason are thought undesirable. For this very purpose the impediments to marriage were greatly widened when matrimonial law was recast and expanded in the Middle Ages. Even in our present law some traces remain, such as the impediment of affinity (can. 1077) and that of spiritual relationship (can. 1079), both of which used to extend much farther than they now do. The reason to some extent for these impediments was a mistaken attitude to physical sexuality: it used to be assumed that becoming one flesh with the marriage partner established a metaphysical bond, in the nature of kinship, with the partner's relatives and that standing sponsor at a baptism (rebirth) also created a quasi-parental bond, the basis for all sorts of metaphysical relationships that ruled out marriage. We must therefore ask how far it now serves any useful purpose to keep traditional impediments in being which a different mental and social context produced and made meaningful. Similarly the impediment of "mixed religion" (can. 1060–4) derives in part from a background of solidly Catholic or Protestant regions (cuius regio, eius religio) and a closed society, that has quite changed today with the great mobility of population and with spiritual pluralism.

The impedient impediments have much the same effects as the prohibitions of marriage, which, for example, forbid marrying lapsed Catholics and members of proscribed societies (can. 1065) and affect the marriage of a public sinner or someone under certain censures. In individual cases a prohibition of marriage may make up for the lack of a matrimonial impediment (cf. can. 1039).

e) The Church's right to determine the *form of marriage* follows from its duty to regulate marriage, including its social aspects, by taking steps appropriate to the nature of the Church to prevent bigamy, arbitrary dissolution of marriage, and the like, so far as may be necessary or desirable; and from its duty to make it clear in fitting ways that marriage is a sacrament and that God joins the marriage partners together. So on the one hand it must beware of abetting moral abuses in the common life of the sexes, such as sometimes prevailed in the Middle Ages, by doing too little; and on the other hand it must not interfere with the freedom to marry, or obscure the fact that bride and groom themselves contract the marriage, by any undue perfectionism. In this connection many question the wisdom of the present regulations for mixed marriages.

Historically speaking, the prescribed form of marriage has evolved from the liturgical rite of betrothal. Its main features are that the bridal pair freely bind themselves together, and that God joins them together as testified by the presence of the Church. The former feature was sometimes so much overstressed in the Latin Church, to the neglect of the form for contracting marriage, that clandestine marriages abounded. But only since the decree *Ne temere* of 2 August 1907 has the active, not merely passive, presence of the priest as the Church's representative been normally necessary. Since then the theology of the Church's necessary part in the contracting of marriage has been considerably deepened. In the Eastern Church, by contrast, so much is made of blessing the bridal pair that they were sometimes not even asked whether they wished to marry, and so a certain clericalist distortion of the sacrament was not excluded. Under the law now in force (can. 1099; motu proprio of Pius XII, 1 August 1948), the Church requires all who were baptized Catholics and all converts to the Catholic Church to use either the ordinary (can. 1094) or the extraordinary form (can. 1098) for contracting marriage. Except in case of emergency, marriage is celebrated according

to the matrimonial rite (can. 1100). Non-Catholics, whether baptized or not, who have never belonged to the Catholic Church are not bound to this form when they marry among themselves. In the ordinary form (can. 1095–9) marriage is contracted before the competent priest and two witnesses. Under Oriental canon law the nuptial blessing is also necessary to the validity of the marriage, except in case of emergency. When marriage is contracted in the extraordinary form, the presence of a competent priest is not necessary: here the Church is present only in its prescriptions. Marriage may be contracted in this extraordinary form only when a competent priest cannot attend, either through physical impossibility or because grave detriment would result for him or Christian people; and, except in danger of death, only when it is prudently judged that the emergency will last at least four weeks.

f) The rules for the *dissolution of marriage* first lay down the circumstances in which the marriage-bond can be extrinsically dissolved — where the main consideration is *in favorem fidei* —, and then what is involved in separation *a mensa et thoro*. There must be grounds for separation so serious that it is too much to expect a person to continue common life, and the interests of the children must be safeguarded so far as possible. Can. 1132 insists that in all circumstances the Catholic education of the children must be guaranteed.

g) Then can. 1960–92 deal with *matrimonial causes in Church courts*. Here many details call for reform. More must be done to safeguard the rights of the person involved, and especially to see that the parties involved take a more personal and responsible part in the exercise of their rights. Oriental canon law agrees with the Latin on all essential points (*Ius Orientale matrimoniale*, can. 1–131; *Ius Orientale judiciale*, can. 468–500).

4. *Pastoral theology*. The most urgent task of pastoral theology is to strengthen the awareness of Christian people that marriage is a saving state which leads those called to it to their due perfection. The existing principles of special spirituality for married people must be further developed. In particular we must not minimize the tension between the "secular" and the sacred in marriage, but rather see that we acquire a

better grasp of its full range — which always involves correlation between the two. Much can be done to that end by overcoming anti-sexual prejudices which are still widespread. We must warmly welcome modern advances in sexual knowledge and sex instruction. It would be a great pity if disagreeable overtones in this accelerating process of enlightenment caused us to suppress the hopeful beginnings that have been made towards banishing a misguided taboo, especially since repressed sexuality would then break out in unruly and unhealthy forms. Many, even many married people, have not acquired the art of speaking and communicating with each other in a way which befits the dignity and realities of sexuality, and this circumstance often creates grave difficulties in marriage. In particular, the notion of woman's role in marriage and the family needs fundamental revision. Moreover, a great many married people will inevitably be alienated from religion unless unnecessary harshness and false emphases in the law of marriage are corrected, and unless a suitable pastoral approach is worked out for couples of different religions and couples who have drifted away from religion. Courses for engaged couples and the development of Catholic marriage-guidance councils, staffed by qualified experts, may be a beginning. The recognition that the multi-dimensional development of society has increasingly involved marriage and the family in a complex social network should help us to acknowledge that it is now more often appropriate to make use of social workers to solve matrimonial problems. The Church should direct more attention to the problems of a choice of partner, early marriage, and the physical and mental health that marriage calls for, even sometimes at the sacrifice of familiar and cherished ideas that do not square with reality. Training of conscience, the practice of the confessional, and methods of pastoral dialogue will all have to be adapted to the deeper insights we have gained in our day into sacramental marriage, which shapes and claims the whole human being.

See also *Education* I, II, *Society* I, II, *Natural Law*, *Sex* II, III.

BIBLIOGRAPHY. MAGISTERIUM: Leo XIII, *Arcanum divinae*, 10 February 1880: *ASS* 12 (1879–80), pp. 388 ff.; Pius XI, *Casti connubii*, 31 December 1930: *AAS* 22 (1930); Pius XII, *Dear Newlyweds*, ed. by J., J., and B. Murray (1961); Vatican II, *Gaudium et Spes*, 7 December 1965; S. Congregatio pro doctrina fidei, *Instructio de matrimoniis mixtis*, "*Matrimonii Sacramentum*": *AAS* 58 (1966), pp. 235–9. LITERATURE: D. von Hildebrand, *Marriage* (1931); G. H. Joyce, *Christian Matrimony* (3rd ed., 1934); J.-M. Perrin, *Perfection chrétienne et vie conjugale* (1946); G. Reidick, *Die hierarchische Struktur der Ehe* (1953); M. Müller, *Die Lehre des hl. Augustinus von der Paradiesehe und ihre Auswirkung in der Sexualethik der 12. und 13. Jahrhunderten bis Thomas von Aquin* (1954); J. Dupont, *Mariage et divorce dans l'évangile* (1959); J. de Fabregas, *Christian Marriage* (1959); P. Grelot, *Man and Woman in Scripture* (1962); G. Teichtweier, *Eheliches Leben heute* (1963); H. Rondet, *Introduction à l'étude de la théologie du mariage* (1960); J. Kerns, *The Theology of Marriage* (1964); H. Doms, *Gatteneinheit und Nachkommenschaft* (1965); B. Häring, *Marriage in the Modern World* (1965); E. Schillebeeckx, *Marriage: Human Reality and Saving Mystery* (1966); B. Häring, *The Law of Christ*, III (1966); D. von Hildebrand, *Man and Woman* (1966); L. M. Weber, *On Marriage, Sex and Virginity*, Quaestiones Disputatae 16 (1966); *A New Catechism: Catholic Faith for Adults* (the Dutch Catechism) (1967), pp. 381–403.

Waldemar Molinski

II. Parents

A. PARENTHOOD

1. When parents bring a child into the world, they make use of their ability to participate in God's creative power, which they do in a human and therefore analogous, but nevertheless unique manner. In giving new life, they share the work of the ultimate giver of all life. They are made more perfect through parenthood, as the child that has been given life opens up the well-springs of maternal and paternal love. Like God, who in his wisdom created us out of pure love, they not only take upon themselves the responsibility of passing on life in wisdom and love, but also the duty to care for their children. God brings his creation to fulfilment by ordaining the infra-human to man, and through his providence self-revelation and grace enables man to work with the help of the Church, freely and responsibly towards his own salvation; similarly, parents must bring up and educate their children, giving them the material things they need and enabling them to make the best use of their physical and mental abilities, so that as the result of parental education, supplemented by that of the Church and society, they become capable of making their own free responsible decisions.

2. In parenthood parents participate in the authority of God as origin "from whom all fatherhood in heaven and earth takes its title" (Eph 3:15). This authority is unique and takes precedence before any other. It is above all the result of actual parental care and is generally greater than any other authority, as is clearly shown by the limited influence of other authorities, such as school or Church. Thus St. Thomas Aquinas, for instance, regards parents as the child's natural and total principle of existence, describing the child as "part of the father" and the family as his "spiritual womb" (*III Sententiarum*, 4, 2, 1 ad 4).

Parents exercise an authority over their children that is subjective and objective, personal and *ex officio,* based on their personal superior position and their educational task. The exercise of parents' authority should, as befits its personal nature, emanate mainly from their care and love, while their *ex officio* authority is primarily and directly a matter of the objective rightness of the institutional aspect and only indirectly personal. This shows that parents have a primary authority, while that of Church and State is secondary, and typologically exemplified in parental authority.

The responsibility of parents arises from the fact that they have given life to the child, which has come helpless into the world, entirely dependent on loving care. Children do not only owe their existence to their parents, but also hereditary traits, and their later development will be decisively influenced by pre- and post-natal factors to which they are inevitably exposed. They need parents to maintain them and help them in their development as human beings. They need particularly their religious example, as faith can only be fostered by bearing witness to it and removing obstacles, as faith is always in danger and unable to establish itself unaided because of our human limitations and sinfulness.

As parents have given the child life, they must *provide* for all his needs. The child will turn spontaneously to those who love and cherish him, to find support and help in taking his place in society. The relationship between creator and creature is therefore the eminent typological example of the parent-child relationship; thus arises the relationship of authority and subordination which is basic to any educational process.

The basis of parental authority is therefore the dependence of the child on its parents. Its content is determined by the needs of the children with regard to their parents. Their authority is therefore substitutional and a guardianship, that is to say, they must try through their independent parental acts to help the children as much as possible towards independence. There must also be an appropriate order and *ex officio* authority because the family community needs a certain "division of powers and functions". But the *specific* parental task is responsible care for their children in their minority. The duties and rights of parents extend as far as is necessary to ensure the development of the children into responsible adults. There are also secondary rights and duties which arise from an ordered communal family life. If for some good reason any parental functions are being exercised by foster-parents, parental rights and duties will pass to them to the same extent.

This exercise of care for their children is the basis of the parents' right to be honoured and cared for by their grown-up children if they should be in need of it and can claim it on the grounds of their own behaviour towards their children.

3. These parental duties and rights, based on the order of creation, are raised to a higher level through grace. Since God wills all mankind to be orientated towards salvation and since marriage is orientated towards participation in grace in God's union with redeemed mankind, the parent-child relationship is thus placed on a supernatural level, giving parents the task of disposing their children, as far as they can, towards salvation. They will receive the grace they need for this, if they do not refuse God's call. This supernatural dimension of parental duties and rights finds its sacramental expression and fulfilment in baptism and matrimony. As God wishes all men to be saved, parents have the duty to give their children a religious upbringing in accordance with God's will and they therefore may count on the necessary grace by virtue of the divine promises. They are, however, unable to give natural life by themselves and even less able to give supernatural life; they can only dispose hearts, for God alone is the source of grace.

By virtue of the call to supernatural

salvation, parental rights and duties have an importance which can be fully grasped only in faith. One cannot therefore expect that non-believers will grasp the gravity of parental responsibility, especially in matters of religion, in the same way as believers.

4. As the children are born of both parents, it follows that in fulfilling their parental functions, both parents have equal duties and equal rights. But as the two parents play a different role in the begetting, rearing and education of their children, a certain division of labour naturally occurs and therefore a certain division of parental duties and rights. This division of tasks between husband and wife which applies only to a limited extent and is not at all easily defined, arises out of the "nature" of fatherhood and motherhood, and also out of the specific function which each status brings with it in their particular society and which, like society itself, is subject to change.

If a division of tasks has not arisen naturally or has not been agreed upon, the necessary decisions must be taken jointly. If no agreement is reached, no one partner has any overriding right, as parental duties and rights derive directly from the parental status and are therefore of the essence of parenthood and inalienable. In such a case the superior communities of Church and State would, as subsidiary authorities, have to render aid and protection. Any precedence on the part of the man, that is, any hierarchical order, can only apply within home and family. The man represents the family unit within family and society, within which the woman is his helpmate (Eph 5:21–33; Col 3:18f.; 1 Pet 3:1); but this in no way affects basic personal rights, including the inalienable right to provide for the education of the children according to the dictates of conscience. Thus one cannot accept, for instance, any exclusive right on the part of the father to determine the children's religion, because both parents have equal rights and because of the tolerance demanded by religious freedom of conscience.

Since rights and duties correspond, and as the duties are not cancelled if one of the partners forfeits his rights because of a neglect of duty, it can happen that one parent loses the right to control education, if by a breach of duty he does not provide a suitable education for his children. However, a breach of duty, in bad faith, cannot be presumed, but must be proved. If the conscience is erroneous regarding education, no compulsion must be used, because of the right to religious freedom, unless overriding necessities of the common good or the welfare of the individual give the State a right to intervene. The Church, in accordance with its spiritual mission, can only use spiritual appeals to the faith of the parents to have the children educated in the faith and can, if necessary, apply suitable sanctions.

If a parent forfeits his rights, he is not thereby absolved from his duties; this can be important in the case of illegitimate children, for instance, or divorce.

B. Parental Duties and Rights

1. As parents participate through their parenthood in God's creative power and since their children depend on them, parental duties (as stressed by *CIC*, can. 1113) imply the following:

a) Responsible assumption of parenthood. This means that they may only bring a child into the world if they have reasonable hopes that they will be able to rear and educate him in a way worthy of a human being. Here the family is the natural framework, willed by God. Thus procreation outside marriage must be regarded as impermissible. One might even say that, because children are dependent on the two parents and the family, procreation outside marriage is a greater wrong than to use illicit methods of birth control, as these do not normally have such far-reaching deleterious effects as illegitimate birth. Hence it would also seem that it would be wrong for a condemned man to beget a child, since the child also has a right to paternal care as far as is reasonably possible.

The problem of how many children one can reasonably bring up and educate depends on so many factors which vary from case to case and family to family, that only the parents themselves can decide when they can undertake the responsibility to bring a new life into the world (cf. Vatican II, *Gaudium et Spes,* arts. 50–51). Church and society can, however, provide valuable assistance in the formation of consciences. It is necessary to pay special attention to the health of the parents — including hereditary factors — and the needs of children already born, but one might also have to consider population factors, the economic and social situation, such as living conditions, professional obligations, etc.

b) Because they have brought children into the world, parents also have a duty to look after them in a manner worthy of a human being, which includes their bodily needs: food, clothing, health, etc. This means that parents must only have as many children as they can hope to feed and they would be doing wrong if they did not make suitable provision for their children. But parents need not take upon themselves any greater — or any lesser — sacrifices than they expect of their children, but should take into account the individual needs of the various members of the family. It is also part of the parental duty to help the children found their own homes when the time comes.

c) But parents have a duty, above all, to educate their children to the best of their ability and to look after their spiritual welfare, for the proper development of the children's personality is the foremost work of care and love and the parents are, because of their status, the immediate representatives of God to their children, though of course analogously. Parents are absolutely bound to provide education and formation, making the best of their children's capabilities and their own opportunities. They must protect their children from moral dangers with which they could not be expected to cope themselves because of their immaturity. They must foster their ability to make moral decisions and support them in the good they do. Hence the right balance must be found in giving children protection and allowing them to fend for themselves.

A special duty in this connection is that of providing religious education. This is because the child is ordained to religion as to the highest fulfilment of man. It is not enough to confront the child with religious problems when he is of an age to make his own decisions, since psychological reasons and God's claim to our religious allegiance demand that religious education must start as early as possible. In any case religious problems and influences cannot be kept from the children.

Of course parents can only provide a religious education within the possibilities open to them, but as it is so important, it should be as comprehensive as possible. Parents will ful-

fil this duty if they are following their sincerely formed conscience, since in this way they are directing their own and their children's lives to God. Parents, of whatever religious creed, who permit or even actively encourage a religious education against their conscientious convictions, fail very gravely. A marriage where husband and wife have different religions or belong to different denominations within Christianity can raise such great problems in this respect that the Church has decided to forbid such marriages in general, reserving dispensation to the competent authorities and making such dispensation dependent on the provision of safeguards (cf. instruction of the Congregation for the Doctrine of the Faith, 18 March 1966). There is, however, some doubt about the pastoral advisability of such legal measures in our present age, considering the modern conditions of faith and marriage, because attempts to force religious decisions on a conscience by law can easily have a deleterious effect on the desired religious education, which today depends more than ever on the personal religious commitment of the parents. This is often more likely to be endangered than fostered by any legalism, especially with people whose links to the Church are not very strong.

d) Parents must not delegate their educational duties and rights without good reason, for example send their children to a boarding school merely for the sake of their own comfort, as their responsibility is basic and inalienable. Nor is it at all easy to replace the natural ties of the parent-child relationship, as is shown, for instance, by experiences in orphanages.

Parents must therefore see to it that anyone who takes their place pays due regard to their wishes. It would be an offence against parental rights if a State or Church institution were to assume that it was carrying out the parents' wishes without having the support of some kind of parental consensus of opinion. Institutions must take care that sufficient regard is paid to parental co-operation in the way they are educating the child. It is of course important to maintain a proper balance between parental wishes and educational expert opinion, for any one-sided influence either on the part of the parents or of the institution would be equally harmful for the child. Clearly, parental influence on institutions will be advantageous only if based on real parental responsibility; a planned schooling for parenthood must be an urgent objective of adult education.

If parents neglect their duties, they can be forced to carry them out. They can, for instance, be obliged to provide higher education, within their means, for children who are apt for it.

If, for reasons beyond their control, parents are not in a position to discharge their duties, they should be helped to help themselves as far as possible, and in the meantime the necessary services should be rendered to the children by the competent "subsidiary" authority. Thus, for instance, the school can give sexual information and education, if the parents have failed to do so and if disadvantages to the children might otherwise result. But the school also has the duty to do all in its power to ensure that the parents themselves can undertake this task.

2. Parents' duties are balanced by rights:

a) Man has an inviolable right to marry and have children as long as he can undertake the responsibility of founding a family. This means that Church and State must not set up arbitrary obstacles to marriage, nor must they demand or enforce a limitation of the number of children, except insofar as is absolutely necessary for discharging their own tasks, for the rights of parents are absolute, though limited by the rights of their children and of the societies within which they live.

b) As the right to marriage is inviolable — although one one may of course decide not to make use of this right — it follows that man also has a right to an income sufficient to maintain a family, insofar as he does not culpably neglect his duty of self-formation and work. The way this family wage is to be achieved will vary with different economic and social systems, but there can be no doubt that there is a parental right to an income sufficient to maintain a family. It is not only a question of personal dignity, but also of the service parents render to society by bringing up and educating their children. It is against distributive justice if responsible parents are expected to accept a lower standard of living than childless people of the same social group. In fact, a higher standard of living for parents would be easier to understand in view of all the additional work and trouble they have taken

upon themselves, especially if those without children are not making any particularly outstanding social contribution.

c) Finally, the parents' duty to bring up children is balanced by their right to do so, and they can decide on the form and content of their education according to the opportunities available. Only in this way can they do what their conscience demands of them. It follows that, to safeguard their basic rights, parents should be associated as far as possible with educational work which they cannot carry out themselves, such as school education. Educational tasks which are beyond parental scope must always be carried out with the rights of the parents in mind. It is therefore a parental right that any task not delegated by the parents, but stemming directly from functions proper to Church or State, should be carried out as far as possible with parental co-operation. To ignore the will of the parents in educational matters without good reason is an offence against a fundamental human right, and the State may only use compulsion as far as this is absolutely necessary in carrying out its own task. The Church too can only play a subsidiary part in religious education, reserving to itself those functions which parents cannot or do not carry out. A monopoly in eduation must therefore be regarded as indefensible, or at best only to be tolerated if sufficient scope is given to all justified parental wishes, in other words, if integration has been achieved freely, and the common good absolutely demands integrated education.

There is a particular parental right to determine their children's religious education, for its foundations must be laid by the parents. The negative reason is that neither Church nor State are in a position to do so on their own. The State is not in a position to do so, because its concern is with man's temporal welfare. It must respect every man's right to religious freedom and must remain neutral in such matters. The Church is not in a position to do so, because religious education must be an integral part of a child's education and it is not the Church's business to provide an integrated education, but only a religious one, and that only as far as men are prepared to open themselves to it of their own free will or through their guardians, as revelation should be accepted with morally legitimate faith. In particular one must remember that the less mature the children are, the more must religion be integrated in their general education, if it is to be at all effective, for the younger the child, the more dependent will it be on an integrated approach. And the older the child is, the more directly must it be led to a personal decision of faith by the discussion of other convictions. From the positive point of view, parents have a right to determine their children's religious education because they brought their children into the world and are therefore responsible for them, a responsibility of which they cannot be relieved by either Church or State, whose responsibilities are limited to their own specific spheres. Neither Church nor State may obstruct any religious education desired by the parents; they may not refuse any help it is in their power to give, if parents want to bring up their children according to their convictions. Thus the State must not place any obstacles in the way of religious instruction in State schools, but must co-operate, without of course interfering with the freedom of religious teaching.

d) When parents exercise their rights, they must bear in mind their obligation to love their neighbour, so that insistence on their own rights does not prejudice the rights of other parents. This could happen if, for instance, one type of schooling, which is perfectly good in itself, were to be given undue preference at the expense of other children's opportunities. Undue preference given to State schools can have this effect just as much as undue insistence on the right of denominational schools, if this would interfere with other educational necessities.

C. Limits of Parental Duties and Rights

Parental duties and rights are directly correlated to the duties and rights of the children, and indirectly to the duties and rights of others, such as the superior communities of Church and State on the one hand and, on the other, school, relatives, etc., who have their own basic responsibilities towards the children. The duties and rights of parents are therefore limited by the duties and rights of others. The inner reason for this limitation of parental responsibility is of course that their basic authority is derivative and therefore limited.

a) Parental authority is limited by the rights of the children, as children are not their parents' property, but in principle equal partners with equal and inalienable human rights. The degree of dependence on their parents determines their duties towards them, and the degree of independence determines their rights. Thus they owe obedience to their parents to the extent to which they are not yet capable of making their own decisions and taking full responsibility for their own actions, but parents may only expect obedience to that extent and no more. Parents must not attempt to limit or influence their children's wills except as far as is necessary in the children's interest, properly understood. This applies particularly to important things, such as choice of occupation and marriage, but also to unimportant matters such as fashion. Physical force may only be used in self-defence or if urgently necessary for the good of the child. In religious matters particularly the child's freedom must be respected to the greatest possible extent, but he must also be faced with the necessity to make a decision, for religious education can only be a shaping of conscience, and any other approach will not only fail to be helpful to a genuine religious development, but will actually be a hindrance. Parents are of course their children's natural guides and advisers and must object in a suitable manner if the children offend against God's law.

b) Church and State also have certain rights within their own sphere, especially regarding education, for the parents are not in a position to provide everything the children need: they must have subsidiary, indirect help from superior communities, especially State and Church, and this gives the helpers corresponding rights. Thus the State is entitled, for instance, to insist on proper schooling, though compulsion must not go beyond what is absolutely necessary. The Church, in order not to go beyond this point, tends to leave preparation for first Communion at the right time as far as possible to the parents (cf. *CIC,* can. 854, § 4). Church and State, in discharging their own functions, also have a direct, basic, natural or supernatural right to influence the children. Thus the State can insist on compulsory schooling and an educational standard appropriate to the age and its culture, without infringing parental rights, as long as it leaves as much free scope as possible within the compulsory framework; similarly the Church is entitled to an appropriate share in religious

411

instruction, and parents do wrong if they refuse. But, unlike the State, the Church must only use moral means of persuasion.

c) School, relatives, etc., apart from any rights delegated by the parents, also have rights of their own which limit parental rights. Thus the teacher in the school carries out his own educational task of integrating the child into the larger community, a responsibility which is not merely based on delegation by parents and State, but is also his own specific task. The same is true of all others who provide some service for the children which only they and no one else can provide within a framework of authority, which is always a sort of relationship of origin.

d) Parental duties and rights, therefore, are to be clearly distinguished from the rights and duties of others, but they cannot be separated from them, as they are all rooted in the indivisible personality of the child in its various aspects. The needs of this personality can be formally decided *a priori,* but the details can only be decided *a posteriori,* as these will depend on continually changing personal attitudes and the resulting needs of the child. The functions and rights of those who stand in some relationship to the child are also subject to change. Thus the actual concrete demands of parental responsibility are continually changing and cannot be described once and for all.

But one can lay down a general rule that the relationship between parental rights and duties and those of other responsible people must be balanced in such a way that any rights over the child are limited as far as possible and extended as far as necessary, because otherwise authority over the child, in the service of the child, turns into manipulation and thus treats man as an object or thing and not as a person. Power over anyone and force can only be justified within the context of genuine preservation and development of the person concerned or of the person exercising the power or force. Only if this truth is understood and observed, is it possible to make a proper assessment of parental responsibilities, their extent and their limits.

As parental rights are subject to historical change under changing conditions, they need to be formulated by *positive law,* which must not, however, be formulated independently of the various holders of authority;

compromises acceptable to all interested parties must be found, as neither parents, nor Church, nor State, nor anyone else has supreme authority over the child, but they all have a common responsibility and are competent within their own sphere.

See also *Creation, Education* I–III, *Authority, Salvation* I, *Social Movements* IV C, *Tolerance, Rights of Man, Birth Control.*

BIBLIOGRAPHY. See bibliography on *Marriage* I, III; also: Pius XI, *Divini illius magistri: AAS* 22 (1930), pp. 49–86; O. Dibelius, *Grenzen des Staates;* J. M. Sailer, *Über die wichtigsten Pflichten der Eltern* (1951); M. Eck, "Autorité et liberté entre parents et enfants", *Études* 292 (1957), pp. 17–32; H. Thielicke, *Elternrecht* (1958); E. S. Geissler, *The Meaning of Parenthood* (1962); H. Thielicke, *Theological Ethics,* I–II (1966 ff.); F. X. Arnold, *Woman and Man* (1964); F. X. von Hornstein and A. Faller, *Sex — Love — Marriage* (1964).

Waldemar Molinski

III. Family

The Church's teaching on the family, if it is to meet present-day needs, must present an up-to-date realistic approach together with a deeper theological outlook. Over-romantic, patriarchal or sentimental ideas of family life no longer carry conviction. Neither can the picture we give be an over-abstract one, divorced from the actual realities of modern families. It must rather take sympathetic account of the nature, difficulties and opportunities of the family as it is.

A. THE FAMILY IN THE ORDER OF CREATION

We lay particular stress on those facts which are of special importance in the Church's preaching and teaching.

1. *Family and marriage.* The family has its origin in marriage; marriage is directed to the family as its goal. In earlier, more primitive times, even in the OT, the emphasis was on the family community, with a view to the continuation and growth of the greater community (clan, tribe), and the individual was almost entirely absorbed in the family (as in ancient China). Nowadays the marriage itself and the personal relationship of the married couple are increasingly seen as the real heart of the family on which the children depend for growth and support. This view of marriage, already clear in Gen 2 and Eph 5,

is expressed too in the pronouncements of Vatican II's Pastoral Constitution on the Church in the Modern World, arts. 47–52. In this important document emphatic and detailed stress is laid on married love, without omitting, however, a corresponding emphasis on its expression and development in the family and the children. ". . . While not making the other purposes of matrimony of less account, the true practice of conjugal love, and the whole meaning of the family life which results from it, have this aim: that the couple be ready with stout hearts to cooperate with the love of the Creator and the Saviour, who through them will enlarge and enrich his own family day by day . . . Marriage, to be sure, is not instituted solely for procreation; rather its very nature as an unbreakable compact between persons, and the welfare of the children, both demand that the mutual love of the spouses be embodied in a rightly ordered manner, that it grow and ripen. Therefore, marriage persists as a whole manner and communion of life and maintains its value and indissolubility, even when, despite the often intense desire of the couple, offspring are lacking" (*ibid.*, art. 50).

2. *Family and community.* The family (not marriage) is the primary unit of community living. It binds the sexes as well as the generations and introduces the young people into the life of the community. It brings into existence on a minute scale an astounding variety of relationships since it encompasses the members entirely and binds them together in love.

The proper development of this variety of relationships needs corresponding need for space (housing!) and time, as well as an alertness and sensitivity of spirit. Pastoral care must help to unfold and realize these riches and must not onesidedly moralize or sacralize — otherwise even the laws of unity and indissolubility of marriage and of piety between children and parents carry no conviction and are not capable of being put into practice.

3. *Family as fellowship.* These relationships include the following:

a) *The sex and blood relationship.* The intimate relationship between husband and wife affects both, physiologically and biologically, but especially the wife, through the exchange of semen and hormones, as well as through the life of the senses. The laws of heredity too have confirmed the experience that the children are physically and therefore in their basic temperaments formed by both parents. The parents pass on life, their life, to the children and see in them both the fruit and the continuation of their own life. Blood relationship in the descent from Abraham *(semen Abrahae)* plays a decisive part in the history of salvation in the OT. Even Christ's own genealogy is given twice in the NT. In the NT, to be sure, blood relationship is no longer of decisive significance, its place being taken by higher bonds (cf. Rom 4; 5; 9). Yet as a fact of the created world it has not entirely lost its meaning.

b) *The primary economic community.* In the family we have an intensive exchange of goods and services which is not commercial but based on love: perfect communism according to the classic formula: from each according to his means, to each according to his needs. Such perfect communism is possible only here, for nowhere else do we find such deep and intimate personal relationships. This "communism of love" carries at the same time an urgent appeal, an earnest demand for selflessness, self-giving, readiness for sacrifice, self-conquest.

c) *Community of mind and spirit.* In daily living, based on love, trust, esteem and respect, there is also an exchange of ideas, convictions, values and attitudes, a sharing of the experience of joys and sorrows, successes and trials, such as we find in no other group. The mysteries of human life have from the earliest times made the family a centre of religious cult (the sacred hearth). Although the essential sacrifice of Christianity does not take place in the family but in a public and specially consecrated community room, since it has its source not in man but in the only-begotten Son of God, yet the family remains a holy place in which religious sentiments and convictions are cultivated in common, passed on to the coming generation and above all carried into the realities of everyday life. In the family the child is baptized and receives the first introduction to the truths and realities of faith.

d) *Educational unit.* Modern psychology and pedagogy confirm the traditional judgment that man's decisive formation takes place in the earliest years of life, long before his intellect is capable of critical discernment, first of all because he is most impressionable at this stage and secondly because it is then that facts and attitudes are conveyed to him in the most intimate and personal way, in love. Man takes in best what comes to him by way of the heart. Thus it is also of decisive importance for pastoral work that the family and family living be shaped and surrounded by a religious atmosphere that is healthy, mature and responsible. Family education, however, relates not only to the children but also to the parents: "As living members of the family, children contribute in their own way to making their parents holy" (Pastoral Constitution on the Church in the Modern World, art. 48).

e) *Meeting of the generations.* The most fundamental and most intensive meeting of the generations comes about through birth, and shared living. Yet in a dynamic society age has not the commanding position it held in earlier times. Nowadays the knowledge and experience of earlier generations are handed on not merely in the family but also in the school, as well as through organizations, books, libraries and museums, press and radio. The older generation has become more independent of the help of the younger generation in material matters. Savings, life insurance, public welfare institutions, hospitals and old people's homes have in many cases taken over the services formerly provided by the children. The duty of children to provide for their aged parents has ceased to a great extent to be a matter of necessity. Nevertheless the meeting of the generations in the family retains its importance, especially in the realm of the mind and the spirit.

4. *The change in family life in industrial society.* Industrial society has made an enormous change in the external form of family living, nor has the inner structure remained unaffected. The essential elements remain, but take on in many ways a new form and undergo a shift of emphasis. For pastoral work and religious education it is important to note these changes and not cling to outmoded images. Careful consideration must be given to the question as to which of these changes represent a decline, which are merely a transition from one historical situation to another, and which even imply genuine progress in the light of true Christian values.

a) *Disappearance of the former economic independence of the family.* On the farm the family produced almost everything that was needed. What was produced was for the most part used by the family itself. This naturally made for a certain simplicity and restricted the circle of acquaintances, but resulted too in a considerable independence of the market and of contact with other people, of competition and the changes of fashion. More than anything else, life on the farm implied a common work and a common destiny. The farm was at once the provider and organizer of work, hospital and health insurance, pension fund and old people's home, vocational guidance (insofar as this was in any sense called for!) and centre for training, marriage counselling and match-making, etc.

This meant that there was a great need for members of the family to help with the work: each child was, even while quite young, an economic asset; large families were economically and socially valuable. Thus in all the rural cultures of the world, in China and Africa as well as in Russia and Patagonia, large families were the normal thing. This was also a necessity because of the high death rate among children and for the growth of the human race. This was not so much a question of morals as of economic and social trends. The present-day family in industrial society has suffered socially and economically a considerable loss of function and has taken a turn in the opposite direction. The consequence is that greater emphasis is laid on the cultural and spiritual functions of the family.

b) *The self-sufficiency of the ancient family was also great in spiritual matters.* At a time when there were no schools, organizations, press, radio or TV, the children learned almost everything from their parents. It was thus comparatively easy for the parents to hand on their views and convictions about life to their children. Today a multitude of outside influences affect the members of the family and the family itself. The force and significance of tradition have diminished. The call for discussion, personal assimilation and independent conviction is incomparably greater.

c) *The number in the rural family* was greater in two respects: the number of children and the number of relatives who lived under one roof or at least in close proximity. The relationship of the generations (parents, grandparents, even great-grandparents and children) was also a matter of course and strengthened the force of tradition. In the nature of things kinship played a greater role socially and politically. Today relationship in both directions plays a far smaller part: the social pressure of the family has grown less, the freedom and independence of the individual has grown greater and more demanding.

d) With the high degree of socio-economic and cultural self-sufficiency came the *very influential position of the father of the family* in respect to his wife and to the children. It was the patriarchal age, based less on moral and religious convictions (these only in a secondary, indirect way) than on social and cultural factors. The father was at once manager of the family business, work director of his "people", master of apprentices, administrator of the family possessions, etc. Today the father's authority rests not so much on his economic functions (these are in fact specifically laid down by law and made legally binding) as on his personal qualities of mind and character.

e) A further factor to consider is *the local, social and mental immobility* of the traditional family in contrast to the mobility of industrial society. This latter in fact weakens tradition or makes it partly impossible. In the city the same life cannot be lived as in the country neither occupationally nor economically, neither from a cultural nor a religious point of view.

f) In addition, partly as a consequence of the changes described above, *the consciousness of individuality and the desire for freedom* have a much greater influence nowadays, bringing a new pressure to bear on the family, even to the extent at times of breaking it up. There is "emancipation" in all spheres and greater exposure to the multiple influences of the larger society. This situation can, however, also lead to a mental development of the individual and to better human relations.

5. *Some characteristics of the modern family.* From all this it follows that the traditional family was anchored much more securely in its economic, social, cultural and traditional functions, whereas the modern family is far more dependent on its mental, cultural, moral and religious powers. This involves a greater vulnerability and insecurity but also a greater opportunity and task from the personal and pastoral point of view.

a) Both for the protection and orderly development of the family, in moral and religious questions as well as in matters of authority, there is need of a more intensely personal commitment. The family is not sufficiently secure, either socio-economically or legally (possibility of divorce). All the more earnestly must those forces be developed which are calculated to strengthen families and hold them together. Pastoral work must also lay less stress on commands and prohibitions and more on the development of the inner forces of selflessness and readiness for sacrifice, of responsibility and fidelity freely chosen.

b) In this respect particular importance attaches to the role of the woman and her training for that role. It is especially the woman's task — and her potentialities make her capable of it — to bring the spiritual forces to their full development. It is a matter for urgent consideration whether the education and training we give to girls take sufficient account of this fact. In our preoccupation with mental and occupational training for girls (not to speak of competitive sport) do we not perhaps give far too little attention to the training of the heart, the sensibilities, the awakening of love? The extension of the education and training of girls, the approach to equality with men in this regard, their increased independence are to be welcomed. But in all this the basic vocation of woman, to be a life companion and mother should not be pushed too far into the background in a reaction against the former patriarchal social order. As well as the similarity, the dissimilarity (not inferiority, not subjection) should not be eliminated or neglected. This would be to subject the special qualities and task of woman to harmful pressure.

c) The man's position and task, as husband and father, call for special qualities of mind and character. Perhaps a new meaning should be found in the saying of St. Paul that the husband is head of the wife, to the effect that man is not so much the head of the wife but rather the natural head of the marriage and of the family community. This gives the justification for his position as well as setting the limits of his task. It signifies no right of precedence but rather an obligation of service. The man has the amount of authority which is called for by the needs of the marriage and family, of the wife and the children. That will vary with age and other circumstances.

d) The children are, through the school and social conditions, State law, and social security, less dependent on their parents. This makes education more difficult but also more human. The basis of education has to be trust and service, rather than authority and obedience.

e) The circle of relatives is smaller, the relationships are fewer and above all less taken for granted. They should not be neglected, especially as a protection against isolation and as an enrichment of life, but they should be cultivated on a new basis and in greater freedom and independence.

f) Similarly, aging parents have become more independent materially of their children and relatives. Young families have a right, indeed a duty, to direct their lives in a freer and more independent way. Yet a warm and intimate relationship between the generations, with respect for freedom on both sides, can be of great human and spiritual value. The duties to the aged must be re-formulated.

6. *The special task of the family in industrial society.* Since industrial society threatens to become a mass society, mechanized, de-spiritualized, anonymous and atomized, increasingly bureaucratic and subject to the extension of public power, the family has a providential task as a place of refuge and protection for the soul and mind of man, for personality and individuality, for freedom and morality, for the direct responsibility for others and for religion.

B. THE THEOLOGY OF THE FAMILY

A specific theology of the family has not yet been written. Yet a beginning has been made in some important respects.

1. Since marriage and the family derive clearly from the order of God's creation, there is a special dignity and sacredness about them. They are much more closely connected with man's nature and existence than, for example, the State. Thus they are also more directly determined and regulated by nature and its Creator.

2. The priority of parenthood over married union is biblically and theologically unten-

able. Gen 2, as well as Eph 5, tells against it. Marriage is a sacrament for the consecration not of parents but of the husband and wife; it refers directly and in the first place to marriage and married love, and only secondarily and indirectly to parenthood. However, since marriage is a permanent sacrament and since married love naturally unfolds in parenthood, the latter shares too in the dignity and grace of the sacrament. Fruitfulness pertains without any doubt to the essential function of marriage in the biblical and theological view.

3. Attempts to deduce the notion of the family theologically from the Blessed Trinity must be regarded as a failure. Life, love, fruitfulness and community living have indeed in a general way their source in the life, love, and fruitfulness in the divine Trinity, but the attempt to establish this in detail is theological speculation, which, however ingenious and even correct and valuable it may be, departs too much from Scripture to be theologically capable of proof.

4. *Order in marriage and the family.* Study of holy Scripture has led to the realization that many directives of Scripture on authority and obedience, on the order of ends in marriage, the position of the wife, etc., contain formulations that are a product of the age in which they were written. Scripture experts are endeavouring to extract the permanently valid core from those elements which merely derive from the culture of the period. Something of this has already been mentioned above under A.

5. *Vatican II* emphasizes both in the Decree on the Apostolate of the Laity and in the Pastoral Constitution on the Church in the Modern World (arts. 47–52) the special significance and mission of marriage and the family for the individual as well as for society and the Church. Art. 47 of the Pastoral Constitution says: "The well-being of the individual person and of human and Christian society is intimately linked with the healthy condition of that community produced by marriage and family." Cf. arts. 50–52, and Decree on the Apostolate of the Laity, art. 11: "Since the Creator of all things has established the conjugal partnership as the beginning and basis of human society and,

by his grace, has made it a great mystery in Christ and the Church (cf. Eph 5:32), the apostolate of married persons and of families is of unique importance for the Church and civil society ... The family has received from God its mission to be the first and vital cell of society." Therefore the family must not close in on itself in an egoistic or timid way, but must exert its influence on the Church and society *(ibid.)* Those who have the care of souls must in their turn have a special care for the family (Pastoral Constitution, art. 52; Decree on the Apostolate of the Laity, art. 11) and help it to overcome difficulties. "It devolves on priests duly trained about family matters to nurture the vocation of spouses by a variety of pastoral means, by preaching God's word, by liturgical worship, and by other spiritual aids to conjugal and family life; to sustain them sympathetically and patiently in difficulties, and to make them courageous through love, so that families which are truly illustrious can be formed" (Pastoral Constitution, art. 52). Pastoral care has in many cases fallen a victim to one or other of two extremes: on the one hand it has been over-individualistic in its care for various groups (children, men, women, young men, young girls) and has only seldom seen the family as a community; one need only think of the arrangements for Mass and the sacraments, of the confraternities and their effect on the family, on the reluctance to make house visitation. On the other hand pastoral work for the family has concerned itself too exclusively with morality (sex morality and number of children), with sacramentality and with the question of authority, while giving too little consideration to the total human reality, especially to the value of married love in its true depth and variety. There are here, especially in the light of the Pastoral Constitution on the Church in the Modern World, big gaps to be filled in preaching and pastoral care.

6. If man is in a certain sense a summary of the variety of existence, so is the family in a special way the living synthesis and harmony of multiple tensions: matter and spirit, natural tendency and free choice, sex and love, personality and community, the past (in the forefathers) and the future (in the children), tradition and individuality,

self-realization and self-giving, nature and grace are brought in the family in a unique, personal and yet socially valuable way to a fruitful unity, both bringing life to be and shaping its development. The seemingly most trivial things in the family come to have the greatest human and spiritual significance as symbols and expressions of love and fidelity. Diversity and tensions are here not so much a source of conflicts as of fruitfulness. Since the sacramental consecration of married love is the foundation of the family and comes in it to full development, the entire order of creation becomes here in a sense the vehicle for sacramental grace and a means of salvation.

See also *Marriage* I, II, *Society* I, II, *Sex* II, III.

BIBLIOGRAPHY. W. Koppers, *La famille chez les peuples primitifs* (1931); E. Burgess and H.-J. Locke, *The Family. From Institution to Companionship* (2nd ed., 1953); C. B. Zimmermann, *Family and Civilization* (1947); R. Anshen, ed., *The Family. Its Function and Destiny* (1949); R. Schlesinger, *The Family in Soviet Russia* (1949); S. de Lestapis, *L'avenir de la famille* (1950); R. Foster, *Marriage and Family Relationships* (1950); H. Günther, *Formen und Urgeschichte der Ehe* (2nd ed., 1951); J. Sirjamaki, *The American Family in the Twentieth Century* (1953); E. R. Groves, *The Family and its Relationship* (1953); A. G. Truxal and F. F. Merill, *The Family in American Culture* (1953); B. Häring, *Soziologie der Familie* (1964); O. Michel, "οἶκος", *TWNT*, V, pp. 122ff.; J. Leclerq and J. David, *Die Familie* (1955); W. Ogburn and M. Nimkoff, *Technology and the Changing Family* (1955); *Semaines Sociales de France 1957* (Bordeaux) (Family 1957) (1958); J. Delcourt, *Famille et civilisation urbaine* (1960); E. McDonagh, "The Moral Theology of Marriage: Recent Literature in English", *Concilium 5* (1965), pp. 70–82.

Jakob David

MARTYRDOM

Etymologically, "martyrdom" means much more than "suffering death for the faith", a restricted sense which the word came to have very early, not indeed in the NT, but attested in the account of the martyrdom of Polycarp, *c.* 150. In the NT it means giving testimony, but in words, by preaching, and not that of being killed *in odium fidei*. It is revealing for the nature of the Christian faith that a word which in general (though not exclusively) meant testimony came to be used in Christianity for that given by suffering death for the Christian faith, while this act of dying for the faith is likewise given the character of testimony.

1. The explanation for this process is usually derived from the formal context, which will be discussed first here, but then completed by a discussion of the material context. When one considers the formal connection between the death of the witness and the faith to which he testifies, one is less directly concerned with the significance of what happens than with the fact that it actually does happen. In the strict sense, death for the faith is martyrdom, when it is freely accepted, in strict "suffering", not falling in battle for the faith and not unconsciously undergone. When a Christian faces death for the faith, he testifies effectively before men to the meaning and truth of his faith. There are two aspects here, one more objective and the other more subjective.

a) Man has nothing more precious than life. If it is threatened or taken away, his faith that existence is simply not blotted out with the end of life on earth does not prevent his feeling death as a deprivation of his selfhood, even when he hopes to waken to eternal life. When death is remembered in the course of man's conscious life, it is felt to be an event which robs man of himself. This sense of being robbed which death always brings with it is particularly acute when death is inflicted by external violence. To accept this willingly, and hence freely to renounce man's greatest possession, surrendering it to men who cannot claim to be the rightful lords of this highest possession of another, presupposes therefore that one is convinced of the existence of a lordship underlying the visible happening, transcending the immediate agents of this robbery. And this lordship is felt to be so real that the highest earthly good, and indeed one's own existence is surrendered without resistance for the sake of it.

Hence the goal to which martyrdom is orientated can only be a reality of the highest value, towering over the person of him who dies a martyr's death. And the goal must be a person, otherwise he could not change being robbed of existence into free, sacrificial dedication. This is not self-destruction in the sense that the martyr kills himself or that death is the annihilation of the person. But it must be experienced as self-destruction in a certain sense, since the person in question loses his earthly existence, all he knew in real experience. Hence martyrdom is the supreme act of love, since it is love which affirms the value of another person. To let oneself be robbed of life for the sake of affirming the person of the incarnate God of faith, is to suffer death "in odium fidei", not just in the sense of testifying to a proposition of faith, but in the personal sense of faith, as happily brought out by Vatican II (Constitution *Dei Verbum*) as a genuine development of the notion of faith given in Vatican I. In martyrdom, the faith attested is vigorously exercised as "I believe you and in you". Martyrdom is loving surrender to the You of God affirmed in faith, and hence is testimony not to an ideology but to religion in the sense of a personal encounter with the divine You of life.

b) The situation thus objectively set up is also capable of impressing people with its force of testimony. Martyrdom is an expression of love of God, for whom one allows one's life to be taken, and to whose love one attributes the pain of this loss. But it need not be the explicit intention of the martyr to bear testimony to his love. His intention is rather the loving desire "to be dissolved and to be with Christ" (Phil 1:23). Nonetheless, the effect on men is that of testimony.

The immediate effect is to make men ask, as they see a fellow-man martyred, what can be so attractive to him that he allows his life to be taken, without defending himself or resisting, though his life must be as dear to him as their own. They learn that the dying man hopes for this prize beyond the bourne of death. Their astonished question may well be choked back or stifled with superficial answers, but it cannot be entirely eliminated. It points to the realm where the true answer is to be found, though for the moment the question remains open.

When the faith which is believed, out of "odium" of which martyrdom is inflicted, expounds the answer, the existenti*el* testimony of martyrdom gives it a credibility which appertains less strictly to a mere verbal affirmation. But of course one must not conclude too hastily from the death of a single martyr or even from a number of martyrdoms to the truth of the faith for which such men have died. After all, it is primarily for his subjective conviction that the martyr dies, not necessarily for its objective truth. But martyrdom is an effective testimony at least insofar as it makes men ready to ask what the martyr died for.

2. The specifically Christian reason for esteeming martyrdom highly, which inspired very early the cult of martyrs in the Church, is to be sought rather in the intrinsic significance of what happens. From the Christian point of view, the significance of martyrdom is not confined to the fact that dying *in odium fidei* points towards and attests the reality of the other life. The great truth is that death by martyrdom definitively seals the Christian's life as one in conformity with Christ's, which ended in death for the sake of the preaching of the message of the Father who sent him.

a) The likeness to Christ in which the martyr ends his life consists of two elements. Firstly, he dies as Christ dies, in unresisting surrender to those who take away his life by violence, convinced that he is thus dedicating himself to God who is ready to take into his love the life which is robbed by force. Secondly, this likeness is not only real participation in the death of Christ. It is also participation in its efficacity. The death of the martyr shares the sacrificial character of the death of Christ and its redemptive power. Hence the Church, from the earliest times, has celebrated the death of the martyr not just as praise of the Christian who died the martyr's death, but also as thankful recognition of the significance of this martyrdom for the whole communion of saints.

The fact that martyrdom is a reflection of the sacrificial death of Christ and participation by grace in this death also intensifies the personal character of martyrdom. The martyr does not die "for a cause". If he did, his martyrdom would of course have "personal" value as the free suffering of death. But in Christian martyrdom the personal character is heightened by the fact that martyrdom is understood and suffered as co-ordination or almost identification with the sacrificial death of Christ in dedication to the Father. The martyr rejoices to share the destiny of Christ, in which he accomplishes with Christ the act of dedication to the Father.

b) This situation explains why from early times martyrdom has been regarded as the "baptism of blood", through which the grace

effected by sacramental baptism is imparted, when this baptism cannot be received. One reason is that martyrdom is the expression of supreme love of God. But another reason is that martyrdom enacts realistically what is done in symbol in sacramental baptism: dying along with Christ, to rise again with him (cf. Rom 6:3–11). Hence according to the ancient conviction of faith, martyrdom has not the ecclesiological effect of baptism, which means nothing to the martyr, since he is not to live in the realm where the Church exists as sign of God's kingship on earth. But martyrdom does possess the grace effected by baptism, as conformity with Christ dying in sacrifice out of love of the Father. Martyrdom as the baptism of blood is not really a substitute for baptism of water, but rather the realistic enactment of what takes place in symbol in the baptism of water — dying and being buried with Christ, to rise with him.

See also *Baptism, Death, Charity* I, *Faith* II, *Communion of Saints, Sacrifice* III.

BIBLIOGRAPHY. H. Delehaye, *Martyr et Confesseur* (1921); O. Casel, "Mysterium und Martyrium in den römischen Sakramentarien", *Jahresbuch für Liturgiewissenschaft* 2 (1922), pp. 18–38; R. Hedde, "Martyr", *DTC,* X, cols. 220–54; H. Strahtmann, "μάρτυς", *TWNT,* IV (1967), pp. 477–520; E. L. Hummel, *The Concept of Martyrdom according to Cyprian* (1946); E. Peterson, "Zeuge der Wahrheit. Christliche Märtyrer", *Theologische Traktate* (1951), pp. 165–224; W. Manson, "Martyrs and Martyrdom", *Bulletin of the John Rylands Library* (1957), pp. 463–84; M. Lods, *Confesseurs et martyrs* (1958); K. Rahner, "Martyrium", *LTK,* VII, cols. 136–8; id., *On the Theology of Death,* Quaestiones Disputatae 2 (revised ed., 1965); N. Brox, *Glaube als Zeugnis* (1966).

Otto Semmelroth

MARXISM

I. System and History. II. Dialectical Materialism. III. Historical Materialism.

I. System and History

1. *Concept and general problem.* a) Marxism is the philosophical term used to describe not only Marx's teaching but also the numerous additions, developments, revisions and immanent criticisms of that teaching. Marxism is thus a collective concept under which many

individual Marxisms may be subsumed, although they differ from one another, sometimes even considerably. Thus the name Marxism-Leninism is given to the modification and application of the Marxist teaching in the Russian Revolution; heretics are called revisionists; there are left and right-wing deviationists, and finally there are numerous national (e.g., Chinese, Yugoslav, etc.) versions of Marxism. Formally this multiple interpretation of Marxism raises a primary fundamental difficulty of Marxism: the problem of an authoritative exposition in practice for any particular historical or social situation. The root of this difficulty lies in the specific nature of Marx's work itself. Theory and practice affect each other dialectically, philosophy does not rest content with the interpretation of historical phenomena, it must be implemented; and vice-versa, every theory must draw into its reflections the concrete social situation in which it is dialectically involved. Thus with a change of historical and material conditions, the theory itself changes. Marx never reflected systematically enough on this scientific method of his for a heuristic principle to be derived from it for the process of the internal revision of Marxism itself.

b) A second problem lies in Marx's choice of the proletariat for the role of revolutionary leadership in the liquidation of the bourgeois-capitalist class-war, and the actual absence of such a revolution. Marxism, it is true, showed itself extremely effective for the international organization of workers, for founding trade unions and for decisive improvements in conditions of industrial work, yet the revolt of the proletariat foretold by Marx did not in fact take place. Rather has the improvement in living standards had the effect of repressing the development of revolutionary thinking. The Russian Revolution was the work of Lenin with a few hard-core professional revolutionaries, and took place in a feudalistic monarchy instead of in a capitalist industrial State; these conditions as well as the early rise to power of cadre and functionary had to have an extensive legitimation. This resulted in large-scale modification of Marxism; Lenin's voluminous writings brought the first justification of national distinctions and a revolutionary doctrine which placed heavy emphasis on the tactics and techniques, more important for the political and strategic application of Marxism

than for its philosophical interpretation. It can be taken as certain that in the modern Western neo-capitalistic countries there is no question anywhere of a revolutionary-minded proletariat, in spite of all the political propaganda which, because of party dogmatism, refuses to accept this. In this respect the Marxist prognostications have been shown to be false, although modern Marxism has not drawn the appropriate consequences from this fact.

c) Through the political developments, above all after World War II, there arose in the opposition between East and West a classical confrontation of capitalism and socialism, which since then, however, has notably diminished, partly as a result of the risk of atomic war if world revolution was pursued, partly because of the rise of a neutral "third world", and finally because of a partial assimilation of capitalism and socialism to each other. This global inter-dependence enforces coexistence at least in practice, and also endangers the permanency of the Marxist doctrine, inasmuch as capitalism, in spite of all prognoses, has not succumbed to its inner contradiction; it has rather endeavoured, by partial assimilation of elements of Marxism, to integrate it and to give it a new function, thereby ushering in a new phase of the class dialectic, the theoretical and practical mastering of which becomes the source of new inner-Marxist controversies.

d) Some philosophical problems, regarded as essential by Marx and the Marxists, have since lost much of their relevance or must be approached from a very different point of view. Thus the opposition between idealism and materialism has become much less important after Husserl, Heidegger and Wittgenstein and the natural philosophy of Planck, Heisenberg and Weizsäcker; the notion of ideology has become in many ways detached from the Marxist context and translated into terms of sociology of knowledge, of psychoanalysis and of positivism; political philosophy and jurisprudence have abandoned the Hegelian position and are rightly uninterested in certain Marxist posing of alternatives about State and society; in social economy the Marxist theory of labour value has not succeeded in establishing itself; the traditional Marxist criticism of religion has been subjected to correction from the point of view of philosophy, theology, and the theory of religion, and this with the approbation of Marxist theoreticians.

These are only a few of the points in which a tension has arisen separating Marxism both from the teaching of Marx and from the realities of modern life. They explain too the reasons for the many versions of Marxism obtaining today.

2. *Doctrine and development*. The philosophical teaching of Marx took shape above all in his grappling with the system of Hegel. Marx took over at first the materialist principle of Feuerbach and some other left-wing Hegelians, to criticize the idealistic assumptions of Hegel, the intellectual monism, the conceptual identity of subject and object, the synthesis of reality and reason as theology; to expose the apparent reconciliation and the abstract ideology; and instead of it to formulate the new task of philosophy after Hegel, namely, to bridge the real gulf still remaining between being and consciousness. To achieve this, philosophy must cease to wish to remain merely philosophy and must rather translate the reality of meaning into meaningful reality. Marx, in the "Eleven Theses on Feuerbach", made an essential modification of the materialism taken over as part of this synthesis from Feuerbach, inasmuch as instead of the uncritical, mechanist, metaphysical notion of matter, he identifies matter as a *social* reality and thus brings being and consciousness into the dialectical process of theory and practice in human society. The gulf between thought and reality, and in particular ideology, is seen to be the consequence of social alienation, the analysis and removal of which becomes thereafter the chief aim of Marxism. At a very early stage Marx entered the sphere of political philosophy and jurisprudence, and in these areas too he attacked the use of Hegelian assumptions found in Prussia; increasingly, however, his attention was given to the classical doctrine of social economy, the results of which occupy by far the greater part of his entire writings. In this, the chief effort was devoted to proving that capitalist society would destroy itself through class war in which the proletariat, being subjected to a progressive pauperization, would carry the banners of revolution and, realizing their momentous role in events, would become conscious agents in the process of world history. Specially characteristic of the Marxist doctrine is the fact that all

empirical economics, sociology and political criticism remain within a systematic philosophical framework, making secure the continuity of earlier and more recent work without at the same time dogmatically pre-empting the empirical analysis. In all his writings the philosophically formulated purpose remains the free self-realization of man and his emancipation from historically conditioned alienation which Marx saw as caused principally by the theory of exchange value, which was raised to the level of an abstract natural law in the capitalist society centred on the market, together with the division of labour deriving from this and from the private ownership of the means of production; in the later writings especially there are extraordinarily sceptical expressions about the power of the "Kingdom of Necessity" in the "Kingdom of Freedom". The first distortion of Marx's doctrine was caused by Engels, partly with the concurrence of Marx. It finds its clearest expression in "Anti-Dühring". Engels applies Marx's dialectic of the historico-social process to nature, thus falling back into the naturalistic materialism previously rejected by Marx. With this Marxism becomes a closed systematic *Weltanschauung,* providing, with the help of materialist metaphysics, a universal, coherent explanation which subsumes the social dialectic under the natural and from then on involves the danger of totalitarianism.

In the succeeding period Marxism was philosophically much neglected; it was swept along in the wake of the factional squabbling and internal rivalries of the Socialist and Communist Parties. Lenin's copious writings too were concerned chiefly with questions of practical politics and of tactics; he was the first to attempt the application of Marxist doctrine to an unforeseen situation, but also gave Marxism an aggressively militant and extremely technological direction. Through the establishment of a corps of functionaries bound to the party and to the orthodox party-line teachings, as well as through his ruthless handling of opponents, Lenin opened the way to Stalinism. Concurrently, the dialectic of theory and practice gradually degenerated to a mere empirio-critical realism, under the formula of basis and superstructure, thus mechanically over-simplifying all tension between subject and object. On this reduction of Marxism, abbreviated to "Diamat", Stalin was able to establish the

Soviet claim to leadership within Communism with the appearance of ideological legitimacy.

Yet, even if there were no other proof, the continuing stream of criticism by Marxists themselves is sufficient to refute the view that a direct line of development leads from the early writings of Marx to Stalin's reign of terror. In *Germany* Rosa Luxemburg and Karl Liebknecht raised severe objections to Lenin's bureaucracy of party functionaries and demanded instead, as orthodox Marxists, the participation of the entire proletariat consciously and willingly in the revolution. Karl Korsch and Georg Lukács attempted to breathe new life into Marxism by reverting to Hegel. The National-Socialist persecution of Socialists and Communists brought Marxist research to a standstill.

In *France* the lectures on Hegel by Kojev resulted in a philosophical acceptance of Marxism, the effects of which are still in evidence and which is represented by names such as Merleau-Ponty, Sartre, Lefèbvre, L. Goldmann, etc. Merleau-Ponty sees in the proletariat a group with inter-subjective authenticity whose action gives meaning to history; the latter is to be brought to realization by creative effort, and thus contingently, not deduced as part of a blind process. It is questionable, however, whether Merleau-Ponty's concept of the historicity of the subject before all history does not remain irreconcilable with the Marxist notion of history, and thus whether an essential limit is placed by Marxism on the transcendental, ontological philosophy of history. Sartre came from an existentialist concept of revolution to an acceptance of Marxism to the extent that he regards existentialism as an essential corrective to Marxism, since this tends to dogmatism and to the reduction of man to a mere object. Severe inner-Marxist criticism is expressed by H. Lefèbvre, expelled from the French Communist Party in 1955: "l'expérience d'aliénation" as a beginning and "l'homme total" as the asymptotic end mark the road of Marxism. The crisis about objectivity affected Marxism also — in place of the flight into rigid dogmatism, Lefèbvre recommends the concrete, critical dialectic of daily life. Besides the confrontation of Marxism with existentialism which has hitherto set the tone, the debate with structuralism begins to take on more significance.

In *Italy* there exists since A. Gramsci (d. 1937) a form of Marxism which is closely tailored to Italian circumstances: undogmatic, nowadays partly pragmatic, it openly advocates parliamentary democracy, dialogue with the Church and ideological tolerance. As L. Lombardo-Radice expressed it, the basic philosophical principle is that men are in a position to recognize their problems and to solve them in the course of history. In *West Germany* there are the hesitant beginnings of a renewal of Marxist research. As well as the investigations into basic sources, Catholic and Protestant theology have made special efforts to come to a right interpretation of the early writings of Marx, with the frequent tendency, it is true, to interpret them in ontological or anthropological terms, as, for example, when the notion of alienation is taken as a basic anthropological category, instead of arising from transitory, socio-economic conditions. The Frankfurt school with Adorno, Horkheimer, Habermas, etc., attempts to understand Marxism as a critical, dialectical social theory, with some emphasis on cultural criticism and psychoanalysis. Habermas in particular takes Marxism as philosophy of history with a practical intent and as a logic of the social sciences. E. Bloch relates Marxism and a cosmological philosophy of history to an utopia of identity strongly reminiscent of Schelling. In *the Communist countries,* above all in Poland, Yugoslavia and Czechoslovakia, a revisionism emphatically existentialist and positivist has won attention as a result of the criticism of Stalinism with its neglect of the individual in theory and practice. Thus Kolakowski distinguishes between institutional and intellectual Marxism, i.e., between its dogmatic form and existential adaptation. However, this revisionism threatens to depart so far from Marxism, that Marxism shrinks to a mere scientific methodology.

A. Schaff poses the question of the place of the individual, of the scientific nature of Marxism and its ability to deal with subjective, personal problems. More remarkable than the results (social eudaemonism, socialist humanism) appears the recognition that even in a socialist society not all conflicts at once disappear, i.e., that the needs of the individual reach beyond the status of unquestioning welfare even in an optimally organized socialist society.

3. *Marxism and Christianity*. Marxist criticism of religion is based on Feuerbach's thesis of the projection of human concepts on God. Marx explained this projection by the social alienation which demands and even enforces an abstract, ideological consolation, since the thought and being of man are torn apart in the wage relationship, instead of being reconciled. Religion protests against the misery, it is true, yet its primary effect is to find, by means of its consolation, a justification and explanation for the present evil, thereby stabilizing it. In the Communist society religion dies of itself; Lenin holds that an extirpation is called for. Even in the early stages of socialism (Fourier, Buchez, Weitling, etc.) and in religious socialism (Tillich, Steinbüchel) the first contacts began between Marxism and Christianity. The weakness of the Marxist criticism of religion is nowadays admitted by the Marxists themselves; it consists above all in its hypothetical character; no precise description of the phenomenon, use of categories false to the history of religion, methodological inconsequence. The thesis about the withering away of religion is established by methods indefensible even by Marxist standards. For Christianity the question arises to what extent the Marxist axiom of the total identity of history and society bears an ideological character. The less true this is, the more easily can Christianity come to a reconciliation with Marxism and in a freer society hope for a form of the faith that would be less endangered by ideology. An acceptance of the permanent difference between the kingdom of the world and the Kingdom of God appears for the moment more possible in practice than in theory.

See also *Religion* I B, *Society* I, II, *Ideology, Materialism, Structuralism*.

BIBLIOGRAPHY. See bibliography on *Marxism* II, III.

Werner Post

II. Dialectical Materialism

1. *History*. One of the specific aims of the Communist Party of the Soviet Union is to train everybody in their territory in the spirit of the Marxist-Leninist ideology. Since the party has full control of all the organs of State, there exists in the Soviet Union — and

the same holds for the other States where Communists hold power — a State-supported ideology. It is made not only the basis of the entire economic, social and political life, but is also intended to dominate the cultural sphere. The whole system of instruction and training is directed towards the imparting of this ideology.

The Marxist-Leninist teaching comprises three chief areas: philosophy (dialectical and historical materialism), political economy and political doctrine. For the ideology of Marxist-Leninism the first section above all is essential. In the second and third sections, means are worked out for achieving the aims enunciated in the first section in the concrete realities of economic, social and political life. For Communism therefore all three sections form an inner indivisible unity.

Dialectical materialism comprises the theoretical philosophy of Marxism as well as its theory of knowledge, whereas historical materialism involves the application of the basic laws of dialectical materialism to the sphere of social development in history.

As far as its historical origin goes, historical materialism is the earlier portion. In the forties of the last century Marx had already worked out his materialist concept of history which forms the nucleus of historical materialism. It was only thirty years later that F. Engels undertook the attempt to prove the application to the natural world of those same dialectical laws of development which Marx had already expounded as an explanation for social development. Engels is therefore the one who, more than anyone else, is to be considered as the real originator of the system known generally today as "dialectical materialism". The contribution of Lenin to its further development was directed chiefly to a more accurate description of the notion of matter. Stalin made no original contribution: he dropped one of the three laws of the natural dialectic formulated by Engels (the law of the negation of the negation), but this was restored to the system of dialectical materialism after Stalin's death.

2. *Materialism*. The term "materialism" is used in Soviet terminology in two senses. Often it is used in the same sense as elsewhere in philosophy: a teaching according to which nothing but matter exists, or, if the existence of non-material things is accepted, matter is at least regarded as the basic reality

which is the source of the non-material. "Materialism", however, is often used as well in Soviet terminology to convey a teaching according to which the object of knowledge is not dependent on the act of knowledge for its existence but exists independently of the knowing subject. With materialism used in this second sense, which is known in philosophy as "epistemological realism", Lenin began his attempt to understand the notion of matter in a new way. Thus the notion of "matter" is for him a philosophical category to denote the objective reality given to man in his sensibilities, copied, photographed and reproduced by these and existing independently of them (W. I. Lenin, *Materialism and Empirio-Criticism* [1953]). On first showing it would seem that according to this definition of matter, Lenin's philosophy is nothing but realism, since matter signifies here "objective reality". But this is not so, for Lenin then restricts objective reality to the reality which is present to us in the sensibilities.

Matter so understood is the basic reality for dialectical materialism. In this theory matter is endless in space and time, capable neither of being produced nor destroyed. This latter conclusion is derived from the principle of physics on the indestructibility of energy. Matter is for dialectical materialism the basic reality, but not the only one. It recognizes that human consciousness is non-material, understanding "consciousness" to mean psychic phenomena as, for example, sensations, thoughts, feelings, acts of will, etc. Nevertheless it is for him nothing more than "a product, function and attribute" of matter, not indeed of all matter but of the matter of the human brain.

3. *The materialist dialectic.* The basic attribute of matter is movement. For dialectical materialism no matter can exist without movement, just as there can be no movement without a material substratum. Movement is to be understood here not only in the mechanical sense, but in the sense of every sort of change. Besides the mechanical type of movement, dialectical materialism indicates as further types of movement: the form of movement known to physics (e.g., electromagnetic processes), then chemical, biological and social forms of movement.

Thus matter is involved in an eternal process. But dialectical materialism does not see this as a perpetual return, but rather a development which is in fact a development to something higher (whereby "higher" is not to be taken in a moral sense but in the sense of a higher stage of being). Once the stage of living things has been reached, "laws" emerge which cannot be reduced to those chemical and physical laws obtaining in the lower order. To a still greater degree this is true of the sphere of man with his non-material consciousness. It is frequently said to belong to the realm of the spirit, though more frequently the term "non-material" is used. The recognition of the various stages of reality can be considered one of the decisive points at which dialectical materialism distinguishes itself from mechanicism ("regular materialism"). While mechanicism attempts to reduce all the phenomena of the higher order to the physical and chemical laws that obtain in the inorganic sphere, dialectical materialism recognizes the formal irreducibility of the higher phenomena to the laws that hold in the lower order.

Nevertheless dialectical materialism steadfastly affirms that the higher orders of existence, as far as the history of their development is concerned, derived from the lower in the course of the development of matter. It is now the task of the dialectic to interpret movement in the world in general and in particular its upward development. According to the meaning of the word, "dialectic" means the art of conversation. Now, just as in a dialogue, according as contradictions between the partners to the conversation arise and are disposed of, progress is made in the knowledge of the truth, so too all movement forward, whether it is in the mental sphere or in that of social development, or finally in the sphere of nature, is due to "contradiction" or to the "struggle of opposites".

In particular dialectical materialism formulates *three laws of the materialist dialectic:*

a) The *law of unity* and of the *struggle of opposites.* It proposes to replace with the dialectic the concept of movement characterized as "mechanistic" according to which the source of movement is to be sought outside the thing being moved. According to the dialectic, the source of the movement is to be found within the thing moving itself, in inner "contradictions" or in a struggle of "opposites" (opposing powers and tendencies, e.g., the struggle between the classes within a particular society). In this way dialectical materialism wishes to avoid the assumption of a "prime mover" (or, when movement is understood in the sense of change in general, of God as *actus purus*) to which the concept of movement derived from the principle *Quidquid movetur ab alio movetur* must lead.

b) The law of the *change of quantity into quality*. This law is to demonstrate in detail how new and often higher phenomena can arise in the process of development. This is said to come about as follows: the process of a change which is at first purely quantitative (increase or decrease of a particular datum) when it passes a certain critical point (determined by the nature of the object in question) leads to a "qualitative", that is, an essential change, whereby the thing ceases to be what it was and becomes something else (e.g., the change of water to steam when it passes the boiling point in the process of heating).

c) The law of the *"negation of the negation"*. It is meant to express more exactly the form of the higher development. This does not always follow a direct course, but often takes the form of a spiral; having turned away from its starting point, it frequently comes back on it again; but this time on a higher level, since the entire positive content of the development up to this point remains "stored away". When, in a qualitative change, the first quality is replaced by a second, the second implies the "negation" of the first. With the next qualitative change, however, this is "negatived" again. Now if the first "negation" is replaced by a second, then the second must lead back to the starting-point.

The materialist dialectic, expressed especially in these three laws, is understood as "the science of the general laws of motion and development of Nature, human society and thought" (F. Engels, *Herr Eugen Düh-ring's Revolution in Science [Anti-Dühring]* [1966], p. 155). Its laws hold for all reality, both for the external world (nature and society) and for thought. Dialectical materialism accordingly distinguishes two series of laws, the objective dialectic (determining the development of the external world) and the subjective dialectic. The latter, the dialectic of thought, is a reflection of the former. The correspondence between the subjective and objective dialec-tic is regarded as being verifiable insofar as thought stands up to the test of practice. Practice is for dialectical materialism the ultimate criterion of truth.

4. *Evaluation.* Through the assumption of the eternity of the material world and through the explanation of upward development with the help of the dialectic, dialectical materialism aims before all else at the exclusion of the existence of God. In this, however, it starts from the false assumption that the proof for the existence of God rests on the fact of the origin of the world in time. The fact is that the basis for the proofs for God's existence is not the beginning of the world in time (a fact neither empirically nor philosophically capable of determination), but rather its contingence, that is, the fact deduced from the changeability of the world, that it does not exist by an inner necessity but is itself indifferent with respect to existence. Since therefore it does in fact exist, it owes its existence to another. Besides, the thesis of the eternity of the world is a mere postulate of dialectical materialism. To prove it, dialectical materialism invokes science, but science, in its present stage of development, is unable to decide this question. And since in addition dialectical materialism does not allow this thesis to be questioned, it shows itself to be an a-prioristic and dogmatic system. The appeal to the law of conservation of energy is a philosophical misunderstanding. This proposition relates to the action of one physical quantity on another, but it says nothing about the relation of the universe to a being outside it. Thus the only basis for the thesis on the eternity of the world is an arbitrary preconception, the result of atheistic attitudes.

In introducing the dialectic into materialism, dialectical materialism wishes to solve the problem of movement, which unlike mechanism, it understands as an upward development. The dialectic derives the origin of movement from the "contradiction" or the "struggle of opposites". Yet contradiction and the struggle of the opposites are not the same thing. A real contradiction (a contradictory opposite, obtaining between an assertion or a determination and its negation, "A" and "Non-A") is possible only as a mental concept; in reality, the non-dog does not exist, but only the cat, the horse, the tree, etc. Movement in reality therefore is not to be derived from contradictions so understood. But if the contradiction is taken in the sense of a "struggle of opposites", movement is explained by means of movement and again there is no explanation. The movement (change) of the total phenomenon (as in the case of society) is to be explained by the struggle of opposing elements within it (e.g., the classes); but the struggle of opposites is itself a movement and therefore the origin of movement as such is not explained.

When, finally, dialectical materialism regards practice as the criterion of truth, this solution is insufficient. The confirmation of an idea in practice can indeed in some cases show us the truth of our idea. Yet it cannot be the ultimate norm of truth, if only because the practical success must itself in turn be grasped through a mental act, which demands a further criterion for its validity. If we wish to avoid a *regressus in infinitum*, we must find, apart from practice, another criterion of truth.

See also *Communism, Ideology, Materialism*.

BIBLIOGRAPHY. F. Engels, *Dialectics of Nature* (1940); J. Stalin, *Dialectical and Historical Materialism* (1940); V. Lenin, *Materialism and Empirio-Criticism* (1953); H. J. Lieber, *Die Philosophie des Bolschewismus* (1957); G. A. Wetter, *Dialectical Materialism* (1959); M. Cornforth, *Materialism and the Dialectical Method* (1960); J. Blakely, *Soviet Scholasticism* (1961); id., *Soviet Theory of Knowledge* (1964); J. M. Bochenski, *Soviet Russian Dialectical Materialism* (1964); G. A. Wetter, *Soviet Ideology Today* (1966); L. K. Dupré, *Philosophical Foundations of Marxism* (1966).

Gustav A. Wetter

III. Historical Materialism

1. *Concept*. While dialectical materialism deals with the ontology and epistemology of the Leninist version of Marxism, historical materialism comprises the philosophy of history and the sociology adopted in the Marxist view of the world. Since Stalin, historical materialism has often been put forward as an application of the basic principles of dialectical materialism to history and society. But in fact dialectical materialism is an extrapolation performed by Engels and can be replaced by other ontologies and theories of knowledge without affecting the basic theses of historical materialism. Hence too

in fact historical materialism has had supporters among Kantians (M. Adler, O. Bauer), Hegelians (G. Lukács, K. Korsch, A. Gramsci) and existentialists (the later Sartre and some "revisionists" of the present day).

The title "historical materialism" is somewhat misleading, since historical materialism is not an effort to reduce all phenomena to material process but a naturalism which seeks to explain all "higher" human attitudes and achievements as "practical" and to reduce them to the economic activities of man. Marx had already constantly used "material" and "practical" interchangeably (in the sense of the Aristotelian ποίησις, making, production). In any case, historical materialism is for the most part completely independent of metaphysical standpoints or such questions as: "Is there a spiritual soul?" or "Are 'things in themselves' accessible to our knowledge?"

2. *History*. Some elements of historical materialism already are to be found in the writings of Guizot, Thierry, Mignet, Hegel, Moses Hess and the early works of Marx. The first systematic outline was *The German Ideology* of Marx and Engels (1845). Up to that date Marx had propounded an "ethical" communism in which communist society had been presented as a moral ideal. It was only as a result of his controversy with Max Stirner and his "critique of ideals" that Marx became a determinist in his approach to history. The only other presentation of historical materialism from the pen of Marx is found in the preface to his *Critique of Political Economy* (1859) and the corresponding preliminary sketches. But most of the historical writings of Marx are applications of the theory which have hardly been improved on since. Engels supported Marx's doctrine with numerous historical studies of particular questions. One of his objects was to prevent the theory being applied too rigidly. Lenin worked out the relevant theory of revolution. But his most important contribution in this line is his adaptation of historical materialism to the special conditions obtaining in Russia with regard to the agrarian question. Stalin's contribution, apart from his dogmatizing of historical materialism which is still influential, was chiefly his thesis of 1950 that language — and hence disciplines like logic and natural science —

was not a product of class distinctions. He also affirmed, in contrast to his predecessors, the continuity of historical development. One of his reasons was to counteract the notion that even in socialist society progress could come about only through a series of revolutions. In contemporary Marxist-Leninism, historical materialism remains along with some fundamental principles of dialectical materialism the dogmatic kernel about which practically no questions may be raised. Nonetheless, important modifications of the doctrine have been proposed, under the cloak of sociological research, especially in Poland.

3. *Doctrine.* a) The basis of historical materialism is a concept of the historicity of man which is rarely considered today, but goes back fundamentally to Hegel. According to this concept, man is a historical being, and history and historical progress only exist because human wants expand with every satisfaction provided and hence constantly demand new means of satisfaction. The satisfaction of needs is provided for by activities which were originally purely biological functions (such as hunting, killing and devouring the prey). But at the very beginning of history, these functions changed to "activity" *(praxis)*, that is, actions by which man alters his environment and brings it into line with his developing wants. Thus the historicity of man is rooted in the labour by which man "humanizes" the world and likewise "puts forth" his own potentialities. Since for Marx, industrial production is "labour at its most perfect", Marx can write that the history of industry is "the open book of the natural powers of man, psychology as accessible to perception" (K. Marx, *Frühe Schriften,* I [1962], p. 602).

b) It follows from what has been said that the most basic determinants both of historical progress and of each historical epoch are the "productive forces". According to Stalin, these include the tools of production (from the axes of the Stone Age to the computer) and man in each age with his experience of production and his ability to work — to which must be added, no doubt, the various amounts and types of raw material present from place to place. These productive forces are in the course of uninterrupted development, corresponding to the development of human wants, their satisfaction and the cor-

responding activities. In any given period, it is these forces which determine the other historical dimensions of human existence.

c) In particular, the "relations of production" are determined by the productive forces. While the productive forces may be described as the relation of man to nature at any given time, the relations of production are the mutual relations of men with each other in the process of production, especially the division of labour, the conditions of exchange and the distribution of material goods. The essence of each type of these relations is the form of ownership of means of production which go with it. And the decisive question is who possesses the means of production (land, raw materials, tools, etc.). A primarily agricultural society brings about relations of production and forms of property which differ totally from those of an industrial society.

d) The unity of productive forces and relations of production forms the "mode of production" which makes up the distinctive essence of a given society in a given period. Further, the relations of production form the basis or infrastructure, in contrast to the superstructure. This latter is formed firstly of the juridical and political conditions obtaining (superstructure I) and secondly of the "forms of social consciousness" such as political, economic, philosophical and religious theories and doctrines (superstructure II). The mode of production determines superstructure I, which in turn determines superstructure II. Hence Marx can say that the social being of men determines their consciousness.

e) Because the productive forces are in a state of continual progress, while relations of production develop at a considerably slower pace, contradictions are constantly arising between the technical and the socioeconomic factors. The relations of production become as it were dead-weights holding back the progress of civilization. A social revolution follows. As soon as the revolution has overthrown existing social and economic structures and introduced new ones, superstructures I and II also begin to change. New forms of political, economic, philosophic and religious thought emerge.

f) The most striking feature of each mode of production is the form of ownership which goes with a given state of the productive forces, i.e., "the form of connection between the producers and the means of production". Ownership is either private property or community ownership. In the latter case the means of production belong to the community as a whole. In the first case they belong only to part of society, which is therefore the ruling class as opposed to the serving or exploited part of the community. For the relationship of men to the means of production determines all other social and economic relationships: the role in production, the exchange and distribution of products.

g) This means that where private property in the means of production is the rule of a society, it is split into classes and characterized by class struggle. Lenin defined classes as "large groups of men distinguished from each other by their relationship to the means of production, by their role in the social organization of work and, consequently, by the way they arrive at their share in the wealth of society and the greatness of their share in it" (V. I. Lenin, *Selected Works,* II [1967], p. 570). Since the actual interests of the different classes in a society always contradict each other, continuous class struggle is the inevitable rule in such society.

h) The first and the last historical societies are classless, because of the absence of private ownership: primitive society, whose productive forces may be described as bow and arrow, fishing and hunting; and the socialist or communist society which is based on a most advanced development of mechanized industry. In between there were three types of society: the ancient society based on slavery, medieval feudalism and modern capitalism. In the first, the corresponding productive forces were metal instruments, cattle-rearing, agriculture and handicrafts. In the second there were the iron plough, the loom, agriculture and handicrafts in a more developed form. In the third there are large factories equipped with machinery. The corresponding classes are slave-owners and slaves, feudal lords and serfs, and finally capitalists and proletarians.

i) Social revolutions are the supreme expression of the class struggle. Such revolutions are not necessarily armed revolts, just as every armed revolt is not a revolution. The essence of a genuine revolution is that it solves social contradictions, especially between classes. While all other revolutions only change the form of exploitation, the last social revolution — the socialist revolution which leads from capitalism to communism — eliminates on principle all exploitation of man by men. Thus the socialist revolution is regarded as the most radical upheaval in the history of mankind.

j) Finally, historical materialism contains a theory of the State and of ideology — the latter doctrine mostly confined to noncommunist Marxists. The State is described as the product of the irreconcilability of classes and as an instrument of the ruling class. The theory of ideology of historical materialism rests on the hermeneutical rule that historical epochs are not to be explained and assessed in terms of their own thinking, but that on the contrary, their thinking is a reflection of the technical conquests and above all of the social and economic relationships of the epoch.

4. *Critical remarks.* a) Historical materialism has undoubtedly made an important contribution to our understanding of history. Since Marx, it is impossible to regard history either merely as a series of kingdoms and rulers with their private ambitions or as a pure process of an unfolding logic. It is also a merit of Marxism to have underlined the significance of the everyday work of the "ordinary" man in the course of history. The latter's course is not regulated only by kings and philosophers but also, and to an important extent, by all those who "put their shoulder to the wheel". And here the private intentions of the so-called "makers of history", the great men of the day, are now accorded far less weight in the long-term view. However, it must be added that these ways of looking at history have long since become common ground to a great extent. The student of history or of the philosophy of history need not be a Marxist now to affirm the importance of technical progress and social-economic relationships in history. Indeed, he need not even appeal to Marx.

b) The fundamental weakness of historical materialism is that it understands the processes outlined above as inexorable laws, and indeed affirms that we can only understand history when we succeed in formulating exact scientific laws for its course. In other words, Marxism here fails to see that while historical research undoubtedly needs heuristic rules, generalizations and even general laws, these all must necessarily remain heuristic instruments. Historical studies, unlike the natural sciences, do not need to establish objective and inviolable laws in order to "understand" their subject.

c) In particular, the following individual points of historical materialism may be called in question: (i) That "relations of production" can change only by virtue of a change in the "forces of production". There was little or no technical progress between 200 B.C. and A.D. 700. Nonetheless, fundamental changes came about in social and economic fields, to some extent under the influence of Christianity. (ii) That the owners of the means of production are always the ruling classes and the exploiters of the poor. For centuries in China the class of exploiters consisted of a bureaucracy which did not own the essential means of production. (iii) That the only decisive historical upheavals are brought about by social revolutions. Neither the barbarian invasions nor the Reformation nor even the French Revolution were primarily "social revolutions". But all three constituted decisive historical upheavals. (iv) That "primitive society" was classless or ideed that there ever was such a classless society. (v) That the essential difference between society in its first and last state, and all the forms of society in between, is that the former are classless while the others are characterized by class struggle. Among other objections, it must be noted that the Marxist definition of "class" is very one-sided. (vi) That it is always social life that determines the thinking of society and not vice versa. (vii) That the thought-forms and doctrines of past epochs were primarily the reflection of historical conditions. (viii) That historical progress can be clearly and definitely traced and that it is irreversible.

d) Finally, it may be pointed out that historical materialism, contrary to some widely held views, is not or at least need not be a determinism in the sense of a denial of the freedom of the will. Marxist-Leninists of the present day rightly note that even inexorable historical laws can be as it were statistical in nature, that is, valid only over long periods of time and with reference to many millions of men. In this case the freedom of individual choice is not necessarily called in question.

See also *Historicism, Invasions (Barbarian), Reformation, French Revolution, Communism, Nature* II.

BIBLIOGRAPHY. B. Croce, *Historical Materialism and the Economics of Karl Marx* (1922); J. Stalin, *Dialectical and Historical Materialism* (1940); M. M. Bober, *Karl Marx's Interpretation of History* (2nd ed., 1950); I. Berlin, *Historical Inevitability* (1954); H. Marcuse, *Soviet Marxism* (1958); J.-P. Sartre, *Search for a Method* (1963); Z. A. Jordan, *Philosophy and Ideology* (1963); J.-Y. Calvez, *La pensée de Karl Marx* (6th ed., 1963); G. A. Wetter, *Soviet Ideology Today* (1966).

Nicholas Lobkowicz

MASS STIPEND

A Mass stipend is an offering, normally consisting of money, which is entrusted to a priest as depository and which is to be ordained by him to an offering of holy Mass.

1. *History*. The Mass stipend was developed as a special use from the offertory of the eucharistic celebration. According to ancient Christian understanding, the eucharistic Communion at table was constituted by an offering of gifts. This was a right and honour which belonged only to full members of the Church, and which was at the same time a duty for all who took part in the sacrifice — laymen, as well as clerics and religious. The introduction of the Mass stipend was based on the conviction that the holy sacrifice could be offered for certain intentions of the individual faithful. The initial stages of such offerings are attested by early witnesses (Augustine, *Ep.,* 111, 8: *CSEL,* XXXIV, 655; Epiphanius of Salamis, *Haereses,* 30, 6: *PG,* XLI, col. 413). The way for the Mass stipend was prepared by the so-called private Masses, especially in the form of votive Masses. Here the sacrifice was originally performed just as in the public liturgy of the Mass. The sick, who could not bring their offerings to the altar themselves, felt a profound need to have their offerings presented by a representative; and the priest was the obvious agent for such an assignment. Foundations were set up for Masses for the dead, the profits of which were intended to serve as sacrificial gifts. In the beginning some particular gift was offered during the celebration of Mass; thus the gift which was proffered *extra missam* was visibly placed within the sacrificial act. The peculiarity of the Mass stipend

is that it does not show visibly the presentation of the offering at the holy sacrifice, though for a long time the connection with the holy sacrifice was made clear at the common offertory. The change in the way of offering gifts was signalled in the canon by the words "pro quibus offerimus", an insertion which is first attested by the edition of the Gregorian sacramentary produced by Alcuin. It quickly prevailed after the 10th century.

2. *Essence and justification*. The Church has acknowledged the proffering and accepting of Mass stipends as a legitimate usage (*CIC*, can. 824, § 1); it has not, however, said how this practice is to be justified. The widely held doctrine that the Mass stipend is a contribution to the support of the priest is not adequate, because it cannot explain the intrinsic connection, suggested by the Mass stipend, between the gift and the graces expected from the holy sacrifice, without laying itself open to the charge of simony. This is particularly clear in the doctrine of the "fruits" of the Mass, which supposes graces (the *fructus ministeriales*), of which the priest alone has the disposal. This is supposed to show what the priest is able to give in exchange. This very material notion of the sacrifice of the Mass, which stems from Germanic jurisprudence, is to be decidedly rejected. The theological justification for the Mass stipend can only be sought by inserting into the Mass the offering given outside the Mass. The Mass stipend is nothing else but the offering which, according to ancient usage, was proffered *infra missam*. In the intention of the giver, it was a gift for the holy sacrifice. The giver strives to share in the sacrifice, which he can only do as a member of the sacrificial fellowship. The priest enrolls him as a donor in a given sacrifice, whether he is present or not. Until this connection is made, the Mass stipend is a gift placed on deposit with the priest as an administrator of the Church (*persona publica*). It reverts to the priest through the altar, i.e., through God, after the gift has passed through the sacrificial action, by being spiritually connected with the holy sacrifice. The lack of clarity in the matter is reflected in the legal terminology of the Church, which speaks of *stipendium, stips, eleemosyna* and, for short, even of *missa* but does not use *oblatio*, in the sense of Mass stipend, though this word would express the historical origin of the Mass stipend as well as its relationship to the holy sacrifice.

3. *Types*. A distinction is made between manual stipends (*stipendia manualia*), which are given a priest in the hand, so to speak; foundation stipends (*stipendia fundata*), which result from the income of an endowment; and manual stipends improperly so called (*ad instar manualium*), which stem from a foundation, but cannot be personally fulfilled by the person obliged to do so (parish priest, holder of a benefice) and are therefore handed on to another priest. The priest is free to accept or decline a manual stipend; foundation stipends are obligatory, on the terms laid down in the articles of agreement.

4. *Canon law*. The legal norms for Mass stipends (*CIC*, can. 824-44) presume the theological justification of the Mass stipend and aim chiefly at guarding against abuses. Only one stipend may be accepted for one and the same Mass. If a Mass must be applied obligatorily for a certain intention, no stipend may be accepted for it; in the case of bination and trination this also holds for the other Masses. It is forbidden to offer Masses for the assumed intentions of future donors and then retain stipends which come in later; it is also forbidden to accept a Mass stipend for the celebration and another for the application. The amount of the Mass stipend is fixed by the local ordinary; the Mass stipend does not become a fee because of this (cf. stole fees). At the time of proffering the Mass stipend special conditions can be attached, e.g., in regard to the church, the altar, the time and similar matters. Mass stipends may be passed on only to priests, and only to such priests who are above suspicion; nothing may be withheld in the transfer. In giving and accepting Mass stipends every appearance of business and trade must be avoided. Trade in Mass stipends and other violations are punishable according to can. 2324.

BIBLIOGRAPHY. M. de la Taille, *Esquisse du mystère de la foi suivie de quelques éclaircissements — Les offrandes de messes* (1924); id., *The Last Supper and Calvary* (1924); id., *The Mystery of Faith and Human Opinion* (1930); J. Jungmann, *The Mass of* the Roman Rite, II (1951); E. Eichmann and K. Mörsdorf, Lehrbuch des Kirchenrechts, II (11th ed., 1967), pp. 44–54; K. Rahner and A. Häussling, The Celebration of the Eucharist (1968).

Klaus Mörsdorf

MATERIALISM

The term "materialist" first appears in Robert Boyle for the older "Epicurean". While some historians of philosophy regard the existence of "materialism" as being as old as philosophy itself (so, for instance, the Marxists), and find it clearly propounded by the ancient Greek philosophies of nature, as in Democritus and Epicure, others date materialism, in the strict sense, only since the concept was "clearly demarcated by Decartes" (R. Eucken). The older philosophies of nature contained so much myth that at the most "only a tendency to materialism can be found there" (A. Müller). According to Eucken, "the English have provided the cleverest, the French the wittiest and the Germans the bluntest defenders" of materialism.

Materialism is an attitude to life and an explanation of the world based on matter. It views matter as corporeal, like the world of bodies which is made from it, and takes various views of what the corporeal is like. This attitude or explanation can be spontaneous and uncritical or thought-out and made a considered theory. Practical materialism, the principle of which is material possessions, comforts and sensual pleasure, is often unreflecting and naive, and can be linked with a theoretical idealism, just as practical idealism is compatible with theoretical materialism. Materialism as a philosophy can be either total or partial. Total materialism considers matter as the principle of all reality, either equivalently or causally, that is, either in the sense that there is nothing but matter, or that matter is the efficient cause (mechanically in metaphysical materialism, dialectically in dialectical materialism) of everything, actual or otherwise. Partial materialism sees matter as the exclusive principle of certain realms of being. It may be an element of a total materialism, but may also be combined with non-materialist convictions. Boyle and Newton were materialists in scientific matters, for which they often appealed to Gassendi, but recognized the limits of this materialism. Boyle compared the universe with the famous clock in the Strasbourg Cathedral. It was a mechanism which presupposed an intelligent cause, like the clock.

The attractiveness of total materialism is due to that of the natural sciences, which rests on the experimental study of matter. In contrast to an infantile and fantastic materialism whose notion of matter is often highly imaginative and which is often the basis of philosophical speculation, this materialism is technically competent and investigates the relationships of matter (Bachelard). It is methodical, and prescinds from other causal factors, in order to test the validity of material explanations.

The question of the structure of the universe was answered by 18th-century science by the principle that it resulted from various combinations of matter which could be analysed and grasped in terms of space and time. The common element of the various materials involved was mass, which is given momentum by energy. The product of mass and momentum gives the amount of the energy acting on mass.

The success of the mechanical explanation of nature led to mechanist materialism, which was accepted by most of the cultured classes and became in the hands of the bourgeois, especially in France, a political instrument, a lever, in the struggle against throne and altar. Confidence, however, that the material world or even reality as a whole could be explained exclusively by matter and the laws of mechanics was shaken by the progress of science. Acoustics, optics and thermodynamics might be amenable to mechanical treatment, but it became clear that alongside of matter, mass and energy there was a physical reality, the nature of which remains obscure to the present day, a something which had to be assumed to render intelligible the action of the various parts of matter on each other. This was the "field" — a field of gravitation, and also an electro-magnetic field which is essentially different from the former, and since the investigation of the atom, a nuclear field, once more essentially different, the existence of which has now to be assumed. It also became clear that the laws of physics which held good for the realities dealt with in classical science and which had seemed to be of universal validity, were actually confined to the level of ordinary quantities and could not be applied without more ado on the cosmic and atomic levels. It was the end of the total domination of mechanistic concepts in physics, where they had gained such brilliant successes and which had been used to build up a universal mechanistic world-view. The physicist, faced with the discovery of infinitesimally small quantities (10^{13}) in the nucleus of the atom, finds himself forced to use concepts which seem to depart definitely from the realm of the mechanistic. Today more than thirty elementary particles are known to exist in the atomic nucleus, appearing and disappearing with extreme rapidity and changing into other particles. Hence W. Heisenberg could say: "All elementary particles are made of the same matter, which we may call energy or universal matter. They are only the different forms in which matter can appear. If we compare this situation with the concepts of matter and form in Aristotle, we might say that the matter of Aristotle, which was essentially *potentia*, i.e., possibility, should be compared to our notion of energy. Energy appears as material reality through the form, when an elementary particle is produced" (cf. W. Heisenberg, p. 131). H. C. Oersted, the discoverer of the relations between magnetism and electricity, pointed to law as the perpetual, unchangeable essential core of things, and hence called for a combination of materialism and spiritualism even for the realm of physics (see his *Soul in Nature* [1852], E. T. of *Der Geist in der Natur* [1850]).

It is still impossible to determine whether matter can be seen as a sufficient explanation for the phenomena of life (changes of matter and form, growth, evolution, perception of stimuli). The nucleic acids (micromolecular combinations) and the proteins (macromolecular combinations) are prerequisites for the coming of life. To explain the appearance of life, some biologists assume the existence of a spiritual principle of organization, while others try to produce life from matter itself. In 1953 Stanley Miller in Chicago used the play of electric charges on an artificially prepared atmosphere to produce amino-acids (micromolecular). Up to the present no such experiments have been successful in the synthesis of the proteins. And even so, amino-acids and proteins are not life. For life, there must also be the major factors of spatio-temporal organization, the co-operation of the various materials in the service of self-sustenance and the preservation of the type. Theologically it hardly seems to matter whether life may be explained on the basis of the intrinsic laws of highly complicated material or the influence of a distinct spiritual principle of organization. God could have produced life equally well through the general laws of nature alone or by means of a special vitalist principle of organization (cf. K. Wacholder, in *Naturwissenschaft heute* [1965], p. 49). Like life, consciousness is also different from matter. Heat as a physical process is "a disorderly movement of the atoms", while heat as sensation is a type of experience which presupposes this movement of the atoms. The eye does not see light-waves but colours. The ear does not hear wave-lengths but sounds. The material basis of the process of consciousness is the nervous system. While sensible knowledge rests on perception, intellectual knowledge becomes independent of its material basis and displays a unity which is alien to matter. Comparison between various impressions, memory, the act of judgment — all surpass the possibilities of material and spatial reality. Taken along with the phenomenon of psycho-physical causality, the nature of life on the higher levels of the soul point to the independence of the physical and psychic spheres.

In their struggle against materialism, philosophers and theologians have often been so much carried away by their zeal that they overlooked the valuable elements which it contains. They forgot that one must often wait patiently to see how much may be accorded to material forces as the explanation of phenomena, that sound material relationships, while not representing the supreme values, still are fundamental, and that the dignity of human existence is often only possible on the basis of their adequate realization. Theology must pay greater attention to the creational character and hence the high value of matter, of the material and sensible world.

See also *Matter, Marxism* II, *Hylemorphism, Spiritualism, Causality*.

BIBLIOGRAPHY. R. Eucken, *Geschichte der philosophischen Terminologie* (1879; reprint 1960); F.

Lange, *History of Materialism and Criticism of Its Present Importance*, with an introduction by B. Russell (3rd ed., 1925); D. Dubarle, "Matérialisme scientifique et foi religieuse", *Recherches et Débats* 4: *Pensée scientifique et foi chrétienne* (1953); A. N. Whitehead, *Science and the Modern World* (1926); G. Bachelard, *Le nouvel esprit scientifique* (1937); A. Einstein and L. Infeld, *Evolution of Physics* (1938); L. de Broglie, *Physics and Microphysics* (1957); W. Heisenberg, *Physics and Philosophy* (1958); id., *Philosophical Problems of Nuclear Science* (1959); R. Schubert-Soldern, *Mechanism and Vitalism: Philosophical Aspects of Biology* (1962); M. Planck, *Philosophy of Physics* (1963); P. Jordan, *Naturwissenschaftler vor der religiösen Frage* (1963); C. von Weizsäcker, *The Relevance of Science* (1964); "Materie und Leben", *Naturwissenschaft und Theologie* 7 (1966).

Marcel Reding

Wds missg
Joy
Happiness

Lange, *History of Materialism and Criticism of Its Present Importance*, with an introduction by B. Russell (3rd ed., 1925); D. Dubarle, "Matérialisme scientifique et foi religieuse", *Recherches et Débats 4: Pensée scientifique et foi chrétienne* (1953); A. N. Whitehead, *Science and the Modern World* (1926); G. Bachelard, *Le nouvel esprit scientifique* (1937); A. Einstein and L. Infeld, *Evolution of Physics* (1938); L. de Broglie, *Physics and Microphysics* (1957); W. Heisenberg, *Physics and Philosophy* (1958); id., *Philosophical Problems of Nuclear Science* (1959); R. Schubert-Soldern, *Mechanism and Vitalism: Philosophical Aspects of Biology* (1962); M. Planck, *Philosophy of Physics* (1963); P. Jordan, *Naturwissenschaftler vor der religiösen Frage* (1963); C. von Weizsäcker, *The Relevance of Science* (1964); "Materie und Leben", *Naturwissenschaft und Theologie* 7 (1966).

Marcel Reding

Wds missg
Joy
Happiness

Wds missg
Joy